RUSSIAN AND EAST EUROPEAN STUDIES

CHARLES JELAVICH, *Tsarist Russia and Balkan Nationalism. Russian Influence in the Internal Affairs of Bulgaria and Serbia, 1879–1886*

NICHOLAS V. RIASANOVSKY, *Nicholas I and Official Nationality in Russia, 1825–1855*

RICHARD A. PIERCE, *Russian Central Asia, 1867–1917. A Study in Colonial Rule*

CHARLES AND BARBARA JELAVICH, eds., *The Education of a Russian Statesman. The Memoirs of Nicholas Karlovich Giers*

SOVIET AND
EAST EUROPEAN
AGRICULTURE

RUSSIAN AND EAST EUROPEAN STUDIES

SOVIET AND EAST EUROPEAN AGRICULTURE

Edited, with a preface, by

Jerzy F. Karcz

UNIVERSITY OF CALIFORNIA PRESS
BERKELEY AND LOS ANGELES
1967

UNIVERSITY OF CALIFORNIA PRESS
BERKELEY AND LOS ANGELES, CALIFORNIA

CAMBRIDGE UNIVERSITY PRESS
LONDON, ENGLAND

LIBRARY OF CONGRESS CATALOG CARD NUMBER: 67–10620

TO THE MEMORY OF

VLADIMIR P. TIMOSHENKO

AND HIS LASTING CONTRIBUTIONS
TO THE STUDY OF SOVIET AGRICULTURE

Preface

In September, 1962, a group of scholars representing various academic disciplines met at the University of Kansas at Lawrence to discuss problems of Soviet agriculture. At the close of the conference (whose proceedings were published in 1963) the participants decided to form a loose interdisciplinary association for the continued study of Soviet agriculture. The action resulted from a conviction that our knowledge in this field was incomplete and that more research was necessary to elucidate further some of the important aspects of farming in a socialist command economy. This field of scholarly inquiry cuts across the boundaries of several traditional disciplines. Experience gained at Kansas demonstrated the value of close contact and the associated exchange of ideas resulting from an interdisciplinary meeting. It was therefore believed that further undertakings of this type would be similarly worthwhile.

The present volume consists of contributions presented at the second gathering of the group, now named Conference on Soviet Agricultural and Peasant Affairs held at the University of California, Santa Barbara, on August 26–28, 1965, under the honorary chairmanship of Naum Jasny. The meeting was sponsored jointly by the Conference and the Center of Slavic and East European Studies at the University of California, Berkeley. This time, the discussion included also some problems of Eastern European agriculture. The decision to enlarge the scope of the conference reflected growing awareness of the need to increase our understanding of agricultural developments in other Communist areas and ultimately to promote comparative studies of agriculture within the Soviet bloc. Indeed, a scholar interested primarily in Soviet developments may often benefit from a more intensive study of related trends in other Eastern European countries, and this is especially true of topics on which the available Soviet evidence is meager. For example, the discussion of the Soviet "employment problem" in rural areas, undertaken in this volume by Miss Nancy Nimitz may be viewed in a much larger perspective in the light of Professor Halpern's contribution on Yugoslav peasant attitudes towards agricultural careers and rural life in general. Some comments made on the same issue by Professor Korbonski on the basis of Polish experience are also relevant in this context.

The importance of agriculture in Soviet society may be illustrated in various ways. The territory of the Soviet Union covers 8.6 million square miles, but climatic and topographical limitations account for the fact that only one-tenth of this total is classified as arable land. Large socialized farms, of a size not encountered in other economic systems, account for 97 percent of total sown area. Yet, the importance of the socialized sector in the production of some major farm products is still rather small. For milk, meat, and vegetables, the share of state and collective farms in total output comes to slightly less than three-fifths; for potatoes and fruit this share amounts roughly to one-third. Of the total Soviet population, 47 percent is still classified as rural. According to a recent calculation, undertaken in the United States by Stanley Cohn, agriculture contributed 29.2 percent to the Soviet gross national product in 1959. Within the past two years, unfavorable weather conditions forced the Soviet government to import substantial quantities of wheat and flour from Western producers and to reduce the volume of Soviet grain exports to other members of the Soviet bloc. Finally, agriculture has played a significant role in the process of Soviet industrialization, and ever since 1928 rapid industrial growth has remained a major policy objective of the Soviet government.

It may be appropriate to discuss briefly the last-mentioned aspect of the problem to provide some background for the discussions that follow. As Adam Smith has once put it, "it is the surplus produce of the country . . . that constitutes the subsistence of the town." A part of the surplus produce may, of course, be exported to provide foreign exchange needed to finance the required machinery imports, while labor transferred to cities from the villages will be used to man the imported or domestically produced machines. A further margin for domestic capital formation may also be provided by restricting consumption in the rural areas. This can be achieved by taxation or by manipulation of prices paid to, as well as those paid by, the agricultural sector.

It is therefore not surprising that problems of agricultural production and those related to farm organization have always been closely linked to major economic policy decisions at crucial junctures of Soviet history. When the leaders of Soviet Russia launched an extremely ambitious industrialization drive in the fall of 1928, they had to come to grips with the problem of extracting the surplus produce of the countryside in terms of either farm products or of human labor. Within the next two years, a drastic and radical transformation occurred in the Soviet countryside as millions of individual households were merged into large collective farms. The decision to collectivize agriculture, supported by ideological and political considerations, was implemented in spite of the human misery that accompanied the process. As reluctant and sometimes rebellious peasants were forced into collectives, livestock holdings were halved, and for a while famine stalked "the land of tomorrow." Yet, insofar as the objectives pertained to the goal of industrialization, the aims of the government were achieved as year after year the engine of growth produced substantial increases in industrial output.

But it was also expected in the U.S.S.R. that agricultural output would rise as a result of collectivization. This did not occur. In 1938–1940, the volume of gross farm output was roughly the same as in the preplan, precollectivization year 1928. As the government concentrated its attention on industry generally and on heavy industry in particular, it neglected those improvements in farming that would have increased agricultural production. The major characteristics of this policy were continued unchanged, broadly speaking, through the period of postwar reconstruction that for present purposes may be taken as ended with the death of Stalin in March, 1953. The results, measured in terms of gross output, were also unchanged, as in the last five years of the late dictator's rule, the index of this output fluctuated narrowly about the peak prewar level achieved in 1940.

To a large extent, the cause of stagnation in output may be sought precisely in those features of collectivized agriculture which had assured its success as the supplier of fuel for the engine of growth. A substantial proportion of what was produced accrued to the government through a complex system of compulsory deliveries and payments in kind for services of state-owned machine tractor stations (MTS). The peasant's claim on collective farm output was limited to the residual remaining after the claims of the state and the requirements of production were satisfied. The level of incentives in the socialized sector was low, as state prices for basic foods remained virtually unchanged since 1932 while urban wages and retail prices were rising rapidly. The resulting burden of taxation in kind detracted much of the peasant attention to the small, individually operated household plot that provided not only the bulk of subsistence but also opportunities to earn cash through sales of products on urban markets. Not enough was done to ensure a volume of capitalization that would have compensated for considerable climatic disadvantages, for the decline in the number of draft animals, and for the transfer of labor to industry.

These features of the collective farm system had many other ramifications. The Soviet government found it difficult—and at times impossible—to reconcile the prime objective of collecting the surplus produce of the countryside with other policy goals that had been equally important for the agricultural sector. Given the considerable limitations imposed on farming activity in the Soviet Union by natural conditions, geographers in tsarist Russia and the Soviet Union have long concerned themselves with the subject of agricultural regionalization. As Professor Jensen notes in his contribution to this volume, this relatively advanced work was abandoned under the impact of cataclysmic stresses of the massive collectivization drive. Although this work has been resumed in the post-Stalin period, continuing pressures from the demand side and the time-honored objective of autarky still conflict with production patterns that would be indicated by the practical application of regional analysis.

It might also be thought that a planned economy of the Soviet type would find it easier to impose rapidly rational cropping patterns on farms that are subject to a vast variety of rules and regulations. However, the ability to impose one's will on the population is not the same thing as the ability to make the correct rational decisions. As Professor Joravsky points out in his stimulating discussion of Williams's grassland rotations, it was an outmoded cropping pattern, derived deductively without proper regard for truly scientific considerations, that received the official sanction. Although the evidence is not complete, it is also interesting to note that under the harsh impact of reality, the officially fostered cropping schemes appeared to have been altered frequently in an effort to adapt them to practical requirements. It still remains to be seen whether the benefits of all scientific achievements will flow fully to Soviet farming in the near and more distant future.

The Soviet system of collectivized farming has not, in the past, led to an efficient use of resources on farms. The existence of payments in kind for the use of machinery and the payment of labor from residual shares presented formidable difficulties to the introduction of simple economic calculations. Indeed, no calculations of production costs were undertaken while Stalin was alive. It would have been embarrassing to do so while, in the words of a highly placed Soviet official, no self-respecting individual would bother to carry potatoes to the truck in return for the then prevailing compulsory delivery price.[1] Since prices set at such discriminatory levels could not direct production into desired lines of activity, the government relied on direct and detailed orders. To ensure that the required deliveries would, in fact, take place, state agencies planned the structure of sowings as well as the level and the structure of livestock herds for each individual farm.

Such policies were hardly calculated to instill the principle of economizing on farm managers and collective farmers. Indeed, the opposite has been true. Since 1953, Soviet farm prices were raised several times. As Naum Jasny shows in his essay, the present level of Soviet farm prices and costs is far above that of most, if not all, other countries of the world. But this was not the only consequence of extracting thoughtlessly the surplus produce of the countryside without reference to peasant welfare. People who must be ordered to produce at a loss cannot be trusted and must be tightly supervised. The Party has never trusted the peasant, but the application of Stalinist policies just described has resulted in further intensification of administrative interference into various affairs of the farm by all kinds of officials at all levels of the administrative ladders of the Communist party and the Soviet government. For obvious reasons, there has been little discussion of this phenomenon in general Soviet economic literature. But a good deal has been revealed in courageous and forthright commentaries of Soviet literary writers. Several examples of flagrant absurdities are given in the typically vigorous essay of Professor Nove, and there can be no question that the attitudes he describes have proved detrimental to the implementation of many reforms introduced in Soviet agriculture after the death of Stalin.

As has been indicated, the policies discussed above brought about a period of virtual stagnation of Soviet farm output during 1948–1952. From 1953 on, the history of Soviet agriculture records many changes in policies and institutions, introduced with the aim of breaking this stalemate and designed ultimately to provide the population with a more balanced and more attractive diet. From 1953 through early October,

[1] Vsesoiuznaia Ordena Lenina Akademiia Sel'skokhoziaistvennykh Nauk im. V. I. Lenina, *Materialy sessii Akademii posviashchennoi dal'neishemu razvitiiu kolkhoznogo stroia i reorganizatsii MTS* (Moscow: 1958), p. 191.

1964, N. S. Khrushchev served as the chief Party and government spokesman on agricultural matters and his own views were very influential in the formulation of agricultural policies. Among the measures permanently identified with his name are the substantial increase in acreage in the New Lands and the attempt to increase the supply of feed through the introduction of corn. (The latter policy is analyzed here by Professor Anderson.) Among other measures introduced in the early post-Stalin period were increases in farm prices, improvements in incentives offered to peasants, changes in administrative and planning procedures, and increased allocations of off-farm inputs. Under the combined impact of these measures and partly as a result of good weather, output rose substantially through 1958. But as Dr. Volin makes clear in his essay, Khrushchev's impact on Soviet agriculture was by no means one-sided. This is particularly well illustrated by agricultural developments under the Seven-Year Plan (1959–1965). Output goals under this plan were set at a high level—by 1965 the level of production was to exceed its high 1958 counterpart by no less than 70 percent. (In 1961, at the October session of the Twenty-second Party Congress, a goal for an increase of 150 percent was enunciated for the decade 1960–1970).

At the same time, however, the government reduced its allocations of machinery to the farming sector. Financial pressures on collective farms grew rapidly following the abolition of the machine-tractor stations, the sale of their machinery to farms and the substantial increases in prices of machinery, spare parts, and fuels. As a result, collective-farm distributions to members declined in 1959–1960. Simultaneously, severe restrictions were placed on the highly productive private sector. The difficulties were aggravated by poor harvest conditions, not only in the nearly disastrous year 1963, but in 1965 as well. The achieved increases in output were moderate. According to official data, the 1965 output was only 14 percent higher than that of 1958, and this was barely enough to keep pace with the increase in total population.

Khrushchev showed some signs of concern about these adverse trends beginning in the fall of 1960. Financial pressures on farms were eased somewhat, there was some increase in state investment in agriculture, and more credit was made available to collective farms. But there was no major significant shift in the allocation of resources to agriculture. On the other hand, procurement goals were raised, the restrictions on the private sector were intensified, and administrative reforms followed each other with great rapidity, leading to increased interference by outsiders in simple as well as complex production problems. For example, farms were often forbidden to reduce the size of herds even though feed supplies were insufficient.[2] Faced with rising urban demand for food and diminishing grain stocks, Khrushchev sought short-term relief in a campaign against Williams's grassland rotations and the existing (rather moderate) use of clean fallow. Thus, once again, the tenets of agronomy were violated in the pursuit of the surplus produce of the countryside to the detriment of peasant welfare. Moreover, as Professor Laird points out in his contribution, the fundamental need for greater autonomy in decision-making on the farm still went unrecognized.

Khrushchev was dismissed in October, 1964, and by March, 1965, his successors had formulated an agricultural program of their own. Its main features are reviewed in some detail in the paper by Professor Judy and Mr. Walters. Restrictions on the private sector were lifted, farm prices of grains, meat, and milk were raised once more, and greater allocations of machinery and other capital inputs have been promised in the near future. Perhaps the most interesting aspect of the new program is a visible change in emphasis: much more attention is now paid to what must be put into agriculture in order to achieve desired results. An effort to limit undue administrative interference with farm management is also being made.

This change in emphasis has been underlined by the formulation of the agricultural goals in the directives of the Five-Year Plan for 1966–1970, approved in April, 1966. In the past, documents of this sort included precise goals for the output of many products in the terminal year of the plan. This is no longer the case, and detailed goals for many products have not been stipulated. In 1966–1970, the *average* annual farm output is to exceed the average output of 1961–1965 by 25 percent.

The projection of output for 1969–1972 undertaken in this volume by Mr. Walters and Professor Judy was of course completed before the new goals of the Five-Year Plan were announced. Their estimating methods, however, did not require any specific knowledge of the official Plan targets. On the other hand, their results depend upon the assumptions made with respect to the supply of inputs to Soviet farming. As far as this aspect is concerned, the projection relied upon the goals of the new agricultural program, announced in March, 1965. These targets

[2] *Plenum Tsentral'nogo Komiteta Kommunisticheskoi Partii Sovetskogo Soiuza 24–26 marta 1965 g.* (Moscow: 1965), p. 50.

have not been altered by the directives approved in the spring of 1966, and the Walters-Judy projection is therefore unaffected by the announcement of the new goals for output. (I very much regret that the pressure of other work made it impossible for Dr. Werner Klatt to revise his valuable contribution to the Santa Barbara Conference for publication. The very useful commentary by Professor Chapman has been revised to fit the contribution by Mr. Walters and Professor Judy.)

In recent years, the volume of statistical information made available by official Soviet agencies has greatly increased, but serious lacunae remain and Western researchers must still compile statistical series of their own. Miss Nimitz, in her essay, constructs one such series, dealing with man-day inputs of labor into the various sectors of Soviet agriculture. Her discussion of problems resulting from the appearance of local surpluses of unskilled labor has recently been confirmed by frequent Soviet references to the need of creating additional opportunities for seasonal or full-time employment in rural areas. Indeed, the intention to develop handicrafts, small-scale processing plants and the production of local building materials on farms has been explicitly included in the directives for the 1966–1970 Five-Year Plan.

If implemented, this eminently sensible policy will represent a major shift in emphasis in the pattern of Soviet industrialization, characterized until now by preference given to large scale, urban enterprises. Some of the consequences of this policy, aimed at the realization of technological economies of scale, are pointed out in Professor Hultquist's essay, dealing with the relation of the sugar-beet processing industry to its raw material base. Excessively long hauls have often led to waste of raw materials and to serious problems in the utilization of capacity. It remains to be seen whether similar pitfalls will be avoided when Soviet planners begin to deal with a new and unfamiliar problem on a relatively large scale.

One of the consequences of rapid industrialization in the U.S.S.R. has been the increased rate of participation of women in the labor force, in agriculture as well as in the other branches of the economy. The essay by Professor Dodge and Mr. Feshbach represents the first Western systematic effort to analyze the characteristics of the feminine component of the labor force and to consider in detail the various factors affecting their participation in various farming activities. The authors find that most of the women employed in agriculture are in occupations requiring little skill but much manual labor. To a large extent, therefore, it is women who are in need of the seasonal employment opportunities referred to earlier.

Agricultural trends in Eastern Europe after World War II did not follow a uniform pattern. The Soviet example of a massive collectivization drive was not repeated. For the most part, gradual collectivization of individual peasant holdings did not begin until 1949 in the aftermath of the Yugoslav schism. Yugoslavia itself, after initiating a drive of its own in 1948–49, disbanded the great majority of its collectives in 1953. In other East European countries, collectivization was gradual and nonviolent, although various forms of compulsion were frequently employed. A moderate relaxation in the drive to collectivize occurred in 1953–1955 in connection with the New Course policies followed in Eastern Europe after the death of Stalin. During the fall of 1956, a dramatic and spontaneous decollectivization occurred in Hungary and Poland in connection with the revolutionary (or quasirevolutionary) developments in both countries. But with the single exception of Poland, the pressures were soon resumed, and the bulk of land in all other countries of the Soviet bloc is now farmed in the socialized sector.

The Polish case is thus unique in that a large private sector in agriculture coexists with socialized enterprises in other sectors of a planned economy. Trends in the performance of this sector are analyzed by Professor Korbonski, whose essay also deals with various proposals advanced in the Polish literature for the ultimate socialization of Polish agriculture. One of these suggestions exhibits a marked similarity with the official Yugoslav thinking on the same subject, elucidated by Professor Halpern.

Dr. Lazarcik's contribution on Czechoslovak agriculture approaches the subject in an entirely different manner. The author is concerned primarily with the measurement of the performance of a socialized agriculture in a relatively highly developed and industrialized economy. His computations lead to the conclusion that it is the present pattern of organization of farming activities that has led to rather disappointing trends in output and productivity. Some changes in this pattern may be forthcoming shortly in connection with the reform of the Czechoslovak economic system undertaken in 1965. No detailed blueprint for agricultural reform has as yet been officially published, but some suggestions for possible improvements have been listed by the author.

Although Professor Halpern's paper deals formally with Yugoslavia, the subject matter of his deliberations transcends the national boundaries of any country. The impact of rapid industrialization affected profoundly the scale of values of rural as well as of urban population and wrought many changes in the attitudes of various groups that make up the developing society. New groups, such as the "peasant workers," emerged in Yugoslavia (as well as in Poland), and their existence poses new problems to the ruling elites. Halpern's investigations in Yugoslavia suggest that agricultural careers are not regarded as attractive by the younger generations. There can be no question that the pull of city life is strong. In the recent past, existing sharp disparities between urban and rural incomes tended to reinforce the tendency to outward migration from agriculture. But as Professor Bićanić suggests it is not yet certain that we are faced here with a continuing trend, and this observation is to some extent born out by Korbonski's observations on the self-image of the Polish peasant.

As these words are written, the Communist command economies find themselves in a state of flux. All Eastern European countries are either introducing or are about to introduce reforms in their economic systems, designed to rationalize their structure through increased scope for market-type incentives. As the Yugoslav experience suggests, the task of rationalizing a command economy is likely to be a hard and protracted one. In view of the existing ideological impediments and of the usual bureaucratic inertia that often reaches formidable proportions in a Communist society, there is no reason to think that progress elsewhere in Eastern Europe will be continuous. But the process of reform, once it is introduced, often develops a logic of its own. As time goes on, official attitudes towards agriculture and the peasants may well be altered. The recent shifts in Soviet agricultural policies and in the underlying attitudes of the Soviet leadership may perhaps be considered as a first, even though modest, step in this direction.

The impact of such changes on Communist societies will undoubtedly be complex. To the extent that it will occur, however, it is likely to result in profound changes in farm organization, methods of management and planning, in the relationships between agricultural and industial incomes and perhaps even in actual—as opposed to nominal—forms of land tenure. In the meantime, of course, socialist agriculture will continue to offer a rich field for dispassionate scholarly study in several academic disciplines.

The conference held in Santa Barbara in August, 1965, was supported financially by the American Council of Learned Societies, the Center of Slavic and East European Studies of the University of California in Berkeley, the University of Kansas, and the University of California in Santa Barbara. A number of other universities and research institutions have also contributed by covering travel expenses of their staff members who took a part in the proceedings. All those associated with the conference join me in extending their expression of gratitude for the support that made the meeting possible.

I am also grateful to Mr. Robert T. Masson for faithful assistance in the preparation of the book and to Mr. Max Knight of the Editorial Department of the University of California Press for the most competent technical editing of a difficult manuscript and for helpful hints and advice in the performance of the editorial task. And I am indebted to Professor Andrzej Brzeski of the University of California at Davis for help in the final stages of proof-reading.

The papers printed in this volume represent more or less revised editions of those originally presented in Santa Barbara. For the most part, the revised versions reached me in February, 1966, but some commentaries not until May, 1966, at which time the manuscript was handed over to the University of California Press. In order to economize space, titles of most East European periodicals, including some weeklies and newspapers, have been abbreviated throughout the volume. This was also the case for the more frequently cited statistical handbooks published in the U.S.S.R. by the Central Statistical Administration and of the eight-volume collection of speeches and writings on agriculture by N. S. Khrushchev. Hopefully, those familiar with the literature will have no difficulty recognizing the relevant titles without further reference to the list of abbreviations which has been provided. We have also omitted the usually lengthy and frequently uninformative titles of Soviet journal articles, though we did retain the names of their authors.

The system of transliteration from the Russian alphabet is essentially that of the Library of Congress, though diacritical marks and ligatures were omitted.

For the tables the following symbols were used: a dash (-) for "not applicable or nonexistent; three dashes (---) for "negligible"; square brackets ([ ]) for estimates; and n.a. for "not available."

It remains to be said that the views and opinions expressed in this book are those of the authors and do not necessarily reflect views held or positions supported by the organizations with which they are associated.

Jerzy F. Karcz

Santa Barbara
May, 1966

Contents

ABBREVIATED SOURCE TITLES

For newspapers, weeklies, and journals the country of origin is indicated in parentheses.

Biull. nauchn. inf.	*Biulleten' nauchnoi informatsii: Trud i zarabotnaia plata* (Soviet)
Ek.	*Ekonomista* (Polish)
Ek. gaz.	*Ekonomicheskaia gazeta* (Soviet)
Ek. nauki	*Nauchnye doklady vysshei shkoly: Ekonomicheskie nauki* (Soviet)
Ek. Pol.	*Ekonomska Politika* (Yugoslav)
Ek. sel'. khoz.	*Ekonomika sel'skogo khoziaistva* (Soviet)
Gosp. Plan.	*Gospodarka Planowa* (Polish)
Itogi-1959-SSSR	Tsentral'noe Statisticheskoe Upravlenie pri Sovete Ministrov SSSR, *Itogi vsesoiuznoi perepisy naseleniia 1959 goda. SSSR: svodnyi tom* (Moscow: 1962)
Ist. arkh.	*Istoricheskii arkhiv* (Soviet)
Izv. Ak. Nauk	*Izvestiia Akademii Nauk SSSR* (Soviet)
Izv. Sib. otd.	*Izvestiia Sibirskogo otdeleniia Akademii Nauk SSSR* (Soviet)
Izv. Timir. Sel'. Ak.	*Izvestiia Timiriazevskoi Sel'skokhoziaistvennoi Akademii* (Soviet)
Kap. stroi.-1961	Tsentral'noe Statisticheskoe Upravlenie pri Sovete Ministrov SSSR, *Kapital'noe stroitel'stvo v SSSR* (Moscow: 1961)

Khim. sots. zem.	*Khimizatsiia sotsialisticheskogo zemledeliia* (Soviet)
Komm. Uzbek.	*Kommunist Uzbekistana* (Soviet)
Kon. tsifry-1929/30	Gosplan SSSR. *Kontrol'nye tsifry narodnogo khoziaistva SSSR na 1929/30 god* (Moscow: 1930)
Kul't. stroi.-1956	Tsentral'noe Statisticheskoe Upravlenie pri Sovete Ministrov SSSR, *Kul'turnoe stroitel'stvo SSSR* (Moscow: 1956)
Lit. gaz.	*Literaturnaia gazeta* (Soviet)
Na agr. fronte	*Na agrarnom fronte* (Soviet)
Narkhoz-. . .	Abbreviation used for the official Soviet statistical handbook, published in Moscow under the title *Narodnoe khoziaistvo SSSR v . . . g.*, usually in the year following that referred to in the title
Narkhoz-RSFSR-. . .	Tsentral'noe Statisticheskoe Upravlenie pri Sovete Ministrov RSFSR, *Narodnoe khoziaistvo RSFSR v . . . g.* (Moscow)
Nowe Roln.	*Nowe Rolnictwo* (Polish)
Part. zh.	*Partiinaia zhizn'* (Soviet)
Plán. hosp.	*Plánované hospodářství* (Czechoslovak)
Plan. khoz.	*Planovoe khoziaistvo* (Soviet)
Pochv.	*Pochvovedenie* (Soviet)
Pos. ploshch.	Tsentral'noe Statisticheskoe Upravlenie pri Sovete Ministrov SSSR, *Posevnye ploshchadi SSSR* (Moscow: 1957), 2 volumes
Prob. ek.	*Problemy ekonomiki* (Soviet)
Prom. SSSR-1964	Tsentral'noe Statisticheskoe Upravlenie pri Sovete Ministrov SSSR, *Promyshlennost'* SSSR (Moscow: 1964)
Rocz. Stat.-. . .	Abbreviation used for the official Polish statistical handbook published in Warsaw under the title *Rocznik Statystyczny* . . . in the year referred to in the title
Sakh. prom.	*Sakharnaia promyshlennost'* (Soviet)
Sel'. khoz.	*Sel'skoe khoziaistvo* (Soviet)

Sel'khoz-1960	Tsentral'noe Statisticheskoe Upravlenie pri Sovete Ministrov SSSR. *Sel'skoe khoziaistvo SSSR* (Moscow: 1960)
Sel'. zh.	*Sel'skaia zhizn'* (Soviet)
Soc. Pol.	*Socijalna Politika* (Yugoslav)
Soc. Sela	*Sociologija Sela* (Yugoslav)
Sots. khoz.	*Sotsialisticheskoe khoziaistvo* (Soviet)
Sots. rek. sel'. khoz.	*Sotsialisticheskaia rekonstruktsiia sel'skogo khoziaistva* (Soviet)
Sots. sel'. khoz.	*Sotsialisticheskoe sel'skoe khoziaistvo* (Soviet)
Sots. zem.	*Sotsialisticheskoe zemledelie* (Soviet)
Sov. Ross.	*Sovetskaia Rossiia* (Soviet)
Sred. spets. obraz.-1962	*Srednee spetsial'noe obrazovanie v SSSR* (Moscow: 1962)
SSSR v tsifrakh-1964	Tsentral'noe Statisticheskoe Upravlenie pri Sovete Ministrov SSSR, *SSSR v tsifrakh v 1964 godu* (Moscow: 1965)
Stat.	*Statistika* (Czechoslovak)
Stat. God.-1964	Savenzi Zavod za Statistiku, *Statistički Godišnjak SFRJ, 1964* (Belgrade: 1964)
Stat. přeh.	*Statistické přehledy* (Czechoslovak)
Stat. Rev.	*Statističke Revije* (Yugoslav)
Stat. roč.-. . .	Abbreviation used for the official Czechoslovak statistical handbook, published in Prague until 1959 under the title *Statistická ročenka Republiky Československé* . . . and thereafter as *Statistická ročenka Československé socialistické republiky* . . . in the year referred to in the title
Stroi. komm.	N. S. Khrushchev, *Stroitel'stvo kommunizma i razvitie sel'skogo khoziaistva v SSSR* (Moscow: 1962–1964) 8 volumes
Trud. Vol'. ek. obshch.	*Trudy Vol'nogo ekonomicheskogo obshchestva* (Russian)
Uchet i fin.	*Uchet i finansy v kolkhozakh i sovkhozakh* (Soviet)
Vest. Ak. Nauk	*Vestnik Akademii Nauk* (Soviet)

Vest. Mosk. Un.	*Vestnik Moskovskogo Universiteta* (Soviet)
Vest. sel'. nauki	*Vestnik sel'skokhoziaistvennoi nauki* (Soviet)
Vest. stat.	*Vestnik statistiki* (Soviet)
Vnesh. torg.-. . .	Abbreviation used for the official Soviet handbook of statistics on foreign trade, published in Moscow under the title *Vneshnaia torgovlia SSSR za . . . god* (or *gody*)
Vop. ek.	*Voprosy ekonomiki* (Soviet)
Vop. fil.	*Voprosy filozofii* (Soviet)
Vop. geog.	*Voprosy geografii* (Soviet)
Vyssh. obraz.-1961	*Vysshee obrazovanie v SSSR* (Moscow: 1961)
Wiés Współ.	*Wies Współczesna* (Polish)
Za soc. zem.	*Za socialistické zemědělství* (Czechoslovak)
Zag. Ek. Roln.	*Zagadnienia Ekonomiki Rolnej* (Polish)
Zem.	*Zemledelie* (Soviet)
Zem. ek.	*Zemědělská ekonomika* (Czechoslovak)
Zem. nov.	*Zemědělské noviny* (Czechoslovak)
Zhen. i deti-. . .	Abbreviation used for the official handbook of statistical data on women and children published in Moscow under the title *Zhenshchiny i deti v SSSR* in 1961 and again in 1963
Zhen.-SSSR-1960	*Zhenshchina v SSSR* (Moscow: 1960)
Życie Gosp.	*Życie Gospodarcze* (Polish)

LAZAR VOLIN

Khrushchev and the Soviet Agricultural Scene

The fall of Khrushchev in October, 1964, brought to an end an era of unparalleled personal influence and impact on Russian agriculture. Never before in Russian history had one as intimately identified with agriculture as Khrushchev by background, experience, and intellectual and political interests so great an opportunity to shape its destiny for so long. Khrushchev's close association with agricultural policy began under Stalin, but it reached its pinnacle after Stalin, when Khrushchev came to be known to the world as Mr. Russian Agriculture. Even after he became the national leader, he remained engrossed in agricultural problems and continued as the chief architect of agrarian policy until the end. In a collectivized society, it is principally government policy that molds the institutional arrangements, the socioeconomic environment and, to a large extent, the technology with which the farmer must work in cooperation with nature to produce food and fibers.

Now that Khrushchev has become an unperson, as a number of other Soviet dignitaries under his regime, it should be worthwhile to take a brief look once more at his stewardship of Soviet agriculture, even though it is too early for a final verdict.

KHRUSHCHEV AS A LEADER

We might begin by setting forth Khrushchev's conception of what leadership in agriculture should not be. His target was, of course, his former master and teacher, Stalin. In his famous "secret speech" at the Twentieth Party Congress in February, 1956, Khrushchev said:

All those who interested themselves even a little in the national situation saw the difficult situation in agriculture, but Stalin never even noted it. Did we tell Stalin about this? Yes, we told him, but he did not support us. Why? Because Stalin never traveled anywhere, did not meet city and collective farm workers; he did not know the actual situation in the provinces. He knew the country and agriculture only from films. And these films had dressed up and beautified the existing situation in agriculture. Many films so pictured collective farm life that the tables were bending from the weight of turkeys and geese. Evidently, Stalin thought it was actually so. . . . The last time he visited a village was in January 1938, when he visited Siberia in connection with grain deliveries. How then could he have known the situation in the provinces?

Perhaps Stalin was not so ignorant of agricultural difficulties as Khrushchev represents and deliberately disregarded them in order to concentrate on advancing the lopsided industrialization and armaments. In any event, Khrushchev knew what the score was in the countryside. Unlike Stalin, he traveled frequently and widely in farm regions and saw things for himself. He completed the last such long agricultural tour in eastern and southeastern regions only shortly before his fall. In addition to informal contacts with farmers, agricultural specialists, and officials, there were the more formal agricultural conferences at different points in the country and in Moscow, including enlarged sessions of the Central Committee, where Khrushchev could engage in a dialogue with knowledgeable local people; though, because of his brusque and domineering manner, the dialogue probably was often not as productive as it might have been. At any rate, it must be gratefully acknowledged that publication of proceedings of these conferences, including Khrushchev's long speeches, provided Western specialists with considerable material on Soviet agriculture—certainly much more than was vouchsafed during the arid Stalin days.

Khrushchev's aggressiveness and flamboyance was bound to make for dynamic leadership in any field. He was helped in agriculture by his peasant background which no other Soviet leader at the *summit* had. Khrushchev was born and reared in the village and worked as a typical peasant boy until his family moved to the Donetsk industrial region, where he was employed as a skilled worker. If he had any sympathy for the peasants, it was no doubt greatly diluted by his primitive Marxism for which peasant agriculture and village epitomize socioeconomic backwardness. But Khrushchev certainly knew the village, knew the peasants, and could talk their language. Perhaps the peasant background accounted for Khrushchev's scorn for what he called the *barski* attitude, which may be translated as gentlemanly disdain for agriculture of *some*

Communist bureaucrats, even in responsible positions, who looked upon it as a kind of a second-rate occupation. He said in this connection: "Such people do not understand the simple truth that without the advance of agriculture the problems of building communism cannot be successfully solved. Communist society cannot be built without an abundance of grain, meat, milk, butter, vegetables, and other agricultural products." [1]

These words from Khrushchev's first speech as a leader in September, 1953, especially those relating to the need of abundance, became the leitmotiv of his utterances during the next eleven years. The same attitude prompted his insistence on bringing agricultural officials and specialists nearer to grassroots, including the shifting of most of the Ministry of Agriculture to a state farm some distance from Moscow (which was later rescinded). But here, as in so many other Khrushchev moves, no proper provision was made for living conditions—housing, transportation, and so on, which resulted in considerable hardships for those affected.

Khrushchev's agricultural background no doubt heightened his interest and curiosity about agriculture. It was inevitable that top Soviet leadership would be concerned with the agricultural problems after Stalin's demise, but Khrushchev, I believe, really liked to immerse himself in such problems and was interested in their technical aspects. This is evidenced from the attention to numerous details of agricultural production and farm practices with which his speeches are filled, even assuming that he had assistance in writing them. To me this interest was brought home more tangibly during a meeting of Khrushchev with the U.S. Secretary of Agriculture, Freeman, and his party in the summer of 1963. I still remember the enthusiasm displayed by Khrushchev, who was generally rather in a low key that morning, when he told us about reading a report of some German farmer of his success in producing meat with an unusually small quantity of feed. Khrushchev became excited over it and also over the prospects of increased production of chemical fertilizer, with which he was preoccupied at that time.

It is undeniable that he acquired considerable technical knowledge of agriculture and took every opportunity to increase his first-hand knowledge by visiting farms and research institutions during numerous trips in the U.S.S.R. and abroad.

Khrushchev was anxious to adopt innovations representing the latest achievements of agricultural science and technology, Soviet and for-

[1] *Stroi. komm.*, I, 77.

eign. Although he wanted to "bury" the United States, he, nevertheless, greatly admired American farm technology and productivity and sought to emulate them. But the coin had a reverse side because of Khrushchev's impulsiveness and lack of systematic scientific training. Khrushchev felt confident that he could judge, and arbitrate between, conflicting scientific and technical proposals and claims. For this, however, he lacked the necessary training and intellectual equipment and often was wrong. The reluctance or inability of Soviet scientists and specialists to criticize freely a position that Khrushchev had adopted or to which he appeared to be veering, made the possibility of wrong decisions and falling for nostrums much easier. Some examples of Khrushchev's wrong choices were: the support of Lysenko, the foe of classical genetics; the excesses of the corn and New Lands campaign; the taboo on perennial grasses in regions where they have long been an important and useful feature of the farm economy; the negative reaction against summer fallow, considered by specialists essential in the dry regions; and a number of other practices on which Khrushchev's views ran counter to many of the best authorities on the subject. This is supposedly what the Soviet spokesmen mean now when they accuse Khrushchev of being "subjective," "unscientific," and displaying the attitude of "knowing it all." Certainly Khrushchev represents a curious amalgam of pragmatism and extremism, of realism and Marxian dogmatism, of modern outlook and an unscientific pie-in-the-sky psychology.

The changing climate for scientific research signalized by Lysenko's dismissal and severe public criticism of his pseudo-scientific theories and methods of operation, after Khrushchev's fall, may prove to be one of the most significant beneficial developments of the post-Khrushchev period, provided, of course, that there will not be another setback. The importance of this change for agriculture stems from the consensus that expansion of agricultural production in Russia depends now primarily on intensification, on increased crop yields per acre, and greater productivity of animals. These, to a considerable extent, are a function of scientific and technological progress, which Lysenkoism impeded.

During Khrushchev's leadership a renascence of agricultural economics and other phases of economic science developed which were neglected under Stalin. This has been manifested in the creation or reestablishment of research institutions like the Institute of Agricultural Economics in Moscow, the increased number of economic studies pursued, and the growing literature on economic subjects. Khrushchev gave an impetus to this development by his cost consciousness, by his insistence that, "it is impossible to carry on farming without a thorough analysis of the cost of commodities being produced and without control by means of the ruble."[2] Shades of Alfred Marshall's "measuring rod of money"! The word *podshchitat'*—to calculate—was a favorite of Khrushchev. This economic calculus which he tried to instill was a new phenomenon in the management of Soviet agriculture, heretofore preoccupied almost exclusively with physical targets. Here is where economists come in. There has been a new interest in research on such subjects as theory and methodology of farm costs, prices, incomes, the size of the farm unit, and others.

But Khrushchev did not hesitate to heap scorn on economists, as he did on other scientists, when they differed with him on a subject on which he held strong views. A case in point was his celebrated slogan of catching up with the United States by the early 1960's in per-capita production of milk and meat. The unnamed economists whom he consulted thought that 1975 was a better target date, but this heresy brought upon them Khrushchev's wrath.[3] Khrushchev often committed the sin of excessive and unwarranted optimism in setting high unrealistic goals which encouraged falsification and other poor practices.

Progress under Khrushchev was less impressive on the statistical front. True, much more statistical information has been published, though there is lack of consistency from year to year, and some important material like farm household budgets is still withheld, while data on incomes and utilization of farm products are fragmentary or nonexistent. But the greatest difficulty is again with the heart of agricultural statistics—production statistics, particularly those dealing with grains. Even the Soviet sources are beginning to admit the inflation of published figures of grain production, confirming the serious misgivings of Western specialists. When will we have reliable Soviet crop statistics?

Khrushchev and his colleagues understood very well that the central domestic problem was Stalin's legacy of a weak agriculture, a sector that was growing too slowly after the devastation of World War II, compared to the rapid strides made by the heavy and war industries that were much more favored by the regime. It is symptomatic that in the same speech in August, 1953, in which Malenkov, then chairman of the Council of Ministers of the U.S.S.R., preceded Khrushchev in disclosing the sad state of agriculture, he also announced the successful development of the hydrogen bomb. When Malenkov and Khrushchev stripped the agricultural picture of the false statistical façade of inflated, so-called biological crop figures, no doubt was left that the country had been

[2] *Ibid.*, II, 419.
[3] *Ibid.*, p. 450.

suffering from serious agricultural underproduction, which had long bedeviled the collectivized Russian agriculture. And this was in the face of a steady increase in the number of mouths to be fed, 3 million a year, not to mention the long-standing expectations by the people of an improvement in the standards of living, which the Communists, including even Stalin, had often promised. Now that Stalin was no longer at the helm, his heirs, and above all Khrushchev, realized that they could not proceed at the Fabian pace of their predecessor who could rely on his prestige—the cult of the personality—and on the fear instilled by terror. But terror had a demoralizing effect on people's morale and productive effort: ultimately it was self-defeating.

Khrushchev was also aware of the favorable effect that an improved standard of living would have on the international image of the Soviet Union, particularly in the underdeveloped societies, for which he made a strong pitch. He considered such an improvement a potent factor in Communist competition with the capitalist world. As he put it: "If we catch up with the United States in per-capita production of meat, butter and milk, we will fire the most powerful torpedo against the foundations of capitalism." [4]

The task of agricultural leadership, then, which faced Khrushchev, was to increase agricultural production greatly, a feat that had to be accomplished as speedily as possible and at a reasonable cost. With this overriding objective in mind, various agricultural reforms were undertaken by Khrushchev. The principal ones were: first, increase of economic incentives for the peasants; second, increase of capital and related inputs; third, introduction of certain institutional reforms to make agricultural operations more efficient or to strengthen the Party-state control over agriculture; fourth, adoption of special programs for increased production of certain commodities or regions—the most important among these programs were, the corn and the New Lands campaigns.

ECONOMIC INCENTIVES

Economic incentives to peasants were notoriously neglected during the Stalin era, especially after World War II. The crux of the matter was heavy government exactions of farm products at extremely low prices, which were far below costs. With the exception of cotton and some specialty crops, it was all a big stick and hardly any carrot for the peasant masses. It was imperative, therefore, to raise the prices paid by the government. This would increase the income of the collectives and

[4] *Ibid.*, p. 451.

make possible larger earnings of the peasants. Much had been done in this direction under Khrushchev. The index of procurement prices for all farm production was tripled between 1952 and 1959; grain prices were increased 7.4 times and livestock prices 12.4 times.[5] This shows, by the way, how ridiculously low prices had been under Stalin.

Yet further price increases were necessary to cover production costs because of the low productivity of labor and low yields per unit of land. Parenthetically, low productivity of labor was partly caused by insufficient incentives, partly by inadequate equipment, by poor farm management, and organization. Insofar as higher prices resulted in larger earnings and greater incentives to farm workers, an important obstacle to higher productivity and lower costs was removed. A number of examples of such an "economy of higher wages" were given in Soviet economic literature.[6]

Some of the additional upward price adjustments, particularly for livestock, cotton, and a few other products, were made in the early 1960's under Khrushchev. For grains, a flexible price system was established in 1958, which provided for variation of prices with annual fluctuations of output in different regions. According to the Minister of Agriculture, Matskevich, the good crop in 1958 led to a general lowering of grain prices, but they were not increased in subsequent years when climatic conditions were less favorable and output decreased.[7] Also, according to Matskevich, when prices were fixed in 1958 for grain and other farm products, it was assumed that the prices of industrial inputs used in agriculture would be stable. But prices of tractors, trucks, and spare parts were raised.[8] Thus, the income of collectives was decreasing as a result of lower prices for the products they were marketing and of increased prices of inputs. While prices of some inputs were lowered in the 1960's, others were not and continued to be high. This was true of so important an input as chemical fertilizer, for which a large expansion program was announced in 1963.[9] Increased capital accumulation in collective farms, which was officially encouraged and often took wasteful forms, exemplified by the highly elaborate barns for livestock—so-called "cow palaces"—also made heavy inroads on the collective-farm income. The liquidation of machine-tractor stations in 1958 placed a

[5] *Sel'khoz-1960*, p. 117.

[6] Akademiia nauk SSSR, Institut ekonomiki, *Material'noe stimulirovanie razvitiia kolkhoznogo proizvodstva* (Moscow: 1963), pp. 19–29, 77–102.

[7] V. Matskevich, *Vop. ek.*, No. 6 (1965), p. 5.

[8] Nancy Nimitz, "The Lean Years," *Problems of Communism*, XIV:3 (May–June, 1965), pp. 14–15.

[9] S. G. Kolesnev, *Izv. Timir. Sel'. Ak.*, No. 2 (1965), pp. 6–7.

serious financial burden on the weak collectives especially because of the speeding up of the payments for machinery purchased from the state, which was supposed to have been paid off gradually on an installment basis.[10] Since labor is in practice the residual claimant to the income of the collectives, it usually has to absorb the depressing effect of these various pressures on income, including the adverse effects of weather on output. And, climatically, the years 1959–1963 were mediocre or outright poor.

The average earnings of collective-farm workers increased considerably between 1952 and 1957; but there are no firm national figures for subsequent years, only conflicting claims. According to one source, average payments in money and in kind to collective farmers did not increase between 1957 and 1960, and even declined in a number of regions.[11] A later source claims that between 1958 and 1962 the average monthly payment to the collective farm workers increased by 23 percent.[12] However, it was admitted that the average monthly earnings of peasants in the collectives in 1962 were from one-half to one-third less than the earnings of state farm workers, who are among the lowest paid strata of state employees.[13] But many weak collectives were converted into state farms and this provided, together with migration to the cities and small private farming on household allotments, the avenue of escape from inadequate earnings in collectives.

The foregoing explains the present criticism of Khrushchev's regime for not devoting sufficient attention to economic incentives. Khrushchev did recognize the importance of such stimuli. From the outset, however, he was reluctant to raise prices and preached the need of increased productivity and reduced costs, which would make possible the lowering of prices. He even published figures which showed exceedingly high labor requirements for production of crops and livestock products in Soviet agriculture as compared with the United States. For production of a centner of grain, for instance, 80 percent more man-hours were required on state farms and 630 percent more man-hours on collective farms than on U.S. farms.[14]

[10] Matskevich, *op. cit.*

[11] V. Khlebnikov, *Vop. ek.*, No. 7 (1962), p. 50.

[12] G. Sarkisian, *Ek. sel'. khoz.*, No. 12 (1964), p. 9. This claim may perhaps be valid if the comparison was made between the reduced number of collectives existing in 1962 and the same collectives in 1958, which would have excluded the many weak collectives converted into state farms during this period. The sharp increase in livestock prices in June, 1962, might also have been relevant.

[13] *Ibid.*

[14] *Stroi. komm.*, III, 420.

What deterred Khrushchev was the inflationary effect of raising prices in the face of the government's policy of according highest priority to the heavy and armament industries as against the expansion of consumer goods output. The latter expanded under Khrushchev but not sufficiently. He recognized that unless an upsurge took place in production of consumer goods of the kind which the population wanted, and at reasonable prices and tolerable quality, the demand resulting from higher incomes generated by increased economic incentives would merely create an inflationary situation of "rubles chasing goods."

On this question of "proportions" as the problem of priorities of different sectors of the national economy is known in the Soviet parlance, Khrushchev, during the early years of his leadership, sided with the heavy industry faction against Malenkov and the school of thought which favored an expansion of the light industry. Thus, Khrushchev's industrial policy, though it was not as extreme as Stalin's, nevertheless conflicted with the agricultural policy insofar as the latter urgently required steadily increased economic incentives to achieve its objectives.

Later, especially during the last two years before his ouster, there were significant indications of a change in Khrushchev's attitude on the question of priorities, in favor of the consumer and of agriculture. This growing consumer-mindedness and the closely related concern with agricultural stagnation were the reason for Khrushchev's strong emphasis on a rapid development of the chemical industry (plastics and synthetic fibers; chemical fertilizers and pesticides). How far Khrushchev would have gone in narrowing the growth gap between heavy and light industries if he remained in power is anybody's guess. I venture to suggest, however, that unless and until the problem of priorities or "proportions" is resolved, the question of economic incentives in Soviet agriculture cannot be solved in a satisfactory manner, though it cannot be denied that progress was made since the lean Stalin days.

There was considerable experimentation under the Khrushchev regime in attempting to improve the cumbersome workday system of remuneration in collectives. This included spacing of payments throughout the year instead of lumping them at the end of the season; introduction of some sort of a guaranteed minimum wage; replacement of payments in kind and in cash by a single cash wage; relation of payments to output, and so on. Some of these schemes were successful in certain collectives but not in others. The nub of the difficulty, however, has been no strict earmarking of the wage fund in the collectives. It would probably also require some definite form of assistance, perhaps through a central intercollective fund, or extension of credit by the state, when the wage bill cannot be met temporarily by a collective.

While dealing with economic incentives to the collectivized peasantry, we should not overlook the improvement in fringe benefits introduced during the last months of Khrushchev's regime. The quality of the free medical service and education should improve with the increased salaries of rural doctors and teachers decreed in July, 1964. Pensions to aged collective farmers, which formerly depended upon the action of individual collectives and often meant inaction, were placed on a uniform national basis by the July-1964 legislation. They are paid out of a central fund created largely by contributions of collective farms, of about 3-4 percent of their income, and a supplementary appropriation by the state (about 800 million rubles by collectives and 500 to 600 million by the state). A survey of seven collectives of the Novgorod province showed the number of pensioners increasing from 79 in 1963 to 491 under the new law; the pension per month increased from 8 to 20.6 rubles respectively; and the total annual payments from 6,338 rubles to 101,313.[15] Paid leave is now provided for expectant mothers in collectives, similar to that of other female workers. The July-1964 legislation must be viewed as a modest step toward diminishing the gap between the city worker and the collective farmer.

CAPITAL INVESTMENT

Another problem also related to the question of industrial priorities and economic incentives is that of capital investment in agriculture. Shortage of capital equipment has been an old weakness of Russian agriculture. Khrushchev himself admitted that, "One cannot demand high productivity of labor and hack corn with an axe." He showed how far short of estimated requirements were the inventories of Soviet farm machinery. There were, for instance, less than 1.2 million tractors on farms on January 1, 1962, although nearly 2.7 million were required to perform the necessary field work during optimum periods.[16] The United States, with a 1962 acreage 45 percent smaller and, on the whole, a more efficient operation of machinery, had on farms 4.8 million tractors.

State agricultural investment, it is true, increased rapidly between 1953 and 1957, when a great expansion of acreage took place, but decreased both in 1958 and 1959, notwithstanding the growth of the state farm sectors. While investment again showed an upward trend since 1960, it constituted a smaller share of the total state investment in

[15] Sarkisian, *op. cit.*, p. 13.
[16] *Stroi. komm.*, VI, 427.

national economy than during the years 1954–1959.[17] Despite the shortages of farm implements, the volume of metal allocated for manufacturing of tractors and other agricultural machinery reportedly was less annually by 20 to 40 percent during the first years of the Seven-Year Plan, 1959–1965, as compared with 1957. Therefore, some of the farm-implement factories shifted to the production of other machinery.[18] These facts point to a rather low priority of agriculture in the Soviet economic scheme. The investments of a decreasing number of collective farms, made from their own income, increased significantly during 1959–1963. If the payment of 1.8 billion rubles for machinery bought from machine-tractor stations is added, the total investment of collectives for 1959–1963 was about 18.3 billion rubles as against 18.2 billion of state agricultural investment. It represented an increase of 7.4 billion rubles over the total collective-farm investment during 1954–1958. But the large investment of the collectives, as indicated before, reduced the funds available for payment to their members, with a resulting decrease of economic incentives.

Much has been said and written in the U.S.S.R. about the gap existing between the so-called "advanced," progressive collectives and the backward ones. The management of the more efficient farms was usually applauded by the press and official statements, while the management of the retarded farms was criticized and told to "pull up" (*podtianutsia*) to the level of the more efficient collectives. What is often overlooked in such pronouncements is the role played by an adequate supply of capital and the quality of land in the performance of the different categories of farms. A Soviet economist estimated that the more efficient collectives in 1962 had 2.45 times greater capital investment per 100 hectares of arable land than the average for all collectives. The advanced collectives also applied 3 times *more* mineral fertilizer and 2.2 times more organic matter per hectare than the average for all collectives; the payment to labor was 2 to 2.5 times higher; the output per 100 hectares was 2.6 times higher than the average for all collectives.[19] The situation was similar with other indicators, which underscores the significance of proper equipment and other inputs.

One illustration of the relation between input and efficiency is the collective Kalinovka in Khrushchev's native village, which he held up on several occasions as having become a model farm, thanks to its efficient

[17] *Soviet Agriculture Today: Report of 1963 Agriculture Exchange Delegation*, Foreign Agricultural Economic Report No. 13 (Washington, D.C.: U.S. Department of Agriculture, December, 1963), p. 67.
[18] M. Terent'ev, *Vop. ek.*, No. 4 (1965), p. 8.
[19] *Ibid.*, p. 9.

management. The capital investment per 100 hectares in Kalinovka was more than 4 times larger than the average for the whole Kursk province where the village is situated. Significantly, the share of the state in capital formation in Kalinovka was 78.8 percent, and for all collectives of the province 44.8 percent. Nearly 7 times as much mineral fertilizer was used in Kalinovka than the average for the Kursk province and production per 100 hectares was 5.6 times greater.[20]

It is interesting to speculate on what might have been the result of a substantially larger investment in agriculture and in industries directly supporting it like those manufacturing farm implements, fertilizers, or pesticides. Such a situation would have made possible a more balanced program of expansion which would have relied to a much greater extent on improvement in crop yields than on expansion of acreage. In other words, considerable headway could have been made on the kind of program that Khrushchev began to pursue actively toward the end of his regime and which his successors are now continuing. The following are some of the more important measures which could have been taken if more capital had been allocated: stepped up use of chemical fertilizer, of which the U.S.S.R. applies only about one-fourth per acre in terms of plant nutrients compared to the United States; increased use of pesticides; liming of acid soils; drainage and other forms of reclamation of land outside the black soil area where considerably higher and more stable yields can be obtained than in the drier regions; irrigation of a substantial area in the dry zone; increased mechanization and electrification which would have made for speedier and more timely farm operations—an important matter in a country with a short season. The results would have been reflected in higher output, though the lack of know-how, faulty farm practices, the built-in shortcomings of the collective-farm system, and the weather would have limited the extent of the expansion, especially in the beginning. But the leverage of the huge acreage in magnifying even a modest increase in the yield per acre also should not be overlooked. If such a program had been initiated early enough, it would have been possible for the Soviets to build up sufficient grain reserves, which would have helped them to cope more adequately with such crop failures as occurred in 1963 and 1965.

EXPANSION OF PRODUCTION

Because of a relatively limited increase in farm investment, Khrushchev jettisoned the large irrigation program adopted toward the end of the

[20] *Ibid.*

Stalin era and resorted to the traditional Russian method of agricultural expansion—more and more acres under crops. This meant a further extension of the sown area in the steppes east of the Volga and the Urals where large tracts of uncultivated land suitable for mechanized farming were available. It involved, however, expansion into a climatically hazardous area. Here severe winters made it impossible to grow high-yielding winter grain. A short and often delayed growing season for spring crops; frequent droughts, accompanied by scorching winds which played havoc with the crops and resulted in soil erosion; and often rain or frost which interferes with the harvest—all these and an abundance of weeds are the conditions which plague the farmers in these marginal regions. At the outset Khrushchev talked blandly of expected yields of 10–11 and even 15 centners per hectare, but said nothing about weather difficulties of which he was doubtless aware. He banked on good crop years compensating for poor harvests. After the poor 1955 harvest, Khrushchev indicated that he would be satisfied if out of every five years there were two good and two poor harvests, and one average harvest.[21] Actually in the beginning weather was on his side, with good crops every other year (1954, 1956, and 1958). But after 1958, there was only one really good harvest, in 1964; it was preceded by the catastrophic 1963 harvest and followed by poor crops again in 1965.

The adverse climatic conditions were aggravated by the neglect of proper farm practices suitable to semi-arid regions. Stubble-mulching, which is widely used in the dry farming areas of the United States and Canada, was an exception in the Soviet New Lands. Even summer fallow, which is such an important and well-known method of weed control and conservation of moisture in the dry regions of the United States and Canada, was little practiced in the Soviet New Lands. The chase of farm managers for more acres to be planted to crops and the fact that Khrushchev, who was persuaded that row crops like corn could replace summer fallow, and came to look upon the latter with a jaundiced eye, militated against a wide use of this valuable yield-improving practice.

Despite the low yields, the New Lands area has become important as the major source of grain for the government, accounting on the average during 1954–1963 for more than 50 percent of the total grain procurements. The good crop in 1964 gave another boost to the region. Khrushchev volunteered the information during the meeting with Secretary Freeman in the summer of 1963, that, if the crop yields should

[21] *Stroi. komm.*, II, 195.

generally increase in the country, a reduction of acreage in the New Lands might take place. Some reduction may also occur in the next few years to give room for more summer fallow. But until there is a substantial increase in grain production in the traditional agricultural regions, the New Lands will continue to be important to the regime as a source of grain despite the vulnerability to weather.

Khrushchev was also intimately identified with the expansion of corn-growing in the Soviet Union, which he began promoting on a large scale in 1955, as a cornerstone in a changing crop pattern. From a minor crop, corn rose to a major place in the Soviet crop structure as a result of Khrushchev's campaign. He insisted on corn being grown practically throughout the vast land, either for grain or, where it cannot mature, for silage. Again, climatic conditions—the fact that in many regions it is either too cold or too dry for corn-growing—did not deter Khrushchev. His attachment to corn, which he called the "queen of the fields" was motivated by the need of increasing the lagging feed supply, a great bottleneck in livestock production. And it is true that corn, where it can be advantageously grown, is a highly productive and nourishing field crop. The American experience with corn constituted the model on which Khrushchev patterned his experiment. The favorable climatic conditions in the American corn belt combined with an abundance of cheap fertilizers, high-yielding hybrid varieties, adequate mechanization—all lacking in the U.S.S.R.—made for a vastly different situation in the United States. But this Khrushchev refused to recognize in pushing his crash program to make corn a major Soviet product.

Because it became a "must" crop in the U.S.S.R., low-yielding corn was displacing other crops more suitable to the climatic and soil conditions of their regions. Oats, rye, and perennial grasses bore the brunt, since they were held in disfavor by Khrushchev. The great expansion of grasses was one of the survivals of the Stalin era, when it was adopted on the recommendation of a Russian soil scientist of American parentage, Robert Williams, who considered perennial grasses absolutely essential to the improvement of the structure and fertility of soils. While Khrushchev had a case against grasses in the drier regions because of low yields, he had none in the more humid northern and central regions; and neither was Khrushchev's negative attitude toward oats or neglect of rye in these regions well founded. The valuable winter (fall-sown) wheat was also displaced in some regions by corn, and it was also adversely affected by the late maturing and harvesting of corn. This led to late sowing of winter wheat when it followed corn with a detrimental effect on yields.

Because of low yields, some deemphasis of corn began already during the last years of Khrushchev's regime, when he recommended pulses, particularly peas, and also sugar beets as useful feed crops. After Khrushchev's fall, corn lost its special status of a queen of the fields but it is still officially recommended—and properly so—for limited regions where conditions are suitable for its growth. The area under corn for mature grain decreased from 17 million acres in 1962 and 1963 to 7.9 million in 1965, or less than in 1953, before the expansion campaign started.

The programs discussed above and those for other crops and livestock, the resulting greatly increased acreage, the favorable weather during several years, and improved economic incentives and capital inputs, compared to those of the Stalin era did bring about a considerable expansion of agricultural production during 1954–1958, variously measured at 40 to 50 percent. (See "Soviet Agricultural Output by 1970," by Harry E. Walters and Richard Judy). After this plateau little progress followed, and in some years retrogression occurred. This was the situation despite Khrushchev's ambitious goals of increasing agricultural production by 70 percent between the very good year 1958 and 1965 and of catching up with the United States by the early 1960's in per-capita production of milk and meat. Inadequate inputs of resources for the needed intensification of agriculture, their inefficient utilization under the collective system, and unfavorable weather developments were the reasons for the retardation. The Kremlin found out that intensification of agriculture, involving increased crop yields per acre and productivity per animal, is a far more difficult and sophisticated task than merely adding more acres to the sown area and animals to the herd.

INSTITUTIONAL CHANGES

Khrushchev introduced significant changes not only in the crop structure but also in the institutional organization of Soviet agriculture. Perhaps the outstanding change was the liquidation of the machine-tractor-stations (MTS) in 1958, and the sale of their machinery to the collectives. It was a measure which Stalin vigorously opposed in his time. Its objective to eliminate "two bosses on the land," as Khrushchev put it, that is, the management of the collective farms and the MTS, was a worthy one. However, the weaker collectives suffered, as pointed out earlier, from the heavy financial burden of paying for the machinery and other supplies. They also experienced difficulties with the repair of machinery, which has not been well organized.

The liquidation of the MTS was to a considerable extent a logical consequence of another major organizational development associated with Khrushchev's name. This was the merger and enlargement of collective farms or their conversion into state farms, which reduced the number of collectives from more than 250,000 at the beginning of 1950 to a little over 38,000 at the end of 1964. This situation sometimes resulted in one MTS serving one large collective farm, or in being absorbed into a state farm together with the collectives it serviced.

The merger campaign, like the corn drive, extended to every region of the vast country—north, south, east, and west—regions with most diverse natural and economic conditions. As a result, the size of the collective farms greatly increased. At the end of 1950, when the merger campaign was in its beginning, a collective farm, on the average, had 165 families; at the end of 1963 it had 411. In 1950 a collective farm had a sown area of a little less than 2,400 acres; in 1963, 7,156 acres. The average number of cattle was 224 head in 1950, and 944 head in 1963.[22] Many collectives were much larger; 29 percent in 1963 had more than 500 families each as against 13 percent in 1958. Less than 16 percent of the collectives included only one village; 48 percent had 2 to 5, and 20 percent had 6 to 10 villages.[23]

The gigantism is even more prevalent in state farms. The number of state farms increased from about 5,000 in 1950 to 9,176 at the end of 1963, and the average sown area increased from 6,400 acres to about 24,000. The number of workers per state farm rose from about 300 in 1950 to 775 in 1963.[24] Most recent statistics indicate some reduction in the size of state farms.

The slogan, "The Bigger the Farm the Better," and the consequent confusion of the largest with the optimum size had long dominated Soviet policy under Khrushchev as under Stalin. This cult of bigness has its roots in the Marxist dogma of the superiority of large-scale production in agriculture similar to that in industry. Giantism may also have some political advantages in the context of the Soviet rule. It tends to widen the gulf between the rank-and-file peasant membership and the collective-farm management, now largely in the hands of outsiders. This gap enhances the driving power of management over labor. The large size may also facilitate central control of collective farms. I believe, however, that the over-all economic effect of the chase after superlarge farms is largely negative. It was one of the great errors

[22] *Sel'khoz-1960*, p. 59 and *Narkhoz-1963*, p. 342.
[23] *Narkhoz-1963*, p. 344.
[24] *Sel'khoz-1960*, p. 49 and *Narkhoz-1963*, p. 359.

committed by Khrushchev in the field of agricultural policy. There was some cautious criticism of giantism in the Soviet Union itself, and experimentation with subdivision for operational purposes of the large farms has been going on. Studies of the proper size of farms, formerly nonexistent, now find a place in the programs of research institutes like the Moscow Institute of Agricultural Economics. The possibility of subdivision of the giant farms in the future cannot be ruled out.

Officially, the coexistence of the collectives and state farms will continue in the foreseeable future. In the meantime, the positive features of either type of organization are to be adopted by both. But there is a school of thought in the U.S.S.R. which is rooting for state-farming as a means of overcoming completely, as one economist put it, the remnants of "anarchism" of individual farming. Another school of thought pins its hope on collective farming, making much of the fondness of the peasant for the soil. It has always seemed to me that the decisive factor in the fate of the collectives will be the willingness of the government to foot their wage and investment bills. When it is ready to do so, wholesale conversion into state farms may take place.

Another institutional change initiated by Khrushchev was decentralization of agricultural planning. The folly of a detailed rigid planning of agriculture from Moscow, as practiced under Stalin, had long been obvious. The criticism of the planning methods voiced by Khrushchev and other Soviet spokesmen sounded similar to those long expressed by Western specialists. In 1955 a reform of the agricultural planning procedure was announced which confined central planning to the task of determining the procurement quotas for farm products and the volume of work to be performed by the MTS. The collectives were supposed to be free to plan their crop and livestock production, provided they were able to meet their quotas. Thus a farm in a cotton region had to plant enough cotton to deliver its procurement allotment, and similarly with other regions and crops. But there were also such universal "must" crops as corn, which interfered with the collectives' freedom of planning. The 1955 decree, moreover, gave the MTS a voice in collective-farm planning, and also accorded certain responsibilities in supervision over farm-planning to other local authorities. As a result, these agencies often interfered or usurped the planning functions of collectives. The reform did not work; the freedom of planning by collectives was mostly a fiction. A similar law was passed by the Khrushchev regime in 1964, eliminating the loopholes which made for bureaucratic interference with the planning by collectives. This policy was reaffirmed by Khrushchev's successors and perhaps strengthened by making procurement targets for grains and some other farm products stable for a six-year period.

Much will depend, of course, on a proper allocation of procurement quotas between collectives, and whether they will be really observed by the authorities. It has been a common practice of local authorities to demand deliveries in addition to the fixed quotas, and this had a demoralizing effect on collectives. A premium of 50 percent would have to be paid now by the government for purchases of wheat and rye above quotas.

The collectivist Leviathan has not swallowed, as yet, the small private farming of the collectivized peasantry and other workers on their kitchen garden plots. This private farming is particularly important in livestock production and in growing potatoes, vegetables, and fruit. In 1962, the private sector accounted for 45 percent of total meat and milk production, 76 percent of eggs, 22 percent of wool, 70 percent of potatoes, 42 percent of vegetables, and 66 percent of fruit.[25] The share of the private sector in total agricultural production was estimated by a Soviet source at more than 36 percent.[26] It should be noted that the peasants obtain part of the feed used for their private livestock from the collectives in payment for their labor or by purchase. In turn, young animals sold by peasants to collectives constitute an important source of livestock for collective farms.[27] Most of the work in the private-farm sector is done by women according to a study of 247 collective-farm families, which indicates that women worked 25.95 hours a week during the summer, and men only 8.43 hours.[28]

Ideologically this private sector has been a thorn in the Kremlin's side —a necessary evil which, according to the Party dogma, will wither with the growth of the collective-farm economy and its ability to satisfy fully the demand for farm products. But the attitude of the Soviet government toward the private sector has fluctuated; now relaxing, now tightening up. When things are not going well with Russian agriculture, the private "acre-and-a-cow" type of farming is encouraged by the regime, and vice versa when an improvement ensues in the agricultural situation. This happened under Stalin in the 1930's, and similarly under Khrushchev in the 1950's. The Khrushchev-Malenkov regime, in fact,

[25] *Narkhoz-1962,* pp. 238, 297.

[26] L. I. Egereva, *Balans proizvodstva i raspredeleniia produktsii sel'skogo khoziaistva* (Moscow: 1963), p. 52.

[27] G. Shmelev, *Vop. ek.,* No. 4 (1965), p. 30.

[28] A. S. Dugal', *Vop. fil.* No. 4 (1965), p. 77.

inaugurated its new agricultural program in 1953 with the announcement of a liberalization of the policy toward the private sector and a reduction and simplification of its taxation. However, the encouragement of private farming in 1953 stopped short of a possible encroachment on the collective-farm economy and was acknowledged as transitory by Khrushchev. The old specter of competition of this small farming with the collective-farm economy for the labor and loyalty of peasants still haunted the Kremlin. By 1958 Khrushchev's attitude toward the private sector stiffened. He began to talk about liquidation of livestock belonging to peasants, which is a key element of the private sector. Even sterner measures were adopted against the fairly considerable ownership of livestock by the population outside farms. A reduction of the small land plots by individual collective farms was legally made possible by a law passed in 1956 and was applied by some farms. The sown area of the private sector decreased from 18.2 million acres in 1958 to 15.5 million in 1964.

Khrushchev advocated, and probably sincerely so, a gradual approach in the elimination of the private sector because he realized the detrimental effect which hasty action would have on the food supply both of the population on and off the farms and on the income and morale of the peasants in collectives. The tie which exists in the U.S.S.R. between small private farming and the free market in the cities is well known.[29] The importance of private farming in peasants' earnings can be judged from a sample survey which indicated that 40 percent of the total income of collective farmers in 1957 and 38 percent in the excellent crop year 1958 was derived from sources other than collectives.[30] The lion's share undoubtedly came from small private farming.

As Khrushchev's policy became more restrictive, it was reported that in some cases local authorities, in their zeal to get on the bandwagon, were quicker in repressing the private farm sector of collectives than was intended by the central government, and corrective measures on its part were necessary. At any rate, Khrushchev is now blamed by his successors for unreasonable curbing of the private sector. Indeed, the post-Khrushchev agricultural policy began with liberalization in this field and, characteristically, it coincided with another period of stagnation in Soviet agriculture. An article in *Voprosy ekonomiki,* an important economic journal, suggested that the withering of the private farm sector and its replacement by the collective sector cannot be expected during

[29] Jerzy F. Karcz, "Quantitative Analysis of the Collective Farm Market," *American Economic Review,* LIV:4, part 1 (June, 1964), pp. 315–333.

[30] A. Kraeva, *Vop. ek.,* No. 4 (1961), p. 77.

the next few years, and criticizes the underestimation of this type of farming in the Soviet theoretical literature and the restrictive tactics of the Khrushchev administration.[31] The more liberal attitude towards the private sector adopted by Khrushchev's successors may not last long, if past experience is any guide. But the small private farmer will not easily disappear.

It is clear, then, that the Soviet Union under Khrushchev did not experience a decollectivization comparable to those in other Communist countries after Stalin, particularly in Poland and Yugoslavia. On the contrary, Khrushchev turned Soviet agriculture organizationally toward supercollectivism. Furthermore, since 1962, new administrative controls portending more regimentation were introduced by him. They resulted in the splitting of governmental and Party organs into agricultural and industrial divisions and involved them more closely in management problems. This reform, upsetting the traditional pattern, apparently provoked a serious opposition among the Party-government bureaucracy, and was the first to go after Khrushchev. It did not help him to solve the problem of agricultural stagnation, which bedeviled Soviet agricultural production between the good harvests of 1958 and 1964, as is now officially admitted by the Soviets. As a consequence, the Soviet Union, which was traditionally a major exporter of grain, became a net importer during the past three years.[32]

Khrushchev, during the last two years before his ouster came to grips with the problem of raising crop yields by focusing attention on such sound but costly remedies as increased use of chemical fertilizers, pesticides, irrigation, and reclamation. He became especially enthusiastic about chemical fertilizer, which acquired top priority in his remedial program, formerly held by corn and New Lands. But the implementation of this program, reinforced by new substantial price increases of farm products, lower taxation and prices of inputs, more liberal credit policies, greater capital investment, and more stable procurement policies, was taken out of Khrushchev's hands in October, 1964. His successors, however, started under a bad omen of a poor 1965 harvest. For they too are unable to control the weather.

It is tempting to look for historical analogies to the Khrushchev phase of Soviet agrarian policy, remembering, of course, the imperfect resemblance of all analogies. The closest example is the quasi-N.E.P., which

[31] Shmelev, *op. cit.*, p. 30.

[32] Lazar Volin and Harry E. Walters, *Soviet Grain Imports*, Economic Research Service, ERS-Foreign 135, (Washington, D.C.: U.S. Department of Agriculture, September, 1965), pp. 1–5, 12–14.

took place in the middle 1930's under Stalin, following the collectivization catastrophe. Then, too, there was no decollectivization, but considerable emphasis on economic incentives, on self-government of collective farms, on small private farming of collective farmers, and so on. Going back farther into history, it seems to me that there is also some resemblance between the Khrushchev era and the Stolypin period, which followed the revolution of 1905, unlike as Khrushchev and Stolypin were—one a Communist party leader and the other a tsarist prime minister, who endeavored to save the throne. Khrushchev, like Stolypin, tried to make significant adjustments in the agrarian order without tampering with the basic principles on which this order was grounded. I think that even many admirers of Stolypin, let alone his critics, would concede today that he might have been more successful in his main objective, of forestalling another agrarian revolution, if he had not stopped in his "wager on the strong," short of assuaging the peasants' land hunger by a moderate land reform—by some compulsory distribution with fair compensation of estate land demanded by the peasant masses in 1905–1906. Similarly, one wonders whether Khrushchev's brand of Soviet agrarian reformism might not have produced greater results, as far as agricultural production and food supply are concerned, and certainly as far as the peasant morale and contentment were involved, if the iron grip of collectivism were more relaxed and more liberal policies pursued with respect to capital investment in agriculture, economic incentives, the supply of consumer goods, and managerial decision-making on the farms.

COMMENT

Anatole I. Popluiko

Dr. Volin presents a clear and exhaustive survey of Khrushchev's activity in matters concerning agriculture. One might say that he paints the panorama of Khrushchev's agricultural policy and its consequences from the vantage point of history's main gate. I would like to enlarge the view while looking at the historical process through its kitchen door.

Khrushchev faced the task of effecting rapid improvements in agricultural production, suffering from great neglect that occurred during the war. The condition of the country after the death of Stalin made it imperative that the task be completed rapidly. Thus Khrushchev worked under constant pressure to show immediate results. He himself often advanced the slogan "produce, produce!" and this cry was heard throughout the immense expanse of agricultural, political, government, and other economic organizations of the cumbersome Soviet system. Everything was done hastily in this atmosphere of pressure. It was expected that the adopted measures would yield immediate results, regardless of the fact that the implementation of such measures might ultimately have detrimental consequences. When the choice among alternative policies, designed to raise the volume of output, was made, preference was given to extensive, and at times predatory, methods of soil cultivation, animal husbandry, or the utilization of labor.

The methods used by Khrushchev to extract agricultural products from the farming sector were not original. Similar solutions were adopted in the course of building socialism in the U.S.S.R. Khrushchev did not invent them; he merely exhibited a seething energy, attempting to be an innovator and discoverer. The essence of Stalinist methods consisted of forceful advances in the main direction of the goal, accompanied by disregard of trivial details. The necessary corrections and improvements were always relegated into the future. This is well illustrated by the slogans: "Do not reduce goals to the bottleneck level," and "Get hold of the main link." Such methods of industrializing led to an uninterrupted emergence of bottlenecks and disproportions among the various branches of the economy. Plants in the processing industry were completed while insufficient attention was given to the production of raw materials, destined as inputs for the completed plants. As a result, planned capacity was frequently not attained for prolonged periods, and feverish activity was a characteristic of the operation of leading enterprises. Throughout the period of rapid industrialization nothing was done to narrow the gap between industry and agriculture. The difficulties arising from this policy of forced growth were euphemistically known as "growing pains."

All of Soviet agriculture, beginning with collectivization, was deeply affected by "growing pains" and endless disproportions among various branches of farming. Another disproportion arose between the socialized—one should really say depersonalized—production in state and collective farms and the necessity to provide personal interest in the growth of agricultural production.

The fundamental defects of Soviet agriculture were not corrected by Khrushchev. To put it in military terms, he enlarged the front of his attack but failed to cover his rear. Although considerable successes were achieved in the first five years of Khrushchev's agricultural decade, it proved impossible to consolidate or at times to maintain the achievements.

As far as the assessment of the second period of Khrushchev's reformist activity is concerned, I happen to disagree with the official view of the Communist Party of the Soviet Union which, unfortunately, is at times accepted without reservations by some Western specialists. The present Soviet leaders attempt to explain the recent failures of Soviet agriculture by Khrushchev's alleged departure from the spirit of the decision of the September (1953) plenum of the Central Committee. It is true that the decline in the rate of growth of farm output coincided roughly with the first years of the Seven-Year Plan. Actually, the real cause of these failures should be sought in the temporary achievements of the period 1954–1958. Subsequent failures may be viewed as logical and inevitable consequences of the earlier successes, achieved by forceful measures applied in a manner resembling a frontal cavalry charge. This may well be illustrated by the methods of settlement of the New Lands, where the future location of state farms was determined with the aid of aerial photography. Today, hundreds of thousands of hectares of arable land in these areas are being abandoned annually. With minor exceptions, a steady reduction of total grain output and of yields occurred in the New Lands after 1956. Even the exceedingly favorable harvest years 1958 and 1964 yielded less grain than was gathered in 1956.

A similar picture emerges when we consider trends in animal husbandry. Within a brief period of time Khrushchev managed to achieve a considerable improvement in this sector as well. In 1957 he seriously suggested that by 1960–1961 the Soviet Union would surpass the United States in the per-capita production of butter, meat, and milk. By 1959, the average milk per cow rose to 2,067 kilograms per year. But then an uninterrupted decline set in, until in 1963 each cow gave only 1,584 kilograms of milk.

Developments in other sectors will not be discussed in detail. Everywhere, however, Khrushchev's measures initially brought a visible improvement, but this was later followed by a retardation of growth rates, by stagnation, and at times by an absolute decline. Every success culminated in a crisis. Khrushchevian measures played about the same role in agriculture that doping does in sports.

Cheerful communiques of achieved successes were not the only consequence of his agricultural offensive. There was also falsification of statistical data. The atmosphere of haste and the desire to achieve immediate successes from any undertaken measures—the increase in corn acreage or improvements in livestock productivity—led to the flourishing of simulation. Some disclosures in the official press reveal deliberate falsification of agricultural statistics and the practice of reporting fictitious increases that permeated agricultural accounting from top to bottom. It is well known, for example, that in the last few years of Khrushchev's administration several interruptions occurred in the supply of the population with food. Yet, according to the reports of the Central Statistical Administration, total farm output grew steadily with the single exception of 1963. According to these reports, the year 1964 set new records in farm production. But already in June, 1964 (if not earlier) the Soviet government concluded additional trade agreements for purchases of grain abroad.

Khrushchev is now subject to Soviet criticism on the ground that insufficient attention was paid to economic calculation during his tenure of office. As Volin has shown, the accusation is not quite valid. The trouble was that whenever objective indicators failed to correspond to Khrushchev's expectations, the relevant figures were adjusted to correspond to the desired objective. At the December, 1958, plenum of the Central Committee, Khrushchev unmasked Malenkov's manipulations of the biological grain harvest. But it was during his term of office that the so-called barn yield of grain was converted into a conventional, unreal magnitude of the bunker weight. The latter includes excessive moisture and other impurities. Before grain is stored in elevators, it must be cleaned and dried. As was noted during the discussions of the conference, the bunker weight must be reduced on this account by at least 6 and at times by 10 to 12 percent. We should also note that in the outlying areas of the New Lands, the weight of grain stored in piles was often determined by eye.

The fact that Malenkov's biological harvest had to be reduced by about 30 percent was first established in the West by Dr. Naum Jasny. But as we have just seen, Khrushchev's bunker weight grain harvest also contains up to 10 or 12 percent of impurities and excess moisture. If we consider that much of the moist grain is also wasted in transport, and that some of the grain produced in the New Lands was in consequence of its condition rendered unfit for either human or animal consumption, we may conclude that Khrushchev's record in grain accounting will not be much better than that of Malenkov.

Similar trends are also noticeable in statistical reporting of animal production. When the goals to surpass American per-capita output within the next few years were announced, the inflation of accounting reports and other indicators began in a systematic fashion. Collective farms bought butter in cooperative stores and delivered it once more to state procurement points. At times one and the same pound of butter was thus counted five or six times as a "newly procured" magnitude. Similar manipulations occurred with respect to other animal products.

When the distortions reached alarming proportions and when it proved impossible to conceal them, the statisticians were forced to adjust various indicators in order to bring them in line with reality. And it was at such times that official statistics reveal the decline in the rate of growth of output. The best example is again afforded by data on milk yields per cow in the second half of Khrushchev's stewardship over agriculture.

I noted that these yields declined after the peak reached in 1959. The annual data are as follows (kilograms per cow per *annum*): 1959: 2,067; 1960: 1,938; 1961: 1,847; 1962: 1,747; 1963: 1,584. In the good harvest year 1964 the milk yield per cow rose by only 100 kilograms. I do not think that it is possible to explain these trends by the decline in available feed supplies in relation to the growing cow herds. The relatively small increase in the 1964 milk yield per cow, in spite of the improvement in the availability of feed, cannot be explained in this fashion. Evidently, the main cause of these trends is to be sought in the correction of statistics on milk yields and milk production and in the reduction of fictitious reporting. But fictitious reporting is still a feature of Soviet agricultural statistics.

Little can be added to the description of Khrushchev's policies supplied by Volin. Khrushchev was fascinated by all new ideas and suggestions. To paraphrase a Russian proverb, he leaped into the water without knowing the ford. He attempted to implement any suggested or insinuated novelty with enthusiasm and energy. He turned out to be a skillful organizer of large-scale campaigns such as the settlement of the New Lands or the increase in the corn acreage. But after initiating a program he would rapidly move to another without tying up all the loose ends. He was always overwhelmed by current affairs or by urgent matters of first priority. The measures he initiated were then relegated to the bureaucratic conveyor belt. The failures of his policies may be partly explained by the inertia and submissiveness of a solidly entrenched bureaucratic apparatus which reduced everything to a stereotyped and automatically followed routine. Many projects remained on paper. Among other things, this explains the fact that the new system of more decentralized planning, introduced in 1955, was actually never implemented in practice.

An important and necessary proposal to form elected and democratically organized collective farm associations in the villages and also a Collective Farm Center was pigeonholed by Matskevich in the Ministry of Agriculture. And yet this idea was propagated by first secretaries of many republics, by many chairmen of republican councils of ministers, by writers, and by society at large. It is difficult to say why Khrushchev, never afraid to implement grandiose projects—even when they were not fully elaborated—capitulated before the agricultural bureaucracy on the matter of the Collective Farm Center.

There were two aspects to Khrushchev's personality. The first was an outstanding man, endowed with practical gumption, who rose from the lower levels of society. The second was an agitator—at the level of the *raion* Party committee. He tried to combine the practical task of administering a huge state with that of implementing dogmatic even though modernized theories. The oscillation between two inconsistent goals—the creation of a strong and productive agriculture and the continuing socialization of the village—led to indecisiveness and to disruption of proper measures. In some instances Khrushchev reversed his attitudes by 180 degrees. At times he restricted the private sector, at times he encouraged it. At times he recommended increases in incentives and then he inveighed against the "unjustifiably high incomes" of collective farmers and state farm workers.

The devotion to the dogmatic goal of progressing towards the stage of communism led Khrushchev to the creation of model farms, better known colloquially as "beacons." The "beacons" were organized as everything else was organized in the Khrushchev era—in haste, in too large a number, and at too large a scale. In consequence, the achievements of many "beacons" turned out to be lower than those of the neighboring ordinary farms. Their privileged position was of no avail—many "beacons" failed to light anybody's way and became burned out stars testifying to the ineffectiveness of the general attitude of grandstand play.

There is no doubt that the latter attitude was the greatest evil accompanying Khrushchev's agricultural policies. It pervaded every aspect of farming. There were model state and collective farms, model chairmen of collective farms, model directors of state farms, model brigadiers, model milkmaids, and model swineherds. There was also the model collective farm—in Khrushchev's native village of Kalinovka. There was a model scientific research institution at "Leninskie Gorki," headed by the model scientific agronom—Trofim Lysenko. There were model crops—corn or peas—there were model, high yielding cows, and so forth down the line.

There were also model arguments, model calculations, and model indicators: the grain yields in the New Lands, additional income from increased sowings of corn or legumes, the reduction of costs after the mergers of state and collective farms, the increase in the profitability of collectives converted to state farms, or the increase in the effectiveness of machinery use following its transfer to collectives. There was much else that occupied space in the long and frequent speeches by Khrushchev, that ultimately filled the eight published volumes of his writings on agriculture.

All economic calculations which supported the introduced policy measures were based on the assumption of maximum possible advantage and often turned out to amount to simple mathematical exercises. The effectiveness of agrotechnical novelties was determined on the basis of early, incompletely analyzed results, achieved on experimental farms in particularly favorable conditions—or, as experience has shown, simply on falsification of results.

It is understandable that measures based on such unstable foundations could not lead to desired results. All agricultural plans and all calculations of agricultural achievements turned out to be soap bubbles—actual achievements were minimal.

While Khrushchev introduced some practical and at times healthy agricultural measures; he also strove to build communism in the fastest way possible. He even indicated a target date for this attempt—by 1980, the Soviet Union was to enter into the kingdom of communism. There is no doubt that he visualized himself as leading the masses into the promised land. He could hardly have supposed that within the next three years he would become a forgotten pensioner whose name would have vanished from the nation's press. But now we may doubt that communism is the promised land, the economic aspects of which in 1980 will correspond to those formulated by Khrushchev at the Twenty-second Party Congress in October, 1961.

ROY D. LAIRD

Khrushchev's Administrative Reforms in Agriculture: An Appraisal

THE MAJOR CHANGES

N. S. Khrushchev probably will be mentioned favorably in future histories for his doctrine of "peaceful coexistence" (surely a fundamental revision of Leninism) and for having presided over the removal of terror as a major means of Soviet rule. In spite of these positive accomplishments, however, in his role as the chief of the Soviet administration, Khrushchev seems to be marked at best for the position of a transitional figure unable to alter the course charted by Stalin. This was certainly the case in agriculture. Although he diminished somewhat the Stalinist austerity, his major administrative accomplishment in agriculture was the completion of Stalin's unfinished "revolution from above." The kolkhozy were finally totally subsumed under the single bureaucratic pyramid that now encompasses the whole Soviet society. Especially on the rural front, Khrushchev left to his successors the task of making the fundamental changes that surely must come.

Khrushchev's leadership was not a failure in the sense that on balance the U.S.S.R. did progress on most domestic fronts during his tenure in office. Yet, when measured in terms of the growing wants and needs of the citizenry, and especially in terms of the lack of progress toward the grandiose economic goals of his Seven-Year (1959–1965) and Twenty-Year (1960–1980) Plan goals he was a serious failure.

Setting the house of agriculture right was the major plank in Khrushchev's campaign to capture the mantle of Stalin. After the original campaign, agricultural problems continued to receive by far the most of

Khrushchev's attention. Within agriculture, administrative reform received the greatest stress; yet his successors' first major administrative reform was the emasculation of the Territorial Production Administrations (TPA's)—Khrushchev's final important administrative cure-all.[1]

Surely there is little room to credit his administrative reforms with having increased production. Most of the output advances must be credited to substantial investment increases and to the tenuous New Lands program (which absorbed much of the new investment).

Indeed, of the claimed 52 percent growth in crop production between 1950 and 1960, a full three-fourths is said to have come from "increased land under crops" and only one-fourth from increased yields.[2] Obviously, Khrushchev's successors also have concluded that his administrative changes were of little production benefit, and his TPA's were a detriment.

If Marx was right—that man is wholly a creature of his material environment—a knowledge of the economic forces at work on the Soviet system would provide the only base necessary for understanding Khrushchev's agricultural administrative reforms. Each of the major changes that have been introduced would be explainable in terms of a new attempt to create the right administrative environment for maximizing output at the lowest cost. However, the need to increase output is not the sole determinant of Soviet agricultural policy-making. The persistence of the collectivized system itself is proof that Soviet agricultural policy is also determined by the need to answer Soviet agricultural problems with Communist formulas. This is so in the face of the reality that, when measured in terms of output per unit of land and per man-hour, the kolkhozy and sovkhozy have proved to be far less productive than the agricultural organizational forms of any of the advanced industrialized nations and many of the less developed nations. Obviously the Soviet leadership has been most eager to maximize production and labor efficiency. Yet, with all of the pragmatism that has been demonstrated by the successive Soviet leaders they have felt constrained to work within the framework of a system conceived outside of the Marxist-Leninist theory that places important restrictions and demands upon policy-making.

[1] Although the TPA seem destined to continue to exist at the time of writing (August, 1965), they are not to be the focal point of local power described by Khrushchev. Thus, their Party committees are being removed, and new *raion* Party committees (*raikomy*) are being created as the focal points of Party control and direction of the farms.

[2] M. Lemeshev, *Plan. khoz.*, No. 1 (1964), pp. 22–23.

THE STALINIST BASE

Granting the importance of strictly economic imperatives, what are the political demands that also have shaped agricultural decision-making? In the U.S.S.R., as in all states, agriculture has been viewed primarily as the source of food for the population and the means of livelihood for those who till the soil and husband the animals. Beyond this, however, at least three additional demands were placed upon the system and the peasants by Stalin and have been unchanged by his successors. Demands similar to the following can be found in other societies, but the difference in emphasis and degree constitutes a difference in kind.

Priority to industry: From the beginning of forced collectivization Stalin made it clear that the "first commandment" of agriculture was not that of maximizing the welfare of the peasant farmers, but rather that of fulfilling state-dictated output plans designed to maximize the amount of investment capital that could be extracted from agriculture in order that Soviet industry could be expanded as rapidly as possible. After Stalin, somewhat greater emphasis was given to agriculture, but the principle of giving first priority to heavy industry (and thus industrial growth) still remained throughout the Khrushchev era.

Maximization of controls: Second only to maintaining first priority for industrial expansion, the agricultural system was seen as providing the means for maximizing the central Party leadership's control over the peasantry. Above and beyond the normal desire for power found in any leadership, or the particular power requirements of a Communist dictatorship, the Bolshevik leadership has had a need for power over the countryside that stems from the knowledge that communism rode to power in Russia in 1917 through its leaders' ability to manipulate what had been fundamentally a peasant revolution. Undoubtedly Khrushchev was confident that the Soviet peasants in the 1950's and early 1960's were not in a mood that could have led to an attempt to overthrow the Communist leadership, but, given the opportunity, most of them certainly would have worked to effect significant changes in the agricultural system—changes that undoubtedly would destroy the centrally planned and controlled character of Soviet agriculture.

The communization of rural society: Although Marx never spelled out precisely how communism was to be brought to agriculture, his successors have all assumed that communism's organizational-administrative forms cannot be confined solely to urban industrial society. Moreover, from the beginning, the peasantry has been viewed (not without reason) as the most backward major element of Soviet society. Therefore all Soviet leaders have agreed upon the necessity to maintain an agricultural system that would train the peasantry to function in a Communist (i.e., industrialized and bureaucratized) rural environment.

Although Lenin had warned against the dangers of forcing the peasants onto the collectives, given the mentioned demands upon agricultural policy, a Stalin was "really necessary in the rural U.S.S.R." [3] unless the experiment with communism was to become a sham. Certainly the imposition of something similar to the kolkhoz-sovkhoz administrative organizational forms (that constitute Stalin's greatest monument) was imperative.

1950–1964: SOVIET AGRICULTURE IN FLUX

Between "the revolution from above" of the early 1930's and the first Khrushchev reforms three decades later, numerous changes and reforms were made in Soviet agriculture. Khrushchev quickened the pace of change, but he fell far short of making the fundamental changes that the seriousness of the Soviet agricultural problem demanded. Khrushchev introduced at least five different, important administrative organizational reforms, but none basically changed the system.

Although Stalin did not die until the spring of 1953, Khrushchev's agricultural leadership really began in 1950, since it was Khrushchev who initiated the scheme to amalgamate the then relatively small collective farms into the huge farms of the 1960's. Therefore any official catalog of Khrushchev's major rural reforms should include the 1950 amalgamations as well as the 1953 elimination of the *raion* governmental administrations for agriculture, the 1955 decentralized planning decree, the 1958 demise of the MTS, and the 1962 creation of the TPA's.

Since several studies have analyzed the earlier reforms, and preliminary evaluations have been made of the TPA, a detailed recounting of the provisions of the various reforms probably would add little.[4] Perhaps, however, an evaluation of the impact of the changes as of the time of the leadership change in 1964 is in order.

THE SITUATION BY 1964

TOTAL BUREAUCRATIZATION

The most far-reaching of all of Khrushchev's administrative reforms in agriculture will not appear in any catalog of legislation. Before 1950,

[3] See Alec Nove, "Was Stalin Really Necessary?" *Economic Rationality and Soviet Politics* (New York: Praeger, 1964), pp. 17–39.

[4] See, for example, Howard Swearer, "Agricultural Administration Under Khrushchev," and the writer's "The Politics of Soviet Agriculture," in Roy D. Laird, ed., *Soviet Agricultural and Peasant Affairs* (Lawrence, Kansas: University of Kansas Press, 1963), pp. 9–40 and 269–286, or the writer's "The Politics of Soviet Agriculture," in Roy D. Laird and E. L. Crowley, eds., *Soviet Agriculture: The Permanent Crisis* (New York: Praeger, 1965), pp. 147–158.

the Party could hardly afford to staff each of the kolkhoz chairmanships with Party-member leaders, much less establish effective Party units on each of the 235,000 collective farms. By 1954, however, the amalgamations already had reduced the number of kolkhozy below 100,000 and, with the infusion of some 20,000 Party members from the cities into farm leadership posts during that year, the bulk of the farms were at long last captured within the Party directorate. As indicated earlier, Stalin's "revolution from above" had left the kolkhozy somewhat outside the total bureaucratic scheme. The hierarchy of Party leadership, held together by Moscow determined rewards and punishments, had not penetrated the bulk of the kolkhozy before 1954. Paralleling the amalgamations, the movement of the Party onto the farms continued, so that by 1958 more than 90 percent of the farms had Party members as chairmen, and the average farm's Party unit comprised about twenty members (see Table 1).[5]

Not only was the entrenchment of the Party on the farms the most important of all of Khrushchev's administrative changes, but all his other administrative reforms depended upon, or reflected, that change.

Thus, for example, the 1958 decision to eliminate the MTS as the all-powerful outside arm of control over the kolkhozy could hardly have been made without a trusted Party leadership fully established on the farms.

SPECIALIZED LEADERSHIP: THE REVOLUTION IN EDUCATION

Before 1950, not only were only relatively few kolkhoz chairmen Party members, but even fewer had specialized or advanced training (Table 1). By 1964, however, virtually all kolkhoz and sovkhoz chairmen were Party members and, according to the then Minister of Agriculture Volovchenko, "two-thirds of the kolkhoz chairmen and virtually all of the sovkhoz directors [also had] higher or specialized and secondary education." [6] In addition, the average farm was said to be staffed with five trained agronomists, animal husbandrymen, and other agricultural specialists.[7]

The magnitude of the revolution in trained agricultural leadership is illustrated by the contrast between Khrushchev's assertion that in 1953 there were only 114,000 specialists working on the farms,[8] whereas by the end of 1963 a total of some 416,000 specialists were said to be working in all branches of agriculture. This included, according to the

[5] *Pravda,* February 28, 1958 and December 16, 1958.
[6] *Ibid.,* February 11, 1964.
[7] *Ek. sel'. khoz.,* No. 10 (1962), p. 1.
[8] *Narkhoz-1963,* p. 365.

TABLE 1

SOME CHARACTERISTICS OF COLLECTIVE FARM CHAIRMEN, U.S.S.R., SELECTED YEARS
(percent of total number of chairmen)

Characteristic	1952	1953	1956	1957	1958	1959	1960	1963
Party members and candidates	79.4	79.6	90.5	91.2	92.6	93.5	95.3	n.a.
Chairmen with completed higher or secondary education	15.1	18.0	37.1	36.0	37.2	50.4	55.6	66.0
Chairmen with completed higher education	n.a.	2.6	7.8	7.4	7.8	11.8	n.a.	n.a.
Chairmen with completed secondary education	n.a.	15.4	29.3	28.6	29.4	38.6	n.a.	n.a.
Serving less than 1 year	23.5	23.8	29.7	16.9	17.3	4.6	4.3	n.a.
Serving 1 to 3 years	36.1	35.6	33.9	41.0	33.7	38.9	39.1	n.a.
Serving more than 3 years	40.4	40.6	36.4	42.1	49.0	56.6	56.6	n.a.

SOURCES: *Narkhoz-1959*, p. 452, *Sel'khoz-1960*, p. 474, and *Pravda*, February 11, 1964, pp. 1–4.

1963 *Statistical Handbook,* 205,000 specialists with higher and secondary training reported to have been on the kolkhozy and another 211,000 on the sovkhozy, TPA and RTS (repair tractor stations) and in other state agricultural enterprises (see Table 2).

DECENTRALIZATION: FROM THE MTS TO THE TPA

Under both Stalin and Khrushchev, each major change in the pattern of kolkhoz-sovkhoz administration was heralded as providing, at long last, the scheme that would solve the problems of agriculture. Both the words of the top Party leaders and the frequency of the reforms provide ample testimony to a vain search. Under Stalin, and especially under Khrushchev, new administrative schemes were designed to sharpen local responsibility (i.e., to pinpoint individuals clearly responsible for local production results). For example, the enhancement of local responsibility was Khrushchev's major argument for strengthening the powers of the MTS between 1953 and 1957. Ironically, the loss of this responsibility with the demise of the MTS in 1958, was given as Khrushchev's major reason for the creation of the TPA in 1962. Thus, as Khrushchev asserted at the March, 1963, conference of agricultural Party secretaries, "For a long time in the past [between 1958 and 1962] no one was concretely answerable for the state of agricultural production. . . . Who is to show concern for all these questions? The production administrations, the party committees." [9]

One of the major, perhaps the most important, hoped-for results of the entrenchment of the Party on the farms was that the presence of such trusted leaders would allow the realization of the advantages of decentralization. Party members living on the farms and directing the production could be trusted to make decisions that at once fit local needs and conditions and at the same time would best serve the needs of the state. A major first move in this direction occurred as early as 1953, when the *raion* state offices were eliminated and the old Stalinist principle of dual, or treble, hierarchies of control, one checking on the other, was largely abandoned in favor of a scheme wherein the Party was granted a monopoly over the administration of agricultural production.

The 1953 changes were followed by such major moves as the 1955 decentralized-planning decree, the momentous decision to abandon the MTS in 1958, and the 1961 demotion of the Ministry of Agriculture to a position of merely directing agricultural research and innovation. As the feature writers of *Ekonomicheskaia gazeta* were to admit in retro-

[9] *Pravda,* March 14, 1963.

TABLE 2

SPECIALISTS IN AGRICULTURE, U.S.S.R., SELECTED YEARS [a]
(thousand persons)

Category	1941	1953	1955	1956	1957	1959	1963	1963 [b]
Collective farms and Machine or Repair Tractor Stations:								
Agricultural specialists [c]	19	69	204	220	211	175	154 [d]	164 [d]
Other specialists	10	14	59	71	67	65	51 [d]	59 [d]
State and institutional farms								
Agricultural specialists [c]	16	27	35	54	70	92	147	158
Other specialists	5	4	10	15	23	34	64	76
Total agricultural specialists [c]	*35*	*96*	*239*	*274*	*281*	*267*	*301* [d]	*322* [d]
Total other specialists	*15*	*18*	*69*	*86*	*90*	*99*	*115* [d]	*135* [d]
Grand total	*50*	*114*	*308*	*360*	*371*	*366*	*416* [d]	*457* [d]

[a] Specialists are defined as persons with a diploma from an institution of higher specialized secondary education.
[b] November 15, 1964.
[c] Agricultural specialists include agronomists, animal-husbandry technicians, veterinarians, and foresters.
[d] Apparently excluding specialists in territorial production administrations and repair tractor stations.

SOURCES: *Sel'khoz-1960*, p. 467; *Narkhoz-1964*, p. 421.

spect, the system up to 1955 "destroyed the initiative of the kolkhozniki and sovkhoz workers, and in a number of cases, resulted in incorrect and economically unadvantageous selection of what to sow and of what type of animals would be suited to the zone of the country involved." [10] Yet, even the 1955 decree on decentralized planning had little initial effect upon administrative practice.

The abandonment of the MTS in 1958 as the focal point of outside control over the farms was clearly the high water mark in the search for a means to encourage the initiative of the farm leadership. As Khrushchev's observation on the lack of local responsibility between 1958 and 1962 emphasized (cited above), outside controls were at a low during the 1958–1962 period. What might have been, had agricultural production continued to climb after 1958 as it had between 1953 and 1958, would make an interesting speculation. Unfortunately, however, what might have been was not destined to be, and the period of experimentation with relaxed controls coincided with the alarming decline in agricultural-production growth that was to culminate in the events of 1963 and the price that had to be paid for the drought of that year. The tendency to meet serious problems by increased controls is overwhelming in the Soviet system, and the TPA were created to recapture controls lost with the abandonment of the MTS. True, the leadership insisted that the drive to advance local initiative continued; repeated complaints in the press reprimanded TPA officials who persisted in issuing detailed orders to the farms. Nevertheless, even in the issuing of official criticisms of bureaucratic actions by the TPA, the TPA's leadership were reminded that they were Moscow's official agents for seeing to the proper planning, production, and procurement of that proportion of the farms' output that is earmarked for state purchases—constituting the largest portion of the farms' output and specifically excluded from the 1955 decentralization decree.

THE TPA

The Khrushchev TPA represented an experiment in bringing the kolkhozy and sovkhozy closer together, and an experiment in separating industrial and agricultural administration. As indicated previously, however, most of all, the TPA provided a means for tightened controls —controls that undermined the post-1963 attempt to place the "production principle" (rather than plan) at the forefront of measuring agricultural success.

[10] *Ek. gaz.*, November 23, 1963, pp. 21–28.

Under Stalin, agricultural administration at the local level had been shared by *raion* Party and state agencies. Khrushchev's elimination of the *raion* state agricultural offices in 1953 was followed by the elevation of the *raion* Party agency, and, particularly, the MTS Party secretary to the key position of local power over the farms. Between the demise of the MTS in 1958 and the creation of the TPA in 1962, the *raion* offices seem to have held the center of the stage, but 1962 witnessed the elimination of the rural *raions* with the substitution of a new kind of dual administrative system (a committee for industry and a committee for agriculture) that extended from Moscow to the individual TPA.

In agriculture, the Khrushchev TPA's served as the final outside agencies under the *oblast'* Party committees but over the some forty kolkhozy and sovkhozy for which they were responsible. As in the case of the MTS earlier, each TPA had its staff of inspectors-organizers, each one personally responsible for the achievements of three to four farms.[11] Even though the TPA's did not share the MTS monopoly over agricultural machinery, by early 1964 their power over the farms probably rivaled that once held by the MTS. Thus, in the Soviet leadership's admission that future output increases must come from greater "intensification" (e.g., largely by increasing yields per hectare and per animal) Khrushchev and his colleagues made it clear that the TPA officials were to be responsible for the successes and failures of the campaign to increase yields. Indeed, although expanding irrigation, production of more herbicides, and so on were seen as crucial to any future advances of agriculture, proper utilization of the huge additional quantity of fertilizer to be made available to the farms was considered the single most important determinant. Therefore, the decisive measure of the importance of the TPA under Khrushchev was that just as the old MTS had held a monopoly over machinery, the TPA's were to be given a monopoly over the distribution of the new fertilizer to all the farms (the MTS had not served the sovkhozy). As noted in the party resolution of February 15, 1964:

> The Central Committee plenary session charges the U.S.S.R. State Planning Committee, the Union-republic Councils of Ministries of Production and Procurement of Farm Products, and the collective farm, state-farm production administrations with effecting the distribution of mineral fertilizers among the zones of the country and the collective and state farms . . . and achieving the best return for the chemical fertilizers applied.[12]

[11] P. Chervenko, *Ek. sel'. khoz.*, No. 8 (1962), p. 34.

[12] *Pravda*, February 16, 1964.

The farm administrators could not escape from the constant realization that the TPA Party bosses were their immediate superiors in the Party hierarchy. True, Khrushchev held up for condemnation a number of TPA officials who issued detailed orders for the farms while sitting in their distant offices. Yet, no farm official or TPA Party boss could read the series of condemnations Khrushchev made in his speech to the February, 1964, agricultural conference without noting that Khrushchev compared the relationship of the TPA official to the farm administrator with that of a superior officer to the inferior officer in the army. In his severe condemnation of the TPA Party secretary who blindly ordered a farm to "mow" a field of ripe grain, there was no suggestion that the Party official did not have such power. To the contrary, the criticisms leveled against the TPA officials were against their failure to get out onto the farms and into the fields in order to acquaint themselves thoroughly with the practical conditions for which they were responsible.[13]

The TPA's were instructed to regard the farms for which they were responsible as a zone. Although the actual working out of the zonal concept of agricultural production is particularly difficult for the outsider to evaluate, this innovation did seem to be important. At the height of the power of the MTS, the "MTS zone" probably did comprise an important administrative-production entity. Although the TPA zone was considerably larger, local authorities were encouraged to reap the benefits of coordinated activities. The creation of inter-kolkhoz and sovkhoz enterprises was encouraged, the stronger farms were charged with helping the weaker, and the TPA and farm administrators were charged with exploiting other advantages to be gained from recognizing the peculiar production demands of the zone. Obviously such innovations could be of value. However, planning production for a TPA zone comprising hundreds of thousands of hectares must surely have posed a conflict with an attempt to adopt the "production principle" (rewarding the farms and the peasants on the basis of the output of crops and livestock produce per 100 hectares of land).

1965 AND AFTER

THE "PRODUCTION PRINCIPLE"

In 1963 Khrushchev renewed his argument of ten years earlier that the "production principle," rather than adherence to plan targets, should be the prime measure of success of failure in production and,[14] at first

[13] *Ibid.*, March 7, 1964.
[14] *Ibid.*, December 10, 1963.

glance, his successors seem to be intent upon emphasizing the concept even more than Khrushchev. However, if the production principle were to be adopted in any meaningful sense, genuine decentralization must result. Adopting this concept as the prime guide for rewarding the peasantry for their efforts would have required changes that were incompatible with the 1964 system wherein the *oblast'* and TPA offices handed out orders to the farms for the kind and quantity of products to be produced for state purchases. Now the TPA's have been emasculated, but putting such a principle into practice runs counter to the Soviet agricultural system itself and thus is doomed to failure for reasons similar to those that caused the abandonment of the frantic pre-1958 campaign to place the MTS on a "cost-accounting" base.

In the case of the MTS, since they were given an economic framework wherein the prices the state paid for output and virtually all of the services rendered by the MTS were dictated by centrally made plans, the Soviet economists charged with devising the scheme found that the built-in rigidities blocked any meaningful attempt to relate MTS costs to farm output. As one Soviet economist noted: "A major feature of the present economy of the MTS is the absence of direct monetary relations between them and the collective farms." [15] Even eliminating the multiple prices that existed in 1957 would not provide any satisfactory means of evaluating the MTS services.

In 1957, 1964, and 1965 Moscow artificially set the prices for agricultural output. In 1957 *oblast'* and MTS offices, and in 1964 *oblast'* and TPA offices, gave out rigid purchase orders for the fulfillment of state plans. In 1965, the newly resurrected *raion* offices seemed destined to fulfill this task. The rigidities of the Soviet system are enormously costly in terms of efficiency. Yet, the alternative is to turn to the farms and the peasants and say: "You are now free to grow what you believe your farms and your talents are most suited to produce." Clearly the advantages of this situation is what Khrushchev was striving for in advancing the production principle, but without really giving the farm administrators freedom to make production decisions and without allowing for the substitution of the only known economic alternative (to planning or chaos)—a market to suggest what is required for society's needs. Barring the decision to let the farmers make their own plans in response to a market as genuine regulator, the Soviet leadership must continue to dictate to the farms through plans in order to be certain that

[15] *Izvestiia,* November 30, 1957.

at least something akin to the quantity and mix of produce required by the cities will in fact be produced by the farms.

THE PEASANT POINT OF VIEW AND THE *Zveno*

In the struggle to create the proper Communist environment for maximizing production, what did the 1950–1964 administrative-organizational reforms mean to the peasant who, after all, is the producer in Soviet agriculture? On the economic side, his wages improved, but even by Russian standards, let alone those of the West, peasant incentives to produce still remained poor.[16]

On the administrative-organizational side, the Khrushchev reforms were of even less benefit to the peasantry. True, bringing more specialists into the farms and into production leadership must have been helpful. However, even if significantly more decisions are now to be made on the farms (and not in distant TPA offices), the huge farms of the 1960's must create a situation in which the peasant worker is nearly as far removed from the decision-making by the farm leadership as the peasant was removed from decision-making monopolized by the MTS. Therefore, there could have been little, if any, increase in the peasant's incentive to work harder and more efficiently through a heightened sense of participation in the affairs of the farms.

By 1964 continued amalgamations had reduced the number of kolkhozy to only 39,500 (while sovkhozy had risen to 9,176) [17] counting several hundred workers each. Very few, outside of the Soviet leadership, even pretend that the huge collectives can practice "kolkhoz democracy" or that the individual peasant worker can have any important impact upon decision-making. When general meetings of the peasant

[16] Professor Nove records that the average collective farmer's cash income per work-day unit increased from 0.14 in 1952 to 0.40 rubles in 1957. However, as both Nove and Henri Wronski have pointed out, by 1960 peasant wages undoubtedly had fallen below the 1957 peak. A measure of the sad state of incentives offered to collective farmers by their farms is provided by Wronski's observation that in 1957 "the wage paid to a collective farmer from a day's work was only half as much as the wage received by a state farm worker, and by 1959 this gap diminished by only 10 percent." Further, according to Wronski, Soviet sources indicate that in 1958 the average daily wage on state farms was 2.24 rubles. See Alec Nove, "Incentives for Peasants and Administrators," in Laird, ed. *op. cit.* (in n. 4), pp. 51–68 and Henri Wronski, "Peasant Incomes," in Laird and Crowley, eds., *op. cit.* (in n. 4), pp. 123–136. According to *Narkhoz-1964,* p. 555, the average monthly money wage in state and institutional farms came to 53.1 rubles in 1958 and 53.9 rubles in 1960. In 1964 it was 73.3 rubles as a result of increases which took place in 1961 and 1962.

[17] *Narkhoz-1963,* p. 226.

membership are called only a few times a year, what influence can one peasant, among 400 or more fellow workers, have on policy? The Soviet press openly reports that all important matters to be decided by the peasants are, in fact must be, carefully prepared by the farm administrators beforehand. Indeed, a new trend is to replace the general meetings by a representative system because of the admitted physical impossibility of getting all members of a single kolkhoz together in one place at one time. By contrast, the sovkhoz worker is but a paid laborer in an even more impersonal setting.[18]

The peasants hardly see a blessing in kolkhoz administrations dominated by Party members who can be trusted to respond to Moscow's wishes. Indeed (although there is no concrete evidence for such an assertion), future histories may well show that the increases in yields claimed for the 1950's could be partly explained by the ability of a tighter Party leadership on the farms to reduce the opportunities for the peasants to exercise their ancient prerogative—appropriating produce from the collectives' (and before them the tsarist landlords') fields and barns for their and their families' private needs.

Although a dominant trend of the Khrushchev reforms seems to have been toward larger, more tightly run farms, and not toward decentralization, the changes did incorporate elements that hold a potential for a fundamental transformation of the Soviet agricultural system in the future. Certainly one change that accompanied the administrative-organizational reforms, which apparently was not planned and certainly has as yet to be widely publicized, could prove to be important. This was the quiet return of the *zveno* (link or team) as an accepted form of organizing the peasants' work.

During World War II, and for some time afterward, a relaxation of the outside direction of the farms was accompanied by rumors that the end of the fighting would be followed by a permanent relaxation in the collectivized system. Peasant hope for reform was reflected in the peasants' expansion of their private plots (at the expense of kolkhoz fields) and the evolution of *zveno* work units instead of the brigades. By the end of the 1940's a Stalin campaign had resulted in a return of the land to the collectives, but the *zveno* continued to persist. Politburo member A. A. Andreev had noted the superior work of the six-to-eight member teams, as contrasted to that of the brigades (averaging 121 workers by 1961)[19] and proceeded to argue publicly for their widespread adoption as a means for the significant increase of agricultural

[18] See, for example, *Ek. gaz.*, October 5, 1963, pp. 21–31.
[19] *Ibid.*, February 1, 1964, pp. 1–6 of the insert.

production. However, an unsigned article in *Pravda* (undoubtedly Stalin's work) took him to task and forced Andreev to reverse his position publicly. At this juncture Khrushchev joined the chorus and offered his amalgamation scheme (incorporating great promises for increasing peasant welfare) as a counter-solution.

As Dr. Schlesinger has pointed out, the *zveno* in the late 1940's were made up of "members of a family or a small group of friends" in a kolkhoz setting that reflected the old precollectivization village and the *mir*.[20] Not only did these teams tend to be family operations, but the team members apparently tended to regard the fields and animals under their charge as their own. No wonder, therefore, that Andreev's critics argued that the *zveno* were anti-kolkhoz and destructive of socialist labor discipline. Now, without fanfare, an article, especially written for the purpose of educating the Soviet citizens in the workings of their economy, includes mention of the *zveno* as basic work units both in the fields and with the animals. In another Soviet article, team leaders are listed among the kolkhoz *aktiv*.[21] In a speech in which Khrushchev stressed the need to increase the differential in peasant incomes, according to yields and labor efficiency (thus the production principle), among the several examples of excellence that he cited for emulation, *zveno* units were most prominent.[22] Finally, in the *Ekonomicheskaia gazeta* series, "School for Rural Economists," the *zveno* is extolled for making possible "the elimination of the lack of individual responsibility" in the brigades.[23]

THE FOURTH DETERMINANT

The implications of the move to adopt the *zveno* and the production principle implies fundamental changes in the system and brings forth the whole problem of economies and policies of size, and in this matter comparative American experience seems to be illuminating.

Whatever the political and economic system, a highly disciplined bureaucratic hierarchy seems to be essential to successful industrial production. Thus, the same basic managerial system that has been the administrative key to the success of General Motors also has been the basis of the relatively successful Soviet industrial record. Communist

[20] R. A. J. Schlesinger, "Some Problems of Present Kolkhoz Organization," *Soviet Studies*, II:4 (April, 1951), 344.

[21] *Ek. gaz.*, October 5, 1963, pp. 21–31 and A. Esin, *Ek. sel'. khoz.*, No. 12 (1963), pp. 16–30.

[22] *Pravda*, March 7, 1964.

[23] *Ibid.*, February 1, 1964.

party rule has been compatible with growth in urban industrial production. However, Lenin called for, and his successors have imposed, the industrial management scheme upon agriculture as well.

Not only Soviet Marxist economists, but perhaps most Western economists as well, evince a conviction that full industrialization is just around the corner for agriculture. True, the industrial revolution has had an enormous impact upon agriculture, but such thinking misses the significance of an essential point made by the American agricultural economists Brewster and Wunderlich of the U.S. Department of Agriculture's Research Service: "There is a fundamental difference in the nature of the 'Industrial Revolution' in agriculture and in industry." As these men point out:

> With minor exception of certain specialized poultry and livestock operations . . . a shift to machine farming leaves relatively undisturbed the sequential pattern of operations that have prevailed in farming since the domestication of plants and animals. In contrast, the same shift to industry transmutes this older sequence of operations into the modern simultaneous pattern characteristic of the factory system. Thus *in farming, the 'Industrial Revolution' is merely a spectacular change in the gadgets with which operations are performed,* [italics added] whereas in industry it is a further revolution in the sequence of productive operations.[24]

Economists have long since established that three crucial elements in all production are land, labor, and capital. Soviet agriculture, although it has serious problems of climate, soils, and training, is relatively well blessed with land and labor. Thus most Western students of the system have agreed that a serious drawback to further advances has been the lack of investment, most particularly the lack of adequate economic incentives for the peasantry. Such an observation is correct. However, does such an observation lead to the conclusion that if the post-Khrushchev leadership significantly increases agricultural investments, production will increase, and costs per unit of output will decrease, at rates proportionate to those in Western agricultural systems? Of course, some improvement will result, but in my opinion the Soviet leadership is in for serious disappointment.

Beyond the traditional triad of economic determinants there seems to be a fourth, equally crucial determinant. This is the factor of organization, perhaps better, administrative dynamism, and here the Soviets have as yet to recognize more openly their agricultural shortcomings.

The nature of production in agriculture is fundamentally different

[24] John J. Brewster and Gene Wunderlich, "Farm Size, Capital, and Tenure Requirements," in *Adjustments in Agriculture: A National Basebook* (Ames, Iowa: Iowa State University Press, 1961), p. 207.

from that of industry, and an examination of agricultural systems will reveal that the production differences demand different administrative forms. Most specifically, the locus and form of what I have described elsewhere as the "focal point of decision making in agriculture" is surely as crucial to success as are land, labor, and capital.[25] Khrushchev was right in his search for local responsibility; only his preconceptions failed to allow him to see what must be done. He was enamored with the success of the American extensive system and cited its technical achievements time and again. Yet, he emphatically rejected any understanding that the successful application of the American technical achievements are inseparable from the American managerial system.

There is a prevalent but incorrect myth that industrial management systems are capturing American agriculture. The growth in size of the average farm and the asserted growth in importance of the huge "corporate farms" (characterized by being dependent upon numerous hired hands) is usually cited as evidence of an American change that the Soviets could profitably adapt to their kolkhoz-sovkhoz system. Such assertions reveal an ignorance of the changes that occurred in American agriculture. A brief review of some of these changes is in order:

While it is true that the traditional family farms in the U.S. are diminishing in number (as are all farms), what might be described "the new family farm" (my term) is actually increasing in importance, relative to the corporate operations. Thus, as defined by Brewster and Wunderlich, these new farms are "any farm on which most of the labor and managerial activities are carried out by the same individual or family." Indeed, even among the most wealthy of farms (those with annual sales above $10,000 a year), which would include most of the so-called corporate farms, it is estimated that while family labor accounted for 31 percent of the production in 1949 the proportion had increased to 39 percent by 1954.[26]

While it is true that the average farm has significantly increased in size, the key limiting factor has been how far new machines and techniques will allow the manager-operated farm to be extended. Thus, various studies made in Nebraska, Iowa, and Illinois show that in recent years maximum economies of size range (according to the type of farm) from 300 to 400 acres with present-day equipment. Indeed, "using least-cost machine combinations for farms of different size in north central Iowa," an Iowa Experimental Station study found that growth between 320 acres and 880 acres added but negligible economies. Furthermore, beyond 880 acres "costs per units of production began to rise somewhat, *'because of lack of timeliness in operations resulting in declines in per acre yields*' "[27] [italics added].

[25] Laird, *op. cit.* (in n. 4), pp. 281 ff.

[26] Brewster and Wunderlich, *op. cit.* (in n. 24), pp. 198, 204.

[27] *Ibid.* The optimum size of farms depends, of course, on the structure and level of both prices and costs. The latter vary with the degree of specialization. Moreover, the time horizon involved in the calculation is also relevant.

In a review of trends, looking to 1975, based upon studies of "organization and structure," H. L. Stewart finds not only that the American literature points to a continued increase in farm size, but also that considerations of efficiency dictate that the manager-operated farm will continue to prevail. Even in livestock raising, which many nonagricultural economists might assume to be most amenable to corporate activity, manager-operation seems to be a decisive key to efficiency. For example, Stewart cites "a recent Indiana study" by G. L. Wilkings that found " 'that a farmer's ability to manage the hog business has more influence on costs than the number of sows and litters raised each year, so long as facilities are used to best advantage.' " [28]

The American farm population was reduced by nearly one-third between 1939 and 1959. Output per man-hour increased "three-fold since 1939," all in a period of significant advances in yields.[29] Measured in absolute terms, the old style family farm may even be described as vanishing from the scene. Nevertheless, the evidence to be gleaned from the American agricultural literature is that "the new family farm" is taking its place, that a combination of "the focal point of decision making" in the hands of the operator (and his immediate family) remains the key to efficient operation on most American farms. Of course, the adoption of factory methods to food production has been realized in some cases in American agriculture. However, the existing literature indicates that such achievement, probably most successful in broiler production, has been limited to a narrow range of outputs.

Given basic differences between the demands of the Soviet economic system as contrasted with the American system, evidence implying that size combined with managerial form is decisive in the U.S. cannot be taken as conclusive proof of the inviability of the Soviet system; yet the American experience casts doubt on the potential efficiency of the kolkhozy and sovkhozy that are huge in area and Leviathan in administration. Under Stalin the Soviet farms already were huge, but as a result of Khrushchev's amalgamations the kolkhozy were expanded some five times. In spite of Khrushchev's protestations in favor of greater on-the-farm responsibility, the logic of the Party control system that he strengthened with his reforms demanded that many production decisions be made at offices far removed from the farms. True, as some Western observers have noted, nothing would be done properly if local production leaders did not in fact seize the bit and go ahead on their own. However, even to the degree that the farm chairmen were able to go ahead on their own, to

[28] H. L. Stewart, "The Organization and Structure of Some Representative Farms in 1975," *Iowa Business Digest*, XXXI:12 (December, 1960), 5.
[29] *Ibid.*

act as the focal point of managerial decision-making the farms that already were too large before 1950 were made unreasonably huge by the 1960's. Thus, whereas the pre-1950 kolkhoz chairman was responsible for directing the operations on 600 sown hectares and the work of 100 able-bodied workers, by 1964 the average kolkhozy (several times smaller than the average sovkhozy) encompassed 3,000 sown hectares and 418 households.[30] This is 7,350 acres as compared to the 300–400 acre American farm.

In recent years Soviet economists have begun to publish studies in which "optimum" farm sizes are cited. Unlike the American studies, however, the Soviet studies had no range, from the very large to the very small, from the small family operation to the huge corporate operation, to examine. Thus, the Soviet "optimum" studies could only conclude, as they have, that with minor suggested variations, the present huge farms are the most efficient. As noted earlier, in the American experience not only do costs seem to rise after a given point, but at least in some cases beyond 880 acres in Iowa, yields begin to drop off. Yet in the Soviet Union there are no 880-acre, much less 300–400 acre, farms to examine.

An example of the blindness to one of the possible costs in efficiency of huge farms is illustrated by the fact that although *Ekonomicheskaia gazeta* has published several studies dealing with optimum size of farms, an article in its February, 1964, issue included approval of the increasing size of kolkhoz brigades in a paragraph that also included the following statement: "In 1957, the average kolkhoz brigade handled 485 hectares of arable land, while in 1961 the figure was 590.5 hectares or 21.7 percent more. The number of able-bodied kolkhoz members assigned to one brigade rose from 89 to 121, or by 35.9 percent." [31]

This is not a questionable American comparison, but the Soviets' own (unquestioned) statistics. The careful reader is left with the implication that the continued growth in the size of the brigades resulted in an increase of 11.7 percent in the labor-versus-land ratio between the two dates. It is true that the transfer of MTS machine operators to the kolkhozy after 1958 (which may or may not be included in the figures given by the source for 1957) may account for the bulk of the increase; no mention of this fact, however, is made in the article. (Trends on labor productivity for agriculture as a whole are given in Miss Nimitz's Table 5 and are discussed by her at greater length.)

[30] *Narkhoz-1964*, pp. 390–391.

[31] *Ek. gaz.*, February 1, 1964, pp. 1–6 of the insert.

Certainly an uncontestable and inescapable price paid for the kolkhoz-sovkhoz system is the high cost of administration. As noted elsewhere,[32] the actual time spent on administration by the manager-operator in the American and European systems may well be as high as that in the U.S.S.R., but since the manager-operator is his own administrator, he does much of his administrative decision-making while on the job, and the paper part of his planning and account work will be done at nights, during unfavorable weather periods, or at off-seasons when field work is at a standstill.

It is unlikely that administrative costs on manager-operated farms in the United States are as high as those in the U.S.S.R.: in state farms wages for administrative and service personnel come to 14 percent and in collective farms to 17 percent of total labor costs.[33]

Beyond administrative and service work, there are minor machine-repair and construction tasks that the manager-operator also will do himself (again mainly in off-season periods). Although no comparative figures for such costs are available, given the nature of the agricultural production process, a conservative estimate would be that in the Soviet system total minor repair and construction labor costs must exceed 10 percent of the total labor costs on the farms—costs that must be paid in terms of wages in the kolkhoz-sovkhoz piecework system. Obviously, therefore, for administrative, service, minor repair, and construction costs alone, the Soviet system carried an inherent outlay for labor that is at least, and probably much more than, 25 percent greater than the Western manager-operator systems. (Given the relatively high cost of labor in the United States, similar additional costs could well be the decisive reason why manager-operated farms seem to be more than holding their own against the corporate farms.)

POSSIBLE PATHS

The dilemma of Soviet agricultural administration (the demands of a bureaucratic farming system versus the need for local initiative) is at the heart of the Soviet agricultural problem, a fundamental flaw that no increase in investments that reasonably could be expected in any system will solve. As the foregoing comparisons demonstrate, the nature of agricultural production is such that with most operations the combination of the focal point of decision-making with the actual production work in the same persons is (unlike in industry) by far the most efficient means of agricultural production. Marx was not right in taking his

[32] Laird and Crowley, eds. *op. cit.* (in n. 4), pp. 147–158.
[33] Esim, *op. cit.* (in n. 21), p. 26.

stand on economic determinism, but economic costs often (indeed, probably most often) are the decisive consideration in a production operation, and the inordinate extra costs of sovkhoz-kolkhoz production will not allow them to compete with Western standards.

Khrushchev campaigned for the mantle of Stalin on a platform that stressed the promise to solve the problems of agriculture. Thus, one of his earliest agricultural speeches, perhaps Khrushchev's most significant speech on the topic, was his *Measures for the Further Development of Agriculture in the U.S.S.R.*,[34] in which he openly acknowledged the serious state of agriculture, including the fact that in some cases the livestock count was below that of the immediate pre-World War I period. Here too, his major stress was upon administrative reforms. Perhaps no more telling measure of Khrushchev's failure was Brezhnev's need to entitle his first major pronouncement on agriculture: *Urgent Measures for the Further Development of Soviet Agriculture.*[35]

Brezhnev's promises stress a significant increase in much-needed investments (and thus peasant incentives) and include favorable price changes, wiping out of the debts of weak kolkhozes, the promise for more on-the-farm authority, and the probable writing of a new kolkhoz charter. If carried through, the implied administrative changes should be of some benefit. However, without knowing what thoughts were behind Brezhnev's remarks that the Khrushchev amalgamations went too far, I can conclude only that the kolkhozy and sovkhozy are such an integral part of the Soviet system and of the vision of a Communist future that they probably will continue to exist without basic change in the foreseeable future. Certainly the restoration of V. V. Matskevich as the Minister of Agriculture and his subsequent revelation that the administrative role of the Ministry of Agriculture has been restored hardly is indicative of a move to fundamental changes.[36] Nevertheless, Soviet leaders often have reversed themselves and often have adopted programs offered by earlier colleagues who were damned. The increasingly desperate situation in agricultural production could lead Khrushchev's successors to the discovery that a combination of the *zveno,* the production principle, as well as the "Leninist principle of material self-interest" (emphasizing individual economic incentives), offer the solution to Soviet agriculture's problems—problems that no reasonable increase in

[34] *Pravda,* September 15, 1953.
[35] *Ibid.,* March 27, 1965.
[36] *Trud,* April 4, 1965. This interview, interestingly enough, was not carried in most of the major national papers. See the translation in *The Current Digest of the Soviet Press,* XVII:17, 10–11.

investments alone can solve, be they in fertilizer or incentives. Soviet conditions built upon a heritage stemming from tsarist times probably are not adaptable to Western individualistic systems, but genuinely cooperative systems of farming are successful elsewhere, and an imaginative Soviet leadership could devise formulas for transforming the kolkhozy and sovkhozy into viable cooperative administrative forms and still argue that such changes are in fact strengthening communism in the rural U.S.S.R.

COMMENT

Howard R. Swearer

Central Committee Secretary M. A. Suslov has substantiated the negative view long held by Western observers of former Premier Nikita Khrushchev's administrative style: "Our cause suffered great harm from the frequent and unjustified reorganizations . . . [they] engendered irresponsibility and nervousness in work." [37] Professor Laird has abundantly illustrated the more egregious cases of this administrative "nervousness" and has indicated its deleterious impact on agriculture.

Soviet commentators have attributed the peripatetic nature of agricultural administration almost solely to Khrushchev's "organizational itch" (as one of his opponents put it in 1957). It would appear useful here to probe more deeply for explanations of the frantic and heavy-handed nature of administration than simply Khrushchev's personal idiosyncrasies (although, in truth, they should not be unduly discounted). The internal dynamics of the Soviet Party-state bureaucracy provide a part of the answer; but they have been examined by Laird and others so that I should like to address myself to two other interrelated sets of considerations, one economic and one political.[38]

When analyzing Soviet agriculture, a political scientist naturally deals with such wares of his trade as cadres, politics, organization, and administrative procedures. However, he must also be aware of the concerns of the economist which tend to center on such matters as investment, prices, and incentives. Investment without the proper institutional capacity to absorb it is wasteful. By contrast, institutional tinkering may have some short-term benefits, but if viewed as a substitute for necessary investment it will be fruitless and usually harmful in the long haul. Thus, it behooves the political scientist to indicate the economic constraints placed on Khrushchev's stewardship of administration.

Historically, the organization of Soviet agriculture can best be seen as the result of a decision to sacrifice the countryside to the purpose of building rapidly the industrial sector. Thus, an administrative-political

[37] *Pravda,* June 5, 1965.

[38] See also Alec Nove, "Soviet Agriculture Marks Time," *Foreign Affairs,* July (1962) and Howard Swearer, "Agricultural Administration Under Khrushchev," in Laird, ed., *op. cit.* (in n. 4).

apparatus was created to extract maximum output from the farms with minimum input. As a consequence, rigid and centralized administrative controls largely replaced market relationships; the habit of command and arbitrary political interference in farm management (most often by urban-recruited cadres) became deeply ingrained; and the industrial revolution in many respects bypassed the countryside.

In the original plan of Soviet economic development, agriculture was to bear the brunt of industrialization for only a few years until the foundations of industry were created and conditions for balanced economic growth restored. Despite faith in their ability, as Marxists-Leninists, to guide consciously and rationally the processes of social and economic development, Soviet leaders have discovered that tactics have a way of evolving into strategies, and means profoundly affect ends. Industry became a greedy goddess demanding ever greater libations from scarce resources. Patterns of planning and thinking arose which vitiated the original development scheme. New branches of industry, buttressed by the growth of powerful bureaucratic vested interests, demanded a continuation of their "fair" share of investments. Habits of administration in agriculture were instilled which proved surprisingly obdurate.

In sum, the legacy of the past continued to weigh heavily on Soviet agriculture even after the Khrushchev regime in the mid-1950's began to stress the need for dramatic increases in agricultural production and accompanying institutional modifications. A bureaucracy designed to keep the peasantry in a straitjacket found it difficult to adapt to the more difficult task of promoting a revolution in agricultural production. The deprivation of the agricultural sector had led to discontinuities between city and country that even the Stalinist command system could paper over only with great difficulty; and steps to dismantle parts of the command economy in agriculture in the 1950's were greatly hindered by the socioeconomic gulf between city and country. Relative underdevelopment of the countryside—manifested not only in under-mechanization of production, but in the backwardness of the whole infrastructure of the agricultural economy as well as the lack of amenities for the rural population—has resulted in low labor productivity and the continuation of an oversized peasant population; while, at the same time, the most ambitious, educated, and capable of the younger people have attempted to escape from the "idiocy of rural life" to the urban meccas. Long-standing distrust and tension between political-administrative cadres and the peasantry have also snarled plans for administrative reforms.

Rapid and sustained growth in agricultural production required major new investments; but agriculture had to compete with powerful vested interests in industry, not to mention an ambitious space program and the insatiable demands of modern armaments. Repeatedly, in the last decade and a half, the Presidium has given indications of being embroiled in dissension over the allocation of resources. Although agriculture has received a larger slice of the budget than under Stalin, resources have not been shifted massively and dramatically into agriculture. Moreover, the discrepancies between investment targets in Khrushchev's pronouncements and actual investments suggest either wishful thinking on the part of Soviet planners or that Khrushchev did not always have his way—or both.

As production failed to reach ambitious targets, especially after 1960, Khrushchev appeared to be attempting to substitute administrative palliatives and political leadership for shortfalls in investment. In so doing, he was conforming to a pattern of leadership well established long before his tenure. Moreover, Khrushchev's administrative reforms in the first five years after Stalin's death had indeed unlocked resources, both human and material, which contributed to improvement in production, and thus he might have expected similar results after 1958. In fact, because of the scope and frequency of the reorganizations, they actually proved to be counterproductive.

If the general economic situation provides the backdrop for an understanding of Khrushchev's administrative problems, specific policies were hammered out on the anvil of political conflict and were fraught with political implications. As the events of October, 1964, make clear, Khrushchev did not make policy in a vacuum: he was opposed at various times by powerful interests and he did not always have his way. We may speculate briefly on the manner in which this political conflict affected agricultural administration.

Khrushchev had staked out agriculture as his special bailiwick even before Stalin's death, and agricultural policy became a major weapon in his political arsenal in the power struggle after 1953. Agricultural successes between 1953 and 1958 inflated his political stock and contributed to his defeat of the "anti-Party group" in June, 1957. However, as production reverses set in after 1958, Khrushchev was so closely identified with agricultural policies that he could not avoid being tarred by these failures. He had compounded his political problems when in propounding slogans about overtaking American production and setting unrealistic targets for food production in the 1961 Party program, he had touched off a revolution of raising consumer expectations.

As disappointments piled up, Khrushchev's reaction was not to back away from his slogans and pare down plans to more realistic proportions in the light of experience; on the contrary, he became ever more activist and demanding. A steady stream of new programs and organizational nostrums was thrown into the battle for production. He repeatedly took to the hustings to goad local Party and state cadres to ever greater efforts. This course of action reinforced the traditional proclivities of local cadres to interfere constantly and arbitrarily in farm management. Moreover, as pressure from above on local cadres grew in intensity, the discipline of the regional and district cadres threatened to crack—as witnessed by the revelations of fraud in reporting on farm production in 1961—and central controls were tightened. Thus, tendencies toward decentralization of administration and granting of greater autonomy to farms in production planning were sharply reversed after 1960—in fact, if not in official pronouncements.

Political conflict afflicted agricultural programs in yet other ways. Disagreements among the top leaders on occasion appeared to lead to policy stalemate and drift, or unsatisfactory compromises. Such was the case in the late 1950's with the widely debated proposal to create kolkhoz-unions. On the other hand, political considerations may also help to account for the hasty and ill-prepared manner in which several major agricultural reforms were implemented. For example, the abolition of the MTS in early 1958 was put into effect more rapidly and more sweepingly than was originally projected. Khrushchev himself had stated that MTS should be retained for a period if they were servicing weaker collective farms. One suspects that Khrushchev may have found it necessary to move with great speed in abolishing the MTS in order to present an opposition with a *fait accompli* before it could launch a counterattack or erode the measure with delaying tactics. Similar considerations may have been at work in the massive and hasty reorganization of the Party and state apparatuses in the fall of 1962. In short, political strife helps to explain the erratic course of Soviet agricultural administration.

Khrushchev's intention—publicly stated in August, 1964—to unveil yet another major reorganization of agriculture at the scheduled November, 1964, Central Committee plenum, served as one of the immediate catalysts for the coup against him. In a broader context the failure of several of his agricultural policies, in addition to the dismal harvest of 1963 and the subsequent wheat purchases abroad, weighed heavily against him. Agriculture came under intense scrutiny and was subject to more far-reaching change than any other sector of public activity in the few months immediately after his ouster. Moreover, high-level personnel changes following on the heels of Khrushchev's political demise were especially marked in agriculture. Central Committee Secretary V. I. Poliakov and First Deputy Chairman of the Bureau for the R.S.F.S.R., L. N. Efremov who bore special responsibilities for agriculture in the Khrushchev regime, were demoted; and former Minister of Agriculture V. V. Matskevich, who had been fired by Khrushchev in 1960, was returned to his old position.

Khrushchev's successors have repeatedly asserted their intention to conduct the economy in a businesslike fashion, eschewing administrative panaceas and utopian thinking. In an attempt to unsnarl the administrative chaos of 1963–1964, Party and state administrations, which Khrushchev had divided into industrial and agricultural branches in 1962, were re-unified. The 1,670 TPA's were replaced by 2,434 *raions*. Although this number of districts is far short of the 3,200 *raions* existing in 1961, nevertheless, the present district is a more manageable size than the unwieldy TPA.

While the C.P.S.U. has gradually expanded its membership on the farms, the proportion of the population deriving its livelihood from agriculture remains badly underrepresented in the "Party of the people." Of the 11,758,000 Communists in January, 1965, only 2,164,000 or 18.5 percent were occupied in agriculture; and only 17 percent were actually working on collective and state farms (1,285,000 on collective farms and 734,000 on state farms). Between 1962 and 1965, the party expanded rapidly by 1.87 million members, but only 17 percent of the newcomers were occupied in agriculture.[39]

The post-Khrushchev leadership has stated its determination to give the farms greater say in the development of production plans and to avoid the past practice of arbitrary and frequent changes in procurement targets. Nationwide discussion campaigns have been held on such topics as kolkhoz democracy and the provisions of kolkhoz statutes in an attempt to provide the peasantry a closer sense of identity with the collective farm. Finally, discussions in the Party press have dwelled on the past errors of Party cadres who indulged in "narrow practicism" and exercised petty tutelage in supervising the farms. Such self-criticism has been accompanied by a spate of articles warning against "administrative rule" which ignores "economic levers" and asserting the need for "political acts and decisions to proceed from the demands of economic development."

[39] *Part. zh.*, No. 10 (1965), p. 15.

It is yet too early to judge whether Khrushchev's successors will be able to implement these intentions. Without being captious, however, one should note that the path of Soviet agricultural history is paved with good intentions and that formidable problems lie ahead. Similar policy statements have been heard more than once in the U.S.S.R.—indeed, they were voiced by Khrushchev himself. Many of the conditions mentioned earlier, which obstructed Khrushchev's fitful gropings for a rationalized administration, still exist. It is difficult to predict whether the newly renovated Ministry of Agriculture can operate with finesse or whether it will revert to earlier patterns and attempt to run the countryside as one huge farm. Many cadres in rural areas will find it difficult to shuck off the operational habits of a lifetime. Finally, the Soviet press indicates that Soviet organizational men are still attempting to carry water on both shoulders. While "definitively condemning" interference by Party cadres "in the daily work of the specialist or replacing him," nevertheless, the *apparatchiki* must engage in "concrete assistance, continuous and thorough supervision of the implementations of decisions." [40]

[40] *Pravda*, June 29, 1965.

ALEC NOVE

Peasants and Officials

The object of this contribution is to discuss the relationship between the local officials and the peasants. It includes the chairmen of the kolkhozes, though they sometimes behave like officials, sometimes like peasant headmen. The emphasis is on the local situation. Needless to say, the behavior of the officials is to a considerable extent conditioned by national policy, by what the leaders want, or by the general priorities of the regime. In these instances, the local secretaries are merely levers, connecting rods. However, it is becoming clear that the methods used by the Party secretaries, though no doubt developed as a consequence of policies insisted on by their superiors, now have a life and logic of their own. It could well be that it represents a major obstacle to the implementation of reforms which the top leadership appears to be considering. Their behavior may have distorted some of Khrushchev's measures, so that they had an impact other than he wished. Finally, the influence of the rural Party officials in the Party itself may affect the kind of proposals which are made. It is never realistic, under the guise of "totalitarianism," to assume that the men on the spot are mere cogs in a machine. Their character, interests, habits, can help to determine how the machine works.

Let us look at some of the characteristics of official attitudes, and then proceed to explain why they arose.

ATTITUDES TO THE KOLKHOZES

The Party secretary has regarded it as his primary responsibility to ensure the fulfillment and overfulfillment of the procurement plan. As Ovechkin's fictional but realistic character, Borzov, put it: *gosudarstvu nuzhen khleb,* "the state needs bread grains." Ovechkin's protest, "it is not merely for simplifying procurements that we created kolkhozes," is in itself significant enough. He describes the Borzov type of secretary as a "procurement agent."[1] Since local procurement plans were seldom fulfilled, and since, even if they were, a deficiency in other regions was probable, farms were constantly under pressure to deliver *all* their surpluses, and more, to the detriment of farms and peasants.

This has led, as is well known, to the repeated dishonoring of pledges about the size of the delivery quota, or promises to return "borrowed grain," or the removal even of seed grain (although there was more than one decree forbidding this), and impossibility of planning even the feeding of the kolkhoz livestock. ("Our concentrates were taken away as overplan deliveries.")[2]

This reflects a deeply rooted feeling that kolkhozes and peasants exist to be exploited, to be prevented from using for their own purposes produce which officials are obliged to secure for the state. There is no equivalent of this in other sectors of the economy.

It is also the practice of the officials in agriculture to issue orders about sown areas, output, livestock holdings, dates of sowing and harvesting, methods of sowing and harvesting, and so on, and this regardless of any legislation, such as the decree of 1955, which instructs them not to do this. Results, as is known, were often deplorable. This is not the place to set out the ample evidence, given by men as varied as Khrushchev and a whole list of contributors to literary journals. To cite one of the latter, Ivanov, who expressed his indignation at orders to increase sowings of corn and sugar beet where there was no means—through lack of labor and machinery—to cultivate them: "What basis was there for the doubling of sowings of corn and sugar beet? Was this not intended for the report, soullessly, without thinking of the consequences, without any economic analysis?"[3]

One sees here, of course, the consequence of pressure from above. This was the meaning of the statement cited by Abramov, that a chairman was reprimanded for "political underestimation of silage."[4] But it is more than this. Some secretaries take the initiative. One sees "a desire to shine," or *blesnut' pered nachal'stvom,* as the Russians say, in much the same way as a company commander wants to show off when an inspecting general comes. This is the way to promotion, or to avoid demotion, and the longer-term effect is ignored; its source may ultimately be unidentifiable, or the official may have been transferred. Some secretaries, with the same motives but less bold, show a tendency

[1] All quotations are from *Novyi mir,* No. 9 (1952).
[2] L. Ivanov, *Novyi mir,* No. 3 (1963), pp. 186–187.
[3] *Ibid.,* p. 191.
[4] *Neva,* No. 1 (1963).

merely to obey others blindly, to be "levers" (*rychagi*), as is so well shown in Iashin's sketch in the almanack *Literaturnaia Moskva*. Sometimes this type of behavior takes the form of simulation. The latter fits into the absurd behavior of the secretary in the Grodno province, criticized by *Pravda,*[5] who fulfills the plan by ordering the delivery of *all* grain, part of which is then transferred back to the kolkhozes in scarce trucks by overworked peasants at the height of the harvest. Asked why, the secretary replied that for him the plan was an order to be obeyed. Other forms of cheating are familiar to students of the subject.

The Party exercises tight control over appointments and also plays an active role in directly controlling agriculture. Local agricultural officials, indeed rural state officials in general, have always been weak. Khrushchev himself described them as the Party secretary's office boys. Whatever had been the intention of creating the Territorial Production Administrations, they seem not to have altered the situation. Ivanov, already cited, remarks that, in his area, the "inspector-organizers" were mainly women who were hardly ever noticeable. One had been on maternity leave without this making any difference.[6]

Historically the Party and the machine-tractor stations (MTS) had the joint function of ensuring that kolkhozes held together, but it seems possible that there was conflict about just who was dominant. In one of Ovechkin's sketches, the *raikom* secretary uses the following language to an MTS director: "You will not succeed in depriving us, the *raikom* of the Party, of the right to rule! It is not you who rule the *raion,* it is us! We will not hand the kolkhozes over to you! The *raikom* of the Party rules and will rule the kolkhozes. We know our obligations! And you, comrade director of the MTS, know your place!" [7] (This suggests that some local party officials favored the abolition of the MTS.)

The priority of "ruling" may help to explain the predilection of many local Party secretaries to amalgamate kolkhozes and sovkhozes too, a process which, as Brezhnev admitted, has gone beyond all reason. As Dorosh has pointed out, not only does it faciliate the exercise of control to have fewer to control, "but the illusion is created that there are no backward kolkhozes in the region." [8] Another form of simulation!

A further familiar feature of Party rule is distrust of kolkhoz officials, table-thumping abuse, cursing, and reprimands. All writers on rural

[5] *Pravda,* November 26, 1964.
[6] Ivanov, *op. cit.* (in n. 2), p. 194.
[7] This and other citations may be found in an analysis of Ovechkin's work by Vinogradov in *Novyi mir,* No. 6 (1964).
[8] *Ibid.,* p. 78.

themes—Ovechkin, Dorosh, Abramov, Ivanov, and Tendriakov—comment on this and deplore it. It constitutes one reason for the reluctance of self-respecting men to become kolkhoz chairmen.

An additional consequence of distrust is the repeated dispatch of "plenipotentiaries," charged with ensuring obedience to current orders about current priority campaigns. Their crudity, ignorance, effect on responsibility of kolkhoz officials, is well known.

This brings me to campaigns in general, and the role of the Party in forcing them on the kolkhozes, regardless of their interests. This, too, is a familiar phenomenon. It is worth emphasizing that not only have the kolkhozes been victims of sharp practice, but in general their needs have been systematically ignored, and particularly so in comparison with MTS and sovkhozes. This helps to explain the increased difficulties which arose with spares and supplies, and even in the production of farm machinery, after the transfer to kolkhozes of the machines in 1958. Similarly, the financial terms of the transfer, the insistence by local officials that the machinery be paid for in a year, despite the more liberal provisions of the law, constitutes one reason among others for the financial difficulties of many kolkhozes.[9]

ATTITUDES TO THE KOLKHOZNIKS

A characteristic, amply documented, of such attitudes is the ignoring of the material interests of peasants. In insisting on deliveries of produce, in financial policy, in ordering the expansion of unremunerative productive activities, the officials seem to have no concern with the peasants, who, they must presumably assume, can devise their own means of keeping alive. Dorosh described such an official in vivid terms. He boasted that "mice would break their heads in the kolkhoz barn searching for just one grain" when he had finished "procuring," and a dismayed chairman is cited as saying: "The hand of such a man would not tremble when he leaves the children without milk—he would not leave a drop." [10]

This leads to ignoring the need to ensure an adequate collective income, in cash and in kind. Gradually this is being corrected, but the correction seems to come from above, not from regional Party level. Thus the Party secretary of the Estonian republic is evidently pleased to be able to report that all "kolkhozes in Estonia pay peasants a regular guaranteed minimum." Others remain prone to ordering loss-making activities, ranging from lavish capital expenditure to the purchase of

[9] See the vigorous criticism by Matskevich in *Vop. ek.*, No. 6 (1965), pp. 4–6.
[10] E. Dorosh, *Novyi mir*, No. 6 (1964), p. 68.

butter (at retail prices) for redelivery to the state "as milk." The cost of simulation often falls on the peasants.

The same neglect extends to the provision of amenities in villages, despite talk about "eliminating differences between town and country." Admittedly the story about an official who was accused of being "an enemy of the people" because he looked after them too well belongs to the thirties. Yet many have noted that little attention is paid to elementary comforts, and that officials who have abundantly proved their inefficiency are apt to be appointed to manage rural cooperatives.

Officials are particularly apt to regard the private plot with suspicion. True, they have been encouraged to restrict it on occasion, but they do not seem to need much encouragement, and the fact that there have been local variations in policies shows that there is no clear and enforceable guidance from the center. The way in which these restrictions are imposed must be a source of endless bad blood between officials and peasants. Instances can be quoted almost *ad infinitum* from Soviet literature. When willing labor is scarce, the obvious way out—to encourage effort by giving a share of it to the peasants—is regarded as almost anti-Soviet, even if the alternative is all-round loss. Abramov raised this issue over hay in his *Vokrug da okolo*. Particularly sharp remarks were made by Dorosh. "Why does this kolkhoz prefer to burn straw rather than to give it to the peasant? And why are potatoes left in the fields, and grass unmown? If the peasant takes them for himself, then he is a thief. Is he in his own kolkhoz, as should be implied by the words 'Collective economy'? . . . Let the straw rather burn and indeed *trudodni* are earned for burning it, let the peasant women rupture themselves dragging all kinds of rubbish from God knows where for manure bedding. The interests of the state, that is, some abstract dogma, are protected thereby." He also remarks: "No one here talks to the peasants, or explains to them what is to be done, what has already been done. . . . It is odd that when [in the *raion* center] the discussion concerns agriculture, people talk about kolkhoz amalgamations, sending chairmen to kolkhozes, on the virtues of corn for fodder . . . and it does not occur to everyone [sic!] to interest themselves in how much a kolkhoznik earns, in whether he would be earning more if the kolkhozes were amalgamated and a new chairman were sent, and indeed what he thinks of all this." [11] There is no need, I think, to labor the point. Recent evidence, published in *Voprosy ekonomiki*,[12] showed that restrictions on the private plot are counterproductive, since all

[11] *Op. cit.*, pp. 56–57.
[12] G. Shmelev, *Vop. ek.*, No. 4 (1965).

additional difficulties in getting fodder compel the peasants to devote *more* time to a smaller number of private livestock. The same, no doubt, applies to the effect of lack of facilities to get to market.

All this must have had a profound effect on the peasants' view of officials. They are usually strangers. As Dorosh once put it, in seven years four *raikom* secretaries succeeded each other, "all arrived from the outside." Each was likely to have "his own special enthusiasms and passions in agriculture." The peasant noted too the relative passivity and total subordination of local state officials. Dorosh paints a picture of such an official, Stepan Pavlovich, who stays for many years in an office known at various dates by a different title, does what he is told, and waits for his pension.[13] The peasant has many reasons to consider himself a second-class, underprivileged citizen. This attitude must be considerably strengthened by what he sees of the way Party secretaries behave toward him and toward the kolkhoz. The peasant is not skilled with the pen, and so he does not write about his feelings. In one of his earlier works, Dorosh warned that the peasant might say to the Party official, as Lenin warned: "if you cannot manage affairs, then get out."[14]

At the same time, many officials seem to have regarded the peasants as untrustworthy, tricky backsliders, always willing to act against state interests, backward technically. This, at any rate, is an integral part of the frequently repeated criticism of the "old methods of work" which are to be (or are being) replaced by a new approach.

THE CHAIRMEN

What about the situation of the chairmen of kolkhozes situated uncomfortably between officials and peasants? And what of directors of sovkhozes? The latter were at one time quite different types of men, though now, with the great increase in numbers of sovkhozes and of the size of kolkhozes, and a tendency to merge the control system, the differences might be less than before. Traditionally, sovkhoz directors received orders from trusts or regional bodies in their own hierarchy, while kolkhozes were ordered about by the *raikom* secretaries. For lack of information, rather than a desire to neglect sovkhozy, I will concentrate on the chairmen of kolkhozes.

Here evidence of great variety is abundant. The sheer size of a kolkhoz makes close human contact impossible. Kuznetsov's vivid

[13] Dorosh, *op. cit.* (in n. 10), pp. 13, 58.
[14] *Novyi mir,* No. 10 (1962), p. 46.

story[15] showed that the chairman appeared in outlying hamlets only when something went seriously wrong, which is scarcely surprising with existing road conditions. He often remains unknown to many of the members; the more so as it has become physically impossible to call a kolkhoz meeting. It follows that his relationship with the peasants, and with his superiors, has greatly changed since the average size of kolkhozes has quintupled, when compared with the period before 1950.

Some chairmen have willingly applied the official line, as they understood it, *against* the peasants. Here is Dorosh again: "He was seized with an irresistible impulse to free the peasants of petty-property instincts, for which purpose he orders them to hand over their cows voluntarily to the kolkhoz . . . promising them all but free milk; and to ensure that the peasants do not refrain from achieving this happy state, he allows them neither pasture facilities nor hay." [16] But against this we have Abramov's "hero" very unhappy with official guidance on this matter, deciding (admittedly with the help of vodka) to defy instructions.[17] There is evidence also, from literature and the experience of individual visitors, of chairmen who are efficient, who do their best for the peasants, and who may be regarded as fellow-victims of officialdom. Here is how Ivanov puts it, in the context of absurd orders to grow corn, eliminate clover, deliver fodder grain to the state, keep cattle alive for statistical purposes, and so on: "There was not a single reproach in respect of the chairman. Said a pig minder: 'He looks after things, but . . . they do not always allow him to do right.' " [18] Ivanov describes a chairman who actually refused to accept some ducklings which were allocated to him by the *raion* official. His comment is interesting: "unheard-of disobedience." But there must be others like him.

Some chairmen, as Dorosh puts it, "tend to introduce all sorts of novelties," others "are quite indifferent." There is a sad account of the first kind, involving, again, ducks. A chairman, described as basically hostile to peasants and anxious to get rid of them and substitute machines, acquires vast quantities of mandarin ducks, which were subsequently killed by pike. The resultant heavy losses were borne by the peasants. The author comments that the large landowners (*pomeshchiki*) also had their brain waves, but at least they paid for the failures out of their own pockets. He also noted the tendency, common also among

[15] *Ibid.*, No. 1 (1963).
[16] Dorosh, *Novyi mir*, No. 10 (1962), p. 13.
[17] *Op. cit.* (in n. 4).
[18] *Novyi mir*, No. 3 (1963), p. 186.

officials, to pick schemes which give publicity to themselves ("Who will be surprised with potatoes or garlic? But a mandarin duck, that's different! They will write in the papers about the ducks.") A similar point was made about a sovkhoz director who, to the horror of his agronomist, ploughed under trees on a hillside and caused many to fall, all to exceed 100 percent of the ploughing plan. "100 percent, that's just average. With just average indicators one will just work on indefinitely, no one will notice." [19]

Then there is another kind of chairman, the skilled maneuverer. One is described by Tendriakov. He once got into endless trouble by growing cabbages to order when other officials had "forgotten" to organize their storage, transport, and distribution. He learned his lesson. His two slogans were: "A reprimand, unlike tuberculosis, can be carried about" and "A wise man does not climb a mountain, he goes around it." He seems to be in league with some at least of his peasants in an endless struggle with the bosses above him. Thus "he met the terrible corn as a wise general," made speeches about the "queen of the fields," and then announced that it had all been killed by frosts and that his fields had to be resown with oats and barley. However, he kept a couple of hectares to show the *raion* officials that, by great efforts, he had managed to save some. He lied shamelessly to the officials, "but in the autumn they had bread grains and were able to pay the peasants." Similarly he dealt with the "Riazan' miracle," the great meat campaign. "In all the country they followed [the Riazan' example], fulfilled and overfulfilled meat sales, slaughtered not only calves and milk cows, but pregnant cows and breeding bulls." This chairman made speeches, and carefully disposed only of his inferior breed of pigs. The point of Tendriakov's story is that the chairman "infected" the heroine with his sly methods, so that she too cheated. But Tendriakov is clear that this chairman, as many others, was himself reacting to campaigns, pressures, reprimands.[20] Others may well be in collusion with Party officials at local level, jointly to mislead those above them. Still others do their best to be honest, although, as is often remarked, circumstances make it difficult not to be in breach of some regulation.

Officials, including senior officials, and also some chairmen, had a predilection for panacea solutions to obtain results. Hence, perhaps, Lysenko was their favorite agronomist. Many of them, as Sharov states in an admirable article on Lysenkoism, "were half-educated guardians of the infallibility of pamphlets." He draws an interesting parallel with

[19] A. Sharov, *Znamia*, No. 4 (1965), p. 170.
[20] *Novyi mir*, No. 5 (1965), pp. 103–104.

what he calls "mighty feudal lords," who also wanted results, and therefore backed alchemy, not chemistry ("alchemy . . . is wholly utilitarian. Its aim is obtaining gold"). Similarly there was more practical value in astrology ("foretells the future!") than in astronomy. Experimental proof was resented, as inconsistent with "blind faith and administrative coercion." And in any case "dogma outweighed millions of tons of grain," as when hybrid corn was rejected. As the Empress Elisaveta Petrovna once said: "From the enemies of Christ I will not take valuable ideas" (*ot vragov khristovykh ne priemliu interesnoi pribyli*, to cite the antique Russian).[21]

CAUSES

These types of behavior have deep roots in history and in institutional arrangements. A two-faced attitude to the peasants is inherent in Bolshevism. H. G. Wells, reporting Lenin's remarks about the socialized agriculture of the future, commented: "At the mention of the peasants, Lenin's manner became confidential . . . as if, after all, the peasants might overhear." [22] Lenin sought to secure peasant support for the revolution and then to change matters somewhat after it.

The problem of procurements was already a vital one in the N.E.P. period. The "Ural-Siberian method" of forced collections was devised by Stalin personally early in 1928. Despite Ovechkin's pained remark, cited earlier, collectivization *was* carried out largely to facilitate procurement. Thus generations of rural Party secretaries were judged by their success in running the procurement campaign. This deeply affected their behavior.

Collectivization itself was a major surgical operation, which affected patients and surgeons deeply. Collectivization was not merely based on large-scale coercion, carried out by local officials, but also on a series of lies, or at best half-truths, concerning what was happening and why it was happening. Officials would not, at least in their official capacity, admit to each other what all knew to be the truth. This habit persisted, and it was this which was so vividly described in Iashin's *Rychagi.* Party officials in rural areas had a tough and unpopular job, and were themselves at the receiving end of reprimands and threats. The efforts they made to show their superiors that they were carrying out orders caused, and still causes, numerous distortions in agricultural planning and in human relations with those below them. All this has been

[21] Sharov, *op. cit.* (in n. 19), pp. 163–168.

[22] H. G. Wells, *Russia in the Shadows* (London: Hodder & Stoughton, n.d.), p. 136.

technically related to overambitious plans, a tendency for the men at the top to ask for the impossible. This has frequently meant that the honest official who aims for the sound and the realistic has been held up to ridicule, while deranged individuals like Larionov of Riazan', the man who promised to treble meat deliveries, were praised by the First Secretary. It is a puzzling matter that the evident harm done by encouraging absurd plans has not been obvious long ago to the top leadership.

The low priority of agriculture was, of course, inherent in the nature of Stalinist industrialization, and in the purpose for which kolkhozes were set up. Therefore the relative neglect of the needs of farming and especially of the peasants was no accidental deficiency of local Party secretaries. Times changed, needs changed, but the habits of officials at all levels lagged behind, and must have contributed to the otherwise inexplicable "reaction" in agricultural incomes, inputs, and investment which occurred after 1957.

Similarly, it was logical to have to substitute orders (and threats of punishment) for incentives when there were no incentives and when prices were confiscatory. When there is no profit in farm activity, then both chairmen and peasants must be ordered to carry out even such elementary tasks as sowing and harvesting, and the production pattern must be the subject of instructions too. One of Ovechkin's characters says: Yes, officials are "pushers and chasers," because "if we leave the whole thing to spontaneity, if we do not press, order, threaten punishment," nothing happens. Hence the value of a plenipotentiary, crude and brutal though he may be, "who, if sent to a district with some kind of concrete task to perform, will run himself into the ground, raise up the living and the dead, but he will carry out his orders." Thus the system developed as a substitute for the nonexistent or misleading economic incentives, and then became a habit. It created a situation in which many junior officials, in offices and in farms, waited for orders, and so the system established its own indispensability.

The lack of economic incentives explains campaigns, which, in part at least, are the *modus operandi* of the Party and provide success indicators for Party officials. The quotation from Ovechkin refers to *raion* officials, who are themselves inactive unless prodded by campaigns, plenipotentiaries, and threats of punishment.

Substitution of commands for incentives also explains the tendency of some officials to resort to various forms of statistical manipulation, since their careers depend on claiming success in the fulfillment of basically unrealistic plans.

Moreover, distrust of private plots has deep roots, since the plots are symbolic of private enterprise, uncontrolled initiative (*samotek*), and other undesirable phenomena. They also visibly take the peasants' attention away from the collective sector, from which, since January, 1958, practically all state procurements have been drawn.

In the historical and institutional circumstances, it seems clear that officials have some basis for thinking that the peasants, their brigade leaders, even at times their "elected" chairmen, have interests other than those of maximizing state procurements; that, left to themselves, they will do the wrong things. Therefore they must be kept on the right track by plenipotentiaries, inspectors, and threats. Some officials presumably also believe that peasants are traditionalist, unenterprising, lacking in initiative. Khrushchev once put it colorfully to an American journalist. Russian peasants, he said, had not been through the capitalist school. (He did not add that those who had were deported as kulaks in 1930.) Therefore it seemed natural that peasants had to be ordered to be modern, to change the old patterns, and the officials who did this may well have reminded themselves of Catherine's insistence on the planting of potatoes in the eighteenth century. The peasants resisted, but they were wrong and Catherine's officials were right about the peasants' own interest. Such reasoning provides cover for a multitude of sins.

Yet there is also an ingrained distrust of peasant initiative which the officials feel may involve actions contrary to the interests of the regime.

The mental makeup of rural officialdom was shaped in the Stalin era. It takes time to make any radical change in their ideas and their methods. They are the local bosses, with special responsibility for agriculture. It is not enough to urge them—as Khrushchev often did—"to work in a new way." How? By persuasion? But if they cannot persuade, they *must* order. No wonder that Ovechkin's Borzov was a much more convincing and human (though nasty) character than his "good" replacement.

Khrushchev's policies concerning local officials were inconsistent and contradictory. He condemned the old crudities, and spoke of the need for a better deal for peasants, more facilities for their private activities, reduced taxes, higher priority for farms, and more autonomy for management. Yet his campaigns and his speeches at the plenum made nonsense of his own recommendations. The unrealistic targets made excesses by local officials unavoidable. It is true that in themselves these excesses were sometimes not desired. Thus Khrushchev was doubtless horrified by the story of a field of growing clover, ploughed in for no better reasons than to show a reduced acreage of grassland. He specifically warned against administrative pressure to sell private cows. Yet he so acted as to cause these local excesses to happen. He added to confusion and irresponsibility by repeated reorganizations of the Party, and by in effect eliminating the powers of the Ministry of Agriculture, especially after 1959. His price reform of 1958 was insufficiently logical, in the sense that price relativities conflicted with the plan; thus a large increase in meat output was desired, though meat production involved heavy loss. This conflict compelled officials to intervene and this, in the campaign atmosphere, led to the excesses of a Larionov in Riazan'.

Let me illustrate, by two quotations, the pressure to which head officials were subjected. One comes from an excellent article by Yu. Chernichenko.[23] He describes an actual meeting in Slavgorod (Kulunda steppe), attended by an unnamed "plenipotentiary from the capital," evidently Khrushchev's right-hand man (Shevchenko?). A *raikom* secretary was speaking, "when the plenipotentiary from the capital interrupted him."

"Why do you fail to keep up the delivery schedule?"

The secretary referred to the weather. Then the mighty visitor, winding himself up, started questioning: have any Communists remained in the *raion* center? Why so? What right have they to stay there when the fate of the grain harvest was being decided? The Slavgorod secretary shrugged his shoulders: these are officials of the *raion* finance office, the posts, railways. What should they be doing in the fields?

It was there that the plenipotentiary blew up. He jumped from the table, he shouted: "Such a capitulator still sits on the *raikom?* Remove him, remove him! What are you afraid of? We removed countless officials in Tula until we found the right man! People like him should be thrown out! Who gave you the right to be so soft [*liberal 'nichat'*]?" . . .

It was not only his rudeness that was so insulting. We were oppressed by the pettiness of the plenipotentary's requirements. We would understand if he were angry because the land was in poor state, because of the wild oats, the roadlessness, lack of grain storage space—because good grain was mixed with rubbish, or because cultivation methods had not changed since the first year of the virgin lands campaign. Sharpness or even rudeness would be explained by the worry of a true husbandman. But the plenipotentiary required only one thing: that this very day, the day of his arrival, grain should be delivered to the elevators and local storage dumps. No matter what kind, dry or in damp lumps, that intended for deliveries or seed grain (later we discovered: he left the Novosibirsk *oblast'* without seed that autumn).

One after another the *raikom* secretaries went up to speak, and were met with the same shouting: "When will there be a plenipotentiary with each combine harvester? Take Communists from wherever they might be, send them to the *machines!* Make them stay there all the time! Let them be

[23] *Novyi mir,* No. 11 (1965), p. 182.

personally responsibile for the threshing! A thousand combine harvesters? Then—a thousand plenipotentiaries. If two thousand are needed, we'll send them."

A young chairman could not refrain from shouting from his seat: "But all our combiners are Communists. Are they also [to have plenipotentiaries attached to them]?"

"What is his name? Consider this at once in the bureau! At once in the bureau,' cried the plenipotentiary, gasping with fury."

The effect on grain quality, and on the morale of officials, hardly needs stressing. The author himself comments: "Crude shouting and directives engendered a reluctance to think. Reluctance to think engendered stereotyped methods. Stereotyped methods make of the harvest the helpless victim of weather conditions, weeds, and pests. The official who deprives himself of the right to act according to circumstances deprives himself of the right to make demands upon others. There arises a vicious circle of irresponsibility. This is the family tree of the standardized scheme."

The same picture emerges from many speeches made at the Central Committee plenum of March, 1965. Here, for example, are the words of I. Gustov, Secretary of the Pskov *obkom*: "Much harm was done by the imposition [from above] of sown-area structures. . . . All of us *obkom* secretaries recall how we were called annually to the Agricultural Department of the Central Committee of C.P.S.U. for the R.S.F.S.R., where the sown-area structure was imposed, we were compelled to put our signatures to this structure, and afterwards it was all presented as proposals from below." [24]

Obviously, this could not but affect the behavior of *obkom* officials.

It must be added in fairness that many speakers at this plenum drew attention in strong language to the necessity of improving pay and amenities in rural areas, pointing to the dangerous loss of labor, especially by kolkhozes. It may well be that they had made these representations in earlier years too, but they were given less publicity.

How far did the policy errors of the period after 1958 also originate with local officials? *They* seem to have pressed for amalgamations of farms, *they* favored lower prices at the winter plenum in 1958–1959, *they* said they were worried about "excessive" peasant incomes in the better-off farms and *they* took the initiative against private plots in a number of instances. It is easy to blame Khrushchev alone. But was he not, in these instances, reflecting the instincts of local Party officials? The point is not unimportant as we look ahead.

[24] *Plenum Tsentral'nogo Komiteta Kommunisticheskoi Partii Sovetskogo Soiuza, 24–26 marta 1965 g.* (Moscow: 1965), pp. 144–145.

WHAT NOW?

The post-Khrushchev era has opened the way for important reforms in agriculture. Among these is to be a change in the *modus operandi* of officials which will affect their relations with peasants and with farm management. At the same time, the leadership principle is maintained, the key role of the Party secretary emphasized. The following quotation gives a fair representation of what appears to be the present policy: "These differences [will be] big! In the place of pressure and arbitrariness has come persuasion, explanation, education, control not over people but through people, relying on people. It is perfectly possible to do without orders, without definitive instructions." (There follows an example of how an argument about whether calves should suckle the cows would have been dealt with by orders binding on everyone, whereas now there was consultation and experiment.) "The way to success lies in the increased role of rural Party organization, the direct influence of Communists on the economics of kolkhozes and sovkhozes. And as for the purely productive side of the work—*and the* raikom *cannot leave it aside, it is still responsible for everything*—this is now decided in far better conditions and by different methods of control." [25] The same point is repeated in other articles. The work is to be done not by campaign methods, but thought out in detail, with the long term in mind, with the *raikom* consulting the experts.[26]

This suggests that the Party will still be very much in charge, but they are to take wise decisions, taking into account local conditions and the ideas of experts, management, agronomists, even peasants. (Whether this will be consistent with the ideas of Matskevich, whose revived Ministry of Agriculture is surely intended to have effective local organs, raises issues not germane to the present subject.) The local Party and state officials are to have a key role in deciding the delivery obligations of farms, and thereby their specialization, if any. They are enjoined not to vary arbitrarily the delivery obligations of farms, to let over-quota sales be genuinely voluntary, to let the farm management have much greater freedom to choose the farming methods, and (within limits) the crop pattern and livestock holdings which they prefer. Private interests of peasants are to be given greater attention, the restrictions on the private plot were relaxed.

Yet these are apparently the same *obkom* and *raikom* officials. There is no sign of any major new broom. On the contrary, the top leadership

[25] *Ek. gaz.*, July 21, 1965. Emphasis mine.
[26] *Ibid.*, July 7, 1965.

has been weakened and seems more dependent than ever on the good will of the intermediate grades of the *apparat.* The latter can therefore largely determine the way in which reforms are implemented. It may well be that they will continue to interfere with farm management and exercise the same pressure as before to overfulfill procurement targets. They are hardly the kind of people to study patiently the demands of specialization, and they might well throw out proposals from below (as has happened often enough in the past) and substitute what they think Moscow wants to hear. Thus skepticism would be in order. The same applies to their reaction to a variety of new proposals and experiments, which are being discussed and (here and there) tried out. The Party secretaries may be, in this respect too, an obstructionist and conservative force.

However, this view may be proved wrong, if Moscow's pressure on local officials is relaxed. One of the causes of "campaigning" pressures by officials, of their neglect of the long-term health of agriculture, and of peasant interest in favor of immediate results, is that they were forced by their superiors to behave in this way. If Brezhnev keeps his promise to have modest delivery quotas for each region, and does not publicly announce excessively ambitious production plans, local officials may after all be able to take expert advice and avoid the stupidities of the past. Many of them may well sincerely desire to do the right thing. If price relativities are improved, then, with the considerably higher general level of purchase prices, incentives could be more closely linked with the pattern of production actually needed, and so the objective need for issuing orders on farming operations could be reduced considerably. Thus, changes toward a less strained relationship between officials and those below them, which seems to be consciously sought by the leadership, might perhaps come about. In this connection the bad weather of 1965 is most unfortunate, since shortage is likely to inhibit relaxation of controls.

But another obstacle to progress must be briefly mentioned in conclusion. The peasants, conditioned to skepticism by many past promises, may not believe Brezhnev, however sincere he may be. The peasant's own status is still that of a second-class citizen, passportless, without assurance of freedom of movement or even of study. Of course, the desire of skilled or ambitious villagers to go to town is a universal phenomenon, and not peculiar to Russia. However, the willing participation of the peasants, the willingness of men to operate and repair farm machinery, these are obviously essential if the new policies are to succeed. Involved in all this is a new spirit between the rulers and the farmers. Evidence of good intention exists. Evidence of the ability and willingness of officials to change long-ingrained habits and methods of work is still lacking. We can just wait and see. The speeches at the March, 1965, plenum are hopeful in that they do indicate a new spirit both among the leadership and among the local officials. However, these same speeches frankly emphasize the magnitude of the tasks.

COMMENT

Basile Kerblay

I find myself in agreement with Professor Alec Nove's statements. So I will restrict my remarks to some differences in emphasis and a few footnotes to his comprehensive analysis.

First the differences in emphasis. There is no denying the fact that the prevailing attitude of Soviet officialdom is arrogance toward their inferiors and submissiveness toward their superiors; their common belief is that the peasants are backward and ignorant, and should be told what is their interest.[27] Moreover, priority is still given to the fulfillment and overfulfillment of specific plans. Still I wonder whether in agriculture as in many other areas of the Soviet economy, there is not some room for various kinds of compromises.

Here are two examples of what I mean: (1) The discussion of procurement objectives between the *raikom* and the chairman of the collective farm sometimes permits even now the substitution of one crop for another;[28] it also permits various deals: for example, as seen in a recent novel, "I'll trade you that *nariad* for timber you wanted if you will transfer part of your cattle to another collective farm";[29] (2) the same kind of compromises are also made inside the collective farm when the kolkhozniks are provided with free transportation for various personal needs—including to the market—or when a traditional village festival keeps the peasant from working.[30] In recent years the possibility of sharecrop farming is emerging not only in Abramov's novel *Vokrug da okolo,*[31] but also in practice: it has been reported that in the Leningrad

[27] As Professor Nove pointed out, such attitudes had been noticed in Russia in the past, and they might also be detected elsewhere. It might be worthwhile to investigate the similarities and contrasts in the attitudes of Soviet agricultural officials and Western agronomists confronted with the task of promoting a new type of agriculture in underdeveloped countries. For example, in Madagascar, where the native peasant stopped working as soon as he earned a few coins, a personal agricultural tax in kind was introduced as a means of extracting a marketable surplus from the peasants living in conditions of subsistence farming.

[28] *Izvestiia,* February 6, 1965.

[29] T. Borisov, *Novyi mir,* No. 10 (1964), pp. 11, 23, 29, 39.

[30] E. Dorosh in *Literaturnaia Moskva* (Moscow: 1956), pp. 571–573. See also *Izvestiia,* March 28, 1965.

[31] *Neva,* No. 1 (1963). In 1956, a 10 percent share was already considered as a "conquest." Cf. Dorosh, *op. cit.* (in n. 30), p. 603.

oblast' 50 percent of the harvested hay on former bushland is given to the sovkhoz workers.[32] Since success is the main criterion for the promotion of rural administrators, top administrators must give some consideration give to the actual possibilities and requirements at the bottom, that is, some kind of compromise.

My second remark deals with the attitude of the peasantry. If we take the problem from the peasant's point of view it makes a big difference whether the boss is an "outsider" coming from town or another region *or* a native related by birth or marriage to the local community. The former is less inclined to compromise, which leads me to the question of factors underlying attitudes. To the comprehensive list of factors given by Nove, I would like to add a footnote: the collectivization of agriculture has deprived the rural community of its real leaders (the so-called "kulaks," clergymen, and so on); therefore there is no longer either a leading rural group playing the role of a buffer for smoothing the relations between the peasants and the authorities or an organized representation of the peasantry, whereas in the West the importance of rural pressure groups and farmer unions tends to increase in spite of the steady decrease of the agricultural population. Communists have always been suspicious of any moves that could enhance the vitality of rural communities. The *agrogorod* proposals for resettling old villages, the reluctance shown toward Strumilin's suggestion for the creation of a pyramidal organization of collective farm unions on the model of *Tsentrosoiuz,*[33] should be viewed as a deliberate policy against the strengthening of rural interests. The tendency now is to go even further and eliminate the collective farm assembly, replacing it by local Party meetings as the locus of decision-making.

Turning now to the short-term perspective, I agree with Nove that the attitude of local officials will depend on pressure from the top. We are now in a situation when the leadership in the Kremlin is yet unsettled, so that there is no emerging trend. (The Party congress has been postponed.) The unified *raikoms* have been reestablished with the same staff and nearly the same functions as they had before.[34] Can we take at face value those promises concerning the autonomy of farm or the independent *economic* determination of delivery obligations? Such speeches have been heard frequently in the past. On the other hand the

[32] G. Vasil'eva, *Kommunist,* No. 9 (1965), p. 127. See also 1. Ivanov, *Novyi mir,* No. 2 (1965), p. 194 where he discusses a similar proposal in the Kalinin *oblast'.*

[33] In *Na puti stroitel'stva kommunizma* (Moscow: 1959).

[34] G. Sizov, *Kommunist,* No. 5 (1965), p. 43; V. Kulikov, *ibid.,* No. 11 (1965), p. 60 and *Ek. gaz.,* July 21, 1965, pp. 3–4.

impact of rapid changes in the professional composition of Soviet officials on their outlook and behavior should also be taken into account. The so-called "professionalization" of rural life tends to increase the number of agricultural specialists in the rank of local hierarchy as well as the number of collective-farm chairmen with an adequate training.[35] At the same time the percentage of professionals becoming members of the Communist party in rural areas is also increasing. One might expect that improved professional education and managerial training will lead towards a more rational type of relationships in the countryside.

Agriculture is not the single factor affecting the relations between local officials and the peasant. The clash between Marxism-Leninism and the traditional peasant-culture *Weltanschauung* is at the root of the problems involved. Is it necessary to recall the intimate relations between agriculture, the family, and religion in the traditional outlook? For the Russian peasant the *raison d'être* of farming is not the seeking of the maximum monetary profit but the securing of the basic needs of its family whatever the costs,[36] and the agricultural work is never completely detached from religion.[37] The old traditions still maintain their vitality in the countryside as is shown in many recent monographs on kolkhoz life.[38] That is why, as in the past, the attitude of the peasantry to a great extent will be affected by the fate of the private plot.

On this issue we find contradictory statements in the Soviet press and publications. The so-called "public discussion" initiated by *Ekonomicheskaia gazeta* [39] on desirable modifications of *artel'* statutes—as shown by the small number of letters published up to the present—reflects a conservative attitude. Chairmen of collective farms are reluctant to abandon the possibility of reducing the size of the plot as a means of

[35] In 1964, 66.4 percent of collective-farm chairmen are reported to have completed secondary or higher education (*Narkhoz-1963*, p. 368). The number of graduates from institutes of agricultural higher education who also worked in agricultural enterprises has increased fom 22,000 in 1950 to 98,000 in 1960; cf. Nicholas DeWitt in U.S. Congress, Joint Economic Committee, *Dimensions of Soviet Economic Power* (Washington, D.C.: Government Printing Office, 1962), p. 265. Nevertheless, 76.6 percent of the total working agricultural manpower consist of unspecialized rank and file collective farmers. Cf. *Kommunist*, No. 11 (1965), p. 44.

[36] See my comments on Chaianov's theory of the peasant economy in *Cahiers du monde russe et sovietique*, V (October–December, 1964), pp. 411–460.

[37] See my presentation of Engelhardt's *Letters from the Countryside*, 1878–1881 in *Le statut des paysans libérés du servage, 1861–1961* (Paris: Mouton, 1963), pp. 265–310.

[38] *Selo Viriatino* (Moscow: 1958); V. Selivanov, ed. *Riazanskoe selo Korablino* (Riazan': 1957); an article by Klebanov in *Voprosy ateizma i religii*, VIII (1960) and IX (1961) and V. Soloukhin, *Kaplia rosy* (Moscow: 1960).

[39] *Ek. gaz.*, No. 13, 21, 22, 30 (1965).

enforcing discipline. On the other hand, we can also point to new trends as they are reflected in some articles where the efficiency of private farming and its complementarity to collective farming is recognized.[40] Finally, the renting of collective farm land to private livestock owners is now permitted.[41]

If the latest trend persists, it is by no means impossible that in the long run a new form of socialized farming will replace the present collective farms. I do not mean a mere restoration of the private farming such as that which existed during the N.E.P. period. At the present time, in many industrialized countries farming is no longer an autonomous activity separate from its processing and marketing. The trend is for a vertical integration in which the private farmer loses his independence for the sake of a stable income.[42] Up to now the emphasis in the U.S.S.R. has been wrongly placed on horizontal integration (that is, big farms) whereas vertical integration has been neglected.[43] Vertical integration in which private farming is closely associated with the cooperative and the state sectors—as in Poland—offers, as pointed out by Korbonski, an alternative for other "socialist" countries. Needless to say such a new organizational framework would imply a complete departure from the present state of relations between officials and the peasant, a vivid picture of which has been presented by Alec Nove.

[40] G. Shmelev, *Vop. ek.*, No. 4 (1965) and Lopatina in *Lit. gaz.*, June 29, 1965.

[41] An article in *Komsomol'skaia Pravda,* August 7, 1965, suggests a sort of share-crop farming with a permanent allotment of collective farm land to small groups of kolkhozniki.

[42] The best example of this western type of vertical integration of private farming can be found in the organization of the Scandinavian firm "Findus." This enterprise operates a number of processing factories (controlling up to 80 percent of the production of frozen foods in Sweden) and a central research unit. Its ties to agricultural producers are organized on a contractual basis. All directives concerning methods of production to be employed by farms are issued by the research unit, while farmers are guaranteed a steady and adequate income. Cf. *Entreprise* (Paris), July 11, 1964.

[43] New trends seem to be emerging in the U.S.S.R. in the form of agro-industrial *kombinaty* where the size of the farm, as well as its location are related to the capacity of the processing plants and their relation to the market.

ROBERT G. JENSEN

The Soviet Concept of Agricultural Regionalization and Its Development

Among the major economic endeavors farming is perhaps the least adaptable to centralized planning. Of this fact the leaders of the Soviet Union must be keenly aware. Yet, barring a fundamental change in the Soviet system, and this seems unlikely, centralized planning will continue to play a leading role in the agricultural sector. Indeed, it is the essence of Soviet agricultural planning that the determination of what is to be grown where and in what quantities cannot be left to chance. On the other hand, it is obvious, if only because of the whims of nature and agriculture's infinite variety, that crop production on each hectare of land cannot be directly planned and supervised by a central authority. Herein lies one of the major dilemmas of Soviet agricultural planning. There must be, as the Soviet regime has so painfully discovered, a balance between the center and the locale, between response to orders from above and the exercise of local initiative, and between all-Union plans and the sum of local possibilities. The problem of achieving such a balance, within the framework of national planning, has been and remains today an important theme in the Soviet agricultural literature.

The Soviets have attempted to inject greater balance into agricultural planning by the process of regionalization. In general terms, the objective is to delineate areas having relatively homogeneous conditions for agriculture and to make generalizations about these conditions that might enable the planner to eliminate what would otherwise be endless detail, describing an infinite number of locations. The region thus strikes a balance between the necessity for detailed central directives at one extreme and the alternative at the other extreme of leaving production decisions in the hands of local authorities. In a sense, then, regionalization may be used in agricultural planning as a substitute for autonomous decision-making at the local level.

The importance attached to economic regionalization in the Soviet Union, even if not fully understandable, is well known. Generally, however, much less is known about the nature of Soviet agricultural regionalization. Therefore, it seems fitting to examine the topic more closely and to consider the role of regionalization in Soviet agricultural planning.

THE AIM OF AGRICULTURAL REGIONALIZATION AND ITS THEORETICAL SIGNIFICANCE

According to Soviet geographers, the task of agricultural regionalization is to make a critical evaluation of existing crop and livestock distributions, to distinguish zones based on a complex of factors, and, finally, to provide the basis for a more "rational" distribution.[1] Unfortunately, the Soviet interpretation of spatial rationality is not readily apparent in either the theoretical literature or in operational procedure. Often, in fact, spatial rationality is defined by mutually exclusive criteria [2]—as, for example, when plans call for regional specialization and regional self-sufficiency in the same area. Nonetheless, the continual plea of Soviet writers for a rational distribution of agriculture suggests, in general terms at least, concern for optimizing the spatial pattern of production. In this essay, therefore, it is accepted that the ultimate goal (and problem) of agricultural regionalization is "to find that variant of the distribution of agriculture by regions of the country which will guarantee, through planning for the country as a whole, the desired volume and assortment of agricultural products at the minimum cost." [3] This objective, although stated in somewhat different terms, was initially put forth at the Sixteenth Party Congress in 1930 [4] and has been used to describe a rational distribution and specialization of agricultural production ever since.

Accordingly, the *raison d'être* of agricultural regionalization, as a tool for planning, rests on the assumption that the spatial pattern of agricultural production is not fully rational. A belief that the agrarian situation could be improved substantially by altering the distribution of produc-

[1] A. N. Rakitnikov in I. P. Gerasimov *et al.*, eds., *Sovetskaia geografiia: itogi i zadachi* (Moscow: 1960), p. 367.

[2] P. J. D. Wiles, *The Political Economy of Communism* (Cambridge, Mass.: Harvard University Press, 1962), pp. 150–152.

[3] V. S. Mikheeva, *Vest. Mosk. Un.: Seriia V Geografiia,* No. 5 (1962), p. 13.

[4] V. V. Matuikhin, *Sots. rek. sel'. khoz.,* No. 7 (1930), p. 78.

tion has long been widespread in the Soviet agricultural literature. It is commonly held, for example, that the agro-climatic resources of the country are poorly utilized.[5] And it is maintained that the potential for improving the use of these resources constitutes a "great reserve" for increasing both the quantity and variety of production. A current variation on this theme is the desire to diversify vegetable production and provide a year-round supply by using successively different climatic areas of the Union.[6] Of course, any significant change in the distribution or regional specialization of agricultural production must be implemented and controlled from the center. The role of agricultural regionalization, according to Alampiev, a prominent Soviet economist, is merely to assure a spatially differentiated approach in the planning process [7]—an approach, it should be noted, for which Soviet agricultural planning has not been known.

In theory, however, the Soviet system is such that regionalization could play a significant role in the planning and development of agriculture. If agriculture is to evolve according to a national economic plan, it is then necessary for the state to exercise deliberate control over the distribution and regional character of agricultural production. Given the total requirements for agricultural products, decisions must be made concerning the location of production. At first this may not require assignment in detail. Later, however, planners must determine what agricultural products are to be raised in specific areas and through the chain of command, in turn, what is to be produced in *oblasts, raions,* and finally on individual farms. In such a process, it is critical that decisions made at each level of the territorial hierarchy conform to reality—that is, with what is possible or desirable from both an agroclimatic or economic-situational point of view. Thus, at each level in the territorial organization of the Soviet Union, planners must be able to comprehend the complex of local conditions (natural, cultural, and economic) if they are to plan rationally the agriculture of larger areas, up to and including the state. A detailed regionalization of the country, which would include generalizations at several territorial levels, based on the computerization of standardized local data could, by reducing gross errors in the assignment of production, contribute significantly to Soviet

[5] F. F. Davitaia and S. A. Sapozhnikova in I. P. Gerasimov *et al.*, eds., *Prirodnye resursy Sovetskogo soiuza, ikh ispol'zovanie i vosproizvodstvo* (Moscow: 1963), p. 43.

[6] F. F. Davitaia, *Soviet Geography: Review and Translation,* IV:2 (February, 1963), 25–32.

[7] P. M. Alampiev in L. M. Zal'tsman *et al.*, eds., *Voprosy razmeshcheniia i spetsializatsii sel'skogo khoziaistva v SSSR* (Moscow: 1962), p. 143.

agricultural planning. However, even under the most ideal conditions, comprehension at the center would be far from perfect. Thus, there would still be, as one writer has noted, a need not only for regions but also for regional authorities.[8]

REGIONALIZATION—A RUSSIAN INTELLECTUAL TRADITION

The concern of Soviet writers with contemporary problems of the regional economy tends to obscure the tradition of regionalization which had developed among the scholars of prerevolutionary Russia. This tradition, apart from the requirements of current national planning, is important if one is to understand the Soviet propensity to regionalize. The delineation of regions, as a method for analyzing the spatial dimension of economic activity, has been a characteristic of Russian geography and economics since the eighteenth century. Schemes for the regionalization of Russia were proposed by leading intellectuals of the period. V. N. Tatishchev, M. V. Lomonosov, P. I. Rychkov, F. I. Soimonov, and N. R. Radishchev, for example, were among those contributing to a growing regional school of thought.[9] It was during this same period that the concept of broad climatic zones stretching latitudinally across Russia first arose. The natural region has ever since been a major factor in the delineation of agricultural regions.

It was not until the nineteenth century, however, that work on the economic regionalization of Russia began to formalize as a methodology. In 1815, K. F. German divided the *gubernias* of Russia into eight regional groupings in order to analyze the "success" (that is, economic life) of Russia's population under differing natural conditions.[10] Three years later, K. I. Arsen'ev published a map of ten regions which, according to Soviet writers, represented the first truly economic-geographic regionalization of Russia.[11] The ten regions were based on several criteria and were highly generalized. But within the major regions he identified subregions of a more specialized nature. Although Arsen'ev was concerned with portraying the regional economy as a whole, his regions, as Jackson has observed, were essentially agricul-

[8] Wiles, *op. cit.* (in n. 2), p. 149.

[9] A. S. Vetrov, *Izv. Ak. nauk: Seriia Geograficheskaia,* No. 6 (1958), pp. 79–87.

[10] N. Baranskii *et al., Otechestvennye ekonomiko-geografy: XVII–XX vv.* (Moscow: 1957), pp. 125–126.

[11] E. N. Pertsik, *K. I. Arsen'ev i ego raboty po raionirovaniiu Rossii* (Moscow: 1960), p. 29. This is a secondary source, and I do not know at this time whether *all* Arsen'ev's views are correctly interpreted by Pertsik. The latter, however, reproduces maps showing Arsen'ev's scheme, and it would be difficult to "quote a map out of context."

tural,[12] and thus reflected the predominantly agrarian character of Russia's economy. Indeed, it was not uncommon for Russian scholars of the nineteenth century more or less to equate general economic regions with agricultural regions. Soviet writers, on the other hand, make a sharp distinction between the two.[13]

Although most nineteenth-century regionalizations were of a general economic nature, the concept of an agricultural region *per se* continued to evolve. An article published in the *Zemledel'cheskaia gazeta* in 1834, which divided Russia into eight agricultural regions based on climatic conditions, evoked comment from the revolutionary philosopher, N. P. Ogarev. He criticized the regional division, pointing out that agricultural regionalization should not be based exclusively on natural conditions but must also consider the general economy as well as the relationship of agriculture to other economic activities. Otherwise, he stated, the regionalization is "one-sided and artificial." [14] Ogarev, then, was one of the first in a long line of critics to attack the natural bias of agricultural regionalization.

Among the early Russian scholars to deal with the regional character of agriculture and the problem of agricultural regionalization, A. F. Fortunatov was particularly significant. The bulk of Fortunatov's work (more than two hundred publications) was concerned with agriculture and particularly agricultural geography. His first major study was an historical survey of agricultural statistics in Russia, published in *Trudy Vol'nogo ekonomicheskogo obshchestva,* 1886, Numbers 1 and 4. More geographical in its approach, however, was his article, entitled "Raiony russkoi polevoi kul'tury," published in *Sel'skoe khoziaistvo i lesovodstvo,* 1892, Number 1, in which he divided Russia into nine regions. Soviet geographers consider the latter study to be the first generalizing work on the agricultural geography of Russia.[15]

In 1896 Fortunatov published an article presenting the first historical

[12] W. A. D. Jackson, "The Problems of Soviet Agricultural Regionalization," *Slavic Review,* XX:4 (December, 1961), 657.

[13] In general economic regionalization all economic activities are supposed to be considered and then integrated into a single territorial complex suitable for long-range planning. However, the nature of general economic regionalization has been the subject of considerable methodological conflict. Apart from polemic, regarding the "objective existence" of economic regions and their number, the major conflict is whether the object of regionalization consists of productive forces (resources, labor, and so on) or production relationships (linkages and interdependencies). Agricultural regions, on the other hand, are not considered to be objective in the ideological sense and hence are subject of fewer methodological disputes.

[14] Baranskii, *op. cit.,* pp. 157–158.

[15] *Ibid.,* p. 272.

survey of the various efforts to divide Russia into economic regions.[16] The article is interesting not only because it is the first to review the Russian regionalization literature, but also because its tenor is so much like that of regionalization studies published even in the most recent Soviet period. To cite one example, Fortunatov states: "There is no question but that the problem of dividing (Russia) into regions has wide practical significance. The expansion of diverse governmental activities throughout the territory of the country must be in accord with different local characteristics."[17] Despite long experience, Soviet writers find it necessary to emphasize precisely the same thing.

Following Fortunatov in the period before the revolution, a host of studies were published which dealt with the problem of regionalizing Russia. Information made available from the census of 1897 made possible more detailed work; besides, the increasingly complex economic landscape, which now included both commercial agriculture and a rapidly developing industry, offered a growing challenge to researchers.

In response to this challenge, the Free Economic Society charged D. I. Rikhter with creating a new regionalization of Russia integrating both natural and economic phenomena. His study was presented in March, 1898. There were at the time, Rikhter noted, many schemes dividing Russia into regions. Each organization, he indicated, had its own division for its own purpose. The Financial Ministry alone, he pointed out, had five separate regionalizations of European Russia, which together had only four regions with similar boundaries.[18] Rikhter complained that the great variety of regional divisions was extremely inconvenient since it eliminated the possibility of making regional comparisons among phenomena. He did indicate, however, that it might be possible with further research to find a single satisfactory system of regions.[19] Nevertheless, the substantive part of his study avoids the major problem—that is, how to relate diverse information in a regional system based on the homogeneity of criteria. Another study published eleven years later indicates that Rikhter had made almost no advance toward a solution of the problem.[20]

Notwithstanding methodological difficulties, work on the problem of agricultural regionalization was greatly facilitated by related developments in physical regionalization.[21] The studies of V. V. Dokuchaev,

[16] A. F. Fortunatov, *Trud. Vol'. ek. obshch.*, No. 5 (1896), pp. 1–12.
[17] Fortunatov, *op. cit.*, p. 1.
[18] D. I. Rikhter, *Trud. Vol'. ek. obshch.*, No. 9 (1898), p. 47.
[19] *Ibid.*, p. 48.
[20] *Ibid.*, No. 2 (1909), pp. 9–20.
[21] N. P. Nikitin, *Vop. geog.*, No. 47 (1959), p. 157.

Russkii chernozem, 1883, and G. I. Tanfil'ev, *Fiziko-geograficheskie oblasti Evropeiskoi Rossii,* 1896, were particularly important in this respect.

By the last years of imperial Russia two divergent schools of thought had developed concerning the nature of agricultural regionalization. A. I. Skvortsov, for example, believed that the natural environment was a determining factor for all economic life.[22] He concluded, therefore, that regions distinguished on the basis of natural conditions should not be termed natural or agricultural regions, but instead economic regions—that is, agricultural regions and general economic regions would in reality coincide territorially. A. N. Chelintsev, on the other hand, believed that agricultural regions existed apart from general economic regions and that in either case the only determining factor was the activity of man within a given area.[23] The Soviets accepted neither view—the first because it was environmental, the second because it was "unscientific."

There is no doubt that Russian scholars, before the revolution, had accepted the concept of regionalization as a challenging academic problem with considerable possibilities for practical application in both education and the administration of the state. Not only had a substantial volume of literature accumulated, but as statistical data became more available the approach to regionalization became increasingly sophisticated. However, as the awareness of the *problem* developed, more questions were raised than were solved. Nevertheless, when the Soviets came to power and were faced with the complex business of national economic planning the concept of regionalization was almost immediately accepted. Indeed, regionalization whether economic or agricultural was declared to be an integral part of national planning. If such was actually the case, Soviet planners had by no means to start at the beginning.

AGRICULTURAL REGIONALIZATION DURING THE SOVIET PERIOD

After the revolution efforts to divide the country into regions were stimulated by a sense of purpose not evident in earlier times. As Saushkin puts it: "Prerevolutionary works on regionalization were written . . . in order to describe the nation. In Soviet times, regionalization has been carried out to reconstruct the nation; it has an active nature . . . and serves as an important weapon in national eco-

[22] Alampiev in Zal'tsman, *op. cit.* (in n. 7) pp. 136–137.

[23] H. Chambre, *L'Aménagement du territoire en URSS: Introduction à l'étude des régions économiques soviétiques* (Paris: Mouton, 1959), p. 165.

nomic planning."[24] The idea of an "active regionalization," despite nineteenth-century allusions to the notion, is one of the few basic contributions to the conceptual development of regionalization that can be attributed to the Soviet period.[25]

Before 1930, however, the territorial planning of agriculture amounted to little more than academic discussion. There were, to be sure, *official* efforts (conferences, and so on) to solve theoretical questions about the nature of agricultural regionalization even before the N.E.P.[26] But these proved not very fruitful. More interesting were the individual studies published during the N.E.P. period, which had not yet become stereotyped by a rigid ideological framework. A. Kotov, for example, drew freely from the ideas of Von Thunen and considered, among other things, the hitherto neglected problem of defining the boundaries between agricultural regions.[27] Kotov, it should be noted, was one of the few writers to interpret agroclimatic conditions in terms of production costs.

With the determined drive to collectivize agriculture numerous editorials and articles were published attacking the previous work on agricultural regionalization.[28] Before 1930, it was claimed, the problem of agricultural regionalization had been studied almost exclusively by "bourgeois economists."[29] In addition to "liquidating the kulaks" the new agricultural policies called for the elimination of "petty bourgeois regionalization" as a real danger to the new order.

The new order in Soviet agriculture was to be based on large collective- and state-farm units, highly mechanized and specialized—truly agricultural factories. Transition to complete "faith in the big enterprise" was rapid indeed.[30] The "reconstruction of Soviet agriculture," as Jackson has noted,[31] however, was not to be accomplished by changes of a social and technical nature only, but also, as contemporary writers stated, by a fundamental change in the distribution of "all crops across the territory of the Soviet Union."[32] This would be accomplished, it

[24] Iu. G. Saushkin, *Novoe ekonomicheskoe raionirovanie* (Moscow: 1963), p. 3.

[25] Even the concept of "objectively existing regions" had been formulated in the nineteenth century.

[26] I. G. Aleksandrov in G. M. Krzhizhanovskii, ed., *Voprosy ekonomicheskogo raionirovaniia SSSR: sbornik materialov i statei* (Moscow: 1957), p. 68.

[27] A. Kotov, *Sots. khoz.*, III (1928), 173–202.

[28] See, for example, *Sots. rek. sel'. khoz.*, Nos. 9–10 (1930), pp. iii–xvi.

[29] Matuikhin, *op. cit.* (in n. 4), No. 9 (1931), p. 32.

[30] Naum Jasny, *The Socialized Agriculture of the USSR* (Stanford, Calif.: Stanford University Press, 1949), pp. 26–30.

[31] Jackson, *op. cit.* (in n. 12), p. 659.

[32] Matuikhin, *op. cit.* (in n. 4), pp. 77–79.

was stated, only on the basis of a thorough analysis of the characteristics of the various regions of the Soviet Union combined with strict planning of the distribution of all branches of agriculture.[33] The ideal distribution was loosely defined as one which took full advantage of the country's agroclimatic resources and at the same time provided for the particular requirements of important economic areas.

At the Sixteenth Party Congress, I. A. Iakovlev, the People's Commissar of Agriculture, presented a map showing ten agricultural zones.[34] The map, based for the most part on natural regions, was highly generalized and was apparently designed only to guide further research on agricultural regionalization.[35] The task of working out a more detailed system of agricultural regions was assigned by the congress to the Lenin Academy of Agricultural Sciences. The academy was directed to delimit more suitable territorial units (regions) based not only on natural differences between zones, but also on such factors as population, the concentration of industry, and the location of mineral-fertilizer deposits. The result was a system of forty-four specialized agricultural regions[36] designed to serve as a guide for the future planning of Soviet agriculture.

The academy's map, however, did not receive Party approval, and a second scheme which had thirty-three regions led to accusations of indecisiveness. Moreover, the regionalization committee was reprimanded for relying on the earlier work of Chelintsev, who had been criticized for supporting small-scale farming. The regions were considered unsuitable for planning purposes since they did not coincide with the plan for industrialization. It was declared, therefore, that the assigned task had not been accomplished—that the "captive tendency" of small-scale peasant-farming had not been overcome.[37]

As announced at the Sixteenth Party Congress, a major objective of Soviet agricultural policy was to promote the regional specialization of agriculture, particularly for commodities such as grains, sugar beets, cotton, and other technical crops. Four years later, however, in his report to the Seventeenth Party Congress Stalin emphasized the need for diversification of agricultural production in all regions of the country:

[33] *Ibid.*, pp. 76–79.

[34] Jackson, *op. cit.* (in n. 12), p. 659. Iakovlev's map is reproduced in Jackson's article.

[35] N. Baranskii, *Kratkii kurs ekonomicheskoi geografii* (Moscow: 1931), p. 214. I am indebted to Professor Jackson for the opportunity to consult his copy of this now rare edition of Baranskii's text.

[36] A map of the Academy's forty-four regions is reproduced and discussed in some detail by Jackson, *op. cit.*, pp. 660–666.

[37] Matuikhin, *op. cit.* (in n. 29), pp. 33–37.

> Development is leading to the point when all our regions will be more or less industrial; and they will become increasingly so as this development proceeds. This means . . . that formerly agrarian districts can no longer supply the industrial centers with as much produce as they supplied in the past because now they have to feed their own towns and their own workers, whose number will be increasing. From this it follows that every region will have to develop its own agricultural base, so as to have its own supply of vegetables, potatoes, butter, and to some extent grain and meat, if it does not want to get into difficulties. . . . The task is to pursue this line to the end at all costs.[38]

In connection with a continuing attempt to reduce long hauls of agricultural products this theme was stressed up to the outbreak of World War II. A governmental decree, for example, stated that a 25-kilometer zone around cities should be reserved for the production of fresh vegetables and milk. It was hoped too that all *oblasts* could produce their own supply of potatoes so that after 1939 the inter-*oblast'* movement of potatoes might be halted altogether. One writer even suggested that the production of sugar beets be handled in the same manner as that of potatoes, even though transport restrictions would be less stringent.[39] Needless to say, fundamental changes in policy toward the regional development of agriculture along with other upheavals during the thirties did not encourage an "active" approach to regionalization. Indeed, there were no significant developments for agricultural regionalization until after Stalin's death in 1953.

At the Twentieth Party Congress in 1956 it was announced that a rational distribution of agriculture would in effect be achieved by establishing in each farm and in each region of the country those crops which in the given local environment would result in the maximum output with a minimum expenditure of labor and materials.[40] The fact that the Lenin Academy of Agricultural Science had been charged by the Sixteenth Party Congress in 1930 with developing a regionalization scheme based on nearly identical objectives was not completely overlooked. Instead it was merely noted that the academy, over the years, had ignored the economic study of agriculture and had failed, therefore, to fulfill the task assigned by the Party.[41] Nevertheless, the more recent declaration had the effect of stimulating further and more intensive research on agricultural regionalization than ever before.

[38] J. Stalin, *Problems of Leninism* (Moscow: 1953), p. 616.

[39] Chambre, *op. cit.* (in n. 23), p. 173.

[40] K. P. Obolenskii in L. M. Zal'tsman *et al.*, eds., *Voprosy razmeshcheniia i spetsializatsii sel'skogo khoziaistva* (Moscow: 1957), p. 21.

[41] *Ibid.*, p. 23.

Editorials in the leading Soviet geographical journals stated again what they had been saying for decades—that the planning of a rational distribution of agriculture could not be considered apart from a thorough analysis of the natural environment. Only through such an analysis, it was declared, would it be possible to develop a more scientific system of agricultural regions which would in turn insure more effective planning.

On that point Soviet geographers and economists seemed to agree. V. Nemchinov, the director of the Council for the Study of Productive Forces, had stated, for example, "that the initial step in planning the future distribution of agriculture should be an inventory of the local characteristics of the principal agricultural regions of the country." [42] In keeping with his notion, the council published a map delineating eighteen specialized agricultural regions. The regions were admittedly based on natural zones for agriculture, which had been described on an earlier map produced by the Academy of Sciences. Upon examination, however, the council's map shows little advance over previous efforts. Certainly it is difficult to see in what way Nemchinov's work could facilitate planning, since the map at best was highly schematic and the supporting text not convincing.[43] Clearly, the council's work was no better than that of Soviet geographers who later conceded the shortcomings of their efforts in the service of agricultural planning.[44]

Although the general objectives for the distribution of agriculture announced after 1953 had been stated before, some differences should be noted. The collectivization of agriculture was complete—the war against the peasant had for all practical purposes been won. In planning agriculture the regime was becoming more concerned with efficiency, whereas before the primary concern had been with control. The call for "decentralization" of authority in 1955 was symptomatic of these changes and of the growing concern for a more efficient system of agricultural planning. According to Party leaders this might be achieved by allowing a greater range of decision-making at the local level. Of course, production could not be left to chance since national goals had still to be met. But it was hoped that control over the distribution of agriculture could be implemented by less direct methods. At any rate, since the Party continued to stress the importance of varying agricultural management according to the realities of local conditions, the Ministry of Agriculture in 1956 set up thirty-nine zonal

[42] V. Nemchinov, *Plan. khoz.*, No. 4 (1955), pp. 60–75.
[43] Jackson, *op. cit.* (in n. 12), p. 676.
[44] A. Rakitnikov, *Vop. geog.*, No. 47 (1959), p. 96.

commissions, with a staff exceeding four thousand, to study and recommend systems of agriculture for different regions of the Union.[45] As will be noted below, similar projects were being recommended at the time of this writing.

REGIONALIZATION AND THE TERRITORIAL PLANNING OF AGRICULTURE

In theory, according to Soviet writers, agricultural regionalization should provide a basis for planning a rational distribution of agriculture in accord with national production goals. Yet after several decades of agricultural planning that goal remains as elusive as ever. While the use of regions has been considered essential, agricultural regionalization appears to have had little connection with what might be considered regional planning. Indeed, one gets the impression that planning organizations have not actually used the materials devoted to agricultural regionalization.[46] If true, one may conclude that the concept of an "active regionalization" has not been a viable one. Regionalization, however, is simply an adjunct of territorial planning. It is necessary, therefore, to examine the other side of the coin and consider the degree to which the actual planning process has been related to the theoretical concept of a rational distribution of agriculture.

The first consideration for any planned system of agricultural regions is the projected needs of the state for foodstuffs and agricultural raw materials. From a regional point of view the problem is to find a spatial pattern of production which will satisfy the plan—presumably in the most effective way. For some commodities, for example, cotton or tea, the problem is minor since only limited areas in the country are reasonably suited for their cultivation. Even here, though, there is a problem, especially if good land is limited, of allocating resources between specialized production for all-Union consumption and the cultivation of foodstuffs for local consumption.[47] For crops which have a greater tolerance for natural conditions the problem is considerably more complex since there may be an infinite number of regional patterns which might satisfy national requirements. But apart from the complexity of the problem itself, the "regionalizer" or planner has been confronted with difficulties inherent in the Soviet system. As one source puts it—"conditions"

[45] V. P. Sotnikov, *Soviet Geography: Review and Translation,* I:10 (December, 1960), 4–5.

[46] K. V. Zvorykin, *Vest. Mosk. Un.: Seriia V Geograffia,* No. 2 (1962), p. 3.

[47] For a discussion of this problem in the Soviet subtropics see Robert G. Jensen, "Soviet Subtropical Agriculture: A Microcosm," *The Geographical Review,* LIV:2 (April, 1964), p. 201.

throughout the country were such that the implementation of a "scientifically based" distribution of agriculture, by regions, was simply not feasible.[48]

The regional planning of agriculture is supposed to take into account the natural and economic conditions of each region, collective and state farms of the country. Yet it has never been determined just how natural and economic phenomena are to be related so as to create a composite index by which "rational" might be defined. Moreover, Soviet writers emphasize that the first criterion for determining what products to produce and where is the best interest of the state. That is, "the (planned) distribution of agriculture must not be approached from the mercenary point of view of a single enterprise." [49] So on the one hand each farm enterprise, *oblast'*, and region are admonished to produce those agricultural products for which natural conditions are most favorable, while, on the other hand, as Evseenko notes, the interests of the state may demand the production of agricultural commodities in regions where conditions might in fact be better for other products.[50]

There is in addition to the double standard just noted the fundamental question how any territorial authority, short of perfect comprehension, can make production decisions which are rational with respect to an area that is larger or smaller than the one for which he is responsible. The greatest difficulty, of course, occurs between the extremes. The planner has an arduous task if he must direct a farm in a manner rational with respect to the country as a whole, just as he would have in devising a national plan based directly on what is most rational for each farm to produce. Indeed, if autarchy is an objective and spatial rationality is defined as *establishing in each farm of the country those crops which in the given local environment give the greatest output,* it is certain that the optimum production on each farm would not result in the optimum distribution of crops for the country as a whole. Under a free-market system, where profit would determine the location of production, this dilemma could not exist and there would be no need for the double standard noted—there would in fact be no need for a national plan.

Thus, one of the more serious obstacles for regional decision-making at any level has been the lack of a valid criterion which would hold for

[48] Ia. G. Feigin, ed., *Osobennosti i faktory razmeshchenii otraslei narodnogo khoziaistva* (Moscow: 1960), p. 461.
[49] P. M. Evseenko, *Ekonomika i organizatsiia sotsialisticheskogo sel'skokhoziaistvennogo proizvodstva* (Moscow: 1961), p. 139.
[50] *Ibid.*

the vast territory of the Soviet Union. The multiple-pricing system used for agricultural products until 1958 not only made it impossible to relate the prices of different commodities produced in the same area, but also presented difficulties when the same commodity was compared among different areas. Prices had no economic validity and therefore could not be used as criteria for regionalization. During the Stalin era, since state procurement prices were low, the analysis of production costs was a highly sensitive subject, avoided by scholars and the state alike. Indeed, it was not until 1955 that the state began to study seriously the level and structure of average costs, and collective farms did not make these calculations until 1958.[51] Therefore, as Nimitz notes, decisions with respect to the regional specialization of agriculture, as well as a host of other alternatives, were made without the benefit of cost criteria.[52]

Generally speaking the regional planning of agriculture was to consist of two separate but related functions: (1) the assignment of production tasks and procurement quotas; and (2) the dissemination of information regarding proper farm practices, crop rotations, and so on. Originally the system of direct planning from above was to include only the major food crops and agricultural raw materials, insuring the basic needs of the state. In a short time, however, a wide range of products were included, thus determining not only the specialized production of a farm or region but to a great extent the total volume and assortment of production.[53] Since, above all else, production and delivery quotas had to be met, approved rotations and other farm practices suffered. Indeed, plans received from above were often incompatible with approved agricultural practices. Success, instead of being measured by efficiency or resource stewardship, was measured by the fulfillment of norms (such as, area sown), creating a set of values among farm managers which negated the theoretical objectives of regional planning.

The pressures which cause plans to be implemented in a manner largely inconsistent with formally stated objectives are evident. Agricultural production often fails to meet the ambitious goals set forth by the regime. Concern with lagging production manifests itself in increased political activity and coercion, and nearly always leads to administrative reorganization. But rather than substituting more realistic goals it has been standard practice to extend and intensify central control. Such a

[51] L. B. Sheinin, *Vop. geog.*, No. 54 (1961), pp. 143–149.

[52] Nancy Nimitz, "Soviet Agricultural Prices and Costs," in U.S. Congress, Joint Economic Committee, *Comparisons of the United States and Soviet Economies*, Part I (Washington, D.C.: Government Printing Office, 1959), p. 241.

[53] Zal'tsman in Zal'tsman, *op. cit.* (in n. 7), p. 156.

turn of events has been evident since the much heralded announcement of decentralization in 1955. Moreover, the party line in agriculture is often carried to an extreme by overzealous local authorities who, rather than risk displeasure from above, may disregard the advice of local experts. These factors and the extent to which Soviet agriculture is a political football subject to the caprice of Party leaders, not to mention inefficiency at the farm level, restricts any potential impact of thoughtful regional planning. Whether the plan to stabilize state agricultural procurements for several years at a time will reduce these pressures substantially, remains to be seen.

As indicated above, there is little evidence of a working relationship between agricultural regionalization and what might be considered operational planning. Indeed, the nature of Soviet agricultural planning would seem to preclude such a relationship. Moreover, the regionalization schemes for agriculture which have appeared during the Soviet period have been highly schematic and based on incomplete data. A leading proponent of applied (active) agricultural regionalization summarizes the situation as follows:

> Most systems of agricultural regionalization now in use do not give enough attention to the spatially exact determination of data about agriculture or to an explanation of the factors that determine regional differences in agriculture. Regionalization work is usually oversimplified on the ground that it plays only a secondary role in determining the distribution of agricultural production. In this connection natural regions are often treated as agricultural regions for convenience. Regional schemes often fail to distinguish between the delimitation of zones (or regions) based on the present state of agriculture and the regionalization of future farm trends. Until recently most authors of regional schemes insisted on drawing boundaries of agricultural regions along administrative frontiers, again in order to simplify their task.[54]

The problem of defining and agreeing on the size of a planning region is more complex than the statement indicates. Ideally, of course, the limits of a region depend strictly upon the purpose for which it is used and the criteria by which it is defined. As a general principle boundaries would be drawn so as to enclose the largest area possible, without averaging out differences relevant to the problem at hand.[55] In practice, however, the size and form of a planning region, whether agricultural or

[54] A. N. Rakitnikov, F. Mukomel', *Soviet Geography: Review and Translation,* V:9 (November, 1964), 24–25.

[55] For a lucid discussion of this problem see E. L. Ullman, "Regional Structure and Arrangement," in Office of Naval Research, Contract No. NR-477 (03), *Report No. 10* (Seattle, Wash., University of Washington: December, 1954, mimeographed).

of some other kind, is influenced by less "scientific" considerations. The planners' perception of a region, for example, may depend upon the means available for implementing policy—for example, the territorial organization of the Party. Most regional schemes, moreover, are based on statistical areas which, even if small, may average out important differences and thus provide poor building blocks for regional analysis. The rule that planning regions may not cut across the boundaries of the Soviet republics only adds to the problem. It is little wonder, then, that the boundaries of agricultural regions are drawn along administrative frontiers. This practice is in effect a practical requirement of the planning process—a requirement, one may presume, which reduces the effectiveness of regional analysis and planning.

AGRICULTURAL REGIONALIZATION AND PRICE ZONATION

In 1958, as a result of changes in the system of state agricultural purchase prices, a new dimension was added to the problem of agricultural regionalization which, for lack of a better term, may be called price zonation. Essentially, the reform replaced the cumbersome system of multiple prices with a uniform procurement price for each agricultural commodity. The uniform prices were differentiated by zones and, in the absence of land rent, were purportedly calculated to correct for sharp variations in fertility and location by removing excess profits from fertile land; and, conversely, to allow farm enterprises in marginal areas to produce at a profit. Under the zonal pricing system, therefore, farms in favorable areas receive a lower price for a given crop than farms producing in areas where conditions are less favorable and where production costs are presumed to be higher.

By definition any area having a uniform price for a product forms a price zone. In areas where certain products are not produced, or where the state does not plan to make purchases, no zonal price is set for those commodities. Such areas, Sheinin maintains, are in effect excluded from production for the state.[56] On the other hand, if a price zone is established it may be assumed that the state considers the area generally suitable for producing the product for which the zone is named—and at a profit! The same consideration is supposed to exist in the establishment of a purchase plan for individual farms. That is, the prices for the products should insure a profit.[57]

There is a fundamental difference between agricultural regionalization and price zonation. Traditionally, agricultural regionalization has had

[56] Sheinin, *op. cit.* (in n. 51), p. 143.
[57] *Pravda,* January 22, 1965.

no direct influence on the distribution and specialization of agriculture—the schemes at best could serve only as a guide for planning. The regionalization of state purchase prices, however, is something considerably more tangible. Indeed, as the welfare of a collective farm depends directly on the price received for its products, price zonation should have a direct influence on the distribution and intensity of agricultural production.

As noted above, one objective of price zonation is to place collective and state farms in a similar economic position irrespective of differences in agroclimatic conditions and locations. The reasoning goes like this: "Since not only the best and average but also poor soils have to be cultivated to meet social needs, labor expended under the relatively poorer conditions is socially necessary. This labor should be given public recognition . . . by means of prices which insure expanded reproduction. Therefore, the influence of natural factors on production costs are calculated zonally." [58] A second objective of price zonation is to promote a more rational distribution and specialization of agriculture, again according to the natural-economic zones of the country. The latter would result from differential profits. But the choice of product mix would in theory still allow each zone to operate at about the same level of profitability.

The requirements for delineating price zones correctly are such that a host of additional problems have been pushed to the fore. Noteworthy among these are the determination of logical price relationships among agricultural products, the economic evaluation of land, and the balancing of site and situational factors as they relate to production costs. It would go beyond the scope of this discussion to explore fully the problem of price zonation. Nevertheless, the major shortcomings of the system may be noted and the impact of the latter on agricultural regionalization (in its traditional form) can be shown.

Given the objectives of price zonation, most price zones are far too large while at the same time the price differentials between zones are not nearly so great as the differences in production costs. As for planning, price zonation is still too crude to provide the automatic production motivators which are apparently sought.[59] Moreover, since the zonal prices are supposed to reflect average natural conditions in the form of production costs, the boundaries of the zones should be drawn in such a

[58] E. Tiapkina, *Vop. ek.*, No. 7 (1961), p. 143.

[59] For a further discussion of this problem see F. A. Durgin, Jr., "Monetization and Policy in Soviet Agriculture Since 1952," *Soviet Studies,* XV:4 (April, 1964), 375–407.

way as to eliminate major physical differences within a zone. Of course, even if the zones were small, and if great care were exercised in determining their geographic configuration, it is clear that equal compensation would be achieved only in the most ideal case. However, when uniform prices are established for large areas one can only conclude that the zones have little logical foundation. In the R.S.F.S.R., for example, only eight zones were delimited for wheat and rye.[60] Zone VI includes twenty *oblasts* and six autonomous republics of the non-Chernozem Center, the Northwest, and the Urals.[61]

Since interzonal price differences have little relationship to actual variations in production costs, the low price zones, where natural conditions are more favorable, have a much greater margin of profit than zones where prices are higher.[62] This has long been recognized and in April of 1965 was partly corrected by the increase in prices for grain in the Northwest and non-Chernozem areas.[63] Of course, within a price zone the marginal areas do not even have the benefit of higher prices. P. Bashkin, using Omsk *oblast'* as an example, shows that farms in the northern section operate at a loss while several hundred kilometers to the south most collectives are able to do much better (see table). As in interzonal comparisons, areas with the lowest production costs obtain the highest level of profitability, but the highest average selling price is instead focused in areas with low production costs. According to Bashkin, this situation results from frost damage in the north along with a grain mix containing less wheat (50 percent wheat in the north as opposed to 90 percent in the south).[64]

However, even if the natural conditions of Omsk *oblast'* were uniform, the zonal price would not eliminate the greater economic advantage of the south. There would still remain, for example, significant differences in profitability related to location with respect to markets (particularly the collective farm market), procurement points, and transportation routes. It is true that the transportation costs for all agricultural products turned in at state purchase prices are paid for by the state purchasing organization and this may reduce the importance of

[60] A. V. Bolgov, *Differentsial'naia zemel'naia renta v usloviiakh sotsializma* (Moscow: 1963), p. 117.
[61] A. T. Zinochkin, *Ekonomicheskaia otsenka sel'skokhoziaistvennykh ugodni* (Moscow: 1963), p. 96.
[62] Cf. A. Soroka, *Ek. sel'. khoz.*, No. 9 (1961), p. 16.
[63] *Pravda*, March 27, 1965.
[64] P. Bashkin, *Vop. ek.*, No. 6 (1961), p. 112.

distance.[65] But apparently the compensation is not adequate.[66] The advantage of a market location is further enhanced by cheaper delivery of machinery, fuel, spare parts, and fertilizers, and this advantage becomes all the greater with more intensive production. Indeed, around most large cities suburban agriculture is encouraged by setting prices somewhat higher than in outlying areas.[67]

GRAIN PRODUCTION IN OMSK OBLAST', 1957–1959[a]

Item	Unit	Taiga	Northern forest steppe	Southern forest steppe	Southern steppe
Number of collective farms		124	34	63	42
Percent of *oblast'* grain production		11.9	21.5	34	32.6
Expenditure per hectare of grain	rubles	970	1,066	1,088	924
Labor-days per hectare of grain		9.5	9.1	8.7	8.4
Average annual yield per hectare	centners	7.1	9.2	13.9	14.3
Average annual production cost per centner of grain [b]	rubles	58.20	39.92	30.09	29.53
Average annual selling price per centner [b]	rubles	43.54	55.00	59.57	60.32
Profit or loss	rubles	−14.66	+15.08	+29.48	+30.79

[a] Based on annual reports of collective farms. Omsk *oblast'* is situated in wheat price zone iv.
[b] 1958–59
SOURCE: P. Bashkin, *Vop. ek.* No. 6, (1961), p. 112.

Along with other defects in the formation of prices the existing system of price zones has been criticized in the Soviet literature. On the whole, however, there appears to have been little official interest in altering the system of price zones. Indeed, according to Brezhnev, the new state purchase prices were set with "due regard for the specific features of the

[65] Outlying farms, for example, are less likely to reduce the bulk or to increase the value of a commodity by local processing than might be the case if distance were a major consideration. Thus, one writer complains that sunflower seeds are hauled over excessively long distances from farms to procurement points. He also notes that the use of processing facilities on farms is neglected. Local processing could reduce the shipping weight by a factor of 3. See Sheinin, *op. cit.*, p. 147.

[66] I. Suslov, *Plan. khoz.*, No. 8 (1963), p. 65.

[67] V. A. Mineev, *Ekonomicheskie osnovy prigorodnogo sel'skogo khoziaistva* (Moscow: 1962), pp. 71–72.

individual zones and regions of the country." [68] Although prices were raised in the non-Chernozem region there is no indication that the geographic configuration of the zones is to be changed. Apparently uniform prices will continue to be applied in large areas where production costs are not uniform.

In connection with the problem of price zonation, there has been a considerable increase in research dealing with the inventory and evaluation of agricultural land. Among the applications most often mentioned are planning the volume of state purchases for specific land areas, improving the distribution of crop production, and evaluating the performance of farms and indeed of whole regions. As one might expect, scholars participating in such research find the existing system of price zones unsatisfactory. A. T. Zinochkin, for example, recommends that state purchase prices be differentiated not only by zones, but also by microzones.[69] In other words he advocates the establishment of a new set of price zones based on much smaller, and presumably more meaningful, areas. He proposed also that the collective-farm income tax be modified so that half the tax would be based on land quality and the remainder on net income. The latter, he proposed, should be based on a progressive scale ranging from 5 to 50 percent of a farm's net income.

A leading geographer, on the other hand, has proposed a new and more comprehensive land cadastre which would facilitate a standard evaluation of land at the all-union level.[70] The cadastre, according to Armand, would make it possible to set procurements and zonal purchase prices that would provide equal incentive for farms in all regions of the country.[71] Of course, the lack of a sufficiently detailed land inventory has long been a major problem in agricultural regionalization. Barring extensive field work, which at best could be completed only in relatively small areas, regionalization schemes had perforce to be schematic. For similar reasons, research on the economic evaluation of lands has been confined to small areas. Furthermore, it has not yet been determined how the economic evaluation of land should be conducted. Until the latter is solved it seems doubtful that a new land cadastre would be as useful as its proponents claim.

The discussion since 1958 concerning the problem of delineating

[68] *Pravda,* March 27, 1965.

[69] Zinochkin, *op. cit.* (in n. 61), pp. 92–134.

[70] D. L. Armand, *Soviet Geography: Review and Translation,* IV:2 (February, 1963), 12.

[71] *Ibid.,* p. 16.

price zones has been closely related to the more traditional problem of agricultural regionalization. Since the methods used and the objectives sought are in many cases the same, the analysis of agriculture from a regional point of view has taken on a more interdisciplinary character than was true before 1958. As a result, the need for a more sophisticated approach to the regional analysis and planning of agriculture has been recognized more clearly and on a broader front.[72] The impact of this change on agricultural regionalization is evident in the more recent literature. For example, there has been a much greater emphasis on the analysis of production costs as a measure of agroclimatic and soil variations and on the use of mathematical techniques in data evaluation. In turn, the concept of the natural region appears to be playing a lesser role. Whether improved methods of agricultural regionalization will in fact contribute to better agricultural planning remains, of course, a matter for speculation.

CONCLUSION

The concept of agricultural regionalization cannot be attributed to the Soviet period. When the Soviets came to power a considerable body of literature dealing with the problem of agricultural regionalization had already been accumulated. However, the demands of Soviet planning, which among other things called for a fundamental change in the geographic arrangement of crops across the country, placed agricultural regionalization in an entirely different context than was the case in imperial Russia. With the advent of almost complete state control over agricultural activities it was declared that regionalization should serve as an *active* tool in agricultural planning. In short, agricultural regionalization was called upon to provide the state with a practical foundation for decision-making which would lead to a rational distribution of production within the framework of centralized planning.

The latter objective, however, has not been achieved. Agricultural regionalization did not become sophisticated enough to meet such de-

[72] It does not follow, however, that the relationship between the state and the agricultural sector will be altered in a fundamental way. As Professor Durgin states (*op. cit.*, in n. 59, p. 407): "Attempts are being made to develop an institutional environment in which centrally planned directives and controls can be transmitted to the periphery via financial and economic levers rather than via a bureaucratic administrative hierarchy. It is, in a word, a search for a more efficient and less costly way of direction and control from the center." One hardly needs to add that this will require a more sophisticated approach to regional analysis of agriculture than heretofore.

mands, nor were sufficient data available to make such a development possible. Moreover, the actual conduct of Soviet agricultural planning was at loggerheads with the stated objectives of agricultural regionalization. For much of the Soviet period a primary concern of agricultural planning has been to maintain strict control over the agrarian sector and to fulfill short-run goals, even if the latter resulted in the irrational conduct of agriculture at the local and regional level.

In recent years, however, the approach to the problem of agricultural regionalization has become more sophisticated. To a great extent, it seems, this change was in response to the voluminous discussion which resulted from the establishment in 1958 of price zones for agricultural commodities. Yet there is still no evidence that agricultural regionalization has contributed measurably to actual planning, despite the continued demand by planning agencies for regionalization to "serve as an active tool of economic planning." [73] Is there any likelihood, then, that agricultural regionalization will play a more significant role in the future? Ironically, this must depend on whether the Soviets will be able to satisfy their growing agricultural requirements. For so long as the major concern is with lagging production, the agricultural sector will be subject to further political pressures, administrative reorganization, and various forms of coercion. Under such conditions agricultural regionalization is likely to remain as before—an academic endeavor.

[73] A. V. Korobov, *Soviet Geography: Review and Translation,* V:9 (November, 1964), p. 11.

COMMENT

W. A. Douglas Jackson

Some years ago, in response to a question concerning the extent to which Soviet economic regions had become truly regions of economic specialization, a student suggested that the Soviets had achieved a very high degree of specialization because the Soviet writers wrote so much about it. There is always the danger, where first-hand impressions cannot be formed, that we may be deceived by what we read in Soviet journals. When the New Lands program was announced and got under way in 1953–1954, some Western observers, noting the fanfare in the Soviet press, concluded that Khrushchev, a farm boy, knew what he was doing and had found a solution to the chronic grain problem. Obviously, in view of the sizable Soviet grain purchases from abroad in recent years, such has not been the case.

Professor Jensen has not fallen into this error. He has examined much of the Soviet literature on agricultural regionalization and has concluded that, despite the statements of Soviet writers about the role and importance of regionalization in planning agricultural activities and patterns, the regime has not achieved its objective. Failure is due, he notes, to a lack of sophistication in regionalization, in part caused by a lack of data upon which to create a satisfactory scientific scheme. Part of the difficulty, he might have noted as a geographer, is that the U.S.S.R. is an immense land, with a crop area of about 500 million acres; it is a northerly land of climatic extremes, and farming is to a large degree subject to the harassments of frost, drought, and other related problems inherent in the natural environment. On the other hand, it is true, as Jensen has pointed out, that Soviet farming is farming by decree and subject to decisions of a highly subjective nature, decisions which might have more political than strictly economic significance. Finally, Soviet agriculture is subject to bureaucratic centralism, conditioned by peasant indifference, if not outright hostility, and a lack of local incentive. At any rate, since collectivization the U.S.S.R. has not produced sizable surpluses, freely or willingly surrendered to the state. Every major Soviet decision, consequently, whether originating with Stalin or Khrushchev, has been a critical one, having serious repercussions throughout the entire economy.

From the beginning of the Soviet regime, regionalization was to form a basic ingredient in the planning mechanism.[74] Scientifically determined regions were to help bring about the planned proportional development of the national economy, which Soviet theorists state is the basic economic law of socialism. Characteristic of capitalism, said Lenin, are imbalances in the economy, both structural and spatial; socialism, on the other hand, permits the working of the law of planned proportional development, an objective law. Through and by it, the state plans production, but if it is to be correctly effective, the plans must reflect its requirements. When plans do not reflect these requirements, disproportions will appear within the economy, leading to interruptions in the normal process of production and circulation.[75] Correct planning will ensure, conversely, that the law works, resulting in correct proportions. Essential to the achievement of correct proportions, especially at the spatial level, is a scientific scheme of regionalization.

Thus, according to Soviet reasoning, the perfunctory performance of Soviet agriculture is due not to socialized agriculture, but to the inadequacies in the planning system and in addition in the regionalization schemes. Jensen affirms that Soviet agricultural regionalization schemes have been weak methodologically and notes that Soviet agricultural planning, lacking any concrete basis for determining what crops to grow where, has therefore not been especially successful. But, it is Premier Kosygin who carries the criticism one step further to demonstrate that Soviet agriculture, in the final analysis, has suffered at the capricious hands of Soviet leaders. In the spring of 1965, he acknowledged what a lack of proportion has led to. More than any other sector of the economy, he said, agriculture has been *affected by the harmful consequences of a subjective approach.*[76] (Italics mine.)

If any fault is to be found with Jensen's otherwise excellent paper, it would be in his omission of concrete evidence to demonstrate Soviet failure to achieve a rational distribution in agricultural production. He might, indeed, have said more about the problem of suburban agriculture, a critical problem in a country whose food-marketing and distribution facilities remain primitive. Take the case of potatoes and vegetables, for example. Though about fifty suburban zones were "established" around Soviet cities between 1937 and 1953, state purchases and

[74] See P. M. Alampiev, *Ekonomicheskoe raionirovanie SSSR* (Moscow: 1963), p. 11.

[75] *Political Economy* (London: Laurence and Wishart, 1957), pp. 526–543.

[76] *Plan. khoz.*, No. 4 (1965), pp. 3–10.

deliveries in 1953 remained below the 1940 level.[77] By the time of Stalin's death, the situation in many regions of the country was critical. Without the produce of private plots there would have been few staples to eat. Some of the difficulties, of course, are due to climate. The Soviet industrialization drive led to the formation, not only of new industrial regions but of many workers settlements beyond the tsarist economic core and especially in more remote parts of the country where growing conditions were less favorable. Thus, as one Soviet writer has noted, the cultivation of potatoes in regions undergoing rapid industrialization was insufficient to reach a balance between production and consumption.[78]

In the assigning of production quotas to suburban state and collective farms, it is not clear what the rational has been. Frequently, farms nearer the cities were assigned lower quotas than those at some distance. Farms, too, were often required to grow such small areas of potatoes and vegetables that the plots or fields precluded mechanization and correct rotations.[79] Little wonder, as a U. N. publication noted in 1955, subsequently confirmed by various editions of the official Soviet *Statistical Handbook,* 70–80 percent of the fruit and vegetables, together with more than 50 percent of the meat and 30 percent of the consumer purchases of dairy products—barring the restaurant trade—are made on the open or collective farm market.[80]

In 1956, some attempt to bring about the materialization of the phantom suburban zones was made by raising state delivery and purchase prices of some commodities to the suburban farms. In 1958, at its August meeting, the Party directed 35 sovkhozes in Moscow *oblast'* to shift entirely to potato and vegetable production. Sovkhozes in Tula, Briansk, Riazan', and Kaluga were also required to produce for the Moscow market. Sovkhozes around other neighboring cities were directed to produce for their immediate urban market.[81] Yet, as late as 1961, Leningrad city obtained only 28 percent of its potatoes from within a radius of 100 km, while more than 50 percent came from a

[77] See, for example, I. Blasov, *Sots. sel'. khoz.,* No. 8 (1953), pp. 3–4 and N. V. Vasil'ev, *Razvitie prigorodnogo sel'skogo khoziaistva* (Moscow: 1954), pp. 12, 20.

[78] *Sel'. khoz. SSSR* (Moscow: 1958), p. 261.

[79] See, for example, M. Rakonovich, *Sots. sel'. khoz.,* No. 8 (1953), p. 30 and Blasov, *op. cit.* (in n. 77), p. 7.

[80] "The Place of Livestock Production in the Agricultural Policy of the USSR," *Monthly Bulletin of Agricultural Economics and Statistics,* UN/FAO, VII:9 (September, 1958).

[81] *Pravda,* August 17, 1958; *New York Times,* November 3, 1958.

distance of 500 to 1000 km.[82] For vegetables the situation was somewhat better. About 68 percent of the vegetables were produced within a distance of 100 km, including 98 percent of the cabbages, 99 percent of the carrots, and 71 percent of beets. The absolute amounts of vegetables available in the state stores of Leningrad, however, are unknown; certainly the quantity is not available when required. At any rate, Sokolev in 1962 noted that the incorrect specialization of farms around cities continues to be a basic problem.[83]

Fresh vegetables tend to be scarce in northerly countries during the winter months. In the U.S.S.R. 80 percent of the fresh vegetables in state stores are available only between June and September. Certainly hot frames or hot houses could help reduce the concentration, by lengthening the growing season; yet this type of cultivation remains weakly developed in the Soviet Union. On the other hand, the production of early vegetables and potatoes in the more southerly parts of the country is handicapped by the sharp increase in temperatures in late spring and early summer, and an inadequate moisture supply (especially where irrigation is not practiced), which in potatoes causes deterioration. Indeed, in southerly regions, potatoes and vegetables suffer absolute shortages, necessitating long hauls from northerly regions. It is not surprising that the total length of haul of potatoes and vegetables has steadily risen. Costs of transportation and losses due to spoilage have both gone up.

Examples of regional imbalances and a lack of proportion may be cited for other crops—and Professor Hultquist has already demonstrated the difficulties faced in the Soviet sugar beet industry. Needless to say, it is just such problems which make agriculture the Achilles heel of the Soviet economy.

Jensen has dwelled at some length on prerevolutionary schemes of agricultural regionalization as well as on the reassessment that occurred during the Khrushchev years. His study might have achieved greater balance, however, had he explored more fully the literature of the 1920's, including in particular the writings of B. O. Bruk and Boris Knipovich,[84] both of whom recognized the role of the market in determining agricultural specialization and regional differentiation. Perhaps,

[82] Mineev, *op. cit.* (in n. 67).

[83] M. M. Sokolev, *Ekonomika sotsialisticheskogo sel'skogo khoziaistva SSSR* (Moscow: 1962), p. 222.

[84] See, for example, B. Bruk, *Vestnik sel'skogo khoziaistva,* Nos. 10–11 (1923), pp. 5–7.

too, the work of Chelintsev requires further examination, especially in the light of his 1928 attempt to arrive at indices of regional intensity (specialization) for the regions of prerevolutionary Russia.[85]

Nevertheless, despite these omissions, Jensen has made a substantial contribution to the Western literature on the problems of Soviet agriculture.

[85] A. N. Chelintsev, *Russkoe sel'skoe khoziaistvo pered revoliutsiei* (Moscow: 1928), pp. 66–67.

JEREMY ANDERSON

A Historical-Geographical Perspective on Khrushchev's Corn Program

One of the most significant measures taken to improve Soviet agriculture since the death of Stalin has been sweeping modifications in the regional pattern of agricultural land use. Key roles have been played by the "New Lands" and corn programs, while subsidiary roles were accorded to programs for increased sowings of grain legumes and other fodder crops. Between 1953 and 1962, with intensive promotion by Khrushchev himself, the area sown to corn in the U.S.S.R. grew from 3.5 million hectares to more than 37 million hectares, increasing its share in the sown area from 2 to 17 percent.[1]

Four facets of Khrushchev's corn program will be explored in the following pages. First, the historical spread of corn cultivation in Russia and the U.S.S.R.; second, the impact of Khrushchev's activity on the aggregate sowings of corn and other fodder crops; third, the geographic distribution of corn utilization; finally, the impact of the corn program on the regional specialization of agriculture.

THE HISTORICAL SPREAD OF CORN IN RUSSIA AND THE U.S.S.R.

Corn was first cultivated in what is today the U.S.S.R. in the late sixteenth or early seventeenth century by non-Slavic peoples in the Carpathian and Caucasian borderlands, having been introduced by way of the Balkan peninsula and the Black Sea.[2] In both Bessarabia and

[1] *Narkhoz-1962,* pp. 247–48.

[2] The discussion of prerevolutionary corn cultivation is based on L. L. Dekaprelevich, "Iz istorii kultury kukuruzy v SSSR," Institut Istorii Akademii Nauk, *Materialy po istorii sel'skogo khoziaistva i krest'ianstva SSSR,* Collection IV, (Moscow: 1960), pp. 366–413, except as otherwise noted.

Imertia (west-central Georgia) it quickly replaced millet as the staple grain of the inhabitants, being higher yielding and more palatable.

Corn was much slower and later in its spread onto the steppe lands being colonized by the eastern Slavs, since the Crimean Tatars remained a threat to colonization of lands over which such diffusion would have to occur until early in the nineteenth century. With the annexation of Bessarabia by Russia in 1812, corn cultivation began to spread slowly into the Ukraine and the Kuban lowlands of the North Caucasus. But the cultural heritage of the Slavs favored broadcast small grains over corn, and an abundance of virgin land precluded any need for more intensive crops.

In the Ukraine and North Caucasus corn did not attract much attention until the "Free Economic Society" and other organizations interested in the economic development of "New Russia" began to promote its cultivation for fodder by distributing descriptive brochures and packets of North American varieties of dent seed during the 1850's. The American Civil War, which cut American exports of feed grains to western Europe, coupled with Russian railroad and port construction in the 1870's, spurred the expansion of commercial corn production in southwestern Russia.[3]

In spite of a lack of detailed statistics for the present area of the U.S.S.R. as a whole before 1906, it appears that from the 1850's to the present the expansion of grain corn cultivation in Russia and the U.S.S.R. has been associated primarily with the intensification and specialization of agriculture (especially fodder-livestock production) in the southwestern steppes, while its cultivation has stagnated in the non-Slavic borderlands where it was originally introduced as (and remains in part) a staple crop (see Fig. 1).

Early in the present century, V. V. Talanov and others engaged in a modest campaign for the introduction of improved varieties of dent corn from the United States into southwestern Russia.[4] Talanov came to the United States in 1908 to acquire seeds of promising crops and models of

[3] See V. D. Mochalov, *Krest'ianskoe khoziaistvo v Zakavkaze v kontsu XIX veka* (Moscow: 1958), pp. 134–144

[4] See V. V. Talanov, *Predvaritel'nyi otchet' seti opytnykh uchastkov po kulture kukuruzy (za 1908–10 godu)* (Ekaterinoslav: 1910) and *Kukuruza i odnoletnia kormovia rasteniia zasushlivoi polosy Soedinennykh Shtatov,* (Ekaterinoslav: 1909); I. V. Rozen and V. V. Talanov, *Kratkoe opisanie pokazatel'nykh posevov v Amerikanskom sevooborote i model' Amerikanskoi fermy* (Ekaterinoslav: 1910); and V. M. Benzin, *Organizatsiia sel'skokhoziaistvennogo obrazovaniia i opytnogo dela v Severo-Amerikanskikh Soedinennykh Shtatakh i eia perspektivy v Rossii* (Tambov: 1913) and *Kul'tura kukuruzy* (St. Petersburg: 1912).

FIGURE 1
REGIONAL DISTRIBUTION OF AREA SOWN FOR GRAIN CORN IN TSARIST RUSSIA, THE U.S.S.R., AND ANNEXED TERRITORIES, 1906–1964

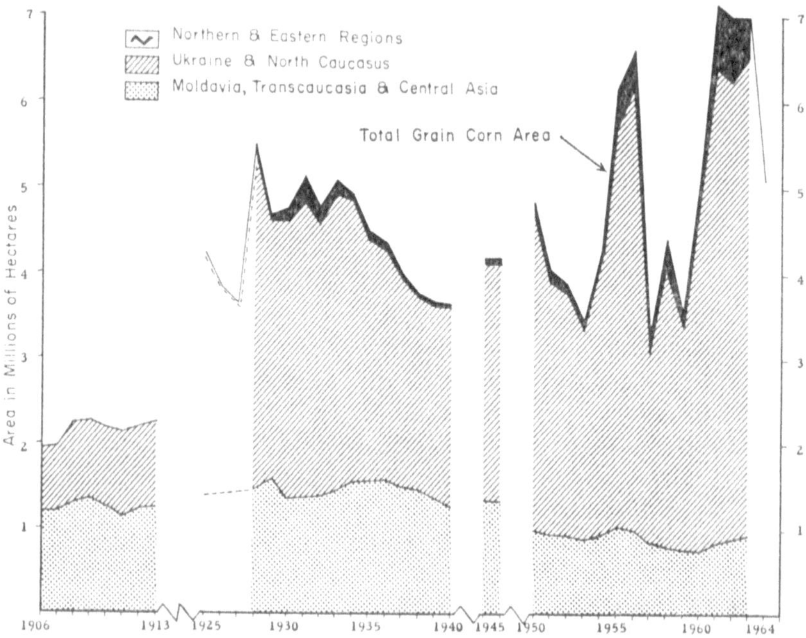

SOURCES: See Table 1. Data on regional distribution were not available for 1925–1927, 1939, and 1964; for 1945 data were partly estimated.

agricultural machinery and to observe American agricultural methods and institutions in general.[5] In his seed-collecting and later, Talanov stressed the selection and use of corn varieties developed in the cooler and drier margins of the North American "corn belt." [6] Thus, Khrushchev's methodology in promoting corn in the U.S.S.R. had prerevolutionary antecedents.

During the early twenties, famine and drought led to widespread sowing of corn since it required less seed than the small grains and gave a higher net yield.[7] Subsequently, land reform and the N.E.P. generally

[5] The results of this trip were published as: *Izvestiia Ekaterinoslavskogo guberskogo zemstva,* Nos. 1–9 (Ekaterinoslav: 1909–1910).

[6] See V. V. Talanov, *et al, Selektsiia i semenovodstvo v SSSR* (Moscow: 1924).

[7] This paragraph is based on V. P. Timoshenko, *Agricultural Russia and the Wheat Problem* (Stanford, Calif.: Food Research Institute and the Committee on Russian Research of the Hoover War Library, 1932), pp. 86–94, 156–195.

favored intensification of agriculture and increased fodder-livestock production. During the late twenties, forced delivery of small grains and a favorable price differential between grain and livestock products also encouraged corn-growing on the southern steppes. Timoshenko regarded the increase of corn production at that time to be a manifestation of agricultural intensification and a healthy departure from the traditional overdependence of southwest Russia on cereal grain production.

TABLE 1

AVERAGE ANNUAL GRAIN CORN PRODUCTION, U.S.S.R.,[a] 1906–1964

Years	Area (million hectares)	Production (million tons)	Yield (centners per hectare)
1906–09	2.1	2.0	9.7
1910–13	2.2	2.5	11.5
1925–28	4.3	4.6	10.6
1929–32	4.9	4.8	9.8
1933–36	4.7	4.5	9.5
1937–40	3.8	n.a.	n.a.
1950–53	4.2	5.3 [b]	12.7 [b]
1954–57	5.1	7.4	14.6
1958–61	5.0	10.7	21.2
1962–64	6.4	13.5	21.7

[a] All figures are for the area presently encompassed by the territory of the U.S.S.R.

[b] 1949–1953 average.

SOURCES: For the method of compilation and sources of data see J. H. Anderson, "The Soviet Corn Program: A Study in Crop Geography" (unpublished doctoral dissertation, University of Washington, Seattle, 1964), pp. 134–156. 1962–1964 data are from *Narkhoz-1964*, pp. 304–305.

While the severe winter of 1928 resulted in a particularly sharp increase in corn sown that year to replace destroyed winter grains, Figure 1 and Table 1 show that the general level of corn production during that period was nearly double its prewar level. As can be seen from Figure 1, the bulk of the increased sowing of corn was in the Ukraine and North Caucasus.

The sustained increase in corn area observed during the early 30's was clearly related to the specialization and intensification of agriculture contemplated by the First Five-Year Plan.[8] A report of the All-Union

[8] U.S.S.R., Gosplan, *Piatiletnii plan narodno-khoziaistvennogo stroitelstva SSR*, II, 3d ed., part 1 (Moscow: 1930), 313–321.

Institute of Plant Breeding called for "significantly increased sowing of corn" to serve as the fodder base for intensive livestock production in the western half of the North Caucasus and in the steppe and forest-steppe regions of the Ukraine, and as a supplementary fodder in the Central Black Soil and dry-steppe regions of the southeastern part of European Russia.[9] Jasny cites a Soviet plan for corn-sowings "in 1930–31 to be at least 10 million hectares." [10] Coming during the chaos of the first all-out drive for collectivization, such an order could not be followed. Nevertheless, between 1913 and the early thirties, the share of corn in the total sown area of the Ukraine increased from 3 to 6 percent, and in the North Caucasus it grew from 3 to 12 percent.[11] Although occupying only a small percentage of the sown area in the cooler Central Black Soil and drier Volga regions, the area sown to corn grew from about 1,000 hectares in 1913 to 250,000 hectares in 1931 in the Volga regions, and to 68,000 hectares in 1933 in the Central Black Soil region.[12]

The crisis of collectivization, resulting in livestock slaughter, capital scarcity, and general chaos, caused Soviet agriculture to falter in its push toward intensification. Accompanying crop failure and food shortages caused schemes of specialization to be abandoned to the basic task of producing enough grain to satisfy delivery quotas and keep peasants alive. With the advent of the transportation crisis, regional self-sufficiency in basic foodstuffs became the official policy for agricultural land use. As one might have predicted, the decline in corn area occurred mainly in Slavic regions where it had been used primarily for livestock feed and declined only slightly in non-Slavic areas where it remained a dietary staple (see Fig. 1 and Table 1).

Almost no information is available concerning corn in the U.S.S.R. between 1940 and 1949. On the basis of limited data, however, it appears that Khrushchev's corn program was given a trial run in the Ukraine, where he was party secretary for a substantial part of the time. As early as 1940, he had noted the potentialities of corn, and in

[9] N. N. Kuleshov, in U.S.S.R., Vsesoiuznyi Institut Rastenievodstva, *Rastenievodstvo SSSR,* II (Moscow-Leningrad: 1933), 233–250. As Lazar Volin kindly recalled to my attention, Kuleshov and other Russian agronomists of the period tended to overestimate the drought resistance of corn.

[10] N. Jasny, *The Socialized Agriculture of the USSR,* (Stanford, California: Stanford University Press, 1949), pp. 502–504.

[11] Russia, Glavnoe Upravlenie Zemleustroistva i Zemledelia, *Sbornik statistiko-ekonomicheskikh svedenii po sel'skomu khoziaistvu Rossii i inostrannykh gosudarstv,* VIII (Petrograd: 1915), 7–57; and *Sel'skoe khoziaistvo SSSR-Ezhegodnik 1935* (Moscow: 1936), pp. 316, 1367, and addenda.

[12] *Ibid.*

an address to the plenum of the Central Committee of the Ukrainian Communist party in 1946, he again pointed out the virtues of corn as a high-yielding grain and as a silage and green fodder crop.[13] Between 1945 and 1950, the corn area in the Ukraine increased by more than a million hectares, while the corn area in the remainder of the U.S.S.R. declined by nearly a half-a-million hectares.[14] Data indicate that the decline was most marked in the non-Slavic borderlands (especially Moldavia), while the extension of corn sowings in the Black Soil regions of European Russia reached as far as Orenburg *oblast'*.

The decline in the grain corn area observed between 1950 and 1953 was due to a general trend in the substitution of bread grains for coarse grains and, especially, increased sowings of winter wheat in the principal corn-growing regions of the southwest. Khrushchev was no longer in the Ukraine; the decline in the all-Union corn area between 1950 and 1953 was accounted for largely by the decrease in the area sown to corn in the Ukraine.[15] This trend was sharply reversed in 1954 by a severe winterkill of fall sown-grains in the winter of 1953–54 in the southwestern U.S.S.R. and the launching of the corn program by Khrushchev at the September, 1953, plenum.

KHRUSHCHEV'S CORN PROGRAM—A CHRONOLOGY

Khrushchev, in his famous keynote address to the September, 1953, plenum, referred to the important role of corn in Western agriculture and livestock production, and calling for the expansion of its sowing for silage in non-Black Soil and eastern regions as well as in the Black Soil regions of the Southwest.[16] His remarks were echoed by the plenum report and the decree "On the Development of Livestock Production," which urged the Ministry of Sovkhozes to "organize an intensive experiment in 1954 for the ensiling of corn ears . . . where natural conditions prevent corn from ripening." [17]

The "Virgin and Idle Lands" decree of March, 1954, went out of its way to attack Williams's "travopol'e" system and urged that more feed grains and succulent fodder crops be grown.[18] As can be seen from

[13] *Pravda,* February 8, 1940, cited by L. A. Zhdanov, ed., *Kukuruza* (Rostov: 1941), p. 11; and Khrushchev, N. S., *Mobilizuvati vsi sili na naishvidshe vidbuduvannia i dal'shii rozvitok sil'skogo hospodarstva* (Kiev: 1946), pp. 33–38.
[14] *Pos. ploshch.,* I (Moscow: 1957), pp. 20–137.
[15] *Ibid.*
[16] *Pravda,* September 15, 1953.
[17] *Ibid.,* September 13, and September 26, 1953.
[18] *Ibid.,* March 6, 1954.

Table 2, these decrees had a modest impact on the areas sown to grain corn, silage, and annual grass crops in 1954 (green fodder corn was included in this latter category that year). The great spurt in the sowing of corn in 1955 was the result of a stronger emphasis on corn-growing contained in the decree on "Increasing Output of Livestock" issued by the plenum of January, 1955, which called for the area sown to corn to reach 28 million hectares by 1960.[19]

The scientific, popular, and educational presses were quick to get the message and amplify it. Editorials appeared in leading agricultural journals lauding corn as "the most valuable fodder crop";[20] numerous pamphlets on how to raise corn were published, and even a schoolteachers' handbook on instruction about corn was issued.[21] During the spring of 1955, Khrushchev made personal appearances at five regional conferences of agricultural workers, urging them to pay special attention to the raising of corn.[22] It made little difference where one's farm was, he implied, since corn could be grown for some purposes nearly everywhere. In his remarks to the January plenum, he had stated that even if silage corn failed to reach milk maturity, the green silage could be put to good use; the livestock decree had stated that "ears ensiled for fodder, are equal, at dry rates, to ripe corn."[23] This false equation of the feeding value of silage corn with that of ripe grain corn early in the corn campaign was probably responsible for part of the ensuing excesses in the sowing of silage and green fodder corn.

The results of the intensive propaganda are clearly evident in the sown-area statistics of 1955 (see Table 2), although yields were disappointing in many regions (especially silage yields in the non-Black Soil regions and all corn yields in the eastern regions). The 1955 failures

[19] *Ibid.*, February 2, 1955.

[20] E. G. *Zem.*, No. 3 (1955), pp. 3–8. and *Sots. sel'. khoz.*, No. 2 (1955), pp. 3–19.

[21] N. N. Kuleshev, *Kukuruza-vazhneishaia zernovaia kultura;* B. F. Solov'ev, *Vyrashchivanie kukuruzy v novykh raionakh,* and M. P. Yelsukov, *Rasshirenie i ukreplenie kormovoi bazy* (all published in Moscow in 1955); and D. E. Gavrilin, *Kukuruza i ee izuchenie v shkole i detskom dome* (Moscow: 1955). Published in the fall of 1955, the latter book outlined the characteristics of corn and corn cultivation, noted its significance for Soviet agriculture, and set forth a number of course outlines and student projects for the practical study of corn.

[22] In the "Southeast" (Saratov), Central Black Soil (Voronezh), Central non-Black Soil (Moscow), Northwest (Leningrad) and Baltics (Riga). In addition he appeared before a plenary session of the Party Central Committee of the Ukraine in February, 1955. Similar appearances were made at conferences of agricultural workers in the Urals (Sverdlovsk), Siberia (Novosibirsk), and Kazakstan (Alma Ata) during a junket in July of 1956. See *Stroi. komm.*, II, *passim,* for complete transcripts of his statements at these appearances.

[23] *Pravda,* February 23, 1955.

TABLE 2

SOWN AREA OF CORN AND OTHER MAJOR FODDER CROPS, U.S.S.R., 1953–1964

(million hectares)

Crop	1953	1954	1955	1956	1957	1958	1959	1960	1961	1962	1963	1964
Barley	9.6	10.7	9.9	11.9	9.2	9.7	9.6	12.1	13.4	16.3	20.5	20.3
Oats	15.3	15.9	14.8	15.1	14.0	14.8	14.3	12.8	11.5	6.9	5.7	5.7
Grain corn	3.5	4.3	6.2	6.6	3.3	4.4	3.5	5.1	7.2	7.0	7.0	5.1
Perennial grass	15.4	15.3	13.0	11.6	13.1	13.5	15.2	15.8	19.4	15.6	13.6	12.6
Annual grass	7.8	9.4	10.5	12.2	15.2	17.0	19.2	19.3	16.7	11.7	17.5	13.9
Ripe-corn silage	(2.3) [a]	(3.9) [a]	2.9	2.7	2.6	3.7	5.2	6.2	6.0	7.2	19.6 [b]	17.9 [b]
Green-corn silage			4.6	6.0	6.5	5.9	7.3	9.2	8.9	13.8		
Green-fodder corn	n.a.	n.a.	4.2	8.7	6.0	5.7	6.4	7.8	3.2	9.2	7.6	4.4
All corn	n.a.	n.a.	17.9	23.9	18.3	19.7	22.4	28.2	25.7	37.1	34.2	27.4
Total fodder area	57.1	62.1	69.5	78.0	74.5	79.1	85.2	94.0	91.8	97.2	104.6	94.0
Total feed grains	28.4	30.9	30.9	33.6	26.5	28.9	27.4	30.0	32.1	30.2	33.2	31.1
Total coarse and succulent fodder [c]	28.7	31.2	38.6	44.4	48.0	50.2	57.8	64.0	59.7	67.0	71.4	61.5

[a] All silage 1953–54.

[b] All corn silage 1963–64.

[c] This figure differs from the total for *kormovye kul'tury* given in the pre-1963 statistical handbooks in that it includes the ripe-corn silage area (lumped with grain statistics by the Soviets until 1963, but utilized for silage in actual practice). "Grain" legumes in excess of the 1950–59 average sown area (2.5 million hectares) have also been included in this figure since it is likely that the largest portion of these are actually utilized as silage, hay, and green fodder. The excess legume figures are as follows: 1960: 0.8, 1961: 1.8, 1962: 4.7, 1963: 8.3, and 1964: 8.1 million hectares.

SOURCES: 1953, 1958–62: *Narkhoz-1962*, pp. 247–48; 1954–57: *Sel'khoz-1960*, p. 133; 1958–61 (green-corn silage and green-fodder corn only): *Narkhoz-1961*, p. 312; 1963–64: *Narkhoz-1964*, pp. 267–268.

were blamed in part on a lack of experience and on the cold spring; but a lack of good seed, proper equipment, cultivation, and storage facilities were all factors responsible for the low yields.[24]

The Sixth Five-Year Plan, published in January, 1956, reiterated earlier calls for further introduction of corn sowings and decreed the organization of large-scale production of hybrid seed.[25] The barrage of propaganda begun in 1955 continued, as an illustrated popular journal devoted solely to the cultivation and utilization of corn was brought into regular publication.[26] Hence, in spite of the problems encountered by corn growers in 1955, 1956 saw further increases in corn-sowings.

That the expansion in the corn area was ill conceived in its magnitude and disruptive to the work of the peasants was reflected by continued low silage yields in 1956 and emphasized by the sharp decline in the corn areas sown in 1957 (see Tables 2 and 3). Khrushchev himself appears to have blown the whistle on further expansion that year when he stated that unless corn yields were at least 200 to 250 centners of green mass per hectare, it would be better to continue cultivation of traditional fodder crops.[27] The sharpest decline, though, was in the grain corn area, in spite of generally satisfactory yields for this crop previously. This was probably due to the fact that the rapid expansion of corn for silage and green fodder diverted critical resources, especially seed and machinery, away from grain corn, for which proper seed and cultivation are most important.

The 1957 setback was only a temporary respite. In January, 1958, the Council of Ministers and Party Central Committee made a plea for more silage production, noting that plans set for meat and milk production would require two to three times as much succulent fodder as was

[24] *Pravda,* April 8, 1956. The Soviet press was full of complaints almost from the inception of the program—see, for example, the Central Committee decree on the results of spring sowing and implications thereof in *Pravda,* June 27, 1954; also *Sel'khoz.,* February 22, September 17, and December 16, 1955; *Pravda,* May 18 and June 28, 1955; and *Izvestiia,* December 16, 1955.

[25] *Pravda,* January 15, 1956.

[26] *Pravda,* May 14, 1956. The journal, *Kukuruza* (*Corn*), is published monthly in Moscow, by the U.S.S.R. Ministry of Agriculture, and features one-half to two-page articles on practical experience and experiments kolkhozes and sovkhozes in the breeding, cultivation, and utilization of all types of corn. A five-volume work, *Kukuruza v 1955 godu,* was hurriedly published in Moscow in January and February of 1956. Organized on a regional basis, it was comprised largely of articles by agronomists relating successes attained in corn-raising in their particular region in 1955.

[27] In a statement made before a conference of agricultural workers from the non-Black Soil *oblasts* in Moscow, March 30, 1957. *Stroi. komm.,* II, 368. Also reported in *Pravda,* April 1, 1957 and *Sel'khoz.,* April 2, 1957.

produced in 1957.[28] At the December, 1958, plenum, Khrushchev gave particular emphasis to the role which ripe corn silage should play in livestock production, while he condemned that growing of corn for green silage and green fodder.[29] He strongly implied that in many regions,

TABLE 3

YIELDS OF SELECTED FODDER CROPS, U.S.S.R., 1949–1964
(Net fodder units in centners per hectare)

Year	Winter wheat	Grain corn	Ripe silage corn	Green silage corn	Fodder beets [a]	Perennial hay
1949–53 average	10.8	15.0	n.a.	n.a.	n.a.	6.6
1953	11.5	12.4	n.a.	n.a.	9.5	6.6
1954	9.4	10.0	n.a.	n.a.	9.2	6.6
1955	14.4	22.8	9.8	2.2	15.0	7.5
1956	12.1	18.2	10.2	2.9	14.9	7.5
1957	15.8	16.9	9.7	4.7	15.4	7.6
1958	17.6	28.4	24.0	9.3	18.4	8.6
1959	16.4	19.2	16.8	9.5	15.8	8.4
1960	16.3	23.3	(13.3)		16.3	7.8
1961	18.5	29.1	(11.6)		14.2	8.0
1962	18.4	26.8	(8.3)		11.6	8.2
1963	13.7	19.0	(7.2)		n.a.	7.3
1964	14.8	31.8	(12.3)		n.a.	7.8

[a] Yield of sugar beets grown for fodder from 1960 on.

SOURCES: For greater comparability, yields were converted to net fodder units using conversion factors from I. S. Popov, *Kormovye normy i kormovye tablitsy*, 14th ed. (Moscow: 1957, *passim*), with silage factors discounted by 40 percent to account for wastage and shrinkage of green mass. Seeding rates (converted to fodder unit equivalents) are from A. I. Smirnov, *Rastenievodstvo* (Moscow: 1958), pp. 54, 124. The formula used was: Seeding rate = gross yield per hectare × fodder-unit factor. For individual crops, the fodder-unit conversion factors and seeding rates are (respectively): winter wheat: 1.20, 1.80; grain corn: 1.26, 0.6; ripe silage: 0.12, 1.0; green silage: 0.09, 1.0; all silage: 0.10, 1.0; fodder beets: 0.135, 0; perennial hay: 0.50, 0.

The underlying data on gross yields are taken from *Narkhoz-1962*, p. 237 (for 1949–1953 average and 1960–1962); *Sel'khoz-1960*, pp. 208–209, 247 (for 1953–1959); *SSSR v tsifrakh-1964*, pp. 76–77 (for 1963–1964).

including those favorable for grain corn, ripe corn silage might be preferable to grain corn since one might secure two crops per year, and since it was "more effective . . . [and] . . . easier to store." [30]

[28] *Pravda*, January 21, 1958.

[29] N. S. Khrushchev, *Agricultural Progress in the USSR* (Moscow: 1959), pp. 124–135.

[30] *Ibid.* The suggestion of two corn crops a year in the Southwest, was first raised by the January, 1955, agricultural plenum. Cf. *Pravda*, February 2, 1955.

But, he continued, green fodder corn was "in actual fact ruined corn," and green silage yielded only "a lot of water and very little nutritive substance." [31]

In spite of the caveats against the green-corn crops, their area continued to grow, spurred on by the goals of the Seven-Year Plan (adopted in February, 1959), and by a decree of the Central Committee of the R.S.F.S.R. urging party workers, kolkhozes and sovkhozes to take vigorous measures to increase the yields and production of corn.[32]

The comparison of ripe corn silage to grain corn may have played a role in the decline of ripe corn harvested in 1959.

The year 1961 appears to have provided a respite after the effort expended to attain the goal of 28 million hectares of corn in 1960. The green fodder corn area contracted by half, while the grain corn area increased sharply in response to the stress laid upon corn as a "main reserve for increasing grain production" by the January, 1961, plenum.[33] However, the contrast between the ambitious goals of the "Twenty-Year Plán" set forth in October, 1961, and the disappointing performance of Soviet agriculture following the record harvest of 1958, seems to have triggered a "great leap forward" in 1962. The plenum of March, 1962, pronounced a death sentence upon the *travopol'e* system, under fire since 1954, as "unsuitable for Socialist agriculture"; low-yielding crops (that is, hay, oats) were to be replaced with intensive row crops for fodder—not only corn, but also sugar beets, and fodder legumes.[34]

The response in the corn-sowings was a staggering increase of nearly 12 million hectares to a total corn area of 37 million hectares. As with earlier increases, the bulk of the increment was comprised of green corn (see Table 2 and Figure 2). As a result of vigorous campaigning against *travopol'e* and for row crops, the situation in 1962 got completely out of hand. By the end of June, Khrushchev was once again

[31] Khrushchev, *op. cit.* (in n. 29), p. 129.

[32] *Spravochnik partiinogo rabotnika,* No. 2 (Moscow: 1959), pp. 371–374. This source was kindly called to my attention by Nancy Nimitz. The principal point of the decree was to stress more intensive and careful cultivation and utilization of the corn crops, although it called for expanded sowings in the North Caucasus, Lower Volga, and Central Black Soil *oblasts.*

[33] *Pravda,* January 20, 1961. The plenum resolution urged that 5 million hectares of the most favorable land in the Ukraine and the R.S.F.S.R. be set aside for raising corn "with a view to obtaining at least 50 centners per hectare of grain from these areas." While the anticipated yield would appear overly optimistic when compared with yields presently prevailing in the United States and western Europe, the scale and location proposed, was more rational than most preceding proposals.

[34] *Pravda,* March 11, 1962.

FIGURE 2
U.S.S.R., AREA SOWN TO CORN CLASSIFIED BY UTILIZATION, 1950–1964

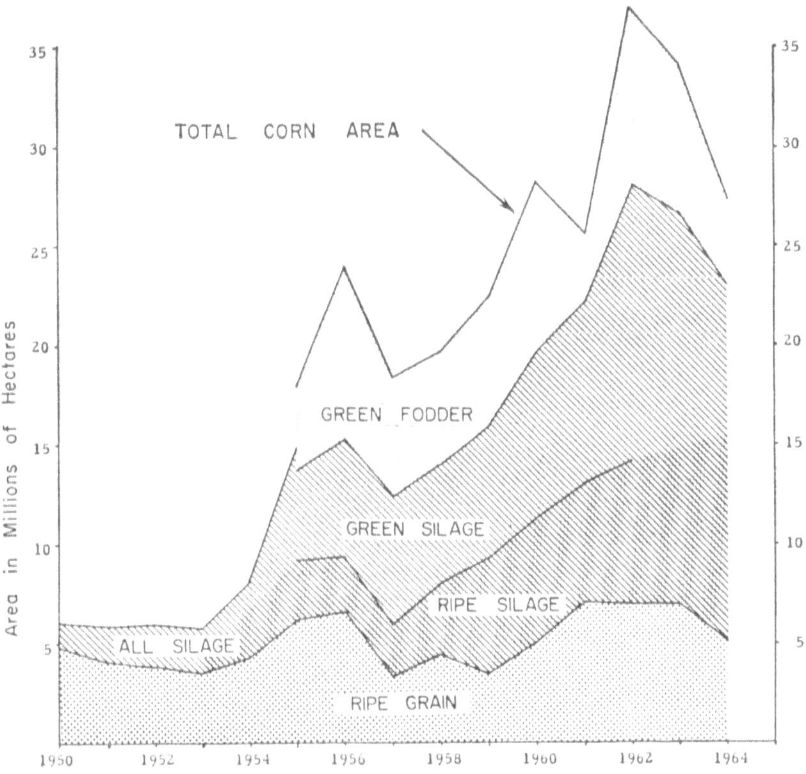

SOURCES: See Table 2.

urging moderation, stating that corn should only be extended within "existing possibilities," that is, to the extent that it could be properly cultivated, harvested, and used.[35]

While the area sown to corn declined somewhat in 1963, any rationalization implicit in the decline appears to have been offset by a doubling in the fodder-legume-sown area. The somewhat greater decline in the corn areas observed for 1964, including a sharp drop in the green fodder corn area and accompanied by improved yields, may have heralded a more positive step toward a rational corn program, again signaled by Khrushchev personally. In his major address to the February, 1964,

[35] *Sel'. zh.*, July 1, 1962: "You can't just urge people on and demand that they sow more."

plenum, he warned against distortion of the corn area, and suggested that decisions on how much to sow should be left to the peasants themselves.[36] Khrushchev was so closely associated with the corn program that even in the absence of detailed data on 1965 sowings, one could predict a sharp decrease in the area sown to the corn crops, especially green corn, although Soviet leaders cautioned in the spring of 1965 against denying corn "its rightful place . . . where it yields a good harvest." [37]

A GEOGRAPHIC VIEW OF THE CORN PROGRAM

Let us now turn to a more detailed consideration of some of the reasons underlying the vicissitudes of the corn-sowings and yields observed above. This may be best accomplished by returning to a consideration of the geographic distribution of the individual corn crops.

GRAIN CORN

The corn program had two immediate effects on grain corn production: it halted a downward trend in corn cultivation observed between 1950 and 1953, but it also brought about a premature and indiscriminate expansion of the grain corn area in regions which were of marginal value for raising it and where it was an unfamiliar crop. As a result of seed and other capital scarcities, low yields in marginal areas, and promotion of corn cultivation for nongrain purposes, the initial increases were followed by rather wide fluctuations in the grain corn area (see Figure 2). Only since 1960 does the cultivation of grain corn appear to have been accorded the position of priority which it deserves among the corn crops.

Of greatest significance, perhaps, is that the pattern of distribution emerging exhibits a continuation of the trend noted earlier. The area sown to grain corn in the non-Slavic borderlands is either stable or declining as the Soviets continue to develop these areas along the line of increased specialization in the production of subtropical crops for which their climates are suited. The relative importance of corn among the grain crops remains high, though, in those areas where it is a traditional staple crop. The greatest absolute gains have occurred in the steppe and

[36] *Pravda,* February 14, 1964.

[37] Moderation with respect to reductions in the corn area was urged by Brezhnev at the March, 1965, plenum (*Pravda,* March 27, 1965) as well as in an editorial in *Ek. sel'. khoz.,* No. 4 (1965), p. 5. An indication of the extent of reductions is that the announced goal for corn sowings in the R.S.F.S.R. this year was 12 million hectares as opposed to 19 million hectares sown in 1963. (*Sov. Ross.,* June 1, 1965, and *Narkhoz–1963,* p. 269.)

FIGURE 3

U.S.S.R., DISTRIBUTION OF GRAIN CORN AND CLIMATIC LIMITS, 1961

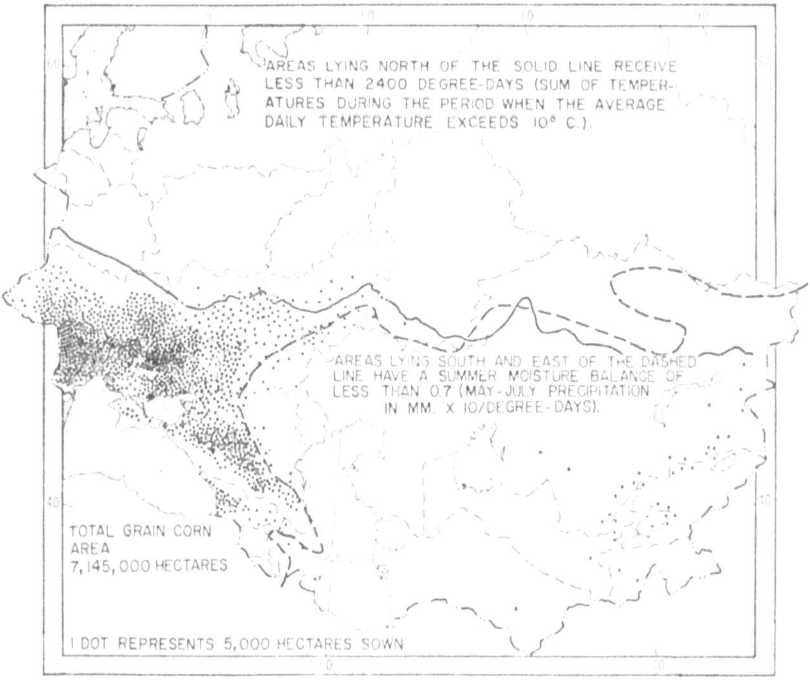

SOURCES: *Narkhoz-1961,* p. 329; *Narkhoz-RSFSR-1961,* pp. 247, 263–264; *Narodne hospodarstvo Ukrainskoi RSR v 1961 rotsi* (Kiev: 1962), pp. 247–248, 265–266; *Atlas sel'skogo khoziaistva SSSR* (Moscow: 1960), pp. 30, 124, and my note 39.

forest steppe of the Ukraine and the North Caucasus and the greatest relative gains in the southern half of the Central Black Soil and the central portion of the Volga region—all areas where Selianinov recommended intensive fodder livestock production more than three decades ago.[38] While the most recent expansion has pushed grain corn up to (and in a few cases, beyond) recognized climatic limits (the 2400 degree-day isotherm in the north, the 0.7 May–July moisture balance in the south),[39] in general, the expanded sowings have been concentrated in those areas best suited for this crop as indicated by average yield data (see Figure 3 and Table 4).

[38] G. T. Selianinov, in *Rastenievodstvo SSSR,* No. I, *op. cit.* (in n. 9), pp. 1–10; see also Kuleshov in *ibid.,* pp. 227–238.

[39] S. S. Andreenko, and F. M. Kuperman, *Fiziologiia kukuruzy* (Moscow: 1959), p. 48, provide all thermal limits incorporated in text discussion and in figures below; the moisture limit is as established by Selianinov, *op. cit.* (in n. 9), pp. 6–10, and Map 1.

TABLE 4

REGIONAL CORN YIELDS, U.S.S.R., SELECTED YEARS
(Net fodder units in centners per hectare)

Region	Ripe grain average 1954–1958	Ripe silage average 1955–1959	Green silage average 1955–1959
U.S.S.R.	19.7	14.1	6.0
R.S.F.S.R.	18.0	11.0	5.9
North	n.a.	n.a.	3.8
Northwest	n.a.	n.a.	6.8
Center	n.a.	n.a.	8.0
Volga-Viatka	n.a.	n.a.	8.9
Cent. Black Soil	15.9	17.3	8.5
Volga	6.7	6.3	4.5
North Caucasus	19.2	11.2	6.2
Urals	7.5	6.0	5.1
West Siberia	14.6	8.8	6.5
East Siberia	n.a.	n.a.	6.1
Far East	17.1	14.0	6.9
Ukraine	20.5	16.0	7.4
Belorussia	n.a.	n.a.	12.6
Lithuania	n.a.	n.a.	10.5
Latvia	n.a.	n.a.	10.6
Estonia	n.a.	n.a.	11.9
Georgia	16.8	13.1	7.1
Azerbaidzhan	16.9	12.8	7.0
Armenia	21.0	18.8	6.9
Kazakhstan	13.5	9.0	3.4
Uzbekistan	26.7	12.4	5.2
Kirghizistan	20.9	15.1	10.5
Tadzhikistan	19.0	10.3	5.2
Turkmenistan	5.6	7.6	4.5
Moldavia	21.7	19.0	10.6

SOURCE: *Sel'khoz-1960,* pp. 221, 248–249. Silage yields are unweighted averages. Grain yields converted to fodder units by multiplying gross yield by a factor of 1.26 and subtracting .6 from the result to compensate for seed expenditure; Silage yields converted by multiplying gross yield by a factor of .12 (ripe silage) or .09 (green silage)—both factors have been discounted by 40 percent to take into account shrinkage and wastage of green mass—and subtracting 1.0 from the result to compensate for seed expenditure. Fodder-unit conversion factors were based on those given by I. S. Popov, *Kormovye normy i kormovye tablitsy,* 14th ed. (Moscow; 1957), *passim.*

Grain corn is the highest yielding grain in nearly all regions in which it is sown, an advantage enhanced by its low seeding rate (less than 0.5 centners per hectare, as opposed to 1.5 to 2 centners for small grains).[40] While stable cropping systems are still lacking in Soviet

[40] Ukraine, Statisticheske Upravlenie, *Valovi zbory i urozhainist' sil'sko-hospodars' kikh kul'tur po Ukrains'kii RSR* (Kiev: 1959), *passim,* provides detailed

agriculture, corn has long been recommended as one of the best crops to precede spring wheat in the cropping sequence, since its cultivation provides weed control and because the stubble and root system left after harvest maximize snow and spring moisture retention.[41] But it depletes the soil too much to precede industrial crops, and its late maturing habit interferes with fall plowing and fall sowing (see discussion below), hence its expansion has conflicted with other development trends in the southwestern regions of the U.S.S.R.

Soviet data on labor productivity and costs appear to lump grain corn with ripe silage corn, and I doubt the validity of comparisons which have been or may be drawn from such data. It is probable, given the contrasts in existing levels of mechanization, that grain corn is more costly to produce than small grains. In terms of land use, however, the substitution of grain corn for other feed grains appears to have increased productivity per unit of crop land input. (My experimental study of the Ukraine indicated that 1953–1961 fodder yields [aggregate fodder units per unit of fodder crop land] increased by about 10 percent as a result of changes in the structure of the sown area, although the bulk of the increase in fodder production was simply due to increased fodder crop area.) [42]

Geographers have done little work about the relationship between production of fodder and livestock specialization in the U.S.S.R. Lack of time and data precludes such an attempt here (the study referred to above did find that increased livestock production in the Ukraine corresponded closely to increased fodder crop production, but also found that regional specialization in fodder production was not accompanied by a corresponding specialization in livestock production.) [43] In the U.S.S.R. as a whole, between 1953 and 1962, the total quantity of concentrates fed to livestock and meat production both increased by more than 60 percent.[44] Increased grain corn production accounted for about 40 percent of the increase in concentrate feeds and probably comprises nearly 20 percent of the concentrates fed to Soviet livestock

---

verification for this. Winter wheat and winter barley appear to outyield corn only along the arid margins of its cultivation in the southern Ukraine and northern Caucasus. Seeding rates are from A. I. Smirnov, *Rastenievodstvo* (Moscow: 1958), pp. 54–144 and I. P. Karnaukov, et al, *Osnovy sel'skogo khoziaistva* (Moscow: 1959), pp. 178–220.

[41] Kuleshov, *op. cit.* (in n. 9).

[42] J. Anderson; "Fodder and Livestock Units in Agricultural Geography: A Case Study of Soviet Land Use," paper read at the annual meeting of the Association of American Geographers, Columbus, Ohio, April 19, 1965.

[43] *Ibid.*

[44] *Narkhoz-1962,* pp. 277, 309, 319, and *Narkhoz-1961,* p. 410.

as opposed to about 7 percent in 1953.[45] Also of significance is the fact that between 1954 and 1963 the Central Black Soil region jumped from sixth to first place in the R.S.F.S.R. in terms of numbers of swine per 100 hectares of arable land, with the largest gains occurring in the three southernmost *oblasts* (Belgorod, Kursk, and Voronezh).[46]

RIPE SILAGE CORN

Jasny noted that modest amounts of corn and sunflower began to be grown for silage during the early thirties, but the area was subsequently reduced as a result of low yields and the return to regional self-sufficiency and semisubsistence agriculture in the mid and late thirties.[47] Since 1950, the area sown for silage in the U.S.S.R. has increased steadily, punctuated by the sharp fluctuations already described in the chronology of the corn program, with the area roughly doubling in 1954, again in 1955, and making large jumps in 1959, 1960, and 1962. Corn for ripe silage has accounted for roughly one-third of the total increase in the all-Union silage area, while green corn silage has accounted for the rest, with other silage crops either remaining static in area or declining slightly.

Like grain corn, the ripe silage corn distribution is compact and appears to be sharply limited by climate (especially by the 2200-degree day isotherm to the north, but less mindful of the 0.7 moisture-balance isoline in the southeast. See Figure 4.) Its greatest relative importance in 1961 was primarily in those regions where it produced above-average yields, although it was overextended in the Urals and Volga regions where both frost and drought hazards affect yields adversely (see Table 4). Its extent in these latter areas was reduced in 1962 in spite of a general increase in the area of this crop. The expanded sowings in the North Caucasus and Ukraine have occurred in part on land formerly fallowed before the sowing of winter grains, since, during a favorable year, the crop may attain sufficient maturity to make good ripe silage and be harvested in plenty of time to allow preparation for fall sowing. The depletion of soil moisture and fertility were outweighed in the mind

[45] In 1953, 35.3 million tons of concentrates were fed, of which corn comprised roughly 2.5 million tons (derived by subtracting 1.2 million tons from total corn production for human use and seed purposes.) In 1962, 61.3 million tons of concentrates were fed, of which 12.5 million tons is estimated to have been grain corn (derived by subtracting 3 million tons from total production for seed purposes and direct human consumption.) Sources cited in note 44, above.

[46] *Narkhoz-RSFSR-1962*, pp. 297–298.

[47] Jasny, *op. cit.* (in n. 10), p. 618.

FIGURE 4
U.S.S.R., DISTRIBUTION OF RIPE SILAGE CORN AND CLIMATIC LIMITS, 1961

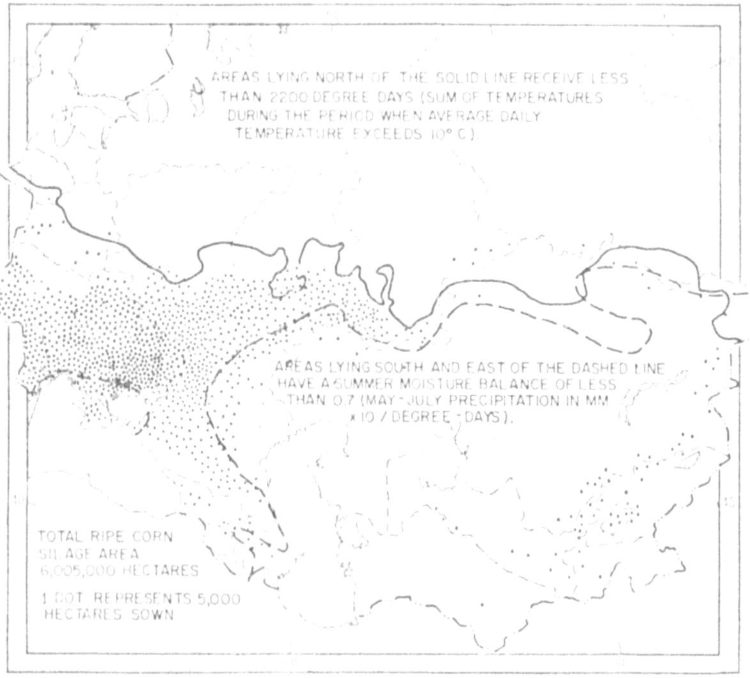

SOURCES: See Figure 3.

of the Soviets by better weed control and increased fodder production.[48] Maniakin has recently condemned this practice, however, noting that corn, "monarch of crop rotation," is harvested so late that it interferes with fall sowing; he lays the blame for increased winterkill of fall-sown wheat in the Ukraine directly upon corn.[49]

GREEN CORN

No detailed (*oblast'*) data are available on the distribution of green silage and green fodder corn as separate crops after 1959. In that year, the green silage corn distribution exhibited two distinct patterns.[50] First,

[48] S. I. Savel'ev, *Vest. sel'. nauki,* No. 2 (1958), pp. 27–31.

[49] V. Maniakin, *Ek. sel'. khoz.,* No. 2 (1965), pp. 2–3.

[50] Detailed data on the separate distributions of green silage corn and green fodder corn up to 1959 is contained in J. Anderson, in R. D. Laird, ed., *Soviet Agricultural and Peasant Affairs* (Lawrence, Kansas: University of Kansas Press, 1963), Table 2, p. 261.

there was a heavy concentration in the steppe Ukraine and North Caucasus where Soviet leaders and others had recommended extensive "second sowings" on land from which winter grain had been harvested (to utilize residual moisture and thermal reserves) in addition to the sowing of corn for silage on black fallow noted above.[51] Second, a belt of production extending from the Baltic to Lake Baikal appeared to comprise all corn sown in those areas which could be harvested with available machines and labor. The areal distribution of green fodder corn is harder to specify—it was sown everywhere, although those areas also engaged in raising grain corn and ripe silage corn had a relatively larger portion of their green corn classed as green fodder than those areas where green corn was the only corn crop and where green silage predominated over green fodder. In other words, those areas with other corn crops where green corn was sown as a catch crop or for "green fallow" were probably faced with machine and labor shortages of sufficient proportions so that the kolkhozniks simply chose to ignore the green corn, much of which may have ended up as green manure instead of green fodder. Figure 2 shows that especially large portions of the increased sowings of corn in 1956, 1960, and 1962 ended up as green fodder rather than green silage. It should be noted that the Soviet data on the "sown" area of the various corn crops appears to be determined in retrospect from harvest and utilization data (thus, in July, 1962, it was announced that 9.7 million hectares had been sown to corn for ripe grain, but official statistics issued the following spring showed the grain corn area to be only 7 million hectares).[52] The fact that the area of green fodder corn has fluctuated most widely and tends to grow during years of expansion and shrink when the total corn area contracts, suggest that green fodder corn has been used by the peasants as a buffer between administrative fiat and feasible practice. Peasants forced to plow up fallow or grassland and sow it to corn could hide a lack of cultivation by dense sowings which would readily pass early-season inspection by officials. In the absence of adequate harvesting equipment and silos, large areas sown to corn simply could not be harvested, hence the residual left in the fields must have simply been classed as green fodder. The low priority accorded the green corn-sowings by the farmers is evident from data which indicate abysmally low silage yields everywhere except in Moldavia, the Baltics, and Belorussia. These latter are regions where high yields of grass and root crops are possible,

[51] Speeches by Podgorny and Khrushchev (*Pravda,* December 23 and 29, 1959) indicated that "second sowings" of corn in the southwestern regions were to be approximately 3.5 million hectares in 1960.

[52] *Pravda,* July 21, 1962; *Narkhoz-1962,* p. 259.

FIGURE 5
U.S.S.R., DISTRIBUTION OF GREEN CORN AND CLIMATIC LIMITS, 1961

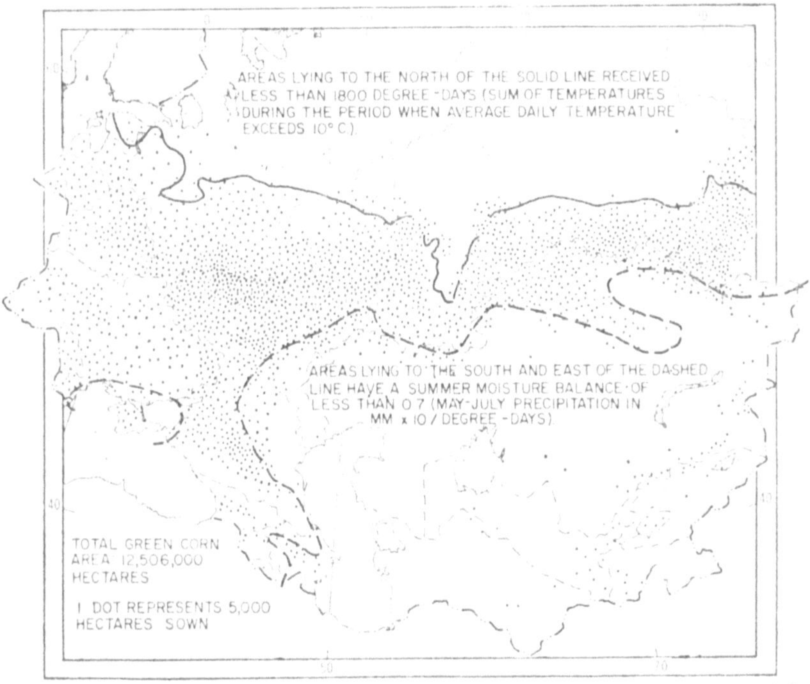

SOURCES: See Figure 3. Green-corn data include both green corn harvested for silage and that classed as green fodder. The distribution of 770,000 hectares of green corn in East Siberia and the Far East is not shown on the map.

however, and green corn may not only represent a less intensive crop, but also be more expensive to produce and use.

The advantages of green corn are its less stringent climatic requirements and, given proper management, its high yield of dry matter. Where the sum of temperatures exceeds 1800-degree days, very early maturing varieties should form milk-ripe ears, and later varieties should reach the tassel stage. That Soviet corn has not performed well is the result of special problems of cold soils, and of shortages of fertilizer and hybrid seed not encountered in Western Europe. The absence of yield data for green fodder corn provides tacit confirmation of Khrushchev's admission that this crop in the U.S.S.R., as in the United States, is largely ruined. The 1961 distribution of green corn was more rational than that of previous years, with sharpest decreases in the southwestern regions where grain and ripe silage corn far outyield green corn (see Figure 5). The year 1962 can only be termed a year of madness in terms of the extent of green corn sowings everywhere. The relative importance of green corn among fodder crops has been especially large in a belt extending from the Central non-Black Soil and northern Central Black Soil regions across the Volga into northern Kazakhstan, Siberia and the Far East. Whether its importance in these latter regions reflects particularly effective Party leadership, or the naïveté of young farmers in the "New Lands" is not known. But it does present an interesting contrast to the resistance to green-corn raising in the areas of intensive dairying in the Baltics and western Ukraine (areas with predominantly non-Russian populations), as well as in the conservative Northwest region of the R.S.F.S.R.

However uneconomic or wasteful the cultivation of green corn may be, the cultivation of corn for silage has had a beneficial effect on Soviet milk production and milk yields per cow. Between 1953 and 1961, the feeding of succulent fodder to livestock increased more than two and one-half times, while the feeding of silage increased nearly five times and accounted for the bulk of the increase in succulent fodders fed.[53] The increased availability of succulent fodder has certainly improved the winter rations of cows, resulting in a lengthening of the lactation period and increased production during the long stall-feeding period when yields had traditionally fallen very low due to poor subsistence rations comprised mainly of coarse fodder.[54] On the other hand, the stress laid on increased production of succulent fodders has brought about a decrease in feeding efficiency, due to the lower protein content of such fodder, especially green corn.[55] The legume program inaugurated in 1960 was clearly in response to this problem, but the Soviet solution stands in contrast to Western practice where increased feeding of succulents has been coupled with increased feeding of concentrates and chemical additives. Unfortunately, yield and cost data for competitive coarse and succulent fodders are lacking, so that firm conclusions about the economics and intensity of green corn cultivation are not possible.

CORN AND REGIONAL SPECIALIZATION OF SOVIET AGRICULTURE

Jackson has recognized and described three major periods of agricultural land use planning in the Soviet era: (1) the first push toward

[53] See sources listed in n. 44, above.

[54] D. G. Johnson and A. Kahan, "Soviet Agriculture: Structure and Growth," in U.S. Congress, Joint Economic Committee, *Comparisons of the United States and Soviet Economies,* Part I (Washington, D.C., 1959), pp. 219–220.

[55] See G. Gaponenko, *Plan. khoz.,* No. 5 (1965), pp. 10–11.

regional specialization and intensification of agriculture during the First Five-Year Plan and during the initial phases of the Second (1930–1934); (2) a period of retreat to diversification and regional self-sufficiency following agricultural failures arising from collectivization, the transportation crisis, and lack of capital due to forced industrialization and World War II (1935–1953); and (3) a return to agricultural specialization and intensification following the recovery from the war and the death of Stalin.[56] Jackson's first period actually represents an extension of the natural specialization of agriculture which was in its infancy when it was interrupted by World War I, the revolution and civil war, but which resumed during the period of the N.E.P.[57]

Although the impact of these three stages of planning on agricultural land use has not been fully explored, the present writer believes that the long-term record of grain corn cultivation (as a specialty crop oriented toward livestock production) serves to demonstrate the general validity of Jackson's periodization of agricultural development in the U.S.S.R. The corn area increased sharply between 1913 and 1928, declined during the late thirties and following World War II, and has increased sharply since 1953. Concomitantly, the area sown to corn in the non-Slavic borderlands of the U.S.S.R. where it was traditionally a subsistence crop has been declining steadily, although it temporarily increased in these areas during the crisis of the thirties.

The expansion of the sowing of corn for grain and ripe silage under Khrushchev was concentrated largely in the steppe and forest steppe of the Ukraine, North Caucasus, and Central Black Soil regions. Here Soviet planners have long urged development of intensive grain-animal agriculture alongside cultivation of appropriate crops. Given proper mechanization, seed, and fertilizer, these corn crops are more intensive and economic fodder crops than traditional hay and oats. These crops have played a role in increasing feed grain and succulent fodder production, although gains from these crops may have been canceled out by poor yields from green corn sowings or reduced yields of other crops neglected in the light of increased capital and labor requirements of corn. The sowing of green corn today is of secondary importance in these southwestern regions, and should decline sharply in the future. Small amounts of green fodder corn may still be sown to supplement livestock feeding in late summer when pastures have been depleted by grazing or drought.

[56] W. A. D. Jackson, "The Problem of Soviet Agricultural Regionalization," *Slavic Review*, XX:4 (December, 1961), pp. 656–678.

[57] See Timoshenko, *op. cit.* (in n. 7), pp. 120, 194, 252.

Green corn has contributed much less to regional specialization, being widely sown everywhere, although of greatest relative importance in the northern and eastern regions where grain and ripe silage corn fail to mature, given cooler climates and greater climatic hazards. While green corn silage has helped to improve the winter rations of dairy livestock, low yields and quality combined with a lack of machines for storing and feeding the crop have probably required more labor on the part of the kolkhozniks, although the increased labor is needed mainly during times when there has traditionally been underemployment (late summer between hay and grain harvest and during the winter). In the non-Black Soil dairy belt, intensive ley-farming and fodder root cultivation hold greatest promise if Western European experience and technology is applicable (and Estonian practice indicates that it is), although modest sowings of corn for silage and green fodder may be retained where physical conditions are favorable and adequate capital and labor supplies exist.

Much of the green fodder corn in these regions has probably ended up merely being plowed under as expensive green manure, because of insufficient development as a result of climatic failure or simply because the farms lacked equipment to use all the crop sufficiently developed to warrant ensiling. In the New Lands beyond the Urals, very low yields of green silage and excessive sowings of corn for green fodder have resulted in a large waste of resources except for minor benefits which may have resulted from grazing livestock on green fodder corn and if seeding plowed fallow with corn has reduced soil deflation. But here properly cultivated summer fallow must be instituted on a large scale, if the Soviet goal of specialization in extensive wheat ranching is to be realized.[58]

In sum, the increased sowing of corn for grain and ripe silage in the southwestern U.S.S.R. has definitely contributed to specialization and intensification of agriculture along lines similar to the grain-animal agriculture of the northwestern cornbelt in the United States. The results of green corn sowings are less positive. While green corn har-

[58] The raising of livestock in the New Lands should probably be based (as it is increasingly in the western U.S.) upon intensive production of fodder on irrigated land. The control of soil erosion, weed control, and conservation of soil moisture is best achieved by modern dry-farming techniques (cultivated fallow and "stubble mulching.") With respect to these matters see C. Zoerb, "The Virgin Land Territory: Plans, Performance, Prospects," in R. D. Laird and E. L. Crowley, eds., *Soviet Agriculture: The Permanent Crisis* (New York: Praeger, 1965), esp. pp. 37–43.

vested for silage has contributed to increased milk production, its cultivation has been so widespread, indiscriminate, and wasteful that it has contributed little to specialization and nothing to intensification.

A more complete appraisal of the effectiveness of Khrushchev's corn program must await publication by the Soviets of more reliable and disaggregated data on the production costs of corn and other crops. Grain corn production costs should be compared with costs of other feed grains (oats, barley, etc.); the costs of the silage and green fodder corn crops should be compared with production costs of other coarse and succulent fodders (hay, potatoes, etc.). Moreover, such comparisons are only valid at the *oblast'* or *raion* level, given the heterogeneity of environments within the Union republics and gross economic planning regions. Available Soviet data appear to lump production costs of grain corn and ripe silage corn together and ignore the cost of green fodder corn; except for the *oblasts* of the Ukraine, no systematically disaggregated cost data have been found by the author.[59] Finally, the present cost data do not reflect the possibilities which would exist if adequate supplies of hybrid seed, machinery, and fertilizer were available, permitting decision makers a more careful choice among alternatives. The net yield data in Tables 3 and 4 do permit limited comparisons concerning the effectiveness of various corn crops relative to each other and to other fodder crops under existing conditions, and do, I believe, justify the conclusions above.

From the foregoing discussion it should be clear that the writer considers the cultivation and utilization of corn (where possible) to be a useful indicator of the development of agriculture in an industrializing nation. It has been seen in the Soviet Union that when economic conditions or government policy have favored specialization of agriculture, the grain corn area has increased, and when conditions or policy have favored subsistence or regional self-sufficiency the corn area has contracted. Khrushchev's corn program, however, pushed the expansion of corn beyond all reason.

The fluctuations in the total corn area, especially during the past decade, but even before that, do reflect the great influence which central planning and political intervention exercise over economic decision-

[59] *Narodne hospodarstvo Ukrainskoi RSR v 1959 rotsi* (Kiev: 1960), pp. 390–413, gives collective-farm production-cost data on an *oblast'* basis, but lumps all grain excluding corn together, grain corn with ripe silage corn, all silage crops together, and annual hay with perennial hay; thus a valid cost comparison on a fodder unit basis cannot be made. Jasny in this volume comments on the difficulty of obtaining even all-Union cost data.

making in even as disaggregated an activity as agriculture in the Soviet Union today. The fluctuations in the utilization of the corn crops also reflect in part the unstable and marginal character of the climate over much of the U.S.S.R, which continues to hamper the specialization and intensification of Soviet agriculture. This instability appears, too, to underlie many of the continual modifications and reversals of Soviet agricultural policy. Finally, one might note that given the problems of political expediency and capital scarcity in the Soviet Union, no crop is given a fair trial as to its legitimate role in any regional agricultural system, and no crop or group of crops can be expected to solve the manifold problems of Soviet agriculture.

COMMENT

Karl E. Waedekin

Special thanks are due to Professor Anderson for his geographic approach to the questions of Khrushchev's corn program. I will try to interpret his geographic evaluation in terms of Soviet reality by using statistics and political science. The result may be a hybrid of scientific methods, but will, hopefully, help to counterbalance some of the distortions inherent in any Soviet statistics, especially in those on corn. The comment can dwell only on a very few points.

The distribution of the sown areas of grain corn, silage corn, and green corn for fodder, as the author shows it in his geographic view, on the whole evokes a picture of a rationality of development, although with some distortions and exaggerations. Anderson takes some notice of the fact that it might be the rationality of nature and not so much of Khrushchev's agricultural planners, which turned Siberia, for instance, or the Central non-Black Soil belt into zones of green corn and not of grain corn. But it seems that he did not fully integrate this fact in his analysis and conclusions. The use of green fodder corn "as a buffer" is only part of the story.

Undoubtedly the regional distribution of the different kinds of corn sowings—fully ripe, milk-wax ripe, green—by 1963 or 1964 had acquired some rationality, more so, at any rate, than in the preceding seven years. But it took too long, and too much damage was caused, before the Soviets acknowledged the facts of climate, labor resources, and technical equipment.

The word "sown area" (*posevnaia ploshchad'*) in Soviet corn statistics and reality does not wholly mean what it should mean. In fact, it often is a substitute for "corn area harvested." Only if we knew exactly and for each year, which areas were sown for grain, ripe and green silage, or green fodder corn, could we judge the accomplishments of the corn program. Here is an example of the *oblast'* level; this lower level is more telling in such questions than the larger territorial units.

AREAS SOWN TO CORN (HECTARES) IN THE KURSK OBLAST', 1957–1959: [60]

	all corn	grain	silage	green fodder
1957	240,800	26,900	74,000	137,900
1958	221,700	72,400	94,100	55,200
1959	220,200	86,400	63,400	70,400

The total area sown to corn in this *oblast'* was fairly constant during 1957–1959, but within the total there were wild fluctuations of silage and green fodder corn sowings. It is hardly possible to explain this by intent or planning of sowings instead of changing weather conditions. Moreover, there is no statistical evidence of those areas which were sown to corn, but later, when the corn perished or could not be harvested, were declared to have been fallow or something else.

For these reasons Anderson's Figures 3, 4, and 5 must be looked at with caution: they do not show the implementation of the corn program as such, but they show the complex outcome of the program and the political pressures and of the weather conditions of each year. This remark is, of course, intended as a caveat, not as a denial of every evidence to be gained from a geographic appraisal of Soviet statistics of sown areas.

The ups and downs of the corn campaign have to be regarded in conjunction with the respective internal political position of Khrushchev. Such synoptics can probably be satisfactorily applied only with the cooperation of the agricultural and political science and geography.

I can only utter a suspicion that the quoted changing and contradictory statements by Khrushchev in regard to the value of silage corn and green corn are not to be tied up in retrospect with the views of the *kukuruznik,* but with the strength of his political position at the given period. Specifically, I would not like to interpret Khrushchev's warning against distortions as "a surer step toward rationality, again signaled by Khrushchev himself," but as a sign of his already weakened position in agricultural politics, which can also be seen from several other indicators of the plenary session. Similarly, this also applies to his statements of March, 1957. "Corn is a political plant"—such a formulation has "a certain threatening sound . . . and nobody dares to protest that it [the corn] flourishes in our latitudes, and that even when it does flourish in a certain year, it becomes very expensive to get ripe." [61] Here lies the most important key to the understanding of how, from some even-in-itself reasonable idea, to increase the sowing of corn in the Soviet

[60] *Narodnoe khoziaistvo Kurskoi oblasti* (Kursk: 1960), p. 22.
[61] E. Dorosh, *Novyi mir.* No. 1 (1965), p. 83.

Union. There originates a campaign, and considerable damage can result. Since Khrushchev was deposed, there has been enough evidence in the Soviet Union of the senseless way in which the planting of corn was enforced nearly everywhere—without respect to the climatic conditions, whether there was sufficient machinery or labor, or if the silage fodder was usable for the cattle in its singularly one-sided composition of ingredients.

It sounds more harmless when Anderson, in conjunction with the spread of corn acreage to Siberia and North Kazakhstam, says: "Whether its importance in these latter regions reflect particularly effective leadership, or the naïveté of young farmers in the New Lands, is not known." In my opinion, neither is the Party leadership very effective in the Soviet agricultural politics, nor are the farmers naïve.

With the exception of a few, all know—and knew—where the corn can be reasonably planted and where it cannot. This fact, very well known to the simple kolkhozniks and the farmworkers, was already stated in another place.[62] The kolkhoz managers and the sovkhoz directors were aware of it, as shown by the fact that they did not want to plant *that* much corn on their own, and that they were forced to do so in many cases.[63] And can one believe that the respective functionaries of the *raion, oblast',* and republic did not know what they were or are doing?

For their behavior and also for the behavior of the kolkhoz managers and sovkhoz directors, who all cooperated in the corn campaign without protest, Alec Nove gave a more persuasive explanation—in a general form: "Typically, Party officials emphasize the campaign of the moment. They aim to report to their superiors the completion of whatever task is currently the center of attention." [64] And: "If he is able to report success at these vital points, approval and promotion await him. . . . If, on the contrary, the principal campaigns fail, dismissal is the common fate of the Party secretary, as numerous examples in recent years show all too clearly." [65]

Concerning the corn acreage in 1962, Anderson says: "The situation

[62] Karl E. Waedekin, "Soviet Agriculture and Agricultural Policy," in Roy D. Laird, Edward L. Crowley, eds., *Soviet Agriculture—The Permanent Crisis* (New York: Praeger, 1965), p. 58.

[63] G. Gaponenko, *Plan. khoz.,* No. 1 (1965), p. 19.

[64] Alec Nove, "Some Thoughts on Soviet Agricultural Administration," in M. Mouskhely, ed., *L'U.R.S.S.: Droit, économie, sociologie, politique et culture* (Paris: Editions du Centre National de la Recherche Scientifique, 1964), p. 271.

[65] Alec Nove, "Incentives for Peasants and Administrators," in Laird, ed., *op. cit.* (in n. 50), p. 66.

in 1962 clearly got completely out of hand." It seems to us that such an explanation bypasses the conditions and driving forces of the agricultural politics—Khrushchev, who himself came from the Party "machine," knew what "campaigning" means, and since he started with the corn campaign he had to accept its "byproducts" beforehand. He probably underestimated the dimensions of the resulting damage, and attributed more in his "holy wishes" to the growers' capabilities and corn than nature could afford.

The campaign will remain an irreplaceable part of the Soviet political economy, for as long as there will be no better indicator of success and a more effective economic incentive, as the elevation in the Party and the State hierarchy, where the ideological faith and an absolute Party discipline is a condition *sine qua non* for the attainment—now as before —of a higher position.

Hence the overextension of the corn planted area in 1962 did not arise from misunderstandings, zealousness, or stupidity of the little Party chiefs and bosses, but simply because all of them, from the lowest to the highest echelon, followed the logic of the system and Khrushchev's directives. Khrushchev probably consciously "bought" these excesses, hoping that after a period of trial and error, an economically defensible distribution of the corn areas in the Soviet Union would "swing into place."

The door to an objective judgment closes when a person makes an apodictical statement: "Grain corn is the highest yielding corn in nearly all regions in which it is sown." No one will argue that corn, in suitable areas, brings high yields, but the question remains: What are the causes for it? Was it sown in the Soviet Union only in such areas or also in other unsuitable ones? To ascertain what corn yields have been achieved under Khrushchev, one must add all the corn areas and correlate them with the grain value units as well as the fodder units, the grain corn, silage corn, and the green corn (as silage and grain corn all summed up together). This is because we cannot judge the yields of the grain corn and silage corn alone, because we do not know, as indicated above, what areas have been sown originally with grain corn, but were harvested as silage corn, or sown as silage corn and used as green fodder and which areas have been plowed under. One can measure the success or failure of the corn program only in respect to the originally intended yields and not to some statistical figures modified in retrospect. Besides, one should, because of the varied weather conditions in different years, take an average of two or three years which overlap mutually, for instance

1957–1959, 1958–1960, and so on, to obtain the yields of the sown areas.

One should not forget, specifically in the case of corn, the question of thefts. These played a major role in the potato harvest—at least in the early postwar years—as was repeatedly testified by returning war prisoners. That something similar was possible for corn was indicated by another source.[66] By how much do such thefts influence the statistics? Accurate statements will probably never be possible in this respect, but, for instance, the "numbers" of hogs in private ownership, which reached high levels in spite of all "administrative actions" and in spite of the poor harvest in 1963, make one wonder. In the notes from 1962, by Troepol'skii, the thoughts of a kolkhoznik from the province of Voronezh are conveyed to us. He likes corn—as food for humans as well as fodder for pigs. "Nobody steals breadgrains. No, it is simply not stolen. So let's now take occasionally some corn . . . and it is so easy to 'take.' Grains, oh no! One would need some sack or container, but corn—it's so simple. Ten ears daily—that's about two kilograms." [67] And besides, tells the kolkhoznik, in the evening when the cows are returning from the pastures one attaches a couple of corn stalks onto their backs, pretending to protect them against flies (in reality to bring the corn home).

Another important aspect of the corn program is the question of available manpower. It happens that the corn harvest comes after the completion of the grain harvest, and the additional labor, which is needed for the preparation and use of the corn silage, relieves the traditional seasonal underemployment. But the story is different during the sowing period and the necessary preparation of the corn fields between the sowing and harvest time. Where, for instance, sugar beets and potatoes are also planted in greater quantities, they will interfere with corn during the harvesting and compete for labor. In Siberia and Kazakhstan, where the early beginning of fall makes it difficult to bring in the grains in time, corn competes with every type of harvest. One also has to take into account that not all labor working during the summer on the kolkhozes and sovkhozes will be available during the fall. In this, one finds a large number of seasonal labor, besides some of the elderly people, invalids, children (during their school vacation), and women with several children, who are not obligated to work (or only during a part of the year). To this it must be

[66] Waedekin, *op. cit.* (in n. 62), pp. 57–58.
[67] G. Troepol'skii, *Novyi mir*, No. 10 (1963), p. 21.

added that the provisioning of labor varies greatly with the regions. In nearly all areas north of the Black Soil zone and east of the Ural, farm labor is extremely scarce today. These are all the areas where Khrushchev wanted to expand the sowing of silage and green fodder corn. In parts of the Ukraine and the Russian Black Soil belt, it means that where the planting of corn had good prospects to play a major role, the labor conditions are more favorable. This does not apply to the Kuban district and to the northern frontland of the Caucasus; people did migrate there, but mainly into the towns. The agriculture here became highly intensified and hence suffers from labor shortages.

There is doubt whether corn does not need more labor proportionally in comparison to other types of grain and other fodder plants. Ten or fifteen years ago this would not have been a problem for the Soviet Union because it did not matter how much more additional labor was needed to increase the agricultural production—much of the population at the time lived on the land, and their wages were low. But since that time the Soviets have recognized the meaning of production costs and, as the wages for farm work rose and are rising further, one must view corn also from the standpoint of the labor cost. Thus, not only is the labor content higher, but it also has increasing cost. Here the two factors are running together and are mutually reinforcing.

Anderson has done a very thorough and useful job in collecting and analyzing the available data on the Soviet corn program and on its implementation. The well-known difficulties in using Soviet statistics are specially embarrassing with regard to corn. All the same, Anderson succeeded in giving us the much-needed basis from which to discuss the hazardous march of this "queen of the fields" through Khrushchev's agrarian empire. At the time when Anderson worked on his study, Soviet periodicals began to publish more realistic and more detailed information on the now past "great decade" and the corn program. One wonders what *Narkhoz-1965* will have to tell us on this account. For any Western scholar preparing an essay on Khrushchev's corn program, the *kukuruznik's* fall would have come either too late or too early. But for Soviet agriculture the deposition of this all too fervent and powerful advocate of corn-growing was a blessing and happened rather too late than too early. This I would like to spell out more pointedly than Anderson did.

WARREN E. HULTQUIST

Soviet Sugar-Beet Production: Some Geographical Aspects of Agro-Industrial Coordination

The Soviet attention to the problems of agricultural production centered, during the Khrushchev era, on increasing the supply of grain, both for animal and human consumption. But other crops, especially the technical crops, were not neglected. Sugar-beet cultivation, whose tradition in Russia reaches back to the early nineteenth century, has continued to be an important phase of Soviet agriculture, and various measures have been taken to stimulate the output of sugar beets and of sugar. However, many of the basic problems, which beset the industry even under optimum conditions, became intensified as a result of the very attempt to achieve new and higher levels of output. This essay considers some problems of a geographic character which have grown out of the Soviet drive for a larger store of sugar.

Concern for the production of sugar was apparent in the Seven-Year Plan of 1959–1965. Though output of sugar had been increasing steadily since the 1950's [1] the goal set forth in the Seven-Year Plan called for the production of enough sugar to provide 41 to 44 kilograms of sugar for each person as against 26 kilograms in 1958, on the eve of the plan period.[2] Attainment of this goal required that the output of sugar be nearly doubled. Thus, in order to meet the goal, 9.2 to 10 million tons of sugar were to be produced in 1965 against the 5.4 million tons obtained in 1958.[3]

The production of sugar from the domestic beet supply has increased

[1] *Prom. SSSR-1964*, p. 427.
[2] *Narkhoz-1959*, p. 103.
[3] *Ibid.*, p. 102.

substantially since 1958. Nevertheless, an output of 7 million tons in 1964 suggests that the high levels set for the end of the plan period will not be reached.[4] On the other hand, if the 1–2 million tons of sugar processed in the Soviet Union from Cuban raw sugar are included in the total production figures, the minimum level envisaged for 1965 may be met.[5] In dealing with the Soviet problem, consideration here is restricted to the production of crystal sugar, a form not fully refined, in which the bulk of the sugar for direct consumption is processed. It excludes refining capacity as well as specific factors associated with increases in Cuban imports.

In order to reach planned levels of output, the Soviet sugar industry has had to be expanded at various stages throughout the entire process. Not only has the sown area been enlarged and wherever possible yields and sugar content increased, but also storage, handling, and transport facilities have had to be improved and factories made larger to handle more abundant sugar-beet supplies. In many cases, new factories had to be constructed. Even so, a major difficulty facing the industry has been the inability to coordinate properly these several phases of the productive process.

The ultimate aim of the beet-sugar industry in any society is to achieve a maximum recovery of sugar from the beet root. Because of the semiperishable nature of the crop, the ability of the factory to attain a satisfactory level of performance depends basically on the speed and efficiency with which the various stages of production are carried out. The problem of coordinating the components of production is, to a large degree, spatial or territorial. Ideally, in any area of sugar-beet production a strong interaction should prevail between the field and the factory. Indeed, the sugar industry is oriented toward raw material. In addition to being relatively perishable, the root is bulky and contains only a moderate amount of sucrose per unit of weight.

Though the farm and the factory need not lie in juxtaposition in space, each gains from close proximity. The farmer gains not only the opportunity of producing a cash crop, but obtains, for livestock feed, the beet tops, foliage, and crowns of the sugar beet, which remain after harvesting; and the pulp, a residue of sugar-beet processing. He receives decided advantages, moreover, from the inclusion of sugar beets in the crop-rotation system. The processor, in turn, may provide to the grower materials and knowledge, conducive to gaining from the latter a crop rich in sucrose. In reality, however, the links between them may

[4] *Sakh. prom.*, No. 1 (1965), p. 2.
[5] *Ibid.*

be weak as a result of adverse natural conditions, affecting the supply and quality of the raw material, the lack of efficient transportation, and the presence of conflicting goals with regard to standards of quality, methods of price determination, and the like.

In the Soviet Union the mentioned factors tend to weaken the connections between the farm and the factory as they do among other producers of the world. Yet in the Soviet Union the factors are intensified because of the Soviet practice of expanding more and more the sown area of sugar-beet cultivation and distributing it among a number of regions of the country, often widely separated from each other. Although there have been substantial additions to the processing base in recent years which may suggest that there are no serious agro-industrial imbalances, these increases, in the aggregate, obscure imbalances on regional and local levels.

The sown sugar-beet area in the Soviet Union grew, within contemporary boundaries, from 0.7 million hectares in 1913 [6] to 3.7 million hectares in 1963.[7] More than 1 million hectares have been added since 1958.[8] This over-all expansion in sown area is the primary reason for the increased output of beets, although yields have been raised to the levels which had been attained before collectivization. At any rate, the output of beets has grown from 11 million tons in 1913 to an annual average of 49 million tons during the years 1959 to 1963.[9] These upward trends in beet hectarage and output have been accompanied by an increase in the daily productive capacity of the beet-processing plants, from 138,000 tons in 1914 [10] to 295,000 tons in 1958.[11] The daily productive capacity in 1964 had reached 480,000 tons.[12]

The traditional areas of sugar-beet cultivation and of sugar production are situated in the north-central Ukraine and the adjacent Central Black-Soil region (Figure 1). Destroyed during the war, these formerly productive areas were rapidly restored so that by 1950 the output of sugar there had reached prewar levels. These centers, accounting for nearly the entire sugar-beet and sugar output in the pre-Soviet period, contribute at present less than three-quarters of that output.[13] While the relative position of these areas has been declining, additional hectarage

[6] *Narkhoz-1959,* p. 341.
[7] *Narkhoz-1963,* p. 263.
[8] *Ibid.*
[9] *Ibid.,* p. 277.
[10] G. S. Benin, *Sakh. prom.,* No. 11 (1957), p. 10.
[11] S. I. Gerasimov, *ibid.,* No. 4 (1961), p. 2.
[12] V. M. Shvarts, *ibid.,* No. 2 (1965), p. 1.
[13] *Narkhoz-1963,* pp. 205 and 278.

FIGURE 1: U.S.S.R. PRODUCTION OF CRYSTAL SUGAR

SOURCES: *Atlas sel'skogo khoziaistva SSSR* (Moscow: (1960), p. 288; *Narkhoz-1963,* p. 205; *Narodne hospodarstvo Ukr. RSR v 1960 rotsi* (Kiev: 1961), p. 99, *Narkhoz-RSFSR-1960,* p. 166.

has been allotted for beet-growing and a larger processing base constructed. Furthermore, in the Ukraine, a pronounced increase in hectarage in the crop within its western *oblasts* has brought about there an essentially new sugar-beet zone. Cultivation of the crop has expanded in the southern *oblasts* of the republic also, but to a decidedly lesser extent. At the same time, the industry has expanded in other areas where it had been introduced during the period of mass collectivization during the early 1930's.[14] Thus, there was further development in the Kazakh and Kirgiz republics, in the Transcaucasus, in Latvia and Lithuania, in western Siberia, and in the Far East. In the North Caucasus, Krasnodar *krai* began producing sugar beets in the prewar period and, in recent years, has become the second most important producing area in the Russian Republic. Its output is more than one-half that of the entire Central Black Soil region.[15] In the postwar years, Belorussia, the Middle Volga basin and the Urals region have been included among the Union's producers of sugar.

Despite the over-all expansion of beet sowings and of processing facilities, serious imbalances exist between field productivity and the factory capacity in the individual producing regions. In several regions, the capacity of beet-processing facilities far exceeds the supply of beets locally available. In others the output of beets outstrips the local capacity to process. These discrepancies are reflected in increasingly longer and larger hauls of material from the fields to the processing centers. And the increasing distance between field and factory is evident in the heavy dependence on the railroad for hauling beets. The relative position of rail in this regard has been declining in favor of truck particularly in short local hauls,[16] but in absolute terms, the average length of haul by rail, remaining steady at approximately 100 kilometers from 1940 to 1950,[17] rose strikingly to 206 kilometers by 1958.[18] Such distances are excessive as indicated by the fact that in the Northern Great Plains of the United States, a major sugar-beet-producing region, the average length of haul by rail from beet farms on the periphery of

[14] For a discussion of prewar expansion of the Soviet sugar industry, see Vladimir P. Timoshenko, *The Soviet Sugar Industry and its Postwar Restoration.* War-Peace Pamphlet No. 13 (Stanford, Calif.: Food Research Institute, August, 1951), pp. 3–7.

[15] *Narkhoz-1963*, p. 205.

[16] *Puti sozdaniia izobil'ia sel'skokhoziaistvennykh produktov v SSSR* (Moscow: 1963), p. 142. See also Shvarts, *op. cit.* (in n. 12), p. 4.

[17] L. V. Opatskii, *Razmeshchenie pishchevoi promyshlennosti SSSR* (Moscow: 1958), p. 233.

[18] *Puti sozdaniia izobil'ia sel'skokhoziaistvennykh produktov v SSSR* (Moscow: 1963), p. 142.

factory supply zones is considerably less than the over-all average length of haul in the Soviet Union.[19] Furthermore, the volume of ton-kilometers in the Soviet Union was 796 million in 1940, increased moderately until 1950, then leaped to 2.3 billion in 1955 [20] and to 5.1 billion in 1958.[21] Suggesting that much of the haul was over long distances, nearly two-fifths of the beets sent by rail in 1958 represented interrepublic or inter-*oblast'* movements.[22]

The heavy rail shipments of sugar beets in 1958 were the result, unquestionably, of serious problems of coordinating farm and factory operations, but these difficulties were intensified by a record harvest and procurement in that year. In subsequent years the indices of sugar-beet transport have been lowered, though remaining exceedingly high by non-Soviet standards. In 1958, 51 million tons of material were procured and, presumably, shipped; for the years 1959 to 1963, the amount averaged 45.3 million tons.[23] Not only were fewer beets hauled, but also the average length of rail haul decreased. In 1962, a year of below-average procurement, the average length of haul was 155 kilometers.[24] In areas of low processing capacity, all material could be processed, conceivably, in the local factories. In places of high factory concentration, much capacity undoubtedly went unused.[25] The decrease in ton-kilometers in 1962—it may be estimated at 2.7 billion—reflected a

[19] See Lee Charles Hopple, "Ecological Crop Geography of the Sugar Beet in the Northern Great Plains," (unpublished master dissertation, Department of Geography, Pennsylvania State University, 1960), pp. 90–95. Data on average length of haul by rail or truck were not available to Hopple. But he indicates that the average length of haul from those farms most distant from factories amounts, for the whole of the Northern Great Plains, to 71 miles. In one of the primary producing centers of the region, namely the South Platte River Valley of Colorado and Nebraska, the average length of haul from the farms farthest removed is 19.5 miles. That the over-all average for the region as a whole is, in fact, 71 miles, is a reflection that some beet-growing farms in Yellowstone County, Montana, are 122 miles from the factory. In a more detailed case study of Yellowstone County, Hopple, (p. 131) is able to show that the average length of haul from all collecting points to the factory, by rail, reaches 22.4 miles and, by truck, from farm to collecting point, 3.05 miles.

[20] Opatskii, *op. cit.* (in n. 17), p. 233.

[21] *Puti sozdaniia izobil'ia sel'skokhoziaistvennykh produktov v SSSR* (Moscow: 1958), p. 142.

[22] *Ibid.* See also *Ekonomicheskie voprosy razvitiia sel'skogo khoziaistva SSSR* (Moscow: 1963), p. 289.

[23] *Narkhoz-1963*, p. 277.

[24] M. I. Galitskii. S. K. Danilov, and A. I. Korneev, *Ekonomicheskaia geografiia transporta SSSR* (Moscow: 1965), p. 161.

[25] Arefiev has written concerning similar conditions in parts of the Ukraine in the 1950's. During periods of poor harvest the many factories concentrated in an area could not obtain sufficient supplies locally nor from sources farther away. Such factories operated at only 30 percent of capacity. See T. U. Arefiev in

relatively small harvest, but it gave evidence, too, of the partial remedy of one of the most glaring imbalances between field productivity and factory capacity—one which existed in the western Ukraine in the late 1950's.[26] Clearly, pronounced expansion in processing facilities in that region in recent years has resulted in a marked decrease in long hauls.

In 1964, an exceedingly high sugar-beet output, reported to be 76 million tons,[27] must have resulted in rail shipments in the nature of those of 1958. Moreover, one may assume that the distance of haul increased, especially if the good harvest occurred in areas with a chronic deficiency in factory capacity. But even with the average length of haul remaining at the 1962 level, it may be estimated, since railroads at present move two-fifths of all procured sugar beets,[28] that the volume of ton-kilometers reached at least 4.7 billion.

Indicative also of the Soviet problem of imbalances between agriculture and industry is the steady increase in the length of the sugar-processing season. The optimum length of season in the Soviet Union as a whole, determined on the basis of the percentage of sugar loss which occurs as the season is extended, ranges from 115 to 125 days.[29] This period varies from one region to another depending upon the climatic effects on stored beets and upon differences in the manner in which beets are stored. Beginning in September, roots are lifted and processed, often before they have reached maturity. In many places the work of processing continues into March and April. Actually, the season of processing averaged 151 days from 1958 to 1962.[30] In the Kirgiz republic, for example, where long seasons are common, the campaign period reached recently as many as 193 days.[31] The Soviet Union average for that period would have been greater but for an extremely curtailed campaign in some areas in 1962. The crop output was especially poor in the Baltic republics, and factories were idle a substantial part of the season. In Latvia they operated only 39 days, and in Lithuania 75 days.[32] The length of the processing campaign in the Soviet Union exceeds, by far, that normally taking place in other producing regions. In western Europe the season extends from October to December or

---

Voprosy razmeshcheniia i spetsializatsii sel'skogo khoziaistva (Moscow: 1957), p. 332.

[26] M. M. Makhinia and V. L. Marianchik, *Sakh. prom.*, No. 2 (1965), p. 9.

[27] Shvarts, *op. cit.* (in n. 16), p. 2.

[28] *Ibid.*, p. 2.

[29] A. Epishin and G. Fedorov, *Sakh. prom.*, No. 4 (1965), p. 72.

[30] *Prom. SSSR-1964*, p. 431.

[31] K. A. Seedanekov, *Sakh. prom.*, No. 2 (1964), p. 13.

[32] *Prom. SSSR-1964*, p. 431.

January—a period of 90 to 100 days.[33] The harvesting and processing period is of similar duration in the Colorado Piedmont, a typical zone of cultivation in the Great Plains of the United States.[34]

Many factors, reflecting conditions both in the field and in the factory, affect the length of the processing season. However, Soviet studies relating to transportation in the sugar industry suggest that the season lengthens as the percentage of beets received by rail increases. For example, for factories which receive 70 percent or more of their sugar beets by rail, and presumably from distant points, the length of the processing season is extended by 20 percent over that of factories receiving less than 10 percent of their beets by rail.[35] Those factories, depending heavily upon rail, have generally a large capacity.[36] Conceivably, they operate at full-scale in autumn, handling beets grown nearby. But as the season progresses the amount from local sources diminishes so that more distant supplies must be sought. Moreover, there are factories of small to moderate size which normally obtain their full supply, locally, by truck and process without prolonging the season. However, these factories are closely spaced and, because the capacity in the area over-all has increased, each must reach farther for its supply.

Harvested sugar beets destined for distant points must remain at the sides of fields, or at rail collecting points, until transportation is available. Since labor and rail equipment are heavily employed in harvesting and shipping other crops, the sugar beet, though requiring rapid delivery, may not be readily picked up. The effect of delays is a rapid loss of sugar, even though improved storage may retard the loss. At any rate there is much evidence to suggest that storage facilities and techniques are highly inadequate.

The lack of good coordination between agriculture and industry is not new in the Soviet Union; the disproportions between the farm and the factory existed in the traditional centers in prerevolutionary days. But the lack of balance of earlier years has been perpetuated and made more severe during the Soviet period.

In the mid-nineteenth century, there were more than 300 factories in

[33] A. N. Duckham, *Agricultural Synthesis: The Farming Year* (London: Chatto and Windus, 1963), p. 372.

[34] M. John Loeffler, "Beet-Sugar Production on the Colorado Piedmont," *Annals of the Association of American Geographers,* LIII:3 (1963) 375.

[35] N. G. Grachev, *Staticheskie gruppirovki v izuchenii ekonomiki promyshlennosti SSSR* (Moscow: 1958), p. 134.

[36] *Ibid.* See also A. E. Probst, *Razmeshchenie sotsialisticheskoi promyshlennosti* (Moscow: 1962), p. 65.

the Ukraine and the adjoining Central Black Soil region,[37] each with raw-material needs sufficiently small to be readily fulfilled from surrounding factory-owned land or from nearby fields of the landed nobility. However, during the course of the second half of the century, a rapidly growing capacity, fostered by high prices for the domestic sale of sugar, a sizable and lucrative foreign market, certain tax concessions to new sugar mills, and growing innovations in processing technology resulted in the formation of a cluster of large factories, especially in the Ukraine. Yet the output of beets did not keep pace with factory expansion. Toward the end of the century, mill owners were, in a manner of speaking, pulling up beets from each other's fields. Indeed, the length of haul increased and factories were forced to draw supplies from more distant small peasant holdings where the practice of sugar-beet cultivation was poorly developed and where, consequently, yields were exceedingly low.[38]

Surprisingly, the disrupting events of the early years of Soviet power hardly lowered the total processing capacity. Few mills were actually demolished, and those which were damaged were quickly repaired. Some were weeded out of the cluster for reasons of low efficiency, but those which remained were enlarged.[39] On the other hand, sugar-beet yields fell to very low levels. The net effect was continuation of underutilized capacity, and, of regional imbalances between beet supply and capacity.[40]

During the industrialization drive between 1929 and 1940 the construction of new factories was begun and the expansion of older ones continued. Gigantism in plant construction was the prevailing tendency in the sugar industry as it was in industry generally.[41] But the construction of larger factories coupled with steady expansion of sown area tended to intensify existing imbalances, although yields remained low throughout much of the period.

At present these disparities continue. The production of sugar beets has risen rapidly in recent years so that substantial additions to total capacity have become necessary. At the same time sugar-industry management, geared to reducing production costs through economies of

[37] V. T. Krasochkin, *Materialy po istorii sel'skogo khoziaistva i krest'ianstva SSSR,* Collection IV (Moscow: 1960), p. 485.

[38] I. Byk, *Sakharnaia promyshlennost v SSSR* (Moscow: 1925), p. 35.

[39] D. V. Gak, *Food Industry of the Ukraine* (Washington, D.C.: U.S. Joint Publication Research Service, 1960), p. 52.

[40] *Ibid.*

[41] *Ibid.,* p. 61.

scale, have created factories of increasingly larger size. The daily processing capacity per factory has increased from 842 tons in 1950–1951 to 1,380 tons in 1963–1964.[42] The larger units of the past few years—some completely new and others additions to existing structures—have been built, seemingly, without regard to local beet-growing conditions. While some factories have been allocated to areas such as the western Ukraine and Krasnodar *krai,* where they are clearly needed, a sizable capacity has been created, nevertheless, in areas where beet yields and beet "densities"—the ratio of beet sowings to total sown area—are low. Moreover, large factories have been constructed in places of high beet concentrations, as in the older centers of the Ukraine, but these areas have sufficient, if not excess, capacity already.

Where many factories are in operation, yields are low (Figure 2). Except for the irrigated districts of Kazakhstan and Kirgizia, they reach their highest levels in the Ukraine, on the right bank of the Dnieper River. There they average nearly 20 tons per hectare, which is below the level of other important world producers.[43] Yields are lower in the Central Black Soil region. Eastward, along the middle Volga, in the Urals and in western Siberia, yields are one-half to one-third the levels of the most favored parts of the Ukraine. They are no higher in the Baltic republics or in Belorussia. Moderately high yields are obtained in Krasnodar *krai,* though, with rapid expansion of cultivation in that area, the trend in yields has been downward.[44]

Sugar-beet densities also vary greatly (Figure 3). It appears that in the expansion of cultivation little attention has been given to concentration of sowings. In many places the sowings, including those in the irrigated districts, are widely dispersed among many collective farms. The Right Bank Ukraine, in addition to having highest yields, contains the highest density of sowing. Although reaching as high as 15 percent of the sown area, densities are not up to European levels.[45] Densities as low as 3 percent are common in the Baltic republics, in Belorussia, and in all producing zones in the eastern region. In parts of western Siberia, in fact, they are less then 1 percent.

Sugar-beet densities reflect the degree to which the crop is given prominence in the land-use structure of the individual collective farm. Because few collective farms serve principally as sugar-beet producing

[42] G. S. Benin, *Sakh. prom.*, No. 12 (1964), p. 65.

[43] D. A. Music, "Sugar: A Review of the Industry in the USSR," *Monthly Bulletin of Agricultural Economics and Statistics of the Food and Agricultural Organization of the United Nations* XI:9 (September, 1962), 14.

[44] *Narkhoz-1963,* p. 279.

[45] I. Buzanov and T. Arefiev, *Ek. sel'. khoz.*, No. 1 (1964), p. 39.

FIGURE 2: U.S.S.R. YIELDS OF SUGAR BEETS

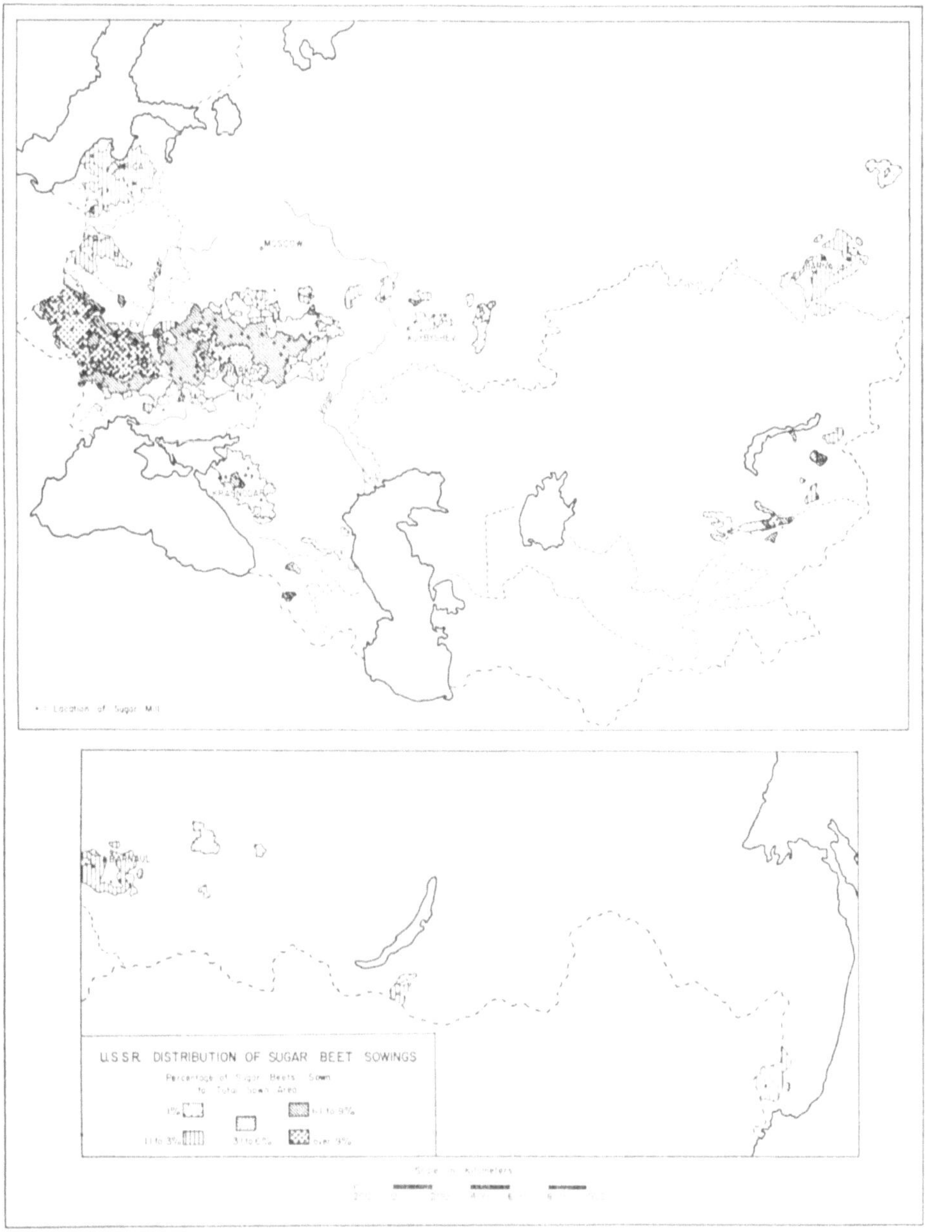

SOURCES: *Atlas sel'skogo khoziaistva SSSR* (Moscow: 1960), p. 155; *Atlas sil'skoho hospodarstva Ukrainskoi RSR* (Kiev: 1958), p. 29; *Atlas SSSR* (Moscow: 1962), pp. 125–128, 130, 134, 136–137; *Geograficheskii atlas: Dlia uchitelei srednei shkoly* (Moscow: 1959, 2d ed.), pp. 122–123, 125–130, 132, 136–137, 140–142.

FIGURE 3: U.S.S.R. DISTRIBUTION OF SUGAR-BEET SOWINGS

SOURCES: *Atlas sel'skogo khoziaistva SSSR* (Moscow: 1960), p. 154; *Atlas sil's'koho hospodarstva Ukrainskoi RSR* (Kiev: 1958), p. 29; *Atlas SSSR* (Moscow: 1962), pp. 125–128; 130, 134, 136–137; *Geograficheskii atlas: Dlia uchitelei srednei shkoly* (Moscow: 1959, 2d. ed.), pp. 122–123, 125–130, 132, 136–137, 140–142.

units and because the generally specialized state farms do not play an important role in sugar-beet cultivation, the crop tends to be spread among hundreds of farms in a given area. In each, the amount of space used for such production often may be limited, precluding, as a result, efficient use of manpower, machinery, and other inputs. Concentration of sowing per farm reaches its highest level in the Ukraine, where upwards of 200 hectares are used.[46] A similar concentration continues into neighboring parts of the Central Black Soil region.[47] To the east the individual farm has less land allotted to beets. In the middle Volga basin, for instance, the allotment is less than 100 hectares, an amount considered a hindrance to effective use of mechanization.[48] But sowings are highly scattered in Belorussia, Latvia, and Lithuania. In fact, in Belorussia at least 70 percent of the farms which grow the crop set aside no more than 20 hectares for that purpose.[49] In these republics extreme fragmentation of sugar-beet hectarage reflects the fact that the soils which are in any way favorable for raising beets are widely scattered. Moreover, there is competition with flax for the same soils.[50] Also, in the Kazakh and Kirgiz republics, a spotty distribution of suitable beet-growing soils on the irrigated tracts, coupled with strong competition with other crops for the land limits the beet sown area of each farm [51] and lessens, to some degree, the effectiveness of these otherwise favorable regions for sugar-beet production.

As a consequence of the wide areal extent of sugar-beet cultivation, together with the upward trend in the size of the factory, a unit of average capacity presently must draw its raw material from as much as 11,700 hectares, contrasted with 2,500 in 1913.[52] Indeed, the factory must reach out much farther for its supply. In 1940, 60 percent of all beet sowings were spread within a radius of 6 to 15 kilometers of a mill. By 1958, 60 percent were as far as 15 to 30 kilometers or more from the mill.[53] These increasing distances add substantially to hauling expenditures. The following data provide an indication of the effect of distance on beet-shipping costs in the Voronezh *sovnarkhoz,* a well-established center of sugar-beet production in the Central Black Soil

[46] *Ibid.*
[47] *Ibid.*
[48] A. A. Nekrasova, *Zem.*, No. 6 (1965), pp. 11–12.
[49] V. F. Medvedev, *Spetsializatsiia v selskokhoziaistvennom proizvodstve* (Minsk: 1961), p. 97.
[50] *Ibid.*, p. 103.
[51] For example, see M. Balbakov, *Ek. sel'. khoz.*, No. 4 (1963), pp. 77–78 and N. V. Zemnukhova, *Sakh. prom.*, No. 9 (1959), p. 33.
[52] T. U. Arefiev, *Ek. sel'. khoz.*, No. 2 (1962), pp. 91–92.
[53] *Ibid.*

region. In that area field and factory connections may be expected to be more favorable than those in many of the Soviet Union's producing zones.

TRANSPORT EXPENDITURES AND LENGTH OF HAUL OF SUGAR BEETS, VORONEZH SOVNARKHOZ, 1961

Length of haul in kilometers	Number of collective farms in group	Transport expenditures per centner of beets in rubles
Less than 30	191	0.10
30 to 50	163	0.24
More than 50	119	0.33

SOURCE: I. Buzanov, T. Arefiev, *Ek. sel'. khoz.*, No. 1 (1964), p. 38.

In areas where railroads are used, losses of both beets and sugar are undoubtedly heavy. But losses are regarded as substantial even when the crop is moved shorter distances by truck. Sugar-industry specialists admit that the conditions of the roads between fields, collecting points, and factories are unsatisfactory.[54] Much delay results from impassable roads. Moreover, poor-quality roads lead to premature wear and tear of the vehicles, preventing further a speedy and continuous flow of material. At present only 1.1 kopeks per 100 tons of procured beets are allocated for road building and repair.[55] Part of this allotment is used for road maintenance in the immediate approach to the factory. It is conceivable that little remains for hard surfacing of sections of the road farther away. At least 10 kopeks per 100 tons of procured beets are considered essential to provide adequate road connections between farms and factories.[56]

Since it appears that costs mount rather steeply, even with relatively short increases in the length of haul, these costs must be especially high in areas of low yields and densities. In such areas the distances covered are particularly great. For example, in Altai *krai* of western Siberia the three mills which are in operation receive their material by rail from 32 collecting points, more than one-half of which are between 100 and 300 kilometers away.[57] In fact, in all areas of low yields rail shipments of more than 100 kilometers of the mill are common. Furthermore, because fields are so scattered, collecting points are widely spread. Truck hauls to these points are known to exceed 100 kilometers.[58]

[54] Shvarts, *op. cit.* (in n. 16), pp. 5–6.
[55] *Ibid.*
[56] *Ibid.*
[57] *Ibid.*, pp. 2–3.
[58] *Ibid.*

Areas of relatively high yields and densities are characterized by many short hauls, but also include long ones. It has been estimated that a factory with a daily processing capacity of 3,000 tons of beets with a processing season of 130 days can draw its supply from within a radius of approximately 25 to 35 kilometers, provided the yields are 22.5 tons per hectare and the sowings occupy 10 percent to 20 percent of the total tilled area.[59] In the Right Bank Ukraine these conditions are met most closely. Yet the close spacing of factories—many are within 10 kilometers of each other—require optimum conditions regarding yields. In reality, when the beet crop is not abundant, the radius of reach is greatly extended. And it must be borne in mind that beet-procurement zones do not form clear-cut radial patterns, but tend toward elongated and often circuitous ones, following the trend of road and rail from farm to mill. Therefore, in recent years many factories in the Right Bank Ukraine have obtained their supply from the western and southern parts where capacity does not yet exceed supply or from areas outside the republic, often 400 or more kilometers away.

A cluster of factories on the left bank of the Dnieper River operates in a surrounding of somewhat lower beet densities and yields. There is considerable evidence that plant expansion has far surpassed expansion in beet sowings in many places. In Lokhvitsa *raion,* in Poltava *oblast',* typical of the entire region, one mill, with a processing capacity of 4,900 tons, draws material from an area of 23,900 hectares.[60] Furthermore, because of insufficient beets within this extensive zone, the mill must supplement its supply from sources in the western Ukraine, Krasnodar *krai* and other places. In Sumy *oblast',* for example, additional modern equipment has been installed, while, at the same time, beet sowings in local farms have actually decreased. Some factories have no local procurement zone, but rely on distant source areas.[61]

The lack of coordination, from a spatial standpoint, between grower and processor has ramifications through the various stages of processing. There are evidences of a worsening of factory production. While some of the reasons may not be associated directly with problems of spatial organization, nevertheless, the ever-extended distance between farm and factory unquestionably plays an important part in current difficulties in factory operations.

Indeed, there has been a declining output of sugar per processed sugar beet in recent years. The downward trend has been steady, ranging from 15 percent sugar extraction in the 1953–1954 season to just over

[59] T. U. Arefiev, *op. cit.* (in n. 25), pp. 421–422.
[60] Arefiev, *op. cit.* (in n. 52), p. 92.
[61] *Ibid.*

11 percent in 1960–1961.[62] As an average of the first four seasons of the Seven-Year Plan period, the indices of sugar output per beet have been lower than at any other Soviet period, except for the years immediately following World War II.[63]

A lowering of the amount of sugar extracted at the mill is apparent throughout the whole length of the processing season. A downward trend has prevailed in the early months of processing and in late winter and early spring. Whereas the extraction levels of the first and the second halves of the campaign were 13.1 percent and 11.6 percent respectively between 1952 and 1957, corresponding figures for the 1958 to 1963 period were 13.1 percent and 10.3 percent.[64] Mass-harvesting in late September undoubtedly results in bottlenecks in the field-to-factory flow. But at this time much of the crop has not ripened. This is particularly the case in the newer zones of production in the eastern regions.[65] It is not until mid-October, in fact, that the optimum sucrose content is reached. But the farmer and the processor alike are prompted to handle an unripened crop because they are concerned with the problem of frost—especially with alternating thawing and freezing—which not only makes root-lifting difficult but also makes fields and roads less passable.

Despite the attempt to harvest the crop and to extract the sugar early in the season, much material is not processed rapidly, especially when the harvest has been good. In the winter and spring of 1958–1959 and of 1960–1961, following a high beet output of the previous autumn, the extraction levels were as low as 10 percent and 7.7 percent respectively.[66] That losses of sugar are heavy in the second half of the season is indicated by the fact that the average sugar yield per beet at the factory, during the first ten days of December, is 1.1 percent lower than in mid-October. By the last week of January, the amount extracted is 1.7 percent below the October maximum and in the latter part of February, 3.3 percent under that level.[67] Where factories work into March and April, as many commonly do, the supply of sugar received must be meager.

The lowering of the output of sugar from each root reflects, in part, losses during the course of processing and the removal of sugar in molasses, the final residue. But it is clear that there is less sugar in the

[62] *Prom. SSSR-1964*, p. 430.
[63] *Ibid.*
[64] *Narkhoz-1958*, p. 305; *Narkhoz-1962*, p. 204. *Narkhoz-1963*, p. 205.
[65] N. B. Pokrovskaia, *Sakh. prom.*, No. 1 (1965), pp. 10–11.
[66] *Narkhoz-1962*, p. 204.
[67] *Sakh. prom.*, No. 9 (1964), p. 2.

root when received at the factory. A lowering of this level in recent years is an indication that heavy loss is incurred in the territorial and time gap between the field and the factory. This is a cogent conclusion in view of the fact that the sugar content of the beet in the field is evidently not declining.

COMMENT

Jacek Romanowski

Professor Hultquist's essay is a concise statement on the inefficiencies of Soviet planning with respect to sugar-beet growing, storage, transportation, and processing as exemplified by the inadequacies of the field-to-factory linkage. Sugar beets are, of course, only one chapter in the tale of Soviet agricultural woes. In the last years, we have had many articles dealing with the political failures of Soviet agriculture. Hultquist's research on the sugar-beet situation promises more insight into its basic inefficiencies.

The Soviet agricultural problem has been apparent in the discrepancies between performance and the bigger-and-better plans, culminating in the daydreams of the Seven-Year Plan. As with most goals, the goal for sugar production was not met. In 1962 only 27 kilograms of sugar per capita was produced and the February, 1964, plenum of the Central Committee of the C.P.S.U. echoed a watered-down plea for the increase of per-capita production of sugar to 40–42 kilograms per year.[68]

There is a whole series of reasons for the low density of sugar-beet acreage, low yields per acre, high spoilage rate, and low efficiency of sugar retrieval from the produced beets. There being little to criticize on the contribution by Hultquist, I feel that I should rather briefly mention some reasons for inefficiency of the Soviet beet-sugar economy.

The distance cost of field-to-factory shipments of sugar beets is very high. So is spoilage cost, caused by excessive time *en route* to the factory, and by inadequate storage and handling facilities. This causes a radical difference from the refined product whose distance, time, handling, and storage costs are minimal in comparison to those of the raw material. This, then, causes the sugar-beet processing industry to be raw-material oriented in its location.

The need to minimize the sugar-beet field-to-factory distance is universal, but is made even more acute for the U.S.S.R. by the traditional inefficiency of Soviet transport in all sectors of agriculture. Thus, for vegetables, a similarly perishable crop, E. P. Kirsanova of the Astrakhan

[68] I. F. Buzanov, *Vest. sel'. nauki,* No. 11 (1964), p. 5.

State Agricultural Experimental Station states that 80,000 tons of vegetables were exported from the Astrakhan *oblast'* in 1964, of which 40–50 percent were lost in spoilage *en route* to the centers of demand.[69] P. V. Goncharov, the chief of the conservation section of the Moldavian Scientific Research Institute of Irrigation Agriculture and Vegetable Farming, states that 90–97 percent of spoiled tomatoes can be saved through shipment by refrigerator vans and aircraft.[70]

Given the somewhat irrational distribution of sugar-beet processing capacity and the dismal state of Soviet transport and storage, it seems that greatest gains in the prevention of vast sugar beet and beet-sugar content losses can be attained through a more rational land-use policy. This involves principally the intensification of sugar-beet production around the processing plants at the expense of shipments from further removed production areas. Sugar beets are a labor-intensive crop, and intensification might require some adjustment in the local labor force, and certainly in its incentives. Beet pulp and fall-off can also be used to enhance the local feed base, which, in turn, may enhance further development of animal husbandry. With better field-to-factory linkage, many sugar beets which now end up in the feed trough could be shipped to the more desirable processing plants for sugar and by-products. Which of these alternatives to be selected (feed versus processing) must be decided by an analysis of the respective costs and benefits.

Hultquist's complaint about the low acreage density of sugar beets is well substantiated by I. F. Buzanov:

> Studies carried out between 1958 and 1962 by the [All Union] Institute [on Sugar Beets] show that the concentration of sugar beets in the zone immediately adjoining the sugar factories enhances the attainment of higher yields of beets and grains and increases the production of meat and milk. However, despite the enlargement of collectives, many farms still disperse beet sowings on small fields which impede the use of mechanization and precludes any decrease in costs of production.[71]

The Soviet Union leads in sugar-beet acreage and production. More than half of the world's sugar-beet acreage is situated in the U.S.S.R.[72] Yet, between 1953 and 1955 it produced only an average of 22 percent of the world's sugar beets.[73] Thus, we do not deal only with low sugar-beet acreage density, but also with low per-acre yield. The efficiency of

[69] *Vest. sel'. nauki*, No. 8 (1965), p. 157.

[70] *Ibid.*

[71] Buzanov, *op. cit.* (in n. 68), p. 6.

[72] *Ibid.*, p. 5.

[73] *The Shorter Oxford Economic Atlas of the World* (Oxford: Oxford University Press, 1959, 2d. ed.), p. 29.

field-to-factory shipments can and should, therefore, be increased, not only through an increase of sugar-beet acreage around the processing plants, but also through an increase in their per-acre yields. Such yield increases should also concentrate around the processing plants, and should be measured in terms of sugar content volume rather than bulk weight.

The yields of sugar beets increased from 148 to 218 centners per hectare between 1953 and 1958, but this trend was followed by a marked decline in the early sixties. The 1959–1963 average yield was only 156 centners per hectare.[74] This decline is now blamed primarily on the removal of incentives for sugar-beet production in 1958, and on the old scapegoat: weather conditions.

The considerations of sugar-beet production location are complicated by the fact that the sugar beet can serve either as a technical plant for sugar extraction, or as a source of animal nutrition, or both. Of the 5.7×10^6 hectares in sugar beets in 1963, 2.4×10^6 hectares were destined for feed.[75]

One would like to hope that the plea for the planting of sugar beets close to the processing plants and in climatically adequate areas will be heeded. In the Soviet command economy, however, it is a common phenomenon to carry programs to extremes. The expansion of sugar-beet cultivation and the "discovery" of sugar beets for feed promised another tale of corn, although, hopefully, not of such dimensions. Already the decline of per-acre yield for the U.S.S.R. implies planting of sugar beets where they should not be planted or where their success has not been correctly ascertained. Culprits in this system are the agricultural experimental stations which manage to attain impressive yields with inputs which are unlikely to be ever equaled in agricultural production proper. Thus the Tiumen *oblast'* agricultural experimental station reports sugar-beet yields of 161 centners per hectare in 1965.[76] Such location of sugar-beet acreage will not be the salvation of the Soviet people's desire for either meat or sugar.

This does not mean that the country should not experiment with new areas. To supply Siberia with sugar requires 610,000 tons of sugar annually which would call for a train of 20,000 car loads between the Ukraine and Siberia.[77] This is a costly operation and renders local

[74] Buzanov, *op. cit.* (in n. 68), p. 5.

[75] *Ibid.*

[76] P. Polishchuk, *Sel'skokhoziaistvennoe proizvodstvo Urala,* No. 3 (1965), p. 49.

[77] N. I. Zhukovskii, *Novoe v sel'skom khoziaistve Sibiri* (Moscow: 1958), p. 49.

production desirable, even if at lower yields. In the mid-fifties, some regions of the Novosibirsk *oblast'* began to grow sugar beets. The absence of a processing plant and the difficulties of transportation caused, however, the abandonment of that effort.[78] Since then, the *oblast'* has obtained a sugar-beet processing plant, and sugar-beet production has been expanding from 1959 on. Even though the promised maximum yields of 300–400 centners per hectare will probably never be reached, the lower goals of 100 centners per hectare may be quite reasonable and economic, considering the cost of shipping sugar from the Ukraine.[79]

Much of the inefficiency of Soviet agricultural production can be blamed on the lack of incentives for the peasant to work at his best. In this, the transition from the work-day to a monetary payment system promises to increase productivity even without any other inputs or improvements. Obviously, this reform alone cannot put Soviet agriculture on a firm base, but it is a necessary prerequisite. Thus, a collective of the Saratov *oblast'* reports that the payment reform has cut the number of peasants who failed to work the minimum of work days for a year by 66 percent, has created a more stable labor force, and has raised sugar-beet yields from 201 centners per hectare in 1961, to 250 centners (1962–1964 average). Both yields are very high for the region. Furthermore, despite the increase in yields, the cost of production of sugar beets has dropped by 10 percent.[80]

Hand in hand with the peasant pay reforms came more equitable prices for agricultural crops. Thus, when the incentives for sugar-beet production were abolished in 1958, the yield and procurements of sugar beets dropped sharply. In 1963, procurement prices for sugar beets were raised from 23 to 26 rubles per ton, and incentives were reestablished. The 1964 sugar-beet yield rose sharply, and the volume of procurements almost doubled.[81] Obviously, much potential improvement lies in a more equitable remuneration to the peasants for their effort. Steps in the right direction are being taken. Perhaps, with time, the Soviets will be able to minimize the losses illustrated by Hultquist.

[78] *Ibid.*
[79] *Ibid.*
[80] P. Krikunov and N. Chernyshev, *Sel'skokhoziaistvennoe proizvodstvo Polvozh'ia,* No. 9 (1965), pp. 24–25.
[81] *Pravda,* March 27, 1965.

DAVID JORAVSKY

Ideology and Progress in Crop Rotation

The relationship between Lysenkoism and Soviet agriculture seems obvious and simple. During the thirties and forties an agricultural policy based on intuition and bluster fostered an agrobiology based on intuition and bluster. During the fifties and sixties the decline of Stalinist agricultural policy has been causing the decline of Lysenkoite agrobiology. (The favorite Soviet pejorative for both is "subjectivist.") But an examination of this relationship turns up perplexing questions about the rational use of irrational incentives, such as enthusiasm and force, in the modernization of Russian agriculture. I shall leave aside the question whether Stalin's decision to industrialize at maximum speed necessitated extreme measures to squeeze produce from the peasants. Let us assume that it did, and ask whether the decision to squeeze the peasants entailed the rejection of rational agronomy and biological science, whether this rejection of science generated gains as well as losses in Soviet agriculture. In theory these questions are absurd, offensive to people like myself, who like to believe that irrationality is not only loathsome but stupid too. The managers of depressed farmers face choices, however limited, among alternative methods of farming. They need sound agronomy and biological science to help them make such choices. Neither the depressed farmers nor their authoritarian managers are helped by flight to pseudo-science. In theory it seems absurd to question these plain truths, yet the historian must wrestle with phenomena that the theorist can dismiss as absurd.

Let us take the case of cropping systems and soil science, the historically evolving methods by which farmers and scientists have achieved a rising level of soil fertility. There have been four major stages in the evolution of European cropping systems.[1]

[1] See D. N. Prianishnikov, *Azot v zhizni rastenii i v zemledelii SSSR* (Moscow: 1945). This excellent popularization exists also in English translation: *Nitrogen in the Life of Plants* (Madison, Wisc.: Kramer Business Service, 1951).

Shifting cultivation (the *zalezhnaia* or *perelozhnaia* system), which restores fertility by allowing land to revert to natural vegetation for ten years or more.

Grain-fallow rotations, often called the two- or three-field system (the *zernoparovaia* or *parovaia* system).

Rotations of grain with green manure (clover or some other leguminous herbage) and with intertilled (*propashyne*) crops such as potatoes, turnips, sugar beets, or maize. This system has many variants and names: the Norfolk system, for example, after the region of England that made it famous in the eighteenth century, or the Thaer system, after the agronomist who popularized it in nineteenth-century Germany. It has also been called mixed husbandry or balanced farming, because the farmer abandons grain monoculture and produces two or more field crops along with meat and dairy products. The systematic use of green manure and dung, the control of weeds by cultivation of the intertilled crops, and the reduction of plant diseases and pests through frequent alteration of crops on a given piece of land, raise yields far above the level achieved by the three-field system and provide a better diet for a denser population. The diversity of the farmer's produce also serves as a hedge against drops in market prices. In Russian the usual term for this type of crop rotation is *plodosmen.*

The diverse schemes that economics and soil science of the industrial age have been multiplying since the nineteenth century. These have ranged from the "mechanically elaborate [but] agriculturally primitive" system of wheat-fallow farming in the American West,[2] through complex systems of balanced farming, to highly intensive monoculture, such as Roswell Garst showed Khrushchev.[3] (He raises seedcorn year after year on the same plots.) Rational farming has ceased to be the calm continuation of a pattern established by long use; it has become an endless quest for the elusive "optimum" in combining land, weather, living organisms, machines, chemicals, and markets. Government intervention—planning as the Soviets choose to call it—becomes ever more important, not least in organizing the development of science and its applications.

From the establishment of the *zemstvos* and the Petrovskaia Agricultural Academy in the 1860's to the collectivization of the 1930's a disturbing anomaly was apparent in Russia: agricultural science advanced ever more rapidly than farming methods. The Russian school of

[2] Charles Singer *et al.*, eds., *A History of Technology,* V (New York and London: Oxford University Press, 1958), 5–7.

[3] For evidence that Khrushchev was deeply impressed, see A. S. Shevchenko, *Kukuruza* (Moscow: 1960).

soil science became the world's pioneer, while the great bulk of Russian farmers were stuck at the second stage of cropping systems, the three-field or grain-fallow rotation. In sparsely settled parts of the country the *first* stage, the *zalezhnaia* system, survived into the twentieth century.[4] One result of this widening gap between science and agriculture was the occasional eruption of nativist obscurantism, denunciations of "Western" science for its uselessness, and demands for a Russian science that would aid Russian farmers.[5]

At the turn of the century Vasilii Robertovich Vil'iams (or Williams, the Russian son of an American railroad engineer) developed a Messianic variety of this nativistic revolt against world science. The dominant school of soil science was wrong, he insisted, not only for backward Russia but for the world at large, for it stressed the chemical elements of soil processes and plant nutrition, while the crucial factor was actually soil structure, the formation of a crumbly texture that provides roots with an optimum of air and water. He worked out a grand theory—grandly oblivious of logic and evidence—to support his insistence on an inevitable, ultimately catastrophic decline in fertility unless farmers systematically restored soil structure by making long courses of perennial grasses the basis of their cropping systems.[6] This kind of speculation was a relic of a dying age in the development of soil science, an age when so many critical factors were obscure that agronomists vacillated between the rival claims of system builders and narrow reliance on the experience of successful farmers. In the 1880's a series of critical discoveries transformed the study of soil processes and plant nutrition into a genuine science, or perhaps one should say into an amalgamated interdisciplinary science with commonly accepted methods and a growing body of significant results. For farmers the first benefit was reliable advice on the use of mineral fertilizers. West European yields began to climb above the levels attainable through the Norfolk system (*plodosmen*), a climb that continues to this day.

Williams remained aloof from these developments. He dismissed

[4] See B. A. Vakar, *Vazhneishie khlebnye zlaki* (Novosibirsk: 1929), pp. 208–213.

[5] The most extreme voice in soil science seems to have been Professor S. K. Bogushevskii and his department at Iur'ev University. See A. A. Iarilov, "'Istinnaia,' 'russkaia,' 'samobytnaia' nauka i eia universitetskie predstaviteli," *Pochv.*, Nos. 1 and 2 (1905). Even such a genuine scientist and cosmopolitan as K. A. Timiriazev commented bitterly on the uselessness to the peasant of Dokuchaev's famous school of soil science. See K. A. Timiriazev, *Sochineniia*, III (Moscow: 1937), 18–19. Timiriazev's comment reflected in part the competition for state funds between the disciplines of plant physiology and soil science.

[6] See V. R. Vil'iams, *Sobranie sochinenii* (Moscow: 1948–1953), 12 vols.

mineral fertilizers as useless, unless their application followed the improvement of soil structure by *travopol'e,* which we may translate as grassland or lea rotations. He refused to admit that the causes of good soil structure and its precise role in fertility were not clearly established. Indeed, they remain obscure to this day. It is doubtful that perennial grasses make such a great improvement in soil structure as Williams thought; artificial soil conditioners developed by chemically oriented soil scientists do the job better.[7] In any case, the best current opinion is that building good soil structure is an important way to raise yields beyond the level of optimum nutrient supply.[8] If that judgment is correct, then Williams was putting the cart before the horse, deferring improvement in the supply of nutrients until optimum soil structure might be achieved. Of course, Williams should not be condemned for mistaken conclusions. His essential flaw was his method: disdain for the limited real achievements of his science, in favor of the limitless triumphs of speculation.

Before the Bolshevik revolution Williams's pretentious speculations were considered beneath criticism by his fellow scientists.[9] His classroom eloquence merely captivated some students at the Moscow Agricultural Institute,[10] as the Petrovskaia Academy was renamed following a political upheaval in the 1890's, in which Williams seems to have been the only staff member to enjoy the trust of tsarist authorities. (All the rest were fired, and he was named caretaker of the empty buildings.) [11] After the Bolshevik revolution this central institution of agricultural education, renamed the Timiriazev Academy, experienced another, and

[7] See M. M. Kononova, *Organicheskoe veshchestvo pochvy, ego priroda, svoistva i metody izucheniia* (Moscow: 1963), pp. 108–110.

[8] See W. H. Allaway, "Cropping Systems and Soil," in U.S. Department of Agriculture, *Yearbook* (Washington, D.C.: Government Printing Office, 1957), pp. 389 and *passim.*

[9] See *Pochv.,* No. 4 (1902), pp. 434–436, for a brief expression of courteous amazement at Williams's views. V. N. Sukachev, *ibid.,* No. 2 (1916), pp. 1–26, gave the only substantial comment on Williams's theories to appear before the revolution.

[10] See *Professor Vasilii Robertovich Vil'iams. K dvadtsatipiatiletiiu nauchnoi, pedagagicheskoi i sel'skokhoziaistvennoi obshchestvennoi deiatel'nosti. Izdanie studencheskoi iubileinoi kommissii* (Moscow: 1914). Sukachev's criticism (*op. cit.* in n. 9) was inspired by the appearance of this collection of student tributes to Williams.

[11] See D. N. Prianishnikov, *Moi vospominaniia* (Moscow: 1957), pp. 154 ff. Compare the bland account of the same events in O. M. Targul'ian, ed., *Akademik V. R. Vil'iams: iubileinyi sbornik* (Moscow: 1935), pp. 14–16. Oral tradition among Russian scientists maintains a memory of Williams as a political timeserver. Khrushchev went out of his way to reject this notion. See Khrushchev, *Stroi. komm.,* VI, 56–7.

sharper, clash with an authoritarian government. Williams was the first professor to support the new regime. "A struggle developed along the line of abolishing the autonomy and independence of the Academy, along the line of struggle with the influence of the peasant parties among the students, among whom the Bolsheviks were then isolated individuals . . . . [This occasioned] a sharp exacerbation of Vasilii Robertovich's relations with the majority of professors, and then also with groups of agronomists, who were hostilely inclined against the Soviet regime." [12] Williams even joined the Party, a very unusual step for a senior scientist in the twenties.[13] He was lionized by the press, but for almost twenty years Bolshevik agricultural officials were no more willing than their tsarist predecessors to endorse his peculiar agronomy.

The recognized leaders among soil scientists and crop specialists, for example D. N. Prianishnikov and N. M. Tulaikov, were slower in coming to terms with the Bolshevik regime, but it was their recommendations that the government endorsed, not only during the twenties, when the actual choice of cropping systems was still made by autonomous peasants, but also during the early thirties, when Bolshevik officials took direct control of farming. To be sure, Williams's political eminence made it impossible for his fellow scientists to go on ignoring him. In repeated debates during the twenties and early thirties, his windy oratory evoked some Bolshevik sympathy, but the chief officials were not persuaded that a revolution in soil science was required to close the gap between science and agriculture.[14] They were convinced that the main obstacle to the development of scientific farming was the backward social organization of agriculture. One of their important

[12] O. M. Targul'ian, ed., *op. cit.* (in n. 11) pp. 24–25. Cf. M. N. Pokrovskii's praise of Williams at the Thirteenth Party Congress, quoted *ibid.*, on pp. 26–27. The journal of the Academy, *Novaia Petrovka,* 1922–1923, reveals a little of the conflict.

[13] See *Izvestiia,* 1928, No. 159, for the celebration of the event. Tulaikov's entrance into the Party in 1930 was not celebrated in the press, for Stalin's "great break" (*velikii perelom*) of 1929 put an end to the view that Bolshevik scientists were a rare breed who deserved special praise.

[14] See various issues of *Puti sel'skogo khoziaistva,* 1926–1929, for repeated discussions of *travopol'e,* which the Commissariat of Agriculture was willing to endorse only in such sparsely settled areas as Siberia. Williams and his small group of followers were repeatedly rebuffed in their efforts to promote a grand *travopol'e* system for the entire country. See especially the record of the Vsesoiuznaia konferentsiia po bor'be s zasukhoi (All-Union Conference on Drought Control), October, 1931, as recorded in its *Biulleten',* Nos. 1–7, and in the newspaper, *Sots. zem.* Molotov and Kalinin, in addressing the conference, approved the free clash of scientific opinions, and implicitly approved the resolutions of the conference, which made only one concession to Williams: a call for a trial of *travopol'e* by twenty state farms and as many machine-tractor stations.

motives in forcing rapid collectivization was the enthusiastic confidence that Russian peasants, once in the new farms, would leap from the medieval to the twentieth-century stage of cropping systems. The experience of the first two Five-Year plans shattered this confidence. Yields did not rise approximately 35 percent, as the planners had forecast; they fell, in the all-important case of grain they fell approximately 14 percent.[15] By the mid-thirties Bolshevik officials were ready to heed aged Williams, ready to close the gap between science and agriculture—by severe retardation of science, as the retrospective outside observer sees it.

It is easy for an outside observer to see why the Bolshevik regime blamed science for its disappointment. They could hardly blame the new social organization of agriculture; it was the most advanced system the world had ever known. To doubt this would be to doubt themselves, a mental process that is usually fatal to political leaders, especially Bolsheviks. The difficult question is why the regime, which was so quick to condemn genuine science for failing to produce immediate gains, was then so slow to recognize the uselessness of pseudo-science. The cropping systems recommended by genuine science were tried in the collective and state farms only seven or eight years, 1929–1936, before they were condemned; *travopol'e* or grassland rotations were given a trial of twenty-four years, 1937–1961, before they were finally discarded. Evidently there was something in Williams's doctrine that satisfied the psyche of Bolshevik officials, something that was lacking in genuine science, perhaps also something that met real needs in their agriculture. Let us try to discover what this was by a closer look at Bolshevik experience with the cropping systems recommended by the two schools.

Genuine soil scientists and crop specialists like Prianishnikov and Tulaikov did not insist on a single scheme of crop rotation. They emphasized the need for individual rotations, adapted to the soil, climate, and economic condition of each farm. Of course they recognized the need for general rules; a single scheme and individualized rotations

[15] For the planned increase of 35 percent, see G. Cherdantsev, *Osnovy sel'skokhoziaistvennoi geografii* (Moscow: 1931), p. 91. For the actual decline of approximately 14 percent, see Johnson and Kahan, "Soviet Agriculture: Structure and Growth," in U.S. Congress, Joint Economic Committee, *Comparisons of the United States and Soviet Economies,* Part I (Washington, D.C.: Government Printing Office) 211. Cf. *Sel'khoz.-1960,* p. 196, where the decline works out to 5 percent. Johnson and Kahan use the average yield for the period 1925–1929 as their base; the Soviet statistical handbook uses the period 1928–1932, thus running together two years before and two years after collectivization.

are not mutually exclusive contradictories but opposite ends of a gradient, and genuine scientists were willing to move toward either end, as the changing situation required. At the beginning of collectivization the emphasis was on regional specialization.[16] The country was divided into regions according to physical and economic geography; cropping systems were to depend on the region and its main products, but in any case were to be worked out on an individual basis by the competent management of each farm. For example, the southeast was to specialize in grain production; since it was dry and sparsely populated, Tulaikov recommended a Soviet version of the mechanically elaborate but agriculturally primitive cropping system that had emerged in the American virgin-lands campaign of the late nineteenth century. Giant farms using little labor and much machinery were to follow simple grain-fallow rotations. Vegetables and meat were to be imported from other regions. Acreage yields were expected to be low, but yields per ruble of investment in machinery, fuel, and skilled labor were to be high. When acreage yields turned out to be much lower than expected, failing to recoup the government's investment, Tulaikov recommended even more primitive methods, such as shallow plowing, hoping to stretch scarce machines, fuel, and skilled labor over larger tracts of land. But administrative chaos and sloppy work held yields at disastrously low levels; the Grain Trust, which was following Tulaikov's plan, got to be known as the Weed Trust. Bolshevik authorities began to denounce shallow plowing as a wrecking scheme, designed to give loafers and enemies of the people an excuse for bad work.[17] Poor management was no longer to be helped by simplified agronomy; it was to be whipped into shape by stern insistence on the most advanced agronomy, which alone was

[16] At the Sixteenth Party Congress in June, 1930, Stalin endorsed regional specialization. See Stalin *Sochineniia,* XII (Moscow: 1949), 325–326. For the plan that the specialists worked out, see G. Cherdantsev, *op. cit.* (in n. 15). Cf. W. A. D. Jackson, "The Problem of Soviet Agricultural Regionalization," *Slavic Review,* XX:4 (December, 1961). For a selection of the large literature on this subject, see *Bibliografiia po raionirovaniiu i razmeshcheniiu sel'skogo khoziaistva SSSR (1818–1960)* (Moscow: 1961).

[17] For a brief review, by K. P. Tulaikova, of the campaigns for shallow plowing and then against it, see N. M. Tulaikov, *Izbrannye proizvedeniia* (Moscow: 1963), pp. 26–27. For Tulaikov's vivid description of the chaos and poor management that prompted him to urge "simplified agronomy," see *Sots. zem.,* October 23, 1931. For his tentative suggestion of shallow plowing, see his article in *ibid.,* May 4, 1932. Early in 1933 the authorities turned against this suggestion. For a vicious attack on Tulaikov as an abettor of wreckers, see M. Strukov, *Na agr. fronte,* No. 2 (1933). For Tulaikov's self-criticism, see *Izvestiia,* June 3, 1933. His colleague, N. G. Samarin, had already been condemned as a wrecker; he himself was repeatedly attacked in the press, and was finally arrested in 1937.

appropriate in the most advanced farm organizations the world had ever known.

By 1933 it was clear to Bolshevik officials that the emphasis on regional specialization was also a scheme designed by wreckers to hurt the Soviet economy. The country's transport network was unable to effect large regional exchanges of surpluses, which were mostly nonexistent anyway. The wholesale slaughter of livestock that attended collectivization—also the work of wreckers and enemies of the people—had created an especially acute shortage not only of meat for consumers but also of manure for the land, while the chemical industry did not produce enough mineral fertilizers to take the place of dung. Clearly, a retreat, or rather an advance, from regional specialization to regional self-sufficiency was called for.[18] The specialists thereupon shifted their recommendations from regional systems of crop rotation to regional variations of a single system: *plodosmen* or mixed husbandry. This had been their choice for some regions from the start. For example, the collective farms of the central non-Chernozem region had been instructed to specialize in vegetables and dairy products, and to raise enough grain to feed their own region in order to cut the nation's transportation bill. Some such rotation as clover, wheat, potatoes, oats, and fallow was to be followed in or eight- or ten-field patterns. (Most of Russia is too dry to dispense with fallow altogether, as the classic Norfolk system did.) In 1933 all regions were ordered to produce their own meat and potatoes, and variants of *plodosmen* were worked out for all. But this new scheme also failed to bring a sharp upturn in yields, if only because it was never seriously tried. Endorsed in 1933, it was officially discarded in 1937, when only one-third of the nation's farms had started rotations in their fields (another third had rotations on paper, the final third nothing).[19] In fact, archival research will probably reveal that the crucial decision in favor of Williams's scheme was made as early as 1934, when public endorsement was being given to *plodosmen*.[20]

[18] For one of the early expressions of official disillusionment with regional specialization, see M. Strukov, *op. cit.* (in n. 17), p. 119. In January, 1934, the Seventeenth Party Congress adopted a resolution condemning "excessive specialization." See *KPSS v rezoliutsiiakh i resheniiakh s'ezdov, konferentsii, i plenumov TsK*, II (Moscow: 1953), p. 752, note, and pp. 759–760, that the Party still endorsed a degree of regional specialization, but insisted that each region should strive to be self-sufficient in basic foodstuffs. On this basis varieties of *plodosmen* became inevitable for all the regions of the country.

[19] See B. Blomkvist, *Sots. zem.*, April 8, 1937, and M. Chernov, *ibid.*, July 14, 1937. The plenary meeting of the Party's Central Committee in June, 1937, in effect gave official endorsement to the *travopol'e* system.

[20] See I. Kantyshev, *Na agr. fronte*, Nos. 2–3 (1934). This heated argument for

Standard science had lent itself to the volatile utopianism, the expectation of a quick leap from medieval to twentieth-century cropping systems, on which the Stalinist agricultural revolution was initially based. When this expectation was disappointed, standard science could only hold out the prospect of following the example of eighteenth-century English farmers. "How can one speak of introducing *plodosmen* rotations in our agriculture, which is the biggest in the world, the most highly mechanized, has the most advanced and progressive structure, in our socialist agriculture?!" [21] Thus spoke the head of the agricultural section of *Gosplan* in 1949, arguing for an intensification of the twelve-year-old campaign for *travopol'e.* In the peak years of that campaign, 1949–1953, the average grain yield was still slightly below the average for 1925–1929,[22] but Bolshevik faith was not broken. In 1950, to be sure, Lysenko called attention to the need for regional variations in *travopol'e,*[23] and in 1954 the stream of decrees imposing it on the nation's farms quietly petered out.[24] But soil science and agron-

---

travopol'e carried the tag, "For Discussion," but the celebration of Williams in *Pravda,* November 18, 1934, endorsed his theories without that disclaimer of official authority. Between these two dates the public record reveals the following sequence: In June, 1934, a plenary meeting of the Party's Central Committee issued an order for rapid increase in all sorts of fodder crops, with a major emphasis on grass. In July, the Council of People's Commissars adopted an unpublished resolution "On the Experimental Verification of the *Travopol'e* System of Agriculture." This was probably the official evaluation of the experiment called for in the resolutions of the October, 1931, Conference on Drought Control (see n. 10). This unpublished resolution of July, 1934, was the first to be rescinded twenty-eight years later, when the Soviet government turned against *travopol'e.* Cf. *Sobranie postanovlenii pravitel'stva SSSR,* No. 3 (1962), p. 47. On November 11, 1934, the Council of People's Commissars ordered a celebration of the fiftieth anniversary of Williams's scientific career, adding five years to the career in order to do so. (Cf. the student celebration of Williams's twenty-fifth anniversary in 1914, as cited in n. 10). The article in *Pravda,* November 18, 1934, followed.

[21] V. S. Dmitriev, *Akademik V. R. Vil'iams, osnovopolozhnik ucheniia o travopol'noi sisteme zemledeliia* (Moscow: 1949), p. 54. For a representative comment on *plodosmen* by Williams himself, see his *Izbrannye sochineniia,* II (Moscow: 1950), 707–708. Consistency was not a characteristic of Williams and his followers. Before nativism reached its peak, in 1948–1953, they sometimes defended *travopol'e* with the argument that it was widely used in Western Europe, in effect identifying *travopol'e* with *plodosmen.* At the same time they condemned the techniques of capitalist agriculture, calling them inapplicable in socialist agriculture.

[22] See Johnson and Kahan, *op. cit.* (in n. 15).

[23] T. D. Lysenko, *Pravda,* July 15, 1950. This article was widely reprinted, as a pamphlet, in magazines, and in other newspapers. Lysenko seems to have been spelling out a decree of the Council of Ministers and the Party's Central Committee.

[24] The last decree to be rescinded in 1962 had been issued in 1954. See *Sobranie postanovlenii pravitel'stva SSSR,* No. 3 (1962), p. 59.

omy were allowed to remain in the grip of Williams's school, which continued to recommend *travopol'e* until 1961, when Khrushchev finally condemned the cropping system and opened the way for basic criticism of the pseudo-science on which it was based.[25]

The psychic or ideological causes of this extraordinary persistence can be discovered in the public record. The volatile utopianism of the First Five-Year Plan gave way in the mid-thirties to a dogged, sullen utopianism, the characteristic Bolshevik style of resignation to painful reality. Williams's doctrine suited the new attitude. He had all along preached that permanently increased yields could be achieved only by massive use of *travopol'e* rotations over a long period of time. The Soviet state had to pit itself against an age-old, worldwide deterioration of soil and climate. (The famous Stalin plan for altering the climate by massive forest planting derives from Williams.) He made it possible to denounce costly twentieth-century methods of raising yields; they were meretricious, the fever of capitalist agriculture preceding its certain death. Soviet agriculture might seem poorer at the moment, but it was following the one sure way to permanent affluence.[26] Williams's doctrine was a tranquilizer for the Bolshevik psyche, soothing its utopian restlessness during a long period of agricultural backwardness.

Was Williams's doctrine, also a harmful drug, as Khrushchev declared in 1961, causing great losses to Soviet agriculture? Until the archives are opened to historians with open minds, the answer to this question can only be surmised. But there is suggestive indirect evidence in the public record. One is struck by the diversity of cropping schemes that acquired the holy name of *travopol'e*. When Williams appropriated the term for his grand scheme, it was generally used to describe the type of dairy- and meat-farming characteristic of Denmark or Switzerland, where half or two-thirds of the sown area are under grass, and grain is imported.[27] In Williams's original version *travopol'e* signified a form of the *zalezhnaia* system: wheat was to be the main crop, rotated with long courses of sown grass, which would support livestock as a subsidiary product. In either case *travopol'e* conflicted with the Soviet government's constant effort to overcome the effects of low grain yields by extending the acreage under grain. In the early thirties there were even charges that *travopol'e* was used by wreckers to subvert the expansion of wheat-farming that accompanied collectivization.[28] Williams was there-

[25] See Khrushchev in *Stroi. komm.* VI, pp. 56 and *passim.*

[26] See, for example, S. P. Anikeev, *Vop. fil.*, No. 1 (1954).

[27] See, for example, V. I. Anisimov, "Sel'skoe khoziaistvo," *Entsiklopedicheskii slovar' Granat,* XXXVIII (1916?), pp. 110–123.

[28] See, for example, *Agrotekhpropaganda,* No. 1 (1933), p. 42.

fore obliged to allow many alterations of his original scheme. He granted the name of *travopol'e* rotations to grass courses of only three or even two years' duration, and therefore reduced his estimate of the amount of land needed for grass to only 22 percent of the sown area.[29] Prianishnikov, the most knowledgeable and persistent critic of Williams, thereupon declared that *travopol'e* would be essentially the same thing as *plodosmen,* if only Williams would recognize the superiority of leguminous herbage to true grass in a country that lacked adequate mineral fertilizer.[30] In 1950 Lysenko placed his imprimatur on further amendments. Not grass but clean fallow must precede grain in dry areas, for grass dries out the soil leaving inadequate moisture for the grain crop. In regions of adequate moisture but considerable density of population, where farms had little spare land, *one*-year courses of grass-legume mixtures were to be used. He even suggested a rough measure of the opportunity cost of keeping land under grass for more than one year: if the first hay-cutting produced less than 30–40 centners per hectare, the meadow was too poor to keep; it should be plowed up for a planting of winter grain. In no case, Lysenko insisted, was a farm to reduce grain acreage to make way for grass.[31]

It is therefore hardly surprising that only 10.7 percent of the sown area was under perennial grass in 1953, the peak year of efforts to force *travopol'e* on the farms; 5 percent was under annual grass.[32] (The word used in the statistical handbooks is *travy,* which includes both true grass and leguminous herbage.) One can only guess how much of this grassland was regularly rotated with other crops, for Williams granted the name of *travopol'e* even to rotations that kept meadowland separate from the basic crops. In short, *travopol'e* was an extremely loose term for many ways of combining a bit of meadow and livestock and intertilled crops with the main business of grain production. The changing structure of the sown area suggests that Prianishnikov was right.[33] The actual rotations in most regions were probably varieties of grain-fallow with increasing elements of *plodosmen.* If this tentative conclusion from inadequate evidence is correct, the *travopol'e* campaign was a great

[29] See, for example, Williams, *Khim. sots. zem.,* No. 10 (1937). In another article of 1937 Williams set the figure somewhat higher. See his *Izbrannye sochineniia,* II (1950), 114.

[30] Prianishnikov, *Sots. zem.,* September 20, 1937. Note that Prianishnikov objects to the sloppy use of the term *travopol'e* to mean any kind of rotation that includes some grass.

[31] Lysenko, *op. cit.* (in n. 23).

[32] *Sel'khoz-1960,* pp. 134–135.

[33] *Ibid.*

mystification. It was a way of pretending to adopt the most advanced system of crop rotation, while Russia was actually making the transition from the second to the third stage of cropping systems, the transition that Western Europe had made in the seventeenth to nineteenth centuries.

To what extent did this mystification help or hurt the transition in Russia? Such a broad question raises a host of subsidiary questions that can be answered only by archival research and economic analysis. One would have to establish what the real alternatives were for Soviet farms, how the *travopol'shchiki* in various regions bent the farm managers' choices in various directions. Then one could assess the gains and losses of the campaign for *travopol'e*. I can only offer some general thoughts. It seems to me unreasonable to expect that depressed farmers can be highly rational in their cropping systems, can show a lively appreciation of their real alternatives, and make carefully calculated choices among them. In collective or private farms, depressed farmers tend to concentrate on crops that are immediately required, whether by the market or the state or their need to keep alive. They tend to neglect such crops as clover or lupine—the green manure that improves grain yields after a few years, at the immediate cost of a reduction in acreage under cash crops or an increase in labor and funds to till extra land. In 1913, after *zemstvo* agronomists had been urging the transition to *plodosmen* for decades, less than 3 percent of Russia's sown area was under *travy*. In 1929, on the eve of forced collectivization, that index of the advance of *plodosmen* had risen only to 4 percent, and it remained low during the terrible years of collectivization, partly because the authorities were trying to overleap *plodosmen* in some regions. In the mid-thirties the campaign for *travopol'e* began. By the eve of World War II the portion of the sown area under *travy* had jumped to 10.8 percent. By 1953, the peak year of enforced *travopol'e,* it had moved to 15.7 percent.

Prianishnikov did not object to the growing portion of land given to *travy;* he figured that 15–25 percent, depending on the region, should be under green manure.[34] What angered him, as we have seen, was the irrational preference that the *travopol'shchiki* showed for true grass. It therefore seems clear that one of the costs of the campaign for *travopol'e* was the loss of the nitrogen that clover and lupine would have fixed in the soil, and the consequent loss of increased grain yields that would have been accumulated, if the authorities had insisted more on legumi-

[34] Prianishnikov, *op. cit.* (in n. 30). For an extended discussion see his *Azot v zhizni rastenii i v zemledelii SSSR* (Moscow: 1945).

nous herbage and less on true grass. At the same time I would suggest that the campaign brought some gain: it generated the enthusiasm and justified the force that jolted Soviet farms away from grain-fallow rotations toward some form of *plodosmen*. What can be established only by archival research is how much pushing there was, and how much was really necessary at one time or another. How many farm managers would have made no serious effort to improve rotations, if the crackpots and timeservers of William's school had not bombarded them with decrees and fines? [35] The Soviet historian who answers questions of that sort will help us toward an answer to the large question: How much did Stalin's reliance on enthusiasm and force, his neglect of material incentives and local initiative, help or hurt the advance of modern farming?

It is my guess that the main cost of the Soviet government's long commitment to Williams's school was the resulting distortion of its investment in higher education and research. Williams had only a few disciples before official support came to him in the mid-thirties, and he died soon after. Official support changed things rapidly. The few disciples were joined by many timeservers, and a genuine school was soon at work, training young people in their image, bawling at scientists who were bold enough to express doubts. The retardation and distortion of Soviet soil science grew especially marked after World War II, when Lysenko threw his support to Williams's school.[36] Lysenko endorsed some sensible criticisms of Williams's agricultural recipes, as we have seen, but he was thoroughly enamored of Williams's grand theory

[35] See G. Pisarev, *Sots. zem.*, June 22, 1937, for an attack on the Commissariat of Agriculture for leaving crop rotation to local authorities; the result, the author claims, has been little or no effort to improve rotations. I. Strakhov, *Vop. ek.*, No. 2 (1962), p. 31, attributes the necessity of administrative orders and fines to "the theoretical groundlessness of the *travopol'naia* system."

[36] After a little friction in 1937 (see *Sots. zem.*, April 18, 1937), Lysenko and Williams began to praise each other in public. In 1938 Williams sponsored Lysenko's candidacy for election to the Academy of Sciences, and in 1939 Lysenko spoke at Williams's funeral. But the major Lysenkoite effort on behalf of Williams's school came after the war. See especially Lysenko's speech at the famous meeting in August, 1948, which made Williams and Michurin twin gods of Lysenkoite agrobiology: *O polozhenii v biologicheskoi nauke* (Moscow: 1948), pp. 7–41. Note especially the speech by V. S. Dmitriev, head of *Gosplan*'s Division of Agricultural Planning, pp. 259–269. See also *Vest. Ak. Nauk,* No. 9 (1948) pp. 75–77 and 119–129, for evidence of the campaign against standard soil science in the Academy's Institute of Soil Science. For evidence of the low state to which the All-Union Institute of Fertilizer and Agricultural Soil Science (*VIUA*) was brought, see *Part. zh.*, No. 13 (1962) pp. 40–44. See also the report of a team of U.S. soil scientists: U.S. Department of Agriculture, Soil Conservation Service, *Soil and Water Use in the Soviet Union* (Washington, D.C.: U.S. Department of Agriculture, 1959).

of a single process of soil formation. (Indeed, Lysenko persisted in this love even after Khrushchev had condemned Williams's school.)[37] He pictured Williams's soil science as a natural partner for his Michurinist biology. One is at first startled by this abrupt discovery of an affinity between two sects that had previously developed quite separately, but reflection confirms Lysenko's judgment. His school of biologists and Williams's school of soil scientists did have a similar method and outlook. Both leaped from speculation to conviction, impatiently brushing aside demands for rigorous proof. Both were ready and willing to use Stalinist methods of suppressing free discussion. Both saw their nativistic isolation from world science as proof of their Messianic role. (At one point Williams compared himself to persecuted Galileo.)[38] And both showed a persistent vitalism, an insistence that chemical methods of analyzing and mastering soil and plants missed the essential quality of living processes.

If Soviet authorities had kept up even a modest investment in standard science during the period when their agriculture was unable to make full use of it, they would now be reaping the benefits. Commercial fertilizers, for example, are beginning to flow into Soviet farms in sizable quantities, but there is an acute shortage of the sophisticated soil maps and properly trained agronomists that would achieve maximum efficiency in the use of these fertilizers.[39]

Standard soil science and agronomy have become ever more necessary as, in the post-Stalin era, careful analysis of farm costs and profits (*okupaemost' zatrat*) have become ever more necessary. But in none of the three fields—soil science, agronomy, and agricultural economics—has progress been smooth and easy. Bemused Stalinists have been struggling to overcome the defects of the system that shaped their whole mentality. Shortly after Stalin died they quietly stopped the flow of decrees by which they had been attempting to force *travopol'e* on the nation's farms, but these decrees (133 all told) were not repealed until 1962.[40] In the meantime soil science and agronomy were allowed to remain in the grip of Williams's school. To be sure, gestures were made in the direction of freedom for scientists and farm managers. Extremists of Williams's school, for the most part unnamed, were criticized for various stupidities in applying the great theories, stupidities that

[37] See Lysenko, *Sel' zh.*, December 15, 1961. Note that Lysenko fastened on a passage in one of Khrushchev's speeches against *travopol'e* where Williams was praised for his theory of soil formation.

[38] Williams, *Pravda*, March 7, 1937.

[39] See, for example, V. Egorov, and B. Dospekhov, *Sel'. zh.*, March 21, 1965.

[40] *Sobranie postanovlenii pravitel'stva SSSR*, No. 3 (1962), pp. 47–59.

Lysenko had criticized in 1950, at the height of the campaign for *travopol'e*. At the same time, though still addicted to Williams's ideology, the government was seized by fits of impatience with low yields. Envy of the dizzily rising yields in advanced Western countries began to break down the tranquilizing effects of Williams's grand theory. In 1955 the great corn campaign was launched, or rather, resumed; twenty-five years earlier Stalin's government had attempted a similar leap to intensive production of fodder. In the early thirties the leap ended quickly in utter failure; in the late fifties it succeeded, which is to say that a considerable amount of fodder was produced on the new corn fields, though it is clear that corn is not the most economical fodder crop for many of the areas and farms that have been obliged to raise it. The devil of the matter is, first, that no one has been quite sure how to measure the relative efficiency of alternatives in fodder production, and, second, that the regime still doubted the ability of farm managers to make decisions beneficial both to themselves and to the national economy. So appeals for individualized rotations based on cost-accounting coexisted with continued preaching of *travopol'e* rotations *and* with insistence on corn as the main fodder crop.

These contrary pressures generated Khrushchev's thunderclap of 1961. Soil scientists and agronomists were set free from Williams's school, and lectured harshly on the duty of the scientific community to stand up for their convictions as Tulaikov had done. (He was rehabilitated posthumously.)[41] Simultaneously, Khrushchev went out of his way to exempt Lysenko from responsibility for the backward state of soil science, and endorsed Lysenko's personal contribution to the subject: a recipe for composting mineral fertilizers with organic matter and soil, which was supposed to make the short supply of mineral fertilizers go further. Farm managers were told that they must choose cropping systems not on the basis of a grandiose single scheme, but on the basis of careful calculation of their real alternatives. At the same time they were harried by a new campaign for a single scheme of crop rotation: the *propashnaia*. This meant a concentration on intertilled crops such as

[41] Khrushchev, *op. cit.* in note 25, pp. 283–285, 383, and *passim*. Khrushchev confined his remarks almost entirely to *travopol'e* as a system of crop rotation. He seemed neutral on problems of soil science. At one point, p. 176, he paid tribute to Williams for his theory of soil formation; but at another point, p. 182, he said that agricultural experience had "overturned many of Williams's theoretical assumptions." As a result, Lysenko and other followers of Williams were able to continue advocacy of Williams's pseudo-science, while genuine soil scientists were able to revive their discipline. See, for example, the discussion of the American system of soil classification in *Pochv.*, No. 6 (1964), pp. 14–48.

Khrushchev's beloved maize, at the expense of fallow, grass, leguminous herbage, and small-grain fodder crops. Once again the Soviet government was trying to push farmers at a rush into the fourth stage of cropping systems, this time into a highly intensive variant, shutting its eyes to the limitations imposed by Russian geography and continuing backwardness. The chemical industry was not able to provide the necessary amount of fertilizers, and in many regions and farms the complex of geographical, economic, and human factors is such that a more extensive type of farming is more economical. In the Baltic region, for example, grass and leguminous herbage are a better source of fodder than corn, as the region's specialists proclaimed in the aftermath of Khrushchev's fall. (They called for *Travy bez travopolia,*[42] but their description makes it clear that they are for the Danish or Swiss type of farming, which was the original meaning of *travopol'e.*)

In the spring of 1965 the Minister of Agriculture of the R.S.F.S.R. boasted that for the first time in more than thirty years no outside authority was trying to impose cropping schemes and methods on farm managers and agronomists.[43] To what extent the boast was justified, and how long Soviet authorities will continue to make it, remain to be seen. It is clear that no government in an advanced country can refrain from interference in the farmer's choice of cropping systems. But it is also clear that the most effective management of farmers rests on official realization that they must have a considerable degree of autonomy within the framework of national controls. The same holds true for management of an advanced nation's scientists, who are not and cannot be the utterly free individualists they often imagine themselves to be, yet cannot be the driven creatures that Stalin, Williams, and Lysenko tried to make of them. The Soviet authorities show a dawning recognition of these elementary truths, but they are still inhibited from full recognition and appropriate policy by their reluctance to apply to themselves the eloquent appeal that a journalist recently addressed to a Lysenkoite agronomist.

Today, at a new stage in our progress, an end has come to subjectivism in the management of agriculture. . . .

Will you have enough strength to argue with yourself every day, and test all you've been doing with great care, to seek with unflagging curiosity to learn what you haven't yet succeeded in learning; will you learn to take a

[42] *Izvestiia,* October 25, 1964.
[43] A. Basov, *Sov. Ross.,* June 1, 1965.

respectful attitute toward the opinion of scientists even if you do not agree with them; will you find your place in science? [44]

When the Soviet press carries similar appeals to the Party chiefs—are they not social scientists?—we will be sure that a proper measure of autonomy has been secured not only by scientists and farm managers but by Soviet citizens at large.

Is that a utopian dream? Fifteen years ago it would have been a utopian dream to imagine that the Soviet press would some day carry such an appeal to the Lysenkoites. At that time it seemed as if intuition and bluster, self-deceiving enthusiasm and force, had permanently suppressed genuine science and free discussion in the Soviet drive for modernization. Evidently there is something in plants, soil, farmers, and scientists that requires rationality and genuine self-criticism of those who would manage them. My hope is that this inherent necessity is limitless in its scope, that it will make itself felt in areas of Soviet life where it now seems utopian to expect it. But I must admit that faith in the necessity of rationality and freedom is not sustained by such studies as I have presented here. A rational plan for the modernization of a backward country likely requires some degree of irrational enthusiasm and force, which are difficult to measure out in usefully moderate doses. It may be that in the modernization of backward countries, as in the nuclear strategy and colonial wars of advanced countries, men of our scientific century need to convince themselves that rationality requires irrationality.

[44] Anatolii Agranovskii, *Lit. gaz.*, January 23, 1965.

COMMENT

Norman Arnheim, Jr.

The few comments that I would like to make concern the future of Soviet biology and its application to Soviet agriculture. The overthrow of Lysenko has been accompanied by discussions in the Russian press on how best to improve the integration of scientific achievement with practical agricultural problems. The following passage taken from the lead editorial in *Pravda* of December 24, 1964, indicates one point of view: "The results of scientific research would have been significantly greater if the All-Union Academy of Agricultural Sciences and the Ministry of Agriculture U.S.S.R. had better coordinated the work of their institutes and directed the efforts of scientists to resolving the most important problems advanced by life and production."

This passage raises a question, whose solution is central to a harmonious relationship between the government and the scientific community. Who should play the major role in deciding which biological problems are important for investigation—the Ministry of Agriculture or the scientists themselves? *Pravda* suggests it is the province of government planners, while most scientists probably feel it is the proper role of the scientific community. The Soviet government's recent recognition that many of Lysenko's practices were derived from invalid scientific principles, and their present embracement of the ideas of modern genetics, should not necessarily be taken as a sign of their increased awareness of the basic dilemma—to what extent should scientists and government officials each be involved in the management and planning of scientific research.

As Joravsky points out, rationality and self-criticism on the part of Soviet leaders is important for the successful modernization of agriculture. What has still to be demonstrated with respect to the agriculturally related sciences is an understanding of the environment needed to nourish a growing scientific discipline so that eventually its principles can be applied to practical problems. With the help of the physicists and mathematicians, who have in the past played an important role in affecting the attitudes of the Soviet government toward the scientific community, a harmonious and fruitful relationship could be established. It may be true as Joravsky suggests that all scientists cannot be utterly free individualists. The achievements of biological science in the Western World, however, are witness to the fact that the scientific community is capable of guiding its own progress and successfully recommending the application of its research to practical problems.

NANCY NIMITZ

Farm Employment in the Soviet Union, 1928–1963

Soviet sources provide fairly complete and consistent data only for state agriculture, where the conditions of employment resemble those in other branches of the economy.[1] Like his counterpart in industry, the state farm worker is a wage earner, and the amount of time he works must be recorded at the enterprise level with at least enough accuracy for wage-accounting purposes. In private and collective agriculture, on the other hand, the farmer is nominally a proprietor whose labor has no fixed price. Hence records of his working time are not automatically generated by the terms of his employment, and they may be complicated by the prevalence of part-time (including part-day) labor.

Where many very small proprietors exist (as in the private sector), the absence of records is inevitable. Like other governments, the U.S.S.R. has kept track of employment trends in household-farming through observation of a representative sample. However, for years since 1928 it has not published satisfactory global estimates derived from the sample, partly, perhaps, because of the conceptual problems raised by part-time labor, and perhaps also because the total amount of labor devoted to this supposedly obsolescent type of production has been embarrassingly large.

In the collective sector enterprises are big and record-keeping is rampant. Yet until recently collective farms kept no record of days

[1] The essay presented here is an abridged version of my memorandum as cited in n. 3, below; sources and methodological details omitted here for the sake of brevity are fully described in the original study.

I am indebted to Barney Schwalberg for advice on the nature and sources of budget sample data for the 1920's, and to John W. De Pauw, Abraham Becker, and Norman Kaplan for comments on an earlier draft.

worked by members. Instead, their participation was measured in synthetic accounting units called labor-days (*trudodni*), which heavily weighted the duration of a task by its arduousness, importance, and skill requirements. The system was intended to secure the incentive advantages of a highly differentiated wage scale without guaranteeing the absolute level of wages: at the end of the year, the unpredictable residual of farm income left after government requirements had been met was distributed to members in proportion to their accumulated labor-days. Conceivably the government could have directed collective farms to keep records of working time even though it required them to distribute earnings on the basis of labor-days. But so long as the returns to collective labor were not only uncertain but also small (compared with what collective farmers obtained from their household plots), any confrontation of earnings with working time was avoided. Accordingly, for the collective as well as the private sector, the government relied upon employment data collected from sample households or farms, and it published official reports of sample investigations only for the years 1933 and 1937.

The household sample data may have yielded reliable estimates of total collective-farm employment, and (in later years) even of labor expenditures in individual branches of production. Hence they may have been adequate for central-planning purposes. But ignorance of labor expenditures severely handicapped management at the farm level, and lack of published employment data precluded serious discussion by Soviet scholars of problems of labor resources and utilization. Thus reticence about employment involved high costs. As collective farm earnings rose following the post-Stalin reforms, the need for secrecy declined while its inconvenience became more obvious. Records of working time were introduced on collective farms in 1957, and official statistical sources have since released considerable information bearing on employment, including collective-farm data for some earlier years, and data for all sectors since 1959.

Presumably the statistical authorities are now committed to publishing current annual data on farm employment. It is doubtful, however, that official sources will soon fill in past gaps. Moreover, the official series are unsatisfactory in two respects: they understate labor inputs to private agriculture (since they disregard part-time labor on household plots by persons also employed in state enterprises and collective farms), and they tend to overstate labor inputs to collective farms (through an averaging method which gives equal weight in any month to the farmer who works 25 days and one who may work only one day). Hence the need for independent estimates.

SCOPE OF ESTIMATES

The present estimates are intended to complement readily available data on employment in nonagricultural branches of the economy. Since the data for nonagricultural branches generally omit nonagricultural pursuits of the farm population, such activities are included here, along with labor inputs to agriculture proper. Thus the collective-sector estimates cover inputs to construction, repair of buildings and machinery, subsidiary manufacturing, administration, and communal services provided by farm members. The employment statistics for workers and employees in state farms are not quite so comprehensive in scope, but even they cover many activities which are only indirect inputs to agriculture (trucking, repairs, materials purchasing, and so on). Because of data limitations, the private-sector estimates are least comprehensive (excluding such indirect inputs to agriculture as processing, marketing, construction, and repair), but they do include a small amount of nonagricultural employment (fishing, hunting, gathering wood and other forest products, and artisan activities).

The choice of a broad or complementary definition of farm employment was dictated by the original purpose of the estimates, an early draft of which provided the farm component of total employment for calculations of labor productivity in the national economy as a whole.[2] For productivity calculations of agriculture alone, a more restricted definition is needed if concern is with absolute labor inputs in particular years. Even in this case, however, the appropriate definition may vary with the specific purpose of the investigation.[3] For this reason (and also because exclusion of nonagricultural activities from farm employment with available Soviet data is unavoidably a rather arbitrary business), those who require an employment series of narrower scope will prefer to make their own adjustments to the present estimates.[4] For trends rather

[2] See Abram Bergson, *The Real National Income of Soviet Russia Since 1928* (Cambridge, Mass.: Harvard University Press, 1961), Appendix K. The early estimates have been revised and extended to cover additional years.

[3] For instance, in comparing agricultural output per man in the Soviet Union and the United States, one might wish to exclude on the Soviet side any activities which in the United States are usually performed by firms outside agriculture (such as repairing machinery, applying fertilizers, preparing seed, cleaning and drying grain, and hauling produce to market). For other purposes it might be desirable to exclude only employment in construction, manufacturing, and communal services.

[4] Information bearing on such adjustments is given in Nancy Nimitz, *Farm Employment in the Soviet Union, 1928–1963* RM-4623-PR (Santa Monica, Calif.: The RAND Corporation, November, 1965). Appendix A and Tables C 3 and D 2.

TABLE 1

FARM EMPLOYMENT IN THE U.S.S.R., 1928–1963

Year	Annual equivalent or average (millions)						Man-days [a] (millions)					
	Private sector	Collective farms	MTS/RTS	State farms	Agric. services	Total	Private sector	Collective farms	MTS/RTS	State farms	Agric. services	Total
	(1)	(2)	(3)	(4)	(5)	(6)	(7)	(8)	(9)	(10)	(11)	(12)
1928	34.2	0.4	[b]	0.345	0.01	35.0	9,584	109	[b]	97	3	9,793
1929	32.6	0.9	[b]	0.416	0.01	33.9	9,140	254	[b]	116	3	9,513
1930	24.7	5.4	[b]	0.795	0.01	30.9	6,912	1,523	[b]	223	3	8,661
1931	15.7	11.8	0.131	1.470	0.01	29.1	4,404	3,313	37	412	3	8,169
1932	10.9	14.3	0.144	2.259	0.01	27.6	3,051	4,009	40	633	3	7,736
1933	9.3	18.6	0.181	2.423	0.01	30.5	2,604	5,195	51	678	3	8,531
1934	10.7	20.8	0.258	2.702	0.02	34.5	3,006	5,823	72	757	6	9,664
1935	12.2	23.3	0.304	2.534	0.02	38.4	3,403	6,522	85	710	6	10,726
1936	11.4	21.9	0.373	2.127	0.02	35.8	3,184	6,129	104	596	6	10,019
1937	12.4	22.7	0.44	1.748	0.03	37.3	3,478	6,361	123	489	8	10,459
1938	13.1	21.9	0.46	1.518	0.03	37.0	3,660	6,134	129	425	8	10,356
1939	11.0	21.8	0.46	1.64	0.03	34.9	3,069	6,096	129	459	8	9,761
1940	14.6	23.3	0.48	1.760	0.03	40.2	4,081	6,537	134	493	8	11,253
1945	16.2	23.6	0.29	2.147	0.02	42.3	4,539	6,604	81	601	6	11,831
1946	15.7	21.2	0.33	2.20	0.02	39.4	4,398	5,940	92	616	6	11,052
1947	16.1	21.3	0.36	2.26	0.02	40.0	4,517	5,969	101	633	6	11,226
1948	16.2	22.4	0.40	2.31	0.03	41.3	4,533	6,272	112	647	8	11,572
1949	16.0	24.9	0.44	2.37	0.04	43.8	4,478	6,961	123	664	11	12,237
1950	16.0	25.7	0.49	2.425	0.04	44.7	4,490	7,197	137	679	11	12,514
1951	15.2	24.9	0.54	2.47	0.04	43.2	4,244	6,975	151	692	11	12,073
1952	13.9	22.9	0.57	2.533	0.05	40.0	3,902	6,413	160	709	14	11,198

1953	15.2	22.3	0.68	2.552	0.06	40.8	4,258	6,257	190	715	17	11,437
1954	15.8	22.7	0.78	2.639	0.07	42.0	4,434	6,362	218	739	20	11,773
1955	15.2	24.0	0.95	2.832	0.09	43.1	4,251	6,708	266	793	25	12,043
1956	13.9	23.6	0.82	2.925	0.10	41.3	3,893	6,619	230	819	28	11,589
1957	14.3	21.5	0.76	3.961	0.12	40.6	3,992	6,031	213	1,109	34	11,379
1958	14.7	20.8	0.54	4.614	0.14	40.8	4,107	5,835	151	1,292	39	11,424
1959	14.3	20.8	0.469	4.957	0.16	40.7	3,993	5,827	131	1,388	45	11,384
1960	16.1	19.0	0.348	6.324	0.17	41.9	4,495	5,311	97	1,771	48	11,722
1961	18.5	17.6	0.003	7.366	0.18	43.6	5,180	4,915	1	2,062	50	12,208
1962	18.4	17.1	0	7.730	0.19	43.4	5,155	4,787	0	2,164	53	12,159
1963	17.8	16.6	0	7.874	0.20	42.5	4,978	4,643	0	2,205	56	11,882

[a] The private sector man-day through 1933 is conceptually identical in length with the average working day on peasant farms in 1928; thereafter it is identical in any given year with the working day on collective farms. On collective farms, the average day worked by collective farmers in budget sample households was 9 hours in 1937 (able-bodied only) and 8.4 hours in 1958 (all age groups); the average in years of less favorable harvest may have been lower (see Nimitz, *op. cit.*, in n. 3, Table C-2). The standard working day in state agriculture has been 7 or 8 hours (8 from 1940 to the last quarter of 1960); whether the actual working day coincides with the standard is not known, since state farms do not record hours worked per day.

[b] Lumped with employment in state farms.

SOURCES: Col. 1: col. 7 ÷ 280; col. 2: col. 8 ÷ 280; col. 3: Nimitz, op. cit. (in n. 3), Table D-3, col. 4; col. 4: *ibid.*, Table D-1, col. 2; col. 5: *ibid.*, Table D-1, col. 7; col. 7: *ibid.*, Table B-1; col. 8: sum of man-days worked by collective farm members (*ibid.*, Table C-1, col. 14) and man-days worked by hired agricultural labor (estimated at 0.75 percent of man-days worked by members, on the basis of evidence cited in *ibid.* pp. 131–133); col. 9: col. 3 × 280; col. 10: col. 4 × 280; col. 11: col. 5 × 280.

than absolute magnitudes, an index of farm employment can probably be equated for most purposes with an index of agricultural employment.

Five components of farm employment are distinguished (Table 1). The *private sector* comprises independent peasant farms, household plots of collective farmers, and household plots and garden allotments of state-employed workers. The estimates for *collective farms* cover all farm members earning labor days in collective production (including those enrolled in the tractor brigades of machine-tractor stations), and also agricultural labor hired by collective farms. *MTS/RTS* estimates refer to personnel of machine-tractor and repair-technical stations who are exclusively state employees (administrative and specialist staff, and the small fraction of production workers who are not also members of collective farms). *State farms* include the large state farms proper and smaller farms operated by various nonagricultural state institutions to supply their own food requirements. *Agricultural services* cover state employees in local agencies providing veterinary and other services to farms.[5]

MEASURES OF EMPLOYMENT

The estimates are presented in terms of both annual averages (or annual equivalents) and man-days.

For comparisons of labor inputs by sector within agriculture, and also for productivity calculations involving agriculture alone, the man-day is the less ambiguous and less artificial measure. There does not seem to be a radical difference between the length of the average man-day on collective and state farms—see note *a* to Table 1—and the private-sector man-day (as derived in this study) is conceptually identical in length with the collective-farm man-day from the mid-1930's on. Furthermore, estimates originally obtained in terms of annual averages (the state-employed) account for a very small proportion of total employment, and since any conversion from one measure to another involves some arbitrariness, comparison in terms of man-days minimizes conversion error.

All state employment is converted from annual averages to man-days

[5] For some purposes, the types of activity represented in the MTS/RTS and agricultural service categories would not be considered farm employment. They are included here because they are classed under "agriculture" in Soviet distributions of workers and employees by branch of the economy. As was noted earlier, the present estimates are intended to complement Soviet employment data for workers and employees in nonagricultural branches; therefore they must exhaust "agriculture" as a branch.

assuming 280 working days per year. The average on state farms from 1959 to 1962 was 282;[6] this figure is somewhat misleading (for reasons to be explained shortly), but it is arithmetically correct, and probably comes close to the average in other types of state agricultural employment where the administrative component is very high.

For comparisons of farm employment with employment in other branches of the economy, the estimates obtained originally in terms of man-days (the collective and private sectors) must be converted to annual equivalents. Since part-time labor predominates in both sectors, it is impossible to convert man-days for either sector by itself into annual equivalents that are more than statistical abstractions. However, since a large part of the labor force of the two sectors is shared, it is possible to define an annual equivalent in such a way that the total for both sectors together bears some relation to the average number of persons employed. That is to say, we can take as the annual equivalent the average number of days worked by a collective farmer on farm and household plot together. When private- and collective-sector man-days are divided by this number, the resulting series for either sector alone will understate the number of persons involved, but when the series are aggregated, total farm employment will not be understated.

In most years since 1940, able-bodied collective farmers have worked between 192 and 208 man-days a year on the collective farm; the long-term average is a little more than 200.[7] In the joint total of time worked by them on farm and private plot together, the collective farm accounted for the following percentages: 1937, 75; 1939, 76; 1958, 72; 1959, 73;[8] the long-term average is assumed to be a little less than 75 percent. Thus their total work on farm and plot together is estimated to have averaged between 270 and 280 man-days per year. Probably the actual average has been closer to the lower end of this range; however, since it is convenient for some purposes to work with annual equivalents which represent roughly the same number of man-days as the state-sector annual averages, the annual equivalent for the collective-plus-private sectors is assumed to be 280 man-days.

Two points about this conversion factor should be emphasized. First, that it refers to man-days, not calendar days. Given Soviet climatic conditions, and also the comparative unimportance (up to now) of nonagricultural or nonseasonal employment in total Soviet farm employment, the average number of calendar days worked per year has proba-

[6] V. Khlebnikov in *Vop. ek.*, No. 10 (1963), p. 56.
[7] Nimitz, *op. cit.* (in n. 3), Table C 1, col. 16.
[8] *Ibid.*, Tables B 5 and B 7.

bly not exceeded 250.[9] In the state sector, the state farmer hired on a year-round basis actually works less than 250 days a year; the average per "annual average" worker reaches 280 only because state farms employ a great deal of seasonal labor whose working days are converted in employment statistics to annual equivalents that contain 307 days.[10] In the collective and private sectors, the average approaches 280 only because able-bodied collective farmers work an abnormally long day, and hence account for more than one man-day in a single calendar day.[11]

The other point is that the conversion factor refers to able-bodied collective farmers. Those not able-bodied (juveniles and the aged), who work considerably less than 280 man-days a year, account for about 10 percent of total collective farm man-days and 30 percent of man-days worked on collective farmers' household plots.[12] In using 280 as the conversion factor, we convert these part-time workers into full-time (able-bodied) equivalents. Since data on state employment in all branches of the economy convert seasonal or temporary workers into some sort of annual or full-time equivalent, this seems a reasonable procedure.

DERIVATION OF ESTIMATES

Private sector.—The man-day series in col. 7 of Table 1 is derived from the following data: (1) a *Gosplan* estimate of farm employment in 1927–1928, when independent peasants accounted for virtually all farm production; (2) estimates of employment on plots of collective farmers in 1934, 1937, 1953, 1958–1959, and 1962;[13] (3) scattered data on

[9] On the unreality of assuming a national average of 280 calendar days for either the collective or private sectors individually, see: M. Sonin, *Voprosy balansa rabochei sily* (Moscow: 1949), pp. 76–77, and *Vosproizvodstvo rabochei sily v SSSR i balans truda* (Moscow: 1959), p. 95, note; K. P. Obolenskii, *Opredelenie ekonomicheskoi effektivnosti sel'skokhoziaistvennogo proizvodstva* (Moscow: 1963), pp. 66–67; S. G. Strumilin in Akademiia nauk, Institut ekonomiki, *Proizvoditel'nost' truda v sotsialisticheskom sel'skom khoziaistve* (Moscow: 1959), pp. 223 ff.

[10] Nimitz, *op. cit.* (in n. 3), pp. 138, 140.

[11] In 1958 the average able-bodied farmer worked about 2,600 hours on the collective farm, on the plot, and as a hired seasonal laborer in state enterprises (*ibid.*, Table B 7, row 9). Given a maximum feasible farm work year of 250 calendar days, this implies an average of more than 10 hours per day.

[12] *Ibid.*, Table B 9, rows 11 and 12.

[13] Given independent estimates of man-days worked on the collective farm, the plot estimates are derived from information on the distribution between farm and plot of hours worked by collective farmers in budget sample households (*ibid.*, Appendix B, Section II).

direct labor inputs per hectare of various crops and per head of various kinds of livestock;[14] (4) information bearing on private-sector incentives to increase plot output (trends in income of collective-farm households, terms of trade, and direct taxes); (5) annual statistics of private-sector sowings and livestock herds.

Item (1) provides the point of departure, while (2) yields benchmarks for the post-collectivization period. Within the constraints set by these aggregates, and guided by the data in (3) and (4), changing estimates of labor inputs per hectare and per animal are derived; these unit inputs include an allowance for labor expended on orchards, poultry production, and other activities for which annual indicators of scale are not available (but which are included in aggregate employment data for benchmark years). Unit inputs are multiplied by the series in (5) to obtain total labor inputs from year to year.

The method of calculation is vulnerable to error on at least three counts, and yields for some years merely hypothetical results. For one thing, the allowance for inputs to orchards, poultry, and so on is obviously crude, since it is responsive to changes in their relative importance only in benchmark years. Another dubious feature is that the unit inputs that fit collective farmers are assumed to be appropriate for the rest of the private sector during much of the period studied. The assumption may be broadly correct, but less correct in some years than others. Finally, benchmark years define only a few points on the curve of effort (unit inputs) over time, and interpolations between points may be wide of the mark. Even if the direction of change in unit inputs is estimated accurately, the fact that the curve has been simplified into a series of steps or levels (each typically taking in a cluster of years around a benchmark year) means that movement from one level to another produces artificial discontinuities. These are serious drawbacks, but the risk of erring on the direction of change and the inevitability of distorting its pace are more acceptable than the assumption of

[14] Unit labor inputs on sample peasant farms in the mid-1920's are available for most crops and for cows, other beef animals, and hogs. Comparison of average data with those for the smallest farms yields clues to the effect on inputs of reduction in plot size in later years. In addition, there are indications of private sector inputs in the 1940's or 1950's to the two most important areas of plot activity: vegetables (including potatoes) and cows. Inputs to sheep and goats are estimated from data for sample collective farms in 1937, when livestock care even in the socialized sector was unmechanized. The effect on inputs to feed crops of the shift from grasses toward feed roots is estimated from planning norms for institutional farms, which are small and technologically more primitive than the rest of the socialized sector.

constant inputs over time, which is plainly incompatible with the available aggregate data.

In interpreting the private sector estimates it should be borne in mind that while private- and collective-sector man-days are identical in length in any given year after the mid-1930's, they may vary in length from year to year. Therefore variations over time in total man-day inputs may reflect changes in hours per day.[15]

Collective farms.—The following information is available: (1) data of varying scope and completeness over time on numbers of farm households and working members; (2) statistics of total labor-days, or average labor-days earned per able-bodied member, in the years 1932–1940, 1945–1948, 1950–1959; (3) sample data on man-days worked per able-bodied farmer in 1939 and 1940; (4) global data on total man-days or man-days per "annual average" worker from 1958 to 1962; (5) data cited by Soviet sources on the average ratio of labor-days to man-days in the years 1932–1937, 1940, 1950–1958.

Estimates for the years 1932–1938 and 1945–1957 rely upon published or estimated labor-day versus man-day ratios. The published ratios are derived from a household sample which increased in size and representativeness over time, and the prewar ratios are less reliable than those beginning in 1950. Because of the complexity of the factors determining ratios,[16] interpolations for the years 1945–1949 are least reliable of all.

The published ratio for 1940 is rejected (in the belief that it has been "deflated" for comparability with the higher work norms and shorter effective working days of the 1950's), and estimates of man-days worked in 1939 and 1940 are derived from (1) and (3).

Collective farm records of days worked by members have improved in accuracy since their introduction in 1957, but through 1959 data taken directly from farm annual reports are quite inflated.[17] Adjusted figures from Soviet sources are preferred for 1958 and 1959; data accepted for later years have apparently not been adjusted, and may still be a little inflated.

It should be noted that estimates for 1957–1961, when conversions of

[15] For example, if collective farms tend to observe the standard on state farms, a decline of 10 to 15 percent in the length of the average working day may have occurred between the late 1950's and early 1960's.

[16] The level of mechanization is not the only or even (in the short run) the main factor. Any increase in work norms or decrease in the length of the effective working day may cause the ratio to decline. Cf. Nimitz, *op. cit.* (in n. 3), Appendix C, Section I.

[17] *Ibid.*, Appendix C, Section II.

collectives into state farms were numerous, are subject to special error connected not with the accuracy of available data but with their completeness. Unlike the collective-farm data published for these years in terms of annual averages (some of which are specified as covering converted farms for the fraction of the year in which they functioned as collectives), data referring to labor-days or man-days appear to originate in annual reports of farms in existence at the end of the year, and presumably exclude labor expenditures on farms converted during the year.[18]

Estimates for the period 1928–1931, for which neither labor-day nor man-day data are available, arbitrarily assume that working members per household and man-days per working member were slightly below the 1932 level. This part of the series (like the private-sector series in the 1930–1933 period) is almost completely hypothetical.

State farms.—Annual average data from official sources are available for all years except 1939, 1946–1949, and 1951. The margin of error in interpolated estimates is probably small.

MTS/RTS.—Annual average data of varying coverage are available in official sources for all years except 1938–1939, 1946–1949, and 1951. Data for 1932–1936 and 1959–1961 refer approximately to the MTS component as defined here (exclusive of collective-farm members earning labor-days). In other years, the official series provide a ceiling over estimates derived from scattered data on administrative personnel and numbers of workers in occupations where the proportion of wage earners is highest.

Agricultural services.—A ceiling is provided by the unspecified residual in official annual average data on agricultural workers and employees. Estimates rest upon a 1941-plan figure, and upon data for specialist personnel (only) in 1940 and later years. The resulting series is quite unreliable, but for present purposes the error is not significant.

COMPARISON WITH OFFICIAL SOVIET SERIES

The state-farm component of estimated farm employment is identical with the official data (row 6 of Table 2). Therefore attention is focused on the collective-farm-plus-MTS/RTS (row 3) and private-sector series (rows 7 or 14).[19] Both differ in scope or methodology from the

[18] Converted farms are, however, included in state farm data for the fraction of the year in which they functioned as state farms.

[19] Row 7 is not official in the strict sense, as it does not appear in published TsSU statistics, but it comes from a Soviet source who seems to have access to unpublished statistics (Karnaukhova). She equates row 14,

TABLE 2

Soviet and Estimated Farm Employment Series, 1940–1963

(annual averages or equivalents in millions, except where specified otherwise)

Item	1940	1950	1953	1955	1956	1957	1958	1959	1960	1961	1962	1963
SOVIET SERIES												
1. Total farm employment	n.a.	n.a.	n.a.	n.a.	36 [a]	36 [a]	36 [a]	n.a.	34.9 [b]	n.a.	33.5 [b]	n.a.
2. Socialized sector	31.3	30.7	29.4	30.7	31.5	30.9	30.8	30.0	29.0	28.1	27.7	27.3
3. Collective farms and MTS/RTS	29.5	28.3	26.8	27.9	28.6	26.9	26.2	25.0	22.7	20.7	20.0	19.4
4. Collective farms	29.0	27.6	25.6	24.8 [c]	25.7 [c]	24.3 [c]	24.9 [c]	24.5	22.3	20.7	20.0	19.4
5. MTS/RTS	0.5	0.7	1.2	3.1	2.9	2.6	1.3	0.5	0.4	0	0	0
6. State farms	1.8	2.4	2.6	2.8	2.9	4.0	4.6	5.0	6.3	7.4	7.7	7.9
7. Private sector	n.a.	n.a.	n.a.	n.a.	5 [a]	5 [a]	5 [a]	n.a.	5.9 [b]	n.a.	5.8 [b]	n.a.
8. Total agricultural employment	n.a.	n.a.	n.a.	n.a.	[34]	[33]	33	33	32	31	31	31
9. Socialized sector	28.1	27.9	26.6	27.9	[28.7]	[27.9]	27.8	26.9	26.1	25.5	25.2	24.9
10. Collective farms and MTS/RTS	26.5	25.7	24.3	25.3	[26.0]	[24.2]	23.5	22.3	20.3	18.7	18.1	17.6
11. Collective farms	26.1	25.1	23.3	22.5 [c]	[23.4] [c]	[21.9] [c]	22.5	22.1	20.1	18.7	18.1	17.6
12. MTS/RTS	0.4	0.6	1.0	2.8	2.6	2.3	1.0	0.2	0.2	0	0	0
13. State farms	1.6	2.2	2.3	2.6	2.7	3.7	4.3	4.6	5.8	6.8	7.1	7.3
14. Private sector	n.a.	n.a.	n.a.	n.a.	[5]	[5]	5	6	6	6	6	6
ESTIMATED FARM EMPLOYMENT												
15. Collective farms and MTS/RTS (280-day year)	23.8	26.2	23.0	25.0	24.4	22.3	21.3	21.3	19.3	17.6	17.1	16.6
16. Percent of row 3	81	93	86	90	85	83	81	85	85	85	86	86
17. Collective farms and MTS/RTS (250-day year)	26.7	29.3	25.8	27.9	27.4	25.0	23.9	23.8	21.6	19.7	19.1	18.6
18. Percent of row 3	91	104	96	100	96	93	91	95	95	95	96	96
19. Private sector (280-day year)	14.6	16.0	15.2	15.2	13.9	14.3	14.7	14.3	16.1	18.5	18.4	17.8

[a] 1956–1958 average.
[b] Erroneously precise (see sources to table).
[c] Excluding MTS tractor brigade workers.

SOURCES:

Rows 1, 7: 1956–1958 average, 1960, 1962: Karnaukhova in Akademiia nauk, Institut ekonomiki, *Puti povysheniia proizvoditel'nosti truda v sel'skom khoziaistve SSSR* (Moscow: 1964), p. 48. The row-7 figures for 1960 and 1962 have obviously been derived by subtracting row 9 from row 8 (treating the rounded total in row 8 as accurate to the nearest 0.1 million).

Rows 2–6: 1940, 1953, 1959, 1961: *Narkhoz-1961*, p. 461; 1950, 1960, 1962–1963: *Narkhoz-1963*, p. 363; 1955, 1958: *Narkhoz-1960*, p. 521; 1956–1957: *Sel'khoz-1960*, p. 450.

Row 8: 1956–1957: row 9 plus row 14; 1958: Karnaukhova, *op. cit.* above; 1959: *Sel'khoz-1960*, p. 450; 1960: *Narkhoz-1960*, p. 521; 1961: *Narkhoz-1961*, p. 461; 1962: *Narkhoz-1962*, p. 368; 1963: *Narkhoz-1963*, p. 363.

Rows 9–13: Same sources as rows 2–6. In the case of collective farms, the source of the 1956–1957 data defines agricultural employment more narrowly than later sources. Accordingly, the *Sel'khoz-60* data for these years were adjusted upward for comparability.

Row 14: 1956–1957: Assumed identical with row 7; 1958–1963: row 8 less row 9.

Row 15: Table 1, sum of cols. 2 and 3.

Row 17: Table 1, sum of cols. 8 and 9, divided by 250.

Row 19: Table 1, col. 1.

estimates of this study, so that the aim of the comparison is not to confirm or disprove them but to see what light they shed upon the estimates and vice versa.

As was noted earlier, the official data in Table 2 on private-sector employment refer to persons working only on the private plot: they exclude collective farmers and workers and employees who also work at all in the socialized sector. Thus they cover only a fraction of total employment. They may not be very reliable,[20] and they are in any case too rounded to be very informative. If the indicated upward trend from 5 to 6 million after 1958 is significant, however, it supports the estimated series in row 19.

The collective-farm component of row 3 covers members of fishing collectives (probably negligible),[21] and also members of collective farms converted to state farms during the year. The series is the arithmetic average of monthly data which include any farm member working one day or more during the month. Thus it tends to give a high weight to the under- and over-aged who work about one-third as many man-days per year as the able-bodied.[22] If these fractional workers were discounted to full-time (able-bodied) equivalent, the averages might be 10 to 15 percent lower.[23] Compared with the annual averages for state farms, the collective-farm series is considerably overstated. The MTS/RTS component also tends toward inflation in the years 1955–1958, when machine operators entered official statistics as annual workers even though they worked only part of the year.

For comparison with row 3, the estimates are given in two variants, equivalent to man-years of 280 and 250 working days (rows 15 and 17). The 250-day variant more closely resembles the official series, but

---

the residual in agricultural employment, with private sector farm employment, agricultural and nonagricultural (row 7). The resulting distortion would appear to be very small: in sample collective farm households in 1963, agricultural work accounted for 95.4 percent and other work (fishing, hunting, gathering, forest products, work as an independent artisan) for only 4.6 percent of private productive activity. Cf. G. Shmelev *Vop. ek.*, No. 4 (1965), p. 35.

[20] The household budget sample yields labor-expenditure data for members of collective-farm households, and possibly for members of some rural-worker and employee households, but not for urban households. See Nimitz, *op. cit.* (in n. 3), Appendix A.

[21] Fishing collectives have varied in number as follows (1,000, end of year): 1940—1.4, 1950—2.3, 1955—1.8, 1963—0.7 (computed as a residual from data on total and agricultural collectives). On January 1, 1955 they included 137,000 households, or roughly 80 per farm (*Bol'shaia sovetskaia entsiklopediia,* 2d ed., XXXVII, 504).

[22] See Table 4, cols. 4 and 5.

[23] B. I. Braginskii, *Proizvoditel'nost' truda v sel'skom khoziaistve* (Moscow: 1962), pp. 59–63.

even it is lower in most years, partly because it omits labor inputs on farms converted to state farms during the year, and partly because the number of man-days actually worked per annual average worker seems to have been less than 250 in most years after 1950.[24]

COMPARISON WITH WESTERN ESTIMATES

Again state farms are ignored, since all estimates in Table 3 accept the official data. The columns headed "Indicators" are from the 1965 edition of a compilation of Soviet economic statistics prepared annually

TABLE 3

WESTERN ESTIMATES OF PRIVATE SECTOR AND COLLECTIVE FARM EMPLOYMENT, 1928–1964
(million man-days)

	Private sector			Collective farms [a]		
Year	Kahan	Indicators	Nimitz	Kahan [b]	Indicators	Nimitz
	(1)	(2)	(3)	(4)	(5)	(6)
1928	6,586 [c]	n.a.	9,584	n.a.	n.a.	108
1933	1,874	n.a.	2,604	4,239	n.a.	5,156
1934	1,662	n.a.	3,006	4,770	n.a.	5,780
1935	1,511	n.a.	3,403	5,360	n.a.	6,473
1936	1,508	n.a.	3,184	5,085	n.a.	6,083
1937	1,659	n.a.	3,478	5,364	6,072	6,314
1938	1,713	n.a.	3,660	5,237	n.a.	6,088
1940	1,907	3,128 [d]	4,081	5,414	7,168	6,488
1950	1,305	2,935 [d]	4,490	5,958	7,143	7,143
1951	1,160	n.a.	4,244	5,575	6,839	6,923
1952	1,030	n.a.	3,902	5,253	6,365	6,365
1953	978	3,006	4,258	5,104	6,210	6,210
1954	1,152	n.a.	4,434	5,225	6,315	6,315
1955	1,248	3,415	4,251	5,429	6,658	6,658
1956	1,262	3,516	3,893	5,558	6,810	6,570
1957	n.a.	3,534	3,992	n.a.	n.a.	5,986
1958	n.a.	3,566	4,107	n.a.	6,840	5,792
1959	n.a.	3,276	3,993	n.a.	6,145	5,784
1960	n.a.	3,117	4,495	n.a.	5,271	5,271
1961	n.a.	3,223	5,180	n.a.	5,350	4,878
1962	n.a.	3,235	5,155	n.a.	4,751	4,751
1963	n.a.	3,114	4,978	n.a.	n.a.	4,608
1964	n.a.	3,192	n.a.	n.a.	n.a.	n.a.

[a] Excluding hired labor; [b] excluding inputs to construction, repair of buildings and machinery, social services, orchards and vineyards; [c] total all sectors, 1926–1929 average; [d] excluding independent peasants.

SOURCES: Cols. 1 and 4: *op. cit.* (in n. 26), p. 453; col. 2: *Op. cit.* (in n. 25), p. 86; Col. 3: Table 1, col. 7; col. 5: *Op. cit.* (in n. 25), p. 83; col. 6: Nimitz, *op. cit.* (in n. 3), Table C-1, col. 14.

[24] See Table 4, col. 7.

for the Joint Economic Committee of Congress;[25] the Kahan estimates were published in 1959.[26]

Both Kahan and Indicators estimate private-sector employment by the same general method used in this study (from unit inputs and annual statistics of sowings and herds). They differ from the present study in assuming no change in unit inputs over time.[27] They differ from each other in the period to which the unit input data refer. Kahan's inputs are described as coming from the 1925–26 peasant budget sample. All of them are in terms of adult male equivalent, and are therefore 20 to 25 percent below actual inputs undiscounted for age or sex.[28] They refer to the average for private farms of all sizes, or to a holding with a sown area more than 10 times the average after collectivization. The resulting estimates are plainly on the low side: Kahan's 1956 figure of 1,262 million man-days barely approaches the official Soviet figure for employment of persons working only on the plot—5 million in terms of annual equivalents,[29] or about 1,260 to 1,540 million man-days (assuming 280 days a year, and allowing for rounding of the figure for annual equivalents).

The unit inputs underlying the Indicators series come from a Soviet source, Gol'tsov, who presents data on employment in man-days on collective farms and on plots of collective farmers in 1958.[30] In the present study, Gol'tsov's figures for total labor expenditures are rejected as inflated.[31] His figures for unit inputs to the plot are rejected because those for livestock production appear to be too low.[32]

The collective-farm estimates in Table 3 are also derived by generally

[25] U.S. Congress, Joint Economic Committee, Congress of the United States, *Current Economic Indicators for the U.S.S.R.* (Washington, D.C.: Government Printing Office, 1965).

[26] Arcadius Kahan, "Changes in Labor Inputs in Soviet Agriculture," *Journal of Political Economy* (October, 1959), pp. 451–462.

[27] This is explicitly stated by Kahan, who recognizes the assumption as unreal. It is inferred of the *Indicators* series.

[28] Nimitz, *op. cit.* (in n. 3), pp. 41–42.

[29] Table 2, rows 7 or 14.

[30] *Ek. nauki,* No. 1 (1961), pp. 46–47. Gol'tsov's figures are partially reproduced in Nimitz, *op. cit.* (in n. 3), Table B–8.

[31] Gol'tsov's collective-farm total, which comes directly from farm annual reports, is 18 percent above the adjusted total implied in another Soviet source (see Nimitz, *op. cit.* (in n. 3), Table C 1, sources to col. 14). Presumably his plot total is inflated to the same degree, since it is evidently derived from the collective-farm total, given the percentage distribution between farm and plot of hours worked by budget sample households.

[32] The household budget sample does not yield data on labor inputs to individual types of livestock on the plot. Gol'tsov's estimates of plot inputs per head of cattle, hogs, and sheep and goats seem to be only notional: they are all exactly double the unit inputs he shows for collective farms. Another Soviet source estimates plot inputs per head of livestock converted

similar methods; Kahan's series, which includes only agriculture and administration, is of narrower scope than the other two. The trend over time in col. 4 does not differ significantly from col. 6.[33] The absolute estimates in col. 5 differ from those of col. 6 by more than 5 percent only in four years: 1940, for which col. 5 relies upon a labor-day versus man-day ratio rejected in this study as deflated; 1958–1959, for which col. 5 accepts data rejected here as inflated; 1961, for which col. 5 derives an estimate by blowing up a figure for the Ukraine alone.

Trends in over-all and sectoral farm employment are related to a number of interesting questions, only a few of which are explored here. Omitted, for example, is any consideration of the growth of state- versus collective-farm employment. The causes of the increase since the mid-1950's in numbers of state farms (largely through conversions of collective to state farms) are many and complex, and not easily treated within the compass of the present study. Nor are the employment estimates for state and collective farms used to test the official Soviet indexes of labor productivity in these sectors. Attention is focused rather upon areas where Soviet data are either nonexistent or manifestly unsatisfactory (over-all productivity, the private sector), and upon problems which currently seem to dominate Soviet concern with farm employment and productivity (utilization of collective-farm labor, the conditions for transfer of labor out of agriculture).

THE INTRACTABLE PRIVATE SECTOR

During the 30-odd years since collectivization was accomplished, the private sector has accounted for a third or more of total farm employment; the share has risen since 1958 to more than 40 percent.[34] What

---

to cattle equivalent as 2.7 times the collective farm level: V. F. Mashenkov, *Ispol'zovanie trudovykh resursov sel'skoi mestnosti* (Moscow: 1965), p. 55. Gol'tsov's estimate of all labor inputs to plot livestock production accounts for less than half of his figure for total labor expenditures on the plot, compared with the proportion of about three-fourths reported elsewhere (Shmelev, *op. cit.* (in n. 19), p. 35; V. F. Mashenkov, *Trudovye resursy sela* (Moscow: 1963), p. 38).

[33] In most years col. 4 of Table 3 amounts to 82 to 83 percent of col. 6. The labor-day versus man-day ratio used by Kahan for 1940 (1.47) refers to Gor'kii *oblast'* alone, rather than to a U.S.S.R. average, but it happens to be close to the ratio (1.44) implied by the estimate of total man-days derived in this study.

[34] Using methods apparently similar to those followed in this study, an unofficial Soviet source has estimated the distribution of employment in 1962 as follows (percent of total): state farms—17.3, collective farms—42.6, private sector—40.1. Cf. Mashenkov, *op. cit.* (in n. 32), p. 43.

explains the continuing importance of this always circumscribed and often belittled form of production?

Distribution of Total Farm Employment in Man-days (Excluding Agricultural Services) 1932–1963
(percent)

Year	Total	Private sector	Socialized sector: Collective farms	Socialized sector: State farms
1932	100	39	52	8
1937	100	33	62	5
1940	100	36	59	4
1945	100	38	57	5
1950	100	36	59	5
1953	100	37	56	6
1958	100	36	53	11
1963	100	42	39	19

Minor discrepancies between totals and components are due to rounding.
SOURCE: Table 1, cols. 7–10.

A merely mechanical answer is that unit inputs have increased. If effort devoted to private crops and herds in 1963 were at the 1928 level, labor expenditures would be on the order of 2,250 million man-days instead of 5,000, as estimated.

The substantive reason is that private agriculture is still indispensable: far from being an anachronism, it has been a necessary condition for the survival of socialized agriculture. The conspicuous advantages of collective farms so far have been the high share of marketings in output, and the fact that marketings were obtained for many years at token prices. Thus the system managed, with all its defects, to feed the rapidly growing cities while at the same time helping to finance industrialization. But farmers also have to eat, and buy kerosene, and pay money taxes. If earnings from the socialized sector do not cover their irreducible requirements for food and cash, there has to be another source. Not only farmers but also nonfarm households have had to rely upon their own efforts for part or all of their consumption of some products: in times of particular scarcity, such as the war and early postwar years, even the urban population has produced much of what it consumed in meat, milk, potatoes, vegetables, and fruit; and even in normal times, the rural nonfarm population has had to obtain these products mainly from the household plot.

Given the limits on plot size, the only way to increase output is to raise yields per hectare or per animal. The only factor affecting yield which the household completely controls is its own labor; this tends to expand to cover deficits in other inputs. Thus policy aimed at reducing plot employment is apt to backfire, as recent experience has shown. In the mid-1950's, when private production was encouraged and collective farmers received a large part of their feed requirements from the collective farm, labor inputs per head of livestock were lower than in the early 1960's, when feed was withheld and farmers were under pressure to sell their stock to the socialized sector. Denied pasture and grain from the collective farm, farmers scrounged hay from distant woods, and pastured their animals along roads, ravines, and railroad tracks where it was not feasible for a single hired herdsman to look after the stock of many families. One way or another, they contrived to feed their herds, but "at what a price!" [35]

The moral is plain. Economic and administrative pressures may succeed in reducing herd numbers and plot size, but so long as the farmer retains any land and any livestock, he will try to extract from them whatever the socialized sector fails to provide.

So far, the socialized sector has not provided very lavishly. In both 1937 and 1958, incomes of collective-farm households from the farm and the plot (including both cash and kind) were about equal.[36] In both years collective farms absorbed roughly two-thirds and the plot one-third of joint total labor expenditures.[37] Thus a day's work on the plot was worth twice as much as work on the farm. Both 1937 and 1958 were bumper-crop years when earnings from the collective farms were relatively high; [38] the differential in more normal years has probably been greater than 2 to 1. The share of plot income in cash earnings of farm households was on the order of two-thirds to three-fourths through the early 1950's, but has since declined to about one-half.

Within the last few years, the traditional role of the private plot has expanded to include a new function: providing employment to persons whose labor is not locally needed in the socialized sector.

Calculations and investigations indicate that while there is a shortage of labor in eastern regions of the country, a considerable quantity of the adult

[35] Shmelev, *op. cit.* (in n. 19), p. 31.
[36] Nimitz, *op. cit.* (in n. 3), Appendix B, Section III.
[37] *Ibid.*, Table B 5.
[38] *Ibid.*, Tables B 11 and B 12.

able-bodied population in some other regions is not involved in socialized production. Their number includes not only women who are fully or partly occupied with housework but a substantial quantity of young people and the adult male population, who are also engaged in housework and the private subsidiary economy.[39]

Pools of surplus labor are said to be largest

in the trans-Caucasus, Belorussia, the Central Black Soil and southwest regions, the Central Asian republics, and also in the Moldavian and Lithuanian republics. In these and other regions, certain groups of workers are encountering some difficulties in finding work at their specialty. Because industry is insufficiently developed in many medium and small cities, workers are forced to find employment in housework and the private subsidiary economy.[40]

UTILIZATION OF COLLECTIVE FARM LABOR

About 30 percent of the *de facto* collective-farm labor force (members who work at all on the collective farm) consists of persons who would not be expected to work in socialized production if they did not live in the country: juveniles 12–15, the disabled, people of pensionable age, and adults who live on the farm but are mainly occupied elsewhere (worker and employee and student family members).[41] The high proportion of these less able-bodied is explained by several related facts: the low level of average earnings (making it necessary for more family members to work),[42] the primitive pension arrangements on most farms until 1964, and the outflow of the able-bodied for many years to better-paid jobs outside agriculture. The less able are not required to work a minimum number of days a year, and in fact contribute a rather small proportion of total man-days worked—10 to 15 percent.

The other 85 to 90 percent are supplied by able-bodied collective farmers (men 16–59, women 16–54) who *are* expected to work a minimum number of labor-days or man-days a year, whether they are

[39] Manvich, *Vop. ek.*, No. 6 (1965), p. 27. "Housework" includes processing and marketing plot-output, constructing and repairing plot-buildings (Nimitz, *op. cit.* (in n. 3), p. 44, n. 3).

[40] Manevich, *op. cit.* (in n. 39).

[41] See Nimitz, *op. cit.* (in n. 3), Table C 1, cols. 3 (total working members) and 4 (able-bodied working members only) for 1940 and later years.

[42] Because of the importance to the household of grain and feed, obtained mainly from the collective farm as earnings in kind, there is an incentive to earn labor-days even though the time so spent may be less rewarding (as conventionally valued) than plot time.

needed or not. The compulsory minimum was first introduced in 1939 to ensure participation in collective production when earnings on the farm were declining sharply. It was raised during the war, and even in that period of labor scarcity the minimum was higher than the level of participation farms in some regions could usefully absorb.[43] While the attempt to substitute compulsion for material incentives to work on the collective farm may have seemed expedient in an earlier economic environment, its tendency is clearly to encourage higher than necessary labor inputs, and it is an anachronism today. Lowering the minimum (let alone abolishing it) is apparently unthinkable.[44]

A second factor conducing to waste has been the tendency of farm management from the very beginning of collectivization to hang onto labor in order to cover peak requirements. Since the cost of labor has been almost infinitely collapsible (being determined not by the quantity used but by the amount of farm income left after meeting fixed obligations), there has been no compelling reason to conserve it.

> The independent peasant didn't have to ask anyone if he could leave the village, but the collective farmer had to have permission from the farm. The managers of many farms, being unable to elicit intensive labor [from members], turned to an easier way of meeting production goals—not by quality of effort but by quantity. . . .
>
> The practice was harmful both to farms and the government. It tended to legitimize less than full use of labor, and did not impel farm managers to

[43] The labor requirements of collective farms in southern and eastern regions, which are devoted largely to mechanized grain production, have never been as high as those of northern regions, where labor-intensive branches are prominent (livestock, flax, potatoes, vegetables). It is for this reason—and not because of differences in the amount of effort diverted to off-farm activities—that the average number of labor-days worked per able-bodied farmer was lower in grain regions on the eve of the war. In revising the compulsory minimum requirements, regional production patterns were ignored: "A memorandum on use of rural labor resources during the war years, prepared by the Planning and Economic Department of the Ministry of Agriculture in 1946, asserts that a high minimum was deliberately introduced in regions where the actual level of participation was low, in order to stimulate it" (Iu. V. Arutiunian, *Sovetskoe krest'ianstvo v gody Velikoi Otechestvennoi voiny* (Moscow: 1963), p. 87).

[44] When farms were authorized in 1954 to establish their own minimum requirements, the proviso was that these be at least as high as the minimum previously established by the government, and that they be approved by the *raion* executive committee (*Sel'. khoz.* August 31, 1954, p. 2, as translated in *Current Digest of the Soviet Press,* October 13, 1954, pp. 9–10). *Komm. Uzbek.,* No. 8 (1962), pp. 56–63, takes collective farm chairmen and local officials to task for trying to lower the minimum. It argues that since the climate in Central Asia permits a work year of 300 days, requirements should rather be increased. Whether individual farms can effectively use larger amounts of labor is evidently irrelevant.

seek out ways of organizing labor more rationally and providing better material incentives.[45]

As the level of earnings and mechanization on collective farms has risen, another feature of labor arrangements which ensures waste has begun to operate: the right to work. Unlike state farms, collectives cannot get rid of surplus members who do not choose to leave, and they are obliged to try to provide work for all members who apply: "A collective farmer cannot be denied work; therefore the number of persons employed is not the minimum required to handle crop and livestock operations but rather the number available on a farm." [46] On farms with large surpluses, mechanization may be resisted, and when introduced does not automatically result in lower labor expenditures: "There is a tendency to perform some kinds of work by hand instead of by machine, and not infrequently the acquisition and use of machinery in farms with surplus labor is not accompanied by increase in work norms." [47]

It is hard to assign weights to these various sources of inefficiency—the compulsory minimum, the tendency to hoard (and squander) labor, and the right to work. However, the general waste from all sources is suggested by the experience on farms converted to state farms in 1959–1960: only 79 percent of the able-bodied members were enrolled as state farmers. Of the rest, 6 percent left agriculture, 12 percent devoted themselves wholly to the plot, and 3 percent found no employment.[48]

Trends in the size and utilization of the *de facto* labor force since 1950 are summarized in Table 4. On a per-household basis, the number

[45] Arutiunian in Akademiia nauk, Institut istorii, *Formirovanie i razvitie sovetskogo rabochego klassa (1917–1961 gg.)* (Moscow: 1964), pp. 107–108.

[46] Karnaukhova in Akademiia nauk, Institut ekonomiki, *Puti povysheniia proizvoditel'nosti truda v sel'skom khoziaistve SSSR* (Moscow: 1964), p. 55. See also: G. Shmelev, *Raspredelenie i ispol'zovanie truda v kolkhozakh* (Moscow: 1964), p. 13.

[47] Karnaukhova, *op. cit.* (in n. 46), p. 53. See also Shmelev, *op. cit.* in n. 46), pp. 41–42.

[48] Gol'tsov in N. I. Shishkin, ed., *Trudovye resursy SSSR* (Moscow: 1961), pp. 92–93. Another source suggests that cuts in the labor force of converted farms have not been drastic enough. "In recent years a substantial number of collective farms have been converted into state farms where labor is still used ineffectively. Some problems of labor utilization [characteristic] of collective farms have arisen also on state farms (in particular, in some regions even state farms have excess workers). This observation is supported by the ratio of workers to land. In 1953 there were 10.5 workers per 100 hectares of arable land on state farms, and 5.8 in 1957; the figure rose thereafter to 7.6 in 1962. The increase . . . is explained only in part by intensification." Mashenkov, *op. cit.* (in n. 32), pp. 43–44.

TABLE 4

UTILIZATION OF COLLECTIVE FARM LABOR, 1950–1962

Year	Working farm members per on-hand household			Man-days worked per:				Ratio of peak workers to:	
				Working farm member			Annual average worker		
	Able-bodied	Other	All	Able-bodied	Other	All		Total working	Annual average
	(1)	(2)	(3)	(4)	(5)	(6)	(7)	(8)	(9)
1950	1.37	0.62	1.99	216	78	176	262	n.a.	n.a.
1951	1.36	0.61	1.97	n.a.	n.a.	174	258	n.a.	n.a.
1952	1.34	0.60	1.94	n.a.	n.a.	164	244	n.a.	n.a.
1953	1.33	0.60	1.93	203	74	163	244	0.86	1.28
1954	1.35	0.58	1.93	203	81	166	249	n.a.	n.a.
1955	1.39	0.60	1.99	206	83	169	254	0.84	1.27
1956	n.a.	n.a.	2.05	196	n.a.	161	244	0.85	1.28
1957	n.a.	n.a.	1.99	193	n.a.	159	237	0.86	1.28
1958	1.42	0.53	1.95	192	65	157	231	0.87	1.27
1959	1.41	0.52	1.93	195	73	162	240	0.86	1.27
1960	1.38	0.51	1.89	197	71	163	243	0.85	1.26
1961	1.34	0.52	1.86	198	64	160	240	n.a.	n.a.
1962	1.30	0.52	1.82	199	63	161	240	0.85	1.27
1958 ÷ 1950	1.04	0.85	0.98	0.89	0.83	0.89	0.88	—	—
1962 ÷ 1958	0.92	0.98	0.93	1.04	0.97	1.03	1.04	—	—

SOURCE: Taken directly or derived from Nimitz, *op. cit.* (in n. 3) Table C-1.

of working members was declining in the early 1950's, rose in the mid-1950's as earnings increased, and is again falling rather rapidly (col. 3); the decline since 1958 is concentrated in the able-bodied component (col. 1). The trend in earnings per man-day since 1958 has been quite unfavorable.[49]

The number of days worked per year per member declined to the mid-1950's and has since been rather stable (col. 6). There has been no significant reduction in seasonality of employment, as measured by the ratio of workers participating during the peak month to the 12-month average (col. 9). Even in peak months, about 15 percent of the *de facto* labor force does not work on the farm (col. 8), partly because peak labor requirements for farm and plot overlap.

Deficit in the supply of member labor in peak periods is made up by hired seasonal labor and by mobilization of the urban population (machine operators lent by industrial and construction enterprises, other workers and employees, students). Both forms of labor are authorized only "in exceptional circumstances" which seem to recur in some regions every year. Use of urban workers has been condemned as disruptive, expensive, and inefficient,[50] and obviously the productivity of such workers is very low relative to their total cost. A rather large number of persons may be involved.[51] In terms of annual averages, however, the ratio of nonmember to member labor is very small—perhaps around 3 percent—compared with the ratio of seasonal and temporary workers to permanent workers on state farms—23 percent in 1960.[52]

So long as the inhibition against hiring seasonal labor remains, sea-

[49] Nimitz, *op. cit.* (in n. 3), Table B 12. It is reported that about 2.5 million workers left agriculture over the four years 1957–1960. Cf. *Osnovy ekonomiki sotsialisticheskogo sel'skogo khoziaistva* (Moscow: 1963), p. 137) and 3.1 million over the four years 1959–1962 (Mashenkov, *op. cit.* (in n. 32), p. 38.

[50] See the party versus government decree of July 12, 1962 (*Pravda*, July 14, 1962). Mobilized urban workers are paid both by the enterprises where they are regularly employed and by farms. Shmelev, *op. cit.* (in n. 46), p. 100, cites the example of an institute of agricultural mechanization where all faculty and laboratory technicians were drafted to a nearby farm for two weeks to help with the corn harvest. "Among them were many candidates of science with monthly salaries of 200 rubles and more. If you count in the cost their pay both at the farm and at the institute, the corn harvested by such a labor force was truly golden."

[51] In September, 1961, 740,000 hired and urban workers were employed on collective farms of the R.S.F.S.R.; this amounted to 7.8 percent of working farm members. In 1960, the comparable ratio in Kazakhstan was 12.5 percent (September) and in Uzbekistan 22.5 percent (November). Shmelev, *op. cit.* (in n. 46), p. 94.

[52] The state-farm ratio probably excludes urban workers. On nonmember labor on collective farms, see Nimitz, *op. cit.* (in n. 3), Appendix C, Section IV.

sonality guarantees underutilization of the collective-farm labor force. During 1950–1959, the ratio of member employment in the December–February quarter to the peak month was about 60 percent.[53] Some improvement may come as employment in nonseasonal or counter-seasonal branches increases (communal and other services, manufacturing), but at best a large part of the labor force will continue to lack employment in winter months.

In areas where the ratio of population to land is particularly high, surplus labor now exists even at peak periods, and in these regions "the presence of a large supply of labor permits and requires a sharp intensification of all branches of agricultural production." [54] But just as diversification cannot completely solve the problem of seasonality, intensification is not likely to sop up all this excess: transfer of labor from the farm to the nonfarm sector must continue.

> Some economists urge an end to the outflow of collective farmers to industry . . . But mechanization of production processes and increase in labor productivity in collective farms make reduction in the number of workers not only feasible but essential. Shutting off such transfers would lead to faster increase in the number of agricultural workers than in industry, since natural increase in the labor supply is higher on collective farms.[55]

Probably for a variety of reasons—the unwillingness of some surplus members to leave farms which offer a tolerable living, the inability of others to find nonfarm employment for which they are qualified, and the avoidance of collective employment by members of very poor farms—utilization of collective labor is not improving: "According to *Gosplan* data, about 69 percent of the labor resources on collective farms were utilized over the three years 1958–1960. By our calculations, 76 percent of the available supply was utilized in 1958 and 66 percent in 1960 and 1962." [56] These data greatly exaggerate underemployment, since they ignore plot labor requirements. But the trend for collective farms is plain.

PRODUCTIVITY

In calculating productivity per man-day (Table 5), the official Soviet index of gross agricultural output is accepted, with some qualms, as the numerator. It is the only published series available for all years covered

[53] E. P. Gubin, *Puti formirovaniia agrarno-promyshlennykh ob'edinenii* (Moscow: 1963), p. 20.

[54] Borodin in Akademiia nauk, Institut ekonomiki, *Ispol'zovanie trudovykh resursov v sel'skom khoziaistve SSSR* (Moscow: 1964), p. 9.

[55] Shmelev, *op. cit.* (in n. 46), p. 13.

[56] Karnaukhova, *op. cit.* (in n. 46), p. 48.

TABLE 5

GROSS AGRICULTURAL OUTPUT PER MAN-DAY, 1928–1963

Year	Gross output	Man-day input	Output per man-day [a]
	(1)	(2)	(3)
		(1928 = 100) [b]	
1928	100	100	100
1929–1933 average	90	87	104
1934	86	99	87
1935	96	110	88
1936	88	102	86
1937	108	107	101
1938	97	106	92
1939	98	100	98
1934–1939 average	95	104	92
		(1940 = 100) [c]	
1940	100	100	100
1945	61	105	58
1945–1949 average	82	103	80
1950	99	111	89
1951	92	107	86
1952	101	100	101
1953	104	102	102
1954	108	105	104
1955	121	107	113
1951–1955 average	105	104	101
1956	137	103	133
1957	140	101	138
1958	155	102	152
1959	155	101	153
1960	159	104	152
1956–1960 average	149	102	146
1961	163	108	150
1962	165	108	153
1963	153	106	145
1961–1963 average	160	107	149

[a] Computed from unrounded index numbers; [b] Prewar territory; [c] Postwar territory.

SOURCES: Col. 1: *Sel'khoz-1960*, p. 79; *Narkhoz-1963*, p. 227; Col. 2: Table 1, col. 12.

by the employment estimates, and although official output data for some products (notably grain) are exaggerated, the trend in aggregate output is not necessarily distorted to the same degree. Comparison with Western estimates available for some years suggests that the official index may be significantly overstated (by 5 to 10 percent) in the mid-1930's and for some years after 1958.[57]

[57] See the estimates of D. Gale Johnson in Abram Bergson and Simon Kuznets, eds., *Economic Trends in the Soviet Union* (Cambridge, Mass.:

Table 5 shows an increase in productivity per man-day in the early 1930's, which is quite improbable. The error lies more in the input than in the output column. As was explained in Section I, the estimates of private- and collective-sector employment in this period are largely hypothetical; the tendency is to understate the increase in both sectors.[58] The estimates for the latter half of the 1930's are better, and they indicate that while productivity in 1937, an exceptionally favorable year, regained the 1928 level, the average for 1934–1939 was roughly 10 percent lower.

Because of the coverage of the output index (which refers in different years to different territory), there is no official datum linking 1939 with 1940. Hence productivity in later years can be compared only with 1940. The obvious trends are the trough in the immediate postwar years, recovery to the 1940 level during the Fifth Five-Year Plan, a whopping increase between 1955 and 1958, and then a leveling off, due (among other things) to a falling off in machinery deliveries and collective-sector incentives.[59]

In appraising this distinctly spotty record, it should be borne in mind that until recently the Russians were much more interested in reducing the seasonal peak (so that people could be transferred out of agriculture) than they were in increasing productivity per man-day or even per man. There was mild interest in productivity in the 1930's, evidenced by the 1933 and 1937 investigations of sample collective farms and by a few journal articles. There was virtually no interest from the war years through 1954.[60] The Five-Year Plan for 1951–1955 was the first to include a specific goal for growth of labor productivity in agriculture,

---

Harvard University Press, 1963), p. 208, and those for recent years in the source cited in note 25, p. 20.

[58] Constancy of unit inputs in the private sector is assumed, though disappearance of the larger and more efficient peasant farms in 1929–1931 should by itself have produced an increase in average unit inputs. Participation in collective production in early years was probably lower than the estimates assume.

[59] For reviews of the factors affecting productivity in the 1950s see Jerzy F. Karcz and V. P. Timoshenko, "Soviet Agricultural Policy, 1953–1962," *Food Research Institute Studies* IV: 2 (May, 1964), 123–163; Nancy Nimitz, "The Lean Years," *Problems of Communism,* XIV: 3 (May–June, 1965), 10–22. In the latter I incorrectly estimated a decline in total man-day inputs after 1958. The present estimates, based on later data for the private sector, show a slight increase.

[60] Almost all entries in a list of works published between 1945 and 1957 on problems of agricultural labor productivity and costs date from 1955–1957 (Akademiia nauk, Fundamental'naia biblioteka obshchestvennykh nauk, *Problemy proizvoditel'nosti truda i sebestoimosti produktsii v sel'skom khoziaistve SSSR posle Velikoi Otechestvennoi voiny; bibliograficheskii ukazatel' knig i zhurnal'nykh statei za 1945–1957 gg.* (Moscow: 1959).

and this had no operational significance (no reference to it appeared in the annual plans).[61] Not until planners became concerned with costs of production, in the mid-1950's, did problems of measuring and analyzing labor productivity come to the fore.

Even then, concern at the top planning level and among research economists was only slowly translated into institutional arrangements and statistical procedures which allowed the individual collective farm to calculate, let alone plan, its own labor productivity and costs. Global data on labor productivity in the socialized sector first appeared in a statistical handbook published in 1956. Calculation at the farm level was not really possible until around 1960, after collective farms had taken over MTS machinery and learned to record working time with tolerable accuracy.

Trends in over-all productivity may be influenced not only by technology, organization, and incentives in the socialized sector, but also by the relative importance of the private sector, where average productivity per man-day in 1937 and 1963 was lower (though not as much lower as most Soviet literature on the plot implies).[62] In 1963 the ratio of private to socialized sector productivity was around 70 percent.[63] Hence the sharp increase in private-sector employment after 1958 may have contributed to the leveling off of total productivity, though this is not self-evident (since marginal productivities are not known).

The rather small decline between 1937 and 1963 in the ratios in row 3 indicates, incidentally, that productivity per man-day increased almost as much on the plot over this period as it did in the socialized sector. This is an astonishing accomplishment,[64] which suggests how much the private sector benefits from conditions the socialized sector has not yet

[61] Braginskii in Akademiia nauk, Institut ekonomiki, *op. cit.* (in n. 9), pp. 127–128.

[62] Productivity per man-day has probably been higher in the private than in the socialized sector in some years, notably the 1945–1952 period.

[63] The ratio reflects differences between the two sectors in composition of output and the average prices at which output is valued, as well as differences in levels of inputs and yields. The technological advantage of the socialized sector lies chiefly in crop production, and crop output accounted for 61 percent of socialized sector output in 1963, compared with 37 percent in the private sector. On this score, comparison tends to favor the socialized sector. On the other hand, nonmarketed output in the socialized sector is valued at cost, while in the private sector it is valued at average realized prices which are strongly affected by collective farm market prices. See Braginskii, *op. cit.* (in n. 23), p. 73.

[64] Between 1940 and 1963, productivity per average annual worker in the socialized sector doubled (*Narkhoz-1963*, p. 65). The increase in productivity per man-day was probably close to this.

been able to duplicate: an exact and predictable relation between effort and reward, complete autonomy in choosing what to produce and how,

PRODUCTIVITY PER MAN-DAY IN THE SOCIALIZED AND PRIVATE SECTORS, 1937, 1963

	1937	1963
1. Share in gross output (percent)		
Socialized sector	72.2	65.8
Private sector	27.8	34.2
2. Share in employment (percent)		
Socialized sector	66.7	57.9
Private sector	33.3	42.1
3. Productivity per man-day		
Socialized sector = 100	100	100
Private sector	77	71

SOURCES:
Row 1: 1937 from TsUNKhU, *Sotsialisticheskoe sel'skoe khoziaistvo SSSR.* (Moscow: 1939, p. 87; 1963 derived from private sector shares in total output of crops and livestock (Shmelev in *Vop. ek.*, No. 4 [1965], p. 28) and the absolute value of crop and livestock output in *Narkhoz-1963*, p. 228).
Row 2: Derived from Table 1, cols. 7 to 10 (agricultural services are excluded).

zero waste of working time from organizational and other failures, zero incentive to employ more labor than is needed.

THE PRESENT FARM EMPLOYMENT PROBLEM

For years there has been an outflow of labor—partly planned and partly spontaneous—from agriculture to other sectors of the economy. As late as 1958 it was assumed that about 3 million workers would have to be transferred to the nonagricultural sector during the Seven-Year Plan to help cover labor shortfalls due to the low birth rate of the war years. But as a Soviet authority on manpower recently noted (in a chapter opening with the question "Does an employment problem exist in socialist conditions?"): "In practice it turned out that our industry has experienced no shortages of labor despite the low natural increase in labor resources. The increase in the nonagricultural labor supply has been higher than anticipated. In fact, in contrast to the prewar period, some enterprises and branches of industry have more than the planned amount of labor." [65]

Like most other Soviet writers on the subject, Sonin affirms that the

[65] M. Sonin, *Aktual'nye problemy ispol'zovaniia rabochei sily v SSSR* (Moscow: 1965), p. 102.

kind of *un*employment problem that plagues capitalist countries does not exist in the U.S.S.R. However, "the problem of achieving a more rational and effective distribution of the employed population by type of activity, branch of the economy, and region . . . is urgent." [66]

If there is a difference between the employment problem and the unemployment problem, it apparently lies in the remedy thus far adopted—feather-bedding in Soviet enterprises,[67] as opposed to unemployment compensation elsewhere. The main cause in the Soviet case appears to be technological progress. The problem has sharply increased since 1962, when the "avalanche" of 17- and 18-year-olds born after the war began to seek employment.[68] Regional shortages of labor persist, and shortages of highly qualified labor are general. But for the nonagricultural sector as a whole, there is now a surplus of less qualified labor.

If there is no longer need for transfer of labor out of agriculture, why are the Russians so concerned about agricultural labor productivity? Their ultimate concern is with expanding agricultural output, but the immediate problem is low agricultural income: "The average annual income of collective farmers is lower than among workers of equal qualification in other branches. In recent years the average income per working day of a collective farmer from farm and plot together has been about three-fourths of a state farmer's daily wage and two-thirds of the wage of a worker in local industry." [69]

Income is low because output per man is low: "Increasing the productivity of collective farm labor is a problem with enormous significance for the national economy [as a whole], because until it is solved, the differences between urban and rural living standards cannot be eliminated." [70]

Largely because earnings in agriculture are low, there is an unplanned outflow of precisely those categories of labor—the young with secondary

[66] *Ibid.*, p. 98.

[67] Managers of Soviet enterprises willingly retain some surplus labor as a reserve. *Ibid.*, p. 106; Mashenkov, *op. cit.* (in n. 32), pp. 130, 133. The bonus system, which relates managerial rewards to the size of the enterprise labor force, may encourage excess. But some of the surplus is clearly involuntary: apparently enterprises have been obliged to retain workers for whom they cannot find employment elsewhere (Manevich in *Vop. ek.*, No. 6 (1965), p. 28).

[68] Shubkin in *Vop. fil.*, No. 5 (1965), p. 58; Sonin, *op. cit.* (in n. 65), p. 102.

[69] R. V. Alekseeva and A. P. Voronin, *Nakoplenie i razvitie kolkhoznoi sobstvennosti* (Moscow: 1963), p. 29.

[70] Karnaukhova in Akademiia nauk, Institut ekonomiki, *Rezervy i puti povysheniia proizvoditel'nosti truda v sel'skom khoziaistve SSSR* (Moscow: 1962), p. 25.

education, the skilled machine operators—who are most needed for a more sophisticated and productive agriculture.[71] As one Soviet sociologist bleakly acknowledges, it is in vain to hope that youth touched by urbanization will ever choose to enter agriculture in significant numbers, regardless of patriotic appeals; therefore it is essential to hold rural youth on the land. Administrative measures will not do it; there must be improvement in economic and social conditions.[72]

The problem is complicated by the coexistence of a socialized and a private sector. If the Russians had no political ax to grind, they could probably achieve significant increases in productivity in the private sector by regularizing feed supply from the collective farm, and by allowing households to use the kind of vest-pocked tractors found in some suburban American backyards and all over Japan. If such privileges were linked to effective participation in collective production, they might even improve the quality of effort on the farm while simultaneously reducing the quantity applied to the plot. But such a course may be considered risky, not only for ideological reasons but also because it might tend to perpetuate the gap between earnings per man-day on the farm and on the plot.

The safer solution—to concentrate on raising productivity and income in the socialized sector—requires more than investment. Farm managers must be free to use labor as effectively as they know how, instead of being handicapped (as they are now) by obsolete institutions like the minimum labor-day requirement. They must be allowed to pursue intensification and diversification in ways that make sense in their particular zone, without interference from ill-informed or irresponsible higher authorities. Unmanageably large farms must be reduced in size. The structure of collective-farm wages must provide more incentives to increase qualifications and reduce costs.

By these and other measures (the list is not exhaustive), productivity in the collective sector can be substantially improved. However, the problem is no longer a "farm" problem alone, and sustained improvement will also depend upon the ability of the nonfarm sector to absorb surplus farm labor. If surpluses are dammed up within agriculture, the collective farmer's right to work will delay or partly nullify the technological and other changes which could reduce labor expenditures and increase earnings per man-day.

[71] Shubkin, *op. cit.* (in n. 68), p. 69, makes the point that material considerations are not the only factor driving youth off the land. Another is the unbalanced sex ratio that results when farm boys after army service go into urban jobs instead of returning to the country. Girls leave for the city partly to find a husband.

[72] *Ibid.* See also Sorokina in *Ek. gaz.*, June 30, 1965, p. 7.

COMMENT

Frank A. Durgin, Jr.

We are indebted to Miss Nimitz for an outstandingly thorough and painstaking study, the complexity of which can be appreciated only by reference to her unabridged Rand Study RM 4623. The unabridged version of the study, which she so frequently cites, is an encyclopedic compilation of interesting facts, figures, and estimates, skillfully cross-referenced and woven into a meaningful and copiously footnoted document. Its reading is mandatory for everybody interested in problems of agricultural manpower and employment, and for anyone interested in the effects of taxation and administrative restraints on the private sector.

I would like to stress that this is a commentary on the contribution of a colleague for whom I have the highest professional regard. If in places I criticize her arbitrary assumptions or choices of data, it must be borne in mind that the void of meaningful data and information (the *raison d'être* of her study) in which she worked, forced these choices. And if I criticize her methodology, I must in the same breath admit that I can conceive of no other manner in which she might have approached the problem.

The degree of uncertainty surrounding all Western estimates of Soviet categories is high. This stems from the uncertainty surrounding the Soviet data which must, in some degree, be incorporated in the derivation of the estimate. In the case of Miss Nimitz's estimates of annual average employment, the degree of uncertainty is particularly high because of the chain nature of her derivations. Her estimate is derived from Soviet estimates of private sown area and head of livestock multiplied by her own estimates of per-unit inputs of labor, all of which is divided by her estimated conversion factor of 280 man-days per year. Her conversion factor is in turn based on her own estimates of total man-days worked in agriculture and Soviet estimates of the percentage of total time worked on the private and socialized sectors.[73] To illus-

[73] As Miss Nimitz tells us, "until recently collective farms kept no records of days worked by members." Hence, Soviet estimates of the percentage of

trate the degree to which this chain dependency reduces the probability of success, if we *assume* that the probability of a successful (plus or minus 5 percent) Soviet estimate of private livestock and sown area is .7, the probability of a successful estimate by Miss Nimitz of per-unit inputs is .8, and the probability of a successful estimate of the man-day versus man-year ratio is .9, then the probability of getting an estimate of average annual employment which falls within plus or minus 15 percent (not 5 percent) [74] of the true figure is less than .5.[75]

The margin of possible error in a chain-type estimate is also large because in the process of multiplying the various links of the chain the percentages of error in each link become cumulative.[76] The frightening extent of possible error from all sources is well brought out by her comparison of her own estimates with those of Kahan and the *Indicators*.[77] In the case of employment on the private sector, for example, her estimates run from 200–400 percent those of Kahan, reaching 435 percent of the Kahan estimates for 1953. Both she and Kahan, as she points out, used the same method.

The magnitude of the differences noted above would seem to be the product, not of random errors, but of arbitrary assumptions and choices of data. And as an indication of the magnitude of the error which can be introduced by arbitrary choices, consider the livestock census, the size of which can vary by 50 or more percent depending on the date of the census.[78] A livestock count of January, 1938, for example, showed the presence of 66.6 million sheep and goats in the U.S.S.R., whereas a count made in July of the same year showed 102.5 million. By differing simply in the choice of census, the estimate of one research could thus reach 160 percent of that of his counterpart.

The weakest link in the Nimitz estimates, in my view, however, is her assumptions regarding the per-unit inputs into the private sector. Whereas Kahan assumed constant per-unit inputs over the period covered in his study, Miss Nimitz assumes rather sharply rising inputs. The assumed per-unit inputs for 1961–1963 expressed as a percentage of those for 1928–1933 are as follows: [79]

---

total time worked on the private and socialized sectors prior to 1957 can only amount to rough guesses.

[74] See below.

[75] Conditional probability: $0.7 \times 0.8 \times 0.9 = 0.5$.

[76] $10 \times 10 = 100$. But $10 + .1(10) \times 10 + .1(10) = 100 + .21(100)$ and not $100 + .1(100)$

[77] Table 2 in this essay.

[78] See *Notes et Études Documentaires* (September 25, 1954) in *La Documentation française*.

[79] Cf. Nimitz, *op. cit.* (in n. 3), Table B–3.

feed	600
grain	250
vegetables	200
industrial crops	166
cows	192
other cattle	160
hogs	160
sheep and goats	120

Given the limited (actually shrinking) [80] dimensions of the private sector and the fact that the degree of labor intensity on that sector has always been high, the marginal-revenue product curve of labor on that sector must fall off steeply. And when one considers this steeply falling marginal-revenue product curve in conjunction with the constant increases over time in the value of a man-day on the collective sector, it becomes apparent that the assumptions of rising inputs into the private sector must be closely scrutinized. Miss Nimitz does not explain how the input estimates were derived, although she criticizes the methods used by Kahan and the indicators.

This lack of information on the derivation of the input estimates is particularly disturbing because of the sensitivity of Miss Nimitz's findings to these inputs assumptions. This high sensitivity to the per-unit input estimates can be seen in the fact that if she had assumed either falling per-unit inputs, constant per-unit inputs, or even rising (but at a slower rate than her present estimates) per-unit inputs, then her findings regarding employment on the private sector would have been the opposite of her present findings (that is, falling instead of rising).

The implications of the Nimitz study are that the supply curve of labor in the agricultural sector of the Soviet economy is a backward one. This is clearly brought to light by an examination of the inverse relationship which exists between the average number of days furnished to the collectives each year by each household and each able-bodied worker and (a) the value of a man-day on the collectives in cash and kind, (b) the amount of cash paid per man day, (c) the increase in the number of farms giving advance payments for work furnished on the collective sector, and (d) the increase in the number of farms shifting to a fixed and guaranteed payment of labor; this backward supply curve is also brought to light by the direct relationship which exists between the number of man-days furnished to the collective by each household and each able-bodied worker and, (e) the dimensions of the private sector,

[80] *Ibid.*, Table B–2.

TABLE 6

RELATIONSHIP OF COLLECTIVE-FARMER EARNINGS FROM THE SOCIALIZED SECTOR TO MAN-DAYS WORKED PER HOUSEHOLD AND PER ABLE-BODIED COLLECTIVE FARMER, U.S.S.R., SELECTED YEARS

Year	Collective farm distributions per man-day		Man-days worked per farm household	Man-days worked per able-bodied collective farmer
	Cash and kind (1953 = 100)	Cash only (rubles)		
1950	n.a.	n.a.	350	176
1953	100	.21	n.a.	n.a.
1956	n.a.	.63	n.a.	n.a.
1958	188	.88	310	157
1959	171	n.a.	314	162
1960	186	n.a.	310	163
1961	216	n.a.	n.a.	160
1962	219	1.33	288	159
1963	n.a.	n.a.	n.a.	n.a.

SOURCES: Index of cash and kind earnings is derived by linking the index numbers given by Miss Nimitz, "The Lean Years," *Problems of Communism*, XIV: 3 (May–June, 1965), 12.

Ruble values are obtained by dividing total cash distributions by the estimates of total man-days worked, given by Nimitz, *op. cit.* (in n. 3), Table 1. Total cash distributions were: 1953: 1.36 billion rubles; 1956: 4.22 billion; 1958: 5.15 billion; and 1962: 6.39 billion. Cf. *Ek. sel'. khoz.* No. 11 (1962) p. 9; A. Nove, *The Soviet Economy* (New York: Praeger, 1961), p. 50 and A. S. Becker, *Soviet National Incomeand Product, 1958–1962: Part I: National Income at Established Prices*, RM–4394–PR (Santa Monica, California: The RAND Corporation, 1965) p. 61.

Total man-days worked per household are obtained by dividing the Nimitz estimates—cf. *op. cit.* (in n. 3) Table 1—by the number of households as reported in the official statistical handbooks.

Man-days worked per collective farm are from Nimitz *op. cit.* (in n. 3), Table 1.

(f) prices on the kolkhoz market and, (g) cash receipts for sales on the kolkhoz market.

Table 6 shows that the trend in earnings per man-day on the communal sector of the collective farms has been upward. Since 1953 earnings per man-day on the collective farms have increased at an average rate of about 9 percent per year and in 1962 stood at about 219 percent of the 1953 level. The trend in both man-days furnished per collective-farm household and per able-bodied worker, however, has been downward. The only significant deviation from this downward trend occurred in 1959, a year in which earnings per man-day fell off. That year, although earnings per man-day fell by about 8 percent from the 1958 level, the number of man-days furnished per able-bodied worker rose by about 4 percent.

Not only did the value of a man-day on the collective farm increase substantially during 1953–1962, but the value of that man-day was further enhanced by its monetization. Cash distributions per man-day rose from 21 kopeks, or 26 percent of the total value of a man-day in cash and kind, in 1953, to 1.33 rubles, or 73 percent of the total value of a man-day in cash and kind in 1962, which is an eleven-fold increase.

The attractiveness of a man-day on the collective farm was further embellished by the speedup which occurred in the timing of its payment. If in the early fifties almost the entire kolkhoz wage fund was paid out only at the end of the year, by the early sixties, as a result of government policies specifically designed to promote this end, 60–70 percent of the total wage fund was paid out during the course of the year in monthly and quarterly advances.[81]

The attractiveness of a man-day on the collective has also been enhanced by shifting its remuneration from a residual to a fixed basis. As of early 1963, more than one-fifth of the kolkhozy of the Union had abandoned the labor-day and instituted fixed and guaranteed rates of pay as is done in the sovkhozes.[82]

With the four factors mentioned in the preceding four paragraphs contributing to the attractiveness of labor on the collective farms it seems that an exceptionally strong case is needed to support the assumptions of rising inputs into the private sector. Such assumptions are legitimate only if it can be shown that the attractiveness of labor on the

[81] V. Karavaev, *Ek. sel'. khoz.*, No. 4 (1963), p. 106.

[82] By early 1963, about 8,000 farms had effected the shift to fixed and guaranteed cash payments. Cf. M. Napolskii, *Ek. sel'. khoz.*, No. 4 (1963), p. 109.

private sector had been enhanced over the period at a faster rate and to a greater extent than the attractiveness of labor on the collective sector. This, however, does not seem to be the case.

Between 1953 and 1963 sown area on the kolkhozniks' private lots fell by almost 30 percent.[83] The significance of this reduction is that, given the high intensity with which the private sector has always been cultivated and the fact that there has been no mechanization or infusions of capital into the private sector, an increase in the number of man-days (or for that matter even a stability in the number of man-days) spent on the private sector would, by virtue of the law of diminishing returns, result in lower returns per man-day on that sector.

This fall in sown area over the period was compounded by a fall in the level of prices on the kolkhoz market. During 1953–1958 (the period during which, according to Miss Nimitz's findings the number of man-days being furnished to the collectives by each able-bodied worker was falling the fastest) the index of prices on the kolkhoz market was falling.[84] As a result of this the kolkhozniks' receipts from sales on the kolkhoz market fell from 3.9 billion rubles (75 percent) of his total cash receipts in 1952 to 2.62 billion rubles (24.1 percent) of his total cash receipts in 1959.[85] The kolkhoznik has in effect (if we accept the Nimitz findings) been working more hours for a smaller reward on the private sector.

[83] From 5.5 million hectares in 1953 to 4.2 million hectares in 1963. Cf. *Narkhoz-1958,* p. 383 and *Narkhoz-1963,* p. 238. Miss Nimitz attempts to justify her assumption of rising inputs into the private sector on the basis of an alleged reduction in the amount of grain distributions to collective farmers in the form of labor-day payments. If this reasoning is correct, we could expect an increase in the sowings of grain in the private sector. The area sown to grain during the period 1950–1963, however declined by 70 percent. Cf. Nimitz, *op. cit.* (in n. 3), Table B–2.

[84] From 100 in 1952 to 92 in 1959; cf. *Vop. ek.,* No. 4 (1965), p. 31.

[85] A. S. Belorukov, L. M. Dobiatkin, *Vestnik Leningradskogo Universiteta,* No. 11 (1961), p. 37.

NAUM M. JASNY

Production Costs and Prices in Soviet Agriculture

The growth of labor productivity is the key to human progress.[1] It is also recognized in the U.S.S.R., at least by D. Laptev, that "all factors affecting the productivity of labor are finding their reflection in the level of production costs." [2]

The production costs of farm products in Soviet agriculture have been high all along the line, for a long time. Production costs of animal products, such as pork, poultry, eggs, and, to a large extent also beef, may even be said to have been excessively high. The prices at which farm products have been procured by the state have actually increased even more in recent years. Most of the costs and prices are now in fact so high as to make a full explanation difficult. The weighted current prices of farm products procured from the kolkhozes in the U.S.S.R. are more than twice as high as in the United States. The Soviet procurement prices of hogs are approximately four times as high as the corresponding producer prices in the United States. The Soviet procurement prices of meat have risen since 1928 about eight times as much as did Soviet steel prices, while during the same period the increase in American farm prices has been substantially smaller than that of steel prices. Taking into account the changes in prices of meat and steel in the U.S.S.R. and the United States, it may be said that since the late twenties Soviet meat prices increased about 12–13 times as much as steel prices.

[1] The present version was revised to include the pertinent data published in the official statistical yearbook of 1964. I received the yearbook at the end of February, 1966, when this essay was about to go to the publisher. The considerable changes and additions in the manuscript were made by the editor of this book to whom I wish to express my sincere gratitude. Thanks are due also to Mrs. Luba O. Richter for comments and editorial help.

Let it be mentioned in passing: It is torture to write for publication at the age of 83.

[2] *Ek. sel'. khoz.*, No. 4 (1965), p. 24. The most recent pronouncement in a similar vein is that of the eminent Soviet mathematician, Kantorovich.

If these calculations are correct, one must conclude that the defects of the Soviet agricultural organization, which are the major cause of those enormous prices and costs, cannot be completely cured. Moreover, not only is the Soviet system of collective farming incurable, but also the Soviet system of state-farming. Production costs on Soviet state farms have been even higher than those in the collectives in recent years, and Soviet state farms emerge as the world's most expensive producers of farm products.

In view of the scarcity of data on prices it is necessary to operate mainly with production costs. The correct methods of calculating costs are not clearly established even for these costs. It also seems impossible to calculate for the U.S.S.R. the weighted prices realized for each farm product. Each of these products usually has three or more different prices: prices realized for the products compulsorily delivered by the collective farms to the state (the so-called procurement prices); similar, prices realized in the same sales by state farms (the so-called delivery prices); and usually much higher prices realized on the collective-farm markets and in the commission trade. It seems impossible to establish all these prices or to obtain appropriate weights necessary to compute average prices.

In view of the shortcomings in the analysis of prices of individual farm products, an attempt is made here to compare the value of farm output as a whole for the U.S.S.R. with the corresponding item for the United States. This comparison will serve as a starting point of our discussion.

One difficulty in this comparison, as well as in the analysis of prices of individual farm products, is the ruble-dollar conversion ratio. The official Soviet rate of exchange equates one dollar to 0.91 rubles. In an earlier work on prices of farm products I equated one dollar with one ruble. The Soviet statistical handbook for 1962 supplied for the first time the value of Soviet national income in both rubles and dollars: 165.1 billion rubles or $198 billion at 1962 prices. This relationship implied a dollar value of only 0.834 rubles.[3]

In view of these uncertainties, I will continue to treat one ruble as equal to one dollar, perhaps without sufficient justification. But it seems that errors caused by this ratio cannot be large.

It is also necessary to state that the composition of officially calculated production costs in Soviet agriculture does not always correspond to the

[3] *Narkhoz-1962*, pp. 74, 482. *Narkhoz-1964* (a source which became available after completion of the study) also shows similar exchange rates for 1964. These come to 0.79 or 0.90 rubles per dollar, depending on the use of either underlying price relationship or the official rate of exchange. Cf. *ibid.*, pp. 89, 577.

usual standards. For example, pension funds are not treated as part of production costs but are obtained from net farm income; the same is true of insurance payments.[4]

These facts should be kept in mind in appraising the discussion that follows. We might also recall that in the U.S.S.R., as well as in the capitalist countries, investment in agriculture is financed from the "surplus" realized by the producers after production costs are covered (defined broadly in the Soviet fashion, that is, without the normal profit margin). In the capitalist countries investments are made voluntarily while under the present arrangements collective farms in the Soviet Union are compelled to invest. Funds allotted for this purpose by the farms are very large, and at times leave little, if anything, for other items which should also be covered by the "surplus" referred to.

THE VALUE OF FARM PRODUCTION AS A WHOLE

According to Stanley Cohn,[5] the share of agriculture in the Soviet gross national product of 1961 was 7.4 times greater than in the United States (31 percent for the U.S.S.R. as opposed to 4.2 percent for the United States). A large part of this excess results from an undue allowance for land rent imputed by Cohn and should not, therefore, be taken too seriously. Another factor responsible for the differences is that the share of farm output in the gross national product (in real terms) is greater in the U.S.S.R. than in the United States. According to the official Soviet statistical handbook for 1962,[6] the Soviet farm output in 1962 amounted to about 75–80 percent of the American farm output, while the Soviet gross national product (according to the same source) came only to "more than 60 percent" of its American equivalent. But the difference in the share of agriculture in the respective national products of the two countries is to a considerable extent a result of the much lower level of agricultural prices (relative to other prices) in the United States as opposed to the Soviet Union.

In terms of 1958 prices, the value of gross farm production in the U.S.S.R. is officially given as 51.3 billion rubles for 1961 and 51.9 billion rubles for 1962. In each of these two years, crop production accounted for 27.6 billion rubles,[7] while the value of output of animals

[4] I. Lukinov, *Ek. sel'. khoz.*, No. 4 (1965), p. 35.

[5] *Soviet Studies*, XVI:3 (January, 1964), 309.

[6] *Narkhoz-1962*, p. 72.

[7] Comments in *ibid.*, pp. 672–673 are not entirely clear on this point, but it appears that the output of natural hay is a part of crop production. It is not clear whether the value of natural pasture is included in the value of gross farm output.

and animal products came to 23.7 and 24.3 billion rubles respectively for 1961 and 1962.[8] In 1961, gross farm production of the United States (redefined in a manner more nearly comparable to the Soviet concept of gross output) came to something more than $40 billion. This figure is composed of (a) the value of crop production: $19.8 billion; (b) cash receipts from farm marketings of animals and animal products: $19.4 billion; (c) the value of farm consumption of animals and animal products: $741.3 million; (d) government payments to farmers: $1.5 billion. The four enumerated items taken together are equal to $41.4 billion.[9]

If the dollar is taken as equivalent to the ruble. the value of gross farm production in the Soviet Union appears to be 25 percent higher than the respective value in the United States. If, instead, we use the rate of exchange implied in official Soviet calculations of national income ($1 = 0.834 rubles), the value of gross farm production in the U.S.S.R. is almost 40 percent above the corresponding figure for the United States.

This great excess of the value of gross farm production of the U.S.S.R. over that of the United States is the result of lower farm prices in the United States, since even according to Soviet calculations the *volume* of Soviet agricultural production in 1959–1963 came only to 70–75 percent of its American equivalent.[10] If we make the necessary adjustment for differences in the volume of output, Soviet prices of farm products appear to have been nearly twice as high in those years than those in the United States.

The price increases which occurred in the U.S.S.R. in 1965 probably raised the over-all, already high, level of Soviet farm prices by a further 20 percent. As compared with the level of American prices, the 1965 price changes amount to an increase of about 50 percent. All in all, these increases probably raised Soviet procurement prices to a level exceeding the farm prices of the United States by more than 100 percent.

The 1965 increases in the level of Soviet procurement prices may well have been inevitable, in spite of the fact that they will make the future needed reductions proportionately larger. But the fact that, for ex-

[8] *Ibid.*, p. 227.

[9] U.S. Department of Agriculture, *Agricultural Statistics 1962* (Washington, D.C.: Government Printing Office, 1962), pp. 534–536, 568. Items (i) and (ii) are a duplication, since farm-produced feed is entered in both of these items. But this duplication is found in all Soviet calculations of gross farm output.

[10] *Narkhoz-1963*, p. 69.

ample, the procurement prices of hogs, which before the recent increases were up to two to three times higher than farm prices abroad, had to be raised substantially is an inescapable testimony that something is basically wrong in the socialized agriculture of the U.S.S.R.

PRICES OF INDIVIDUAL PRODUCTS

Only the prices paid by the state to the collective farms [11] (procurement prices) can be considered here. A special study is needed to analyze the delivery prices paid to state farms. For some products, such as rice, the delivery prices have lately been the same as the procurement prices.[12] But it is quite different with reference to most other products. It is for example difficult to understand the "wisdom" of having state farms of the Krasnodar *krai* turn their oats over to the government at a price of 14.25 rubles per ton (which certainly did not cover production costs), while the same price is being paid to collective farms for the delivery of a ton of such a mediocre product as spring-grain straw (other than spring-wheat straw) in the R.S.F.S.R.[13]

Prices of Crops Other Than Feed—Grain is the relatively cheapest important farm product in the U.S.S.R. Technical crops are in general more expensive than grain. But grains used for groats, that is rice, buckwheat, and millet, carry high prices and may be ranked with technical crops in this respect. Dry legumes, although classified as grains in the U.S.S.R., are also relatively more expensive than the technical crops; the same is true of potatoes.

The average procurement price for grains other than corn (but including dry legumes as well as buckwheat, millet, and rice) came to 65 rubles per ton in 1962.[14] The 40 percent premium paid for durum wheat and high-protein common wheat was probably considered in the calculation of this average. The price paid for corn, which was not included in this average, was higher in 1962 than the average price of all grains (76 as opposed to 65 rubles per ton).[15]

The March, 1965, plenum meeting of the Central Committee of the Communist Party of the Soviet Union raised the procurement (and delivery) prices of wheat, rye, rice, buckwheat, millet, and (in some

[11] For a useful compilation of Soviet prices of farm products see Jerzy F. Karcz, *A Compendium of Soviet Farm Prices in 1961* (Berkeley, Calif.: Institute of International Studies, 1964, mimeographed). Section III of the compendium contains information on price changes since 1961.

[12] *Ibid.*, pp. 6, 8, 81, 83.

[13] *Ibid.*, p. 51.

[14] *The 1965 Eastern European Agricultural Situation*, Economic Research Service, ERS-Foreign-115 (Washington, D.C.: U.S. Department of Agriculture, 1965), p. 8.

[15] *Ibid.*

areas only) of feed barley and oats.[16] It would be difficult to calculate a weighted average price abroad for the same composition of grains as entered the U.S.S.R. weighted average price before March, 1965. And it would be impossible to calculate weighted prices abroad for the Soviet grain "market basket" after the March, 1965, plenum meeting.

According to Khrushchev,[17] the average procurement price of wheat, paid in 1963, came to 75.60 rubles per ton. As already noted, prices paid for durum and high-protein common wheat were considerably higher than this average. The average price paid to collective farms for wheat in 1958 was approximately 81 rubles per ton.[18]

According to Brezhnev's report of March 24, 1965, procurement prices for wheat were raised by about 12 percent, or to 86 rubles, per ton in the better areas of the R.S.F.S.R., to 76 rubles per ton in the Ukraine and in Moldavia, and to 80 rubles per ton in Kazakhstan. But in Belorussia, the Baltic republics, the northwestern areas of the R.S.F.S.R., and the Polesie in the Ukraine the wheat-procurement prices were raised by more than 50 percent, namely to 130 rubles per ton. The newly established procurement prices of wheat may be compared with the following prices of wheat abroad in 1960–1962 (U.S. dollars per metric ton):[19]

Argentina, f.o.b. Buenos Aires	43
Australia, for domestic consumption, f.o.b. station of origin	65
Canada, No. 1 Northern, f.o.b. Fort William–Port Arthur	66
U.S., producer price	68
European ports, c.i.f., from Argentina	70
European ports, c.i.f., from Australia	70
France, domestic, fair quality	88
United Kingdom, producer price	74
Netherlands, producer price	83

If the value of a dollar is the same as that of a ruble, the data in the tabulation indicate that even before the 1965 price increases the level of Soviet farm prices for wheat was moderately high. In fact, the Soviet

[16] *Pravda*, March 27, 1965, and similar decrees published in the central press.

[17] *Ibid.*, March 7, 1964.

[18] *Spravochnik bukhgaltera kolkhoza* (Moscow: 1961), pp. 338–339. This may have been the price for standard-quality wheat.

[19] Food and Agriculture Organization of the United Nations, *Production Yearbook 1963* (Rome: Food and Agriculture Organization of the United Nations, 1964), pp. 294 ff.

procurement price for wheat was about double that of Argentina, if we deduct from the latter the cost of transportation and handling to Buenos Aires. The Soviet price was about one-third higher than the Canadian, when the latter is similarly adjusted for transportation and handling charges to the respective ports. But the Soviet procurement price was only about 10 percent higher than the American price and was not even as high as the price in the European importing countries. After the March, 1965, increase, however, the procurement price of wheat in the expensive areas of the U.S.S.R. became about 50 percent higher than the wheat prices in European importing countries. If we assume instead a lower ruble-dollar ratio, the disparity of Soviet wheat prices, relative to those abroad, becomes correspondingly larger. The same applies to other farm products, of course.

The newly established procurement prices for rye are only a little lower than those for wheat on the average.[20] The difference between wheat and rye prices in the U.S.S.R. is smaller than in the other countries, and thus the excess of Soviet procurement prices for rye over the prices paid in other rye-growing countries is also larger than in the case of wheat.

Buckwheat is a minor crop, but it merits attention here because trends in buckwheat prices and buckwheat production reveal the chaotic state of Soviet agricultural organization with particular force. In 1925/26 and 1927/28 and on the average, the Soviet farm price for buckwheat was 5.45 rubles per centner, as compared with the then effective prices for wheat and rye of 6.55 and 5.18 rubles per centner respectively.[21] Before March, 1965, collective farms received 200 rubles per ton of buckwheat, or more than twice as much as they were paid for a ton of wheat or rye. In spite of these relatively high prices, acreage under buckwheat declined drastically in recent years,[22] and its output remained far below the level of domestic requirements. The Brezhnev government then decided to increase the price paid for buckwheat to collectives by 50 percent (or to 300 rubles per ton); the new level of buckwheat prices is more than three times as high as that of the new prices for wheat.

A similar situation prevails with respect to millet. In the nineteen

[20] U.S. Department of Agriculture, *Soviet Agriculture Today: Report of 1963 Agriculture Exchange Delegation,* Foreign Agricultural Economic Report No. 13 (Washington, D.C.: U.S. Department of Agriculture, December, 1963), p. 52.

[21] *Kon. tsifry-1929/30,* p. 581.

[22] The acreage under buckwheat was 3 million hectares in 1950 and 2.7 million hectares in 1957. By 1964 it declined to 1.4 million hectares. Cf. *Pos. ploshch.,* I, 6–7 and *Narkhoz-1964,* p. 284.

twenties, millet was the cheapest grain.[23] Currently, the procurement prices of better grades of millet are 110 rubles per ton (as against 80 rubles per ton paid previously). Thus, better grades of millet are now the third most expensive grain (following buckwheat and rice). Thus millet, which was grown extensively in the south Russian steppes already some 2,500 years ago, proves to be too delicate a crop to be grown at a sensible price by the socialized agriculture of the U.S.S.R.[24]

The price of rice was raised recently to the same level as that of buckwheat. The price of feed barley was raised to 90 rubles per ton and that of oats to 75 rubles, but these increases were limited to the less favorable areas of the northwestern R.S.F.S.R., the Polesie regions of the Ukraine, Belorussia, and the Baltic States.

The average procurement price paid by the state to collective farms for potatoes was 47 rubles per ton until 1963 exclusive. Since then, the prices of potatoes are (rubles per ton):

Large, choice, September–December	100
Large, choice, January–August	120
Ordinary, food and industrial:	
September–December	60
January–August	80
Average	72

[23] *Kon. tsifry-1929/30,* p. 581.

[24] The inability of Soviet socialized agriculture to solve even the simplest tasks is not limited to the failure to produce the needed quantities of buckwheat and millet. Since 1959 a huge premium of 40 percent is paid in the U.S.S.R. for the delivery of hard wheat (known in the U.S.S.R. as "strong") and of durum wheat (known in the U.S.S.R. as "hard" wheat). Hard spring wheat was developed in the early years of the nineteenth century from the so-called RED FIVE variety originating in the former Saratov *guberniia* (now *oblast'* of the same name). In the United States, durum wheat and the successors of RED FIVE—long since replaced by better varieties—command a premium of 10 to 20 percent. Even smaller premiums are paid for these wheats on the world market. Cf. U.S. Department of Agriculture, *Agricultural Statistics 1963* (Washington, D.C.: Government Printing Office, 1963), p. 15.

A. Stepanov, *Ek. sel'. khoz.,* No. 2 (1965), pp. 21–22 provides the following data for Saratov *oblast',* the home of the famous Red Five. In 1964, 1,889,000 hectares were sown to wheat, of which 161,000 was hard spring wheat, and 713,000 durum wheat. The procurement plan called for the delivery of 175,000 tons of hard spring and 500,000 tons of durum wheat. Actually, only 500 tons of hard spring wheat and 390,100 tons of durum wheat were delivered. The best year for the procurement of hard spring wheat so far was 1962, when 26,000 tons were sold to the state.

Many other such phenomena can be cited. Rye is fostered in the post-Khrushchev era, although rye is a crop of the past. See N. Jasny, *Die Zukunft des Roggens* (Berlin: 1930).

The average of the prices is about double the average price of potatoes in other countries with large potato outputs.[25]

Until 1963, the procurement price of sugar beets averaged 23 rubles per ton; it was then raised to 28.70 rubles per ton. This is almost double the price of sugar beets in European countries with a large output of this crop. For purposes of comparison, we list the following prices of sugar beets (U.S. dollars per ton): [26]

Belgium	13.30
Netherlands	13.30
France	14.30
Italy	14.00
West Germany	18.00

Even in the United States (where labor is considerably scarcer than in the Soviet Union) the price of this labor-intensive crop came only to $16.70 per ton in 1960–1962.

The average production cost of sugar beets in the U.S.S.R. was 16 rubles per ton in 1962. In western Europe, the same costs are only about 75 percent of this amount. For the late fifties, a German professional journal has listed them as follows (U.S. dollars per ton): [27]

Country	Prices	Production costs	
		Direct	Total
West Germany	17.50	8.50	13.00
Belgium	11.40	9.00	13.50
France	14.80	8.60	13.00
Netherlands	15.70	8.40	12.60
Switzerland	18.60	9.20	14.00

[25] In 1959–1961 (average), potato prices in U.S. dollars per ton were: United States—41; West Germany—36; Denmark—33; Netherlands—36. Cf. Food and Agriculture Organization of the United Nations, *op. cit.* (in n. 19), p. 308.

[26] The Soviet prices are from *Ek. sel'. khoz.*, No. 4 (1965), p. 5 and from *Pravda,* March 7, 1964. In addition to the price paid, some quantities of sugar are sold at privileged prices to collective farmers participating in sugar-beet production. Cf. Karcz, *op. cit.* (in n. 11), p. 12. Other prices are averages for 1960–1962 taken from the Food and Agriculture Organization of the United Nations, *op. cit.* (in n. 19), p. 306.

[27] Soviet costs are from *Narkhoz-1962,* p. 338 (calculated with labor charged at actual cost to farms). Western European costs are from *Landbauforschung,* No. 4 (1960), p. 95 recalculated by the writer to U.S. dollars. Data on direct costs are based on detailed calculations, those for indirect costs are more crude. They include the land tax.

Soviet cotton is also expensive, but more moderately so. Until 1963, the average procurement price paid by the state to collective farms was 341 rubles per ton of *seed* cotton. Since 1963, the average price has been 382 rubles. The average producer price for *lint* cotton in the United States in 1960–1962 was $700 per ton, or about two-thirds of the average Soviet price when the latter is recalculated to a comparable basis.[28] The price of short-staple lint cotton in India was $496.7 per ton, while various varieties of Egyptian long-staple cotton sold for $816.7 to 916.7 per ton.

The relatively highest procurement price paid for a crop (relative to other crops within the U.S.S.R. and also probably relative to prices in foreign countries) is that paid in the Soviet Union for sunflower seed. Although the cost of production of sunflower seed is less than that of cereals under comparable conditions,[29] the procurement price for the former is double that of the latter (also under comparable conditions). According to Khrushchev, the 1963 procurement price of sunflower seed was 181 rubles per ton. In the United States, the average producer price of soybeans in 1960–1962 was less than half as much, or $84.80 per ton.[30]

For all crops sold, whether for food or industrial uses, the procurement prices paid in the U.S.S.R. around 1963 exceeded comparable foreign prices by more than 50 percent. After the price increases introduced in March, 1965, the weighted Soviet procurement price for crops may have become double that effective abroad. These price relationships would be still less favorable to the U.S.S.R. if we used a lower ruble-dollar ratio in our comparisons.

The high procurement prices in the U.S.S.R. are rendered necessary by high production costs in Soviet collective farms. For 1962, a favorable harvest year, production crops for these farms have been given in an official source (rubles per ton): [31]

[28] Actually, the excess of Soviet prices is somewhat less than indicated here because of smaller proportion of long-staple fibers in the United States.

[29] Production costs of sunflower seed for the U.S.S.R. come to 30 rubles per ton as opposed to 37 rubles per ton for grain. Cf. *Narkhoz-1962,* pp. 338–339. In 1964, the relevant figures were 30 and 44 rubles per ton respectively. Cf. *Narkhoz-1964,* p. 396.

[30] U.S. Department of Agriculture, *op. cit.* (in n. 24), p. 134. In the U.S.S.R. soybeans are grown only in the Far East, and their procurement price is 260 rubles per ton, or three times as much as the U.S. price.

[31] *Narkhoz-1962,* pp. 338–339. Comparable cost data for 1964 are as follows: grain (excluding corn)—44; sugar beets—17; potatoes—35; sunflower seed—30; seed cotton—281 (all in rubles per ton). Cf. *Narkhoz-1964,* pp. 396–397.

Grain (excluding corn)	37
Sugar beets	16
Potatoes	38
Sunflower seed	30
Seed cotton	224

Grain and potatoes and possibly some other crops to which these costs refer apparently include the weight of excessive impurities or moisture.

The production cost of corn has been concealed as long as corn was the queen of the fields. Corn is harvested in three forms: as grain, as earcorn harvested by machine, and by hand. Only about 10 percent of all corn was harvested as grain. The cost of harvesting is not high, but the average crop being harvested with a high water content results in a high breakage of the kernels. The harvesting costs of corn are high, when it is harvested by machine as earcorn and even higher if it is harvested as earcorn by hand.[32]

To compare Soviet production costs of wheat with the cost of producing wheat, say, in Canada, the Soviet figure for grain quoted above would have to be raised to account for the weight of impurities and excess moisture present in the Soviet grain. Similarly, the Canadian wheat prices quoted in our first list would have to be lowered to account for (a) the difference between the price of No. 1 Northern wheat and that of average-grade wheat, (b) freight and handling charges to Fort William–Port Arthur, and (c) the profit and land rent, which are, of course, included in the Canadian prices. When all these elements are taken into account, it appears that production costs of Canadian wheat are likely to be substantially lower than those of producing comparable wheat in the U.S.S.R.

Production costs of reasonably clean potatoes in the Soviet collective farms are unlikely to be much less than 50 rubles per ton. This is about as much as the full price of potatoes in many countries, including land rent and profit.

Production costs of Soviet sugar beets are about equal to their full price in many countries with large production of this crop, where land rent represents a substantial component of the price. P. Rintelen and H. Neumann of the Institut für Wirtschaftslehre des Landbaues, Weihenstephan, Germany, show the following income figures (in German marks per hectare) for Lower Saxony: [33]

[32] G. Shefer, *Ek. sel'. khoz.*, No. 5 (1965), pp. 63–68.
[33] *Zucker*, October 15, 1959, p. 15.

Type of farm	Gross income	Net income
Large	3,678–3,762	1,478–1,562
Small	4,200–5,145	1,790–2,735

Hence, even for the less profitable larger farms, net income accounts for about 40 percent of gross income. On small farms, the return from by-products (tops and stems) alone is said to exceed the total production costs (that is, material expenses and labor).

Price of Crops Used For Feed—Soviet accounting practices distinguish between the value of feed crops sold and that of the same crops used on the farm. The former are valued at realized prices while the latter are appraised at the production cost on the farm. In the United States, feed is presumably valued in all calculations at prices which could be obtained for it on the market. In spite of these differences in valuation practices, the cost of feed appears to be higher in the U.S.S.R. than in the United States.

As already noted, the officially computed production costs of all grains other than corn in Soviet collective farms were 37 rubles per ton in 1962. The figure may possibly be used also for those grains other than corn which are grown as feed to be used on the farm. The production cost of corn is substantially higher than the average of the other feed grains, and one may estimate the average cost of producing all feed grains (including corn) at something more than 40 rubles per ton.

The producer price of corn in the United States was $43 per ton in 1960–1962, or somewhat more than the production costs of feed grains grown in the U.S.S.R. Part of the feed grains fed in the U.S.S.R. are purchased by the farms from the state at high prices. According to A. Soroka, purchased feed grains accounted for 15 percent of total grain fed to livestock on the collective farms and for 36 percent of all grain so fed on state farms. For this feed, farms paid prices exceeding their own production costs by 50 to 100 percent. Hence, total feed costs for Soviet farms must be greater than those of American farms.[34]

In the United States, or in the other free countries, it would make little sense for farms to use in large quantities feed that was more expensive than feed grains, except when such action is dictated by quality considerations. But in the U.S.S.R., according to Soroka, the cost of feed other than grain exceeded in 1960 the costs of producing

[34] *Ek. sel'. khoz.*, No. 6 (1962), p. 24. Soroka's prices are roughly in agreement with prices paid to collective farms. Percentages of purchased feed given in *Vest. stat.* No. 12 (1964), p. 14, are higher than those quoted in the text.

grain in the R.S.F.S.R. and in the Ukraine by 74 percent. The same author gives the following data on the cost of feed in the important Soviet republics, presumably for 1960 (rubles per ton of feed units): [35]

Republic	Collective farms	State farms
R.S.F.S.R.	55	68
Ukraine	43	47
Belorussia	83	106
Kazakhstan	38	56
Estonia	68	99

The average feeding value of a ton of feed units is 15–20 percent below that of a ton of average feed grain. When an adjustment for this factor is made, the cost of feed for hogs in the R.S.F.S.R. turns out to be more than 50 percent greater than the producer price for corn in the United States.

There is no feed in the U.S.S.R. which can be considered as cheap. Soviet silage is expensive, and when the green mass going into it does not reach the milk stage, it is definitely very expensive.

According to Silin and Pravdin, the average collective-farm production costs of feed for beef cattle, cows, and hogs in 1960–1962 was 40.4 rubles per ton of feed units and 31.7 rubles per ton of silage. As already noted, the nutritive value of feed units is less than that of an equivalent weight unit of feed grains. Moreover, storage losses in silage are much greater than storage losses for grain, while it is also likely that the feeding value of a unit of silage is exaggerated in Soviet calculations. All in all, the production costs of silage for feed are higher than those of grain. In view of low yields, hay is not cheap in the U.S.S.R. either, though it may be a little cheaper than grain.[36]

Khrushchev showed enthusiasm for the use of sugar beets as feed, but it was soon recognized that sugar beets are a very expensive form of feed. According to the authors just cited, the cost of a feed unit of sugar beets in 1960 came to 60.2 rubles per ton. The same study also shows some data on the costs of milk used to feed young cattle and on the

[35] *Ek. sel'. khoz.*, No. 6 (1962), p. 23.

[36] *Vest. stat.*, No. 12 (1964), p. 14. The authors quote a price of 40.4 rubles per ton of feed which is not easily reconciled with Soroka's data cited earlier. Presumably they do not include all types of feed. Production cost of hay per ton of feed units, and used to feed cattle and hogs in 1960–1962, is given in the same source as 32.7 rubles per ton (as opposed to 40.4 rubles per ton for the average ton of feed units).

amounts so used, but the reliability of this information seems to be questionable. On the collective farms, milk fed to young cattle is said to amount to 5.4 percent of total feed unit value of rations, but milk accounts for 45 percent of the total *cost* of the rations. For state farms, the corresponding figures are 3 and 27 percent.[37] In any case, however, milk is very expensive in the U.S.S.R. and a great deal of it is used for feeding young animals.

The quality of Soviet feed leaves much to be desired, and this is also true of mature feed grains, especially of corn. The quality of hay is much more adversely affected by poor organization of farm work than is the quality of feed grains. The quality of a large part of silage is very poor, and cattle and hogs suffer from this—cattle more so. When these quality differentials are taken into account, the cost of feed in the U.S.S.R. is presumably higher than the official data show. Soroka says that the value of feed used for hogs is to account for more than one-half of the total cost of raising hogs. Hence, the high feed costs are important but not the decisive factor in the formation of meat costs. But this topic cannot be discussed here in detail.[38]

Prices of Livestock and Livestock Products—As was shown above, the average procurement prices of most crops are considerably higher than their production costs.[39] By contrast, the corresponding prices of animal products hardly ever exceed production costs. For some products, and in many areas, they were indeed lower even after the drastic (35 percent) increase in the procurement prices of meat enacted on June 1, 1962. The substantial additional increase in the prices of animal products in March, 1965, improved the situation.

While the procurement prices of animal products, but especially those of meat, had been recognized as being too low before the March, 1965, increases, the prevailing prices were nevertheless considerably higher than those effective abroad for comparable products. This is shown by data assembled in Table 1.

While precise comparisons are precluded by the nature of these data,

[37] *Ibid.*, pp. 12, 14. For a statement that sugar beets are used for this purpose and that they are very expensive, see Lemeshev's article in *Plan. khoz.*, No. 1 (1964), p. 28.

[38] This is obvious from the fact that Estonia, one of the highest-cost feed producers, is among the lowest-cost producers of pork. On the other hand, Kzakhstan with low feed costs (suspiciously low as quoted in the source) is among the most expensive pork producers. Cf. *Ek. sel'. khoz.*, No. 6 (1962), p. 21.

[39] Production costs of grain in the northern and northwestern areas of European Russia are, however, extremely high and exceeded procurement prices before the March, 1965, price increases.

TABLE 1

PRICES OF ANIMALS AND ANIMAL PRODUCTS, U.S.S.R. AND OTHER SELECTED COUNTRIES
(in U.S. dollars per ton; rubles for U.S.S.R.)

Country	Cattle (live)	Hogs (live)	Hogs (slaughtered)	Chickens (live)	Milk	Eggs
U.S. (average producer price)	455	354	n.a.	237 [a]–340 [b]	94.5	52.3 [c]
Canada, Toronto	513	n.a.	573	383 [d]	108.5	74.9
Argentina, export	169	231 [e]	n.a.	n.a.	n.a.	36.0
Netherlands	450	463 [f]	n.a.	n.a.	78.5 [g]	44.8
West Germany	550	626 [h]	n.a.	630	89.8 [g]	66.3 [i]
Denmark	400	n.a.	563 [j]	400 [k]	53.5 [g]	44.2 [g]
U.S.S.R., procurement price, 1964	799	980	n.a.	1,322	129.0	70.0 [l]
U.S.S.R., procurement price, April 1965	1,309 [m]	1,294 [m]	n.a.	n.a. [n]	155.0 [o]	n.a. [n]

[a] Farm chickens; [b] Commercial broilers; [c] Extra large, Chicago; [d] 3 to 4 lbs. per bird; [e] Hogs of 140 kilograms per animal, Buenos Aires; [f] Meat hogs, leading markets; [g] Producer price; [h] Well-fleshed, 100–119.5 kilograms per hog, 24 markets; [i] Class B, 55–60 grams per unit; [j] Meat hogs, 60–70 kilograms live weight, price at slaughter houses; [k] Slaughtered weight; [l] Price per thousand eggs; [m] *Ek. sel'. khoz.* No. 6 (1965), p. 10; [n] No increase in this price has been announced so far; [o] Prices raised by 22 percent on the average on Jan 1, 1965. In April, 1965, the standard butter fat content for milk was reduced.

SOURCES: Data for countries other than the U.S.S.R. are from Food and Agriculture Organization of the United Nations *Production Yearbook 1963* (Rome: Food and Agriculture Organization of the United Nations, 1964), converted from local currency units. The U.S.S.R. procurement prices are those paid to collective farms. The data are from various sources, such as reports by Khrushchev or are implied in the article by V. Venzher in *Ek. sel'. khoz.*, No. 9, 1962. The 1965 procurement prices are from Brezhnev's report as printed in *Pravda*, March 27, 1965, or similar sources.

it is certain that even before March, 1965, the American farmer was supplying nearly 2.5 times the amount of meat per capita of American population (and for considerably less money) than the socialized agriculture of the U.S.S.R. was able to deliver to the Soviet consumer. In 1962, per-capita consumption of meat in the United States was equal to 201.1 pounds of all meats excluding lard; including lard, the figure is 212 pounds or 96 kilograms. The official Soviet data for 1962 show a meat output of 9.46 million tons (of carcass weight), but this must be adjusted downward because all official Soviet meat series include (while the American counterparts exclude) offal. With this adjustment, the total Soviet meat production amounts to at most 8.6 million tons, yielding a per-capita consumption of about 40 kilograms a year. Data in Table 1 as well as the subsequent comments show that (after the 1965 price increases) no category of meat would be sold in the United States for more than 40 percent of the Soviet procurement price.

Let us now turn to the prices of individual animal products. Argentina, with its particularly low prices of animal products may as well be ignored. The procurement prices of hogs in the U.S.S.R. were (until the recent increase) almost three times as high as the farm prices in the United States, Canada, and Denmark. Even in West Germany, with its high import duties on grains and other farm products, the prices of hogs were not much more than half as high as the Soviet procurement prices of 1963/64. After March, 1965, the procurement price of "live weight" hogs in the U.S.S.R. is four times or more the price paid to the producer in the United States. Per-capita consumption of pork in the United States in 1962 was about twice that in the U.S.S.R. Hence, after consuming twice as much pork for less money, the American consumer is free to use the remainder of the money he would have to spend on pork in the U.S.S.R. for covering other consumer needs.

The per-capita consumption of poultry in the United States is about five times that in the Soviet Union.[40] Before the increases, the price of chicken in the U.S.S.R. was about five times as high as the American price for broilers (farm chickens, of course, are even less expensive). We thus have a five-fold per-capita consumption for about the same outlay.

The producer price of beef cattle in the United States exceeded that of

[40] The per capita consumption of chickens and turkeys in the United States in 1962 was 16.8 kilograms; cf. U.S. Department of Agriculture, *op. cit.* (in n. 24), pp. 418, 425. The Soviet output of poultry in 1962 came to 800,000 tons or to 3.6 kilograms per capita. By 1964 output declined to 600,000 tons or 2.6 kilograms per capita. Cf. *Narkhoz-1962*, p. 238 and *Narkhoz-1964*, p. 251.

hogs in 1961 by slightly more than 20 percent (in spite of a greater yield of meat from hogs). Even then, however, the American producer price of beef cattle was not half as high as the Soviet procurement price before the latest price changes; thereafter, of course, it has been much less than half this price. Per-capita consumption of beef in the United States is about 2.5 times that in the U.S.S.R.; thus, the value of the much greater per-capita consumption in the United States may be somewhat larger than the value of (the smaller) Soviet per-capita consumption. The advantage of the American consumer is nevertheless large, and this was also the case even before the March, 1965, increases in Soviet procurement prices for cattle.

The procurement price of wool in the Soviet Union is about double the price of wool realized in the world markets.[41]

Among animal products, the smallest difference between Soviet procurement prices and world market prices is that encountered in milk. Even there, however, the Soviet procurement price is about one-third greater than the producer price in the United States, which is the highest among all non-Soviet milk prices shown in Table 1. Soviet prices are double those effective in Denmark. Reference has been made, of course, to Soviet prices of milk effective before the January 1, 1965, increases in milk prices and before the enactment of measures which reduce the standard butterfat content of Soviet milk (April, 1965).

A kilogram of eggs contains about 17 units of average size. Under the circumstances, the procurement price of eggs in the U.S.S.R. (which is far below their production cost) is about 50 percent higher than the price of eggs in Denmark.[42]

MAJOR FACTORS IN ANIMAL HUSBANDRY

Despite my mistrust in the conditions of livestock-raising in the U.S.S.R., Soroka's statement to the effect that "total losses from death of hogs in 1960 amounted to 16 percent of production costs" came as a surprise.[43]

Size of Herds and Production of Animal Products.—An important adverse factor in Soviet animal husbandry is the large size of the herds

[41] See my "The Failure of Soviet Animal Industry—II," *Soviet Studies,* XV:3 (January, 1964), 304.

[42] We abstract from the fact that Danish, Dutch, Swedish, and some other eggs are larger and that the number of these eggs per kilogram is correspondingly smaller.

[43] *Ek. sel'. khoz.,* No. 6 (1962), p. 22.

TABLE 2

SIZE OF HERDS AND OUTPUT OF ANIMAL PRODUCTS, U.S.S.R. AND U.S., 1962

Number or output	Unit of measurement	U.S.S.R.		U.S.	
		Herds [a]	Output	Herds [a]	Output
Cattle	million heads	82.1–87.0		100.0–103.8	
Meat, live weight	million tons		6.6 [b]		13.6
Milk, per cow	kilograms		1.710		3,340
Hogs	million heads	66.7–70.0		57.0–58.7	
Meat, live weight	million tons		6.6 [b]		9.3
Sheep and goats	million heads	137.5–139.7		31.3–30.2	
Meat, live weight	million tons		1.6 [b]		0.7
Chicken [c]	million heads	542.6–550.7		368.5 [d]	
Meat, live weight	million tons		1.07 [b]		3.7 [e]
Eggs, hen	billion		30.1		

[a] The lower figure refers to January 1, 1962, the higher figure to January 1, 1963; [b] including fat and offal; [c] or poultry; [d] January, 1962; [e] all poultry slaughtered under Federal inspection, including condemned (0.22 percent of inspected tonnage).

SOURCES: Data for the U.S.S.R. are from *Narkhoz-1962*, pp. 303–304, 309, 317. Distribution of meat output other than pork is an estimate. Data for the U.S. are from U.S. Department of Agriculture, *Agricultural Statistics 1963* (Washington, D.C.: Government Printing Office, 1963), pp. 310, 315, 325, 329, 335, 340, 381, 409, 419, 427.

relative to meat output. To a considerable extent, targets for the former variable have continued to be imposed on the farms by higher authorities.

According to Table 2, the United States produces 50 percent more pork than the U.S.S.R., although the size of its hog herd is about 15 percent smaller. (The difference is actually greater, because Soviet output data include offal, omitted from American figures.) The relationship between the size of the herds and the meat output is even greater for cattle and particularly so for sheep and goats. The U.S.S.R. has 4.5 times as many sheep and goats, but produces only about twice as much mutton and goat meat. The Soviet output of milk per cow is almost exactly half that of the American, but the superiority of American agriculture shows clearest in the productivity of chickens. With two-thirds as many chickens as in the U.S.S.R., the United States is producing four times as much poultry meat and twice as many eggs.

Table 3 shows the ratio of hog numbers (1960/61) to the 1961 pork output for most important hog-raising countries of the world. Intensive hog-raising returns about one ton of (slaughter weight) pork for every 10 hogs in the herd. This ratio is found in virtually all countries of central and northern Europe (with the exception of Denmark where the explanation is to be sought in the small size of the animal at the time of slaughter). Of all socialist countries, the same relationship is to be found only in East Germany, and in Poland (where the bulk of land remains in the hands of individual peasants). In all other Eastern European countries, the output of pork in relation to the herds is much smaller.

After making the necessary correction for the inclusion of offal in official Soviet output data we find that the production of pork in the U.S.S.R. comes to less than 0.5 tons of (slaughter weight) meat per each 10 hogs in the herd. Two other East European countries with a socialized organization of agriculture for which data are available—Czechoslovakia and Hungary—were characterized by even smaller output relative to the size of the herd.[44]

The Soviet figure just referred to applies to the U.S.S.R. as a whole. When the data are broken down between the socialist and the private sector, the resulting relationships are particularly striking: [45]

[44] Data for these countries do not include offal and probably lard neither.

[45] Cf. *Narkhoz-1962*, pp. 303, 309 and *Narkhoz-1963*, pp. 312, 314, as well as Carl Zoerb, "The Pig Gap," *Studies of the Soviet Union*, No. 3 (1964), pp. 159–163.

Year (January)	Socialized sector Herd (million head)	Output of pork (million tons)	Private sector Herd (million head)	Output of pork (million tons)
1960	39.5	1.8	13.9	1.5
1961	43.2	1.9	15.4	1.8
1962	49.4	2.1	17.3	1.9
1963	53.9	2.4	16.1	1.9
1964	27.7	n.a.	13.2	n.a.

TABLE 3

HOG HERDS AND SLAUGHTERINGS, SELECTED COUNTRIES, 1960/61 OR 1961

(herds in thousand heads; slaughterings in thousand tons, slaughter weight)

Country	Herds	Domestic slaugh-terings	Total slaugh-terings [a]
U.S.S.R.	58,674	3,700 [b]	n.a.
Finland	484	n.a.	61
Poland	13,434	1,250	1,319
East Germany	8,316	748 [c]	n.a.
West Germany	15,776	1,652	n.a.
Denmark	7,095	614	641
Sweden	2,034	207	216
Norway	534	n.a.	56 [d]
Netherlands	2,860	334	337
Belgium	1,772	236	246
Great Briitan	6,043	695	694
Ireland	1,056	95 [d]	95 [d]
France	8,603	n.a.	1,167
Italy	4,335	n.a.	235
Austria	2,990	237	277
Czechoslovakia	5,962	483	n.a.
Hungary	5,921	276	280
Rumania	4,300	n.a.	n.a.
Bulgaria	2,553	141	150
Yugoslavia	5,818	275 [b]	276
United States	55,443	5,176	5,176
Canada	5,528	470	470

[a] Includes slaughterings of imported animals; [b] too high because part of the offal is included; [c] 1958; [d] 1960.

SOURCE: F. A. O. *Production Yearbook 1962*, pp. 167, and 188–194.

Hog-raising in the private sector, in spite of its relatively small size of herds per enterprise, reveals an output to animal ratio which exceeds one ton of pork per 10 hogs.[46] The private sector of Soviet agriculture thus falls into the same category as the farmers of Western European and other capitalist countries. Hog-raising in the socialized sector is correspondingly less efficient or less intensive than that of the U.S.S.R. as a whole. For that sector, the relationship between meat production and the size of herds is indeed very low and about the same as that prevailing in Czechoslovakia and Hungary.

Maintenance of large herds relative to the output of animal products is reflected in high production costs of animal products. The costs of feed, labor, and housing are boosted in proportion to the size of the herds, but only maintenance, not weight-gaining or milk-producing feed, must be counted. The great length of time needed to bring the animals to maturity may be the decisive factor which accounts for the high costs in the Soviet animal-raising industry. Another factor which may be worthwhile discussing is that of breeds.

Breed Cattle—Here, we are quoting only the evidence on the proportion of beef breeds of cattle which struck me as particularly significant. According to a volume written by *Gosplan* experts on "ways to create abundance of farm products" in 1963, Russian livestock herds before the revolution included 16 to 17 million heads of beef breed cattle. Since then, beef breed cattle has virtually disappeared, since there are at most 2 million heads of such cattle in the U.S.S.R. at present. According to the same source, beef breed cattle amounts to more than 50 percent of total beef cattle in the United States.[47] How long will it take to regain the more favorable situation that existed in the backward tsarist Russia before the revolution?

More on Feed—It may not be out of place to refer again to the high figures on the cost of feed for hogs listed above. Only in Belorussia were the costs of a unit of feed used on farms lower than local costs of producing feed grains.

Excessively large herds lead to a deficiency of feed. Still, more feed is used in the U.S.S.R. than would be needed with a proper organization of feeding. According to two Soviet experts, "the thing involved is not only the deficiency of feed; it is necessary to note the poor organization of feeding in the majority of enterprises." [48] The same source also reports

[46] One cannot be certain of the correctness of data on livestock holdings and output in the private sector, but there is no reason to assume that a lower ratio is in order for this sector than that indicated by official data.

[47] *Puti sozdaniia izobil'ia sel'skokhoziaistvennykh produktov* (Moscow: 1963), p. 190.

[48] *Vest. stat.*, No. 12 (1964), p. 15.

that while the number of cows rose by 30 percent between 1959 and 1962, the utilization of feed increased by only 2 percent. Yet, 172 kilograms of feed units (138 kilograms if we exclude the use of pasture) were still used to produce 100 kilograms of milk, although, with rational use of feed, only 1.1 to 1.3 kilograms of feed are needed to produce a kilogram of milk.

A further reason for the high cost of feed in the U.S.S.R. is the improper composition of the rations. These do not contain as much protein on the average as is required. While Soviet leaders often talked of overtaking the United States in all branches of the economy, and while much progress was made in this direction in some branches, the protein content in Soviet feed rations actually declined in recent years. It should also be noted that the resulting increase in the feed-versus-output ratio is necessarily reflected in higher than necessary labor inputs. Unfortunately, it is not possible to make detailed estimates.

LABOR

Soviet farms may properly be called giants even when they are compared with farms in the United States or Canada. Yet, until recently, the size of farms seemed much too small to Soviet officials in position of power, and the average size of farms had been rapidly increasing.

One would expect that large farms would operate at least as efficiently as small ones, and the amount of labor employed per unit of product would tend to reflect this efficiency. As a result of the great inefficiency of the socialized farming, the amounts of labor needed to produce a unit of various farm products in the U.S.S.R. are immense.

According to Silin, the 1960 input of labor on collective farms alone was equal to 5.3 billion person-days (the term "person-day" rather than man-day is used to indicate that no attempt was made to convert a day of woman or child labor to their man-day equivalent). The same source also lists the share of labor in total production costs as follows (percent of total cost):[49]

Product	Total labor	Direct labor
All farm products	47	36
Crops	54	41
Livestock and livestock products	41	31

Silin, furthermore, states that "if it is considered that the input of labor also represents about 50 percent of total production costs, the share of

[49] *Ek. sel'. khoz.,* No. 6 (1962), p. 40.

total labor that may be imputed to the output of farm products on collective farms amounts to 62–65 percent of total production costs." Silin draws the conclusion that a decline in the labor input in Soviet agriculture represents the principal reserve for reducing production costs of Soviet farm products.

In 1960, the input of labor in American agriculture was equal to 9,974 million man-hours. Farm wages (excluding room and board) amounted to $0.97 per hour. Hence, the total labor cost in farming was about $10 billion. Since the value of gross farm output in the United States is roughly $40 billion, the cost of labor amounts to about one-quarter of this total. This, then, is half, or less, of the Soviet counterpart.

The great differences in the magnitude of the labor input between the U.S.S.R. and the United States are shown in greater detail in Table 4, which lists data for the Soviet Union in terms of "person-days" and those for the United States in terms of "man-hours."

As would be expected, fewer man-hours are used in the production of a unit of meat in the United States than are person-days in the U.S.S.R. Even where the number of *hours* in the United States is greater than the number of *days* in the Soviet Union, the difference in labor inputs per unit of product is at least large and frequently very large. Obviously, the use of labor on Soviet collective farms is especially large.

Official Soviet sources emphasize that the simple comparison of the official data on the use of labor measured in terms of hours or days in the U.S.S.R. and the United States tend to exaggerate the resulting difference. The Soviet Central Statistical Office made a special comparison between labor inputs for the United States in 1956 and the Soviet Union for 1956/57 after performing a number of adjustments and recalculating labor inputs to terms of units of male labor. The resulting ratios of Soviet to American labor inputs per unit of product are as follows: [50]

Product	Collective farms	State farms
Grains	7.3	1.8
Potatoes	5.1	4.2
Sugar beets	6.2	4.2
Seed cotton	2.3	1.6
Milk	3.1	2.1
Cattle (live weight)	14.2	6.6
Hogs (live weight)	16.3	6.8

[50] *Sel'khoz-1960,* p. 449. The correctness of these computations cannot be checked at present. It appears, however, that only direct labor was included for the U.S.S.R. while total labor was included for the United States.

TABLE 4

LABOR INPUT PER TON OF MAJOR FARM PRODUCTS, U.S.S.R., BY TYPE OF FARM, SELECTED YEARS; AND U.S., 1960

Product	U.S.S.R. (person-days)								U.S. (man-hours)
	Collective farms				State farms				
	1960	1962	1963	1964	1960	1962	1963	1964	1960
Grain, excluding corn	8.6	7.0	7.7	6.0	2.6	2.6	3.0	2.2	n.a.
Corn	n.a.	n.a.	n.a.	n.a.	n.a.	n.a.	n.a.	n.a.	3 [a]
Cotton, seed	68	69	61	60	61	61	51	49	107
Sugar beets	3.8	4.0	4.2	3.0	4.0	4.0	4.8	3.4	2.8
Potatoes	8.0	9.2	8.3	6.4	7.0	8.4	7.5	5.9	5.5
Vegetable	21.3	21.4	21.6	18.1	12.1	12.1	11.8	10.4	n.a.
Milk	26	27	28	27	18	18	18	17	29
Cattle (live weight)	147	143	152	136	82	85	93	84	62
Hogs (live weight)	166	145	162	138	71	70	78	56	48
Sheep (live weight)	113	102	103	103	66	68	65	69	n.a.
Wool	525	472	473	481	300	346	304	311	n.a.

[a] For wheat, the United States figure is 2.8 man-hours.

SOURCES: Data for the U.S.S.R. are from *Narkhoz-1964*, p. 416. They refer to direct labor inputs only. Data for the United States are from U.S. Department of Agriculture, *Agricultural Statistics 1963* (Washington, D.C.: Government Printing Office, 1963), p. 463.

Although the adjustments made in the Soviet calculation were probably excessive (at least in part), the Central Statistical Office still came to the conclusion that "in agriculture as a whole, productivity of labor in the U.S.S.R. was in 1958 about three times lower than in the United States." It was subsequently acknowledged that in 1959–1964, productivity of labor in Soviet agriculture was about four times lower than in the United States.[51]

In the United States, the cost of producing one ton of hogs in 1960–1962 (average) came to $354; 48 to 49 man-hours of labor were used in their production at an average wage of almost $1 per hour.[52] In 1960 the cost of *direct* labor alone used for the production of hogs in the R.S.F.S.R. state farms was 21.4 percent of total production costs—a much larger total relative to that shown for the United States. Besides, indirect costs in the U.S.S.R. amounted to an additional 7.1 percent of total cost; these costs consisted almost exclusively of payments to labor.[53]

Since the total labor cost of producing hogs in the U.S.S.R. is much greater than in the United States, and since the share of labor in this cost is similarly much higher in the Soviet Union, it turns out that the cost of *indirect* labor alone used in the U.S.S.R. to produce hogs is greater than the *total* comparable labor cost in the United States.

According to official data for 1953–1958, productivity of labor in Soviet agriculture increased by 50 percent in collective farms, and by 51 percent in state farms. In 1958–1962, however, the increase in collective-farm productivity of labor was much smaller, amounting only to 16 percent; on state farms, productivity of labor rose only by 2 percent, a rise so small as to amount to virtual stagnation.[54] Were we to consider a slightly longer period, such as 1958–1963, we would observe an increase in labor productivity on collective farms of 10 percent, while trends on state farms would show a decline of 8 percent. If, as is well possible, the volume of 1953 output has been underestimated in official Soviet statistics, the subsequent increases in productivity would be correspondingly smaller. In any case, official data on the volume of farm output for 1953–1963 overstate the growth in production and, consequently, also in the productivity of labor.

[51] *Ibid.*, and *Narkhoz-1964*, p. 87.

[52] Food and Agriculture Organization of the United Nations, *op. cit.* (in n. 19), p. 344 and U.S. Department of Agriculture, *op. cit.* (in n. 24), pp. 450, 463.

[53] Implied in *Ek. sel'. khoz.*, No. 6 (1962), p. 21.

[54] *Sel'khoz-1960,* p. 439 and *Narkhoz-1962,* p. 362. No data exist for 1963.

Data on the labor input for individual farm products disclose the picture even more clearly, and they further illustrate the uncertain nature of the evidence. This is shown by direct labor requirements per ton of product, expressed in person-days, for 1953 (1956 for collective farms), 1958, 1962 and 1964: [55]

Product	Collective farms				State farms			
	1956	1958	1962	1964	1953	1958	1962	1964
Grain, excluding corn	13	9	7	6	4.5	2.6	2.6	2.2
Potatoes	9	9	9	6	n.a.	8	8	6
Milk	27	25	27	27	19.4	18.2	18	17
Cattle, live weight	213	176	143	136	89	89	85	84
Hogs, live weight	196	175	145	162	89	75	70	56

The growth of labor productivity was greatest in grain chiefly because of the relatively greater degree of mechanization and also because of the development of grain production in areas with relatively small inputs of labor per unit of grain (such as Kazakhstan). At the same time, however, we should keep in mind that the extent of exaggeration in the official statistics of output is probably also greatest with respect to grain.

State farms have a greater proportion of their area under crops in grains than collective farms. If this were not so, the increase in labor productivity on state farms would have been smaller than on the collective farms. The absence of any increase in productivity of labor in the production of milk and largely also in that of potatoes is significant.

SOME PROBLEMS OF PRICES AND PRODUCTION COSTS

Feed Grain versus Animal Products Price Relationships—It is common practice in the United States, but also in some other countries, to calculate ratios of prices of animal products to those of feed grains. Such calculations are made *inter alia* by the Food and Agricultural Organization of the United Nations. The price of feed grains is used in this context because one would not normally grow more expensive crops for use as feed when such crops can be replaced by feed grains. The practice of calculating these price relationships is particularly widespread with respect to hogs and poultry, because both types of animals are fed primarily with feed grain. When such price ratios are calculated

[55] *Sel'khoz-1960,* p. 446 and *Narkhoz-1962,* Data for 1964 are from *Narkhoz-1964,* p. 416.

for the U.S.S.R., they turn out to be immensely higher than elsewhere.

Ratios of hog prices to those of feed barley and corn for various countries in 1961/62 are shown in Table 5. The typical relationship between the price of hogs and that of feed grain is 6:1–6.5:1. The relation of 8.2:1 shown for the United States for 1962 is rather high. In 1955, the corresponding ratio was 6.6:1 in the United States. It was at 7.3:1 in Poland—the only member of the Soviet bloc without socialized agriculture but it was as low as 3.2:1 in Poland when free market prices were used for Poland. Czechoslovakia, however, a country with socialized agriculture, shows much higher ratios than the other countries in Table 5. For the U.S.S.R., the ratios are even greater, approaching a

TABLE 5

RATIOS OF HOG VERSUS FEED PRICES, SELECTED COUNTRIES, 1961–1962

Country	Hog [a] versus feed barley	Hog [a] versus corn
Austria	5.7	5.7
Denmark (slaughtered weight)	8.1	8.9
Finland (slaughtered weight)	11.2	7.3
Germany, Federal Republic	5.5	4.8
Ireland	6.0	5.2
Italy	7.8	8.2
Netherlands [b]	5.3	5.7
Norway	5.5	5.3
Portugal	6.3	8.3
Sweden	6.8	5.1
Switzerland	6.3	6.9
United Kingdom	8.8	7.0
United States	n.a.	8.2
Yugoslavia	6.3	n.a.
Czechoslovakia	14.7	10.0
U.S.S.R.	19.2 [c]	17.8 [d]

[a] Live weight unless stated otherwise; [b] the price of meal rather than grain was used in the calculations in this case; [c] prices applied to most of the Ukraine; [d] based on price of yellow or white corn; the price of mixed color corn was 10 percent lower.

SOURCES: F.A.O. *Production Yearbook 1963*, and F.A.O. *Prices of Agricultural Products and Fertilizers in Europe 1962/63*, pp. 31, 58, 83 and Annex p. 10. The Soviet prices are from J. F. Karcz, comp., *A Compendium of Soviet Farm Prices in 1961*, Berkeley, Institute of International Studies, mimeographed, 1964, pp. 7, 9.

level of 20:1, or almost three times as much as is shown by most Western European countries. Moreover, reference is to ratios prevailing before the recent price increases of March–April, 1965, when hog prices rose by about 33 percent, while prices of feed grain (with the exception of the prices of feed barley and oats in the unfavorably situated northwestern part of the European Russia) remained unchanged.

Farm Prices and Prices of Nonfarm Products—The abnormally high production costs and prices of animal products in the U.S.S.R. are *inter alia* revealed in the relationship between prices of farm products and certain industrial goods.

In 1928, typical Soviet steel prices, such as the price of structural steel or round steel (20–40 mm diameter) were 118.75 to 125 old rubles per ton; the cost of rails to railways was 108.75 rubles per ton. In 1964, the price of steel (that is, construction steel, rails, and so on) in the U.S.S.R. varied between 61.6 and 64.4 new rubles per ton. The new low level of prices is of course the result of the revaluation of the ruble (at the ratio of ten old rubles for one new) on January 1, 1961. In terms of ruble values prevailing at the beginning and the end of the period, steel prices in the U.S.S.R. declined from 1928 to 1964 to little more than one half.

The changes in prices of farm products in the U.S.S.R. during the period 1927/28 to 1963 are shown in Table 6.

In contrast to prices of steel and indeed of many other nonfarm products, there is not a single important farm product in the U.S.S.R. which shows a decline in price during the same period. Of the products listed in Table 6, wheat shows only a small price increase, though any increase is of course significant when steel prices declined by almost 50 percent. The increase in prices of milk and eggs is large, but that in the price of meat is enormous and implies a 7.5 times increase in meat prices relative to those of steel. Should we also consider the additional increase in meat prices legislated by the March, 1965, plenum meeting, the increase in meat prices, relative to those of steel is ten-fold. Yet, only a short time ago, Khrushchev spoke of overtaking the United States in the production of meat, and this prediction was repeated and acclaimed by the Soviet press.

The situation in the United States was different. No revaluation of the dollar occurred in the United States between the late twenties and the sixties, and indices covering this period have a more conventional meaning. From 1929 to 1961, American prices of steel rails rose by 171 percent, but those of No. 2 hard wheat at Kansas City increased by

TABLE 6

PRICES OF SELECTED FARM PRODUCTS, U.S.S.R. 1927/28 AND 1963

(rubles per ton or per thousand eggs)			Index (1927/28
Product	1927/28 [a]	1963 [b]	= 100)
Wheat	68.4	75.6	105
Meat [c]	402.0	1,570	391
Milk	69.6	121.8	175
Eggs	31.5	70.0	222

[a] Old rubles; [b] new rubles (each new ruble = 10 old rubles); [c] slaughter weight; it is assumed that in 1927/28 two-thirds of the total meat output was beef and mutton, and that one-third was pork. The prices in the source for 1963 were originally in terms of live weight. They were recalculated to slaughter weight assuming extraction coefficients of 45 percent for beef and mutton and 65 percent for pork. The rates are approximately those given in J. F. Karcz, *Soviet Agricultural Marketings and Prices, 1928/1954*, RM-1930 (Santa Monica, Calif.: The RAND Corporation, July, 1957), p. 288. Actually, somewhat lower extraction rates should have been assumed for a comparison with 1927/28. Karcz describes these prices as the average prices realized in all marketings for beef, mutton, and pork. An idea about the proportions of the various meats included in the aggregate can be obtained from the extraction rate of 54.3 percent for all these meats taken by Karcz from a book by Nifontov (cf. Karcz, *op. cit.*, p. 343). This rate implies a substantial proportion of the more expensive pork. Since March, 1965, the price of wheat was raised to about 85 rubles per ton, while the prices of beef went up by 36 percent and those of pork by 32 percent. Milk prices were raised as of January 1, 1965, and again in April, 1965 (through a reduction in the standard butterfat content).

SOURCES: Data for 1927/28 are taken from *Kon. tsifry-1929/30*, pp. 581–582. Data for 1963 are taken from *The 1965 Eastern Europe Agricultural Situation*, Economic Research Service, ERS-Foreign-115 (Washington, D.C.: U.S. Department fo Agriculture, 1965), p. 8.

only 71 percent, while prices of beef rose 86 percent, and of hogs 74 percent.[56]

Steel was the product which showed a large price change in the United States in the specified period; increases in the prices of wheat and hogs were only half as large. Only for beef is the increase in prices as great as 50 percent of the increase in steel prices.

Thus, in the United States the price of steel increased from the late twenties to the early sixties by about one-third in relation to meat prices. In the U.S.S.R., meat prices rose 7.5 times as much as steel

[56] Data obtained from various volumes of the *Statistical Abstract of the United States.*

prices in the same period. In relation to the changes in prices in the United States, meat in the Soviet Union became 11 times as expensive as steel. If we take into account the increases in Soviet farm prices of meat in March, 1965, meat in the U.S.S.R. has become 14 times as expensive as steel.

Trends in Production Costs in the Recent Decade—While the production costs of Soviet farm products are high, their level in the past decade did not improve. The reverse may have been true, but the available data are not reliable.

Table 7 shows trends in state-farm production costs for 1950, for selected years in the fifties and annually for the more recent period. Data for the years through 1957 are those supplied by Benediktov. For 1950–1953, they show a sharp decline in state-farm production costs for grain and pork, but the information for this period is of particularly uncertain reliability.[57] As far as other products are concerned, Table 7 shows no substantial changes in state-farm production costs during this period. The moderate decline in production costs of animal products and cotton indicated for 1953–1957 seems more reasonable.

From 1958 through 1964 (whenever the data are available) Table 7 indicates a strong upward trend in state-farm production costs with the exception of cotton, for which the rise was relatively small.

During 1953–1963, over-all production costs in state farms probably increased moderately. Some cost data have recently become available on the magnitude of production costs in 1964. Since 1958, these costs rose by 35 percent for grain, 12 percent for potatoes, 9 percent for cotton, 46 percent for milk, 42 percent for eggs, 25 percent for hogs, 45 percent for cattle. and 69 percent for wool.[58] Table 7 shows also that costs in state farms in 1964 were higher than they had been in 1961.

Official calculations of production costs in the collective farms began only in 1958. For 1953–1956, we have the results of Terent'ev's calculations, but these were based only on data supplied by a limited number of farms. His figures indicate high production costs for grain in 1953, amounting to 69 rubles per ton. For 1956, Terent'ev still shows a figure

[57] Thus, for example, Benediktov shows a production cost of 38.2 rubles per ton of grain for 1953 while A. N. Malafeev, *Istoriia tsenoobrazovaniia v SSSR, 1917–1963* (Moscow: 1964), p. 268, shows a cost of 62 rubles per ton. Conceivably Benediktov's figure refers only to state farms in the former Ministry of State Farms, while Malafeev deals with costs for all state farms.

[58] *Vop. ek.*, No. 4 (1965), p. 26 shows somewhat different percentage increases based, presumably, on earlier and preliminary evidence.

TABLE 7

STATE-FARM PRODUCTION COSTS, U.S.S.R., SELECTED PRODUCTS, SELECTED YEARS

(rubles per ton or per thousand eggs)

Product	1950	1953	1954	1957	1958	1959	1960	1961	1962	1963	1964
Grains, excluding corn	50.8	38.2	39.88	43.03	37	n.a.	41	45	n.a.	n.a.	50
Potatoes	41.71	n.a.	46.44	48.50	56	n.a.	n.a.	51	n.a.	n.a.	63
Seed cotton	n.a.	n.a.	187.88	158.23 [a]	259	n.a.	253 [b]	246	n.a.	n.a.	282
Sugar beets	n.a.	n.a.	n.a.	n.a.	17	n.a.	18	21	n.a.	n.a.	23
Cattle, live weight	651.3	664.0	665.5	597.6	806	820	878	925	1,006	1,148	1,167
Hogs, live weight	1,509	999.4	998.2	943.4	1,007	1,049	1,167	1,218	1,272	1,508	1,261
Sheep, live weight	n.a.	n.a.	n.a.	n.a.	372	n.a.	430	462	n.a.	n.a.	662
Poultry, live weight	n.a.	n.a.	1,390.4 [a]	1,302.8	1,436	n.a.	n.a.	1,558	n.a.	n.a.	n.a.
Milk	117.0	117.0	117.1	116.6	124	127	132	143	160	171	181
Eggs	87.2	65.3	64.5	59.3	57.6	n.a.	65	80.6	n.a.	n.a.	82
Wool	n.a.	n.a.	n.a.	n.a.	1,833	n.a.	2,800	2,228	n.a.	n.a.	3,096

[a] 1956; [b] Uzbek S.S.R. only.

SOURCES: Data for 1953 are taken from I. A. Benediktov, *Sovkhozy nashei strany* (Moscow: 1956), p. 66, and from his article in *Vop. ek.*, 1958, No. 1, p. 34; those for 1950 and 1954 and 1957 are taken from Benediktov, *Puti snizheniia sebestoimosti produktsii sovkhozov* (Moscow: 1957), pp. 46, 74, 92, 98, 121, 130, 148. Benediktov's data may refer to costs on state farms administered by the former Ministry of State Farms; otherwise the substantial increases between the 1957 and 1958 costs for cattle and cotton are difficult to explain. Data for 1958 and 1961 are from *Ek. gaz.*, February 9, 1963, Supplement, p. 5. Those for 1960 are from *Ek. sel'. khoz.*, No. 6 (1962), pp. 45–48 and No. 9, p. 53. Those for 1959, 1962, and 1963 are from *ibid.*, No. 2 (1965), p. 10. Data for 1964 are from *Narkhoz-1964*, pp. 412–13.

TABLE 8

COLLECTIVE-FARM PRODUCTION COSTS (LABOR VALUED AT 1958 STATE-FARM WAGES), U.S.S.R., SELECTED PRODUCTS, SELECTED YEARS
(rubles per ton)

Product	1953	1958	1959	1960	1961	1962	1963	1964
Grains, excluding corn	65	44	44	40	37	37	46	39
Potatoes	44	34	33	32	31	41	40	32
Seed Cotton	241	210	200	208	210	216	210	214
Sugar beets	17	12	17	14	14	15	17	12
Cattle, live weight	932	941	913	913	847	866	875	781
Hogs, live weight	1,870	1,309	1,165	1,230	1,152	1,152	1,257	1,152
Sheep, live weight	500	500	510	530	485	485	485	520
Milk	167	133	131	133	129	130	130	129
Wool	2,613	2,456	2,481	2,603	2,333	2,333	2,407	2,628

SOURCES: Calculated from official data on the magnitude of costs (as defined here) for 1962, given in *Narkhoz-1962*, pp. 338–339, and from official indices of costs "with comparable valuation of labor," given in *ibid.*, pp. 332–337, and *Narkhoz-1964*, p. 393. Results are rounded to the nearest ruble. As explained on page 678 of *Narkhoz-1962*, comparable labor cost is that calculated in terms of 1958 state farm wages. This is done explicitly for the period since 1958; nothing is said explicitly about the comparability of data for 1953, but it appears that this is the case for that year as well.

of 56 rubles per ton even though Zverev gives a more reliable cost of 40 rubles per ton for 1958, and a decline of this magnitude between two years (both characterized by good harvest conditions) is unlikely.[59]

Thus, although Terent'ev's absolute cost figures may be too high, the moderate decline he shows for 1953–1956 appears reasonable. According to his later calculations, production costs on collective farms declined in these years by 15 percent for grain, 12 percent for cotton, 9 percent for meat, and 15 percent for milk.[60]

Official production-cost indices, which served as a basis for information compiled in Table 8, show a strong decline in collective-farm costs between 1953 and 1958, except for costs of raising cattle and sheep. These indices are based on costs which value the labor component in terms of 1958 state-farm labor renumeration. As will appear shortly, the data for 1958–1962 shown in the same table leave an incorrect impression, and it may well be that they distort trends also in the earlier period. A certain decline in production costs in 1953–1958 seems nevertheless probable, because the number of collective farmers, engaged in work on collective farms, declined from 23.3 million in 1953 to 22.1 million in 1959, in the face of a substantial increase in output.[61]

For 1958–1962, the official indices of production costs in collective farms show moderate cost declines for some products and equally moderate increases for others (Table 8). A slightly more favorable picture emerges from the comparison of the data for 1958–1964. Additional evidence on 1958–1963 was published early in 1965 by Maniakin and is shown in Table 9. Maniakin's cost data appear to value labor partly in terms of 1962 state-farm expenditures and partly in terms of 1958 state-farm expenditures (employed for the same purpose by sources on which Table 8 is based). They are limited to three products. The trends shown by Maniakin's data for 1958–1961 are the same as those shown in Table 8. For 1962, however, there is substantial rise in the cost of milk and more moderate upward trends for the costs of cattle and hogs, while Table 8 registers for these years declines for these products.

All in all the costs shown for 1963 by Maniakin are substantially higher than those in Table 8.

[59] M. L. Terent'ev, *Sebestoimost' kolkhoznoi produktsii* (Moscow: 1957), p. 260. See also A. G. Zverev, *Natsional'nyi dokhod i finansy SSSR* (Moscow: 1961), p. 306. Miss Nimitz, who collected all data available in 1959, reproduced (in the absence of better information) Terent'ev's figures in her "Soviet Agricultural Prices and Costs," U.S. Congress, Joint Economic Committee, *Comparisons of the United States and Soviet Economies,* Part I (Washington, D.C.: Government Printing Office, 1959).

[60] *Vop. ek.*, No. 3 (1958), p. 61.

[61] *Narkhoz-1962,* pp. 226, 368.

TABLE 9

COLLECTIVE-FARM PRODUCTION COSTS (AS CITED BY MANIAKIN [a]), U.S.S.R., 1958–1963
(rubles per ton)

Product	1958	1959	1960	1961	1962	1963
Cattle, live weight	945	917	916	847	1,014	1,040
Hogs, live weight	1,305	1,165	1,226	1,149	1,347	1,462
Milk	133	132	133	129	156	157

[a] *Ek. sel'. khoz.*, No. 2 (1965), p. 10. Maniakin, perhaps motivated by the desire to show a trend unfavorable to Khrushchev, appears to have manipulated the data. While his 1962 costs are in terms of labor valued at 1962 state-farm wages, his figures for 1958–1961 appear to be the absolute figures in terms of labor valued at 1958 state-farm wages (they differ from those I show in Table 8 by amounts that can be explained by rounding. My figures in Table 8 are derived from the Soviet index and the known figure on 1962 costs, obtained in terms of 1958 state-farm wages). The meaning of Maniakin's figure for 1963 is not clear, but apparently reference is to costs using 1962 state-farm wages to value the labor component. See *Narkhoz-1962*, pp. 333, 338–339 and *Narkhoz-1964*, p. 393.

A still different picture emerges from Table 10, which uses costs obtained with the aid of actual labor expenditures of collective farms for 1958, 1961, 1962 and 1964. For 1958–1961, the data show moderate cost declines; for the more inclusive period 1958–1962, the picture is mixed. For 1958–1964, costs rise for all products other than eggs.

All in all, collective-farm costs declined moderately from 1953 to 1962; since state-farm costs in the same period showed a moderate increase, there were no significant changes for Soviet agriculture taken as a whole. By 1964, actually incurred costs increased in both sectors, and in many instances in a very pronounced manner. The picture is more favorable for the collective-farm sector when comparison is made in terms of Table 8.

The Helplessness of State-Farming—It was shown that production costs on Soviet collective farms range from high to very high. It is therefore particularly significant that the huge farms owned by the Soviet state are unable to produce even at these high, or very high, costs.

The calculation of production costs for collective farms with the aid of state-farm wage rates to value the labor component is widely used in the U.S.S.R. Terent'ev's calculations for 1953–1956 employed this method as did those of the Central Statistical Administration shown in the 1961 and 1962 statistical yearbooks. Malafeev's calculations for 1958–1963, published in 1964, continued to employ the same method. Calculations of production costs with the use of actual collective-farm labor payments are indeed rare. Yet the practice of using state-farm wage rates for this purpose is objectionable even so far as intertemporal

TABLE 10

COLLECTIVE-FARM PRODUCTION COSTS (LABOR VALUED AT ACTUAL EXPENDITURES), U.S.S.R., SELECTED YEARS
(rubles per ton or per thousand eggs)

Product	1958	1961	1962	1964
Grains, excluding corn	38	36	37	44
Potatoes	28	28	38	35
Seed Cotton	219	206	224	281
Sugar Beets	12	14	16	17
Cattle, live weight	798	740	834	927
Hogs, live weight	1,148	1,081	1,146	1,250
Sheep, live weight	386	466	512	609
Poultry, live weight	1,030	1,172	n.a.	n.a.
Milk	116	116	129	151
Eggs	84	81	n.a.	82
Wool	2,635	2,178	2,504	2,939

SOURCES: Data for 1958 and 1961 are taken from *Ek. gaz.*, February 9, 1963, Supplement, p. 5. Data for 1962 are from *Narkhoz-1962*, pp. 338–339. Those for 1964 are from *Narkhoz-1964*, pp. 396-397.

comparisons of collective-farm costs are concerned. The practice is misleading when comparisons are made between production costs of state and collective farms. Collective-farm production costs, calculated with the aid of state-farm wages to value the labor component, are obviously exaggerated.

According to official calculations published in the annual statistical yearbook for 1962, production costs on collective farms, obtained with the use of 1962 state-farm wages to value the labor component, exceeded the costs calculated with the use of actual collective-farm labor expenditures by 19 percent for grain, 20 percent for cattle, and 21 percent for milk.[62]

A direct comparison between the state-farm production costs and costs actually incurred on the collective farms may be made for 1958, 1961, 1964, and (to a limited extent) 1962. The relevant data are shown in Table 11. In 1964, state-farm production costs were higher than collective-farm costs for all products with the exception of eggs. For cotton and hogs costs were virtually identical. In several instances state-farm costs are considerably higher than collective-farm costs.

[62] *Narkhoz-1962,* pp. 338–339. For 1964, the corresponding figures are: 9 percent for grain, 6.6 percent for cattle, 14.3 percent for potatoes, 7.3 percent for milk, 6.1 percent for hogs, and 3.8 percent for wool. Cf. *Narkhoz-1964*, pp. 394–397.

TABLE 11

RELATIONSHIP OF STATE-FARM AND COLLECTIVE-FARM PRODUCTION COSTS, U.S.S.R., SELECTED YEARS
(Collective-farm costs = 100)

Product	1958	1961	1962	1964
Grain, excluding corn	97.4	125.0	n.a.	113.6
Potatoes	200.0	182.1	n.a.	180.0
Seed Cotton	118.3	119.4	n.a.	100.4
Sugar Beets	141.7	150.0	n.a.	135.3
Cattle	101.0	125.0	120.6	125.9
Hogs	87.7	112.0	111.0	100.9
Sheep	96.4	99.1	n.a.	108.7
Poultry	139.4	132.9	n.a.	n.a.
Milk	106.9	123.3	124.0	119.9
Eggs	68	99.5	n.a.	100.0
Wool	69.6	102.3	n.a.	105.3

SOURCES: Calculated from data in Tables 7 and 10.

Thus, for sugar beets and cattle, state-farm costs exceeded those incurred on the collectives by 35 and 26 percent respectively. The production costs of potatoes on state farms was 80 percent higher than on the collective farms. As already noted, in the United States, the price for hogs in 1961 was $354 per ton. Their cost of production on Soviet state farms in 1961 came to more than 1,200 rubles per ton, and this cost did not include the profit and rent elements which are present in the American price. Thus, in this sector, Soviet production costs are more than four times as high as the prices in the United States.

Average costs of production for the country as a whole can sometimes be misleading because of pronounced regional differences. Fortunately, N. V. Tsogoev published a detailed tabulation for the Stavropol' *krai,* covering state- and collective-farm production costs for 1963. As it turns out, only the costs of producing grain (as an aggregate) are the same for both types of farms. For the other fourteen products (or product groups) listed, state-farm costs of production exceed those of the collective farms by margins varying from 3.8 percent (wheat) to 81.2 percent (potatoes).[63]

From 1958 to 1961, production costs in state farms changed less favorably than on the collective farms. Consequently, a comparison for 1958 is less favorable to the latter. In 1958, production costs of producing grain were even slightly lower on state farms than on collec-

[63] V. N. Tsogoev, *Statistika sebestoimosti produktsii sel'skogo khoziaistva* (Moscow: 1965), p. 119.

tives. For pork, eggs, and wool, the state-farm cost of production was decidedly lower than that on the collectives, while the costs of producing cattle and sheep were about the same. For crops other than grain, as well as for milk and poultry, collective farms enjoyed an advantage. All in all, however, state-farm production costs in 1958 appear to have been somewhat higher than costs on collective farms.

While appraising trends shown in Table 11, several factors need to be borne in mind. As already indicated, state-farm wages were raised in 1961 and again in 1962. Collective-farm earnings per man-day are estimated to have risen by 14.7 percent between 1958 and 1963; the issue is beclouded, however, by the problem of valuation for income in kind which declined by about one-third during this period (when measured at state retail prices).[64] There was a further increase in man-day earnings in 1964. Finally, collective-farm costs other than labor were affected by increases in prices charged to farms for machinery, spare parts, fuel, lubricants, seeds, fertilizers, as well as weed and pest killers. Some of these increases took place in mid-1958, others occurred in 1959. The extent to which state-farm costs were also affected by these price changes cannot be measured at present.[65]

If trends for collective-farm costs in 1953–1958 are shown correctly in Table 8, it would appear that in the same period state-farm production costs would have been lower still, especially at the beginning of the post-Stalin era. But the data are too uncertain for conclusions.

Some explanations or justifications may be found for the high production costs in collective farms. But what can be said of the respective costs in state farms except to accept them as acknowledgement of ignorance and irresponsibility of the Communist dictatorship?

The amount of labor per unit of product used on the state farms is much smaller than on the collective farms, but part of the saving of labor is compensated by higher wages on state farms. The value of feed spent per unit of animal products, is also greater on state farms. According to

[64] Nancy Nimitz, *Farm Employment in the Soviet Union, 1928–1963,* RM-4623-PR (Santa Monica, Calif.: The RAND Corporation, November, 1965), pp. 97–98.

[65] Nancy Nimitz, "The Lean Years," *Problems of Communism,* XIV:3 (May–June, 1965), 14–15 and Jerzy F. Karcz, V. P. Timoshenko, "Soviet Agricultural Policy, 1953–1962," *Food Research Institute Studies,* IV:2 (May, 1964), 144. See also *Plenum Tsentral'nogo Komiteta Kommunisticheskoi Partii Sovetskogo Soiuza 24–26 marta 1965 g.* (Moscow: 1965), p. 228. Little is known of the extent to which these price changes affected state farms. So far as machinery is concerned, prices paid by state farms for some items rose less than those paid by the collectives. But the opposite was also true for other items. The available evidence on this aspect comes from unpublished Soviet sources (made available by J. F. Karcz) and refers to the increase implemented on July 1, 1958.

A. Soroka, the cost of feed fed to hogs in 1960 was as follows, stated in rubles per ton of feed units: [66]

	State farms	Collective farms
R.S.F.S.R.	68	55
Ukraine	47	43
Belorussia	106	83
Kazakhstan	56	38
Estonia	99	66

In 1960–1962, the cost of a feed unit used in the production of milk, beef, and pork is said to have been 50 percent higher on state farms than on the collective farms.[67]

The Soviet reluctance to acknowledge the deplorable condition of state farms is not surprising. Possibly this is one of the main reasons for the disinclination to give up the use of state-farm wage rates in the calculation of collective-farm costs. The prevalent view in the U.S.S.R. is that production costs on collective farms are higher than on state farms. This is even repeated by Malafeev in his 1964 book, though the data he shows indicate the contrary.[68]

The desire to maintain the proposition that production costs in collective farms are higher than in state farms is presumably the reason for withholding data on the costs in the latter until January, 1966. While for 1953–1957 much information on state-farm costs was available in the writings of Benediktov, nothing comparable has been published for subsequent years before the appearance of the 1964 statistical year book, which includes detailed regional data on state-farm costs in 1964. The 1962 statistical yearbook contained seven and a half pages on costs in collective farms, but nothing on state-farm costs.

Data discussed in the next section show that Soviet state farms are thousands of times as large as the average farms elsewhere. The fact that production costs on state farms are four-fold (hogs) or five-fold (chicken) greater than costs on much smaller private American farms, reveals an inefficiency of Soviet farming creditable only because proved by Soviet data.

CAUSES OF HIGH PRODUCTION COSTS

Unfavorable soil and climate conditions are among the causes for the high production costs of farm products in the Soviet Union, but the

[66] *Ek. sel'. khoz.*, No. 6 (1962), p. 23.
[67] *Vest. stat.*, No. 12 (1964), pp. 13–14.
[68] Malafeev, *op. cit.* (in n. 57), p. 268.

negative effects of this factor should not be exaggerated. Only crops are directly affected. The livestock industry is not touched by it, except to the extent that crops are used as feed. Yet, it is precisely in the livestock industry that production costs are the highest in the U.S.S.R.

The United States has the great advantage of possessing the corn belt where an enormous amount of corn can be obtained at a low cost. But the high temperatures in a large part of the American South are unfavorable for animal husbandry.

If the natural conditions of Canada are at all more favorable for agriculture than those of the U.S.S.R., this is because of a relatively higher land-to-population ratio. Large parts of arable land of Kazakhstan and of the territory beyond Lake Baikal are so poor that they probably would not be used for this purpose in Canada. This factor is likely to be offset—at least to a large extent—by long stretches of relatively warm, good, land with a long frost-free period in the Ukraine, Moldavia, North Caucasus, and Central Asia. Land of similar quality is not available in Canada. The fact that in Canada grain, its predominant crop, must be grown exclusively as a less-yielding spring crop is an important, unfavorable factor for Canada.

One can guess that crop production in the U.S.S.R. is affected by adverse soil and climatic conditions to an extent not exceeding 25 percent. This percentage, however, would probably be too large as an average.[69] In prerevolutionary times, Russia exported 10 million tons of grain and large amounts of other farm products. It occupied the first place among the world's grain exporters. This would hardly have been possible if natural conditions were greatly unfavorable.

If we assume a 25 percent cost differential in the production of crops as being due to adverse soil and climatic conditions, and if we apply this differential to the production of feed crops specifically, then (on the strength of an additional assumption that feed constitutes not much more than one half of the total cost of animal production), the maximum adverse effect of soil and climatic conditions on the costs of animal production should be taken as approximately 15 percent.

Since Soviet production costs in agriculture are at least twice as high as those of the United States, the importance of the organizational factor, the other negative factor in Soviet agricultural production, emerges as very large. An improvement of 10 or even 20 percent in the operation of socialist organization of agriculture would still leave Soviet

[69] The great deterioration in the condition of Soviet soils which took place under the Soviet rule may not be sufficiently taken into account in this appraisal.

farming as immensely expensive, as a great handicap to progress. In view of the fact that the socialist organization of agriculture in the course of a half century only succeeded in making Soviet agriculture one of the most expensive—if not the most expensive—producer of farm products in the world, it seems unlikely that production costs in the U.S.S.R. can be cut by anything approaching a half.

The topic of socialist organization of agriculture is a big one and cannot be discussed here in detail. A very few aspects cannot be bypassed, however. One of them is that Soviet farms prove to be very inefficient in spite of their large size. To this, there is no parallel anywhere else in the world.

Gigantomania with respect to farm size proves actually one of the sources of inefficiency. A very strong, detrimental tendency to enlarge individual enterprises has continued to operate for years with only a small modification in most recent times. From 1958 through 1964, the number of collective farms declined from 69,100 to 38,300. Most of this decline was due to collective-farm mergers, but conversion to state farms was also an important factor. At the end of 1964 there were as many as 418 households per collective farm as opposed to 275 in 1958. Only 5.2 percent of all collective farms had fewer than 100 households in 1964, while each farm had an average of almost 3,000 hectares of sown area, 967 heads of cattle, and almost 600 hogs. In the state farms, the average cropped area per farm in 1958 was 8,700 hectares; by 1962 the figure reached a peak of 10,100 hectares, declining to 8,600 hectares in 1964.[70]

Recently the official attitude toward the size of farms changed somewhat, but very large farms are still believed to be indispensable. A. Rumiantseva shows in an article that collective farms in the Kirov *oblast'* after a series of mergers in 1958–1959, are averaging 7,000 hectares of sown area per farm. According to her, two-thirds of the farms in the northern part of the province are unmanageable because of their excessive size. The same reason is cited for the deterioration in productive conditions of the *oblast'* as a whole. Nevertheless, she believes that it is difficult to organize rational management on *fermy* (parts of a farm) which include less than 300 heads of cattle or 200 hogs, 100 cows, or 500 sheep each.[71]

The same writer also provides approximate estimates of the optimum size of collective farms. She recommends the smallest size (800 to

[70] *Narkhoz-1962*, p. 359; *Narkhoz-1963*, pp. 341–343 and *Narkhoz-1964*, pp. 390–391, 398, 411.

[71] *Ek. sel'. khoz.*, No. 5 (1965), pp. 29–30.

1,500 hectares) for the western part of Kalinin *oblast'* (an area of expanded flax-growing). For the eastern and central parts of the same *oblast'* her recommendation is 1,700–3,000 hectares. The optimum size of farms for the right bank part of the Saratov *oblast'* is given as 6,000–8,000 hectares; on the left bank of the Volga the optimum size, according to Rumiantseva, rises to 8,000–14,000 hectares.[72]

The recommended optimum size for the state farms is naturally still much greater. For grain state farms in the southern part of the Ukraine, G. Kotov recommended a size of 12,000–16,000 hectares of sown area; for Kazakhstan, he has 18,000–38,000 hectares. The optimum size of a division (*otdelenie*) of a state farm should, according to Kotov, correspond in the same natural conditions and for the same type of farm to the optimum size of a whole collective farm.[73]

Such a large concentration of farm holdings occurs, moreover, without a corresponding concentration of the farming population, or, more specifically, of farm labor. At the end of 1963, the U.S.S.R. had 48,700 state and collective farms, but also 700,000 inhabited settlements in rural areas. In 1964 only 14.8 percent of collective farms had only one settlement; 47.9 percent of such farms included from 2 to 5 settlements, 21.2 percent were spread over 6 to 10 settlements. At the top of the distribution 1.5 percent of farms had more than 75 settlements per farm.[74]

In the United States, California is believed to be the state of the large farms, but it cannot match the size of Soviet farms. In 1959 California had 99,232 farms. Of these, only 29,556 reported hired labor for a total of 145,215 persons in this category. A total of 76,784 farms reported a harvested crop acreage, with an average of a little more than 100 acres per farm. Only 1,201 Californian farms reported a harvested crop acreage of more than 1,000 acres per farm.[75]

In his study of optimum size of corn-livestock farms in northeastern Nebraska, O. J. Scoville of the U.S. Department of Agriculture found that virtually no additional economies of scale were realized beyond the size of two-men, two-tractor farms representing 440 acres. Under 1935–1945 price relationships, the total costs per dollar's worth of output on

[72] *Ibid.*, pp. 42–43.
[73] *Ibid.*, No. 2 (1964), p. 54.
[74] M. Osmolovskii in *ibid.*, No. 3 (1963), p. 35; *Narkhoz-1963*, pp. 341, 358 and *Narkhoz-1964*, p. 398.
[75] U.S. Bureau of the Census, *U.S. Census of Agriculture: 1959*, I, *Counties: California* (Washington, D.C.: Government Printing Office, 1960), 6, 36, 132–133.

such a farm came to $0.87 compared to $0.86 for a seven-tractor, five-man farm, covering 1,760 acres.[76]

Farms in California, and indeed in the United States in general, are, of course, very large when compared with farms in western Europe. This is well illustrated for sugar-beet producing farms for which some cost evidence is on hand. Data on the size of arable land per Soviet collective farm in sugar-beet-growing areas indicate that such farms have 500 or more hectares of land under this crop per farm. The optimum size recommended for Soviet sugar-beet-growing state farms is 3,500 to 5,500 hectares for the Ukraine, between 6,000 and 8,000 hectares on irrigated land in Kazakhstan, and so on. The acreages just referred to apply of course to the over-all size of total farms.[77]

A detailed German study shows that among the western European countries by far the greatest average acreage in sugar beets per enterprise is found in the Paris area of France (47.1 hectares in 1957–1958). This is considerably more than the average French acreage of 1954 (3.3 hectares). Even smaller acreages are reported for other western European countries: in Germany in 1958 the average acreage was about 1 hectare per farm; in Switzerland in 1959, it was slightly more than half as much.[78] In southern Germany, the average sugar-beet acreage per producing enterprise was only 0.81 hectares. The crop was marketed at a price of 62 DM per ton, which left a generous margin for rent and profit. Yet, a similar sum would not even cover the direct cost of producing beets on the huge sugar beet farms of the U.S.S.R. There is no doubt that conditions in southern Germany are favorable to sugar-beet production.[79]

Even an acreage of sugar beets of about 40 hectares per sugar-beet-producing farm, or about the same as in California in 1959, would be believed unacceptable in the U.S.S.R.[80]

[76] As quoted in *Adjustments in Agriculture: A National Basebook* (Ames, Iowa: Iowa State University Press, 1961), pp. 208–209.

[77] *Vop. ek.*, No. 12 (1963), p. 48.

[78] Forschungsgesellschaft für Agrarpolitik und Agrarsoziologie, *Die wirtschaftlichen Grundlagen des Zuckerrübenbaues in der Europäischen Wirtschaftsgemeinschaft,* Part I (Bonn: 1961), 11–12 and Part II (Bonn: 1961), 38. See also Agrarwirtschaftliches Institut der Hochschule für Bodenkultur, *Zuckerrübenbau in West Europa* (Vienna: 1959), pp. 30, 44, 53.

[79] Forschungsgesellschaft für Agrarpolitik und Agrarsoziologie, *op. cit.* (in n. 78), I, 10. This is shown by the increasing acreages which nearly doubled in Bavaria between 1954 and 1959.

[80] U.S. Bureau of the Census, *op. cit.* (in n. 75), p. 14. The largest sugar-beet acreages in California come to 100 hectares per farm. There were only 202 such farms in California in 1959.

The gigantic size of farms is, of course, not the only reason for the immense amount of labor used to produce a unit of product in the U.S.S.R.

The mediocre state of Soviet agriculture is also illustrated by the poor quality of output, even if comparisons were to be made with primitive, small-scale individual peasant producers of precollectivization days. We have already referred to the inability of the U.S.S.R. to produce hard and durum wheat, of which enough was produced before the revolution, or to produce buckwheat and millet at reasonable prices, or to grow good potatoes fit for consumption. The list could be expanded, but it is sufficient to say that the Soviet technical press recognizes that, with minor exceptions, the quality of products produced on individual peasant household plots is better than that produced by the socialized sector.

The feed produced in the U.S.S.R. is both expensive and of inferior quality. The unfavorable effect of these features on the cost of animal products is enhanced by the faulty composition of the feed, especially with respect to protein content.

The expensive animal products are mostly of poor quality. This is due not only to the deficient composition of feeding rations, but also to other negative factors, such as shortages of feed during the winter. Large amounts of high-cost feed are needed under existing conditions to produce a unit of animal products. In 1962, the cost of feed per ton of live hogs on state farms came to the huge sum of 812 rubles,[81] or to more than twice the total level of American prices of hogs. On collective farms, the corresponding figure was 698 rubles per ton of hogs, or nearly twice as much as the total American hog price.

Other factors resulting in high production costs are discussed in the proceedings of the international symposium on Soviet agriculture, held in February, 1964, in Munich.[82]

CONCLUSIONS

Khrushchev repeatedly pointed to the target of increasing Soviet labor productivity in agriculture above the level found in capitalist countries. Judged by the level of production costs, recognized by Soviet writers as indicative of productivity of labor, Soviet agriculture occupies an exceptional position in the world precisely because of the high level of its

[81] *Vest. stat.*, No. 12 (1964), p. 17.

[82] Reprinted in Roy D. Laird and E. L. Crowley, eds., *Soviet Agriculture: The Permanent Crisis* (New York: Praeger, 1965).

production costs. It is particularly significant that these are high not only on collective farms, but on state farms as well. There may be special reasons in the organization of the collective farms which are reflected in high production costs. But the production costs are even higher on state farms where these special reasons do not exist. Moreover, it would seem that the possibility of substantial cost reductions are smaller for state farms than for collective farms.

Production costs in farming continued to decline in most countries in recent years, but they were increasing in the Soviet Union.

As a result of senseless farm policies pursued by Khrushchev, Soviet agriculture is in such a dismal situation that a substantial improvement would not be difficult to attain. It seems indeed reasonably certain that Khrushchev's dismissal will improve agriculture. Some good results will probably be attained because of the restoration of summer fallow, of the restrictions of the size of livestock herds to the level allowed by available feed supplies, and of the putting of corn, perennial grasses, and dry legumes in their right place. In addition, there will undoubtedly be the impact of intended ample supplies of commercial fertilizers, of the considerable expansion of irrigated acreage, of other land improvements by drainage and liming, and last, but not least, of the more sensible procurement policies (though the plan order [*plan zakaz*] for several years ahead, the new form of the procurement organization, is hardly the last word in this respect).

What will be the over-all result of these changes? It is clear that a moderate improvement will help, but would it solve the problem? A reduction of 20 percent in the level of production costs would only compensate for the price increases introduced by the March, 1965, plenum. An immense, indeed an unattainable, reduction in the level of production costs to 60 percent of their present level would only bring them to the level of costs of capitalist countries. But such ambitious targets are not even voiced by the Soviet rulers. Now socialist organization of agriculture will continue to be combined with high, possibly even very high, production costs and, consequently, with high prices in both collective and state farms. These prices will be much higher than those that suffice for enterprises in capitalist countries.

The measures incorporated in Brezhnev's March 24, 1965, report have been described as revolutionary.[83] Such drastic characterizations may be found time and again in the Soviet press, although the measures

[83] Even Miss Nimitz called the program announced by Brezhnev "vague on details, but so far as it goes . . . admirable." *Op. cit.* (in n. 65), p. 21.

consist to a considerable extent of the elimination of Khrushchev's panaceas, such as growing corn almost at the North Pole, the sharp curtailment of summer fallow and of the acreage under grasses, further strangulation of individual farming on private household plots, and so on. Some of Khrushchev's measures (as for example, the insistence on growing sugar beets for feed) were so absurd that a reaction against them began even before his dismissal. This was also partly true of his corn-expansion program. But the most necessary measures are also at the same time too difficult to accept for Communist leaders. Among these is the real autonomy for state and collective farms in the field of planning and conduct of farming operations, particularly with the participation of the rank and file of collective farmers.

A decisively negative feature of the Soviet system may be preserved. The following is a quotation from the journal of the Central Statistical Administration commenting upon the decision of the November, 1962, plenum meeting of the central committee (which provided for the reorganization of Party leadership in the economy into separate agricultural and industrial branches):

The Soviet people met with gigantic enthusiasm the decision of the plenum of the Central Committee of the Communist Party of the Soviet Union, made in accordance with the report of N. S. Khrushchev. . . . The unanimously approved decision of the plenum on the reorganization of the system of control of the economy is fully in accord with the present period of the unfolding of the construction of communism. . . . The resolution of the plenum of the Central Committee . . . is imbued with the spirit of really creative Leninist approach to the solving of the tasks of further development of socialist society and the building of communism.[84]

Two years later, the organization of the Party along productive principles was rejected, again unanimously, and was branded as "subjective" or otherwise defective. The "really creative Leninist approach" was declared to be illiterate, and the acceptance of it was labeled as involving *podkhalimazh*.[85]

The rejection of Khrushchev's ideas was unanimous as was their acceptance while he was still in office. Recent editorials of agricultural press are all full of statements such as these: "All Soviet people see in the decisions of the March, 1965, plenum, a vivid incorporation of the gigantic, creative activities of the Party, of its entire care for the well-

[84] *Vest. stat.*, No. 12 (1962), p. 3.

[85] See Kosygin's speech in *Ek. gaz.*, April 21, 1965. The word *podkhalim* means bootlicker; the word *podkhalimstvo* means bootlicking. Kosygin made the word harsher by substituting a crude and in any case unusual ending of *-azh* for the usual *-stvo*. He may have coined the word himself.

being of the population. . . . All the Party, the whole Soviet people, both in town and in the village unanimously approved the decisions of the March plenum." [86]

And so it goes. Yesterday, the party, the government, and the whole Soviet people unanimously accepted Khrushchev's agricultural policies. Today, the party, the government, and the whole Soviet people unanimously are rejecting Khrushchev's agricultural policies. There has not been in the Soviet Union much change in the past half a century in the matter of treating things.

It would be a great achievement to bring Soviet agriculture in some order, even with those "yesterdays" and "todays" disposed of. So long as they are preserved, so long as they will continue, so long as forced unanimity remains as an inherent feature of the Soviet system, Soviet agricultural production is likely to remain in a poor shape, though probably in better shape when compared to its recent past.

Interesting comments on this issue have recently been made by A. M. Rumiantsev, former editor of *Pravda,* who writes: "It is not a secret that many are tired of reforms and that their trust in innovations has been undermined. Moreover, they are tired not so much of innovations as of the parade drumming that has always accompanied them." [87]

I do not dare to predict whether an economic system with an immensely weak link, such as that represented by the important agricultural sector, can continue to exist for long. But I have serious doubts.

[86] The first quotation is from *Sel'. zh.,* April 14, 1965; the second from *Ek. sel'. khoz.,* No. 4 (1965), p. 1.

[87] *Iunost',* No. 1 (1966).

COMMENT

Philip M. Raup

It is appropriate to begin by paying homage to the remarkable achievement of Dr. Naum Jasny represented by his contribution which deserves serious attention at an age when most men have ceased productive work. The highest tribute that can be paid is to review it as a professional work, by a respected colleague, with no concession for the author's age. Dr. Jasny, as scholar and scientist, would not want it otherwise.

First, an overall judgment: A strong case has been weakened by overstatement. This can be illustrated by reference to the comparisons made between trends in meat and steel prices in the U.S.S.R. and the United States from 1928 to 1964. The steel industries of the U.S.S.R. and the United States were not at comparable levels of development in 1928. Most of the cost advantages of large scale were still ahead of the Soviet steel industry in that year. In contrast, the United States by 1928 had gained a large measure of the economies in production that can be achieved by increasing the plant scale. And the cost-increasing influences deriving from unionization of labor in the steel industry did not exercise a marked influence in the United States until after the depression of the 1930's. To use U.S.S.R. and American steel prices in 1928 as a base for the construction of a time series of meat versus steel price ratios is misleading. It invites memories of similar uses of percentage changes from questionable bases by those who sought to conceal rather than to analyze.

A similar minor but distracting twist to the argument is given by references to the decline in acreage sown to durum wheat and buckwheat in the U.S.S.R. Declines in farmland area devoted to these two crops are not confined to the U.S.S.R. It has been difficult in some recent years to interest American farmers in durum wheat, and buckwheat has all but disappeared from American land-use statistics. The reasons are rising labor costs, changes in the relative risk of crop failure among competing crops, and perhaps inadequate investment in scientific seed-breeding work. In the United States, changes in acreages of buckwheat or durum wheat have reflected clear-cut shifts in comparative advantage among crops. A possible interpretation of the Soviet data for these two crops is to conclude that forces affecting land use in the United States are also at work in the U.S.S.R., and that Soviet farm managers are also economic men.

Jasny is on firmer ground in his revealing comparisons of relative prices for major agricultural products in the U.S.S.R. and in other producing nations. The continuing high cost of food is perhaps the most remarkable evidence of the blockages in the Soviet system that prevent the generation of a structure of incentives that will bring forth added output in response to price.

For as long as prices were bookkeeping entries only, the pattern of the motivating forces that guided Soviet farm managers yielded a generation of men insensitive to price signals. With the return to price policy as a tool to achieve output increases, a period of trial and error lies probably ahead.

The possible nature of future agricultural adjustment problems in the U.S.S.R. can be illustrated by reference to hogs. It is largely true that the Soviet Union is still on a "fat standard" in the pricing of farm products. This is apparent in the relative prices of beef and pork, of fat and lean hogs, and in extremely high prices for sunflower seed and (in the Far Eastern maritime provinces) for soybeans. Criteria for breed selection and development in the swine industry are clear-cut indicators of the shortage of fat and of drabness in the diet.

The geographic position of the Soviet Union is a partial explanation of this price premium on fat. The U.S.S.R. has been largely unable to take advantage of recent advances in the production of vegetable oils. The corn that Khrushchev saw in Iowa in 1955 could be promoted with some success in the Soviet Union. The soybean could not.

There are grounds for doubt, however, that the current high prices for pork in the U.S.S.R. can be maintained. The relative level of Soviet hog prices is not as high as indicated in Jasny's essay. The years chosen for comparison have yielded misleading data. The sharp increases in 1965 in hog prices in the United States mark a phase in the hog-price cycle that carried American hog prices (live weight) to more than $600 per ton in February, 1966. This is in sharp contrast to the 1963 figure of $354 per ton shown in Table 1, and used by Jasny elsewhere in his comparisons of costs of production.

As a consequence, the statement that "no category of meat would be sold in the United States for more than 40 percent of the Soviet procurement price" must be amended. Hogs in midwinter 1965/66 in the United States sold for approximately 50 percent of the post-March, 1965, Soviet procurement price of 1,294 rubles per ton.

A similar overstress is placed on differences in producer prices paid for hogs in the United States and U.S.S.R. After the March, 1965, raise, the Soviet procurement price for hogs was not four times the American farm price but was approximately 2.7 times the 1965 American average price for slaughter hogs (barrows and gilts) at Chicago, of $475 per metric ton live weight.[88]

In spite of these amendments to the data, Soviet hog prices are still surprisingly high. So high, in fact, that one is tempted to speculate on the possibility that the Soviet Union may be generating its own unique version of the classic hog cycle.

The recent drop in Soviet hog numbers was dramatic, from 70 million head in 1963 to 41 million head in 1964. In addition to all the errors of agricultural policy, this was a physical response to a biologic and climatic situation. It had little to do with prices or profits. In the economic literature it has always been assumed that the hog cycle was a price-induced phenomenon, peculiar to a market economy. But cycles occur in lemmings, moles, rabbits, and other animals, without benefit of price inducement. It seems possible that the trough in the Soviet hog cycle of the mid-1960's was generated primarily by weather, feed supply, and other "natural forces," only weakly related to farm-management plans or central-government farm policies.

This reasoning suggests that the Soviets may have set hog prices too high in the March, 1965, price reform. The U.S.S.R. may now have reached the stage in its development at which it is capable of generating a true price-induced hog cycle, rooted in the traditional lag between price signals and production responses.

The stress placed by Jasny on the exceptionally high level of hog prices in the U.S.S.R. may be less a reflection of true costs of production and more an indication of the extent to which Soviet agricultural price trends must be interpreted by the tests of a market economy. The available evidence suggests that in basing comparisons on post-March, 1965, Soviet prices and 1963 American prices, Jasny was unfortunate enough to hit the trough of an American hog-price cycle and the peak of the Soviet administered-price cycle.

One of the strengths in Jasny's paper is his emphasis on the misleading nature of the practice of valuing collective-farm labor at the wages paid on state farms, in computing production costs on collective farms. There are several reasons why state-farm wages may be inappropriate.

All available evidence suggests that the collective-farm worker has an

[88] U.S. Department of Agriculture, *Livestock and Meat Situation,* LMS-148 (Washington, D.C.: U.S. Department of Agriculture, March, 1966), p. 15.

advantage over a state-farm worker, in the greater opportunity to utilize his private plot or to obtain feed for his livestock. The impairment of this advantage on a state farm would require that the wage level be higher on the state farm, as partial compensation for this deficient "fringe benefit."

In the U.S.S.R., for a significant array of goods and services, regional graduations in prices are just the reverse of the patterns that prevail in more developed economies, where transport costs are incorporated into prices on the basis of a central market structure.

In the United States farm prices are usually based on central market prices, minus freight. Prices in central Montana are lower than those in North Dakota, North Dakota prices are below Chicago prices. In the U.S.S.R. the pattern is reversed, with the higher prices in the more remote or disadvantaged areas. This also tends to be true of labor wages.

If state farms are situated at greater distances from population centers, or in areas where working and living conditions are relatively unfavorable, then the wage rate on state farms may be higher as partial compensation. School teachers and medical technicians in remote areas of the U.S.S.R. get higher wages than do those in more stable, long-established communities.

The state farms tend to be clustered in these more marginal, remote, and newly settled areas. Their wage structure is thus a reflection of the general characteristic of Soviet regional prices. This is an added reason why the use of state-farm wage rates to calculate the cost of labor in collective farms is apt to be misleading. The greater concentration of collective farms is in areas of relatively lower prices, including wages.

An additional and major reason why state-farm wage rates are invalid in valuing labor on collective farms is due to differences in sex composition of the two labor forces. Women perform most of the work on the collective farms. In 1959, Soviet data show that women comprised 60 percent of the total collective-farm labor force. By job classifications, women made up 87 percent of all field team leaders, 71 percent of all workers in plant-breeding and feed production, 90 percent of all workers in the hog enterprises, 93 percent in poultry, and 99 percent in milking.[89]

At the risk of being misinterpreted, it seems necessary to point out that the labor output of women in Soviet agriculture cannot be equated

[89] U.S. Congress, Joint Economic Committee, *Current Economic Indicators for the USSR* (Washington, D.C.: Government Printing Office, 1965), p. 101.

with that of men. The state-farm labor force has a larger proportion of males and includes many who are specialized machine operators. They have been given favored treatment in many direct and indirect ways, not the least in wages. To use state-farm wage rates in valuing collective-farm labor can only be interpreted as a desire to cast collective farms in an unfavorable light.

Jasny cites the interesting study of collective farms in the Kirov area, by A. Rumiantseva, *Ekonomika sel'skogo khoziaistva,* 1965, No. 5, pp. 29–30, in which the author concludes that for rational management farms should be large enough to include 300 head of beef cattle, or 200 hogs, or 100 cows, or 500 sheep.

It is illuminating to compare these norms with the results of current research in the United States. A recent publication by Harold E. Barnhill, of the U.S. Department of Agriculture, uses linear programming techniques to determine the resources needed in selected type of farming areas in order to yield farm operator incomes of $2,500, $3,500, $4,500, and $5,500 per year.[90]

In order to yield $5,500 of operator income, Barnhill found that major enterprises on the following scale would be needed:

Wheat, north-central Montana	1,058 acres in wheat
Cotton, Oklahoma rolling plains	592 acres in cotton,
	1,303 acres in wheat,
	207 stockers
Beef ranching, south-central Okla.	465 cows
Beef ranching, northern Nevada	249 cows
Poultry, eastern Connecticut	5,234 laying hens
Dairy, eastern Wisconsin	60 cows
Hogs, west-central Illinois	33 sows
	495 fattening hogs, and
	48 beef cows

In terms of the livestock enterprises, these figures are not greatly different from those used by Rumiantseva. The important difference is that in the American estimates, each of the farms was designed as a family-type unit, with family labor in most cases accounting for more than half of the total labor input.

Among the many reasons for high costs of production in Soviet agriculture are those that reflect a failure to adjust production plans to

[90] Harold E. Barnhill, *Resource Requirements on Farms for Specified Operator Incomes,* Economic Research Service, Agricultural Economics Report No. 5 (Washington, D.C.: U.S. Department of Agriculture, November, 1964).

reduce seasonal demands on the labor force. This is illustrated by the highly seasonal nature of milk production in the U.S.S.R. Labor costs are excessive since the labor force to handle peak milk production in June, July, or August must be on hand the rest of the year, when output falls to less than 60 percent of output in the peak months.

This can be illustrated by comparing the seasonality of milk production from two herds in 1958—one near Kiev, of 143 cows, and one near Fergus Falls, Minnesota, of 120 cows. The following proportions [91] are available from the herd records:

		Peak-month output as percent of lowest-month output.	
Herd location	Number of cows	Peak months	As percent of low
Kiev, Ukraine	143	June–July	172
Fergus Falls, Minnesota	120	December–January	126

The months of peak output in the Kiev herd came at a time of year (June–July) when other farm enterprises also had peak labor demands. The peak months for the Fergus Falls herd came at a time of year when other demands on farm labor were at the lowest level for the year.

A further reason for high costs of production in Soviet agriculture is rapid depreciation of machinery and equipment. A part of this rapid depreciation is due to the fact that equipment is cannibalized for spare parts as soon as it breaks down, reflecting long delay and inadequate distribution in parts supply.

The average age of tractors on American farms is in excess of 10 years. Many are more than 20 years old. The average age of tractors in the U.S.S.R. is only about one-half that in the United States. This results in a much greater demand on tractor producing capacity in the U.S.S.R. in order to maintain a given level of power input.

The unsatisfactory nature of the supply and maintenance of farm machinery calls attention to another dimension of the task of cost reduction in U.S.S.R. agriculture. Developments in nonagricultural sectors play an important role in determining the speed and extent of any reductions in cost of production. This is obvious for prices and stocks of machinery, spare parts, feeds, and fertilizer.

[91] Data for the Kiev herd I obtained from the barn records of the Red Partisan Collective Farm, Kiev *oblast'*, in September, 1958. Data for the Minnesota herd are from the records of the Fergus Falls State Hospital, as reported to the Minnesota Dairy Herd Improvement Association. Average output was about 9,500 pounds of milk per cow per year in both herds.

It may also be important in less direct ways. The speed with which urban housing demands are met will influence the attitudes of families toward life on collective farms as a base for multiple job-holding. In a number of agricultural areas it has been rewarding for a family to retain a base in a collective farm, as a solution to housing and food-supply problems, while able-bodied members of the family worked in nonfarm jobs.

In this sense, many collective farm-families would be classified as "part-time farmers" in noncollectivized economies. The qualitative contribution of these families to the agricultural labor force is surely below average. Qualitative improvement in this labor force will come about when urban housing, and urban food supply improve to the point at which labor is no longer held in agriculture by the strength of the fringe benefits. At that point labor productivity in Soviet agriculture will begin to improve.

The Role of Women in Soviet Agriculture

NORTON T. DODGE AND
MURRAY FESHBACH

Soviet industry has expanded at a record pace during the past four decades and today ranks second only to the United States. Nonetheless, at the time of the 1959 census the majority (53 percent) of the 56.6 million women who worked in the Soviet Union were still in agriculture, and the bulk (84 percent) of these were engaged in unskilled, nonspecialized work. Thus, a woman working in a field brigade on a state or collective farm or selling her hard-earned produce at collective-farm markets is still more representative than the woman factory worker or the highly trained and more enlightened professional woman who is so often publicized in Soviet literature and the press. The pattern and rhythm of the lives of Soviet farm women, trapped in the backwaters of the agricultural economy, have been little touched by the twentieth century. Their fictional counterparts are vividly portrayed in Abramov's *Vokrug da okolo,* Solzhenitsyn's *Matrenin dvor,* and Iashin's *Vologodskaia Svadba,* and the isolation and archaic cultural patterns of their villages have been strikingly described in recent sociological studies such as *Selo Viriatino v proshlom i nastoiashchem.*

Our fundamental objective here is to set forth the facts of female participation in the agricultural labor force and from these to deduce Soviet policy on the utilization of women in agriculture. Although we shall focus on the present, some speculations regarding the future will be ventured. Our approach will be primarily statistical and economic since the space at our disposal forces us largely to neglect the sociological.[1]

EMPLOYMENT OF WOMEN IN SOVIET AGRICULTURE

MAJOR TRENDS

In prerevolutionary Russia when all but a very small proportion of the working population were engaged in agricultural pursuits, the work of

[1] For an interesting sociological background and for earlier estimates based on preliminary results of the census, see Demitri Shimkin, "Current Characteristics and Problems of the Soviet Rural Population," in Roy D. Laird, ed., *Soviet Agricultural and Peasant Affairs* (Lawrence, Kansas: University of Kansas Press, 1963), pp. 79–127. Our study is based on final census results which were not available to Shimkin in 1962.

TABLE 1

TRENDS IN THE AGRICULTURAL AND NONAGRICULTURAL LABOR FORCE, BY SECTORS, SOCIOECONOMIC CATEGORY, AND SEX, U.S.S.R., CENSUSES 1926, 1939, 1959

Sector of the economy and socioeconomic category	1926				1939				1959			
	thousand persons				thousand persons				thousand persons			
	Both sexes	Males	Females	Percent females	Both sexes	Males	Females	Percent females	Both sexes	Males	Females	Percent females
Total labor force	*84,500*	*45,300*	*39,200*	*46.4*	*89,800*	*49,300*	*40,500*	*45.1*	*108,995*	*52,440*	*56,556*	*51.9*
Nonagricultural labor force (including Armed Forces)	12,800	9,200	3,600	28.1	34,800	23,700	10,900	31.2	60,704	33,864	26,841	44.2
Agricultural labor force	71,700	36,100	35,600	49.7	55,000	25,400	27,600	53.8	48,291	18,576	29,715	61.5
Private farmers [a]	70,500	35,300	35,200	49.2	12,600	4,400	8,200	65.1	9,957	946	9,011	90.5
Collective farmers	—	—	—	—	36,300	16,600	19,700	54.3	31,723	13,731	17,992	56.7
Agricultural workers and employees	1,200	800	400	33.3	6,100	4,400	1,700	27.9	6,611	3,898	2,713	41.0
	(percent)											
Total labor force	*100.0*	*100.0*	*100.0*	—	*100.0*	*100.0*	*100.0*	—	*100.0*	*100.0*	*100.0*	—
Nonagricultural labor force (including Armed Forces)	15.1	20.3	9.2	—	38.8	48.5	26.9	—	55.7	64.6	47.5	—
Agricultural labor force	84.9	79.7	90.8	—	61.2	51.5	73.1	—	44.3	35.4	52.5	—
Private farmers	83.4	77.9	89.8	—	14.0	8.9	20.2	—	9.1	1.8	15.9	—
Collective farmers	—	—	—	—	40.4	33.7	48.6	—	29.1	26.2	31.8	—
Agricultural workers and employees	1.4	1.8	1.0	—	6.8	8.9	4.2	—	6.1	7.4	4.8	—

[a] Includes individual farmers and persons occupied solely in subsidiary agriculture.

SOURCES: 1926 and 1939: Warren W. Eason, "Labor Force," in Abram Bergson and Simon Kuznets, eds., *Economic Trends in the Soviet Union* (Cambridge, Mass.: Harvard University Press, 1963), p. 84. *Itogi-1959-SSSR*, tables 30 and 33, pp. 96–97 and 104–105.

planting, cultivating, and harvesting were as much a part of a woman's life as a man's. However, the industrialization drive in the late 1920's induced important changes in the pattern of male and female employment. Owing to the long agricultural heritage of Russia, the share of women in the agricultural labor force (49.7 percent) was already high in 1926 and had increased by a dozen percentage points to 61.5 by 1959 (see Table 1). In 1926, approximately nine-tenths of the women in the labor force were in agriculture, which then meant private agriculture. Men, also, were primarily employed in agriculture although the proportion (80 percent) was somewhat smaller. By 1939, as a result of the demands of industry, the proportion of working women employed in agriculture had declined to 73.1 percent while the proportion for men was only a little more than half. Further industrialization and the effects of World War II reinforced these trends. By 1959, only 55.3 percent of employed women were in the agricultural labor force and 42.7 of employed men. The shift from a concentration of women workers in agricultural employment to a rough balance between agricultural and nonagricultural employment reflects, of course, the vast economic transformation in the Soviet Union which has converted from a largely backward and agrarian society into a comparatively highly developed and complex one, possessing an advanced industrial sector along with a large agricultural sector still relatively backward and insulated in many ways from modern industrial civilization.

WOMEN IN THE POPULATION—EMPLOYMENT BALANCE IN 1959

Data from the 1959 census are used to describe the structure of population and employment because they provide detailed socioeconomic characteristics not obtainable in regular employment statistics based on establishment reports or sample surveys.

Females made up 49 percent of the underaged, 54 percent of the able-bodied, and 74 percent of the overaged population. Among those employed in the labor force, women made up 52 percent of the total, 50 percent of the able-bodied group, and 68 percent of the overaged group.[2]

The large proportion of agricultural workers in the civilian labor force (46 percent), the high ratio of women in the agricultural labor force (54 percent in the socialized and private independent sector and 91 percent

[2] U.S. Congress, Joint Economic Committee, *Annual Economic Indicators for the U.S.S.R.* (Washington, D.C.: Government Printing Office, 1964), Table V-A-1, pp. 44–45.

TABLE 2

CIVILIAN LABOR FORCE, BY SECTOR, SOCIOECONOMIC CATEGORY, AND SEX, U.S.S.R., JANUARY 15, 1959

Category	Total (in thousands)	Males (in thousands)	Percentage distribution	Females (thousands)	Percentage distribution	Percent females
Total civilian labor force	*105,372*	*48,817*	*100.0*	*56,555*	*100.0*	*53.7*
Agriculture	48,291	18,576	38.1	29,715	52.5	61.5
Collective farmers	31,723	13,731	28.1	17,992	31.8	56.7
Workers and employees	6,611	3,898	8.0	2,713	4.8	41.0
Individual peasants	92	32	0.1	60	0.1	65.2
Private subsidiary sector	9,865	914	1.9	8,951	15.8	90.7
Industry, construction, transportation and communications	36,575	22,423	45.9	14,152	25.0	38.7
Trade, public dining, etc.	5,171	1,993	4.1	3,178	5.6	61.5
Education, science, and public health	9,793	2,864	5.9	6,928	12.3	70.7
Housing, communal economy, administration, financial system	4,660	2,385	4.9	2,275	4.0	48.8
Other branches	882	575	1.2	306	0.5	34.7

SOURCES: *Itogi-1959-SSSR*, Tables 30 and 33, pp. 96–97 and 104–105.

in the private subsidiary sector), and the high proportion of employed women who are in agriculture (53 percent) are some of the most striking characteristics of the Soviet economy shown in Table 2.

Four categories of workers are employed in agriculture. In 1959, the largest category (31.7 million) was made up of those who are members of, and contribute most of their labor to, collective farms. A second group, 6.6 million in 1959, are the workers and employees engaged in agriculture primarily on state farms.[3] A third group are those engaged primarily in private subsidiary farming. Numbering more than 9.8 million in 1959 they are mostly members of collective farm families. In addition, this last figure includes members of families of workers and employees in the state-farm sector who raise livestock and work private garden plots producing vegetables and fruit for their own use and the local market. The fourth category of agricultural workers—individual peasants—has almost passed out of existence, for only 92,000 were left

[3] The combined term "worker and employee" has a very special meaning in Soviet terminology. Persons so designated are paid wages or a salary by the state or by (state-owned) enterprises and are entitled to a specified set of fringe benefits, including pension rights and rights to an annual vacation.

FIGURE 1
AGE DISTRIBUTION OF MALES AND FEMALES EMPLOYED IN "PHYSICAL" OCCUPATIONS IN AGRICULTURE, U.S.S.R., JANUARY 15, 1959 [a]

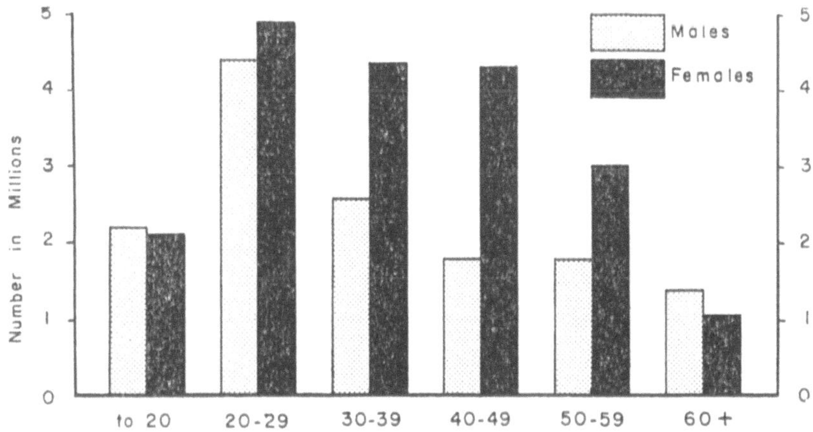

[a] Excluding private subsidiary agriculture.
SOURCE: Appendix Table 1.

in 1959. Of the three significant categories of agricultural workers, women made up 57 percent of the collective farmers, 91 percent of the workers in private subsidiary agriculture, and 41 percent of the workers and employees in the agricultural sector.

WOMEN IN NONPROFESSIONAL AGRICULTURAL EMPLOYMENT

Women still perform most of the "physical" work in agriculture. A comparison of the proportion of women engaged in primarily physical occupations in agriculture (excluding those in the private subsidiary economy) for the years 1926, 1939, and 1959 reveals a deterioration in the position of women over the years.[4] In 1926 the proportion was 50 percent, and in both 1939 and 1959 it stood at 58 percent. By 1959, however, the absolute number of women had declined to almost half the 1926 level, corresponding, of course, to the over-all decline in the number of persons employed in agriculture. Many younger rural women have entered industry, construction, trade, and the professions, while older women lacking mobility have remained behind.

Older persons remaining in agriculture, and the younger shifting into industry and other expanding sectors of the economy, is a phenomenon often observed in economic development. Figure 1 shows the age distribution of males and females employed in "physical" occupations in

[4] *Itogi-1959-SSSR,* p. 168; *Zhen. i deti-1961,* pp. 114–119; *Zhen. i deti-1963,* pp. 94–99.

TABLE 3

CONTRIBUTION OF ABLE-BODIED WOMEN TO COLLECTIVE-FARM LABOR, U.S.S.R., SELECTED YEARS

Year	Number (thousand)	Index (1940 = 100)	Percent of all able-bodied workers on collective farms	Percent of total labor days earned by women	Index of average number of labor days earned by women (1940 = 100)
1936	17,896.2 [a]	104	46.2 [a]	n.a.	n.a.
1938	18,705.8 [a]	108	52.7 [a]	n.a.	n.a.
1940	17,275.0 [b]	100	54 [c]	42 [c]	100 [c]
1941	8,485.1 [d]	49	52 [g]	40 [d]	n.a.
1942	8,913.7 [d]	46	60 [d]	n.a.	n.a.
1943	9,191.6 [d]	53	72 [d]	n.a.	n.a.
1944	8,575.9 [d]	50	76 [d]	70 [d]	n.a.
1945	8,216.0 [d]	48	76 [d]	n.a.	n.a.
1950	(18,306) [e]	106	64 [f]	n.a.	n.a.
1953	(16,859) [e]	98	63 [c]	52 [c]	122 [c]
1955	(17,336) [e]	100	61 [c]	50 [c]	139 [c]
1957	(16,342) [e]	95	59 [c]	48 [c]	138 [c]
1958	(15,950) [e]	92	58 [c]	47 [c]	140 [c]
1959	(14,916) [e]	86	57 [c]	49 [c]	n.a.
1961	(12,264) [e]	71	56 [g]	48 [h]	n.a.
1962	(11,872) [e]	69	56 [i]	49 [h]	n.a.
1963	n.a.	n.a.	56 [j]	n.a.	n.a.
1964	n.a.	n.a.	55 [k]	n.a.	n.a.

NOTE: By census definition able-bodied women are 16 to 54 years of age, and able-bodied men are 16 to 59. This is also used for employment statistics. Figures in parentheses are derived.

SOURCES:

[a] *Prob. ek.*, No. 7 (1940), p. 119.

[b] *Istor. arkhiv*, No. 6 (1962), p. 30.

[c] *Zhen. i deti-1961*, p. 129. The figure for 1959 in column 3 is in terms of man-days.

[d] Iu. V. Arutiunian, *Sovetskoe krest'ianstvo v gody Velikoi Otechestvennoe voiny* (Moscow: 1963), pp. 66–67.

[e] Estimated by multiplying the percentage of women able-bodied participants in column 3 times the total number of able-bodied participants in corresponding years. For 1950 (28,603,000), 1953 (26,761,000), and 1957 (27,699,000) from Iu. V. Arutiunian, *Mekhanizatory sel'skogo khoziastva v 1929–1957 gg.* (Moscow: 1960), p. 271, excluding able-bodied farmers working in state industry, transport, etc.; for 1955 (28,419,000) and 1956 (29,382,000) estimated by multiplying the average number of able-bodied collective farmers from V. G. Venzher, *Voprosy ispol'zovaniia zakona stoimosti v kolkhoznom proizvodstve* (Moscow: 1960), p. 73, by the number of agricultural collective farms from *Narkhoz-1956*, p. 140, and *Narkhoz-1959*, p. 423; for 1958 a total of 27,500,000 was reported in Iu. G. Feigin, *et al.*, eds., *Osobennosti i faktory razmeshcheniia otraslei narodnogo khoziaistva SSSR* (Moscow: 1960) p. 404, excluding members working in state establishments and institutions and full-time students; for 1959 (26,168,000) the total number was estimated by multiplying the total number of collective farmer participants by the percentage of able-bodied collective farmers (35,411,100 × 0.739)—N. I. Shishkin, ed., *Trudovye resursy SSSR* (Moscow: 1961), pp. 98–99; for 1961 and 1962, total number of able-bodied participants of 30,400,000 and 29,559,000, respectively, are given in E. S. Karnaukhova and M. I. Kozlov eds., *Puti povysheniia proizvoditel'nosti truda v sel'khom khoziaistve SSSR* (Moscow: 1964), p. 56.

[f] *Zhen.-SSSR-1960*, p. 42.

[g] *Zhen. i deti-1963*, p. 109.

[h] Estimated as follows: *Ibid.* gives 171 and 173 man-days worked by able-bodied women in 1961 and 1962, which when multiplied by the number of able-bodied women (col. 1) yields 2,097 and 2,054 million man-days worked by able-bodied women. Total number of man-days worked by all able-bodied collective farmers was obtained by multiplying the average number of able-bodied participants (21,900,000 and 21,200,000 in 1961 and 1962, Karnaukhova, *op. cit.*) and the average number of man-days worked by each (198 and 199, *ibid.*, p. 63). Thus, in 1961, 2,097 million man-days divided by 4,336 million man-days equals 48 percent and in 1962, 2,054 million man-days divided by 4,219 million man-days equals 49 percent.

[i] G. I. Shmelev, *Raspredelenie i ispol'zovanie truda v kolkhozakh* (Moscow: 1964), p. 113.

[j] *Vest. stat.*, No. 2 (1965), p. 93.

[k] *Ibid.*, No. 1 (1966), p. 92.

agriculture (excluding the private subsidiary sector). Here the proportion of men and women in the older age groups is higher than in other sectors.[5] Furthermore, women engaged in agriculture tend to be older than men; approximately 42 percent were 40 years of age or older versus 35 percent of the men.

WOMEN ON COLLECTIVE FARMS

Before World War II the proportion of female able-bodied collective farmers showed an upward trend. According to Table 3, women made up 46 percent of the total number in 1936 and 53 percent in 1938. During the war, owing to the draft and the transfer of men into industry and youths into labor-reserve schools, the proportion of women among able-bodied collective farmers climbed to a record high of 76 percent. The postwar high of 63 to 65 percent was reached in 1950–1953, when, as a consequence of the Korean conflict, the government was drafting men into the army or shifting them to industry. In 1963, the date of the last available information, the proportion had declined to 56 percent.

The contribution of women to collective-farm labor can be measured in several ways: in terms of absolute numbers; the proportion of the total which are women; the proportion of labor-days (*trudodni*) earned by women, and the proportion of man-days worked by women. We find that the female contribution in absolute numbers over the past decade (Table 3, col. 1) shows a substantial decline from 1938 when the number of women collective farmers was almost 4 million higher than in 1959. The percentage of women among able-bodied farmers working on collective farms still remains several points higher than in the late 1930's, despite the steady decline since the peak of 76 percent during the war. The decline since 1950 in both the number of collective-farm women working and their proportion of the total reflects, of course, the increased efficiency of labor on collective farms in the decade of the 1950's.

In applying the third measure, we must remember that the labor-day is not a measure of time worked but a composite yardstick that reflects the type and quality of work performed. A tractor or combine driver, for example, earns more labor-days per shift than a worker in a field brigade. Local rates are based upon national minimums for certain occupations but still vary from region to region. The situation in the Ukraine in 1957 can be considered fairly typical: able-bodied males received on the average 1.91 "labor-days" for every "man-day" while

[5] See the forthcoming study by Norton T. Dodge, *Women in the Soviet Economy* (Baltimore: The Johns Hopkins University Press, 1966).

women received only 1.68. As a rule, the coefficient for men is higher because they do more complicated and harder work.[6]

The different expectations for the two sexes are reflected in the minimum number of labor-days or man-days required. Typically, the number of days which must be worked by women is considerably smaller than the number required of men. For example, in 1957, at the "Kirov" collective farm in Kharkov *oblast'*, the minimum for males 18 to 50 years of age was 300 labor-days and for males 50 to 60 years of age, 250. For women 18 to 40 years of age the minimum was 200 days, and for women 40 to 50 years of age and for nursing mothers the minimum was 150.[7] An indication of the smaller contribution of women also is given in Table 4. The situation had not improved in 1959: 4.1

TABLE 4

UTILIZATION OF COLLECTIVE FARM LABOR RESOURCES, BY SEX, U.S.S.R., 1953

Number of labor-days earned	Percent		
	Total	Men	Women
None	2.6	1.4	3.3
Up to 50	5.8	2.5	7.6
51 to 100	7.0	3.0	9.3
101 to 200	26.4	15.9	32.3
201 to 300	21.8	20.7	22.3
301 to 400	15.7	20.9	12.8
More than 400	20.7	35.6	12.4
TOTAL	100.0	100.0	100.0

SOURCE: N. I. Shishkin, ed., *Trudovye resursy SSSR* (Moscow: 1961), p. 109.

percent of the women collective farmers who were required to earn the minimum number of days did not work even one day, while 14.1 percent did not earn the obligatory minimum.[8] Further increases in the proportion of nonparticipants occurred in 1961 and 1962 when 5 and 5.3 percent, respectively, did not participate in the socialized economy.[9] Women fail to fulfill the norm principally because they devote their

[6] I. Paskhaver, *Balans trudovykh resursov kolkhozov* (Kiev: 1961), p. 74.

[7] *Ibid.*, p. 264.

[8] N. I. Shishkin, ed., *Trudovye resursy SSSR* (Moscow: 1961), p. 109. A collective farmer's income from the collective farm is typically reduced by 10 percent for failure to work the required minimum number of labor-days per year. Cf. O. D. Dubinskaia, *Prava i obiazannosti chlenov kolkhoza* (Moscow: 1957), p. 34.

[9] U.S. Congress, Joint Economic Committee, *Current Economic Indicators for the U.S.S.R.* (Washington, D.C.: Government Printing Office, 1965), Table VI-8, p. 83.

energies to private garden plots and the home. Both the smaller labor-day versus man-day coefficient and the fewer man-days worked have the result that women, on the average, contribute less work measured in labor-days than men and as a result of this smaller number of labor-days, the series showing the percent of labor-days earned by women collective farmers (Table 3) is, on the average, about ten percentage points or approximately a fifth below the percentage of women collective farmers.[10] The importance to the economy of female participation in the agricultural labor force is, therefore, exaggerated unless allowance is made for the difference between the number of available women laborers and the work they actually perform.

National data available for 1959 show that able-bodied females required to earn the minimum number of days averaged 67 man-days less work than males.[11] The 1956–1958 data for Krasnodar *krai,*[12] a fairly typical agricultural region, are similar in their internal distribution to the 1959 national data. Although women constituted 57 percent of the able-bodied collective farmers in the U.S.S.R. in 1959 (see Table 3), in Krasnodar *krai* they contributed only 46.4 percent of the total man-hours expended in all types of activity—on the collective farms, in the state sector, for other individuals, and on their own garden plots.[13] By far the largest share of their time was contributed to the collective farms where for the four-year period 1956 to 1959 they devoted approximately 58 percent of their work time.[14] The next largest claim on their time was work in the private subsidiary economy—on private plots, in wood-cutting, fishing, hunting, and as independent artisans. In no year for which data are given did women work less than a third of their time in private activity.[15]

Because female collective farmers devote substantially more of their time to private plots than do men, women accounted for 80.6 percent of

[10] However, the 1959 figure of 49 percent applies to man-days worked. A shift to this form of reporting collective-farm labor inputs was made in this year.

[11] M. P. Vasilenko, *Puti preodeleniia sezonnosti truda v kolkhozakh* (Moscow: 1962), p. 53.

[12] B. I. Braginskii, *Proizvoditel'nost' truda v sel'skom khoziaistve: Metodika ucheta i planirovaniia* (Moscow: 1962), p. 194.

[13] Vasilenko, *op. cit.* (in n. 11), pp. 23–24.

[14] *Ibid.*, and Braginskii, *op. cit.* (in n. 12).

[15] The closer a collective farm is situated to an urban center, the fewer the number of labor-days worked in the socialized sector, especially by female labor. This is the result of higher returns from work on private plots. See V. Komarovskaia, V. Luzgina, V. Shatskii in I. A. Borodin, ed., *Ispol'zovanie trudovykh resursov v sel'skom khoziaistve SSSR* (Moscow: 1964), p. 211.

the labor time spent in the private subsidiary agricultural economy. Men, on the other hand, devoted over more than a third again as much of their time as women to work on collective farms. Women's share in the work of state and cooperative organizations was slightly smaller. However, when all agricultural activities are taken together, including work on private plots, women accounted for 55.5 percent of the total labor inputs, measured in man-hours, of able-bodied men and women in 1959.[16] This total is close to the share of able-bodied women on collective farms (57 percent).

In appraising the contribution of women to collective farm work, we must consider not only the quantitative but also the qualitative aspects of their contribution. Among women collective farmers, 17.4 million, or 97 percent, are engaged in "physical" labor.[17] Of these, 14.5 million, or 83 percent, are employed in nonspecialized and unskilled work compared with 66 percent of the male collective farmers engaged in physical labor (see Table 5).

Of the two major branches of collective farm activity—crop-growing and animal husbandry—the former is highly seasonal whereas the latter requires constant attendance throughout the year. According to the 1959 census, women comprised 51 percent (2,221,000) of the 4.4 million animal-husbandry workers. Most of them, and especially the milkmaids and poultry workers, are girls and young women with children of preschool age.[18] However, the proportion of collective-farm women employed in animal husbandry in 1959 was small (12.8 percent).[19] The overwhelming proportion of collective-farm women (87.2 percent) were employed in seasonal field work—the planting, cultivating, and harvesting of crops—where they made up 66 percent of the workers.[20] Data from Rostov *oblast'* show wide monthly variations in the rates of female participation in collective farm work—in 1960, fewer than 57 percent of the women employed in July worked during January–February and November–December.[21] Therefore, many women are able to devote much time during slack periods to their private plots, the care of their children, and other household duties. Such irregular partici-

[16] Calculated from data in Vasilenko, *op. cit.* (in n. 11).

[17] *Itogi-1959-SSSR,* Tables 23, 46, pp. 104–105, 160.

[18] G. Shmelev, V. Ladenkov, *Ek. sel'. khoz.,* No. 10 (1962), p. 30.

[19] *Ibid.* According to Shishkin, *op. cit.* (in n. 8), p. 99, the corresponding percentages for both sexes from collective farm annual reports are: 1956—11.7; 1958—12.1, 1959—12.6 percent.

[20] For both sexes, Shishkin, *op. cit.* (in n. 8), p. 99, gives the following percentages: 1956—79.8; 1958—78.8; 1959—78.2 percent.

[21] Shmelev, Lazenkov, *op. cit.* (in n. 18), p. 29. For earlier and similar figures see B. Babynin, *Prob. ek.,* No. 2 (1940), p. 71.

TABLE 5

NUMBER AND PERCENT OF WOMEN AMONG COLLECTIVE AND STATE FARMERS ENGAGED IN PREDOMINANTLY PHYSICAL LABOR BY OCCUPATION, U.S.S.R., JANUARY 15, 1959

Occupation	Collective farmers			State-farm and other workers		
	Number		Percent female	Number		Percent female
	Total	Female		Total	Female	
Total employed in physical labor	*28,728,425*	*17,420,143*	*60.1*	*5,071,233*	*2,261,473*	*44.6*
Administrative and supervisory personnel:						
Heads of livestock and poultry subfarms	134,983	20,227	15.0	8,114	2,046	25.2
Brigadiers of field brigades	232,772	19,295	8.3	26,364	3,396	12.9
Brigadiers of livestock brigades	31,697	4,043	12.8	42,790	7,718	18.0
Other brigadiers	195,940	10,256	5.2	66,948	6,243	9.3
Skilled workers and junior supervisory personnel:						
Bookkeepers	23,443	4,363	18.6	6,671	1,835	27.5
Tractor and combine drivers	1,259,261	9,571	0.8	1,130,031	7,669	0.7
Implement handlers and workers on agricultural machinery	124,751	1,774	1.4	25,481	1,296	5.1
Field-team leaders	149,666	130,664	87.3	6,839	5,845	85.5
Specialized agricultural workers:						
Workers in plant breeding and feed production	524,606	374,167	71.3	86,661	58,297	67.3
Cattle farm workers	701,449	423,786	60.4	260,014	122,178	47.0
Milking personnel	1,150,363	1,136,923	98.8	281,126	278,686	99.1
Stablemen and grooms	716,017	50,708	7.1	299,274	34,852	11.6
Swineherds	420,541	381,145	90.6	142,601	132,682	93.0
Herdsmen, drovers, shepherds	550,657	96,356	17.5	202,958	44,655	22.0
Other livestock workers	113,874	23,920	21.0	74,681	38,812	52.0
Poultry workers	116,557	108,886	93.4	45,596	42,996	94.3
Beekeepers	62,603	9,497	15.2	17,383	4,085	23.5
Orchard and vineyard workers	50,854	20,887	41.1	55,541	34,441	62.0
Vegetable and melon growers	56,539	45,546	80.6	28,290	22,118	78.2
Irrigators	7,975	861	10.8	11,635	2,154	18.5
Nonspecialized agricultural workers	21,991,868	14,523,178	66.0	2,130,267	1,350,240	63.4

SOURCE: *Itogi-1959-SSSR*, pp. 159–60.

pation has tended to keep women from developing the knowledge and skills required for the more attractive kinds of work in agriculture. Furthermore, it is young men rather than girls who are encouraged or sent by collective farms to obtain specialized training. For example, in 1960 only 1.7 percent of all students entering agricultural mechanization schools were girls.[22] As a result, most collective-farm women spend their lives doing the least interesting and least challenging work.

After the abolition of the machine tractor stations in 1958, the bulk of the MTS workers were transferred to the collective farms, and by the

TABLE 6

SHARE OF WOMEN IN MTS PERSONNEL, BY OCCUPATION, U.S.S.R., 1948, 1954
(percent of total personnel)

	May 1, 1948	May 5, 1954
Personnel servicing tractors and agricultural machinery	7.5	3.9
Drivers	1.1	0.7
Repair workers	4.4	3.3
Workers employed on construction	n.a.	35.7
Wage workers of subsidiary units, dining halls, kindergartens, and others	44.5	34.6

SOURCE: Iu. V. Arutiunian, *Mekhanizatory sel'skogo khoziaistva SSSR v 1929–1957 gg.* (Moscow: 1960), pp. 296–297, 299, and 303.

time of the 1959 census were classified as collective farmers. The jobs performed by the MTS workers—who numbered 3 million in 1954—were usually among the more highly skilled and better paying jobs in agriculture. As Table 6 indicates, the proportion of women in these occupations was very small. Despite the ubiquitous sturdy girl tractor driver in Soviet fiction, she remains largely a creature of the propaganda mill. Only during World War II did women make up a significant percentage of those employed in the machine tractor stations as drivers or mechanics. For example, in Rostov *oblast'* in 1943, 41 percent of the tractor drivers and 50 percent of the combine operators were women.[23] However, the important role women played in the machine

[22] Only 1 percent of all students entering such schools in the R.S.F.S.R. were girls. The corresponding percentages for other major republics were: Ukraine—0.7; Belorussia—0.5; Kazakhstan—4.3 percent. Cf. G. I. Shmelev, *Raspredelenie i ispol'zovanie truda v kolkhozakh* (Moscow: 1964), pp. 121–122.

[23] *Izvestiia,* August 18, 1943.

tractor stations diminished drastically with the passing of wartime exigencies.

WOMEN IN THE PRIVATE SUBSIDIARY ECONOMY

The second group of agricultural workers are those engaged in the private subsidiary sector. In 1959 almost 10 million persons reported work in the private subsidiary economy as their principal occupation. It consists almost entirely of work on private garden plots [24] with only a negligible amount of handicraft work included.[25] These activities constitute a major remnant of private enterprise in the Soviet Union which continues for very practical reasons. As a result of intensive cultivation, private plots, which occupied only 3.7 percent of the sown area in 1959, accounted for a substantial share of total farm output, particularly of certain key products such as potatoes (64 percent), meat (41 percent), milk (47 percent), and eggs (81 percent).[26] By 1961, the sown area of the plots had shrunk to 3.3 percent but the production continued to be very nearly as important as previously.[27]

The plots are cultivated by members of families of collective farmers, of state-farm workers, and of other workers and employees. The first is the largest group, accounting for 58 percent of the total number reported employed in this sector by the 1959 census. The allocation of the remaining 42 percent between families of state-farm workers and of other workers and employees may be estimated at 30 and 12 percent, respectively.[28] When employment is converted to man-year equivalents,

[24] The 1959 census data on employment in the private subsidiary economy are considered to be the least reliable data in the census by Soviet as well as non-Soviet demographers. The reason is that it was the respondent who determined himself whether this was his principal occupation.

[25] Evidence on the distribution of labor inputs (for men and women) among the various aspects of the private subsidiary economy is available for the Rostov *oblast'* during 1957–1960. In this period, 75 to 82 percent of the total number of man-hours were spent in animal husbandry, 16–23 percent in crop production and only 1–3 percent in other activities. The latter include procurement and collection of forest products, fishing, hunting, independent artisan and handicraft work. Cf. Shmelev, *op. cit.* (in n. 22), p. 131.

[26] These figures are for the year 1959 and are calculated from data in *Sel'khoz-1960*, pp. 235–238, 240–243, 348, 350–351, 354–356, 359.

[27] Calculated from *Narkhoz-1961*, pp. 300, 319, 321, 376, 391.

[28] In making this estimate, it is assumed that the proportion of workers not in state farms and employees in the private subsidiary sector is fairly accurately reflected by the percentage of urban element employed in this sector. The presumption is that the number of members of families of collective- or state-farm workers who live in urban areas is more or less exactly offset by the number of members of families of other workers and

so that labor inputs from all sources are taken into account, the share of families of collective farmers (including the labor of persons classified as collective farmers but who work on the plots in their spare time) is estimated to have been 71 percent of total labor inputs in the subsidiary economy.[29] No further breakdown of the remainder has been attempted.

Women account for the great majority of the workers in the private subsidiary economy: in 1959 almost 9 million women made up 91 percent of the workers of both sexes (Table 1). Among the able-bodied age groups, their share was even larger (96 percent) since men in this age group were usually engaged full-time in the socialized sector. Their share among over- and under-age workers was slightly smaller (86 percent). A very high proportion of the persons employed in the private subsidiary sector is in the overage group (60 and more for men and 55 and over for women). Among women of all ages employed in this sector, the majority are more than 45 years of age,[30] and 46 percent are in the overage group.[31] Typical would be the grandmother who leaves the socialized labor force to take care of grandchildren and the garden plot because the daughter or daughter-in-law is likely to be a better earner in the socialized sector.

---

employees who live in rural areas and who are engaged in private subsidiary agriculture. The relevant data are not provided by the 1959 census. Even if such a breakdown were available, reservations about the validity of the data would be in order. It may be presumed that many collective farmers, who devote much of their time to their plots, are listed by census takers as working on the collective farm, although they earn only a small number of labor-days. The importance of cultivation of urban or suburban garden plots by families of workers and employees is provided by data on the city of Saratov (1959 population: 581,000): more than 2,000 acres were reported as cultivated by 13,339 families. Cf. S. A. Osipov, "Flowering Gardens," *Soviet Women,* No. 4 (1960), p. 11. See also data on the share of the private nonagricultural plot in per-capita consumption in the nonagricultural sector as a whole in 1956, quoted by Jerzy F. Karcz, "Quantitative Analysis of the Collective Farm Market," *American Economic Review,* LIV:4, Part I (June, 1964), 332.

[29] M. Weitzman, M. Feshbach, L. Kulchycka, "Employment in the U.S.S.R." in U.S. Congress, Joint Economic Committee, *Dimensions of Soviet Economic Power* (Washington, D.C.: Government Printing Office, 1962), p. 662.

[30] M. Ia. Sonin, *Aktual'nye problemy ispol'zovaniia rabochei sily v SSSR* (Moscow: 1965), p. 195.

[31] The number of underage workers in the private subsidiary sector is small and is consequently ignored in our discussion. It should be remembered that the census would not classify a pupil, working on the family plot during the summer months, as employed in private subsidiary agriculture. This is a major reason why census data are not very helpful in analyzing labor inputs into the subsidiary sector.

WOMEN ON STATE FARMS AND IN OTHER STATE AGRICULTURAL ENTERPRISES

The third group of agricultural workers are those on state farms and in other state agricultural enterprises such as repair-technical stations. These workers and employees, numbering 6.6 million in 1959, have the same employment status as those in industry and other nonagricultural branches of the economy.[32]

The proportion of women among state-farm and related workers is smaller than among collective farmers, only 41 percent.[33] Like women collective farmers, women working on state farms are primarily assigned to the less skilled jobs. Of the 2.7 million women employed in this sector, almost 2.3 million, or 92 percent, were reported by the 1959 census as engaged in "primarily physical" labor. Approximately three-fifths of these were nonspecialized workers who made up 63.4 percent of total employment in this category.

The percentage of women differs widely among the different agricultural occupations, but the pattern shown for workers and employees in Table 5 is similar to that for collective farmers. If we combine the collective-farm and state-farm sectors, we find that 80.7 percent, or 15.9 million of the 19.7 million women wage workers and collective farmers, are unskilled. These women represent 66 percent of the total of unskilled farmers of both sexes. Of those engaged in administrative work of the limited type shown in Table 5, women number only about 20 percent of the total. Only among field-team leaders do they have the majority (87.3 percent), and this job is basically a foreman-type position where the workers supervised are predominantly women. The remaining areas of employment of women in specialized categories are not necessarily those of highly skilled occupations.

Since the three categories of agriculture which we have discussed utilize well over half of the women in the Soviet labor force, it is evident that the majority of women who work are still engaged in heavy, physical labor. We should not forget that for every woman pursuing a challenging or stimulating career, there is a brigade of farm women bent to their tasks in the fields.

WOMEN ADMINISTRATORS AND SPECIALISTS IN AGRICULTURE

In the economy as a whole, women have made up an increasing proportion of the administrative, managerial, and specialized personnel. In 1941, 31 percent of these personnel were women and in 1957, 50

[32] *Itogi-1959-SSSR*, Tables 30, 33, pp. 96–97, 104–105.
[33] *Ibid.*

TABLE 7

ADMINISTRATORS AND SPECIALISTS ON COLLECTIVE AND STATE FARMS, BY OCCUPATION AND SEX, DECEMBER 1, 1956

	Men and Women		Women		
	Number (thousands)	Percentage distribution	Number (thousands)	Percentage distribution	Percent Women
Total	*566.7*	*100.0*	*119.0*	*100.0*	*21*
Collective farm chairmen and directors of state farms	89.9	15.8	[1.7]	[1.4]	[1.9]
Agronomists	106.2	18.7	42.5	35.7	40
Animal-husbandry technicians	69.1	12.2	30.4	24.5	44
Veterinarians veterinary feldshers, veterinary technicians	73.9	13.0	13.3	11.1	18
Unspecified	227.5	40.1	[31.1]	26.3	[10]

SOURCES: *Zhen.-SSSR—1960.* p. 49. N. I. Shishkin, ed., *Trudovye resursy SSSR* (Moscow: 1961), p. 140, reports that about 1,000 of the more than 52,000 chairmen and directors of collective and state farms at the beginning of 1960 were women. This percentage (1.9 percent) is applied to the number of collective and state farms at the end of 1956 (89,900) to derive the estimate of 1,700 women chairmen and directors at the end of 1956. See *Narkhoz-1958*, pp. 494 and 514.

percent. Gains were made in every field for which information is available, but the role of women varies widely from one branch of the economy to another. The highest percentages are found in public-health institutions (88 percent) and educational-cultural services (66 percent). In trade and distribution, women comprise 46 percent and in government administration 44 percent. Much lower are the proportions in industry (31 percent), transportation and communications (28 percent), and construction (22 percent). Our particular concern, agriculture, has the lowest proportion of the major branches of the economy—21 percent.[34]

At the highest managerial level—chairmen of collective farms and directors of state farms and other state agricultural enterprises—women are rare (see Table 7).

Only during World War II did the proportion of women in these posts become significant, rising from 2.6 percent at the end of 1940 to 14.2

[34] The exceptions are public health where women make up 85 percent of the workers and employees and 88 percent of the managerial personnel and specialists; and educational and cultural services where the respective percentages are 69 and 66.

percent at the end of 1943. At the close of 1944, however, their share had declined to 11.8 percent and a year later to 8.1 percent.[35] With demobilization, government policy encouraged experienced officers to return to their home villages to serve as chairmen. The drive to consolidate farms launched in 1950 also caused a further shrinkage of opportunities for women since a man was more likely to emerge as chairman of combined farms. At the end of 1956 less than 2 percent of the chairmen and directors were women, and at the present time 2 percent of the chairmen and 1 percent of the directors are reported to be women.

Khrushchev has remarked on the absence of women in executive posts. On December 26, 1961, he is reported to have said at a regional farm conference in Kiev: "We all know what an enormous role women play in all the sectors in the building of communism. But for some reason there are few women in this hall. Just take a pair of binoculars and have a look around. What is the reason for this? It will be said that it is mainly administrative workers who are present here. It turns out that it is the men who do the administrating and the women who do the work." [36]

Despite official concern for the small role of women among administrators, little progress appears to have been made in increasing their importance. Women do, however, make up a large percentage of the agricultural specialists on state and collective farms (see Table 7), and the growth in the number of women professionals with a secondary specialized or higher education in agriculture has been rapid (see Table 8). Among agronomists they account for 40 percent of the total; among livestock specialists, 44 percent; and among veterinary doctors and technicians, 18 percent. These three occupational groups account for almost 75 percent of the women employed as agricultural managerial and specialized personnel.

How does the productivity of male and female agricultural specialists compare? Have women contributed as much to agricultural technology as their male counterparts? Although data which would permit definite answers to these questions are almost entirely lacking, some inferences from one kind of measure regarding the relative productivity of male

[35] Iu. V. Arutiunian, *Sovetskoe krest'ianstvo v gody Velikoi Otechestvennoi voiny* (Moscow: 1963), p. 289. The proportion of women chairmen of collective farms and women directors of state farms has varied considerably among the different republics. It is usually much lower in more backward areas, such as Transcaucasia and Central Asia than in the R.S.F.S.R. and Belorussia, where at the end of 1944 women made up almost 15 percent of the total.

[36] *Izvestiia,* December 26, 1961.

TABLE 8

WOMEN SPECIALISTS EMPLOYED IN AGRICULTURE, U.S.S.R., SELECTED YEARS[a]

Year	With a specialized secondary education		With a higher education	
	Number (thousands)	Percent	Number (thousands)	Percent
1941	n.a.	n.a.	18	25
1954	n.a.	n.a.	55	41
1955	116	46	65	41
1956	117	40	70	39
1957	123	40	74	38
1959	147	41	87	39
1960	155	41	94	39
1961	166 [b]	43	100	41
1962	180 [b]	44	107	42
1963	176 [b]	43	109	41

[a] Only specialists with a specialized secondary or higher education in the fields of agronomy, animal husbandry, veterinary science, and forestry are included; "practicals" are excluded; [b] excludes forestry specialists whose number is insignificant.

SOURCES: *Zhen. SSSR-1960*, pp. 58–59; *Zhen. i deti-1961*, pp. 138–39; *Zhen. i deti-1963*, pp. 118 and 1920; *Sred. spets. obraz.-1962*, p. 42; *Narkhoz-1956*, pp. 210–11; *Narkhoz-1959*, pp. 615–16; *Narkhoz-1962*, p. 472; *Vyssh. obraz.-1961*, pp. 52 and 66.

and female agricultural scientists can be made from an examination of the contributions of men and women to the scholarly literature. Clearly, the contribution of women to scholarly journals is much less than would be expected from their numbers (see Table 9). This disparity may be largely, perhaps wholly, explained by the fact that professional women are not exempt from burdensome and time-consuming home responsibilities and are often less strongly motivated in pursuing their professional careers than men because of their dual commitment.

FACTORS AFFECTING THE EMPLOYMENT OF WOMEN

Of primary importance in encouraging female participation in the agricultural economy is the shortage of males in the rural population. Although a shortage existed before World War II, the problem became acute during the war and has continued to be a serious problem. Of primary importance in discouraging women from participating in the labor force, in agriculture as in other branches of the economy, is the conflict between responsibilities to a husband and children and to a job. Attempts to reduce this conflict have resulted in a number of measures

TABLE 9

COMPARISON OF THE SHARE OF WOMEN IN VARIOUS AGRICULTURAL OCCUPATIONS WITH THEIR SHARE IN AUTHORSHIP OF ARTICLES IN RELATED PROFESSIONAL JOURNALS, U.S.S.R., 1940, 1960

Specialty	Percent of women in Specialty		Percent of articles by women authors		Ratio		Sample size	
	1940	1960	1940	1960	1940	1960	1940	1960
Agronomists, animal husbandry technicians, veterinarians, and foresters	25	39	15	24	.60	.62	430	676
Agronomists	n.a.	41	16	25	—	.61	156	345
Veterinarians	16	31	6	16	.38	.52	274	331

SOURCES: The method followed has been to count the number, based on surname suffixes, of male and female contributors to leading professional journals in agricultural fields for which information on the percentage of women professionals is known. The percentage of contributions by women has then been compared with the proportion of women in a given field. Only articles of a substantial nature were included in the sample. In instances where two, three, four, or more authors were listed, fractional credit was given to each author. The journals sampled included *Sovetskaia agronomia*, *Sovetskaia veterinariia*, *Zemledelie*, and *Vestnik Akademii sel'skokhoziaistvennykh nauk* (in 1940, *Doklady Vsesoiuznoi Akademii sel'skokhoziaistvennykh nauk*). The few articles by women animal husbandry technicians or foresters have been allocated under agronomists or veterinarians.

such as the enactment of protective legislation and the provision of child-care facilities. Still a third factor affecting female participation is educational attainment. Agronomy, veterinary medicine, and other specialized fields, require much training while agricultural field work demands a minimum. Therefore, availability of education to women and the extent of their motivation to obtain this training largely determine the extent and nature of their participation in the agricultural labor force.

THE MALE DEFICIT IN THE RURAL POPULATION

The acute shortage of males in the rural population at the time of the 1959 census, particularly in the age groups over 35 years, is dramatically shown by the population pyramid in Figure 2. The shortage will remain a problem for at least another two decades at the end of which time the imbalance in the sexes will be largely righted in the able-bodied age group. This shortage of males in the rural population is primarily the cause of the high proportion of women in the major branches of agriculture shown in Figure 1.[37] This proportion reaches a peak of 70 percent in the 40-49-year age group and exceeds the proportion of males in all other age groups, with the exception of the under-20 and over-60 age groups.

The imbalance of the sexes in rural areas has had other important effects. Although according to 1959 data a higher proportion of rural men than urban men are married, there are simply not enough men to go around. In fact, if all rural males in the most depleted age groups married, no more than 50 to 60 percent of the females in that age range could marry. The significance to agricultural employment of the low proportion married among rural women is that about 12 million women in the age range 20 through 59 years (more than one-third the number of women in the rural labor force) do not have husbands upon whom they may depend for their livelihood. The implications of this for female employment cannot be overemphasized for it is reasonable to assume that virtually all these women must work for a living. As the numbers of men and women become more balanced, the proportion of unmarried women will probably decline, and, although marriage does not afford the Soviet woman immunity from employment, married

[37] The rural population does not, of course, include all those who are employed in agriculture. Nor is that portion of the rural population which is employed engaged exclusively in agricultural pursuits. The basic relationships between urban, rural, and total agricultural employment are shown in Appendix Table 2.

FIGURE 2
AGE DISTRIBUTION OF MALES AND FEMALES IN "PHYSICAL" OCCUPATIONS IN AGRICULTURE, U.S.S.R., JANUARY 15, 1959[a]

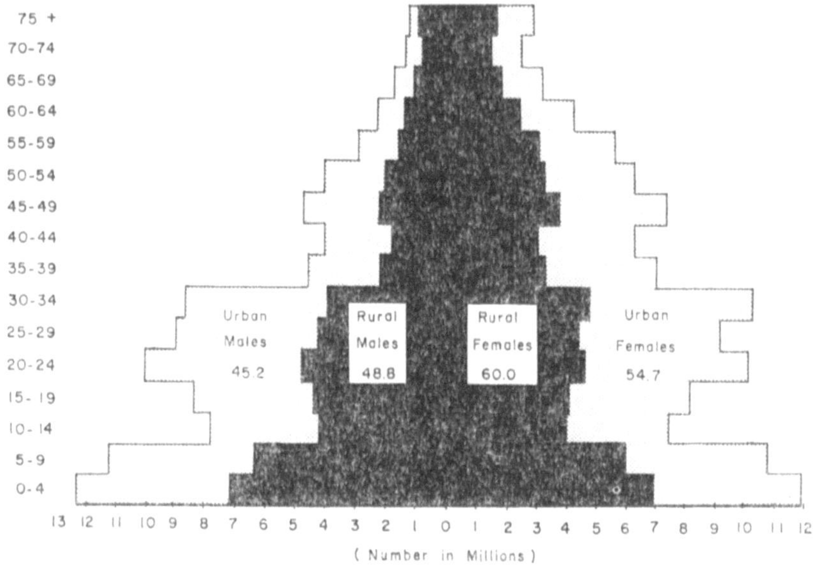

[a] Excluding private subsidiary agriculture.
SOURCE: Appendix Table 1.

women are not as likely to be in the labor force as their unmarried counterparts.

FAMILY VERSUS WORK

Family demands play an important role in determining the extent and nature of the participation of women in the labor force. The burden of domestic duties may deter a woman from entering or remaining in the labor force especially while her children are young. According to the 1959 census, 45 percent of women in the able-bodied ages outside the Soviet labor force had children under 7 years of age, and 59 percent had children under 14 years of age.[38] Although we do not know the exact corresponding proportions for women in the able-bodied ages who work, it is expected that these would be smaller. Not unexpectedly, sample data for Siberia show that there is a negative correlation between family size and desire to work.[39] However, circumstances force many women

[38] *Itogi-1959-SSSR,* p. 251.
[39] A. N. Gladyshchev, *Izv. Sib. otd. Ak. nauk,* No. 11 (1962), pp. 16–17.

with large families in both urban and rural areas to work, a fact reflected in the high participation rate of women in the Soviet labor force.

The second effect of the heavy burden of housework is its debilitating influence upon the energies, and, consequently, upon the productivity of many women workers. According to figures cited by Shishkin, a working woman with a family will be busy three more hours a day than the full-time housewife. The woman worker-housewife typically has two hours less time for self-education, reading, entertainment, and rest and gets one and one-half hours less sleep.[40] Men share little of the burden as sample data for four collective farms show:

TABLE 10

TIME SPENT BY COLLECTIVE FARM MEMBERS IN HOUSEWORK, BY SEX AND TYPE OF DAY, U.S.S.R.

(percent of total housework done)

<table>
<tr><th rowspan="2">Length of time</th><th colspan="2">Workdays</th><th colspan="2">Days off</th></tr>
<tr><th>Men</th><th>Women</th><th>Men</th><th>Women</th></tr>
<tr><td>Up to 1 hour</td><td>77</td><td>3</td><td rowspan="2">85</td><td>10</td></tr>
<tr><td>1 to 2 hours</td><td>12</td><td>11</td><td>23</td></tr>
<tr><td>2 to 4 hours</td><td>8</td><td>20</td><td>9</td><td>26</td></tr>
<tr><td>4 hours or more</td><td>3</td><td>66</td><td>6</td><td>41</td></tr>
<tr><td>TOTAL</td><td>100</td><td>100</td><td>100</td><td>100</td></tr>
</table>

SOURCE: L. Bibik, *Biull. nauch. inf.*, No. 6 (1961), p. 49.

The time spent by women in household work on work days is characteristically between 35 and 40 minutes less on advanced collective farms than on backward farms, due to the existence on the former of more facilities such as electricity, child-care centers, dining halls, and bakeries, which lighten the women's burden.[41] Thus, any significant reduction in the burden of housework for Soviet farm women will depend primarily upon three developments: (1) a marked improvement in public utilities, such as running water and electricity; (2) the more widespread provision of labor-saving household devices on both a private and communal basis; and (3) the provision of more child care facilities. To the present, progress in all these areas has been remarkably slow. In 1956,

[40] Shishkin, *op. cit.* (in n. 8), p. 146.

[41] L. Bibik, *Biull. nauch. inf.*, No. 6 (1961), p. 50. More than 80 percent of the collective farms are reported to have been electrified at the beginning of 1963. See G. Sarkisian, *Ek. sel'. khoz.*, No. 12 (1964), p. 15. On many of these farms, however, electricity was available only for lighting.

two-thirds of the urban families had to carry their water in buckets from a communal tap or pump. In rural areas, where conditions are even more primitive, a household with running water is a rare exception. Hot water is practically unavailable even in the cities, where it is estimated that less than 3 percent of the population has hot water.[42] Thus, for a working woman the family washing alone can take the equivalent of two strenuous days a week which must be fitted into the evenings and days off.[43] Public facilities for laundry and dry cleaning exist only in the cities and even there they are entirely inadequate.

RURAL CHILD CARE FACILITIES

Only 40 percent of the collective farms are equipped with nurseries or kindergartens and half of these are of a seasonal character—inadequacies which restrict the participation of many women in the labor force and which the government naturally hopes eventually to eliminate.[44] From the meager data available for the postwar years, we can estimate that only 6 percent of rural nursery-age children (2 months to 3 years) can be accommodated in permanent nursery facilities (the percentage is double for the cities). However, when the largely rural seasonal nurseries are taken into account, the situation is improved, and in the periods of peak labor demand in agriculture a substantial proportion of nursery-age children can be accommodated in some sort of facility.

Kindergartens admit children aged three to six, and, like nurseries, their capacity is insufficient to accommodate more than a small percentage of kindergarten-age children. Reported enrollment of 3,800,000 children in 1962 represents 20 percent of an estimated 19.3 million children in the three-to-seven-year age group.[45] Because of the unequal distribution of facilities in urban and rural areas, however, an estimated 37 percent of urban, but only 7 percent of rural children of kindergarten

[42] Even in Moscow, only 10 percent of the apartments had hot water in 1956. See Timothy Sosnovy, "The Soviet City," in U.S. Congress, Joint Economic Committee, *op. cit.* (in n. 29), p. 337.

[43] Elena Whiteside, "For Soviet Women: A 13-Hour Day," *The New York Times Magazine*, November 17, 1963, p. 28.

[44] V. F. Maier, P. N. Krylov, eds., *Planirovanie narodnogo potrebleniia SSSR* (Moscow: 1964), p. 64. The number of places in Soviet nurseries during 1913–1962 will be found in the forthcoming book by Norton Dodge, *op. cit.* (in n. 5).

[45] The number of children from 3 to 7 years old is based on estimates of the Soviet population by year of age for each year from 1950 to 1981, prepared by the Foreign Demographic Analysis Division of the U.S. Bureau of the Census in June, 1962. Statistical data on the number, enrollment, and staff of urban and rural kindergartens during 1913–1962 are given in Dodge, *op. cit.* (in n. 5).

age can be accommodated in kindergarten facilities.[46] Collective farmers in particular have to rely on summer playgrounds for the care of their children. In 1955, only 30,400 children were accommodated in collective-farm kindergartens, while 523,700 children of kindergarten age were cared for at collective-farm playgrounds.[47] Although the precise number of seasonal kindergartens and summer playgrounds in 1962 is not known, their capacity was probably sufficient for more than a million children.[48] If so, they provided facilities, admittedly often makeshift, for an additional 10 to 12 percent of the rural children of kindergarten age. Nonetheless, most rural children of kindergarten age are of necessity cared for at home.[49] The capacity of rural child-care facilities of all types still falls far short of the number needed to permit women with young children to rely upon them rather than upon other arrangements to free themselves for participation in the labor force. The day when the Soviet farm woman is freed from domestic responsibilities appears to lie many decades in the future. In the interim, these responsibilities will continue to conflict with the full participation of women in the labor force.

EDUCATION OF WOMEN IN AGRICULTURE

The third major factor affecting the character and extent of female participation in the agricultural labor force is education. Although males and females theoretically have equal access to education in the Soviet Union, in practice there are some significant differences in the proportion of male and female enrollments at different eduational levels and in different fields, reflecting primarily the divergent motivations and

[46] The estimate of the number of urban and rural children of kindergarten age was made by dividing the total for this age group into the proportions of urban and rural population of children in the new-born to 9-year age group given in the 1959 census. Cf. *Itogi-1959-SSSR,* pp. 60–66.

[47] *Cultural Progress in the U.S.S.R.* (Moscow: 1958), p. 198.

[48] In 1955, a total of 971,000 children were cared for in summer playgrounds. See *ibid.,* p. 199. Of these, 815,000 were in rural areas; 771,000 of the latter were at playgrounds of the collective farms. Of these, 524,000 (68 percent) were 3 to 7 years old. Accordingly, we may assume that some 550,000 of the 815,000 children in rural areas were of kindergarten age. By 1959 the total number of children accommodated had increased by more than 50 percent (or to 1,155,000; cf. *Narkhoz-1959,* pp. 738–739). It is not unreasonable to assume that further expansion has occurred since then, given the expansion of other child-care facilities.

[49] The cost of kindergarten care is given in Decree No. 1314 of the Ministry of Higher Education of the U.S.S.R., dated September 10, 1948, as quoted in *Vysshaia shkola: Osnovnye postanovleniia, prikazy i instruktsii* (Moscow: 1957), p. 487.

interests of each sex. There are also important differences between the proportions of both sexes enrolled in urban and rural areas.

Through the first seven grades the proportion of boys and girls is approximately equal in urban and rural areas. In grades eight to ten, however, the proportion of girls in rural areas is six percentage points below that of urban girls, although the rural girls in these grades outnumber the boys.[50] In the republics with a Moslem tradition, many girls, particularly the rural, marry young and leave school. In the Uzbek Republic in 1955, for example, girls made up 48 percent of the urban enrollment in grades 8 to 10 but only 26 percent of the rural.[51]

Training in agriculture is carried out at four types of institutions: state vocational-technical schools and trade schools for the mechanization of agriculture; specialized secondary educational institutions; higher educational institutions; and graduate programs at research institutes (and at higher educational institutions).

Vocational-technical schools train youths aged 14 to 17 in a variety of skills, including tractor-driving and repair work. The proportion of girls in all vocational-technical programs has declined since the war, when it was 25 percent, to less than 15 percent in recent years.[52] The percentage of girls in specifically agricultural training programs probably has been much smaller since few women are engaged in repair work and tractor-driving.

Specialized secondary educational institutions in the agricultural field train assistant agronomists, breeding technicians, mechanics, veterinary aides, bookkeepers, and so on. These are not among the most popular occupations for girls as Table 11 indicates. Nevertheless, in 1959, more than 100,000 girls are estimated to have been enrolled in agricultural technicums.[53] The distribution of women among the broad fields of specialization in specialized secondary educational institutions has remained essentially the same since the 1920's. Women have predominated in health and medicine (83 to 90 percent of the total); the proportion enrolled in education, art, cinematography, economics, and law has also been high (more than 75 percent). In industry, construction, transportation, and communications the proportion of women students, initially less than one-tenth, has remained relatively low, averaging about a third of the enrollment. Agriculture has been slightly more popular,

[50] *Kul't. stroi.-1956*, pp. 176–177.

[51] *Ibid.*

[52] See Nicholas DeWitt, *Education and Professional Employment in the U.S.S.R.* (Washington, D.C.: National Science Foundation, 1961), pp. 157–161.

[53] *Ibid.*, p. 179. DeWitt estimates that total enrollment in agricultural technicums in 1959 was 300,000.

TABLE 11

SHARE OF WOMEN IN STUDENT ENROLLMENT IN SPECIALIZED SECONDARY AND HIGHER EDUCATIONAL INSTITUTIONS, U.S.S.R., SELECTED YEARS[a]

(percent)

Year	Specialized secondary educational institutions: Total enrollment	Specialized secondary educational institutions: Enrollment in agricultural fields	Higher educational institutions: Total enrollment	Higher educational institutions: Enrollment in agricultural fields
1926	n.a.	n.a.	30.9	16.3
1927	37.6	15.4	28.5	17.4
1928	n.a.	n.a.	29.1	18.4
1929	n.a.	n.a.	29.2	20.4
1930	38.8	31.0	28.3	25.4
1931	n.a.	n.a.	30.8	28.1
1932	44.7	33.5	33.3	30.6
1933	43.9	30.1	36.5	32.1
1934	44.1	31.6	38.0	31.8
1935	43.0	30.2	39.5	30.2
1936	46.7	29.3	41.0	29.3
1937	51.6	28.7	43.3	30.2
1940	54.6	37.0	58.0	46.1
1945	67.1	66.0	77.0	79.0
1950	43.6	41.0	53.1	39.3
1955	54.8	43.0	52.3	39.3
1956	52.0	44.0	51.0	39.0
1957	48.0	38.0	47.0	31.0
1959	46.0	36.0	45.0	28.0
1960	47.0	38.0	43.0	27.0
1961	48.0	38.0	42.0	26.0
1962	49.0	38.0	42.0	25.0
1963	49.0	38.0	43.0	25.0
1964	49.0	37.0	43.0	25.0

[a] Day as well as evening students are included in enrollment figures on which the calculations are based.

SOURCES: *Specialized secondary educational institutions:* Data for 1927, 1940, 1945, 1950, 1955, and 1958–61: *Sred. spets. obraz.-1962*, p. 92; for 1930, 1932–37, and 1956–57: Nicholas DeWitt, *Education and Professional Employment in the U.S.S.R.* (Washington, D.C.: National Science Foundation, 1961), p. 613; for 1962: *Narkhoz-1962*, p. 573; for 1963: derived from *Narkhoz-1963*, pp. 566 and 578; for 1964: derived from *Vest. stat.*, No. 2 (1965), p. 95.

Higher educational institutions: Data for 1945 are inconsistent with those in the rest of the table. Data through 1956, except 1945: DeWitt, *op. cit.*, p. 654; for 1945: *Vyssh. obraz.-1961*, p. 86; for 1956–58: *Narkhoz-1959*, p. 751; for 1959–61: *Narkhoz-1961*, p. 699; for 1963: *Narkhoz-1963*, pp. 566 and 578; for 1964: derived from *Vest. stat.*, No. 2 (1965), p. 95.

the percentage of women ranging between 29 and 44 percent except during the war when the proportion of women was dramatically higher.

The percentage of women enrolled in higher educational institutions before the revolution was severely limited. Since then, however. Soviet higher educational institutions have become genuinely coeducational. Health and education have been the fields most favored by women. In the mid-1920's women accounted for only 16 percent of the enrollment in agriculture and 7 percent in engineering. Apart from a doubling of the percentage of women in engineering and smaller increases in the agricultural and socioeconomic fields, the situation changed little during the remainder of the 1920's. However, as the drive to industrialize gained momentum in the early 1930's, special efforts were made to expand the enrollment of women in higher educational institutions. primarily in institutions in the agricultural, engineering, and socioeconomic fields where female enrollments were low.

By 1935 the proportion enrolled in agriculture had risen to 30 percent while the over-all proportion of women in higher education approached 40 percent, owing to the large numbers of women in health and education. The proportion of women continued to increase in the late 1930's up to 58 percent of the total in 1941 when the proportion in agriculture was 46 percent. As a result of the war, women accounted for 77 percent of total enrollment in 1945 and 79 percent of those enrolled in agriculture. However, by 1950, the proportion of women in higher education was well below the 1940 level, and beginning in 1955, when the proportion was 52 percent, a rather sharp decline set in. Each year the proportion dropped one or two percentage points until it reached 42 percent in 1961 where it appears to have stabilized. Women continue to predominate in health and education, but in the health field they dropped from 69 percent in 1955 to 52 percent in 1964 and in the educational-cultural field from 72 to 64 percent. In engineering the decline was from 35 to 29 percent. In agriculture, which now had the lowest percentage of women of any major field, the decline was from 39 to 25 percent.

Whether these downward trends have stopped cannot be definitely determined since the reasons for the change are not clear. Undoubtedly changes in the admission regulations for higher education which followed the school reforms in 1958 have had an effect on the enrollment of women since they gave preference to ex-servicemen and persons with two or more years of work experience. Further changes made in the spring of 1965, however, would seem to have largely restored the earlier situation of equal access.

An extensive sampling of candidate degrees (roughly comparable to a Ph.D. degree) in selected years (see Table 12) shows that at the graduate level the proportion of women in agriculture and veterinary medicine has been close to the average for all fields and also close to the proportion of female undergraduates enrolled in agriculture.

TABLE 12

ESTIMATED PERCENTAGE OF WOMEN RECIPIENTS OF CANDIDATE AND DOCTORAL DEGREES, AGRICULTURAL AND VETERINARY FIELDS, U.S.S.R., SELECTED YEARS

Degree and field of study	1936–37	1941–45	1956–58	1959–61	1962–64
Candidate degrees, all fields	20.5	n.a.	32.8	30.0	27.9
Agricultural and veterinary fields	19.5	n.a.	36.1	33.1	28.6
Doctoral degrees, all fields	9.6	5.5	14.8	17.7	21.2
Agricultural and veterinary fields	n.a.	2.7	12.5	11.1	13.0

SOURCE: Norton T. Dodge, *Women in the Soviet Economy* (Baltimore: The Johns Hopkins Press, 1966).

The percentage of women earning Soviet doctoral degrees in agriculture is much smaller, however, both in comparison with other fields and with the percentage receiving candidate degrees. The declining proportion of women at higher levels of education accounts in part for the smaller proportion of women occupying the more responsible and highly specialized jobs in agriculture.

LEVELS OF EDUCATIONAL ATTAINMENT

Reflecting the history of enrollments and the smaller number of jobs in agriculture which require advanced educational training, the educational attainment of rural women is not only substantially below that of rural men but also is below that of urban women.[54]

Before World War II these male-female and urban-rural disparities were particularly marked, but since then the gaps have been significantly narrowed. For example, in 1939 two and one-half times as many rural men as women in the able-bodied age group had a higher education, whereas in 1959 men outnumbered women by only 50 percent. The proportion of all persons with a higher or secondary education, including incomplete secondary education, increased 3.5-fold between 1939 and 1959 (see Table 13). The greatest improvement (19.8 times) was achieved by women collective farmers in the rural population. But in spite of the educational gains made by collective farm women, they remain educationally the most backward of the major socioeconomic groups in the Soviet Union. In 1959, nearly half of these women had less than a four-year education (see Appendix Table 3). The level of their education varied greatly with age. Among women over 40 years of age, from 70 to nearly 100 percent have less than a 4-year education.

[54] *Itogi-1959-SSSR,* p. 81.

TABLE 13

WORKERS, EMPLOYEES, AND COLLECTIVE FARMERS WITH HIGHER AND SECONDARY EDUCATION, BY TYPE OF RESIDENCE, U.S.S.R., 1939, 1959[a]
(number per thousand of total population in a given group)

Residence group and sex	Total		Workers		Employees		Collective farmers	
	1939	1959	1939	1959	1939	1959	1939	1959
Total population	123	433	82	386	519	893	18	226
Male	136	434	100	393	455	859	26	261
Female	104	431	44	377	639	921	11	198
Urban population	242	564	96	424	555	898	50	241
Male	235	537	122	430	496	872	63	287
Female	255	597	54	413	641	918	26	193
Rural population	63	316	60	311	454	879	17	226
Male	81	337	73	320	394	828	24	260
Female	42	294	27	296	632	927	10	198

[a] Including those with incomplete secondary education for all groups and both years.
SOURCE: *Itogi-1959-SSSR*, p. 116.

This is indeed a lost generation so far as education is concerned. It is evident that the government has concentrated its educational efforts elsewhere, where expected returns were higher. In the lower age groups, where real effort has been made, substantially more women have achieved higher levels of education.

Further information on the level of male and female educational attainment in the various major agricultural sectors and branches is given in Table 14. It is interesting to note that the select group of women engaged in the technical or administrative side of agriculture is, for the most part, as well educated as the men. At the administrative level, 17.7 percent of the women have a higher education and 21.6 percent a secondary specialized education. The proportion of women with a higher (14.5 percent) or secondary (24 percent) specialized education employed in veterinary and other establishments serving agriculture also is high and exceeds that of men. The educational level of women exceeds that of men in repair-technical and related stations as well.

Many more years will be required before the average educational level of women in agriculture is appreciably raised. Until that time, lack of education will continue to reduce the contribution of women and inhibit the role which they play. The older women, in particular, will continue to perform the least skilled and least attractive tasks while men will dominate the more responsible and skilled occupations in spite of the exhortations of Soviet leaders to recruit more women for such posts.

CONCLUSIONS

A number of conclusions regarding Soviet manpower policies in agriculture can now be ventured. The past three censuses show that agriculture has become increasingly dependent upon female labor. The number of women as a proportion of the agricultural labor force increased from 50 percent in 1926 to 62 percent in 1959. During the same period, as a result of the growth of industry, the proportion of the female labor force engaged in agriculture has declined from 91 percent to 53 percent. Thus, although agriculture remains the major occupation of Soviet women, and the bulk of the women in agriculture are still engaged in unskilled, backbreaking work, many women have shifted into more attractive occupations in other sectors of the economy or have entered careers in agriculture which require specialized training and offer substantial satisfactions.

The policy of the government has clearly been to let the older generation of women continue working at unskilled, low-productivity jobs in

TABLE 14

EDUCATIONAL LEVELS OF PERSONS EMPLOYED IN AGRICULTURE, BY BRANCH AND SEX, U.S.S.R., JANUARY 15, 1959
(persons per thousand employed)

Branch	Completed higher education		Specialized secondary and incomplete higher education		General secondary and incomplete secondary education		Elementary and incomplete seven-year education		Less than a four-year education	
	Male	Female	Male	Female	Male	Female	Male	Female	Male	Female
All agriculture	5	2	20	9	258	198	415	310	302	481
State farms	10	5	29	16	265	233	436	332	260	414
Collective farms	2	1	14	6	249	192	411	308	324	493
Repair technical stations (RTS), machine-tractor stations (MTS), machine-livestock stations (MZhS), drainage stations (LMS)	17	32	50	110	417	406	435	228	81	224
Other agricultural enterprises and establishments	15	14	46	43	210	247	425	317	304	379
Organizations servicing agriculture and veterinary institutions	140	145	235	240	260	299	233	163	132	153
Administration of agriculture (trusts, offices, etc.)	148	177	171	216	311	361	282	123	88	123
Individual peasant farming	0.4	0.2	3	2	95	65	278	188	624	745

SOURCE: *Itogi-1959-SSSR*, pp. 125 and 127.

agriculture, and little effort has been made to educate or train this group. On the other hand, men and younger women were drawn into industry in large numbers up to the outbreak of World War II. Since 1939, the number of men employed in agriculture has shrunk further—by 7 million—largely due to war losses. The 18.6 million men (versus 29.7 million women) who remained in agriculture in 1959 were for the most part employed in the more productive and skilled occupations. Thus, the government "placed its wager on the strong"—on men and younger women—providing them with the education and specialized training required for the more appealing and remunerative jobs.

From a purely economic standpoint, the neglect of the older generation of women would seem logical. The seasonality of much of their work, the shorter period during which investment in their training could be recouped, and the smaller learning capacity of older women prevents as high a return as from effort devoted to men or young women. Similarly, the difference in the proportions of women employed in the three major sectors of agriculture—41 percent of state farm workers, 56 percent of collective farmers, and 91 percent of those working the private plots—would seem to reflect differences in the productivity of men and women in the varying kinds of work required by these sectors.

The relative share and importance of women with a secondary specialized or higher education in agriculture has increased significantly since 1926, although little relative improvement has been shown in recent years, and the share of women remains below that of men. The smaller proportion of women enrolled in secondary specialized and higher educational institutions also has its economic justification. The distractions of family responsibilities and related factors result in the productivity of women professionals being less, on the average, than that of men. However, since agriculture has not been so attractive a field for women as medicine or education, a process of self-selection has kept the proportion of women receiving specialized training in agriculture relatively low, and Soviet manpower planners have never felt the necessity to restrict the proportion of women enrolled in agricultural fields. Indeed, during the 1930's they successfully increased the proportion. But should a higher proportion of women be engaged in the more responsible agricultural occupations? If discrimination against hiring women in these jobs exists, and it undoubtedly does to some extent, a higher proportion would seem desirable on economic grounds. Nevertheless, the conflict between job and family mentioned above, which becomes more acute as the burden of professional responsibilities increases, can be expected to continue to restrict quite legitimately the role of women in administrative work.

In favoring the extensive utilization of women in agriculture—witness their paeans to champion tractor drivers and pig raisers—Soviet leaders seem to be attempting to make a virtue of necessity. However, as the older generation of farm women dies off, as mechanization and modernization in farming methods advance, and as the shortage of males in the Soviet working age population diminishes, we can expect a decreased reliance on women as the "work horses" of agriculture. A slow shift of women out of the marginal and archaic types of work in which so many are now occupied—gleaning after the combine, tending loose cattle, hand-hoeing corn—can also be expected. Past experience has shown, however, that evolution in Soviet agriculture is a slow and uncertain process. Like the horse, women are likely to coexist with the tractor, yielding useful service to Soviet agriculture for many decades to come.

APPENDIX TABLE 1

AGE DISTRIBUTION OF MALES AND FEMALES EMPLOYED IN "PHYSICAL" OCCUPATIONS IN AGRICULTURE, U.S.S.R., JANUARY 15, 1959[a]

Age group	Number (in thousands)		Percentage distribution		Percentage	
	Males	Females	Males	Females	Males	Females
All ages	*14,150*	*19,743*	*100.0*	*100.0*	*41.8*	*58.2*
to 20	2,206	2,132	15.6	10.8	50.9	49.1
20–29	4,391	4,896	31.0	24.8	47.3	52.7
30–39	2,585	4,363	18.3	22.1	37.2	62.8
40–49	1,796	4,304	12.7	21.8	29.4	70.6
50–59	1,778	3,001	12.6	15.2	37.2	62.8
60 plus	1,394	1,046	9.8	5.3	67.1	42.9

[a] Excluding private subsidiary agriculture.

SOURCE: Calculated from *Itogi-1959-SSSR*, pp. 136, 143, 162–63, and 168.

APPENDIX TABLE 2

DISTRIBUTION OF POPULATION BY RESIDENCE, AGE, AND SEX, U.S.S.R., JANUARY 15, 1959

(thousands) [a]

Age	Total			Urban			Rural			Percent females	
	Total	Males	Females	Total	Males	Females	Total	Males	Females	Urban	Rural
All ages	*208,827*	*94,050*	*114,776*	*99,978*	*45,208*	*54,769*	*108,849*	*48,842*	*60,007*	54.8	55.1
0 to 4 years	24,328	12,388	11,940	10,158	5,176	4,982	14,170	7,212	6,958	49.0	49.1
5 to 9 years	22,034	11,220	10,814	9,538	4,860	4,678	12,496	6,360	6,136	49.0	49.1
10 to 14 years	15,309	7,770	7,539	6,996	3,554	3,452	8,313	4,226	4,087	49.3	49.2
15 to 19 years	16,499	8,296	8,203	8,062	3,975	4,087	8,437	4,321	4,116	50.7	47.5
20 to 24 years	20,343	10,056	10,287	10,892	5,295	5,597	9,451	4,761	4,690	51.4	49.6
25 to 29 years	18,190	8,917	9,273	9,505	4,694	4,811	8,685	4,223	4,462	50.6	51.4
30 to 34 years	18,999	8,611	10,388	10,269	4,702	5,568	8,730	3,909	4,820	54.2	55.2
35 to 39 years	11,591	4,528	7,062	6,039	2,352	3,687	5,551	2,176	3,375	61.1	60.8
40 to 44 years	10,408	3,998	6,410	5,514	2,219	3,295	4,894	1,779	3,115	59.8	63.6
45 to 49 years	12,263	4,706	7,558	6,221	2,518	3,703	6,042	2,187	3,855	59.5	63.8
50 to 54 years	10,447	4,010	6,437	5,094	2,004	3,091	5,352	2,006	3,346	60.7	62.5
55 to 59 years	8,699	2,905	5,793	3,896	1,359	2,537	4,803	1,547	3,256	65.1	67.8
60 to 64 years	6,697	2,348	4,349	2,781	953	1,828	3,916	1,395	2,521	65.7	64.4
65 to 69 years	5,039	1,751	3,288	2,092	717	1,376	2,947	1,034	1,913	65.8	64.9
70 to 74 years	3,805	1,273	2,532	1,392	401	991	2,413	812	1,601	71.2	66.3
More than 75 years	4,167	1,268	2,899	1,525	438	1,086	2,642	889	1,752	71.2	66.3
Age unknown (error of closure and rounding)	8	4	4	[5]	[2]	[0]	[5]	[3]	[3]		

[a] Minor discrepancies are due to rounding.

SOURCES: Total population: U.S. Bureau of the Census, *Projections of the Population of the U.S.S.R., by Age and Sex*, International Population Reports, Series P-91, No. 13 (Washington, D.C.: Government Printing Office, 1964), p. 21. Urban and rural population: *Itogi-1959-SSSR*, pp. 50–51; and P. G. Pod'iachikh, *Naselenie SSSR* (Moscow: 1961), p. 34.

APPENDIX TABLE 3

EMPLOYMENT IN AGRICULTURE BY RESIDENCE, SOCIOECONOMIC CATEGORY, AND SEX, U.S.S.R., JANUARY 15, 1959

Residence and sex	Total	Workers	Employees	Collective farmers	Individual peasants, independent artisans	Private subsidiary agriculture
Total employment	*48,290.768*	*5,918,418*	*693,004*	*31,722,834*	*91,671*	*9,864,801*
Males	18,575,560	3,458,342	439,938	13,731,230	32,147	913,903
Percentage male	38.5	58.4	63.5	43.3	35.1	9.3
Females	29,715,208	2,460,076	253,106	17,991,604	59,524	8,950,898
Percentage female	61.5	41.6	36.5	56.7	64.9	90.7
Total urban employment	3,263,435	810,197	200,138	1,169,552	11,055	1,072,493
Urban males	1,264,674	509,500	121,454	571,436	3,912	58,372
Percentage male	38.8	62.9	60.7	48.9	35.4	5.4
Urban females	1,998,761	300,697	78,684	598,116	7,143	1,014,121
Percentage female	61.2	37.1	39.3	51.1	64.6	94.6
Total rural employment	45,027,333	5,108,221	492,916	30,553,282	80,616	8,792,308
Rural males	17,310,886	2,948,842	318,484	13,159,794	28,235	855,531
Percentage male	38.4	57.7	64.6	43.1	35.0	9.7
Rural females	27,716,447	2,159,379	174,422	17,393,488	52,381	7,936,777
Percentage female	61.6	42.3	35.4	56.9	65.0	90.3

SOURCE: *Itogi-1959-SSSR*, p. 104.

APPENDIX TABLE 4

EDUCATIONAL LEVEL OF THE EMPLOYED POPULATION, BY RESIDENCE, SOCIOECONOMIC CATEGORY AND SEX, U.S.S.R., JANUARY 15, 1959

(Persons per thousand in a given group)

Residence and socioeconomic category	Higher, incomplete higher, specialized secondary education		General secondary education		Seven-year and incomplete secondary education		Primary and incomplete seven-year education		Less than a four-year education	
	Male	Female	Male	Female	Male	Female	Male	Female	Male	Female
Total population										
Total	103	116	60	68	271	247	386	272	180	297
Workers	23	16	56	63	314	298	459	353	148	270
Employees	508	476	124	161	227	284	121	69	20	10
Collective farmers	14	6	29	18	218	174	413	308	326	494
Urban population										
Total	153	184	82	109	302	304	362	243	101	160
Workers	27	19	67	76	336	318	449	350	121	237
Employees	533	459	129	169	210	290	110	71	18	11
Collective farmers	28	10	38	23	221	160	420	292	293	515
Rural Population										
Total	56	60	40	34	241	200	408	295	255	411
Workers	14	9	36	34	270	253	480	361	200	343
Employees	450	523	113	139	265	265	146	64	26	8
Collective farmers	13	6	29	18	218	174	412	309	328	493

SOURCE: *Itogi-1959-SSSR*, p. 115.

APPENDIX TABLE 5

EDUCATIONAL LEVEL OF THE COLLECTIVE-FARM POPULATION BY SOCIOECONOMIC CATEGORY, AGE AND SEX, U.S.S.R., JANUARY 15, 1959

(Persons per thousand)

Socioeconomic category and age	Higher, incomplete higher, and specialized secondary education		General secondary education		Seven-year and incomplete secondary education		Elementary and incomplete seven-year education		Less than a four-year education	
	Male	Female	Male	Female	Male	Female	Male	Female	Male	Female
Total population	10	4	24	14	148	112	285	209	533	661
10 years and older	13	5	33	18	203	139	390	260	361	588
10 to 19 years	1	2	42	43	312	335	402	375	243	245
20 to 24 years	30	26	118	76	386	367	398	372	68	159
25 to 29 years	20	11	22	12	201	171	598	515	159	291
30 to 34 years	25	10	18	13	266	232	530	497	161	248
35 to 39 years	32	9	28	14	252	160	465	424	223	393
40 to 44 years	28	5	17	4	131	43	465	245	359	703
45 to 49 years	15	2	8	1	49	10	347	118	581	869
50 to 54 years	8	1	5	1	27	6	291	104	669	888
55 to 59 years	5	—	5	1	20	5	271	82	699	912
60 to 64 years	3	—	4	1	14	4	234	61	745	944
65 to 69 years	2	—	3	—	11	3	202	49	782	948
70 years and older	1	—	2	—	7	2	134	29	856	969

SOURCE: *Itogi-1959-SSSR*, pp. 113–114.

COMMENT

George S. Murphy

The foregoing essay presents much interesting material, such as the attempt to measure differences in the productivity of male and female scientists. Footnote 24 deserves attention. It suggests that the high participation rate for women in private subsidiary agriculture is not very reliable. If this is so, then the estimates of the total contribution of Soviet women to agriculture may well be on the high side, for they hardly could be revised upwards. And if this is true, then the contribution of Soviet women to agricultural labor may not be surprising in a country where most women work, and where the deficit in males of working age is large. So much for descriptive issues.

Dodge and Feshbach's welfare and analytical judgments require qualification. The tone of the article implies that they view the results of the Soviet planners' policies as bad. Soviet women in rural areas in the 1930's, 1940's, and 1950's made their own choices about education. Typically they made the traditional choice of leaving schools for marriage. Later, they made the traditional choice of reentering the workforce, generally in manual occupations. Given such traditional choices, they might have felt keenly that their welfare had declined if they had been constrained to take more education, delay marriage, or aim for more demanding jobs.[55] In these matters, persons were essentially deciding according to their own tastes and preferences.

Russian women clearly do a great deal of agricultural labor and work at the worst jobs. How far are Soviet planners responsible for this? The rationale which Dodge and Feshbach give explains why once this state of affairs exists the Russian planners cannot change matters. It does not make sense in terms of direct economic payoff to send an old peasant woman to school! But this is not to present any evidence that the Soviet planners in the past wanted this state of affairs to come about or that present Soviet planners want it to continue in the future. The authors

[55] This is not to argue that, in general, rural people did not feel constrained by restrictions on their employment opportunities (i.e., private enterprise was forbidden). I am merely trying to isolate the welfare effect of a particular policy rather than discussing that of the entire set of policies adopted by Soviet planners.

quote Khrushchev to the effect he wanted to change at least one aspect of this situation. The educational statistics for younger rural women suggest that they are headed for more of the better jobs. What was the policy of the planners in the thirties, forties, fifties? I am not aware of any conscious policy to disadvantage rural women. Many must have left rural occupations for urban ones. Many must have been educated. Educational opportunities do seem to have favored urban people relative to rural, but there may have been no specific denial of educational opportunity to rural women. Thus their tastes for early marriage, the lower educational opportunity for all rural people, and the effects of male deaths in World War II have some role to play in explaining Soviet female agricultural employment. These factors are more a mixture of policy, historical accident, and unintended effects of other policies, than a result of actions taken to implement the preferences of planners.

Is there occupational discrimination against women in agricultural regions or in the Soviet Union generally? Dodge and Feshbach seem to think so. I would suggest that we perhaps should start with a presumption in favor of the reverse: that there is discrimination for women. Under an equal wage policy with rational entrepreneurs we should expect fewer women than men in given posts, for, assuming a normal distribution of ability of a given supply of a given grade of labor, the employer will hire women of sufficiently greater marginal physical productivities than men to offset the smaller expected returns due to the employment of women.[56] This is to say that the average expected marginal revenue productivity of women is less than for men. It is not discriminatory then to hire fewer women than men.

Are Russian managers rational in the sense of adjusting their hiring to maximize profits? It has generally been thought that they are output maximizers. If they are, and if women have lower average expected marginal physical productivities than men, the rational manager will tend to hire fewer women than men at a given wage fund, and this is not discriminatory in the economic sense. He will, then, hire the more efficient women. This, of course, is in a situation where equal pay is paid for equal work. This situation prevails in the Soviet Union. We may look at it another way. Agriculture typically has seemed a sector of the Soviet economy where the proper calculation of cost and best use of resources have seemed weakest. Suppose the extreme case where managers ran farms at whim in a way to maximize their own utility func-

[56] Data cited by Dodge and Feshbach on the relative productivities of male and female scientists confirm the belief that the expected returns from female labor are less than those from male labor in the Soviet Union.

tions. Discrimination would exist if one argument in such functions was a positive benefit for not hiring women. But this case certainly does not exist. Due to Soviet policy and Party pressure, it is more likely that the average Soviet farm manager sets a positive benefit for hiring women rather than not. Hence it is hard to believe that occupational as opposed to educational discrimination exists. In addition, the problem of whether occupational discrimination exists can hardly be settled by examining agriculture alone.

Dodge and Feshbach have two types of explanation for the present situation. They look at planners' preferences for given policies to try to explain matters. They also look at certain variables affecting occupational choice and distribution: educational attainment, home responsibilities, shortage of males. These two types of explanation can be integrated. If one were to reduce the variables mentioned to economic ones affecting the net stream of income to the average household and to view the planners as attempting to manipulate such variables, the explanations are then tied together. Such an approach would suggest further relevant variables. The approaches of labor economists might be helpful in this.[57] Such an integrated explanation would be more useful, for example, to explain the distribution of rural women by type of occupation than the authors' explanation of productivity differences. If one works on a private plot the costs of gaining an income—baby-sitting, transportion or travel time to work, home maintenance, and so on—are clearly lower than if one goes to the collective farm. In areas where there is a good truck farm market the expected returns from private work are undoubtedly greater than those from collective-farm work. Women thus try to turn to private farming from collective farming if they legally can. Essentially, in terms of contribution to household income they get more in private farming. Yet their average physical productivity might be less in private farming than in collective, rather than greater as the authors suggest.

[57] See especially Stuart Harold Altman, "Factors Affecting the Unemployment of Married Women" (unpublished doctoral dissertation, University of California, Los Angeles, 1964); Arnold M. Katz, "Cyclical Unemployment and the Secondary Family Worker" (unpublished doctoral dissertation, Yale University, 1961); Thomas A. Mahoney, "Factors Determining the Labor Force Participation of Married Women," *Industrial and Labor Relations Review,* XIV:4 (July, 1961), 563–578; Jacob Mincer, "Labor Force Participation of Married Women," in National Bureau of Economic Research, *Aspects of Labor Economics* (Princeton, N.J.: Princeton University Press, 1962), pp. 63–105 and Richard Rosett, "Working Wives: An Econometric Study," in Thomas F. Dernburg *et al.,* eds. *Studies in Household Economic Behavior* (New Haven, Conn.: Yale University Press, 1958).

HARRY E. WALTERS AND RICHARD W. JUDY

Soviet Agricultural Output by 1970

When originally suggested, the idea of projecting agricultural output in the Soviet Union by 1970 seemed, if not attractive, at least bearable. Since then, however, we have come to appreciate, rather ruefully, why Professors Johnson and Kahan could say that "anyone who attempts long-term projections of agricultural output in the U.S.S.R.—in any country for that matter—could be called foolhardy and perhaps should be." [1] It may, indeed, seem ironic that at the very time when "subjectivism" and "hare-brained scheming" are being so strongly condemned in the Soviet Union we should undertake a project which ultimately involves large doses of both.

THE PRESENT ENVIRONMENT FOR PROJECTING SOVIET AGRICULTURAL OUTPUT

In attempting to project Soviet agricultural output at this time the following considerations appear to us to be self-evident. First, this is a potential turning point in the development of Soviet agriculture—output has stagnated for seven years, wheat is being imported in large quantities, Khrushchev has been deposed, agricultural policy has undergone significant changes, and a new agricultural program has been put forward. Second, whether it will be a turning point or not depends heavily upon the degree to which the new programs for agriculture are implemented. Third, how fully they are implemented will determine, in great measure, how much reliance we can put upon the output trends of the past decade as an indication of trends in the future. Fourth, past trends

[1] D. Gale Johnson, Arcadius Kahan, *The Soviet Agricultural Program: An Evaluation of the 1965 Goals,* RM-2848-PR (Santa Monica, Calif.: The RAND Corporation, May, 1962), p. 110.

TABLE 1

INDEXES OF GROSS AND NET AGRICULTURAL OUTPUT, U.S.S.R., 1958–1965 (1950-100)

Year	Gross agricultural output		Net agricultural output
	Official Soviet [a]	Johnson [b]	Willett [c]
1950	100	100	100
1951	93	98	91
1952	102	104	103
1953	105	108	104
1954	110	113	107
1955	122	128	123
1956	138	146	139
1957	142	145	139
1958	158	166	157

SOURCES:
[a] *Narkhoz-1962*, recalculated with 1950 as the base year.
[b] D. Gale Johnson, "Agricultural Production," in A. Bergson and S. Kuznets, eds., *Economic Trends in the Soviet Union* (Cambridge, Mass.: Harvard University Press, 1963), p. 208, recalculated with 1950 as the base year.
[c] Joseph Willett, "The Recent Record in Agriculture," in U.S. Congress, Joint Economic Committee, *Dimensions of Soviet Economic Power* (Washington, D.C.: Government Printing Office), p. 98.

in output, especially grain yields, are obscure and cannot be determined with accuracy from the available Soviet data. Furthermore, students of Soviet agriculture do not always agree on this important matter.

The first two considerations suggest that any projection of Soviet agricultural output at this time must rest heavily upon subjective evaluations, especially with respect to the second point. After observing developments in Soviet agriculture over the past half decade, when the actions of the Soviet government made increases in output difficult if not impossible, few would be willing to offer more than speculative guesses.

Even if these factors did not have to be considered, trends in output during the past decade would provide a very questionable foundation upon which to base projections. In terms of total output, the period 1953–1964 can be divided into two distinct halves. From 1953 through 1958 agricultural output increased at an unprecedented pace. This increase in output was led by the grain sector, and within that sector by the production of wheat. The Soviet index of gross agricultural output and all other indices of Soviet agricultural output, presented in Table 1, indicate an increase of 40–50 percent during this period.

As is shown in Table 2, agricultural output has more or less stagnated

TABLE 2

CHANGES IN AGRICULTURAL OUTPUT, U.S.S.R., 1950–1958

Year	Soviet indexes[a] Total gross agricultural output	Crops	Live-stock	U.S.D.A. index of net agricultural output[b] 1958/59 = 100	
1958	100	100	100	1958/59	100
1959	100	95	108	—	—
1960	103	99	107	—	—
1961	106	101	112	1961/62	100
1962	107	101	115	1962/63	101
1963	99	92	108	1963/64	94
1964	110	117	101	1964/65	103
1965 plan	170	—	—	—	—

SOURCES:
[a] *SSSR v tsifrakh-1964*, p. 68.
[b] *The 1965 Eastern Europe Agricultural Situation*, Economic Research Service, ERS-Foreign-115 (Washington, D.C.: U.S. Department of Agriculture, March, 1965), p. 2.

since 1958 whereas it was planned to increase 70 percent, and the situation in 1965 suggests that the Seven-Year Plan will draw to a close while gross farm output remains approximately at the level of 1958. During this second period the sector of agriculture which lagged the most was the grain sector, or the one that grew fastest in the preceding five years. Since 1963, the Soviet Union has become one of the world's leading wheat importers, with gross imports of about 11 million tons in 1963–64, 3 million tons in 1964–65 and over 9 million tons in 1965–66. Historically the Soviet Union has been a major net exporter of wheat.[2] In some sectors of Soviet agriculture—primarily the industrial crops and livestock numbers—output continued to grow during this period, but for the most important sector, grain, the situation today is little better, if as good, as in 1958. In other words, seven years ago Soviet agriculture also appeared to be at a turning point, and a grandiose program was announced with great plans for increases in output. Yet output has increased very little since 1958. In some areas grain output has decreased.

[2] *Vneshtorg-1963*, pp. 32, 46; Theodora Mills, *Soviet Agricultural Trade, 1955–61*, Economic Research Service, ERS-Foreign-47 (Washington, D.C.: U.S. Department of Agriculture, June, 1963 and *Soviet Foreign Agricultural Trade, 1962–63*, Economic Research Service, ERS-Foreign-120 (Washington, D.C.: U.S. Department of Agriculture, March, 1965). The exact amount of imports during 1965–1966 depends upon the treatment of contracts to import and scheduled imports, the former being around 7.5 million and the latter close to 9 million tons.

These factors alone are sufficient to make one agree with professors Johnson and Kahan, and therefore ask for some other less foolhardy topic. But projecting Soviet agricultural output at this particular time faces one final, and this may prove to be the most disturbing, problem. We cannot say, with any degree of certainty, what the exact level of output of certain crops has been in recent years. During the past decade Soviet agriculture has been meticulously studied, and the flow of information and data from the Soviet Union has been incomparably superior to that of the thirties and forties. We now have area, yield, and production statistics for most major crops, and the output of livestock products for the entire period from 1953 through 1964 is also known. Nevertheless, virtually every leading student of Soviet agriculture has expressed doubts about these statistics, especially for the past half dozen years.

Although doubts exist about many of the output statistics, the primary burden of these doubts falls upon Soviet statistics of grain output and yields. With the publication of a number of articles in the Soviet press and Soviet journals,[3] and the dropping of the term "barn yield" from the unchanged official grain output statistics (the term "barn yield" has been replaced by a note: "the harvest and yields of grain are measured in terms of the originally harvested weight") there is now little dispute that Soviet grain output and yields, as reported, are in terms of "bunker weight" and are, therefore, inflated.[4] How much grain statistics are inflated and how this inflation has affected the data for various years of the past decade, however, is not a matter upon which students of Soviet agriculture agree.

The grain sector lies at the heart of present Soviet agricultural difficulties as it did in 1927/28. It was the primary concern of the past decade and it is the primary concern now. Upon developments in the grain sector depends the level of livestock output, the quantity and quality of the Soviet diet, and ultimately the question of whether the Soviet Union will regain her grain exporter status or become increasingly a grain

[3] *Sel'. zh.*, February 28, 1965; *Ek. gaz.*, February 10, 1965; *Uchet i fin.*, No. 6 (1965), pp. 9–10. These articles indicate that the difference between barn yield (i.e., clean and dried grain) and bunker weight (the weight of the uncleaned and undried grain) could range from less than 1 to 15 or more percent. Hence, in some regions, the difference may range from less than 1 to as much as 3 quintals per hectare. The waste obtained from drying and cleaning of grain has been variously described as both utilizable and unutilizable. Some of the waste may be fed to livestock. On the basis of the available information it is impossible to determine the grain content of such feed.

[4] *Narkhoz-1963*, p. 273 and *Narkhoz-1964*, pp. 295, 814.

importer. Virtually all Soviet and Western specialists agree that the dominant factor in increased grain output from 1953 to 1958 was the increase in sown area and that any significant increases in future grain production will have to come from increases in yields.

The present program announced by the new Soviet leaders in March, 1965, is designed to bring about such increases; and if this goal is not achieved, the future of Soviet agriculture looks bleak and the prospect of the Soviet Union's becoming a progressively more important grain importer increases significantly.[5] Therefore, the grain sector is *the* major unknown in projecting Soviet agricultural output at this time, and the future level of Soviet grain output depends upon what happens to yields.

This obscurity about yields poses basic problems for a projection of grain output in the U.S.S.R. today. Every agricultural region in the U.S.S.R. has a certain production horizon determined by climate, soils, the existing level of technology, and agronomic experience. With a given quantity of inputs, each crop can be expected to reach a certain yield under average conditions. The area of potential yield increase is encompassed by the existing level of average yields and that which is obtainable with given inputs.

If the existing yields are known with confidence and the obtainable level is also known within certain margins, then the range of potential increase can also be determined. If, on the other hand, the existing yields are not known with confidence, the area of potential increase is widened and the basis for projecting weakened. In the Soviet Union certain crops present greater problems in this regard than others. One of the major problems is that of winter wheat, a crop of crucial importance within the context of present Soviet food-grain difficulties and in the new program for increasing food-grain output.

At the aggregate level of total grain output, the problem is simple: the higher the yields are now (given a fixed level of potential increase) the smaller is the possibility for increasing yields with a given quantity of inputs. The lower the existing yields the greater the potential for increase. Studies of the potential yield increase in the Soviet Union for most crops in most regions have been completed both in the U.S.S.R. and in the West. These set a limit upon the potential for an increase of the grain output. With the ceiling thus established, the floor—the

[5] This subject is discussed in greater detail in Lazar Volin and Harry E. Walters, *Soviet Grain Imports,* Economic Research Service, ERS-Foreign-135 (Washington, D.C.: U.S. Department of Agriculture, September, 1965).

existing level of yields and output—assumes an even greater significance.

WHAT IS TO BE DONE?

To undertake a meaningful projection of Soviet agricultural output it is necessary to explain the stagnation since 1958; to show how the present programs, if implemented, will or will not alter the factors which were responsible for that stagnation; to explore the production possibilities of Soviet agriculture—in order to determine what is possible if the new program is carried out—and to make explicit the area of doubt surrounding the question of Soviet grain output and yields. Only after these questions have been explored in some detail, can we attempt to fulfill our obligatory deliveries, that is, projections of output to 1970. We put the question of grain-output statistics first because it is crucial to anything said about the past twelve years and because it arises at many points in the analysis before we come to the actual projections of grain output.

SOVIET STATISTICS OF GRAIN OUTPUT AND YIELDS

By now, most students of Soviet agriculture have expressed themselves on the subject of the Soviet statistics of agricultural output.[6] There are a number of published estimates of total grain output and these, the comments of other authors, and statements in Soviet statistical handbooks indicate that the statistics of grain output and yields are inflated. The various estimates are of two types. The first type encompasses those obtained by estimating the crop independently on the basis of

[6] *The 1964 Eastern Europe Agricultural Situation,* Economic Research Service, ERS-Foreign-73 (Washington, D.C.: U.S. Department of Agriculture, March, 1964), pp. 9–14; Arcadius Kahan, "Soviet Statistics of Agricultural Output," and "Commentary" by Luba O. Richter in Roy D. Laird, ed., *Soviet Agricultural and Peasant Affairs,* Lawrence, Kansas: University of Kansas Press, 1963), pp. 134–168; D. Gale Johnson, "Agricultural Production," in Abram Bergson and Simon Kuznets, eds., *Economic Trends in the Soviet Union* (Cambridge, Mass.: Harvard University Press, 1963), p. 233; Nancy Nimitz, *Soviet Government Grain Procurements, Dispositions and Stocks, 1940, 1945–1963,* RM-4127-PR (Santa Monica, Calif.: The RAND Corporation, November, 1964), p. 6; Werner Klatt, "Output and Utilization of Foodstuffs in the Soviet Union," *Studies on the Soviet Union,* New Series, III:4 (1964), 99–109; Jerzy F. Karcz and V. P. Timoshenko, "Soviet Agricultural Policy, 1953–1962," *Food Research Institute Studies,* IV:2 (May, 1964), 157; Abraham S. Becker, *Soviet National Income and Product,* Part I, RM-4394-PR (Santa Monica, Calif.: The RAND Corporation, June, 1965), pp. 88–89. See also the contribution by Walters and Judy.

weather data and other relevant information.[7] The other, more recent, type, includes those based upon deductions from officially reported Soviet production figures.[8] Many students of Soviet agriculture do not use any of these independent sets of estimates, preferring to work with the figures published in the Soviet Union while indicating their deficiencies. Most of those in the last category have made it clear, however, that the grain figures are inflated by a percentage at least as great as the minimum deductions in some of the independent estimates.[9]

The differences between these estimates and the figures officially reported by the Soviet Union are explained by the fact that Soviet grain output is given in terms of bunker weight and that reported grain output has been further inflated, in recent years, because heavy pressure has been exerted to report high yields. Of the estimates which have been published, those of Kahan are designed to exclude only the inflation due to bunker weight.[10] The other estimates all assume that inflation exists for both reasons.[11] The yields which are implied in several of these estimates, all of which accept Soviet figures on sown (really a combination of sown and harvested) area, are presented in Appendix Table 1.

The views of these authors and organizations are clear, and little purpose could be served by repeating them here. No amount of discussion here will compensate for a careful study of all available evidence on the output and utilization of agricultural products in the Soviet Union and, as is indicated in Appendix Table 1, not all have come to the same conclusion. However, some general conclusions are possible.

First, since official Soviet statistical agencies have recently changed the description of their published figures on grain output from barn yield to bunker weight, there can now be little dispute on this point. As indicated above and in the notes, students of the subject assume that the difference between the two concepts could amount to anywhere from 10 to 15 percent of total grain output.[12] The lowest estimates of Soviet total grain output excluding grain equivalent of immature corn use a deduction of slightly more than 20 percent. Second, explicit in the U.S. Department of Agriculture (USDA) estimates and implicit in all others

[7] These include the U.S. Department of Agriculture estimates found in the source cited in n. 6 above and the estimates of the Central Intelligence Agency, *Production of Grain in the USSR,* CIA/RR ER 64–33 (Washington, D.C.: Central Intelligence Agency, October, 1964).

[8] These include those of Kahan, Laird, and Klatt (see n. 6).

[9] Most have indicated a range of from 10 to 15 percent.

[10] Kahan, *op. cit.* (in n. 6), p. 149.

[11] Roy D. Laird, "Agriculture Under Khrushchev," *Survey,* No. 56 (July, 1965), p. 107 and sources cited in n. 7.

[12] Cf. n. 6.

is the assumption that the degree of inflation is greater for some grains, especially wheat and corn, than for others.[13] Third, the degree of inflation has increased since 1957. Before that date, few appear to have strong objections to the official Soviet data on total grain output or to corresponding data for individual grains. Fourth, the smallest deduction amounts to 1 centner per hectare (which amounts to 13 million tons of grain on the present grain area) and the largest deduction amounts to 2 centners per hectare (or to 26 million tons). These are not insignificant amounts. They all exceed the amount of grain imported by the Soviet Union in 1963/64.[14]

The upshot of all this is that an aura of vagueness pervades the question of output and yields of certain crops *at the farm level,* despite the fact that detailed time series have been published by the Soviet Union in recent years. In an effort to gain precision in their analysis, some have made adjustments in the figures published by the Soviet Union, others have estimated the output of certain crops independently, yet others prefer to use the published Soviet data, indicating that they have flaws. None of these approaches is wholly satisfactory, and presumably those using one or another approach would readily agree that room for error exists.[15] Anyone who has studied the question in depth —either in an effort to come up with sound estimates, derive appropriate deductions, or simply to understand Soviet grain statistics—knows that questions of judgment enter into the analysis. Judgments differ, but by now disagreement exists only over the degree of inflation in Soviet official statistics.

Nevertheless, official Soviet statistics exist, many of us use them daily, and many prefer to base their work on them initially while making their own deductions ultimately. Furthermore, the estimates which have been published usually deal with total grain output, with the single exception of those of the USDA which are published for five major grains.[16] None of the published estimates compare in detail, either by

[13] Most estimates which show a rising degree of inflation for the bunker weight attribute this phenomenon to the spread of wheat into the new lands as well as to the increase in corn output.

[14] Soviet grain imports in 1963–1964 amounted to 10–11 million tons depending upon the method of measurement. It should be obvious by now that precision on the entire matter of grain yields and output cannot be attained, given the magnitude of gaps in our knowledge on this important subject.

[15] The U.S. Department of Agriculture assumes that its estimates are only "rough" and Kahan (*op. cit.* in n. 6) indicates that he is not seeking "purity."

[16] Wheat, rye, barley, oats, and corn.

crop and by region, with the official Soviet output or yield series. For these reasons, we use Soviet official figures and supply the estimates of the USDA wherever they apply. As the USDA has already indicated,[17] its estimates might be considered as the lower limit of Soviet grain output. As we have explained, Soviet official figures cannot be considered as the upper limit of the actual barn yield. This does not resolve the crucial question of the output of specific grains, such as winter wheat, where presently reported yields in the Ukraine are now almost at the level they might be expected to attain only under heavy fertilization and optimal farm practices.[18] Nevertheless, it helps to narrow the area of controversy. For most other products the problems posed by the Soviet statistics are not as crucial.[19]

CHANGES IN SOVIET AGRICULTURAL OUTPUT 1953–1964

Because of the planned character of agricultural production in the Soviet Union we tend to think along the lines of Soviet "benchmark years." Since Stalin died in 1953, all progress is measured from that point, or from 1949–1953. The Seven-Year Plan established goals for 1965 based upon the level of output in 1958, and as a result we tend to measure progress from that year also. As an indication of goals and of success in achieving them, or as an indication of progress since 1958, this framework is valid.

Trends in the output of major farm products between these (and some other) benchmark years can be supplemented by various indices of Soviet agricultural output, including the official Soviet index of gross output, the gross output index compiled by D. Gale Johnson, and net output indices constructed by Joseph W. Willett and the USDA. These last three indices (which are also presented in our Tables 1 and 2) are based either upon adjustments of official Soviet data or on independent estimates of the output of individual products.

Progress made from 1953 through 1958 was spectacular when compared with that of earlier decades, but progress since 1958 has been minimal. Gross output in 1965 was planned to be 70 percent above that of 1958, whereas it was only 10 percent above that level in 1964,

[17] *Op. cit.* (in n. 6). See also Volin and Walters, *op. cit.* (in n. 5).

[18] P. M. Zemskii, *Razvitie i razmeshchenie zemledelia po prirodno-khoziaistvennym raionam SSSR* (Moscow: 1959), p. 105. See also *Narodne hospodarstvo Ukrainskoi RSR v 1963 rotsi* (Kiev: 1964), p. 245.

[19] Oilseed output is also reported in terms of the bunker weight; see *Ek. sel'. khoz.*, No. 6 (1959), p. 32. Meat output, as reported by the Soviet Union, includes fat and offal, which the U.S.D.A. attempts to eliminate in its estimate of red-meat output.

and 1964 was an exceptionally good year for most crops. Crop output in 1965 will undoubtedly fall short of the 1964 level, and livestock production can only be expected to increase slowly. On the whole in 1965 the Soviet index is not likely to exceed its 1964 level.

Such a comparison, however, is primarily the result of peculiarities inherent in the practice of measuring trends in output against certain fixed periods in time. Few years can be expected to be as favorable in terms of weather as was the case of 1958; it is therefore hardly appropriate to make it a point of departure for judging progress in terms that are not primarily concerned with the extent to which plan targets have been met. Trends in output for major crops and livestock products since 1953, computed in terms of four year averages, are presented in Table 3, together with planned goals for a most distant future and a Soviet projection of achievable potential output (for an unknown date). Similar data are also presented in Appendix Table 2 for additional individual products, where we also contrast Soviet official estimates with those of the USDA. (Trends in livestock herds are shown in Appendix Table 3.)

Table 3 provides a more balanced picture of change for the period 1953–1964, but not necessarily a more favorable one for the attainment of 1965 goals. Average output in 1961–1964 compares much less favorably with 1965 goals than does output in 1964. As we have indicated 1964 was an exceptionally favorable weather year; moreover, the output of certain crops, such as cotton, sugar beets, oilseeds, and potatoes increased exceptionally either in 1963 or 1964, or both, whereas in the earlier years 1959–1962 their output grew more slowly. At the same time, the period 1961–1964 includes a year of crop failure, one exceptionally good year, and two average years.

Total grain output increased during each of the three periods, but the increase was much less during the third period than during the second, and it was due entirely to increases in the output of corn, barley, and pulses. Production of major food grains declined. Potato output during the third period was smaller than in the second, and only insignificantly higher than in the first period. Vegetable output was substantially higher in each period, but especially in 1961–1964.

In the industrial-crops sector, the output of sugar beets increased in each period, but more rapidly in the second than in the third. Most of the increase in 1961–1964 was due to the near doubling of output in 1964 over 1963. The output of oilseeds increased more rapidly in the third period than in the second. Cotton output showed modest improvement in each period, but the average for the last period was raised by the exceptionally high outputs of 1963 and 1964. Flax fiber output

TABLE 3

OUTPUT OF SELECTED AGRICULTURAL COMMODITIES, U.S.S.R., FOUR-YEAR AVERAGES 1953–1964, 1964, FUTURE PLANS AND GOALS
(million tons, except eggs)

Commodities	1953–1956	1957–1960	1961–1964	1964	1965 plan	1970 goal	Output projected by Zemskii	1980 goal
Grain:								
Excluding immature corn	98.8	120.3	132.1	151.1	—	—	—	—
Including immature corn	100.6	126.6	n.a.	n.a.	164–180	229	228	295–311
U.S.D.A. estimate, excluding immature corn	92.4	99.5	107.9	121.3	—	—	—	—
Sugar beets	26.6	48.9	55.7	80.3	76–84	86	86	98–104
Cotton	4.1	4.4	4.8	5.3	5.8–6.1	8.0	9.8	10–11
Oilseeds	3.9	4.3	5.6	6.5	5.5	8.0	(7.4)	9–10
Potatoes	78.8	86.3	79.7	93	147	140	187.7	156
Vegetables	12.9	15.3	16.5	18.5	30–31	47	39.4	n.a.
Meat	6.3	8.2	9.1	8.2	16.0	25	—	30–32
Milk, official	41.7	59.2	62.7	63.1	100–105	135	—	170–180
U.S.D.A. estimate	39.2	50.3	53.5	54.0	—	—	—	—
Wool	.246	.331	.366	.352	.550	.800	—	1.0–1.1
Billions of eggs	17.8	24.5	28.6	26.7	37.0	68	—	110–116
Flax fiber	.320	.406	.387	.337	.580	n.a.	.978	n.a.

SOURCES: *Narkhoz-1964*, pp. 251, 295, 309, 311, 316, 318, 321, 361. See also Appendix Table 2. Oilseeds estimated on the basis of data for sunflower, whenever other official data are lacking. Plan and goal figures are from Jerzy F. Karcz and V. P. Timoshenko, "Soviet Agricultural Policy 1953–62, *Food Research Institute Studies*, IV:2 (May, 1964), 157. Zemskii's projected output is from Zemskii's, *op. cit.* (in n. 18), pp. 105, 114, 116–117, 120–121, 145–147, 154–159, 170, 180, 185, 204, 207.

declined significantly in the last period by comparison with the second, but was much above the level of 1953–1956.

The output of livestock feed crops other than grain, with the exception of corn silage, fell in the third period compared to the second, but was still well above the level of 1953–1956. Corn-silage output grew rapidly throughout the period. Livestock numbers during the third period exceeded their 1953–1956 levels by about 40 percent. The growth in output of livestock products—meat, milk, eggs, and wool—declined in the third period when compared with the second, but their output in 1961–1964 was still 40 to 60 percent above the level of 1953–1956 during the last period. For meat, much of this increase was due to heavy slaughterings in 1962 and 1963.

If the Soviet index of gross output is recalculated to correspond with our three periods, it would have come to 100 in 1953–1956, to 130 in 1957–1960 and to 140 in 1961–1964. A roughly similar pattern of progress would be indicated in the USDA index and that of Willett for net output, but possibly at a somewhat lower level.

The period as a whole cannot be described as a failure. By comparison with agricultural progress in most countries of the world, during a comparable period, it would have to be considered a success, although the initial level of output was low.[20] In terms of goals and in terms of demand for agricultural products in the Soviet Union at the existing price levels, however, it fell far short of expectations and requirements. The impact of the 1963 crop failure upon the domestic bread supply, the livestock sector, imports, and indeed the entire economy indicated how precarious the situation was during the first part of this decade.

Perhaps no other set of data is more revealing in this context than information supplied by trends in actual and planned government procurements of farm products (see Appendix Table 4). In the Soviet command economy, planned procurements are to a large extent a reflection of demand for farm products for consumption and other uses of the nonagricultural sector (as far as consumption is concerned, demand also manifests itself through the collective-farm market).

[20] See any of a number of studies on trends in agricultural production and consumption such as the Food and Agriculture Organization of the United Nations (FAO), *The World Food Surveys,* including its *Third World Food Survey,* Basic Study No. 11 (Rome: FAO, 1963); *The World Food Budget, 1970,* Economic Research Service, Foreign Agricultural Economic Report No. 19 (Washington, D.C.: U.S. Department of Agriculture, October, 1964) as well as earlier editions of the same document; Lester R. Brown, *Land, Man and Food,* Economic Research Service, Foreign Agricultural Economic Report No. 11 (Washington, D.C.: U.S. Department of Agriculture, November, 1963).

Although total grain procurements during 1962–1964 exceeded the original 1965 plan goal by about 2 million tons, they were demonstrably insufficient to satisfy the needs of the government. The pattern of grain procurements and their utilization has been analyzed in great detail in several studies.[21] The essential point as far as grains are concerned, is that *wheat* procurements have failed to cover the requirements of the government. At no time have they attained the level of 1958, and yet the U.S.S.R. has been exporting large quantities of wheat. Furthermore, it has had to provide the food for an urban population which increased by more than 21 million between 1959 and 1965. Although these people consume less grain than those in the countryside, they still require large quantities on a per-capita basis, especially since they have not been supplied with increasing quantities of potatoes, meat, vegetables, and other foods which tend to reduce urban consumption of grain products. For this and other reasons, principally connected with the decline in the volume of collective-farm-market sales (in turn a function of policies affecting the private sector), the state is now required to feed a larger share of a larger population.[22] We have some difficulty in accounting for grain used for industrial purposes in addition to alcohol and beer, but we know that it is used for other purposes.[23] We also know that the return flow of grain to farms has been heavy in recent years, because procurements have impinged upon seed or feed requirements at the farm level.[24] For all these purposes it is wheat, not total grain, that matters most; wheat has been the real laggard in the past few years, and it is wheat that is being imported.

The procurement situation with respect to other crops is readily apparent from a more detailed examination of Appendix Table 4. Oilseeds have exceeded the original 1965 plan level. Cotton has come close to that level in 1963 and 1964. Sugar beets have come close to the planned level for 1965 only because of a greatly expanded area and excellent growing conditions. For the other crops and livestock products the gap between the present level of procurements and the 1965 plan goals is still large, even though livestock products in general have increased substantially since 1958.

[21] Nimitz, *op. cit.* (in n. 6) as well as Volin and Walters, *op. cit.* (in n. 5).

[22] Nimitz, *op. cit.* (in n. 6) Table 2, p. 58 and Volin and Walters, *op. cit.* (in n. 5), p. 11.

[23] Khrushchev cited a figure of 4 million tons of grain for industrial usage out of the 1955 harvest. Virtually every Soviet statement on industrial uses of grain published after that date indicates that the absolute amounts of grain so used are increasing. See *Stroi. komm.*, I, 90.

[24] *Ibid.*, IV, 365 and *Izvestiia*, December 10, 1964.

CAUSES FOR THE TRENDS IN AGRICULTURAL OUTPUT 1953–1964

Recent developments in Soviet agriculture and the numerous causes of stagnation since 1958 have been intensely studied.[25] Certain points are worth repeating, however. Although the Seven-Year Plan established high goals for agricultural output from 1959 to 1965, the policies followed by the Soviet government from 1958 through 1961 had the effect of retarding growth in this output. Most students of Soviet agriculture interpreted the impact of these policies correctly and few anticipated significant increases in Soviet farm output. Certainly none assumed the 1965 goals would be attained, with the possible exception of some industrial crops.[26] To some extent, Khrushchev himself reached similar conclusions by the end of 1961. A number of measures designed to change the situation were undertaken in 1962; but only some of these could be considered as helpful; others only complicated matters.

Table 4 shows that during the period 1953–1957 trends in the supply inputs of capital, labor, land, machinery, and fertilizer were rising steeply. After 1957 these trends were either reversed, or gave evidence of a significant deceleration. Roughly the same pattern is followed by trends in farm incentives, although this was in part a function of stagnation as well as a cause.

The expansion of sown area into the New Lands permitted the rapid increase of grain output in those regions, while other nongrain crops and corn moved into the areas where grain had been traditionally grown. Deliveries of chemical fertilizer slowed down significantly after 1958, even though rapid increases had been planned, and exports of fertilizer increased.[27] If 1957 rather than 1958 had been used for comparison in Table 4, the absolute decline in machinery deliveries, especially those of trucks and combines, would have been much greater. The big increases in state capital investment in agriculture came in 1954 and 1955: this

[25] Roy D. Laird and E. L. Crowley, eds., *Soviet Agriculture: The Permanent Crisis* (New York: Praeger, 1965), Karcz and Timoshenko, *op. cit.* (in n. 6), Nancy Nimitz, "The Lean Years," *Problems of Communism,* XIV:3 (May–June, 1965), 10–22, *Soviet Agriculture Today: Report of 1963 Agriculture Exchange Delegation,* Foreign Agricultural Economic Report No. 13 (Washington, D.C.: U.S. Department of Agriculture, December, 1963); Volin in Chapter 1 of this volume.

[26] Johnson and Kahan estimated that 1965 output would exceed that of 1958 by about 24 percent. See *op. cit.* (in n. 1), p. 107. See also the publications of the U.S. Department of Agriculture cited in notes 2, 6, 25.

[27] *Vneshtorg-1959–1963,* pp. 46–47 indicates that fertilizer exports increased substantially throughout the period (from 2.15 million to 4.08 million tons between 1958 and 1963).

TABLE 4

TRENDS IN INPUTS AND INCENTIVES, U.S.S.R., 1953–65

	1953 = 100	1958 = 100						
	1958	1959	1960	1961	1962	1963	1964	1965
Sown area [a]	124	100	104	105	110	112	109	106
Chemical fertilizer [b]	159	105	107	110	126	146	202	265
Deliveries of machinery [c]								
Tractors	207	92	100	118	131	152	n.a.	n.a.
Trucks	148	75	65	68	81	67	n.a.	n.a.
Grain combines	158	82	88	108	122	123	n.a.	n.a.
Productive investment [d]								
State	266	89	108	131	148	184	(212)	(249)
Collective farms	239	126	111	112	121	125	n.a.	n.a.
Employment in man days [d]	112	97	93	93	91	(88)	n.a.	n.a.
Output per man day [d]	135	104	111	115	118	n.a.	n.a.	n.a.
Procurement prices [d]	192	101	101	103	112	n.a.	n.a.	n.a.
Money income of collective farms [e]	266	104	101	103	115	121	n.a.	n.a.

SOURCES:

[a] *Narkhoz-1962*, p. 247 and *SSSR v tsifrakh-1964*, p. 69. 1965 is mid-year plan fulfillment figure.

[b] *Vest. stat.*, 1964, No. 5, p. 83 and *Ek. gaz.*, No. 1, 1965.

[c] *Narkhoz-1958*, p. 493, *Narkhoz-1962*, p. 329 and *Narkhoz-1963*, p. 340.

[d] Nancy Nimitz, "The Lean Years," *Problems of Communism*, XIV:3 (May–June, 1965), except for 1964 and 1965 investment plans which come from *Pravda*, 10 December 1964.

[e] *Narkhoz-1960*, p. 492, *Narkhoz-1962*, p. 330, and *Narkhoz-1963*, p. 346.

type of investment increased from 881 million rubles in 1953 to 1.5 billion in 1954 and 2 billion in 1955. It remained fairly constant at a level of 2–2.5 billion rubles until 1961. Collective farm investment rose more slowly until 1955 and then fluctuated between 1.8 and 1.9 billion rubles until 1957. It increased sharply in 1958 and 1959 to a level of 3 billion rubles per year but fell afterward. Thus, in terms of the allocation of investment funds, there was some reorientation of priorities in favor of agriculture during the 1954–1957 period, but afterward there was a return to previous priority scales within the all important state sector of the Soviet economy.

Incentives which grew rapidly from 1953 to 1958 because of greatly increased procurement prices, either did not increase thereafter, or declined considerably because of less favorable crop conditions, of no further significant increase in procurement prices, and of increased costs of operating equipment. Furthermore, in spite of the great increase in procurement prices through 1957, prices did not cover the costs of production on many farms, and for livestock products they were below cost of production for *most* farms.[28] Nancy Nimitz has pointed out that

> peasant incentives were poor and investment inadequate on almost all farms (in 1953). Given the universality of these conditions, no great discrimination was needed to do good. . . . Any price increase which swelled the income of the average farm was an improvement. (After 1958, when prices were much closer to cost and therefore more of an incentive to produce a particular product, their interrelationship became a more delicate matter.) [29]

Costs of production were increased significantly by the transfer of the machine-tractor stations (MTS) to the collectives and the sharp increase in prices of spare parts.[30] As we have already noted, trends in the allocations of machinery after 1958 were distinctly unfavorable to farms. Since prices were also increased, weak farms, especially those not located in the Black Soil zone, were effectively deprived of opportunities to increase, or modernize their machinery stocks. By manipulating the farm terms of trade, the government was able to increase the share of state farms in its productive investment in agriculture from about 33 percent in 1957 to about 60 percent in 1960, while raising total investment of this type by only 5 percent (it should be noted in this connection that sown area in the state-farm sector increased—partly as a result of conversions—by about 35 percent).[31]

The corn program was pushed, although output of grain corn was small and even though corn was impinging upon such a crucial crop as winter wheat.[32] The New Lands were being exploited beyond their long-run carrying capacity as a result of insufficient use of fallowing and neglect of other dry-land farming practices.[33] In the livestock sector the policy of increasing numbers to and beyond the limits of adequate feed supplies was pursued throughout the period, although the supply of feed, especially concentrates, was growing only slowly. The operation of

[28] For livestock products, prices were far below the costs of production throughout the period, and Brezhnev made it clear that this was also the case for grain in many areas. See also *Soviet Agriculture Today* (as cited in n. 25) and Jerzy F. Karcz "The New Soviet Agricultural Programme," *Soviet Studies,* XVII:2 (October, 1965), 135–146.

[29] Nimitz, *op. cit.* (in n. 25), p. 11.

[30] *Ibid.,* pp. 14–15.

[31] *Kap. stroi.-1961,* pp. 155, 167.

[32] V. Maniakin, *Ek. sel'. khoz.,* No. 2 (1965). See also Naum Jasny, "Low-and-High Yielding Crops in the USSR," in Laird, ed., *op. cit.* (in n. 6) and "Commentary" by Jeremy Anderson in *ibid.,* pp. 215–265.

[33] Carl Zoerb, "The Virgin Land Territory: Plans, Performance, Prospects," *Studies on the Soviet Union,* III:4 (1964), 29–43.

private plots was rendered more difficult by administrative measures which reduced both output and individual incentives.[34] Furthermore, application of scientific innovations in agriculture was stifled by the dominance of Lysenko, or arbitrary choices of agronomic techniques imposed from above.

We must also mention the wide variety of administrative and organizational changes which took place during this period primarily to enforce compliance with procurement and production goals which were not being met.[35]

It seems futile to attempt to find *the* factor which accounted for the stagnation in output during the period since 1958. Any one of them—the corn program, overextension of the New Lands, the downward trend in inputs and incentives, the administrative and organizational practices—would have had a significant impeding effect on output after that date. All of them combined made significant increases in output impossible. Thus, we need not have expected output to increase. Furthermore, since output in 1958 was unusually high because of weather factors, there was no sound reason for expecting that this level could be maintained.

Although the changes which came about after the March, 1962, plenum had some beneficial effects—inputs of capital, machinery, and fertilizer were increased, meat prices raised, and some costs reduced; the other features of the program—the downgrading of oats, fallow and grasses, the increased party role in agriculture, and the unrelenting pressure on procurements at a high level—were harmful. All these measures had little chance of showing their impact upon agriculture in 1963, but they do deserve some of the credit for the increase in the level of output in 1964.

It should not be forgotten that, although wheat imports in the past three years have been exceptionally large and the over-all situation in agriculture looks bleak at this time, much of the present predicament is a result of unfavorable weather. Weather conditions in general in 1963 and 1965 were exceptionally bad in large areas of the country and two such bad years following two years of only average performance would have had a serious impact on grain output even if the best or the most rational policy had been adopted. Furthermore, yields of winter wheat

[34] G. Shmelev, *Vop. ek.*, No. 4 (1965), pp. 27–37.

[35] Karcz and Timoshenko, *op. cit.* (in n. 6), pp. 146–147; Nimitz, *op. cit.* (in n. 25), pp. 16–19; *The Agricultural Situation in 1961–62 in the Soviet Union and other Eastern European Countries,* Economic Research Service, ERS-Foreign-29 (Washington, D.C.: U.S. Department of Agriculture, September, 1962).

and winter rye in the Soviet Union during 1963 and 1964 were low by comparison with yields in the years 1958–1962. For these reasons bread grains were affected most seriously in 1963 and, although the 1964 output was large, it was not as large as it would have been had better conditions existed in the winter grain regions. At the same time the livestock sector, in terms of livestock numbers or the output of livestock products, is well above the level of 1958. The present situation, therefore, obscures in part the benefits of some of the policy changes which were instituted by Khrushchev in 1962–1964 and those of his successors.

THE NEW PROGRAM

Certain positive policy measures, including the fertilizer program, the pension plan for collective farmers, the increase in investment and somewhat greater machinery deliveries, initiated under Khrushchev were tampered with initially by his successors. Between October, 1964, and March, 1965, the new leadership implemented a few innovations of their own: milk policies were raised, policies governing private agriculture were relaxed, government credit was extended for private purchases of livestock, and feed was supplied to private individuals. All these policies, supplemented by the new program for agriculture announced in March, 1965, add up to an impressive array of measures designed to halt the trend of the past *quinquennium* and to raise the level of agricultural output. Although one need not agree that they will cure all the ills of Soviet agriculture, there is considerable truth in Matskevich's comment that they "open up a new stage in the development of agriculture" in the Soviet Union.[36] How new a stage it will eventually prove to be obviously depends upon the degree to which the new policies will be implemented.

The main features of the program are familiar, and it has already been analyzed, especially with respect to its price and cost features.[37] One of the most striking elements of the new program and of numerous articles which have been published in the U.S.S.R. since the fall of Khrushchev, is the change in tone and the emerging new approach to agricultural problems. In many respects the policies announced now are similar to those that many Western observers might have suggested as necessary to

[36] V. Matskevich, *Vop. ek.*, No. 6 (1965), p. 4.

[37] Keith Bush, *The New Plan for Soviet Agriculture,* Radio Liberty Research Paper No. 4 (Munich: 1965, mimeographed); Karcz, *op. cit.* (in n. 28), pp. 129–161; G. Stanley Brown in *Foreign Agriculture,* May 3, 1965, pp. 3–4.

overcome the basic difficulties of Soviet agriculture. As one would expect, past errors have been condemned and possibly overstated a little, but in general the criticisms have been valid, and the measures put forward to correct them point in the right direction. One cannot help but agree with Brezhnev when he says that "in practice very little was done [since 1958] to raise agricultural methods to a higher level or to increase yields." [38]

The instability and excessive nature of grain procurements has been altered by fixing permanent procurement figures for 1965–1970 at a level approximating that of 1958.[39] The prices to be paid in procurements of basic food grains, and some other grains as well, have been increased; for purchases above the planned quota of wheat and rye, a 50 percent premium is to be paid. Procurement prices for livestock have been increased, and the present procurement goal for 1970 is 11.4 million tons of meat (in terms of live weight), or about the level planned originally for 1965, and considerably below that indicated as "needed" by Khrushchev (see Appendix Table 4). Milk, eggs, and wool-procurement plans are also reduced. As is the case with meat, most of these plans for 1970 are at about the level planned originally for 1965 and well below that called for by Khrushchev in 1962 for "the near future." It would appear that in the livestock sector the new leaders are listening to the economists who, much to his displeasure, told Khrushchev in 1957 that it would be 1975 before the Soviet Union could catch up with United States output of livestock products.

For livestock, as for grains and milk, the presently increased prices appear to cover the cost of production for the average farm, even in some high cost areas.[40] Some six years ago, Miss Nimitz noted that a positive correlation appears to exist in the Soviet Union between profitable procurement prices and the level of output of these crops.[41] Although inadequacies persist, the new price levels continue the process begun in 1953 and aiming at the increase of prices paid by the government for food products to a level which will cover production costs on the farm. They also appear to correct some of the more obvious disparities in the price structure.

[38] *Izvestiia,* March 27, 1965.

[39] 55.7 million tons. Taken from Brezhnev, *ibid.,* which serves as a source for all other comments on the new program.

[40] Karcz, *op. cit.* (in n. 28), pp. 135–146.

[41] Nancy Nimitz, "Soviet Agricultural Prices and Costs," in U.S. Congress, Joint Economic Committee, *Comparisons of the United States and Soviet Economies,* Part I (Washington, D.C.: Government Printing Office, 1959), p. 255.

Capital investment in agriculture is planned at 71 billion rubles during the period 1966–1970 and the government will account for 41 billion rubles. Investment in agriculture will aproximately double during the coming five years over that of the past five years.[42] As opposed to 1,092,000 tractors delivered in 1961–1965, 1,790,000 are to be shipped to farms in 1966–1970. In comparable terms, truck deliveries are scheduled to increase by 119 percent and shipments of spare parts and agricultural machinery by about 50 percent or more.[43] Repair facilities are to be expanded as well.

The list of improvements on the input side is impressive, including the opening of 3 million hectares to irrigation and drainage of 6 million hectares. This compares with only 2.3 million hectares opened to irrigation and 3 million drained during the past twenty years. These measures are accompanied by the writing off of much of the debt which burdened economically weak collective farms and by changes in the income tax levied on collective farms from gross to net income. The amalgamation of farms is to be halted, but "at the same time it would be no less rash to solve the question of the breaking up of amalgamated farms with the same haste." [44] Even a reduction in prices of consumer goods in the countryside is taking place, at least gradually. The reemphasis on agriculture in the non-Black Soil zone, where weather conditions are more consistent and favorable to crops, is one of the most important features of the new program.

More interesting, however, than any specific measure is what can only be described as a changed "approach" to agriculture which is revealed in the program. The emphasis is upon what has to be put into agriculture, not what should be taken out of it, and in many ways the program shows a willingness to do what has to be done first, and await the results. As announced, the program suggests strongly that much of the general framework within which Soviet agriculture will operate by 1970 will be significantly different from that which has been in operation for the past few years, provided, of course, that the program is fully implemented.

This does not mean that the system of socialized agriculture in the U.S.S.R. will be altered significantly. There is no indication that basic changes of this type are being contemplated. It does mean, however, that given the existence of that system, much more will be put into agriculture in the form of investments, machinery, fertilizer, and other

[42] By our calculations it has more or less doubled from 1950–1955 through 1960–1965.

[43] P. Koshevnikov, *Ek. sel'. khoz.*, No. 6 (1965), p. 29.

[44] Brezhnev, *Izvestiia*, March 27, 1965.

inputs, as well as higher prices, while less will be extracted in the form of procurements. Furthermore, the new program suggests that the management of agriculture and the nature of procurements within the existing system will be changed.

Certainly the significance of all this is a matter of debate, first with respect to implementation and, second, with respect to effectiveness. As to the first point we cannot say whether the program will be fully implemented, modified downward, or even upward. At the present time, however, it is *the* existing program and much of it has been implemented already. It could be pointed out that the fertilizer goals for 1970 have been reduced from the original 70–80 to 50–55 million tons, but by comparison with the quantities of fertilizer delivered in past years, this amounts only to a shift from the unattainable to an impressively realistic target.[45] It should also be noted that we have not been told what the output goals of the new Soviet leaders are. Although this makes our task a little more difficult, it is more an indication of the new approach on the part of the present leaders compared to that of Khrushchev. We do not know either exactly how much grain will be purchased by the government on a year-by-year basis. Procurement plans have been fixed, but these are a minimum which all farms are expected to fulfill, and purchases above this level are not only expected but apparently planned. The government frankly admits that the procurements will not satisfy its needs for grain.[46] The manner in which these "above-plan" procurements are handled could alter the fixed nature of procurements.

One final feature of the new program is worth considering: the setting in which it was announced. When the Seven-Year Plan was formulated, the trend in agricultural output was rising steeply, and Khrushchev evidently felt this trend would continue even though efforts to stimulate output would be reduced. The consequences of a reduction in government efforts to increase output have been serious, and the new leadership appears to be well aware of this elementary economic phenomenon. The point of departure for the present program or any other program undertaken by the Soviet Union at this time, is drastically different. The existing "state of Soviet agriculture" must be viewed with serious concern. Even if 1964 levels of output were maintained, the Soviet Union would face a progressively deteriorating situation with respect to domestic food supplies and its balance of payments. Under these conditions there is every reason to assume that the present program will be carried out at least until significant improvements are

[45] Matskevich, *op. cit.* (in n. 36), p. 7.
[46] N. Gusov, *Ek. sel'. khoz.* No. 6 (1965), p. 10.

achieved. There is also some justification for assuming that the present efforts to increase output will be continued until some reasonable margin against another crop failure of the 1963 magnitude has been accumulated.

THE OUTLOOK FOR THE FUTURE

In this last section we propose to suggest, in somewhat less than precise terms, the area of potential change between now and 1970, taking into consideration certain immediate problems facing the Soviet Union, its long-run production possibilities, and some of the obscurities involved in the grain sector. We have divided the period from 1953 to 1964 into three four-year periods and are concerned with a range of likely levels of output during the period 1969–1972, that is, an average level of output eight years after 1961–1964.

Since we do not know the present output goals for 1970 we use as our benchmarks the previous goals for 1965 and 1970. These goals were obviously unattainable in the time allowed, but they are assumed to reflect the general requirements of the Soviet Union, in terms of the quantity and composition of output, and can therefore be taken seriously as indicators of long-run objectives. In addition, we rely heavily upon the study of Soviet agricultural production possibilities by P. M. Zemskii [47] and an evaluation of that study based upon North American analogs.[48] These output goals and the obtainable levels of output assumed by Zemskii were presented earlier in Table 3. In view of the importance of Zemskii's study for our projections, we reproduce his estimates of "attainable future output" in much greater detail in Table 5, which also shows corresponding figures for some other time periods of the recent past. Zemskii's output projections are obviously the result of his projections of sown areas and yields. Since these two magnitudes are to a certain extent interrelated, they are also shown separately in Appendix Table 5.

Some other comments about the Zemskii study need to be made here because of its unique features in the present context. There is much to indicate that the present leadership in the Soviet Union is more or less attempting to reintroduce policies forsaken in 1958. Mr. Matskevich, the Minister of Agriculture, has indicated that for a period of five years in the past, careful studies had been carried out on the production

[47] Zemskii, *op. cit.* (in n. 18).

[48] *Future Crop Yields and Fertilizer in the Soviet Union* (Washington, D.C.: U.S. Department of Agriculture, February, 1964, mimeographed). Hereafter cited as *Zemskii's Evaluation.*

TABLE 5

OFFICIAL AND "ATTAINABLE" OUTPUT OF SELECTED CROPS, U.S.S.R., SELECTED YEARS (million tons)

Crop	1953 production	1959–1962 production	1964 production	Zemskii's attainable production
Grains:				
Wheat	41.3	67.8	74.2	84.3
Winter	[19.8]	[25.9]	[26.3]	31.1
Spring	[21.4]	[41.5]	[47.9]	53.0
Rye	14.5	16.7	13.5	36.6
Barley	7.9	14.8	28.5	15.7
Winter	[0.4]	[2.3]	[2.5]	1.8
Spring	[7.5]	[12.5]	[26.0]	13.9
Oats	10.1	10.0	5.5	38.0
Corn, grain	3.7	12.0	13.3	42.6
Millet	2.68	2.55	3.47	6.7
Buckwheat	0.76	0.69	0.71	2.8
Rice	0.22	0.23	0.46	1.6
Pulses	1.12	4.1	11.08	2.8
Total grains	*82.3*	*128.1*	*150.7*	*228.3*
Technical crops:				
Sugar beets	23.2	50.0	80.3	86.0
Cotton	3.85	4.44	5.28	9.8
Flax fiber	0.162	0.405	0.337	0.978
Oilseeds	3.11	4.65	6.50	n.a.
Sunflower	2.63	4.14	5.99	7.4
Potatoes	72.6	81.3	93.0	187.7
Vegetables	11.4	15.9	18.5	39.4
Feed crops:				
Annual grasses	8.2	22.4	17.3	66.8
Perennial grasses	16.2	23.8	15.7	96.2
Corn other than grain	n.a.	186.1	238.0	64.0

SOURCES: 1953, 1959–1962: *Narkhoz-1962*, pp. 234–235; 1964: *SSSR v tsifrakh-1964*, pp. 72–73; Zemskii's attainable production: *Razvitie i razmeshchenie zemledeliia po prirodno-khoziaistvennym raionam SSSR* (Moscow: 1959), *passim.*

possibilities of Soviet agriculture, and such research was later abandoned. Work along these lines, he said, "is highly important and must be resumed." [49] It is interesting that in the introduction to the Zemskii study reference is made to studies begun in 1954 on the production possibilities of Soviet agriculture, and Zemskii's own book is indicated to be an outgrowth of that work.[50] The Zemskii study was published in 1959, more or less five years after 1954, and, until now, it has been generally neglected in the Soviet Union. Although many trends pro-

[49] V. Matskevich, *Sel'. zh.* June 24, 1965.
[50] Zemskii, *op. cit.* (in n. 18), p. 3.

jected by Zemskii are debatable (this is especially true of his projected areas under corn and oats), a glance at Table 5 and Appendix Table 5 indicate that his projections were much more realistic than those followed by Khrushchev in the past few years.

The structure of sown area has changed drastically during the years since 1958 and especially since 1962, with sharp decreases for oats, fallow, and grasses, and rapid increases in corn, barley, and pulses. Since October, 1964, these trends have been criticized vigorously in the Soviet Union and many of them are being reversed, especially with respect to lands under fallow, grasses, and corn. For all these reasons the Zemskii study, in spite of certain drawbacks, is a valuable tool for analyzing the future possibilities of Soviet agriculture, not only for our present purposes, but also for anyone concerned with a particular crop or region. Its usefulness is further increased by the careful scrutiny it received at the hands of a group of American agricultural specialists with the aid of North American analogs. Furthermore, Zemskii's output projections were designed to match the composition of future planned output of crops and livestock products.[51]

Although only a careful look at the Zemskii study and its evaluation will make it clear in which particular areas and for which particular crops the American specialists disagreed with his findings, their general conclusion is noteworthy:

> On the basis of the available evidence, we feel that the projections do show, on the whole, an understanding of the potentialities and limitations of the different parts of the Soviet Union. We also feel that the author displays an understanding of the potential increases of output to be expected through the application of technology in conjunction with fertilization. The projected fertilizer rates appear to reflect a sensitiveness to the relationships among soils, climate, and crop requirements as regards response to fertilization.[52]

The Zemskii study is not used here as an indicator of the composition of sown area or the level of output in the Soviet Union by 1970, but only as a crutch to lean upon in an obscure situation. Zemskii assumed a

[51] *Ibid.*, p. 5. "Our task consisted in establishing, on the basis of the Party's and government decisions, an approximate level of prospective agricultural production . . . which would assure fulfillment of the people's requirements for food, based on scientific norms, the required supply of the necessary state surplus and export stocks." As long as it can be assumed that the Soviet government output goals for 1965 and 1970 still roughly reflect the desired composition of output, no matter whether they are attained (or when), the Zemskii study has the added advantage of reflecting an appropriate composition (though not necessarily the level) of output.

[52] *Zemskii's Evaluation* (as cited in n. 48), p. 1.

fertilizer availability of from 70 to 80 million tons in gross weight, or about 17.6 million tons in terms of plant nutrients.[53] He further assumed that this fertilizer would be applied correctly and appropriately, and that adequate machinery and equipment would be available.[54] We postulate that 50 to 55 million tons of fertilizer will be available to agriculture in 1970, and that the composition of this supply of fertilizer will differ somewhat from that anticipated by Zemskii. We also assume that the machinery deliveries now planned will come fairly close to those which Khrushchev indicated would be necessary to carry out production at peak periods.[55] We do not assume that this fertilizer or machinery will be used to its full capacity,[56] but that the availability of machinery will assist in improving sowing and harvesting at more appropriate times, even though the supplies of these inputs will not be adequate to meet all needs of Soviet agriculture.

One final but important feature of the Zemskii study is that it was carried out without reference to the existing reported Soviet yields. Zemskii used the yields of crops before the revolution and yields obtained on test plots as a guide, but did not mention existing yields—[57] probably because such data were not published by the Soviet Union until 1958. It also suggests that his estimated yield levels are free of whatever bias now exists in the Soviet statistics.

This, unfortunately, brings us back to the subject of Soviet grain yields mentioned earlier. Appendix Table 5 shows that the reported yield of winter wheat in the Soviet Union averaged 16 centners per

[53] Zemskii, *op. cit.* (in n. 18), p. 266.

[54] Zemskii makes this point on several occasions, e.g., in *ibid.*, pp. 73–74, 104.

[55] *Pravda,* March 6, 1962. For a further discussion of these goals see *Soviet Agriculture Today* (as cited in n. 25), pp. 33–37 and 72–73. Given the rates of retirement implied in Soviet handbooks (net additions on an annual basis), the presently planned deliveries of machinery will more or less match these levels by 1970.

[56] Examples of waste of fertilizer and of poor utilization of machinery are often published in the Soviet press and have been mentioned frequently by Khrushchev. For example, A. N. Efimov, ed., *Ekonomika SSSR v poslevoennyi period* (Moscow: 1962), p. 194, indicates that in some of the central *oblasts* the loss in transport and storage alone amounted to 39 percent for phosphate fertilizers, 18 percent for nitrogen, and 28.5 percent for potassium fertilizers. In addition, there is a loss in application. Presumably, such losses will decline in the future, but they constitute a serious problem at this time.

[57] The anticipated yields projected by Zemskii and cited in Appendix Table 5 are not those that could be obtained on test plots. Zemskii makes substantial reductions in order to obtain yields that could be realized on regularly operated farms. *Cf. ibid.*, pp. 73–74.

hectare during 1959–1962 compared to only 11 in 1953. On a somewhat larger area, Zemskii projected a level of 18 centners. When the Ukraine is analyzed, the presently reported yields for 1959–1962 are less than one centner per hectare below those projected by Zemskii in the future with the fertilizer, machinery, and farm practices he anticipated.[58] It is also interesting to note that his anticipated yield for total wheat is only 13.8 centners per hectare while the presently reported yield for 1959–1962 was 10.7 centners per hectare (Appendix Table 5). In other words, according to the Soviet yield figures, more than two-fifths of the potential increase in yields (over 1953, or 1949–1953) which might be expected from the entire complex of inputs and techniques anticipated by Zemskii, was obtained more or less without them. For the other grains the gap between the presently reported yields and those anticipated by Zemskii is quite large. For the most part, those who evaluated the Zemskii study found it to be correct about wheat, and especially about wheat in the Ukraine.[59]

This point is important since the new program is "devoting particular attention to the development of grain production, the basis and pivot of the whole of agriculture," [60] and wheat is the crop now being imported in such great quantities. Furthermore, wheat prices have been raised, and the trend in production is now heavily toward winter wheat in such areas as the Ukraine.[61]

There are many reasons for believing that fairly substantial yield increases did take place in the Ukraine and in certain other regions during the period from 1953 to 1959–1962 due to increases in the application of manure, more machinery, higher yielding seeds, the residual impact of chemical fertilizer applied to other crops, some increases in fertilizer applied to grains, increased irrigation, and a general improvement in crop practices. Furthermore, anyone who has worked with analogs knows that the margin for error is substantial. Nevertheless, the basic question is whether the yields of winter wheat in the Ukraine could have increased from 11.9 to 18.9 centners per hectare between 1949–1953 and 1959–1962, when in 1959 Zemskii anticipated an attainable level of only 19.6 centners per hectare, and when the

[58] *Ibid.*, p. 105. Zemskii projected a yield of 19.6 centners per hectare while the reported yield of winter wheat in the Ukraine was 18.9 centners per hectare in 1959–1962. See *Narodne hospodarstvo Ukrainskoi RSR v 1963 rotsi* (Kiev: 1964), p. 245.

[59] *Zemskii's Evaluation*, pp. 49, 52, 55.

[60] Brezhnev, *Pravda*, March 27, 1965.

[61] G. Kotov, *Ek. sel'. khoz.*, No. 6 (1965), p. 42 and *Pravda Ukrainy*, August 12, 1965.

evaluation of his study found this figure to be substantially correct. In the light of our preceding discussion it seems more likely that the reported increase in yields for this period is exaggerated than that both Zemskii and his evaluators could have erred so substantially.[62]

But one is still left with uncomfortable feelings about this matter. If we assume that the reported Ukrainian yields for winter wheat in 1959–1962 are exaggerated, and if we attempt a correction of 15 percent to account for this exaggeration, then the "real" yield (comparable conceptually to the one used by Zemskii) turns out to be 16.1, instead of the official 18.9, centners per hectare. It still turns out that the Ukrainians would have succeeded in obtaining more than one-half of their potential increase in yields of winter wheat without the benefit of additional fertilizer and machinery, and with agronomical techniques that would have left much to be desired (if for no other reason than because of pressures on land and resources associated with the corn program). On the other hand, Zemskii was writing at a time when the expansion of corn acreage in the Ukraine was still proceeding. He assumed that this policy would continue and may also have assumed that winter wheat would be treated less favorably in terms of both land and other inputs within the time horizon encompassed by his study.[63]

It is not possible here to examine in detail each of several disturbing points, and the reader is directed to the two basic studies, especially if he is interested in the more complex aspects of the impact on yields of shifts between various crops and regions (on Zemskii's many assumptions) or if he prefers to alter the assumptions of this study. In the remainder of this study we shall deal only at the aggregate (i.e., all-union) level.

GRAIN PRODUCTION

The present difficulties with grain suggest that the greatest emphasis in the remainder of this decade will be upon grain production and espe-

[62] Research by the writers with weather data (monthly temperatures and precipitation for the years 1953–1963) suggests that a large share of the increase in yields in the Ukraine cannot be explained by weather factors alone. Most of the increase in yields occurred before 1958, when the amount of fertilizer applied to wheat could only have been minimal. Much has been published recently in the Soviet press and in Soviet journals on the discriminatory treatment of winter wheat with respect to fertilizer application. See, for example, Maniakin, *op. cit.* (in n. 32) and *Pravda Ukrainy*, August 12, 1965.

[63] Zemskii, *op. cit.* (in n. 18), p. 106. Given the continuing expansion of corn, Zemskii may have assumed that wheat will not receive the most suitable land or other inputs. The situation within the next five years may well change in this respect.

cially the basic food grains—wheat and rye—and the less, but still, important millet, buckwheat, and rice. Prices for all of these have been increased significantly.[64] Their production will shift as much as possible to regions where weather is more favorable, consistent, and where yields are higher. This will facilitate the use of fertilizer. Grain production will be reduced wherever possible in regions where yields are low.[65] This means greater concentration of grain production in the Central Black Soil zone, the Baltic region, the North Caucasus, the Ukraine, Moldavia, and even the non-Black Soil zone of the R.S.F.S.R. However, in the new and semi New Lands regions of Kazakhstan, the Volga region, and the Southern Urals, grain production will continue, despite low yields, because these regions are heavily committed to grain production and because the country needs the grain produced there.[66]

Wheat, especially winter wheat, will be given first place in such areas as the Ukraine, the North Caucasus, and Moldavia. Rye production will increase, and the crop will be given preferential treatment in the Baltic regions, White Russia, the central Volga region, and in the central and northern Urals regions.[67] Corn will be treated with some degree of rationality: neither abandoned where yields are good and full maturity is possible, nor pushed where yields are low or where it impinges upon other grains.[68]

A winter-grain area of around 40 to 45 million hectares seems likely. Of this, between 20 and 25 million hectares could be in winter wheat. There is no indication, as yet, that a significant reduction in the sown area in the New Lands will take place until yields in other areas are increased, and the present policy seems to be, as in 1965, to sow in anticipation of a harvest, even if one does not materialize. A spring-wheat area of from 45–50 million hectares, decreasing toward 1970,

[64] *Pravda,* March 27, 1965.

[65] Kotov, *op. cit.* (in n. 61), p. 42.

[66] *Ibid.* It cannot be ruled out that a rapid increase in yields in European Russia will facilitate greater use of fallow in the New Lands, or that a series of dry years will drive the government to the adoption of this solution. Greater use of fallow in the New Lands is to be expected and may eventually reach the 40-percent level commonly encountered in comparable areas of Canada. This, we assume, will take place slowly under any circumstances. It may also depend on yield and output trends in other wheat producing areas.

[67] *Ibid.,* pp. 42–43.

[68] *Ibid.,* p. 43. A large number of statements in the Soviet press as well as in journal articles suggest that corn is being credited with its virtues and that there will be no massive retreat from corn, regardless of its association with Khrushchev. Certainly, the long-range possibilities for corn production in the U.S.S.R. are better than its recent record.

does not seem unlikely. In part this will be due to greater sowing of spring wheat in regions which are not, strictly speaking, New Lands areas.[69]

Feed grains will most likely be expanded at the expense of immature corn.[70] Some return of oats might materialize, but the present barley area will probably be maintained or reduced slowly.[71] Pulses could decline. The area projected by Zemskii for millet, buckwheat, rice, and rye seems appropriate for the period 1969–1972. Corn for grain will probably range from 4 to 7 million hectares.[72] The direction of change indicated in Zemskii for grasses and fallow appears reasonable; considerable changes in that direction have already taken place and are under discussion.[73]

Thus the following distribution of area under grains might be anticipated by 1969–1972:

Type of grain	Possible range	Assumed likely
	million hectares	
Winter wheat	20–25	23
Spring wheat	45–47	46
Barley	20–22	20
Oats	6–7	7
Corn	6–7	7
Rye	19–20	20
Other grains	10–13	12
Total	126–141	135

This assumes that pressure from the demand side will still be forcing a greater sowing of food grains than might be optimal in terms of Zem-

[69] There has been much discussion (primarily in *Sel'. zh.*) about the increase in the cultivation of spring wheat in such areas as the Ukraine. This, we would anticipate, would take place as a regular sowing and as a crop to replace winter kill of winter wheat.

[70] Kotov, *op. cit.* (in n. 61), p. 39.

[71] It seems clear that procurements of feed grains have recently run above plan targets, while those of food grains were underfulfilled. As a result of these developments, the area under barley could decline for some time while that under bread grains will increase. But by 1969–1972 we would assume that the projected areas under oats and barley will materialize under the impact of demand for feed grains.

[72] *Zemskii's Evaluation* expressed some doubts about the projected level of corn yields in some regions. It nevertheless came to a conclusion that there was room for an increase in the present area under *grain corn.* This would seem reasonable as the pressure for production of food grains declines in the future.

[73] *Sel. zh.*, July 27, 1965, and a large number of articles in the same newspaper in recent months.

skii's appraisal. In the long run, if yields of these grains increase, their area can be expected to decline.

What could the yield be on such an area and what is it likely to be by 1969–1972? Obviously this depends upon one's assumption about the impact of the program and its implementation, and upon what one assumes the present yield level to be. On the basis of the Zemskii study an average barn yield of 16.8 centners per hectare could be obtained, but the conditions upon which that yield level rests will not be present in the U.S.S.R. by 1970, even with the full implementation of the new program. If grain yields of 1953 or 1949–1953—yields which few are inclined to dispute—can be taken as those obtained in the U.S.S.R. without application of fertilizers and with only limited inputs of other factors (except labor and land) then the problem resolves itself to one of determining where yields might fall by 1969–1972. The limits of the range are given by actual yield in 1949–1953 and the level projected by Zemskii. For all grain the difference between these two points is 9.1 centners per hectare. We assume that if the present program is fully implemented, at least one half of the response projected by Zemskii could be expected. The inputs would exceed one-half of those required, but allowances for the present pressure for production of food grains, difficulties in shifting the patterns of sown area, and a lag in response necessitate some pessimism at least until 1970.

Such a yield (12 to 13 quintals per hectare) would produce, on an area of 135 million hectares, a grain crop of from 162 to 175 million tons of grain, in terms of "more or less" barn yield (see Table 6). If area under grains should fall below that assumed, we assume a compensatory increase in yields. Such an increase in output is large by comparison with any of the estimates and even by comparison with the "bunker weight" output of 1961–1964. It would nevertheless be only 4.3–5.3 centners per hectare above the average 1949–1953 yield when farms had no fertilizer to apply to grains, when there were no incentives, little machinery, and little reason (except coercion) for producing grain. Furthermore, the grain situation is critical at this time, and a sizable proportion of the output would consist of food grains.[74] Assuming that the grain sector will be given top priority in the next few years, such a level of output is not impossible, given *full* implementation of the

[74] We assume that more than one-half of the difference between Zemskii's projected yield and the 1953 actual yield of winter wheat is obtainable. Less than one-half of the corresponding difference with regard to spring wheat is believed to be attainable. Zemskii's study indicates that the present emphasis on rye may lead to substantial increases in output, as well as yields. In general we assume that wheat and rye will be favored in the near future.

TABLE 6

GROSS OUTPUT OF SELECTED FARM PRODUCTS, U.S.S.R., SELECTED YEARS
(million tons, except eggs)

Commodities	1953–1956	1957–1960	1961–1964	1969–1972 (projected)
Grain:				
Total grain (Soviet)	98.8	120.3	132.1	n.a.
Total grain (U.S.D.A. estimate)	92.4	99.5	107.9	n.a.
Projected High assumption	—	—	—	162–175
Low assumption	—	—	—	148–162
Sugar beets	26.6	48.9	55.7	86
Cotton	4.1	4.4	4.8	6.5–7.5
Oilseeds	3.9	4.3	5.6	8.0
Potatoes	78.8	86.3	79.7	120–130
Vegetables	12.9	15.3	16.5	25–30
Meat (Soviet, including fat and offals)	6.3	8.2	9.1	n.a.
High assumption	—	—	—	13–14
Low assumption	—	—	—	12–13
Milk (Soviet)	41.7	59.2	62.7	n.a.
High assumption	—	—	—	90–100
Low assumption	—	—	—	80–90
Wool	.246	.331	.366	.500
Billions of eggs	17.8	24.5	28.6	37
Flax fiber	.320	.406	.387	.550–.585

SOURCE: for 1953–1964: Table 3.

present program. Should the program fall short of full implementation or the response be inhibited for other reasons, an output of 148–162 million tons would still seem possible. In terms of yields, this implies an increase of 3.3–4.3 centners per hectare above the level achieved in 1949–1953.

How such a yield should be compared to the various estimates and to the reported "bunker weight" output is a problem that cannot be resolved here. "Bunker weight" output in 1964 was 151 million tons, or well within the range of our "low" projection. It has already been indicated, however, that this figure is assumed to be from 10 to 20 percent inflated according to virtually all students of Soviet agriculture. By comparison with any of the estimates for 1961–1964 and the reported "bunker weight" figure, both the low and the high projections represent very substantial increases in grain output. What the "bunker weight" output might be, if the Soviet Union does not further change its reporting system, is a matter which we cannot determine, but it would certainly be well above the levels projected here.

A significant increase in the output of perennial and annual grasses can be expected from the present reemphasis on these crops. This, together with an increase in the use of grain as feed for livestock, will further production of livestock products in general. It should also be noted that, although pig and sheep herds declined significantly in 1963, other livestock herds were not seriously affected and are well above the level of earlier years. Furthermore pig herds increased significantly since 1963.[75] During 1969–1972, therefore, a level of from 14 to 15 million tons of meat (Soviet concept, including fat and offals) does not seem impossible. A lower range of output for meat, fat, and offals of 13 to 14 million tons would correspond to the lower range of grain output. Milk output of from 90 to 100 million tons (in terms of the Soviet concept) for a high assumption and 80 to 90 million tons for a low assumption seems likely. To a large extent, this would result from the recovery of the loss in yields during the past half-dozen years, but some increase in cow herds, and a considerable increase in feed of one kind or another, can also be expected to occur. More favored treatment of the private sector will facilitate increases in livestock output. Present problems with sheep suggest that a level of output of 500,000 tons of wool might be high, but sheep-raising has been given some special priority by the new leaders. An increase in egg production to about 37 billion eggs is projected because of increased use of grain for feeding and also as a result of greater specialization in this area.

The output of livestock products projected here is large by comparison with the level of 1961–1964. This is explained in part by the fact that livestock numbers are still at a relatively high level despite the low level of output in 1961–1964. On the other hand, this level of output is below that originally planned for 1965 (Table 3) and much below the output level previously planned for 1970. We assume that the combination of relatively large livestock numbers and a better feed supply will facilitate fairly substantial increases in output, but that bottlenecks in improving feeding efficiency and improving herds will still impede its growth.

Whatever the reason for the rapid expansion of sugar beets and oilseeds in recent years, we assume that price increases and application of additional fertilizer will facilitate the increase in yields. Any shortfalls in yields could be compensated for by expansion of area under these crops.[76] A sugar-beet output of 80–86 million tons seems quite

[75] *Sel'. zh.*, July 27, 1965.

[76] The expression "whatever the reasons" is used to indicate the apparent contradiction between import contracts with Cuba, and present plans for a large domestic production of sugar beets and sugar. So far there are no

likely, and an oilseed output of 8 million tons is not unattainable. This, in turn, means that the 1970 goals for these two crops may well be reached. The potential for yield increases allowed by Zemskii does not prohibit such levels of output, and both crops have been given special priority before as well as after the departure of Khrushchev.[77]

Cotton, which showed a very unimpressive trend until 1963, could increase in area to 3 million hectares or more by 1969–1972. The greater availability of fertilizer, machinery, and irrigation facilities could result in a yield of 25 centners per hectare. We assume that 25 centners would be the outside possible yield level and that any shortfalls in area would bring the crop down. An output of between 6.5 and 7.5 million tons of cotton is therefore considered attainable. The present gap between yields of flax fiber and Zemskii's projected yields suggests that a yield of 3.5 centners per hectare by 1969–1972, on an area of 1.6 to 1.7 million hectares, would produce from 550 to 585 thousand tons. This, we assume, is possible.

Trends in potato output and yields are most difficult to assess. That both could increase significantly is obvious from Zemskii's projection and from the depressingly low yield level of the past few years. Nothing as yet indicates that the area is to increase, but we assume a combination of yield and area increases sufficient to sustain output at 120–130 million tons. It is clear that the potato output could be raised sharply, but the fact that it has not done so in the past, does not warrant optimism. The upward trend of the vegetable output throughout the period 1953–1964 suggests further increases resulting from over-all benefits of the program and should result in an output of 25–30 million tons or more by 1969–1972.

CONCLUSIONS

Implicit in our "projections" is the assumption that the program as announced will be largely implemented. The benefits are expected to lag behind the implementation of various policies, so that the rate of

indications that the heavy pressure to increase the output of sugar beets and oil seeds is being relaxed. Should the Soviet Union find itself with large stocks of sugar as a result of the fulfillment of its present trade agreement with Cuba, a reduction in the area under sugar beets (through the shift to fodder crops) is quite possible.

77 It should not be assumed, however, that exports of these or other food products would increase as a result of such developments. For most of these products, consumption is much below the planned level. In the long run, of course, trends in exports will be a function of government decisions with respect to the allocation of output between consumption and exports.

growth of output should increase as 1970 is approached. It is also assumed that the program, if implemented, will bring about a significant change in the economic environment in which Soviet agriculture will operate by 1969–1972 but the existing institutional structure will not be altered. One significant retarding factor is the fact that increased output must come from increased productivity. In the past, this has not been an outstanding characteristic of Soviet agriculture.

We assume a continued downward trend in labor inputs, and some gradual, but expensive, increases in land. Although we have not calculated an index, the assumption that the 1965 planned level of output will still not have been reached for some important commodities by 1970 is implicit in our projections. This is particularly true of meat, milk, and potatoes. Grain output is likely to approach the lower limit of these goals, but for certain crops, such as sugar beets and oilseeds, the 1970 goals could well be reached. We do not rule out the possibility that the 1965 goals may be achieved for many crops by 1969–1972.

Our projected levels of output, especially those of grain and meat, may seem high in relation to the achievements of 1961–1964. It should not be forgotten, however, that these achievements were clearly inadequate in relation to the present policy of raising living standards, the need to replenish depleted grain stocks, and the demands that may again be placed upon the U.S.S.R. by other members of the Sino-Soviet bloc. To repeat a statement made earlier, the present state of Soviet agriculture is so unsatisfactory that stagnation cannot be tolerated for a longer period of time, since other sectors of the economy might be seriously affected. In a sense, the Russians are now forced to pay a heavy price for the policies pursued in the distant as well as the more recent past. Given the present posture of the Soviet economy as a whole, the opportunity cost of purchasing more than 20 million tons of "capitalist" wheat during the past three years may well turn out to be higher than the cost of the new program. It is interesting to note in this context that the present leaders have thought it advisable to condemn even minimal expenditure of foreign exchange for imports of rice.

Two things should be watched closely between now and 1970: the weather and the implementation of the presently announced programs. We have assumed, as we must, that weather conditions in 1969–1972 will be "average." Much of the current spectacular troubles in Soviet agriculture—especially imports of wheat—can be explained primarily by weather. The year 1963 must be put down as a virtually complete agricultural failure due to exceptionally bad weather. For winter grains, mostly wheat and rye, there was no great improvement in 1964 or 1965.

Should these conditions occur two or three times again in the coming five years, there is little chance that the current difficulties will be overcome, regardless of the efforts exerted to increase output. On the other hand, average weather conditions should result in the increases in output as roughly projected here, while better than average conditions, such as those of 1956 and 1958 bunched in the next five years, could raise output very substantially above these levels.

In the recent past, the sharp downturn or virtual stagnation in such indicators as the levels of capital investment, fertilizer production and machinery allocation, farm price levels, and trends in farm incentives provided Western observers with most reliable devices for predicting

APPENDIX TABLE 1

GRAIN YIELDS OFFICIAL AND IMPLIED IN INDEPENDENT WESTERN ESTIMATES, U.S.S.R., 1953–1962

(centners per hectare)

	Including immature corn Implied yields			Excluding immature corn Implied yields		
	Official	Estimates		Official	Estimates	
	Soviet statistics [a]	CIA [b]	Laird [c]	Soviet statistics [a]	Kahan [d]	U.S.D.A. [e]
1953	7.7 [f]	7.7 [f]	7.7	7.7	7.7 [g]	7.5
1954	7.7	7.8	—	7.7	7.2	7.2
1955	7.5	8.1	—	8.4	7.8	8.0
1956	10.0	8.2	—	10.0	9.0	8.8
1957	8.4	8.0	—	8.4	7.8	7.7
1958	11.3	10.0	10.2	11.1	10.0	9.5
1959	10.5	8.4	9.5	10.4	9.4	8.2
1960	11.0	8.2	9.9	10.9	9.8	8.2
1961	10.8	9.0	9.1	10.7	[9.6] [h]	8.9
1962	10.9	8.5	9.2	10.9	[9.8] [h]	8.7
1959–1962 average	10.8	8.5	9.4	10.7	9.7	8.5

[a] *Sel'khoz-1960*, pp. 202–203, *Narkhoz-1962*, pp. 234–235, *Narkhoz-1963*, p. 73 and *SSSR v tsifrakh-1964*, p. 72. [b] *Production of Grain in the U.S.S.R.* (Washington, D.C.: Central Intelligence Agency, October 1964), p. 16. [c] Roy D. Laird, "Agriculture under Khrushchev," *Survey*, No. 56 (July, 1965), p. 107. [d] Roy D. Laird, ed., *Soviet Agricultural and Peasant Affairs* (Lawrence, Kansas: University of Kansas Press, 1963); p. 149. [e] *The 1965 Eastern Europe Agricultural Situation*, ERS-Foreign-115, (Washington, D.C.: U.S. Department of Agriculture, March, 1965), p. 10. [f] The sown area for 1953 was 106.7 and total grain output reported as 82.5 million tons. This results in a yield of 7.7319 centners per hectare compared to the reported yield of 7.8. The 1949–1953 average yield was also 7.7 centners per hectare. [g] Kahan indicated that a deduction of 5 percent is appropriate for 1953 but does not actually estimate 1953 output. [h] Kahan does not estimate 1961 or 1962. His 10 percent deduction for the years from 1958 through 1960 is applied to the reported output for these two years.

APPENDIX TABLE 2: OUTPUT OF AGRICULTURAL PRODUCTS, U.S.S.R., FOUR-YEAR AVERAGES 1953–1964 (million tons except eggs)

Crop	Soviet official [a]			U.S.D.A. estimates [b]		
	1953–1956	1957–1960	1961–1964	1953–1956	1957–1960	1961–1964
Grain, total:	*98.8*	*120.3*	*132.1*	*92.4*	*99.5*	*107.9*
Wheat	49.5	67.0	65.3	42.3	52.6	51.1
Rye	15.2	15.9	14.8	15.2	14.7	13.4
Barley	9.7	11.9	20.3	9.1	9.5	17.3
Oats	11.5	12.9	6.0	11.4	11.6	5.5
Corn	7.2	7.6	14.3	7.0	6.2	10.1
Millet	3.3	2.2	2.7	—	—	—
Buckwheat	1.1	0.6	0.7	—	—	—
Rice	0.2	0.2	0.3	—	—	—
Pulses	1.1	2.0	7.7	—	—	—
Potatoes	78.8	86.3	79.7	—	—	—
Vegetables	12.9	15.3	16.5	—	—	—
Industrial crops:						
Sugar beets	26.6	48.9	55.7	—	—	—
Oilseeds	3.9 [c]	4.3 [d]	5.6	—	—	—
Sunflower seed	3.1	3.6	5.0	2.9	3.2	4.6
Cotton	4.1	4.4	4.8	—	—	—
Flax fiber	0.320	0.406	0.387	—	—	—
Feed crops:						
Perennial grasses	16.3	21.9	20.0	—	—	—
Annual grasses	10.1	23.9	16.9	—	—	—
Natural hay	66.4 [e]	90.6 [f]	76.8 [f]	—	—	—
Corn silage	77.4 [g]	142.2	196.1	—	—	—
Meat production [h]						
Beef and veal	2.2	2.9	3.4	1.9	2.5	2.9
Pork	2.6	3.4	3.7	2.0	2.6	2.8
Mutton, lamb and goat	0.8	1.0	1.1	0.6	0.8	0.9
Poultry	0.5	0.7	0.8	0.5	0.7	0.8
Other meat	0.2	0.2	0.1	0.3	0.3	0.3
Milk	41.7	59.7	62.7	39.2	50.3	53.5
Billions of eggs	17.8	24.5	28.6	—	—	—
Wool	0.246	0.331	0.366	—	—	—

[a] Soviet official output figures in "bunker weight" for grain and oilseed. [b] For grain, U.S.D.A. estimates of usable grain. For oilseeds, the U.S.D.A. estimate is 8 percent below Soviet reported output. [c] 1954–1958 average. [d] 1958–1960 average. [e] Excludes that harvested by individuals. [f] Includes that harvested by individuals. [g] 1954–1958. [h] Soviet reported meat output including fat and offals. U.S.D.A. estimates exclude fat and offals.

SOURCES: *Sel'khoz-1960*, pp. 206–207, 334–336; *Narkhoz-1962*, pp. 234–235, 238; *SSSR v tsifrakh-1964*, pp. 72–73, 82; *Zhivotnovodstvo SSSR* (Moscow: 1959), pp. 157, 159; estimates of the U.S. Department of Agriculture.

failure in the agricultural component of the Seven-Year Plan. There is no reason to expect that the reliability of these indicators will decline in the future. Should they fail to follow the path charted in present plans within the next year or two, there would be a good deal of justification for pessimism. This would also be true if the present policy concerning farm management and procurement practices were abandoned in favor of methods followed by Khrushchev in the last few years of his tenure of power.

These things will tell us more about the possible level of agricultural output in the Soviet Union by 1970 than this study or any programs announced by the Soviet government. With respect to the weather there is little the present leadership can do except to take what comes. The implementation of the present program is, within broad limits, up to them. We would assume, however, that backsliding on the present program at a time like this would lead to very serious consequences which the present leadership would not be inclined to accept.

APPENDIX TABLE 3

LIVESTOCK HOLDINGS, U.S.S.R., SELECTED YEARS
(millions)

Livestock	1953–1956	Soviet official 1957–1960	1961–1964
Cattle	57.0	68.3	82.6
Cows	25.9	31.9	36.9
Hogs	31.7	46.8	59.1
Sheep	99.1	123.6	136.0
Horses	14.5	11.7	9.2

SOURCE: *Narkhoz-1964*, p. 352.

APPENDIX TABLE 4

State Procurements of Major Farm Products, U.S.S.R., Selected Years
(million tons except eggs)

Product	1953	1958	1959	1960	1961	1962	1963	1964	1965 (plan)	"Needed"
Grain	31.1	56.6	46.6	46.7	52.1	56.6	44.8	68.3	[56.6]	68.8
Wheat	19.2	41.9	34.2	30.7	33.3	34.6	22.7	38.7	n.a.	n.a.
Cotton	3.9	4.3	4.6	4.3	4.5	4.3	5.2	5.3	5.7–6.1	n.a.
Sugar beets	22.9	51.0	41.4	52.2	47.7	43.9	41.5	76.1	81.0	n.a.
Oilseeds	2.1	2.9	2.1	2.5	3.3	3.6	3.5	4.2	3.9	n.a.
Potatoes	5.4	7.0	6.8	7.1	7.0	5.7	8.0	10.7	11.7	n.a.
Flax fiber	0.145	0.392	0.333	0.369	0.369	0.395	0.368	—	0.530	n.a.
Livestock, live weight	3.6	5.7	7.5	7.9	7.3	8.6	9.3	8.3	11.0	13.0
Milk	10.6	22.1	25.0	26.3	27.5	29.2	28.5	31.4	40.6	50.0
Wool	0.197	0.315	0.354	0.358	0.369	0.374	0.380	0.352	0.540	n.a.
Billions of eggs	2.6	4.5	5.7	6.5	7.4	8.5	8.7	8.3	10.0	n.a.

SOURCES: 1953: *Narkhoz-1958*, p. 357; 1958–1962: *Narkhoz-1962*, pp. 239, 288–291, 315–317; 1963, *Narkhoz-1963*, pp. 273–293; 1964: *SSSR-v tsifrakh-1964*, pp. 83–89; 1965 plan: *Narkhoz-1959*, p. 323; "Needed": said by Khrushchev in 1961 to be required to satisfy the need of the government in the nearest future (see Jerzy Karcz, "The New Soviet Agricultural Program," *Soviet Studies*, XVII:2 (October, 1965), p. 149.

APPENDIX TABLE 5

SOWN AREAS AND YIELDS, OFFICIAL AND "ATTAINABLE" LEVELS FOR SELECTED CROPS, U.S.S.R., SELECTED YEARS

Product	1953		1959–1962		1964		Zemskii's "attainable" levels	
	Area	Yield	Area	Yield	Area	Yield	Area	Yield
Grains:								
Wheat	48.3	8.53	63.4	10.7	67.9	10.9	61.1	13.8
Winter	17.8	11.1	16.2	16.0	19.0	13.8	17.3	18.0
Spring	30.5	7.0	47.2	8.8	48.9	9.8	43.8	12.1
Rye	20.2	7.2	16.9	9.9	16.8	8.1	19.9	18.4
Barley	9.6	8.2	13.0	11.4	2.17	13.1	10.1	15.5
Winter	[0.4]	9.8	[1.6]	14.3	[2.0]	12.9	1.0	17.5
Spring	[9.2]	8.1	[11.3]	11.1	[19.7]	13.2	9.1	15.3
Oats	15.3	6.6	11.4	8.8	5.7	9.6	21.1	18.0
Corn, grain	3.5	10.6	6.2	19.4	5.1	26.0	14.1	30.2
Millet	4.1	6.6	3.65	7.0	3.5	9.7	4.73	14.2
Buckwheat	2.6	2.9	1.7	4.1	1.4	5.1	2.86	9.8
Rice	0.1	16.1	0.1	23.0	0.2	24.2	0.486	33.9
Pulses	2.4	5.4	4.3	9.5	10.6	10.4	1.7	16.3
Total grains	*106.2*	[*7.7*]	*120.6*	[*10.6*]	*132.9*	[*11.3*]	*136.0*	[*16.3*]
Technical crops:								
Sugar beets	1.57	148.0	3.0	166.6	4.11	195.0	3.21	268.1
Cotton	1.88	20.5	2.27	19.6	2.46	21.5	3.02	32.7
Flax fiber	1.24	1.3	1.63	2.5	1.57	2.1	1.88	5.2
Oilseeds	n.a.	n.a.	5.43	8.56	n.a.	n.a.	7.3	n.a.
Sunflower	3.90	6.7	4.17	9.93	4.61	13.0	5.34	13.9
Potatoes	8.3	87.0	9.1	89.3	8.5	109.0	10.2	186.0
Vegetables	1.4	87.0	1.5	106.0	1.5	125.0	2.34	168.5
Feed crops:								
Annual grasses	7.8	11.9	16.7	13.4	13.9	12.9	21.976	30.5
Perennial grasses	16.9	13.1	16.97	14.0	12.6	15.5	27.4	35.1
Corn other than grain	0.0	n.a.	22.2	83.8	22.3	133.0	18.8	7.1
Fallow	29.6	n.a.	16.1	n.a.	11.6	n.a.	28.0	n.a.

SOURCES: 1953, 1959–1962: *Narkhoz-1962*, pp. 234–237, 247–248, 256–265; 268–287; 1964: *Narkhoz-1964*, pp. 249–250, 267–268; 279–324; Zemskii's "attainable": P. M. Zemskii, *Razvitie i razmeshchenie zemledeliia po prirodno-khoziaistvennym raionam SSSR* (Moscow: 1959), pp. 105, 114, 116–117, 120–121, 145–147, 170, 180, 185, 204, 207.

COMMENT 1

Janet G. Chapman

My role here, I understand, is to comment on the implications for consumption of projected Soviet agricultural output in 1970 rather than to venture into the intricacies of Soviet agricultural statistics and the complex problems of Soviet agriculture. Expectations concerning progress in agriculture must be taken into account in policy decisions on the rate of growth of consumer income and on the distribution of income. Similarly, policies on the level and distribution of income have important implications for the adequacy of food supplies. I should like to explore some of the questions the Soviet planners must face in relating income policy to prospective food supplies, with emphasis on the question of income distribution.

The present Soviet leaders have inherited Khrushchev's "income revolution" and are now facing the question of how soon to make good Khrushchev's promise of a minimum monthly wage of 50 rubles for all wage earners and salaried workers. Khrushchev's original promise, it will be recalled, was for a minimum wage of 40 rubles by the end of 1962 and a minimum wage of 50 rubles by the end of 1965. The 40-ruble minimum wage had been introduced in industry and other "productive" branches by 1961 but it was only at the end of 1964 and in January 1965 that the 40-ruble minimum wage was extended to wage earners and salaried workers in the "nonproductive," or service branches. The establishment of the 40-ruble minimum wage and other wage reforms in the productive branches may not have had a very significant effect on income distribution. Relatively few in these branches, it is believed, were earning such low wages as to be affected by the rise in the minimum wage, though this is probably less true of light industry.[78] But the recently completed wage reform in the service branches, which was to increase wages of more than 18 million workers in services by an average of 21 percent,[79] and the extension of the 40-

[78] See my "The Minimum Wage in the USSR," *Problems of Communism,* XVII: 5 (September–October, 1964), 76–79 and Murray Yanowitch, "The Soviet Income Revolution," *Slavic Review,* XXII: 4 (December, 1963), 683–697.

[79] *Pravda,* July 14, 1964.

ruble minimum wage to these workers must have meant a substantial increase in income for a large number of low-paid service workers. Wage rates in services were below the rates for jobs requiring comparable skill in industry, and there are large numbers of unskilled workers, such as waiters and charwomen, in services. Evidently the Soviet leaders are now beginning to face the first major consequences of the "income revolution." [80] In planning relations between food supplies and income policy, the effects of changes in income distribution are becoming increasingly important. This is all the more true if the new program in agriculture is to mean higher incomes for the kolkhozniks.

On an average per capita basis, the data indicate that the Soviet consumption of a little more than 3,000 calories is probably adequate but that a large proportion (more than 60 percent) of the calories are consumed in the form of the cheap starches and that the diet is "deficient" in comparison with the American (of today or of 1900) and in relation to Soviet consumer tastes and to Soviet planners "rational norms of consumption" in meats, fats, milk, eggs, vegetables, and fruit.[81] The trend in recent years has been for only a modest increase in calorie consumption and for some decline in the consumption of grain and potatoes. This decline is evident in absolute terms, as a share of total calorie consumption, and as a share in expenditures on food. Also the share of food in total consumption has probably declined during the past decade as consumer income has risen.

On the basis of these average per-capita figures and past trends, it would appear that the Soviet consumer's demand for calories is largely satisfied and that demand for food will reflect primarily a desire for qualitative improvement, a substitution of the more costly foods for the cheap starches. Soviet goals for agriculture stress qualitative improvement and the substantial increases projected here in the output of meat, milk, eggs, and vegetables should help considerably in satisfying this demand. It would appear also that expenditures on food can be expected to increase in connection with the improvement in diet but that

[80] The increase in the average earnings of all wage earners and salaried employees during the twelve months when the wage reform was carried out in services (June, 1964 to June, 1965) is reported to have been 6 percent, an unusually large annual increase (cf. *Pravda,* July 26, 1965). The estimated increase for the calendar year 1965 was 4.5 percent. The average annual increase between 1958 and 1964 was 2.4 percent (*Pravda,* December 10, 1964).

[81] U.S. Congress, Joint Economic Committee, *Current Economic Indicators for the USSR* (Washington, D.C.: Government Printing Office, 1965), p. 121. See also P. S. Mstislavskii, *Narodnoe potreblenie pri sotsializme* (Moscow: 1961), pp. 141–142.

the increase in food expenditures should continue, as in the past, to be less than the increase in consumer income. If this is so, purchasing power could be increased by substantially more than the increase in the retail value of food output without creating serious pressures on food supplies or food prices.

Would it make a difference to these conclusions if the increase in income during the next five years were to be received mainly by those in the lowest income groups? Introduction of a 50-ruble minimum wage would mean a 25 percent increase in income for the considerable numbers now at the minimum wage rate and substantial increases also for those earning wages not much above the minimum. Presumably this would mean a larger share of incremental income would go to food.[82] How adequate is the projected supply of food and how appropriate is the projected "mix" of the various types of food under these circumstances? This is a question the Soviet planners must ask themselves. And indeed, as Murray Feshbach pointed out here, Soviet economists have lately shown a great interest in the pattern and elasticity of consumer demand. We are hampered in our inquiry by lack of adequate published information about income distribution and patterns of consumption, but there are a few things that can be said.

Kolkhoznik real per-capita income, it seems clear, is on the average well below worker income,[83] and a much larger share of the kolkhoznik's real income is consumed in the form of food. This is a reflection of the lower level of kolkhoznik income but it may be true even at comparable levels of income.[84] How will the peasants react to the new fixed delivery

[82] This trend may already have started. Between 1960 and 1964 the volume of retail sales, at "constant prices," of foods increased by 25 percent, while the volume of sales of nonfoods increased by 16 percent. In both instances, reference is to sales in state and cooperative shops, including restaurants. Cf. *Narkhoz-1963*, p. 507; *SSSR v tsifrakh-1964*, p. 139; S. Partigul, *Vop. ek.*, No. 1 (1965), p. 3. A decline in sales on the collective farm market offsets partly, but probably not completely, the relatively greater rise in food sales in the state and cooperative retail trade network.

[83] Just how much lower, we do not know. But see the comparison from a Soviet source cited by Miss Nimitz.

[84] It is reported that 1961 budget data show that among families with equal per-capita income the share of total consumption accounted for by food was 58 percent for families of collective farmers, 43 percent for families of industrial wage earners, and 44 percent for families of industrial office employees. See N. Kirichenko, *Ek. nauki*, No. 5 (1963), pp. 40–46 as cited in N. S. Lagutin, *Problemy sblizheniia urovnia zhizni rabochikh i kolkhoznikov* (Moscow: 1965), p. 14. Consumption in kind of foods is included though it is not explained (at least in the secondary source) how this consumption is valued.

quotas and to the higher prices they will receive? Will they improve their diet? Or will they be lured by the high prices for above-quota deliveries into selling more food and buying more manufactured consumer goods? The peasant's freedom of choice concerning the disposal of his produce has apparently been increased. While this is expected to increase his incentive to produce, it may make the prediction of food supplies for the urban population more difficult.

To turn to the urban population, we are rather in the dark about the consumption patterns of the lower-income worker families. The published data on urban worker budgets indicate that expenditures on food increase as income increases though the proportion spent on food decreases and the share of the food budget devoted to the cheap starches declines as income rises. However, we do not know at what level of income these trends set in, and it may be fairly high. In the published samples from the budget survey the lowest income class for which data are given is that with a monthly per-capita income of "up to 40 rubles." An income of 40 rubles a month per family member—given the typical family structure of just over one dependent per worker—implies an average income per working family member of more than 80 rubles. This is somewhat above the average monthly wage of all wage earners and salaried workers of 79 rubles in 1959 (the date of the budget study I refer to below). Roughly half of all wage earner and salaried worker families must have fallen into the "under 40 ruble" per-capita monthly income class. We should like to know more about differences within this group when considering how those at the lower income levels are likely to respond to a significant increase in income.

Some clues may be found in a study of the budgets of 92 industrial wage-earner families in Moscow, Gor'kii, and Ivanovo conducted by the Institute of Labor in March, 1959. This, too, lumps together all with per-capita incomes up to 40 rubles but it does provide more details on food consumption than are usually published. In this study average per-capita calorie consumption was 2800 calories in the less-than-40-ruble per-capita income group, 3132 calories in the 40-to-70-ruble income group, and more than 3,500 calories in the more-than-70-ruble per-capita income group. It is reported that a "considerable difference" in the pattern of consumption of food products is observed only between families in the under-40-ruble income group and those in the 40–70-ruble income group. Details are not given but the implication is clear that the considerable difference refers primarily to meat. The difference in the consumption of food products between the 40-to-70 ruble income group and the over-70-ruble income group is "less considerable" and there is "almost no difference" in the consumption of meat. The over-70-ruble income group, however, consumes 22 percent more butter, 33 percent more milk and milk products, 36 percent more vegetables, and twice as much fruit as the 40–70-ruble income group. It is pointed out also that the cost per calorie consumed increases with income level, being 2.3 kopeks per 100 calories in the under-40-ruble income group, 2.7 kopeks per 100 calories in the 40–70-ruble income group, and 3.2 kopeks per 100 calories in the over-70-ruble income group.[85]

These data, to the extent that they are representative of consumption patterns at the different income levels, suggest that there is still an unsatisfied demand for food among Soviet families with below-average income. If per-capita consumption is below the Soviet average and below the Soviet physiological norm of about 3100 calories on the average for all families with less than 40 rubles per capita monthly income, for some in the low income group it may be considerably lower. And it is significant that calorie consumption appears to increase with income up into the highest income levels. The quality of the diet of the families in the lower-income group is evidently poor in many respects but their major demand appears to be for more meat.

One might well expect that the lower-income groups would spend quite a large proportion of an increase in income on food.[86] Many will be less interested in increasing their caloric intake than in improving the quality of their diet—primarily by increasing their purchases of meat. This, in addition to expenditures on meat of the higher-income groups, may well put considerable pressure on supplies for even the rather substantial increase of 32 percent to 54 percent in the output of meat projected by Walters and Judy would mean a per-capita meat output of

[85] N. Kuznetsova, *Biull. nauchn. inf.*, No. 12 (1960). I was unable to consult the original source and have relied on the translation of the Joint Publications Research Service. This issue contains a series of articles on this budget study and gives more details than are usually published elsewhere. The study is not free of major shortcomings. The distribution of income in the sample is possibly representative of the particular area and industries covered, but it is certainly not representative of income distribution among all Soviet wage earner families. Only 15 out of the 92 families investigated were in the "under 40 rubles" per-capita income class. The figures on caloric consumption are apparently not adjusted for age and sex. The comparisons between 1959 and earlier years are based on the identical 92 families and for this reason seem dubious as an indication of expenditure trends in the population at large.

[86] The budget study showed that among families with "under 40 rubles" income in both 1951 and 1959, expenditures on food increased by more than did expenditures on manufactured goods during this period. Cf. F. Aleshin, Ia. Kabachnik, *Biull. nauchn. inf.*, No. 12 (1960).

only 49 to 58 kilograms a year.[87] Some in the low-income groups, one can suppose, must still wish to increase their calorie consumption and, given the extremely high prices of meat, may find themselves purchasing more bread and potatoes. With one ruble the Soviet housewife can purchase almost 15,000 calories if she spends it on rye bread or over 10,000 calories it she spends it on wheat bread but, even before the 30 percent increase in meat prices of June, 1962, she could obtain only 1,267 calories from a ruble's worth of pork or 1,172 calories from a ruble's worth of beef.[88] This would increase the pressure for production of food grains.

It has been suggested at the Conference that the high and increasing costs of production may necessitate a further increase in the retail price of meat. The function of Soviet retail-price policy is to equate consumer demand with the available consumer goods, and retail-price structure need not reflect very closely relative production costs. If the income policy adopted increases the demand for meat beyond foreseeable supplies then indeed an increase in the retail price of meat might be expected. An alternative presumably open to the Soviet price setters would be to raise the price of bread for, owing to its quality of "inferior good," an increase in the price of bread leads to larger expenditures on (and probably larger consumption of) bread and tends to reduce the effective demand for other products such as meat.[89] While an increase in the price of bread is never politically palatable, perhaps a further increase in meat prices would be even less so.

In conclusion, the projected increase in food output, if achieved, would support a considerable further improvement in real consumer income. How large an increase in total consumer income a given increase in food supplies will support evidently depends in large part on the distribution of income. The pressures on food supplies—particularly on meat, but possibly even on bread—will be greater the greater is the redistribution of income from the better-off to the kolkhozniks and to the lower-paid workers. Presumably Soviet policy concerning the pace

[87] The Walters-Judy estimate for 1969–1972 is 12–14 million tons of meat; I assume a 1970 population of 243 million. The Soviet rational consumption norm is 73–91 kilograms per capita; Mstislavskii, *op. cit.* (in n. 81), p. 141. The American consumption was 89 kilograms in 1890 and 91 kilograms in 1958; cf. Janet G. Chapman, "Consumption," in Abram Bergson, Simon Kuznets, eds., *Economic Trends in the Soviet Union* (Cambridge, Mass.: Harvard University Press, 1963), p. 252.

[88] V. T. Konienko, *Tseny i potrebitel'skii spos* (Moscow: 1964), p. 26.

[89] "Raising the price increases and reducing the price decreases the consumption of bread," according to a Soviet writer in a discussion of the elasticity of demand. *Ibid.*

at which to proceed with the "income revolution" will be influenced by such considerations. They are perhaps already committed on kolkhoznik income. For the workers, they appear to be committed to raising the minimum wage to 50 rubles a month but they have a choice as to timing and as to the pattern of increases in wages at above-minimum levels. It took, after all, seven years to put the 40-ruble minimum wage into effect. If, as under Khrushchev, the minimum wage is raised first where it has least effect (heavy industry) and last where the greatest numbers will be affected (services), the effects can be spread out and the major impact delayed for a number of years. Other considerations, of course, will enter the decisions on income distribution policy, and probably overriding will be the assessment of the present structure of wages in light of current labor requirements. Possibly on these grounds the Soviet leaders feel the income revolution has been carried far enough for the time being.

COMMENT 2

Keith Bush

I welcome that section of the study by Messrs. Walters and Judy which compares Soviet claims with Western estimates of past and present agricultural production in the U.S.S.R. Most Western observers, and an increasing number of Russian specialists, must be aware of the fact that Soviet official statistics of agricultural production have been and are, to varying degrees, inflated and must be treated accordingly. However, since only the Central Statistical Administration makes available extensive data on all aspects of agricultural production within the Soviet Union, Western specialists are forced to use the official handbooks as primary sources. A virtue of this particular study is that it has assembled some of the best Western estimates into a compact and accessible guide for skeptical readers of the publications of the Central Statistical Administration.

I find myself in agreement with virtually all of the authors' findings on past and present production levels and practices, especially with their views that grain is the key to the success or failure of the agricultural sector, that extensive farming must now give way to intensive farming, and that four- to five-year averages are more meaningful bases for comparison than the results of a single year. Some qualification may be in order concerning two of their assumptions, namely the "continued downward trend in labor inputs and some gradual, but expensive, increases in land." On the first count, it seems to me that the provisions of the new economic reforms, combined with the increasing application of automation in industry, will result in a slowing down of the recent very high growth rate of the urban labor force and, correspondingly, in the flight from the land. This will also depend to a large extent upon the success of the agricultural reforms in keeping the skilled and able-bodied cadres down on the farm. What we may see by 1970 is not so much a sizable decline in the rural labor force but a considerable improvement in the utilization of existing farm manpower. As for an increase in arable land, it is true that the scheduled program of land improvement, irrigation, and drainage will provide an increase in the total acreage under cultivation. However, this increase may be more than offset by the considerable share of the new lands which must be left to summer fallow every year if these regions are to provide stable and economic average annual yields.

My sole regret is that the authors have not devoted more space and energy to the central topic under discussion, namely a projection of Soviet agricultural output by 1970. An informed estimate of future Soviet capability in this area is surely one of the most useful contributions which can be made by such an assembly of specialists, for the future performance of Soviet agriculture will have a considerable effect not only upon the shape of Soviet society and the future standard of living in that country but also upon the U.S.S.R.'s relations both with her socialist neighbors and with the rest of the world.

In their projection, the authors have, it seems to me, leant somewhat too heavily upon the Zemskii study and its American critique. Since few of us have had access to either of these sources, a meaningful evaluation of the projection is difficult to make. For this reason, I would like to restrict my own comments to the subject of the March, 1965, agricultural plenum, for Soviet agricultural performance by 1970 will depend, to a large extent, upon the degree to which its resolutions are implemented.

The March, 1965, plenum, as Walters has intimated, represents a potential turning point for the fortunes of Soviet agriculture. During the period of the Five-Year Plan, it provides for not only 41 billion rubles of state investments in agriculture but also an estimated additional 22 billion rubles of budgetary resources reallocated into the farm sector, which should go far to provide for the financing of envisaged kolkhoz investment and for a more meaningful level of material incentives. After a third of a century during which the peasant has been milked almost dry to provide much of the accumulation for rapid industrialization, the Soviet government is now committed to a policy of price support which probably goes farther than in any other country. The above-plan procurement price (i.e., for kolkhozes) for one ton of wheat ranges from 114 to 195 rubles, while the planned procurement prices for beef cattle (inclusive of the temporary surcharge) vary from 1,080 to 1,395 rubles a ton, liveweight. For the sake of comparison, the *U.S. Statistical Abstract* for 1964 gave the average prices to farms in March of that year as $68 a ton for wheat and $411 a ton for beef cattle. The financial commitments to the farm sector during the course of the coming Five-Year Plan thus represent something approaching the maximum feasible concessions at this time.

The lifting of "unjustified restrictions" upon the size of private plots and livestock holdings, the measure of ideological acceptability conferred upon the private sector (albeit reluctantly), and the practical steps taken to aid this sector, such as the provision of credits, the lifting of taxes and the sale of feed—all these have already produced encouraging results.

As has been pointed out, grain is the key to success for Soviet agriculture. Now there is some current speculation in the West that the Soviet grain purchases of 1963–1964 and those taking place in 1965 herald a permanent shift in the direction of the international grain trade. This I believe to be unrealistic, for in the near future the Soviet Union must, for strategic, economic, and political reasons, regain and retain the virtual autarky in the supply of foodstuffs which she enjoyed until 1963. A regular pattern of grain imports from the West, the only possible source, is out of the question. Strategically, the U.S.S.R. cannot afford to be dependent upon the West for staple foodstuffs. Economically, the Soviet gold reserves are, according to the best Western estimates, down to less than 2 billion dollars' worth, and the U.S.S.R. is finding it increasingly difficult to export enough to the developed nations in order to pay for the imports of the equipment and technology which she so urgently needs. Politically, the Soviet Union can hardly proclaim, with any conviction, the superiority of socialist agriculture to her own subjects and to underdeveloped nations whose greatest enemy is hunger, when it must import grain from the West. The new leaders must, therefore, solve the "grain problem" where their predecessors have failed.

Provided that the inputs of capital, machinery, fertilizer, weed killer, drainage, irrigation, ground clearance, and the other measures envisaged by the March plenum are supplied in full or in large part, and allowing for only moderate response in view of the still formidable problems of production, storage, transportation, and application—not to mention apathy—I believe that by about 1969–1972, the Soviet Union should be able to count upon an average annual grain harvest of between 155 and 170 million tons (barn yield), which is roughly at the level indicated in the essay under review. This level would provide enough grain for human consumption, for an annual increment to the grain reserves, and to a small export surplus. If and when an assured sufficiency of food grains is attained, increasing emphasis will have to be laid upon feed grains in order to promote the average Soviet diet from its present excess of starchy carbohydrates. But a long haul is in prospect, for it will be after the year 1980, which is the presently scheduled threshold of material abundance, before the Russians will be able to enjoy the current Western European per-capita consumption levels of such staples as meat and eggs, and it is probable that we shall not be hearing any further Soviet pledges to catch up with the U.S. in this respect for many years to come.

A renewed upsurge in Soviet agricultural production will not, however, come from massive capital inputs and financial concessions alone. As I see it, there are three major obstacles to the attainment of the more modest and realizable agricultural goals for 1970 which have been set by Khrushchev's successors.

The first is the excessive grain-procurement targets which have been fixed for the New Lands in general and for Kazakhstan in particular. Increasingly in the past few years—if one excludes exceptional harvests like those of 1956 and 1964 which seem to occur about once every five years—the over-all yields from these regions have borne depressing witness to the aftereffects of ten years of monoculture. Irrigation is feasible for only a small portion of the New Lands, and the low annual levels of precipitation preclude the effective use of mineral fertilizer over much of the area. Western experience of grain production in regions with similar climatic and soil characteristics has shown that the best results are obtained when a large proportion of the land is left to fallow every year. Yet the high procurement goals for the New Lands areas set by the March plenum militate against the immediate adoption of extensive fallow, despite the explicit support given this practice by leading research institutes and its implicit acceptance by official spokesmen. The perennial and harmful practice of sacrificing the long-term average yields for the sake of fulfilling the procurement plan in a given year was evidenced yet again in 1965 under the new leadership. After an early spring in Kazakhstan, it was evident to the local farmers that they were in for a dry season and a low yield. If the choice had been left to those who till the land, many of them would doubtless have opted to leave a considerable portion of the land to clean fallow in the hope of better harvests in the future. But the available evidence suggests that, once again, *this* year's sowing plan had to be fulfilled to the detriment of future crops. Until the authorities can find the courage to cut back on sowing in these regions and to leave more land in fallow, even if this were to mean importing Western wheat for another year or more, the New Lands cannot be relied upon to provide stable and economic yields and to justify the enormous volume of productive and nonproductive investments lavished on this project.

A second obstacle is the inferior ideological, social, and economic status of the kolkhoznik. Much should be done to remedy this injustice at the Third All-Union Congress of Kolkhozniks in 1966.

The third, and perhaps most deeply rooted, impediment is the state's and Party's petty tutelage over every phase and aspect of the farmer's activities. Lip service was paid at the March plenum to the necessity for ending this stifling and bumbling supervision by state and Party officials, but instructions continue to pour from above which demand detailed meddling by outsiders. The habits ingrained during a third of a century die hard, and there has been little evidence during the past few months of any significant improvement in the operational independence and autonomy of the farmer.

These three brakes upon progress in this weakest sector of the Soviet economy will have to be removed or eased if the considerable financial concessions of the March plenum are to yield commensurate returns.

JOEL M. HALPERN

Farming as a Way of Life: Yugoslav Peasant Attitudes

The village and the city, the farm and the factory, the developers and the developed—these are the too frequently evoked dualities used to describe some of the complex processes of change being acted out in our time.[1] In those countries which have experienced the major portion of their industrialization since World War II, we cannot easily draw any firm lines separating villager from urbanite because they are both changing, although not always at the same rate or in identical ways.

The pre-industrial city which served as an administrative market and religious center, or a combination of these, has undergone enormous changes, but the continuity with the past has usually been more clearly

[1] This essay draws on two of my articles published earlier: "Yugoslav Peasant Society in Transition—Stability in Change," *Anthropological Quarterly,* XXXVI (July, 1963) and "Peasant Culture and Urbanization in Yugoslavia," *Human Organization,* XXIV:2 (Summer, 1965). It is based on research carried out in Yugoslavia during 1961–1962 and in the summer of 1964, supported by grants from the National Science Foundation and counterpart funds from the Department of State. The present discussion includes a preliminary survey of some of the field data, a more complete analysis of which will be published later. Part of the field data was gathered by Yugoslav students, with organizational support from university authorities in Belgrade, Zagreb, Ljubljana, and Sarajevo. Vida and Theodore Tarnovsky assisted in the United States, and helpful comments on a preliminary version of the essay were received from Dimitri Shimkin and Jozo Tomasevich. To these varied sources of assistance appreciation is gratefully expressed. A fuller discussion of the general question of social change in Yugoslavia may be found in the author's study "Yugoslavia: Modernization in an Ethnically Diverse State" in Rex Hopper, ed., *Social Change: Studies of a World in Transition* (New York: Macmillan, 1966).

evident than in the village community, although there is considerable variability. Even the most revolutionary governments do not seek to obliterate the traditions of the preindustrial city. Rather, these traditions are regarded as a key factor in asserting national identity. By contrast, village-based values and traditions are almost uniformly regarded as obstacles to progress, or at best provide incidental subordinate embellishments to the national tradition.

The village is certainly being urbanized, and we can also with some legitimacy speak of the contemporary "peasantization" of the town. Specifically the pressure on limited urban facilities and the carry-over of rural habits become strongly manifest, as in the maintenance of public housing. While these negative effects on the quality of urban life are apparent, to some degree they have been offset by the lessening of population pressures on the land. Further, geographic and occupational mobility are by no means synonymous, as attested to by the phenomenon of the peasant-workers who commute daily from their village residences to their places of work.

The reciprocal influences of village and town concern not only economic ties through jobs and marketing but also social ties, particularly those of kin, and ceremonial obligations. These patterns are especially important in eastern Europe where a large majority of the population is at most a few generations removed from a rural environment.

The mass exodus from the land for the attractions of the city is happening on a worldwide scale with a variety of local manifestations. An important insight into this process can be gained by considering peasant attitudes toward farming as a way of life. This is a difficult matter for generalization, especially in a country as ethnically varied as Yugoslavia.

There are, however, some shared features. First, whether as a serf, owner, or pastoralist the peasant was primarily involved with his land and livestock. Not only were there no other alternatives available, but his way of life was also sanctioned by religion and tradition. This is not to say that submission was unquestioned, as peasant revolts demonstrate, or that toil was given without hardship, as folk sayings bear out, but that in general the peasant accommodated himself to his lot while simultaneously fearing and mistrusting the city and its people. Farming was the only way of life he knew. He could know no other.

This situation is well illustrated by the situation in Serbia at the beginning of the nineteenth century. Writing in 1827 the pioneer Serb ethnographer and linguist Vuk Karadžić said:

There are no members of the Serbian nation but peasants. The small number of Serbs who live in town as traders and craftsmen are called townsmen. They wear Turkish costumes and live according to the Turkish way of life; during rebellions and wars they shut themselves up with the Turks in the towns, or run away to Germany with their money; for this reason they are not called Serbs by the people and are despised by them. The Serbs, as peasants, live only from land and livestock.[2]

Today, despite the often traditional appearance of the countryside, national policies of industrialization have in some areas depopulated the land and in other areas drawn away much of the youth. Thus in 1961 Tito could speak of a national objective being the reduction of the proportion of the population dependent primarily on agriculture from 50 to 40 percent.

Among the most telling statistics are those of the sex and age ratios of the farm labor force in eastern Europe and how these have noticeably changed in the postwar period, with an increasing preponderance of older people and women in agricultural labor. Further, not only has the composition of the agricultural labor force changed, but in some areas their numbers have declined in relative and absolute terms compared to the total population.

In eastern Europe, a number of negative features, often associated with modernization and industrialization in other parts of the world, are directly linked by the peasant to Communist ideology, so that in some measure peasant resistance has been a general resistance to change as much as it has been to specific value connotations of communism.

Change in a rural or village context is not a new phenomenon. House types, clothing, social structures, customs, and agricultural technology have all changed through the centuries, reflecting migration patterns, ecological developments, conquest, style evolution, improved techniques and technologies, and varying governmental forms. But because of the limited opportunities in towns, in crafts, trade, administration, the military, or the religious hierarchy, a focus on the village prevailed. Further, in times of frequent wars and epidemics, the preindustrial town offered only limited attractions and these to only a limited number of people. Villages were not immune to plunder and plague, of course, but their

[2] Vuk Karadžić, in *Danica,* II (Vienna: 1827), 79–83, republished in *Istoriska Citanka* (Belgrade: 1949) pp. 84–85. The English translation is from Doreen Warriner, ed., *Contrasts in Emerging Societies* (Bloomington, Indiana: Indiana University Press, 1965), p. 298. This quotation from Karadžić implies a village orientation but not economic isolation, since livestock trade with Austria was important at this time. See "The Commerce in Swine," in Warriner, *op. cit.,* pp. 300–302.

closeness to the food supply and their ability to survive for prolonged periods without urban trade goods, gave them a basic viability which the inhabitants of preindustrial cities lacked. One might add that they lacked mobility as well, because it was much easier for farmers to migrate with their families, herds, and tools and to establish a new village in a different locality than it was for the inhabitants of preindustrial cities to transport themselves *en masse* to a new area. Evidence of this situation was dramatically provided during World War II in East Europe when many city dwellers sought refuge in the countryside. If ready access to education, manufactured goods, mass amusements, sophisticated medical care, a guaranteed income, and avoidance of adverse natural phenomena be considered desirable ends—in short, a life of prestige, diversity, and comfort—then these can be more easily obtained in the city than the countryside.

The most stirring testimonial to the attractiveness of the modern city is the extraordinary extent to which people have voted with their feet, to borrow a phrase from another context, giving rise to the world-wide growth of cities in the past century. This development has continued despite the great problems of urban growth and crowding. As a result, the prestige of traditional small-scale farming has declined, as have handicrafts, but the problem of replacing the village weaver or blacksmith has been much easier than that of replacing the peasant farmer. The problems of urban growth, however, have demonstrated that the absorptive capacity of the city is finite. It may well be that what is often cited as the peasant's innate conservatism or attachment to the land represents his desire to achieve security within the limited opportunities available.

Much has been written of the deadening effect of mass production on the factory worker. Others have commented on the banalities of rural life even during the nineteenth century when it was being romanticized. But the problem is usually conceived of in terms of modifying the urban environment and not, as the slogans for the rural areas would have it, of transforming the countryside. To borrow a phrase from an American context, we often hear of urban renewal, but not of rural renewal. If one can view the relationship between rural and urban subcultures as one of reciprocal patterns of influence, then it seems clear which way the equilibrium point is shifting. Items derived from rural subcultures may be used in an artistic and recreational context to provide a degree of specific national identity (folk art, crafts, literature, song and dance). This is harder to do for aspects of industrialization. It is easier to identify with a folk song than with a steel mill. But it would seem that, generally speaking, in terms of contemporary national cultures these village-derived elements tend to be overshadowed by their urban counterparts as, for example, folk crafts versus painting and sculpture or folk dance groups versus a *corps de ballet*. There are more subtle ways in which village-derived value patterns influence urban and national life, but these generally tend to be part of a large shared tradition which existed in the preindustrial city as well as the countryside, such as in religious beliefs and patterns of family structure and behavior.

Significantly, when speaking in terms of urban influence in the village as opposed to peasant influence on the town, society tends to regard the former as positive and the latter as negative. In short, the peasant has been adapting to industrialization much more than industry to the peasant (although this, too, has occurred, mostly in short-range tactical accommodations). The reference here is primarily in terms of the evolution of patterns and values and not of administrative accommodation, even when this may be of long-standing duration. For example, the retention of the private garden plot in the Soviet Union, or the private farm in Yugoslavia and Poland may not be evidence of the future viability of peasant society; rather, it may be possible to regard this situation as a temporary accommodation to an urban focused society in an interim transitional period. Communist planners have, indeed, spoken in these terms when referring to the transformation of the countryside. With the increasing mechanization of agriculture, the diffusion of urban amenities, the related progressive disappearance of the peasant farmer, and the consequent increase in wage labor on large farms run as modified industrial enterprises, there arises the crucial question of the status of rural workers and their future useful role in an evolving industrial society.

Few village youths voluntarily choose farming as a career. Those who have remained in farming seem to be persons who have been unwilling or unable to make the transition to some city-oriented activity. If we exclude from consideration the former leadership group, there seems little doubt that the segment of the population most drastically affected by the introduction of Communist governments in East Europe has been the peasant. When viewed over generations, it is conceptually much easier for the children of the former bourgeoisie to make the social and even ideological adjustment than for those of peasants. It is true that the question of competing ideologies is present. But in a broader sense there is also a question of the role of abstract ideas derived from an intellectual tradition that is foreign to the village. The child of bourgeois or middle-class parents may be in conflict with his parents over specific ideas and values, but the child of peasant parents must reject many of the values in his background to succeed in an urban environment. The child of working-class parents may wish to see his children progress in the social scale, but there need not be a complete break in the same way that is forced on the village child. Certainly this shows clearly in the official attitudes of Communist governments toward workers as a group who are in general idealized as opposed to farmers. These attitudes are reinforced by the schools and mass media, as well as by the disadvantaged position of the farmer in a nation placing emphasis on industrial growth.

There then naturally arises an antipathy and contempt with regard to farming as a way of life or even as an occupation. It is possible and indeed likely if present trends continue, that agriculture will employ fewer, and more highly skilled, people, but there remains the problem not only of finding useful employment for the surplus agricultural workers, but of being able to house and provide other amenities for their families. An interim solution exists where the worker remains on the land and commutes to his job. The ultimate urbanization of village life takes place when no heirs remain to inherit the land, and the countryside becomes depopulated.

The village and town are changing. The village subculture is being reformulated while urban subculture is undergoing modification. This is clearly shown in that urban traditions are venerated even by revolutionary regimes, while rural traditions are viewed usually as a bar to progress, or at best as quaint specimens for museums. The tragic and perhaps foredoomed efforts of peasant parties in the interwar period in East Europe show some of the difficulties in attempting modernization under the auspices of a rural-oriented political system. (The reference here is to the ideal programs which were formulated and not to the ruthless ways in which these parties were dealt with, but, significantly, they receive little support from any organized urban group.)

One of the greatest problems of the rural peoples of eastern Europe is their own negative self-image. Also, they lack the ability to come to terms with their own past in any reassuring way; there is a negation of the past, a frustrating present and an uncertain future. Although their *raison d'être* has not been totally destroyed, the fundamental problem of rural areas appears to be that of its inhabitants attaining a meaningful stake in society, not only in economic terms but even more importantly in terms of a positive social role. Despite a generally rising standard of living in rural as well as urban areas, the degree of frustration has increased because of the more rapidly mounting level of aspiration.

From an over-all viewpoint there is presently more hope, however, because there now are vastly greater opportunities than existed a generation ago.

YUGOSLAV DEMOGRAPHIC DATA

How do these generalizations apply to Yugoslavia? As in the other countries of eastern Europe the rural population of Yugoslavia has been generally declining in both relative and absolute terms since Yugoslavia became a nation at the end of World War I. The percentage decline has been continuous from 79 in 1921, to 75 in 1938, and to 49 in 1961.

TABLE 1

DISTRIBUTION OF POPULATION, YUGOSLAVIA, 1921–1961

	Total population (thousands)	Agricultural population (thousands)	Nonagricultural population (thousands)	Percent of Agricultural Population
1921	12,545	9,885	2,660	79
1931	14,534	11,132	3,401	77
1938	16,657	12,027	4,030	75
1948	15,842	10,696	5,196	67
1953	16,999	10,352	6,647	61
1961	18,549	9,170	9,173	49

These figures are intended to show only general trends and are not strictly comparable since varying criteria were used in the different census periods. The 1960 census has revealed some of the complexities; see Table 2 where the population living on the land is broken down into categories which include those who earn their living outside of agriculture.

SOURCE: D. Marković, *Soc. Sela*, No. 1, 1963 Table 1, p. 44.

Trends in absolute terms have been somewhat different: agricultural population first increased to a peak of 12 million in 1938 but declined by 1961 to 9 million (Table 1).

However, these statistics reflect only the portion of the village population engaged primarily in agriculture. A more comprehensive view of the total village-dwelling population is given in Table 2 which is based on a special 1960 agricultural census. Assuming for the moment that the populations of Yugoslavia for 1960 and 1961 were roughly equivalent, we see that the total population living on agricultural holdings was more than one-third greater than the number of agriculturalists listed in Table 1 for 1961, or somewhat greater than the agricultural population in 1938. These figures include an important component of the Yugoslav industrial labor force, namely 1,306,000 peasant-workers, who commute from their agricultural holdings to their jobs, out of a total number

TABLE 2

MEMBERS OF AGRICULTURAL HOUSEHOLDS BY OCCUPATIONS AND REPUBLICS, YUGOSLAVIA, 1960

	Yugoslavia	Serbia			Croatia	Bosnia Hercegovina	Macedonia	Slovenia	Montenegro
		All Serbia	Vojvodina	Kosmet					
Population living on land (thousands)	12,590	5,204	1,124	755	2,775	2,503	947	822	339
Agriculturalists	5,585	2,489	498	278	1,259	956	384	363	134
Men	2,533	1,185	238	156	528	440	183	140	56
Women working primarily on land	1,244	543	76	27	275	207	85	106	27
Women working part-time on land	1,809	761	184	95	456	309	116	117	51
Peasant-Workers	1,306	452	142	49	351	244	94	139	27
Housewives	830	347	96	72	156	224	62	22	19
Others [a]	4,869	1,916	388	356	1,009	1,079	407	298	159

[a] Children, pupils, elderly and infirm.

SOURCE: *Stat. God.-1964* (Belgrade: 1964), after Table 205–230, p. 415.

TABLE 3

MIGRANTS FROM RURAL AREAS, YUGOSLAVIA, 1949–1960

Year	Number (thousands)	As a percentage of natural increase
1949	121	70
1950	131	76
1951	139	81
1952	146	85
1953	154	89
1954	164	95
1955	172	100
1956	184	106
1957	198	114
1958	216	122
1959	235	134
1960	262	152
1949–1960	2,162	107

SOURCE: *Jugoslovenski pregled,* No. 11–12, November-December, 1962, p. 422, reproduced in Andrew Elias, *The Labor Force of Yugoslavia,* International Population Statistics Reports, Series P-90, No. 22 (Washington, D.C.: U.S. Bureau of the Census, 1965), Table 9, p. 15.

of 2,985,000 employees in 1960. In addition to this large number of peasant-workers who have made a partial transition to urban life, the total village population has been declining because in recent years the number of migrants from villages has exceeded the natural increase (Table 3). In a decade more than 10 percent of the population of Yugoslavia, or 2,162,000 people, have left their agricultural holdings.

These migrations, both permanent and daily, have altered significantly the age structure of the full-time agricultural labor force. Between 1953 and 1961 the 50-to-64-year age group increased its proportional representation in the total agricultural labor force from 15 to 22 percent, while the 15-to-19-year age group declined from 18 to 12 percent.[3] Even more striking is the contrast in age structures of the agricultural and industrial labor forces. Of the total number of male workers (miners, industrial workers, and craftsmen) in 1961, 54 percent were 20–34 years of age, 22 percent were 35–49 years of age, and only 12 percent were 50 or more, as contrasted with 33 percent, 21 percent, and 35 percent respectively for agricultural workers.[4] Those who were

[3] Danica Marković, *Soc. Sela,* No. 1 (1963), Table 4, p. 47.

[4] Andrew Elias, *The Labor Force in Yugoslavia,* International Population Statistics Reports, Series P-90, No. 22 (Washington, D.C.: U.S. Bureau of the Census, 1964), Table 12, p. 16.

TABLE 4

PERCENTAGE DISTRIBUTION BY AGE OF AGRICULTURALISTS AND EMPLOYED PEASANT-WORKERS, YUGOSLAVIA, 1960

Age	Agriculturalists	Peasant-Workers
10–14 years	2.1	.1
15–19 years	9.8	7.6
20–29 years	25.2	38.3
30–39 years	21.1	26.7
40–49 years	14.2	14.1
50–59 years	16.8	11.0
60 years and over	10.8	2.2

SOURCE: P. Marković, *Soc. Sela,* No. 2, 1963, Table 3, p. 25.

employed outside their holdings were by and large the younger men (Table 4). Households without adequate manpower have been increasing in rural areas, constituting 8 percent of all agricultural households in 1960, and approximately 3 percent of all agricultural households were composed of elderly people exclusively.[5]

OFFICIAL YUGOSLAV POLICY

Before turning to the attitudes of rural people on farming it is necessary to identify the official policies which in part condition these attitudes. The Yugoslav constitution, as revised in 1963, states that farmers have the right to own arable land up to a maximum of ten hectares per household. However, the ultimate ideological desire for the socialization of the land is clearly set forth in a preceding statement in the same article: "The social community shall provide the material and other conditions for the establishment and development of agricultural working organizations based on social ownership of land and socially organized work, and for cooperation of farmers with the cooperatives and other working organizations." [6]

This policy has been specifically outlined by the leading Yugoslav theorist Edvard Kardelj, who states that the Yugoslav government has not applied the classical type of collectivization practiced in the Soviet Union. Without doubt this is in part due to the unfavorable experience of 1949 to 1951 when an abortive attempt was made to emulate Soviet policies. Kardelj gives as the main reason, however, the fact that unlike

[5] Petar Marković, *Soc. Sela,* No. 2 (1963), Table 1, p. 22.

[6] *Constitution of the Socialist Federal Republic of Yugoslavia* (Belgrade: Secretariat for Information of the Federal Executive Council, 1963), article 21, p. 19.

in tsarist Russia, where the land belonged to feudal landlords, in Yugoslavia the peasant was attached to his own land.

Although the statement would not seem to apply to the areas ruled by Austria-Hungary and Turkey, it was substanially valid for nineteenth-century Serbia. Kardelj continues that two-fifths of Yugoslavia is mountainous and mostly unfit for modern agricultural techniques and the development of large-scale farming, a point which appears to be more rationalization than reason since large-scale herding could be undertaken in these areas.

The long-range objectives are clear, however. Kardelj points out that although most of the land "appears" to be in the hands of private owners, the socialist sector markets a higher percentage of agricultural products than one might assume from the amount of land at its disposal. (The socialized sector is more productive because it has a virtual monopoly on modern machinery, and peasant agriculture is preserved in a somewhat forcedly archaic condition. Artificial fertilizer and other supplies are made available to socialized farms at subsidized prices. Because of the high cost to them, peasants hesitate to use some of these products. Nevertheless items such as improved seed and veterinary services are relatively easily available and are extensively used by peasants.)

It is planned that by 1970 the socialist sector will become predominant in the marketing of agriculture goods. Currently the "socialist transformation of agriculture" is seen as proceeding in two ways: The first is by the enlargement, through purchase, of land in the socialist sector, including a transitional phase in which the peasant receives "a larger or smaller rent" and then is employed by the cooperative or industry. The second is when the peasant and the cooperative enter into an agreement for services to be performed by the cooperative.[7] These services may include plowing the private holding by tractor or harvesting by combine. It is the government's hope that these arrangements will eventually lead to a more intimate relationship between the private peasant and the cooperative. Considerable progress appears to have been made in this direction, particularly in the flat wheat plains of the Vojvodina where jobs in industry are relatively easily available. More than one-tenth of individually owned arable land was worked by machinery drawn from the socialist sector (600,000 out of 5,346,000 hectares); of this, 239,000 hectares were in the Vojvodina, where

[7] Edvard Kardelj, "Some Current Questions in Yugoslavia's Development" in *Interviews with Edvard Kardelj, President of the Yugoslav Assembly with Foreign Journalists* (Belgrade: Federation of Yugoslav Journalists, 1964), pp. 13–15.

184,000 men worked outside of their holdings, whereas 498,000 were agriculturalists working on their own land.[8]

These policies have been reaffirmed at the Eighth Yugoslav Party Congress in 1964. There has been a claimed growth in agricultural production of 50 percent over the 1930–39 average (from 1956 when the prewar average was regained there has been an annual growth rate of 4½ percent over-all and 17 percent in the socialist sector). "However," says Kardelj, "these results still do not satisfy our growing needs in feeding the population, and agriculture is still constantly lagging behind. . . . The problem is first of all that within the framework of the adopted agricultural policy, which has been absolutely confirmed by practice, more should be invested in agriculture.[9]

This seems a rather predictable analysis and solution. The related exodus of labor, particularly youth from the countryside generally and from agriculture specifically, is seen by the government as a positive development albeit one that raises some problems: "The young generation is quitting the countryside and wants to work outside agriculture, in urban settlements and industrial centers. Every year a larger number of people have to be provided with work. Thus we have a constant and strong pressure on the employment front." Kardelj points out, however, that merely to absorb these people into industry with a built-in low productivity would be detrimental to the economy. Nevertheless he states: "It is quite clear that relatively speedy transfer of the labor force from the countryside to non-agricultural activities will continue to be not only our task but also a condition of economic progress." [10]

Kardelj conceives of the problem in broad terms, mentioning automation and the relative decline of the number of industrial workers while at the same time foreseeing new jobs, services, and social activities. He concludes this discussion by observing: "Neither must we lose sight of the fact that this problem is solved, or at least reduced, by speedier development of agricultural production, given the ever-expanding and comprehensive cooperation of the socialist sector with individual producers, and given the improvement in general economic conditions of life and work in the countryside."

[8] *Stat. God.-1964*, p. 415.

[9] "The Social Economic Tasks of Economic Development in the Coming Period," Report of Edvard Kardelj, Secretary of the League of Communists of Yugoslavia to the Eighth Yugoslav Party Congress, December 7, 1964 in *Foreign Broadcast Information Service: Daily Report, Supplement, U.S.S.R. and East Europe*, No. 13 (Washington, D.C.: Foreign Broadcast Information Service, December 14, 1965, mimeographed), p. 6.

[10] *Ibid.*, p. 8.

Unemployment, particularly of unskilled workers from rural areas, is a growing issue in Yugoslavia. According to official statistics, it increased from 82,000 in 1953 to 230,000 in 1963 and[11] to 288,000 in 1964, of whom 86 percent were unskilled.[12] Significantly, while figures remained stable in Slovenia, greatest increases occurred in the less developed areas during the past decade—five times in Montenegro and four times in Bosnia-Hercegovina. There is also much concealed unemployment, since those who cannot find work in the towns often return to the land without formally registering with the government. A semi-official estimate for 61–62 characterized 10–15 percent of job holders as potentially surplus.[13] In 1959 an official publication estimated the number of underemployed in industry to be 300,000.[14] In addition, there are Yugoslavs working in western Europe, more than half of these in West Germany. No official statistics are published and precise estimates are difficult, varying for those in West Germany alone from 50,000 to 80,000.[15] Many of those working abroad are unskilled or semiskilled workers from peasant villages, particularly from underdeveloped parts of Croatia.

The underemployment of industrial workers reflects one aspect of the heavily burdened urban resources attempting to absorb migrants from rural areas. One report describing the process of urbanization in a town of above-average economic standards estimated that 70 percent of the immigrants were of working age and without skills. To provide jobs for each one it was necessary to invest up to 3,000,000 dinars in industrial capacity and social services in order to retain present standards. However, the commune in which this town is situated did not have these resources. Consequently both working and living standards were lowered. It was also found to be difficult to decrease the number of unemployed, for as fast as new jobs were created additional migrants arrived from the countryside.[16]

This is one aspect of the "peasantization" of the town. Another is the

[11] *Stat. God.-1964,* p. 380 and Elias, *op. cit.* (in n. 4), p. 27.

[12] *Indeks,* No. 5 (1964), p. 3.

[13] As quoted in Robert G. Livingston, "Yugoslavian Unemployment Trends," *Monthly Labor Review,* LXXXVII:7 (July, 1964), 756.

[14] "People Leaving Agriculture—How and Why?" translated from *Ek. Pol.,* No. 362, March 7, 1959 in *Joint Translation Service,* No. 2738 (Belgrade: U.S. Embassy, April 17, 1959), p. 7.

[15] For more on this question see Livingston, *op. cit.* (in n. 13), p. 762; Anthony Sylvestre, "Yugoslavia's Triumphant Reformers," *East Europe,* XIV:2 (February, 1965), 4; Irwin Ross, "European Slogan—Go North Young Man," *The New York Times Magazine,* May 9, 1965, p. 34.

[16] Rikard S. Stajner, *Ek. Pol.,* No. 364, March 21, 1959, pp. 299–300.

form of new towns and the ways in which older settlements expand. In many areas, in addition to new industries, apartment houses and stores a large number of private homes have been built, particularly in the outskirts. These are most often the homes of families who have moved to town from villages in the area. The men are urban workers in the sense that they are permanently employed in a local factory or enterprise, but their cultural and social ties with the village remain strong. This is reflected in house plan, furnishings, and other material ways, and in social patterns such as sleeping arrangements, kinship bonds, and modified gardening and stock-keeping within town limits.[17] The process is reciprocal, of course, and the rural migrant alters his ways at the same time that he is changing the urban setting.

The negative attitudes of villagers toward hard agricultural work and toward their way of life appear to encompass an aversion to farming in general, including the state-supported and mechanized variety. The basic problem, then, goes far beyond a question of increasing investment in agriculture or of providing more amenities for villagers. Although manual work in industry has gained greatly in prestige in postwar years, the prewar attitude of idealizing the life of the white-collar worker who was not required to perform hard manual labor has continued. Education, whether technical or academic, is highly valued as a means of achieving mobility, despite the fact that the sons of peasants are in a disadvantaged position relative to the children of industrial and white-collar workers and especially professionals. These status differences are also reflected in Party membership which, as would be expected, includes but a small proportion of peasants. Aleksandar Ranković, vice president of Yugoslavia, recently discussed these questions and commented on the desirability of attracting more workers and peasants into the party but spoke of

> objective difficulties resulting from their material position and the need of some workers for a supplementary income and participation in schools for professional education, and because of the special position of the so-called worker-peasants, who still live in the village and are tied to their property.

[17] For a detailed description see Halpern, "Yugoslav Peasant Society in Transition—Stability in Change," *op. cit.* (in n. 1), pp. 167–168. The problem of rural-urban transition has begun to be investigated seriously by Yugoslav scholars. In addition to the pioneering work of Cvetko Kostić, *Seljaci Industriski Radnici* (Belgrade: 1955), significant articles have also appeared in the journals *Sociologija* and *Sociologija Sela*. The following monographs are also of note: *Strukturne Promene na Selu kao Resultat Ekonomskog Razvitka, Period 1900–1960* (Belgrade: 1963) and *Socijalna Struktura i Pokretljivost Radnicke Klase Jugoslavije* (Belgrade: 1963).

. . . It is also necessary to refer to the admission of farmers, the individual producers. Many organizations have been rather passive and reserved toward admitting them, and the result of this is that some rural organizations contain the smallest number of peasants. The content and method of work of many basic organizations are such that they do not attract peasants, and even make passive those who are already members.

Ranković contrasts the small number of peasants admitted to the Party with the growth of cooperatives in the countryside and states that poor peasants should not be especially favored but that peasants should be admitted on the basis of their attitude "toward processes which contribute to the strengthening of socialism in the countryside." He also points out that the strengthening of the socialist sector has involved peasant members who became workers on state farms.[18]

ASPIRATIONS OF VILLAGE CHILDREN

With this much background on official policies and attitudes, we can turn now to those of the villagers themselves. In the course of investigations in Orašac, a village in central Serbia, in 1953–1954 I was able, with the cooperation of the principal of the eight-year village elementary school, to sponsor an essay contest among the thirteen- to fourteen-year-old eighth graders, whose theme was "What I Want to Be and Why." The boys typically desired to become workers, "inspired," as they put it, by the examples of the founders of the Communist party in Yugoslavia, especially Tito, about whom they had read at school. Others expressing patriotic motives said they wanted to join a military service or become a border guard to protect their country. A few with more personal motives wanted ot be sailors in order to travel and see the world. The girls often wrote about becoming teachers, emphasizing the social service implied. None of the pupils considered careers involved in any way with agriculture, even in a professional sense. Only one mentioned agriculture, but this was in the context of his wish to become a writer. He felt compelled to justify the role that peasant farmers can play in the development of a modern state: "If a conscientious man cultivates the land in the proper way, he helps the rebuilding of the country. If it weren't for agricultural products, all factories would stop. So it is clear

[18] "The Further Work and Role of the Yugoslav League of Communists," Report of Aleksandar Ranković to the Eighth Party Congress, in *Foreign Broadcast Information Service: Daily Report, Supplement, U.S.S.R. and East Europe,* No. 17 (Washington, D.C.: Foreign Broadcast Information Service, December 17, 1964), pp. 22–23.

that a man is a man whether he works in a village or in a city, and one can't live without the other." [19]

In a survey of educational and job aspirations conducted in the nearby market town of Arandjelovac in 1962, among the sixty-two students in their final year of the gymnasium forty-two were born in local villages, the fathers of nineteen of whom were still farmers (of the other twenty-three, the parents had moved to town or the father had died; a few were children of teachers in village schools). Only one student mentioned as a desired occupation one related to agriculture—the boy said his parents wanted him to become a physician while he preferred to be an agronomist. Three students (two of whom were born in town) whose parents also lived in town chose advanced education in forestry. The ten boys and nine girls whose fathers were farmers, the following occupational aspirations were given: among the girls, teachers (2), lawyers (2), engineers (2), doctor, reporter, economist (1 each); among the boys, lawyers (3), engineers (3), high-school teachers (2), technician and agronomist (1 each).

Despite the relatively great potential for mobility most university students are of urban white-collar class origin. According to data available, in 1957–1958 at Sarajevo university 38 percent of the students in the Agriculture-Forestry Faculty were of peasant origin, while children of white-collar workers composed 44 percent of the enrollment in this school. Students of peasant origin made up only 24 percent of the total full-time enrollment in the university (children of white-collar workers accounted for 53 percent).[20]

These figures reflect nationwide university enrollments. O' total of 69,000 university students in Yugoslavia during the sarr academic year, 26 percent were of agricultural origin, 48 percent r white-collar background, 12 percent from workers' and 7 percent from craftsmen's families.[21]

In 1962, pupils in village elementary schools in areas other than central Serbia were asked to write essays about their plans for the future. Most participants were eighth-graders who would soon face turning points in their careers. As with the Orašac group earlier, none of these wanted to remain in the village or pursue a career related to farming. It should not be inferred that their attitudes toward village life

[19] See Joel Halpern, *A Serbian Village* (New York: Columbia University Press, 1958), p. 258.

[20] A. Fiamengo, *Pregled,* September, 1959, pp. 215–216.

[21] Vojin Milić, *Stat. Rev.,* No. 1–2 (1959), p. 71.

were wholly negative. On the contrary, many expressed real affection for the place where they were born and raised, acknowledging at the same time that they would eventually leave. A Montenegrin youth said: "I love my village because here I was born and first heard my mother tongue. I will remember the beautiful meadows, the hills on which shepherd boys watch their flocks and autumn, which I awaited with great anticipation, because of the beautiful fruit." Others expressed the joy of running through fields looking for flowers or watching lambs. Another declared affection for his village in terms of his ancestral roots. Some mentioned the increasing attractiveness of their village in terms of electrification, improved roads to town, the presence of a new store or school or better-constructed peasant homes.

One girl (who had repeated the grade) from a remote mountain village expressed fear of the city, with its tall buildings and factories, and a reluctance to leave her friends. Few seemed to fear the city as she did and most were keenly aware of the limitations of village life. A boy from the same mountain village recognized education as a channel of mobility, aided by kin ties in town: "I do not want to become a peasant or agricultural worker, for I want to be somebody. This can be done only by going to the city. Those who remain in the village have a difficult life, with much hard work. When I complete eighth grade this year I will go to live with my brother in Tuzla. There my life will be better, but if I do not get good grades now I will not be able to enter high school there. I must therefore study." Another wrote: "My desire to continue my studies becomes greater when I see how hard workers have to labor with a pick-axe. If I graduate from a higher school I would become a *gospodin* [gentleman, a bourgeois word frowned upon by the government]. This is my greatest wish."

Others were less concerned with status and more with the possibilities of consumption and travel. One boy in southern Serbia said he would like to become an engineer, have a comfortable apartment, buy a television set, go to the movies, get a motorcycle, travel to cities throughout Yugoslavia, and learn foreign languages. Another put it succinctly, "I wish to dress nicely in city clothes and be able to eat my fill."

Youthful fancies may run wild, but peasant school children have no illusions about the difficulties which face them or about the very real possibilities of failure to realize an urban career. Because of the scattered nature of most Yugoslav rural settlements and the frequent lack of dormitory facilities in towns it is often necessary to walk long distances to school, especially for those who go on to higher grades (in some villages past fourth grade and in others past eighth grade). Boys and girls in Serbia, Montenegro, Bosnia, and Macedonia wrote about getting up before sunrise, pasturing the livestock, and setting out for school on foot. Sometimes the schools were as far as ten kilometers away. They wrote of arriving too early or too late and of snowy or rainy days when part of the school hours had to be spent thawing and drying out around the wood stove.

An interesting conjecture, although the data are not conclusive, is that in those regions where material conditions are poorest occupational aspirations are highest. Montenegrin and Serbian shepherd boys dream of exploring the moon or at least of becoming airplane pilots, even though they live in homes without electricity and may never have been on a train. Children from a Slovene village near a town with electronics and textile industries and whose usual activities include watching television, sports events, and illustrated travel lectures, aspire to become skilled workers (some of the girls want to be shop clerks). These aspirations are paralleled by those of children in a village near Zagreb. The closest approach to continuing contact with the village is found among those pupils, particularly girls, who indicate a career in teaching, possibly in villages. The situation is not as strange as it might appear, since in the more marginal agricultural communities a certain proportion of the youth must leave the land. Factors of accessibility and contact are also significant, and it is true that some of the richest farm land in Yugoslavia is now being abandoned.

In interviews conducted among members of youth brigades engaged in highway construction, in a sample of 650 which included 391 young workers (361 males and 30 females) and 259 peasant youths (252 males and 7 females) of whom 75 percent of the total were of village origin, the most favored occupations among both workers and peasants were found to be those of chauffeur, craftsman, and mechanic. The closest to an occupation related to agriculture (other than agronomist, which was listed among a miscellany including actor, photographer, reporter, and lawyer) was that of tractor driver, favored by 3 percent of the young workers and 8 percent of the young peasants. Significantly, 9 percent of the workers and only one percent of the peasants said they were satisfied with their occupations. Relatively few appeared to aspire to professional occupations such as engineering (4 percent of the workers and one percent of the peasants) or to the arts (3 percent of each group). When asked why they desired a particular occupation the most frequent reply (a third of the workers and half the peasants) was: easier work followed by better pay. There seems to be a greater reality orientation among these young adults than among the school children, but their basic feeling toward farming as a way of life appears unchanged.[22]

INTERVIEWS WITH VILLAGE ADULTS

The more realistic aspirations of the children are reinforced by those their parents have for them. Included in a questionnaire which was used for interviewing adult villagers in Serbia, Bosnia, and Slovenia were these questions:

What do you think about educating children beyond the eighth grade?
What do you think is the best occupation for young men and young women, and why?
If it were possible to live your life over would you like something to be different, would you choose the same occupation, would you live in the same place?

(Under normal circumstances it is of course desirable to prepare an initial questionnaire, test it out, and on the basis of the responses formulate the final version. It is also desirable to preselect according to certain criteria the group of individuals to be interviewed and to have trained interviewers to do the job. For a combination of reasons the field conditions were not ideal, and pretesting was not possible. Further, the population interviewed was a random sample of those people who were available at the time the interviews were to be conducted. However, the questionnaire was based on extensive background experience in conducting unstructured interviews in depth in many villages. It was devised with the active advice and support of Yugoslav sociologists. The interviewers were sociology students, in most cases in their final year of university studies, and with some previous interview experience. A number of them were of village origin. The villages in the over-all sample represented a diversity of ethnic and religious groups, occupations, education, and income levels, and data from three of the ethnic areas are summarized below. Generally, most questions were readily answered. There was, however, some resistance to the abstract nature of the question concerning repeating one's life experiences, many replying that such a thing was impossible. A few responded to this question on the level of personal emotional experiences; one old man replied that he would pursue and seduce beautiful girls; several women said they would never have married.)

[22] Krsto Kilibarda, *Soc. Pol.*, XV:7–8 (July–August, 1960), pp. 60–64. Five of those in this sample had less than four years of schooling, 214 completed four grades, 260 had from four to seven grades, 115 completed eight grades and 52 had more than eight years of school.

Perhaps most typical for Yugoslavia as a whole were responses to interviews conducted in Šumadija in central Serbia in villages clustered near the town of Arandjelovac. This town had a population of approximately 10,000 in 1961, having increased greatly in size since the war and more than doubling since 1948. Much of its growth can be attributed to the expansion of fire-brick and electro-porcelain factories which draw on local clay resources. Unlike some western parts of Yugoslavia, with an industrial tradition of several generations, the labor force in the Arandjelovac factories was recruited from the surrounding villages primarily within the last decade. (It should be added, however, that mining has an older tradition than manufacturing in this region, so that among the families interviewed there were a number of pensioned miners and clerks.) [23]

Interviews were conducted with eighty-five household heads in nine villages (not including Orašac) in the vicinity. Five of these villages are basically agricultural, and four, because of their proximity to town and the fact that a large proportion of villagers from them work in town, have a mixed economy. Thirty-seven interviews were conducted in the agricultural villages and forty-eight in the mixed settlements. Of the heads of households questioned, sixty were full-time farmers and twenty-five were workers or were on pensions but practiced agriculture to some degree.

Twelve of those who farmed exclusively indicated that they would repeat their careers. Their average age was considerably greater than the average in the total sample, all of them being more than 50 years old at the time (nine were over sixty). One 48-year-old farmer said he would like to have been an agronomist, providing the sole case where a professional occupation related to agriculture was mentioned. In these twelve cases, at least one son in each household has remained on the land, the one exception being a family where the son was attending an agricultural school. Seven of the twelve were from villages with a mixed economy (of a total of twenty-eight full-time farmers in the sample from the mixed villages); the remaining five, from the purely agricultural villages, were part of a total of thirty-two full-time farmers questioned in those villages.

In prescribing ideal career patterns for boys and girls most of the

[23] It is significant to note that in Serbia in the 1880's, approximately 5,000 Italians were working on railroad construction. Evidently, there was not a sufficient number of Serbian peasants interested in wage labor. See Jozo Tomasevich, *Peasants, Politics and Economic Change in Yugoslavia* (Stanford, Calif.: Stanford University Press, 1955).

twelve household heads expressing a preference for agriculture as a way of life nevertheless highly valued education and urban careers, in some cases for women as well as men. One man related schooling to inheritance of land, saying that those who have land should stay in the village, while if there are many children and little land they should be educated. This attitude, which is increasingly common, represents a change from the traditional pattern where sons generally remained on the land. A 67-year-old farmer was moved to be defensive, saying that he was never ashamed of his work, for in it he had found satisfaction and happiness. He agreed that schooling was a good thing but claimed that it was best to be a farmer.

Among the 80 percent of the full-time farmers in the sample who explicitly rejected agriculture and in most cases life in the village as well, the most common response was that they wished they had learned a craft or continued in school. Five would have become workers but would have remained in the village, and an equal number who would have liked to become workers said it would not have mattered where they lived. However, seventeen of those responding to the part of the question about place of residence indicated a desire to leave the village. Twenty-one expressed a wish for change in terms of a different occupation only, although the nature of the job change appeared to carry with it an implicit desire to move. It seems clear, however, that the main dissatisfaction was with farming as an occupation rather than residence, especially in the villages nearer Arandjelovac. A number of replies explicitly rejected agriculture: "I would search for an easier life. A peasant's life is hard. I have had enough of the land." An illiterate 60-year-old woman said, "I would go to school and wouldn't even look at a peasant." A villager whose son had completed law school remarked, "No one brags about being a farmer," and a middle-aged man who had had one year of school said, "I would study day and night. I'm tired of working the land." (However, his 30-year-old son went to school for two years only.)

The latter case is but one of twenty-two from both types of villages where the household head expressed a desire for a life other than farming but where sons have either remained on the land or become peasant-workers at unskilled manual work which is supplementary to the agriculture-based household economy. Thus those twenty-two individuals all stated that they would study or learn a craft, in most cases would move to a town, that children should be educated beyond elementary school, if possible for a white-collar job or profession—but the fact remains that their own children have done none of these things. However, these men are mostly in their late fifties and sixties, and since the extended families of most of them are composed of three-generation households, many of their grandchildren show promise of achieving a career outside the village. In nine out of the ten cases where applicable, the grandchildren have already surpassed the educational experience of their parents and grandparents. Most of these grandchildren are now in their teens, and so the extent of their careers cannot yet be determined. Some have already reached the university or skilled technican level of training. Undoubtedly some will remain on the land, but the implications for increasing depopulation of rural areas, qualitatively as well as quantitatively, are evident.

From 1890 to 1948 the population of the primarily agricultural villages in this region remained approximately stable. During 1948 to 1953 village populations declined slightly in a number of cases. Significantly, if we analyze the population living entirely or partly from agriculture in 1890 and in 1960 in ten comparable villages, including most of those in which the interviews were conducted, six showed a decline in population and four an increase. With one exception, the increases have occurred in villages adjacent to Arandjelovac which have large numbers of peasant-workers.[24]

Of the twenty-five household heads in the total sample who are peasant-workers or pensioners, only three (one over 50 years of age and two over 60) indicated satisfaction with the ways their careers had turned out, and two said they would have liked to get further education and changed jobs but remain in the village. The majority indicated that they wished they had been able to have more education and a different job. They also expressed a desire to live in Arandjelovac, Belgrade, or some large town. The peasant-workers' ages ranged from the late twenties to the early fifties. They were generally younger than the farmers and their households were smaller, usually composed of two generations. In two of the twenty-five cases sons were farmers. In six households children had achieved schooling or jobs superior to those of their fathers.

Another view of the peasant-worker is obtained from data from a Moslem village near a coal-mining and steel complex about an hour's train ride from Sarajevo. This Bosnian sample included 118 interviews with heads of households, of whom only ten were farmers. Most of these peasant-workers worked in the mine or on the railroad, and some

[24] Joel M. Halpern, *Social and Cultural Change in a Serbian Village* (New Haven, Conn.: Human Relations Area Files, 1956), p. 125, and *Popis Poljoprivreda,* I (Belgrade: 1964), 343–344.

were on pension. All of them cultivated their own land in the village, which is situated in relatively fertile rolling hills. Only one of the ten farmers in the sample (all of whom were more than sixty) said he would repeat his life experience. The others said they would like to have had more schooling and another occupation. Four of these said they would have moved to town. Among the 108 peasant-workers ranging in age from 20 to late sixties, less than half (thirty-seven) expressed a desire to remain in the village, but only four of these said they would choose the same careers; the others would have liked more education and to have entered a more highly skilled occupation. In some cases the children of peasant-workers achieved the goal of moving to a job in town. More frequent in this area are cases of three-generation households where fathers and sons are or have been workers. Here as in Serbia most movement can be looked for in the generation now in school.

Studies conducted in other areas of Yugoslavia corroborate the Serbian and Bosnian peasant-workers' great desire for occupational and spatial mobility. This is not universal, however, in all parts of the country, particularly in village communities in prosperous regions situated near towns. An example is the Slovene village of Šenčur, a short bus trip from the industrial town of Kranj. This alpine area combines a highly prosperous farming, tourist, and industrial economy. Of sixty-seven peasant-worker household heads interviewed, thirty-six indicated that they would prefer to continue living in Šenčur, and only nine said they would have liked to move. Five of the six farmers in the total sample of seventy-three indicated a preference for remaining in the village. However, there was markedly less occupational satisfaction, since only eleven of the peasant-workers and two of the farmers wished to repeat the same experience. (The attitude of rural Slovenes in less favored regions matches that of villagers in other parts of the country: among sixteen heads of households in a relatively remote and backward region of Slovenia, all of whom are farmers, thirteen indicated a desire to change both occupation and place of residence.)

CONCLUSIONS

The survey data and personal accounts presented here suggest trends not intended to be conclusive. It is not possible to see this evolutionary stage in the development of a total society as simply involving a peasant attaining an education, developing new skills, and learning urban ways of life. All these factors are only part of the total nineteenth- and twentieth-century modernization process.

An integral aspect of the process has been modern warfare. The peoples of today's Yugoslavia generally, and Serbs in particular, have been deeply involved in the major wars of this century. A peasant's closest contact with modern technology and a modern state organization has been his army service, making a greater impact on village youth than a few years' attendance at the local school. Many peasant soldiers were prisoners of war. It is no accident that in autobiographies obtained from villagers often 80–90 percent of the narrative relates wartime experiences (although this might have been done, in part, to interest or impress a foreigner). Many Croats and Slovenes who were taken prisoner by the Russians during World War I were witnesses to some of the more dramatic moments of the Bolshevik Revolution. Those from Serbia, especially, who spent several years in both world wars in Austrian or German prisoner-of-war camps, returned with lasting impressions of an industrialized society and of more advanced agricultural techniques than they had known before.

Undeniably they lacked the technical background, financial resources, and national leadership which would have enabled them to use their experiences comprehensively in order to raise their standard of living. Various innovations did come about, however, and, more importantly, despite the traditional appearance of the countryside, the peasants' view of the world was receptive to change. This attitude was reinforced by a self-consciousness of their own relative backwardness. The Communist revolution has been opposed on ideological grounds but much less so with regard to its schemes for economic development.

Particularly in Serbia the concept of a peasant state is pertinent. That is, the successful achievement of independence growing out of armed revolt, with Serbia's coming into existence as a country composed mainly of peasant small holders, developed in the individual villager a high degree of national consciousness.

These developments provide something of the background for a statement often heard in the countryside: "Give us twenty years without a war, and we will make our country into a little America." This and the frequently uttered village axiom, "A man must work," reflect attitudes radically different from those which have been written about elsewhere with regard to European peasantries. There are surely elements of Slav Messianism, an early twentieth-century immigrant view of America, and the more recent future-oriented Communist ideology—but the particular historical experience of the villagers is also important.[25]

[25] These interpretations have been suggested in conversations with Asen Balicki and Eugene Hammel.

The villager does not see himself as a passive element in change. He seeks active involvement. Despite an early tradition of mistrust of the city, especially with regard to urban merchants and creditors, migration to towns and social and economic advancement is eagerly sought regardless of the difficulties encountered. Peasants' attitudes toward change can be a series of interrelated and often contradictory views. In speaking of the Yugoslav rural population as a whole differences among regions has been stressed. Differences between individuals must also be borne in mind. A villager may make great sacrifices to send his children to school and prepare them for a professional occupation, be willing to try improved varieties of seed, or experiment with better breeding stock, and at the same time cling to traditional religious observances and the virtues of home cures as opposed to modern medicine. The concern of the preceding pages has been the attitudes toward agriculture and associated village residence. Therefore many values and practices which the rural migrant carries with him when he settles in town have not been discussed other than to indicate the existence of the broad phenomenon of the peasantization of the town, which implies a continuity in many types of behavior and not a complete psychological, economic, or social break with his rural past.

In Serbia, which lags significantly behind the former Austro-Hungarian areas of Croatia and Slovenia, developments have been particularly dramatic within the past half century. Taking 1921 as an index of 100, the rate of growth of the urban population of Serbia proper by 1953 was 295, compared to 221 for Croatia and Slovenia.[26]

Other factors have aided the transition. The rural areas of Yugoslavia have long lacked experience with wage labor in the extractive industries of logging, mining, and quarrying. In addition, there has been the even older tradition of peasant migrant workers known as *pečalbari,* who left from areas such as Macedonia to work in Turkey, Egypt, or the United States for months or years before periodically returning to their villages. Within Yugoslavia peasant traders and craftsmen have also ranged widely in disposing of their wares. These various activities have all served to acquaint the villager with the town.

A village-based peasant subculture is not about to disappear from Yugoslavia. In fact, the situation in Šenčur suggests how some peasant villages are being incorporated in the suburbs of expanding industrial towns, promoting the peasantization of the towns. But the consequences of the negative attitude toward farming as a way of life for the

[26] Dolfe Vogelnik, *Urbanizacija kao Odraz Prevrednog Razvoja FNRJ* (Belgrade: 1961), Table 8, pp. 44–45.

future of the agricultural labor force on both private and state farms is already evident. Providing increased economic incentives to villagers alone would not appear to make a career in agriculture more attractive.

The villager has strong ties to his native place and to his family's plot of land, and at the same time he is attracted to a job in the town. The current resolution of this dilemma is the transitional phenomenon of the peasant-worker. The equilibrium is a dynamic one, with movement both ways. Developments in 1965 indicate that with greater stress on economic efficiency in industry numbers of unskilled factory workers may have to return to the land.[27] Under such conditions it would seem that the transitional status of peasant-worker will not soon disappear. The ultimate security which the land offers in time of crisis is not lightly abandoned. However, this is not synonymous with permanent, unyielding attachment to village life.

The peasant has stubbornly resisted collectivization, but it seems he is even more determined to gain access to the seeming attractiveness of urban life. His attachment to his land appears to vary inversely with the degree to which other opportunities become available. This has not always been so, and it is not true everywhere in Yugoslavia today, but the general long-term trends are clear.

[27] David Binder, "Price Increases Pain Yugoslavs," *New York Times,* August 1, 1965, p. 13.

COMMENT

Rudolf Bićanić

In the first, general, part of his presentation Professor Halpern rightly stressed that changes are taking place both in the rural and urban society; therefore it is not logically correct to talk about transforming a rural way of life into an urban one under the presupposition that all rural is old and traditional and all urban new and modern. Perhaps it would be more correct to compare urbanization to ruralization rather than to "peasantization" as Halpern prefers to say.

The concept of peasant as different from that of rural inhabitant should be linked with five characteristics: agriculture as the main activity (including auxiliary and additional services); family production relations, i.e., members of the same family working together on family land in order to secure common consumption for all members living together and with the expectation of continuity of the family consumption unit over generations through inheritance; working ownership—owners being at the same time operators doing physical work on the land; a high degree of income in kind; multifunctional services, economic and non-economic (cultural, educational, health, recreational). This rationalized picture, tending to isolate different components in what is commonly called "the peasant way of life," obviously provides a composite concept far from the romanticized idea of an "eternal peasant."

The second point made in Halpern's general remarks is the influence of the Communist ideology and attitude towards the peasants. This also may be subject to change, and, if I read the signs properly, such change is already taking place. One major factor of influence here is the shortage of agricultural products in almost all Communist-controlled countries. Another one is that the peasants are leaving agriculture faster than the substitution of capital goods for labor is taking place. Therefore there is an increasing deficit in the agricultural labor force. Under the influence of such and similar facts Communist policies towards agriculture gradually change, and so does their attitude towards the peasant. In the sixties the policy has been to stimulate the peasants to remain on the land and not to leave agriculture.[28] One might call

[28] These changes were discussed in my paper "Problems of Socialist Agriculture," *Indian Journal of Agricultural Economics,* XIX:3–4 (July–December, 1964), 173–185.

such changes transitional or temporary but no one has so far estimated how long this transitional period will last. Only dogmatists of all creeds can believe that factors and objectives of agricultural policy do not and cannot change. Attitudes change under pressure of facts in many countries and so they do in Yugoslavia too, as Halpern's essay has demonstrated.

My third remark with regard to the general part of Professor Halpern's paper refers to the notion of urban and rural subcultures. Some consider both as subsets of a set of a national culture; in fact both are parts of much wider sets. Therefore, the comparisons Halpern has produced are very interesting. They are based on the antagonism of agriculture versus industry, where each is considered as a separate subset with some interconnections. The town influences the village, and the village the town. But if we talk in terms of agriculture influencing the manufacturing industries and those industries influencing agriculture, the perspective for the future is subject to an accelerated change, and the contradiction is being fast overcome. It might therefore be more appropriate to talk today about traditional agriculture and traditional industries based on physical labor and financial capital—and modern agriculture and modern industries based on scientific research and development.

Already people have been compelled to admit that the industrial society is far from being ideal, that industrial advance in closed urban settlements brings with it problems comparable to some of the worst effects of rural backwardness. Such problems as air and water pollution or juvenile delinquency gravely affect both capitalist and socialist societies although in somewhat different forms and to a different degree. But the roots are the same; and in addition to the problem of the alienation of man from labor there is a problem of the alienation of man from nature.

The process of revision of values of the industrial society is already taking place, and more and more students of society write today about the postindustrial society. It has not yet been given a proper name, but it is obvious that in this society the affluence of material goods will not be considered as the final state of human happiness. The progress of human society should enable all to return to nature and enjoy its immeasurable riches. From this point of view both urban and rural life are developing a new dimension and a new scale of values. The dilemma of agriculture versus industry already belongs to the past, and new avenues are opening to the exploration of development of human institutions.

In the second part of his presentation, Halpern deals with Yugoslavia, giving some examples of how this research fits into his general scheme. Perhaps in his analysis of migration and age structure of the labor force, the sex structure should also be taken into account. I find his section dealing with the aspirations of village children of particular interest, although in a mixed country like Yugoslavia any generalization calls for caution. The motivation to leave the village can be influenced by many push-in and push-out, as well as pull-in and pull-out factors. The further distinction as to how far the motives are world-wide and to what extent they are specific conditions within Yugoslavia, is of great importance. To take just one example—the influence of the pressure of agricultural overpopulation on the one side, and the receiving capacity (absorption capacity being somewhat different) on the other side, are different not only in different parts of the country but also in short periods of time. In the years 1963 and 1964 employment increased by 230,000, but in the years to come an annual increase of 100,000 is expected. Halpern is right in stressing that the problem of exodus is not a matter of aspirations of young people which can be solved by education, skill, and urban living; it is a much more complex and many-sided matter. The examples he gives about aspirations and attitudes are interesting indeed, and his research provides some valuable contributions to the problem. Official statistics, and many sample surveys already carried out, give some answers. But in this varied country we do not know how representative such surveys are so that much more work on the same lines would be required before any general conclusions can be reached. In view of the changing situation in economic perspectives, the influence of school, army, press, politics, and the technological extension service there may soon be a different focus. Prejudices may fall on both the industrial and the agricultural side. Indeed they are falling already as the new economic policy of the 1965 reforms indicates.

The motivation of the village children is also being altered. It is true that there will be fewer of the old values left among the younger generation, but what is new to them may well be different from what the present adult generation thinks is new. In a multinational state at different levels of development, with different family structures and different ecological and technological conditions, the new may take very varied forms.

GREGOR LAZARCIK

The Performance of Czechoslovak Agriculture since World War II

The socialist economic system prevailing in Czechoslovakia as well as in other East European countries has achieved substantial progress in industrial development since World War II.[1] Although Czechoslovakia was already one of the ten most industrialized countries in Europe before the war,[2] her industrial output increased by 153 percent from 1937 to 1962.[3] From 1962 to 1964, however, her industrial growth was brought to a complete stagnation because of a series of errors and inefficiencies in the planning mechanism and leadership.

In agriculture, the socialist economic system in Eastern Europe has been unable to show a progress comparable to that in industry. Although the population of Eastern Europe has been increasing at a faster rate than in Western Europe since World War II, agricultural production has increased at a slower rate than in West. The agricultural output between 1935–1939 and 1962–1963 in Western Europe and the United States rose by 52 and 70 percent respectively; in Eastern Europe including the Soviet Union, it rose by 45 percent.[4]

[1] I am indebted to Thad P. Alton, Director, Project on National Income in East Central Europe, for helpful suggestions and comments.

[2] Gregor Lazarcik, *Le Commerce en matière agricole entre l'Europe de l'Ouest et l'Europe de l'Est* (Paris: Librairie Marcel Riviere & Cie, 1959), p. 11.

[3] George J. Staller, "Czechoslovak Industrial Production Indexes, 1937–1962," unpublished, Columbia University, Project on National Income in East Central Europe (1965), Table 1.

[4] Food and Agriculture Organization of the United Nations, *Yearbook of Food and Agricultural Statistics: Production, 1957,* II (Rome: Food and Agriculture Organization of the United Nations, 1958), 25–26 and *Production Yearbook 1963,* XVII (Rome: Food and Agriculture Organization of the United Nations, 1964), 27–28.

A few words need to be said about general conditions and changes in the organization of Czechoslovak agriculture since prewar years. Agriculture, the second-largest sector of the economy after industry in Czechoslovakia, is diversified because of the different quality of soil at different altitudes, a climate suitable for many crops, and a demand for a large variety of agricultural products. The main products are wheat, barley, rye, oats, corn, sugar beets, potatoes, pork, beef, milk, eggs, and fruits.

Before World War II, the typical unit of production in Czechoslovak agriculture was a privately owned "family" farm. In 1937, there were 1.5 million private farms owning 98.3 percent of total agricultural land; the remaining 1.7 percent was owned and managed by the state or local government. Most farms were very small. About 71 percent of all farms were less than five hectares and occupied only 23 percent of the total agricultural land. The medium size "family" farms, 5 to 20 hectares large, amounted to 25 percent of all farms and 42 percent of all agricultural land. Only 4 percent of the farms had more than 20 hectares, but their share of total agricultural land was 35 percent. Between the two world wars, the Czechoslovak government reduced the inequality of land ownership through land reform, which redistributed the land of large estates to small farmers amounting to 17 percent of total agricultural land. Despite the land reform, the problem of small farms with insufficient capital remained the dominating factor of the country's agricultural policy. Except for the government's fixing prices of the main crops through the "grain monopoly" after 1934, the agricultural sector was organized and operated along the lines of a private-enterprise system.

Since the thirties, Czechoslovak agriculture has fundamentally changed. Its contribution to the national income (Marxist concept) declined from 23 percent in 1937 to 13 percent in 1963. Because of labor shortage, agriculture entered a phase of rapid mechanization. The mechanical power replaced horse power and the labor force employed in agriculture decreased by about a half between 1937 and 1964. In 1949 the rapid reorganization of the social and economic structure of agriculture was begun by collectivization and socialization of private ownership of land. By 1963, more than 90 percent of agricultural land had been socialized and private farms produced only 6 percent of total agricultural output. There was a spectacular increase in the average size of farms in collective agriculture by the integration of more than one million formerly private farms into some 7,500 collective farms.

The socialized agriculture, however, did not bring about the increased supply of food needed to meet the increased demand for food in rapidly growing urban and industrial areas, especially in Slovakia. During most of the postwar years the agricultural output was stagnating below the prewar level. Before World War II, Czechoslovakia was just about self-sufficient in food supply; her exports of food approximately balanced the imports. After the war there was constant pressure by consumers to obtain a higher quality of food. According to official sources, per-capita consumption of meat increased from 34 kilograms in 1936 to 58 kilograms in 1963, of eggs from 138 to 185. of fats from 14 kilograms to 20 kilograms. This divergent movement of demand for and supply of agricultural products from domestic production resulted in greater dependence on net food imports, especially butter, eggs, meat, wheat, rye, fruits, and feed grains. The net import of food and feed increased by about 60 percent between 1948 and 1963, and the share of all agricultural products in total import increased from 16 percent in 1937 to 34 percent in 1963. Rapidly increasing food import undoubtedly contributed to Czechoslovakia's recent balance-of-payment difficulties. The reasons given above compel the planners and leaders of Czechoslovakia to desire an increase in agricultural output and efficiency since this will decrease the country's dependence on food from abroad and will increase per-capita food supply.

The following discussion will attempt to measure and appraise more systematically the performance of Czechoslovak agriculture since World War II; it will attempt to provide answers to the following questions about the agricultural sector of the Czechoslovak economy during 1934–1938 and 1948–1964: (1) How did different production measures behave during this period? (2) What changes occurred in the productivity of land, capital, labor, and total productivity? (3) What were the most significant economic and noneconomic influences affecting production and productivity? (4) How did Czechoslovak performance compare with that of Western Europe? (5) What is the position of agriculture in the New Economic Model of Czechoslovakia?

Czechoslovak postwar agriculture is of particular interest as an example of economic performance of agriculture in a socialist economic system characterized by a high level of individual development. This study thus provides a comparison between the 1934–1938 base period, during which a private-enterprise system prevailed, and the 1948–1964 period, during which Czechoslovak agriculture was reorganized into a centrally planned socialist system.

The official Czechoslovak statistical agencies publish an index of value added in agriculture,[5] but detailed calculations of these indexes

[5] *Stat. roč.-1960,* pp. 37, 211.

have hot been released, although the general methodology concerning the construction of these indexes was discussed in the Czechoslovak economic literature. One of the purposes of this contribution is to check the official indexes against our measures.

To insure the comparability of the statistical series developed in this discussion with those available for agricultural sectors in other countries, the standard definition and methods of classification and presentation developed by the United Nations organs [6] are followed.

The weights used in the calculation of index numbers of the volume of agricultural production and input measures are 1936 and 1956 weighted average prices received, or paid by farmers.

A modified index formula was employed in computing the indexes using 1956 prices as weights. In those instances where 1936 price weights were used, an approximation of Laspeyre's formula was used in making index computations.

The base chosen for the calculation of all indexes is the prewar five-year average, 1934–1938. Five-year averages seem to be adequate to smooth out seasonal fluctuation caused by weather conditions.

PRODUCTION AND INPUT MEASURES

Total Crop and Animal Production.—This measure comprises the production of all crops and pasture and all animal products including livestock inventory changes, before any allowances are made for utilization of agricultural production (e.g., fodder). The production is measured at farm level (adjusted for harvesting losses) for each calendar year.[7]

On the whole, the technique used by the Czechoslovak official authorities in estimating crop and animal production does not differ significantly from the techniques used in Western European countries and in the United States. No major deficiency was found in cross-checking the official data. It seems that the State Statistical Office in Prague processes the collected data with care and impartiality. However, the basic raw data are collected by local government agents. The reliability of measures developed in this study depends on the impartiality and com-

[6] United Nations, Economic Commission For Europe, Food and Agriculture Organization, *Output, Expenses and Income of Agriculture in Some European Countries,* Third Report (Geneva: United Nations, 1958) and United Nations, *Statistical Papers,* Series M, No. 4, Rev. 1 (New York: United Nations, 1958), p. 6.

[7] The detailed method of estimation of crop production is described in Státní úřad Statisticky, *Methody zjustovani zemedelskych plodin* (Prague: 1956), pp. 4–32.

petency of these primary sample-taking agents. Available food balances seem to support the reliability of our data.

Agricultural Output.—In this study agricultural output is defined as end-use output from the nation's farms available for human consumption and industrial use, plus changes in stocks, and work in progress on farm.

This definition is used by the U.N. economic organs to calculate agricultural output in Western European countries.[8] The U.S. Department of Agriculture uses a similar concept under the term "farm output," differing from the one used in this study in that it omits miscellaneous output and farm investment in kind.[9] The Czechoslovak official statistics have not hitherto used the concept of agricultural output in this sense.

The output in agriculture was calculated by subtracting from total crop and animal production (see above) all intermediate products utilized on farms in further production, which consist of feed, litter, manure, seed, inventory losses and by-products of food processing.

Current Operating Expenses and Depreciation.—Current operating expenses are defined here as total value of all goods and services bought by the agricultural sector from all non-agricultural sectors and used up in production of agricultural output.[10] The items included in expenses are: expenditures on imports of feed, including feed manufactureed from imported commodities; handling charges on inter-farm sales which include merchants' margins and transportation provided by the nonagricultural sector; fertilizers; pesticides; fuel and lubricants; electricity; maintenance and repairs of farm buildings, machinery and equipment provided by the nonagricultural sectors; and miscellaneous expenses.

Depreciation is the current charge to take account of wear and tear and obsolescence of capital goods in agriculture. The annual charge is based on the cost of replacing the assets at the end of the estimated economic lifetime of each asset.

Calculation of expenses and depreciation is necessary for the estimation of the gross and net product of agriculture. Trends in the magnitude of production expenses provide a useful indication of the extent to which the agricultural sector is dependent on nonagricultural sectors for production requisites.

[8] United Nations, Economic Commission for Europe, Food and Agriculture Organization, *Agricultural Sector Accounts and Tables: A Handbook of Definitions and Methods* (Geneva: United Nations, 1956), p. 12.

[9] U.S. Department of Agriculture, *Agricultural Statistics 1952* (Washington, D.C.: Government Printing Office, 1952), p. 661.

[10] United Nations, *op. cit.* (in n. 7), p. 10.

Gross and Net Product.—The gross product of agriculture is the gross value added by productive activity within the agricultural sector to the value of materials and services which are obtained from nonagricultural sectors including the foreign sector.[11]

In this study the gross product of agriculture is obtained from output by subtracting current operating expenses. The gross product is directly affected by prices paid by farmers for production requisites. These prices contain elements of indirect taxes and subsidies.

The gross product valued at 1936 prices is, in fact, the gross product at factor cost, because the subsidies are included and the indirect taxes excluded. The gross product valued at 1948 and 1956 prices does not include all subsidies, especially those given to collectives and state farms.

The net product of agriculture is the gross product as defined above minus an allowance for using up fixed capital in the process of production.

Results.—The various measures of production and cost in Czechoslovak agriculture calculated according to outlined methods are summarized in Table 1. The findings show the following patterns:

1) Total crop and animal production and agricultural output remained below the prewar level until 1958. In the three subsequent years the figures increased slightly above the prewar level. Both measures showed similar patterns, which indicates that the share of intermediate products used on farms in total production remained about the same for the most part of the period. From 1958 on, however, the output began to rise faster than the total production because of increasing import of feed.

2) Inputs into agriculture from other sectors increased sharply since the war. The most spectacular increase occurred in the consumption of fuel due to rapid mechanization, followed by consumption of electricity and consumption of fertilizers and imported feed.

3) Because of stagnating output and rapidly increasing operating expenses, the gross product and net product decreased significantly since the prewar period.

4) The choice of price weights does not affect significantly the production and output measures.

5) Significant changes occurred in the composition of output of animal products. From 1934–1938 to 1963, the share of meat output increased from 28.7 to 36.2 percent while that of eggs and milk de-

[11] *Ibid.*, p. 7.

TABLE 1

INDEXES OF AGRICULTURAL PERFORMANCE, CZECHOSLOVAKIA, SELECTED YEARS

Item	1934–1938 average	1948	1953	1958	1960	1961	1962	1963 [a]
A. My Calculations:								
Total crop and animal production:								
at 1936 prices	100.0	77.9	89.9	97.7	101.7	99.3	92.3	99.9
at 1956 prices	100.0	76.6	88.6	100.2	104.8	102.0	94.8	102.9
Agricultural output:								
at 1936 prices	100.0	76.4	86.9	102.7	108.5	105.1	98.7	106.0
at 1956 prices	100.0	74.3	85.4	104.9	110.3	106.9	100.3	107.8
Current operating expenses:								
at 1956 prices	100.0	141.8	188.8	252.1	342.9	347.9	385.2	413.7
Gross product (at factor cost):								
at 1956 prices	100.0	68.5	76.6	92.4	90.5	86.3	76.0	84.0
Capital consumption allowances:								
at 1956 prices	100.0	103.4	113.1	127.3	135.5	149.2	166.0	185.0
Net product (at factor cost):								
at 1936 prices	100.0	65.4	73.3	89.2	86.4	80.6	67.9	79.0
at 1956 prices (1948 = 100)	152.9	100.0	112.1	136.4	132.1	123.2	103.8	120.8
Meat output in percent of total	28.7	22.9	31.4	33.2	33.0	34.6	37.9	36.2
Eggs and milk in percent of total	33.9	24.3	28.6	26.5	25.8	27.1	27.1	25.7
B. Official Data: [b]								
Total crop and animal production	100.0	74.8	87.5	99.3	104.2	103.1	95.3	102.3
"Net product"	n.a.	100.0	127.6	129.2	119.0	114.6	94.2	109.8

[a] Preliminary data.

[b] Valued at 1955 prices, for 1961–1963 valued at 1960 prices, *Stat. roč.-1958*, pp. 29–30, *ibid. 1961*, pp. 38–39, 230 and *Stat. přeh.*, 1964, No. 4, pp. 136–137.

SOURCES: 1934–1961: Gregor Lazarcik, *The Performance of Socialist Agriculture . . .* ,(New York: L.W. International Financial Research, Inc., 1963), Tables 7, 11, 14–15; 1962–1963 calculated from *Stat. roč.-1964*, pp. 233–280.

creased from 33.9 to 25.7 percent of total agricultural output. The ratio of crop output to animal products output decreased from one-half to one-third from 1948 to 1963.

6) A comparison of our figures with official Czechoslovak calculations show close agreement in crop and animal production. Although the general pattern in the official and in our series of net product is to a certain degree similar, the year-to-year differences between the two measures are in some years very large. The abrupt, significant, upward and downward jumps in official net-product series are caused by institutional changes affecting the scope of the agricultural sector and its series. Therefore, the official measure of net product does not express correctly the net product generated in agriculture, and hence its contribution to national product.

7) Although a few small items of output and expenses had to be estimated, the result of a test indicates that the maximum error in our data is less than ± 1 percent and in the net product the error is most likely less than ± 2 percent. Technical literature and abundant information on procedures used and problems encountered in the calculation of output and input measures in other countries (i.e., Western Europe and the United States) were helpful in deriving acceptable measures of the Czechoslovak agricultural performance.

All measures derived in this article are interdependent. They all, however, ultimately reflect the amounts. quality, and combinations of factors of production used and on the effectiveness of their use or productivity.

PRODUCTIVITY

Measures of productivity in agriculture are usually derived from the relationship between the volume of output and the volume of input of one or more of the factors of production (see Table 2).

Yields.—Although the yields of some crops increased 25 to 50 percent (e.g., grains), the yields of other crops (e.g., potatoes and hay) remained about 30 percent below the prewar level. As a result, total crop production per hectare remained around the prewar level. Yields in Slovakia, however, increased at a faster rate than for the whole country.

Yields per head of livestock of three most important products—milk per cow, meat per pig, and eggs per hen—remained during most of the postwar period 15 to 25 percent below the prewar level.

Output, Gross and Net Product per Unit of Capital.—These measures are ratios of output, gross or net product to total input at 1936

TABLE 2

PRODUCTIVITY INDICATORS AND RELATED INDICES, CZECHOSLOVAKIA, SELECTED YEARS

Item	1934–1938 average	1948	1953	1958	1960	1961	1962	1963[a]
Output per man-year	100.0	80.3	111.2	144.3	182.3	187.9	182.4	197.8
Gross product per man-year	100.0	74.1	99.7	127.1	149.6	151.7	138.2	154.1
Net product per man-year	100.0	70.7	95.4	122.7	142.8	141.7	123.5	145.0
Machinery and equipment per man-year	100.0	123.6	154.9	188.9	238.7	284.5	330.4	373.0
Capital input per man-year	100.0	120.5	168.2	217.7	309.9	340.6	380.7	410.0
Total capital per man-year	100.0	102.3	127.0	138.1	171.7	186.3	196.5	207.0
Output per unit of capital	100.0	80.0	88.6	101.3	103.5	99.2	91.3	97.0
Output-input ratio	1.05	0.78	0.89	0.94	0.92	0.88	0.78	0.87
Output-input ratio, as index	100.0	74.3	84.4	89.5	87.6	83.8	74.3	82.9
Man-years, index	100.0	92.5	76.8	72.7	60.5	56.9	55.0	54.5
Total input, index	100.0	102.6	102.6	114.8	121.9	124.5	131.1	135.0
Total crop and animal production per man-year, adjusted	120.8	100.0	139.4	166.5	209.2	216.5	208.2	228.1
Total crop and animal production per man-year, official	n.a.	100.0	157.9	176.9	221.0	231.7	220.8	240.0

[a] Preliminary data.

SOURCES: Gregor Lazarcik, *op. cit.*, Tables 19, 20; for 1962–1963, calculated from *Stat. roč.-1964*, pp. 233–280.

prices. Capital here includes all assets engaged in productive activity in agriculture, estimated in terms of its replacement value.

The output per unit of all capital remained below the prewar level for all years except 1958 and 1960. The gross and net product, however, remained very much below the prewar level. The reason for this sizable decrease is to be found in the great increase of expenses in the postwar year.

Output, Gross, and Net Product per Unit of Labor.—Labor accounted for about one-fourth of the cost of all inputs into agriculture in 1960. Output per unit of labor depends on the effectiveness of the labor unit which, in turn, is determined by the combination of several elements.

The indexes of output, gross, and net product per unit of labor are ratios of indexes of output, gross, and net product to the index of labor input expressed in man-years of work.[12]

There are some data available which indicate a change in the quality of man-years in the period under study. The age structure shifted toward older age groups,[13] and this shift affected efficiency adversely.

The output, gross, and net product per man-year is shown in Table 2. The 98 percent increase in output per man-year is attributable mainly to increased use of capital in the postwar period. Increased mechanization reduced the man-years' requirement by almost one-half from the prewar period to 1964 while the quantity of capital (including land) per man about doubled. Thus, the increased output per unit of labor was mainly the result of substituting capital for labor.

The indexes of gross and net product per man-year show a much smaller rate of increase than those of output because of the great increase in production expenses. The quantity of all inputs increased 35 percent from prewar to 1964 (see Table 2).

Output-Input Ratio.—The output-input ratio developed in this study is the relationship of agricultural output to all production inputs used to produce that output at 1936 prices. This ratio measures average aggregate productivity of all inputs together (operating expenses, depreciation, interest on capital and cost of labor). The cost of labor includes all labor—that is, hired workers, farmers, and unpaid family helpers—in agriculture expressed in full man-years, valued at 1936 average annual earnings per hired worker in agriculture. The output-input ratio indicates whether the agricultural sector would operate at a "net loss" (if the

[12] One man-year is equivalent to one adult person working full time in agriculture.

[13] *Stat. roč.-1959,* p. 260.

ratio is less than 1) or a "net profit" (a ratio of more than 1), if the prevailing "market prices" had to be paid for all inputs.

In Czechoslovakia the ratio for 1934–1938 indicates that had the farmers purchased all inputs at prevailing 1936 "market" prices, they would have realized a net entrepreneurial profit amounting to 5 percent of the value of all inputs; after the war, however, they would have realized a net loss amounting to more than 10 percent of the value of all inputs for most years (Table 2).

Changes in the output-input ratio over time are of greater significance than magnitude of the ratio in any given year. An increase in the ratio indicates a rise in "total productivity" due to one or a combination of several factors, such as improved technology, enterpreneurship, and (possibly) the effects of increasing returns to scale. Conversely, a decrease in the ratio indicates a decline in "total productivity" and may be the result of deterioration of technology, detrimental changes in the organization of production, and eventually of decreasing returns to scale of individual farms. While changes in the ratio over time are in part due to the "index number problem," [14] they have, nevertheless, been used in recent years to provide a measure, however imperfect, of changes in efficiency or technological progress, in the economy as a whole or in individual industries.[15]

Provided that the quality of output or of input does not change over time, changes in the output-input ratio are here presumed to be the result of: (1) changes of one or, more likely, several intangible inputs (i.e., changes in basic science, technology, education, training, and economic organization); (2) the effects of all other indogenous causes (i.e., increasing or decreasing returns to scale, nature of tax system, character of government subsidies, regulation of prices, and all other government regulations affecting the efficiency of the use of resources); (3) the effects of other exogenous factors (e.g., weather). All these factors are related in a complex way and constitute integral determinants of changes in "total productivity." [16]

[14] Vernon W. Ruttan, *Technological Progress in the Meat Packing Industry, 1917–1947* (Washington, D.C.: U.S. Department of Agriculture, 1954) pp. 15–20. Among other things, the author discusses the bias in output-input ratio, caused by changes in relative prices.

[15] George J. Stigler, *Trends in Output and Employment* (New York: National Bureau of Economic Research, 1947), pp. 49–53; G. T. Barton, Martin R. Cooper, "Relation of Agricultural Production Inputs," *Review of Economics and Statistics,* XXX:2 (May, 1948), 117–126, and "Changing Efficiency of the American Economy," *ibid.,* XXXIV:3 (August, 1952), 214–232; and numerous other writings on this subject.

[16] Moses Abramovitz correctly characterizes productivity as a "measure of our

In Czechoslovak agriculture, sizable changes in "total productivty" have occurred from year to year. In the early postwar period productivity was improving, but since 1952 it remained below 90 percent of the prewar level, except for 1958 and 1960. Because the data were not available, the ratios could not be calculated in 1956 prices. Despite its limitations, the output-input ratio is a useful measure for the researcher who is examining the causes affecting the productivity changes.

FACTORS AFFECTING PRODUCTION AND PRODUCTIVITY

The more significant factors which affected Czechoslovak agricultural production and productivity can be divided into three groups: War damage and weather conditions; Production inputs; and Organization of production and entrepreneurship. We shall examine their impact only in general qualitative terms.

War Damage and Weather Conditions.—The war losses in agriculture were officially estimated at 44 billion crowns at 1947 prices, that is, over one-fifth of the value of capital excluding land in agriculture in 1947. The number of pigs was reduced by one-third and the number of poultry by one-half. Damages to farm buildings and inventories were great, particularly in Slovakia. As a consequence, immediate productive capacity was substantially diminished. In 1945 agricultural production amounted to only 56 percent of the prewar level.[17]

Weather conditions affect agricultural production more than production in any other sector. Unfavorable weather in 1947 caused a sharp drop in crop production amounting to 32 percent of the low 1946 level. The sharp decrease in production in 1952 was also due largely to bad weather. The effect of these noneconomic factors cannot be eliminated, though they introduce an exogenous element into the pure economic relationship described.

Production Inputs.—Brief observations are made below concerning changes in the more important inputs (land use, mechanization, improvement in farming methods, capital investment, and labor) which affected production and productivity.

Although the agricultural land decreased by about 7 percent from 1934–1938 to 1964, the productivity of the remaining land rose due to

ignorance" concerning the causes of economic growth and "an indication of where we need to concentrate our attention." See Moses Abramovitz, *Resource and Output Trends in the U.S. Since 1870,* Occasional Paper No. 52 (New York: National Bureau of Economic Research, 1956), p. 11.

[17] United Nations, Economic Commission for Europe, *Economic Survey of Europe in 1948* (Geneva: United Nations, 1949), p. 11.

increased application of fertilizers. The increased yields helped to increase output per man because increment in the yield is proportionately much greater than the increment in man-hours attributable to fertilizer-spreading and harvesting work.

Acute shortage of labor in postwar years gave an impetus to rapid mechanization of agriculture. To a large degree, human and animal power were replaced by mechanical power. The number of tractors increased greatly from 1934–1938 to 1964 and the volume of all machinery and equipment rose by 120 percent. This development is reflected in higher output per man-year.

Mechanization, however, was concentrated on state and collective farms, while on privately owned farms there was probably no change. The allocation of machinery to various segments of agriculture seemed not to have been made in all instances according to the principle of equalizing the marginal productivity of machinery in all segments.[18]

Scientific research for improvement of crops and livestock breeds, highly developed in Czechoslovakia, undoubtedly contributed to the increase in yields and quality of products. The number of students at vocational and agricultural colleges increased from 9,915 in 1948–49 to 55,000 in 1963–64.

The volume of investment in agriculture increased greatly since 1948. In private farms, however, a net disinvestment was noticeable since 1950. In this year the gross new investment in buildings on private farms amounted to less than 100 million crowns valued at 1956 prices, but the depreciation charge was estimated at about 500 million crowns. There were many critics in the Czeshoslovak press who declared that the productivity of new investment in state and collective farms was decreasing because of unnecessarily costly installations. The productivity of new investment in stables, for example, decreased by 68.5 percent from 1952 to 1957.[19]

A substantial decrease in labor input was possible by the substitution of capital for labor. On the whole, the quality of labor changed adversely after the war because of the rapidly aging labor force. In 1963, about 26 percent of workers in agriculture were more than 60 years of age.

In summary, the total volume of all measurable inputs increased 35 percent between 1934–1938 and 1963; some of the nonmeasurable inputs, such as technology and available knowledge, probably increased at an even higher rate than the measurable inputs. Yet the volume of

[18] *Zem. ek.*, No. 2 (1959), pp. 107–112.

[19] *Za soc. zem.*, No. 12 (1957), p. 702; *Zem. ek.*, No. 2 (1959), pp. 107–112.

TABLE 3

INDEXES OF AGRICULTURAL INPUTS AND OUTPUT IN WESTERN EUROPE AND CZECHOSLOVAKIA, 1934–38, 1956

Item	1934–38	1956	
	Czechoslovakia and western Europe	Czechoslovakia	Western Europe
Agricultural land	100	96	97
Labor force	100	78	80
Tractors	100	836	1,002
Fertilizers	100	409	178
Horses	100	83	65
Imported feed	100	436	190
Output	100	99	125
Output per man-year	100	124	156
Output-input ratio	100 [a]	96	112

[a] 1950.

SOURCES: Gregor Lazarcik, *op. cit.*, and U.S. Department of Agriculture, *Expansion of Agricultural Production*, pp. iv–v and 46.

output reached the prewar level only in 1958 and it stagnated thereafter. As a result, the "total productivity" remained below the prewar level in the whole postwar period. One major factor, organization of production and "entrepreneurship," remains to be considered as a possible cause of the deterioration in "total productivity."

Organization of Production and Entrepreneurship.—Organization of production has undergone basic changes since the war. A hypothesis that these changes were mainly the reason for deterioration in "total productivity" may be tested empirically by comparing Czechoslovak agricultural performance with that of Western European countries having broadly similar natural and economic conditions in agriculture. The private enterprise system, however, remained in Western Europe, while in Czechoslovakia it was replaced by a centrally planned socialist system.

Since the war, the trend in major production inputs of these two areas has been almost parallel (Table 3).

The output in West Europe rose 25 percent, but in Czechoslovakia decreased by about 1 percent. The "total productivity" between 1950 and 1956 increased by 12 percent in West Europe and decreased by 4 percent in Czechoslovakia. Since there is only one major variable of any significance, organization of production and entrepreneurship, the relatively less efficient performance in Czechoslovakia must be attributed largely to this change. To a certain degree, however, the price system might also have been the reason for showing an unfavorable performance in Czechoslovakia.

The increase in "total productivity" in West Europe was chiefly the result of improved technology used on farms.[20] In Czechoslovakia, however, the probable positive effect of improved technology seems to be more than offset by the negative effect of basic structural changes in organization of production, changes imposed by the state in the ownership of land, entrepreneurship, and rewards of agriculture.

The success in agricultural production is dependent upon technical knowledge and skills which are specific to each particular area and they require long experience to attain. In a privately owned family farm system, much of this specialized knowledge is passed from father to son who traditionally inherits the management of the farm and continues to improve agricultural methods in order to achieve the greatest possible output with a given amount of input.

With the advent of collectivization and of the rapid expansion of the state farms, this traditional pattern was changed. The farmers, who were pressured into joining the collectives, or hired workers in the state farms, had no authority to influence or to make decisions concerning the organization of production. Such decisions were made by managers whose selection was influenced by the Communist government with more emphasis on loyalty to the regime than on managerial ability. This political element in the managerial aspect of farming resulted in inefficiencies in collective-farm production. The inexperienced managers failed to recognize that state-prescribed farming plans disregarded the optimum cropping patterns for certain crops in specific areas, and this resulted in yield decreases (e.g., oil crops and fibers).

Central planning and collectivization affected adversely the personal incentives of farmers. Private farmers lost their interest for improving their farms because of continuing government pressure for collectivization; collective farmers already had lost their ownership of land and their economic independence, and they had been reduced to the role of laborers. The incentives of private farmers were further diminished by governmental manipulation of prices which affected their rewards.

In 1949, discriminatory multiple prices directed against private farmers were introduced to force them into collective farms. As a result the average money income of private farmers amounted to only 47 percent of that of collective farmers in 1953. The limited income of private farmers did not permit them to purchase machinery, fertilizers, and

[20] United Nations, Economic Commission for Europe, Food and Agriculture Organization, *European Agriculture* (Geneva: United Nations, 1954), pp. 42–43.

other production requisites, even if they desired to improve production. Although the inputs into agriculture as a whole rose substantially, their diversion from private to collective and state farms resulted in a less efficient allocation of productive resources and hence in lower over-all output to input ratios.

In 1953, the government had recognized that if agriculture were to supply the growing population and the growing urban areas, the allocation of productive resources to farms and manufactured consumer goods to farmers had to be increased. Therefore, a new agricultural policy was initiated consisting of: first, a diminished pressure to collectivize; second, increased incomes in a variety of ways—by decreased prices of agricultural inputs, by increased prices of agricultural products, and by reduced taxation in cash and kind; third, allocation to the agriculture as a whole of greatly increased volume of productive resources. As a result of these measures the terms of trade of farmers improved significantly between 1953 and 1964.

This favorable development of price relationships had a perceptible effect on output in later years. With the renewed government pressure for collectivization after 1956, however, the favorable effects of the new policy were partly reduced by again diminishing incentives of private farmers. Stagnation of production between 1956 and 1964 was the consequence.

THE NEW ECONOMIC MODEL OF CZECHOSLOVAKIA AND THE POSITION OF AGRICULTURE

Until 1962 Czechoslovakia's economic growth was satisfactory. averaging about 5 percent annually in rate of growth in her gross national product for the period 1948–1961.[21] In 1962–1964, however, a real economic depression struck the country's planned economy. According to official data, the national income in 1962 (Marxist definition) increased only 1.4 percent; in 1963, it decreased 2.5 percent;[22] and in 1964 it remained at the depressed level of the year 1963.[23] The output of usable goods probably fell more drastically.

The New Economic Model.—The economic collapse led to major criticism of the effectiveness of the centralized planning policies, which

[21] Gregor Lazarcik, George J. Staller, Vaclav Holesovsky, "Czechoslovak Gross National Product by Sector of Origin and by Use, 1937, 1948–1962," unpublished, Columbia University, Project on National Income in East Central Europe (1965), Table 3.

[22] *Stat. přeh.*, No. 2 (1964), p. 70 (Supplement to *Stat.*, No. 7 (1964).

[23] *Stat.*, No. 4 (1965), p. 145.

had been heretofore patterned on those of the Soviet Union. Under the influence of leading economists the government undertook at the plenary meeting of the Central Committee of the Communist Party, January 27–28, 1965, to change the economic system radically.[24] The changes, extending over a period of years, are intended to create a more liberalized market system in which the law of supply and demand would be given a greater role. The new economic policy was to be introduced in the main sectors of the economy over several years, beginning in 1966.

In the new system, the central planning agencies are supposed to elaborate long-range forecasts for 10–15-year periods, from which more detailed five-year plans will be prepared. Actual annual plans will, in fact, implement in broad guidelines the tasks drawn up in the five-year plans. It is not as yet clear to what degree the annual plans will depend on proposals submitted by the enterprises and the regional trade unions. The central planners will continue to plan: capital investments; the relative position of the various branches of industry (light and heavy industry); balanced growth between the various regions of the country. Prices of basic raw materials and the fundamental necessities of life (e.g., bread, meat, housing) will remain fixed by central planners, and prices of other goods will be allowed to fluctuate between set minimums and maximums.

The managers of enterprises, trusts or branch concerns will be vested with great economic power and relative freedom in decision making. They will have the power to hire, transfer, and dismiss subordinates. They will be free to bargain prices within allowed limits with their suppliers and also set the prices of their products between limits specified by the government. In certain fields (e.g., some fruits, seasonal vegetables, certain intermediate products) the prices will be governed by the supply and demand and free agreements between producers and marketing organizations. The prices, in general, should reflect production costs both at home and abroad. The wage policy will become more flexible and the employees' remuneration will depend on profits. The performance of an enterprise will be judged by its profitability rather than on its ability to meet quantitative plans. The State Bank is to play a more important role than heretofore by using credit policy as an economic lever.

Economic experiments with the new model are already in effect in several industries. Enterprises producing almost one-half the output of

[24] *Rudé Právo,* January 30 and February 2, 1965.

iron, steel, and building construction and about one-fourth of the total production of heavy engineering, chemicals, power generating, and consumer goods are experimenting with the new economic model.

The enterprises run by local administrations will be charged to produce badly needed services of better quality and will compete with cooperatives. There will be a stimulation of competition between the state, cooperative, and local government network of retail stores.

It should be noted that the Communist party is to play a leading role as a chief unifying force in carrying out the reforms which are to correct old deficiencies rather than to set up a whole new path. The Party is to combat the "incorrect" view that the new policies represent a victory of liberalism in the communist economy.[25]

It remains to be seen whether the reforms will work. In the past there were many reforms too, but the optimistic projections never materialized.

The Position of Agriculture in the New Economic Model.—In the nonagricultural sectors the economic reforms are being introduced as a reaction to the three-year-long economic slump. In agriculture, however, the crisis arose ever since the inception of collectivization in 1949. During the past 15 years, all efforts of the Communist regime to expand agricultural production by large-scale investments in agriculture, by raising prices of some agricultural products, and by providing health services and social security for agricultural workers proved unsuccessful.

The gravity of the agricultural problem requires a bold and thorough study of ways how to achieve finally a real improvement in production and productivity. Thus far the government has not revealed details on its new economic policy for agriculture. General proposals have been elaborated in several research institutes in agricultural economics and submitted for discussion to agricultural specialists at universities and research institutes and to managers of the state and collective farms.

These proposals of the new economic model in agriculture may be summarized as follows.[26]

Role of Planning.—In agriculture, just as in other sectors of the economy, the central planners are to prepare perspective, economic forecasts for 10–15-year periods in general terms; the macroeconomic five-year plans should be the result of the coordination between the central long-term forecasts and the actual annual plans. The general level of prices of agricultural products and production requisites would

[25] *Ibid.*, February 3, 1965.
[26] *Zem. ek.*, No. 5–6 (1965), pp. 247–339.

become an integral part of five-year plans to which one-year plans would be linked. The preparation of the annual production and investment plans would be made by the agricultural establishments instead of central-planning agencies as heretofore. The state authority would directly prescribe to collectives and state farms only the percentage of gross income tax to be levied by the state. It is evident that these proposals, if accepted, will mean a great stride forward in liberalization from regimentation of the organization of agricultural production.

Function of Prices.—The proposals are in favor of improvement in the level of agricultural prices which would create incentives for agricultural workers to increase their gross income. According to official Czechoslovak sources, agricultural prices about doubled from a low level in 1953 to 1964,[27] and the real net income of collective farmers rose 21 percent from 1958 to 1964 while that of workers in the socialized sector of the economy rose only 11 percent in the same period. Nevertheless, the net annual income of a collective farmer from all sources averaged only 85.5 percent of that of a worker in the rest of the socialized economy between 1961 and 1964.[28] The average number of working hours the collective farmer works in a week is, however, 14 percent higher than per worker in nonagricultural sectors. The differences in earnings per hour are, therefore, greater than the average yearly earnings in agriculture and nonagricultural sectors would suggest. For example, a tractor driver earns 4.50 crowns an hour in agriculture and 6.75 in industry, or 50 percent more.[29] Thus the main reason for the shortage of labor in agriculture has been substantially lower earnings than in industry.

The economic model proposals aim at adjusting the agricultural prices upward to the extent that the net income of an average collective farmer and worker in agriculture will be equal to that in nonagricultural sectors. Also, the earning differences now existing between state farm workers and collective farmers will be eliminated by a uniform pricing policy for the whole of agriculture. As in the other sectors of the economy, in agriculture there are also to be three categories of prices: fixed, fixed within minimum and maximum limits, and free market prices. The fixed prices are proposed for major staple commodities, such as wheat, rye, barley, sugar beets, hops, potatoes, beef cattle, hogs, milk, eggs, and production requisites from other sectors. Prices which could change within maximum and minimum limits would be applied to

[27] *Stat. roč.-1959*, p. 389 and *Stat. roč.-1964*, p. 394.
[28] *Stat.*, No. 4 (1965), pp. 157–161.
[29] *Zem. nov.*, December 6, 1963.

vegetables and fruits. The free market prices would apply to products of minor importance, such as aromatic and medical plants, forest fruits, game, and all intermediate products transacted between agricultural enterprises. The over-all structure and level of prices should reflect the actual production costs.[30]

New Position for Agricultural Enterprise.—In the new model, the agricultural production units—individual collective farms and state farms—are to enjoy much greater independence from central planning in deciding what to produce and how much to produce. The yearly production plans are to be prepared by the managements of these farms. The existing differential rent resulting from different productivity of land would be eliminated through special levies by the state. The total gross income would serve as a base for normal levies by the government. The remaining gross income would be at the disposal of each enterprise for its expansion and for distribution to employees in the form of wages and profits, if any. New investment would be financed largely from retained profits of enterprises. Bank credit should become more liberalized to provide flexibility in its use by agricultural enterprises at their own discretion.

It is hoped that the differences in the organization of production and management between the collective and state farms will be eliminated and that uniform principles for management will be elaborated. The proposals favor increased specialization within individual enterprises through merger into larger units. The individual enterprises should be organized into syndicates which would perform functions beyond the capability of individual enterprises or which could be performed better by them. There is a great interest in the application of modern mathematical methods in finding the optimum solutions for production and management of agricultural enterprises.

Most of these proposals seem to go in the right direction. It remains to be seen, however, in what form they will be adopted and what will be their effect of agricultural production and income of farm workers.

CONCLUSIONS

The materials presented bear on questions central to the appraisal of an economic system in agriculture. One of the basic tests of performance of any economic system is: How large a quantity of economically useful goods and services has it produced per unit of productive inputs? The

[30] *Zem. ek.*, No. 5–6 (1965), p. 272.

findings of this study show that the output per unit of productive inputs has been less under predominantly socialist agriculture for most of the postwar years than under the prewar predominantly private ownership of agriculture. In Western Europe and North America where private ownership has remained, agricultural output increased 52 and 66 percent, respectively, between 1934–1938 and 1963,[31] while in Czechoslovakia output rose only by 6–8 percent for the same period. In Western countries, there are also governmental controls and influences, but many of them, such as governmental research, extension services, education programs, and land reform, are effecting a rise in productivity of agriculture. In other East European countries where agriculture was collectivized, the performance of agriculture was similar to that of Czechoslovakia. In Poland, however, where collectives account for only 1.1 percent of agricultural land, the agricultural output rose 48 percent between 1949 and 1961–1962.[32]

In Czechoslovakia, one of the most important reasons for the stagnation seems to be of sociological origin. As the result of historical development of rural life, the Czechoslovak farmer has a deep-rooted sense of private ownership, individual freedom, religious feeling, and family farming. All these were challenged by the Communist government through the imposition of the socialist system of farming. Most farmers reacted by passively resisting to cooperate with this new system. It remains to be seen whether the passive resistance of farmers will be broken in the future. During the 1950's and early 1960's, however, it was one of the major factors negatively affecting Czechoslovak agricultural output and net product.

Why was agriculture collectivized in Czechoslovakia, when it had been accompanied by lower performance? The planners probably anticipated a temporary decrease in output but believed that in the long run, the collectives would be more productive than the small private farms. The deciding factor in the government's decision to collectivize agriculture, besides Soviet pressure, may have been that the country's economy could afford "temporary" difficulties, even a decrease in agricultural output, without seriously impairing the fulfillment of industrial plans.

The relatively strong position of Czechoslovak industry on the world market makes it possible and, for some products, even advantageous for the country to exchange the industrial goods for agricultural products through international trade. Before the war, exports of food from

[31] Food and Agricultural Organization of the United Nations, *op. cit.* (in n. 3, 1958), pp. 27–28 and *op. cit.* (in n. 4, 1964), pp. 27–30.

[32] *Rocz. stat.-1963,* p. 203.

Czechoslovakia approximately balanced imports, while after the war the country became a net importer of agricultural products. It seems that the comparative advantage of the Czechoslovak economy lies more in industry than in agriculture—an advantage that causes a rapid decrease of the labor force in agriculture. The economy's performance in other sectors has been more satisfactory. According to the official data, the net product in industry increased 194 percent, in construction 260 percent, in the whole economy 165 percent—but only 5 percent in agriculture from 1948 to 1963.[33] Even if we accept a very significant upward bias in the stated data, the performance would still be satisfactory since Czechoslovakia was already industrialized before the war. Despite the emphasis on industry, the government desires much to increase agricultural output since this will decrease the country's dependence on food from abroad. In recent years Communist-bloc leaders have recognized the failure of their policies in agriculture. Major steps have been taken toward decentralization of the organization of production and relaxation of price discrimination. In 1958 the Soviet Union abolished machine-tractor stations and obligatory deliveries at low prices fixed by the state. In Czechoslovakia machine-tractor stations were liquidated in 1959–1960. Their machinery was sold to collectives. The discriminatory multiple-price system was repealed in 1960, and uniform higher prices (15 percent higher on the average than the weighted average of preexisting prices) are being paid to farmers.[34] Planning is being regionally decentralized with management receiving greater freedom concerning detailed decisions of production. The government is channeling more resources into agriculture. The Third Five-Year Plan provided for 35 percent increases in "real" income of collective farmers and a 40 percent increase in gross production between 1961 and 1965. In the 1961-1964 period, however, the agricultural production remained below the 1960 level.[35] It remains to be seen whether the proposed new economic model will bring radical improvement.

Whatever the future performance may be, our findings show that up to now, under the Communist system of government, the agricultural sector has been producing less efficiently than agricultural sectors under predominantly private enterprise systems in other countries.

[33] *Stat. roč.-1964,* pp. 23, 42.
[34] *Plán. hosp.,* No. 7–8 (1959), pp. 495–522.
[35] *Stat.,* No. 4 (1965), p. 145.

COMMENT

Maurice Ernst

The postwar performance of Czechoslovak agriculture is a poor advertisement for Communist agricultural policies and institutions and a source of considerable difficulties for Czechoslovakia. Dr. Lazarcik's able and useful study leads inescapably to this conclusion, which evidently was also arrived at by the Czechoslovak government. I will first remark on various aspects of Lazarcik's estimates of production and productivity in Czechoslovak agriculture and then turn to the broader question of international comparisons of agricultural performance.

The measures of production seem both careful and thorough. We are indeed fortunate that the primary Czechoslovak data on harvests, animal numbers, and so forth, are considered reliable enough to be used without adjustment. Not having to estimate or adjust the basic production data made it possible to move rapidly to the calculation of different types of output measures and to estimates of productivity.

The productivity estimates are useful, although many lines of analysis remain to be explored before the specific causes of the poor postwar performance of Czechoslovak agriculture can be pinpointed. It would help to know how sensitive are the estimates of "total productivity" to changes in the weights assigned to individual inputs. Further study of changes in the quality and utilization of individual inputs also suggests itself, especially an analysis of labor inputs by age, sex, and, if possible, hours worked. Finally, information on the distribution of output and inputs among the various types of farming units—state farms, collective farms, private plots of collective farms, private farms—is likely to give new insights into some of the specific effects of collectivization.

The "new Czechoslovak economic model" in agriculture, the subject of the next to last section in Lazarcik's essay, has not yet been introduced, and we do not know how it will operate. Even if a serious attempt is made to increase the independence of collective farms, there is no guarantee that the Communist party cadres will reduce their interference. And it remains unclear what kinds of incentives are envisaged to encourage hard and efficient work on collective land. The partial forms of share-cropping that Hungary has introduced would be difficult to use in the more mechanized agriculture of Czechoslovakia and there is in any case no indication that the Czechoslovaks are prepared to imitate the Hungarians. No doubt some improvement can be made in the operation of agricultural institutions, but it seems best to reserve judgment on the "new economic model" until the Party has resolved for itself some basic questions about the relationship of political control to economic efficiency.

In regard to international comparisons Lazarcik calculates that total productivity declined in Czechoslovak agriculture while it rose in Western European agriculture as a whole between prewar years and 1956. Some readily available indicators suggest that in most other Eastern European Communist countries also, productivity trends were less favorable than in Western Europe. According to U.S. Department of Agriculture estimates,[36] agricultural output in all of Eastern Europe, excluding Yugoslavia, had barely surpassed the prewar level by the early 1960's. By contrast, output in Western Europe had risen about 50 percent from prewar levels. Since the early 1950's Eastern European output has grown, but more slowly than Western European output. Although the output trends were very different in the two areas, the pattern and rates of growth of various input indicators appear to have been roughly similar—for example the use of chemical fertilizer increased rapidly, and tractors were substituted for agricultural labor. The input indicators, of course, are quite inadequate for any firm conclusions on comparative trends in productivity. It is clear that consumption of chemical fertilizer on the whole increased at least as rapidly in Eastern Europe as in Western Europe, but many other current inputs, on which data are lacking, are important. The data on agricultural employment differ a great deal in definition and reporting. There are practically no comparative statistics of the growth of fixed capital, except for the stock of tractors, which has risen at roughly similar rates in both areas but does not reflect the full range of mechanization, much less the use of other types of agricultural capital. There is, however, another approach to comparisons of capital inputs—the comparisons of expenditures on agricultural investments.

[36] *The 1963 Western Europe Agricultural Situation,* Economic Research Service, Supplement No. 2 to *The 1963 World Agricultural Situation* (Washington, D.C.: U.S. Department of Agriculture, 1963), p. 4; *The 1963 Eastern Europe Agricultural Situation,* Economic Research Service, Supplement No. 3 to *The 1963 World Agricultural Situation* (Washington, D.C.: U.S. Department of Agriculture, 1963), p. 2; *The 1964 Western Europe Agricultural Situation,* Economic Research Service, ERS-Foreign-72 (Washington, D.C.: U.S. Department of Agriculture, 1964), p. 3; *The 1964 Eastern Europe Agricultural Situation,* Economic Research Service, ERS-Foreign-73 (Washington, D.C.: U.S. Department of Agriculture, 1964), p. 2.

Investment statistics clearly show that the Eastern European countries since the mid-1950's have spent relatively more on agriculture than the Western European countries.[37] In 1955–1963, Bulgaria put about 28 percent of its gross fixed investment into agriculture and forestry, Rumania and Hungary 18 percent, and Czechoslovakia 16 percent. These are considerably higher shares than in Western Europe, with very few exceptions, and differences in the contribution of agriculture to GNP do not account for the differences in the investment shares. It is interesting to note that the Polish share was only 12 percent, less than in many Western countries, but Poland still has a predominantly private agriculture. The relatively high expenditure for agricultural investment in Eastern Europe is even more striking if we allow for the fact that the Eastern countries tended to invest a larger share of their GNP at factor cost than the Western European countries. Using estimates of the share of gross fixed investment in GNP at factor cost,[38] I calculate that Bulgaria devoted nearly 10 percent of its GNP to agricultural investment (5 times more than Greece); Czechoslovakia, and Hungary nearly 4½ percent (3 times more than France and 75 percent more than Italy); and Poland more than 3 percent. No Western European country which publishes appropriate data used as much as 3½ percent of GNP for this purpose, and nearly all used considerably less than 3 percent.

These investment statistics are not entirely comparable. For some Eastern European countries, they include investments for purposes not normally classified as agricultural—for example, construction of housing and some food-processing plants by Bulgarian collective farms, and of servicing facilities by machine-tractor stations. It is also possible that unit costs in the Communist countries are relatively unfavorable to agricultural investments. However, the differences in relative investments are so striking that other explanations appear to be needed. Part of the explanation may lie in the heavy requirements for new construc-

[37] *Statisticheski Godishnik Na Narodna Republika Bulgaria* (Sofia: 1963), p. 228; *Annaurul Statistic Al RPR 1965* (Bucarest: 1965), pp. 344–345; *Statisztikai Evkonyv 1964* (Budapest: 1965), p. 42; *Stat. roč.-1965*, p. 151 and *Stat. roč.-1966*, p. 103; *Rocz. Stat.-1964, p. 78.* Data for the OEDC countries are from *OEDC Statistics of National Accounts, 1950–1961* and *OECD General Statistics*, January, 1965.

[38] Thad P. Alton and associates, *Czechoslovak National Income and Product, 1947–48 and 1955–56* (New York: Columbia University Press, 1962), p. 234, *Hungarian National Income and Product in 1955* (New York: Columbia University Press, 1963), p. 229, *Polish National Income and Product in 1954, 1955 and 1956* (New York: Columbia University Press, 1965), p. 227, and "National Income and Product in Bulgaria," occasional paper (unpublished) of the Project on National Income in East Central Europe.

tion that result from collectivization. In Czechoslovakia, for example, the construction of common shelters for livestock is closely correlated with the rate of collectivization—such investments are a kind of overhead cost of collectivization. Moreover, they were often poorly planned and executed. Much analysis of the investment statistics is needed, but these data are additional indications that collectivization was very expensive. Indeed, together with the input indicators, these data strongly suggest that the postwar lag in Eastern European agriculture was not the result of inadequate inputs by Western European standards, but of inefficient use of inputs.

ANDRZEJ KORBONSKI

Peasant Agriculture in Socialist Poland since 1956: An Alternative to Collectivization

In contrast to other sectors of the economy, agriculture in the Soviet bloc can be said to constitute both a political and economic problem. It is with this in mind that the situation in Polish agriculture will be discussed here. This is perhaps one factor which makes the Polish case unique in the bloc. Everywhere else, to a greater or lesser degree, agriculture lost its political connotation, retaining its predominantly economic character. This is not to imply that the former disappeared with the completion of the collectivization program. The border line between politics and economics in the Communist bloc is tenuous, and economic decisions have usually a strong political flavor (and vice versa). What is meant here is simply the fact that collectivization in its initial stages can be considered primarily as a political measure; only when it has been accomplished does the economic factor assume the main role.

This is not the case in Poland and we will, therefore, discuss both the economics and politics of Polish agriculture. The economic performance, at the present time, as it has been since 1956, seems to occupy the attention of the Communist rulers, and it will receive more attention in this study. Nevertheless, one of the most interesting elements in the Polish situation is the continuing search for a solution of the agricultural problem which has been going on since the mass dissolution of the collective farms in the fall of 1956. Although couched in economic terms, the fascinating dialogue carried on by a number of top Party and non-Party agricultural experts touches on the basic issue, namely, how a professedly socialist country can encompass an individually owned agriculture which provides livelihood for almost 40 percent of its population. The last part of the study will be devoted to the discussion of that dialogue.

It should be stated what will not be discussed. I shall ignore the knotty subject of optimum farm size, as this cannot be treated here with the care and attention it deserves. Nor will the socialized sector in Polish agriculture be discussed extensively. To begin with, collective farms ("producer cooperatives" in Polish terminology) are a marginal factor in Poland. At the end of 1964 there were only 1,246 of them, representing a decline of 288 since the fall of 1956. They cultivate 1 percent of agricultural land and account for 1 percent of total output and 1.2 percent of marketable production.[1] These figures show that the collective farms did not recover from the debacle of 1956 and that the Party in the past 9 years has made no attempt to reintroduce them as the sole form of socialized agriculture by pushing them down the peasants' throats.

Those farms that do exist can hardly be called collective in the usual (i.e., Soviet) sense. In the words of one of the experts they are in fact "private associations of individual peasants farming common land."[2] They are characterized by the absence of rigid limits with regard to the size of the household plots and by the fact that many farms raise livestock only on private plots. The post-1956 collectives, eager to achieve independence from the state-owned machine-tractor stations (MTS), managed to purchase their own tractors and tractor-driven machinery, thus strengthening their position vis-à-vis the government. Altogether, one has the impression that the existing collective farms serve the same purpose as cooperatives in industry and other sectors: they provide a convenient shield for private enterprise which is thus protected from discriminatory taxation or other restrictive government measures.

The situation is somewhat different with regard to state farms. Almost immediately after October, 1956, in accordance with the general trend to stress the importance of high output and efficiency, the state-farm sector was thoroughly reorganized. The separate Ministry of State Farms was abolished in December, 1956, and the entire network of farms was put under the supervision of the Ministry of Agriculture. The system was also largely decentralized, highly detailed annual output

[1] Appendix Table 1 and *Rocz. Stat.-1965*, pp. 217, 219, 223.

[2] S. Pasko (chairman of the National Council of Producer Cooperatives), *Zag. Ek. Roln.*, No. 2 (1960), p. 134.

plans were abolished, and the method of accounting, which had precluded any rational economic analysis, was changed.

The reorganization seemed to work well, and by 1964 the state farms began to show the results of the new policy.[3] With 1956 as base, their total production in 1964 increased by 16 percent and their marketable output by 74 percent; the latter accounted for about 15 percent of total marketable production in the country.[4] Their performance in crops and animal products was now roughly comparable to that in individual farms, the major exceptions being potatoes and sugar beets. Nevertheless, despite various measures taken to improve the financial position of state farms, they still had to be subsidized. In general, state farms are a long way from becoming what they were supposed to be in the first place, namely, examples of socialist farming which would impress the peasants so much that they would organize collective farms on a mass scale.

The third element in the pre-1956 socialized agriculture, the MTS, lost their main *raison d'être* with the dissolution of the collective farms. After long debates concerning their future it was decided to retain them, albeit in a different form. Today they are engaged primarily in rural transportation activities and also serve as repair shops for tractors and other equipment owned by individual farmers and agricultural circles.

This short review covers all that Polish socialized agriculture deserves today. For all practical purposes, Polish agriculture of 1965 is an individually owned agriculture which, in many respects, resembles agriculture in Western and Southern Europe and is subject to similar forces which are shaping their future. As stated above, in this respect the Polish situation is unique in the world. Poland, together with Yugoslavia, provides a fascinating field for study of such problems as the relationship between individual farmers and the rest of the state and of the changing role of private agriculture in the process of economic development along Communist lines. There is not enough space in the context of this article to discuss all these topics, and only selected issues will be touched upon.

ECONOMIC PERFORMANCE

Obviously, the first question to be asked concerning possible alternatives to collectivization (which in the Polish case turns out to be private agriculture) is this: does it work out and does it represent an improve-

[3] For a recent account, see Z. Karczewski, *Gosp. Plan.* XIX:8–9 (August–September, 1964).

[4] *Rocz. Stat.-1965*, pp. 217, 219.

ment over the past? This is the crucial problem, since the collapse of collectivization in 1956 was due primarily to the failure of collective farms to expand output. The future of individual farming is closely related to its ability to provide increasing quantities of foodstuffs during years to come. One can even venture a statement that as long as individual peasants are able to produce the required volume of output, there is little chance that the Party would impose a rapid transformation of the existing system.

According to fairly complete statistical data up to and including 1964 (i.e., the eight-year period after decollectivization), the performance of individual peasants was generally impressive. The two major categories of production (total and marketable) showed the respective increases of 14 and 24 percent in 1964 as compared with 1957. Average yields also showed considerable improvement and so did the output of milk and eggs. The successes were particularly striking in crops, less so in meat. Although the production indices look impressive, the per-capita growth appears less spectacular. The corresponding indexes for 1964 (1957 = 100) were 4 percent for total and 13 percent for marketable production.[5] The population of Poland was still rising at a fast rate, and it is only in the last two years that a visible deceleration could be observed. To round up the picture one should also mention livestock. The number of cattle was increasing rather slowly; this is particularly true of cows where herds are still below the prewar level. On the other hand, the hog population was growing rather rapidly. Figures for horses show some stability in the last few years, which could not help but disappoint the planners who hoped (and are still hoping) to reduce rapidly the number of horses.[6]

The relative successes, however impressive in comparision with the pre-1956 performance, provided only a partial solution of the economic problem. Problem number one, that of acquiring sufficient amounts of foodstuffs to feed the growing population, remained largely unsolved, especially with regard to animal products. Consumption of grain and potatoes appeared to have reached its peak and for the last several years showed hardly any change.[7] While the same is roughly true for meat and fats, the per-capita consumption of which in 1964 reached a respectable figure of 54 kilograms, there is no sign that demand has been

[5] *Ibid.*, pp. 13, 217, 219. The base year of 1957 was taken instead of 1956 because no separate data are available for 1956 on individual farms (which were lumped together with cooperatives in the official data). The corresponding figures for agriculture as a whole were 4 and 18 percent.

[6] *Ibid.*, p. 230. The number of horses in 1963 was almost the same as in 1957.

[7] *Ibid.*, p. 483.

satisfied. On the contrary, according to Polish estimates, the income elasticity of demand for meat, sugar, and other foodstuffs is so high that the planners expect continued pressure on supplies likely to be available for many years to come.[8] Attempts to induce the people to divert some of their income increments to other goods, especially consumer durables, proved unsuccessful thus far.

It is this constant growth in demand for meat and animal products which presents the Poles with their second most difficult problem, that of imports of grain. The country switched from its traditional role of exporter of grain to that of an importer in 1949 and it remained in that position ever since.[9] Despite considerable improvement in grain production, the import of wheat, rye, and barley showed an almost uninterrupted growth for the past ten years, and various experts predict the presence of continuing imports of grain at least until 1970, the terminal year of the forthcoming Five-Year Plan, or even beyond that date.[10] The main difficulty concerning imports is, of course, that of payment. Initially it was assumed that increased imports of grain could be transformed into meat which could then be exported, and some Polish economists began to compare Poland with Britain and other advanced countries which import foodstuffs and export manufactures. As it turned out, however, meat instead of being exported was largely consumed at home, and other means of payment had to be found. Even though Polish meat exports did show considerable increase since 1956, the net balance of Polish foreign trade in foodstuffs showed a negative figure for a number of years and only the most recent data on exports of meat, sugar, and butter indicate that an improvement might be in the offing.[11]

Ever since 1956 part of the repayment problem was solved by an agreement with the United States which permitted Poland to take advantage of Titles I and IV of Public Law 480, the "Food for Peace" program. Nevertheless, in September, 1964, the Congress removed Poland from the list of countries participating in Title I of the law, and from now on the Poles had to pay for their import in dollars which thus

[8] According to Polish estimates the current income elasticity of demand for food is about 0.6–0.7. This, in addition to the more equal distribution of income and migration from the countryside to the cities, was the reason for the growing demand. Cf. W. Herer, *Nowe Drogi,* XVIII:5 (May, 1964), 182–183.

[9] *Rocz. Stat.-1960,* p. 290; *Rocz. Stat.-1965,* p. 341.

[10] Appendix Table 2. For an interesting discussion of the entire problem, see W. Misiuna, *Wieś. Współ.* VII: 2 (February, 1963) and H. Olszewski, *Zag. Ek. Roln.,* No. 5 (1962).

[11] The index of agricultural exports in 1964 (1956 = 100) was only slightly below that of 1961. Cf. *Rocz. Stat.-1965,* p. 335.

far they have been largely able to avoid.[12] The repayment problem remains acute, since the country has no reserves to speak of and nothing much to offer in exchange for import of grain from non-Communist countries.

It is the latter problem which presumably prompted Gomułka to announce at the Fourth Congress of the Polish United Workers Party that a way must be found to reduce the import of grain. Leaving aside the general problem of socialist transformation of agriculture as *the* key to success, Gomułka and others followed the Soviet example in concentrating mainly on investment and chemicals.[13] In line with other Communist countries Polish agricultural investment lagged behind in comparison with investment in other sectors even where the new agricultural policy was proclaimed after 1956. Despite the introduction of some innovations such as the Agricultural Development Fund (*FRR*), total funds available from state sources were still pitifully small. True, they were being supplemented by investment undertaken by individual peasants, but the extent of the latter, although growing, was still insignificant. Before the Congress, in March, 1964, the Party announced that in the new Five-Year Plan starting in 1966, agricultural investment would be increased 60 percent as compared with the current plan and that it will amount to 18 percent of all investment expenditures.[14] While the figure looks impressive it must be remembered that previous much smaller investment figures were never fulfilled, and there is no reason to suspect that the new program will turn out to be different.

With particular regard to chemical fertilizers, Gomułka announced a substantial planned increase in the production of nitrogen with three new plants to be built in the course of the next five years. Actually the input of fertilizers per hectare exhibited a striking increase since 1956 and, no doubt, contributed to an improvement in crop production. In this respect, however, Poland still lagged behind some other members of the bloc, especially Czechoslovakia and East Germany, and considerable room for improvement remains. Interestingly enough, despite official pleas for more fertilizers at home, Poland did export them abroad. Nevertheless, after a significant dip in domestic sales in 1957, due to a

[12] *The 1965 Eastern Europe Agricultural Situation,* Economic Research Service, ERS-Foreign-115 (Washington, D.C.: U.S. Department of Agriculture, March, 1965), p. 24.

[13] Gomułka's address at the 4th Congress of the PUWP, *Nowe Drogi,* XVIII: 7 (July, 1964), 36–37 and 42 ff.

[14] *Ibid.,* XVIII: 4 (April, 1964), 8 and 47.

sharp increase in the price level, purchases by individual farmers increased substantially.[15]

So much for the over-all picture of the economic performance. It can thus be said that the improvement was significant although not spectacular. The important thing, however, is that individual farming was able to accomplish what collectivized agriculture could not do, and for that reason no attempt has been made so far to change the existing state of affairs. It might be useful to examine the current situation in greater detail in order to provide a background for the discussion of the model of Polish agriculture in the final section of this study.

THE POLISH PEASANT TODAY

The Polish peasants today still account for a very large share of the total population. Gone are the days when the peasantry equaled more than two-thirds of the population, but, according to the 1960 census, the number of persons deriving their main income from agriculture still accounted for 38.4 percent of the population. The average size of a holding is still relatively small amounting to 4.8 hectares.[16] This makes Poland a country of predominantly medium peasants.

Both preceding statements, however formally true, call for an explanation. The still fairly large percentage of agricultural population and relatively small average size of farms are influenced by the presence of peasants occupying holdings ranging from 0.5 to 2 hectares. This category of farmers (accounting for 32.8 percent of total agricultural population) are known in Poland as "worker-peasants." They are usually included among farmers in the official statistics although they derive most of their income from working in industry and other nonagricultural sectors. Space does not permit a full discussion of this fascinating group which introduced a completely new element into the whole discussion of agricultural change, throwing a monkey wrench in the Communist declarations about capitalist differentiation and progressive impoverishment of peasants.[17] Once this category is removed from agricultural statistics, the percentage of farm population in total population declines to 36.7 percent and the average size of holding rises to 6.7

[15] *Rocz. Stat.-1964,* pp. 263 and 468; *Rocz. Stat.-1965,* p. 273.

[16] *Rocz-Stat.-1964,* p. 31 and 229.

[17] A. Korbonski, *Politics of Socialist Agriculture in Poland. 1945–1960* (New York and London: Columbia University Press, 1965), pp. 285–286. According to some estimates by 1965 2.2 million peasants, accounting for 56 percent of the total agrarian population would have derived their main and partial incomes from sources outside agriculture. A. Bodnar, *Wieś Współ.* VI: 6 (June, 1962), 32.

hectares.[18] While our main conclusions are not altered significantly, this adjustment permits us to concentrate on peasants proper.

Next to its economic performance, the crucial question in discussing the role of individually owned agriculture is that of the welfare and standard of living of the peasants. Collectivization collapsed in Poland because it was identified with stagnation in agriculture and the lack of incentive to join cooperatives which offered no improvement in the standard of living. Does private farming as an alternative to collectivization provide better incentives to expand output and ensure higher incomes for the peasants? Judging by the experience of the last eight years, the answer must be an unequivocal yes. Looking back at the period 1949–1956 it can be estimated that the only element in peasant income which remained relatively untouched was consumption in kind. Compulsory deliveries, high taxes, and other financial obligations kept the money income at a minimum level and eventually resulted in considerable dissaving reflected in a serious disinvestment in agriculture. There was obviously no incentive to expand production and such increments in output as did occur were consumed on farms.

The situation changed drastically in 1956, although the harbingers of new things to come began to appear in 1953–1954 as part of the Malenkovian "New Course." Since 1956 the following measures have been taken by the government: the volume of compulsory deliveries was substantially reduced, particularly in the case of grain, and prices raised so that only in meat is the share of procurements in total output still very high.[19] Land tax rates remained unchanged until 1962 when they were revised upward. Smaller volume of deliveries permitted the peasants to divert more produce to city markets. On the input side, prices of fertilizers, building materials, and equipment were increased considerably but, at least, these products became available to individual peasants. Official estimates of real income of the peasants show an increase of 18 percent in 1964 over 1956.[20] This increase was and is reflected in a large expansion of private farm investment and consumption which contributed to an improvement in the standard of living.

The rapid increase in peasant incomes proved embarrassing to the regime since it continued the trend which originated in the early 1950's. At that time, farm incomes rose faster than those of workers, and the Party leadership had a difficult time explaining this phenomenon to the

[18] *Rocz. Stat.-1964*, pp. 31, 37, and 229.
[19] *Rocz. Stat.-1965*, p. 285.
[20] *Ibid.*, p. 289.

rank and file of the "vanguard of the working class." [21] In 1962, the government finally decided to take steps in order to slow down the growth of agricultural incomes and new tax rates were imposed on the peasants.[22] It should be added that, in spite of the rapid increase, farm incomes in general remain considerably below the incomes in industry on a per-capita basis.[23]

The question of the standard of living in agriculture is closely related to the problem of employment. Before the war, Poland, together with many other agricultural countries suffered from the so-called "hidden unemployment." After the war, and particularly at the close of the Six-Year Plan in 1956, the Communist leaders boasted that the problem was solved by a massive increase in nonagricultural employment.[24] Shortly afterward, however, in the course of a far-reaching debate concerning Poland's economic situation, the same people rediscovered "hidden unemployment" in many parts of the country. They used its alleged presence to support the argument in favor of either continuing collectivization or introduction of some other form of socialization in farming. They pointed to an increase in the number of farms which supposedly reflected a growing subdivision of holdings, expansion of small, inefficient farms, and growth of overemployment.

It is true that the number of holdings has been increasing fairly steadily for a number of years.[25] According to research conducted in Poland, however, this increase did not reflect a growth of unemployment. Insofar as the increase in the number of farms affected primarily the category of smallest holdings (0.5–2 hectares) it simply represented an increase in the number of "worker-peasants" who no longer treated farming as their main occupation. The number of medium and larger farms remained relatively unchanged, and in some categories (10–15 hectares) the increase actually contradicted Communist claims. The general conclusion which emerged in a number of recent studies is that hidden unemployment has been eliminated throughout most of the coun-

[21] Korbonski, *op. cit.* (in n. 17), p. 236.

[22] For a criticism of the tax policy, see S. Ignar, *Wieś Współ.* IX: 4 (April, 1965), 20.

[23] According to official and semiofficial estimates, farm incomes per head are equal to 60–80 percent of comparable incomes in industry. M. Czerniewska, in Appendix to *Zag. Ek. Roln.* No. 6, (1960); W. Herer, *Rolnictwo a rozwój gospodarki narodowej* (Warsaw: 1962), pp. 22–23; L. Rzendowski, Ek. No. 5. (1964), p. 1102; *Rocz. Stat.-1965,* pp. 249–250 and 484–489.

[24] K. Kowalska, *Zag. Ek. Roln.,* No. 1, (1957), p. 32, estimated rural unemployment in 1956 at about 1.5 million persons.

[25] *Rocz. Stat.-1964,* p. 229.

try and that it was encountered on a significant scale only in two or three of the least developed districts in southern and southeastern Poland.[26]

It appears that the various mentioned surveys were responsible for the toning down of official statements which emphasized the danger of a growing subdivision of holdings and called for government action restricting it by law or in some other fashion.[27] Nevertheless, a number of measures taken in the last few years dictated that the planners were still concerned with this problem. In 1961, a plenary meeting of the Central Committee called for a forcible sale of small, inefficient holdings to the state in return for a fixed pension; two years later the government announced the introduction of the so-called "agrominimum" which meant that all peasants had to perform a fixed number of minimum necessary tasks in order to qualify for state aid.[28] Both regulations aimed at reducing the number of poorly run farms which then could be transferred to the state.

There is little doubt that the danger of overemployment and subdivision still exists on the Polish countryside. Although until now it has been possible to absorb most of the increase in agricultural population, the over-all picture does not look as impressive as one might have expected. Even though nonagricultural employment rose considerably, it was the unemployed or underemployed labor in the cities which got the first crack at industrial employment, and the movement from the country to the city was not as overwhelming as the official statements would like us to believe.[29] Obviously, the number of able-bodied persons in agriculture did decline and shortages of labor in some parts of the country appeared but these phenomena did not occur at a scale comparable with Czechoslovakia or East Germany. The most significant change was that in the age structure of agricultural population which begins to show a rapidly growing predominance of higher-age groups.[30] This, in turn, is related to the growth in the number of farms run by old, often ill, peasants, unable to devote their full energies to farming or to hire agricultural labor.

The worst, however, is yet to come. During the next five years

[26] A. Szemberg, *Zag. Ek. Roln.*, No. 3 (1963) and *Ek.*, No. 5 (1964).

[27] Korbonski, *op. cit.* (in n. 17), p. 301.

[28] For a discussion of this problem, see K. Smoleński, *Gosp. Plan.* XVIII: 4, (April, 1965). A law passed in June 1963 restricted subdivision by prohibiting transfer of land (usually by bequest) to persons without agricultural qualifications.

[29] Net outflow in the period 1946–1960 is estimated at over 2.5 million persons, or 61 percent of natural increase in agricultural population. M. Pohoski, *Migracje ze wsi do miast* (Warsaw: 1963), pp. 53 ff.

[30] According to the 1960 census 23.9 percent of individual owners of farms were over 60 years old, as compared to 18.5 percent in 1950. *Rocz. Stat.-1964*, p. 36.

Poland will reach the so-called "demographic summit" when young people born in the early 1950's will enter the labor market. It must be remembered that at that time the farm population alone was growing at the rate of close to 2 percent annually, and already in the last four years 1961–1964 the economy had to absorb some 1.2 million persons.[31] Signs of unemployment begin to appear in the cities, and unless the nonagricultural sectors are able to continue absorbing well over half a million persons annually, hidden (and open) unemployment may appear again in full force.[32] This is one of the reasons for the strong emphasis laid on the expansion of labor-intensive agricultural tasks such as livestock-breeding, production of industrial crops, and so on.

At the present time, however, the problem does not exist on a mass scale, and peasants are enjoying a relative prosperity. The Polish village has been undergoing considerable transformation since 1956. This can be witnessed by the fact that by 1964 over 70 percent of all farms have been electrified and neither a radio set, motorcycle, nor even television appear today as a novelty. The improvement in means of communication and transportation means that the gap between the city and the village is being narrowed rapidly. Various surveys conducted by rural sociologists indicate interesting changes in the status of the peasants and in their value systems. The social prestige of peasantry appears to be rising on the scale of occupations, and the age-long contempt of the peasants seems to be disappearing. Undoubtedly, this is partly due to the growth of a new intelligentsia of peasant origin.[33] The old value system also appears to be giving way to new ideas. In the past, the position of an individual peasant in his village was associated with the amount of land he owned, and almost invariably all increments in his income were devoted to acquisition of additional land. This, allegedly, is no longer true. According to a number of sociological surveys, purchase of land no longer occupies the first place on the peasants' scale

[31] *Rocz. Stat.-1965*, p. 59.

[32] About 65,000 persons were registered in employment exchanges in December, 1963. *Ibid.*, p. 67. According to estimates made in the West actual unemployment in 1964 reached 500,000. M. Gamarnikow, "Niektóre aspekty sytuacji gospodarczej w Polsce," in *Dylematy Gospodarki Polskiej* (London: 1965), p. 21. The latter figure appears highly exaggerated.

[33] The peasants apparently occupy nineteenth place on a scale of twenty-nine occupations ranked by prestige by the urban population. This gives the peasants the same rank as professional army officers. W. Wesołowski, A. Sarapata, *Studia Socjologiczne*, No. 2 (1961), pp. 91 ff. This is a rather interesting comment on the extent of social change in Poland since 1939. When the views of the rural rather than urban population are taken into consideration, the social prestige of peasantry is still higher (thirteenth place out of twenty-one occupations). Pohoski, *op. cit.* (in n. 29), p. 188.

of preferences: its place has been taken by a desire to acquire a profession or education.[34]

Politically the peasantry seems to retain its indifference. Before 1956, peasant membership in the Communist party, in the satellite Peasant party, and in the Young Communist League was extremely small. This did not change after Gomułka's return to power, in spite of significant increases in over-all membership of both parties. After the collapse of the Young Communist League, a separate Association of Rural Youth was formed to serve as a transmission belt linking young peasants to the Communist party. According to latest figures the membership embraces a fairly high percentage of eligible youth.[35]

There is little doubt that the absence of significant representation of peasants in the various parties and associations must be of some concern to Communist party leadership. If nothing else, it makes it difficult for the *apparat* to influence peasant thinking, to spur the peasants to greater productive effort, and, last, but certainly not least, to induce them to give some thought to the abandonment of individual farms and to entering a new phase of the socialist transformation of agriculture. Since all Communist leaders (from Gomułka down) assure the peasants that no force would be used for that purpose, the Party must rely on its powers of persuasion in addition to some other measures which it took in the past few years.

HOW TO SOCIALIZE AGRICULTURE WITHOUT ANTAGONIZING THE PEASANTS

It must be kept in mind that Gomułka and the rest of the Party leadership, while willing to accept the dissolution of collective farms in 1956, still firmly believe in the ultimate socialist transformation of agriculture. Since collectivization had proved a failure, another vehicle had to be found to bring the peasants closer to socialism. It was apparently believed that this vehicle could be in agricultural circles.

The circles had an old and honorable tradition in Poland. They were

[34] B. Gałęski, *Nowe Drogi*, XVIII: 8 (August, 1964), 150–151.

[35] In 1964, 168,000 peasants belonged to the Communist party and 228,000 belonged to the Peasant party. Altogether they accounted for 17 percent of all peasants, excluding worker-peasants. *Wieś Współ.*, VII: 10 (October, 1964), 7. According to official statistics, the Association of Rural Youth in 1964 accounted for about 80 percent of actively employed peasants between 14 and 24, and for about 48 percent of all peasants in that age group. *Rocz. Stat.-1965*, pp. 32 and 526. This rather high membership ratio would indicate that the Party abandoned strict adherence to ideological principles and instead concentrated on attracting young peasants in a variety of nonpolitical ways. Korbonski, *op. cit.* (in n. 17), p. 276.

resurrected in 1956 to provide a convenient name shield for an institution of cooperative-machinery centers, which Gomułka saw as an instrument of mechanization of agriculture and its eventual socialization. The idea behind the recreation of the cooperative-machinery centers under the guise of agricultural circles—to avoid the hated word "collective"—was a relatively simple one. With the failure of collectivization, there was no longer any reason to continue the prohibition on sales of heavy machinery and equipment to individual peasants, and the prohibition was abolished. The MTS, whose role had to be adjusted because of the dissolution of collective farms, never proved to be very successful: in any case they could never service the hundreds of thousands of peasant farms. On the other hand, Gomułka firmly believed in the blessings of mechanization and considered it almost the sole palliative for all the evils in Polish agriculture. The prices of the individual items of equipment were still very high and few individual peasants could afford to buy them. Thus the only way to expand mechanization of private farms was to induce the peasants to get together and buy equipment on a cooperative basis. The voluntary character of the circles was strongly emphasized.

It appeared initially that the peasants took Gomułka's words seriously: some 320,000 joined the circles during 1957.[36] The Party, however, never intended to let the matter get out of control, and the spontaneous activity of the peasants was not looked upon favorably. To some extent, the situation resembled the development of workers' councils which were growing like mushrooms until the Party at one point decided that the situation was getting out of hand since no room was left for the *aktiv*. Roughly the same happened to the circles, the growth of which after 1957 became much more moderate.

A relatively new interpretation of the role of the circles was provided by Gomułka at the Third Party Congress in March, 1959, and at the Central Committee Plenum in June of the same year.[37] According to Gomułka, the circles could become a foundation of socialism only if they contributed to the growth of agricultural production and became at the same time a mass organization of the peasants. The initial performance of the circles apparently proved disappointing: both the membership and funds collected by the circles were growing rather slowly. Upon reflection the Party realized that it would take years for the organizations to accumulate sufficient funds, that mechanization would affect only a part of the agricultural sector, and, finally, that ownership of

[36] *Rocz. Stat.-1964*, p. 234.

[37] *Nowe Drogi*, XIII: 4 (April, 1959), 522–523 and *Trybuna Ludu*, June 23, 1959.

machinery would be concentrated among groups of wealthier peasants, thus increasing the danger of "exploitation." In June, 1959, Gomułka announced the creation of a special Agricultural Development Fund which was to finance the purchase of tractors to replace that perennial troublemaker, the horse, which consumed some 800,000 tons of grain annually (or about one-half of total grain imports).[38] The capital of the Fund, contributed by the state, was to amount to the difference between the actual value of compulsory deliveries of grain, potatoes, and meat made by the peasants and the calculated value of the same amount of produce in terms of free-market prices.

As stated by Gomułka, the rationale upon which the idea of the Fund rested amounted to the desire to convince the peasants that the Party and the government had only their interest in mind. The Fund could have been financed by raising the land tax but that idea apparently was discarded as being antagonistic to the peasants. The latter still treated compulsory deliveries as an extraordinary obligation imposed on them for the purpose of accelerating the industrial but not the agricultural growth of the country. From now on the deliveries were to benefit both the peasants and the state. The peasants would receive their money back in the form of tractors and other equipment while the government would secure basic supplies for the urban consumers.

Despite this rather attractive idea, the growth of the circles since the creation of the Development Fund left some room for concern. In numerical terms the increase was fairly impressive. By the end of 1964 the circles' membership reached a total of about 1 million embracing some 40 percent of holdings above 2 hectares, and there was a circle in 77 percent of all parishes (*solectwa*).[39] At the same time, total actual investment undertaken by the circles and financed from the Agricultural Development Fund was not impressive. While some 16.5 billion zoltys were deposited on the circles' account in the period 1959–1964, only 7.1 billion were actually spent.[40] Farm experts believed that the structure of this investment was distorted. Even though the funds were to be spent mainly on tractors and tractor-driven equipment, the planners

[38] *Trybuna Ludu*, March 15, 1959.

[39] *Rocz. Stat.-1965*, pp. 239 and 244. The increase in membership, at least until 1962, was due not to the expansion of the existing circles (which the Party favors) but to the creation of new ones. This is understandable since the attractiveness of joining an existing circle declines when the membership is growing. Every new member reaps less benefits than his predecessors and he also hurts the position of the current membership. Z. Kozłowski, J. Rajtar, *Gosp. Plan.*, XVII: 7 (July, 1963), 19–20.

[40] *Rocz. Stat.-1965*, p. 279.

hoped that other types of investment, such as repair shops, experimental stations, schools, and training centers would not be neglected. This, however, was not the case, and 97.6 percent of available funds was invested in tractors.[41]

What were the reasons for the rather disappointing performance of the circles, particularly in the field of investment? No clear-cut answer can be discovered thus far. Initially the slow growth of investment was apparently due to the fact that in order to benefit from the Development Fund the members of the circles had to put up some of their own money. This they were unwilling to do, and the respective provision of the law was eventually modified in 1962.[42] Moreover, the low level of compulsory deliveries in many villages resulted in small allocations to the Development Fund; this in turn made significant investment impossible. In recent times permission was given to combine funds of several circles and this apparently contributed to some increase in investment activity.[43] The lack of repair facilities and spare parts may also have contributed to the slow expansion of capital formation by the circles. The latter had no repair shops of their own and were forced to rely on MTS for this purpose. Conflicts began to arise between the circles and the MTS with each side accusing the other of bad faith and dishonesty.[44] In general, the activity of the circles themselves consisted almost as much of purely agricultural work as of such peripheral tasks as transportation; the degree of the circles' influences on output of the membership and the increase in the number of tractors did not result in any significant decline in the number of horses. Apparently the peasants remained attached to their horses as a reliable source of power.[45]

While all these factors should be taken into consideration, the chief reason for the apparent lack of interest and initiative on the part of the circles was the basic change in their role as proclaimed by the Party shortly after the creation of the Development Fund. It must be remembered that, for a number of years following Gomułka's return, the role of the circles as instruments of socialization of agriculture was kept in the background. Gomułka himself appeared to be quite pragmatic and realized that there was little sense in bringing back the question of socialist transformation so soon after the debacle of 1956. The first harbinger of change was the Agricultural Development Fund in 1959,

[41] T. Wyszomirski, *Nowe Drogi,* XVIII: 10 (October, 1964), 129.
[42] M. Mieszczankowski, *Życie Gosp.,* No. 11 (March 17, 1963), p. 6.
[43] Wyszomirski, *op. cit.* (in n. 41), pp. 121–123.
[44] T. Hunek, *Nowe Drogi,* XIX: 2 (February, 1965), 94.
[45] J. Tepicht, *Ek.,* No. 5 (1964), pp. 1075–1077.

but even then the purely voluntary and limited character of the circles was emphasized, and there was relatively little talk about socialization. A new approach to the circles was announced some time in the early 1960's. The actual date is hard to pinpoint but the change in emphasis and direction is unmistakable.

For the past three or four years the circles largely replaced collective and state farms as the most frequently discussed institution in Party meetings and journals. There was no longer any attempt at pretending that the circles were created mainly for the benefit of individual peasants and that their role as a tool of socialization was to be confined to education and spreading of good will. From now on the circles were to become unequivocally the spearhead of socialist transformation even though no force or other "administrative measures" were to be applied to induce the peasants to join them *en masse*. The circles were no longer to limit themselves to a selected number of tasks connected with ownership of tractors. They were officially encouraged to take over cultivation of land, initially to be supplied by the state and eventually by the members. They were told to engage in a variety of collective production tasks such as milk-processing, livestock-breeding, drainage, and other.[46] By virtue of their ownership of tractors they were to perform various tasks which in the past belonged to MTS. In the most recent period, it appeared that the circles might soon absorb the existing MTS repair facilities. For all practical purposes this would put an end to the separate existence of that institution.[47] Actually when one considers the present character of the circles, their similarity to MTS is inescapable. While MTS were primarily an instrument of control and only secondarily performed economic tasks, the role of the circles thus far has been the reverse. Both institutions, however, were acclaimed as vanguards of socialism in the countryside, and they were also to be staffed by devoted members of the *aktiv,* spreading the message of socialist transformation among the peasant masses.

In view of all this one might suspect that the enthusiasm of individual peasants with regard to the circles was likely to diminish appreciably. It is one thing to belong to a circle and another to strengthen it. Membership itself meant little since the facilities of the circles were available to members and nonmembers alike. The peasants were probably aware of the fact that mass organizations in the past often proved quite weak, as witnessed by the Young Communist League which collapsed overnight in the fall of 1956. Consequently, as long as the circles confined them-

[46] *Ibid.*, p. 1093.
[47] Hunek, *op. cit.* (in n. 44), p. 95.

selves to the ownership and utilization of tractors, they did not present a danger to individual farming. On the other hand, once the circles were to invest on a large scale in other production facilities, or to acquire land and to engage in various other collective activities, the character of the organization was qualitatively changed and the circles became as serious a threat to private agriculture as collective farms used to be in the past. Actually the danger this time was greater, because collective farms never became economically attractive to the peasants. On the other hand, the circles, well equipped with machinery and money, could become a real Trojan horse in Polish countryside.

This, in brief, was to be the role of the circles as agents of socialization, combining vertical integration of production and horizontal integration of producers. This is how the circles were seen by Gomułka and some of the agricultural experts engaged in a continuing dialogue concerning the future of Polish agriculture. The dialogue itself is not new. It began sometime during 1956 preceding Gomułka's takeover, and it continued ever since. Initially it was devoted primarily to the criticism of the pre-1956 period. After 1956 it concerned itself with the role to be played by private agriculture in a socialist country.[48] In recent years it began to discuss once again the ways and means of socializing agriculture, and also this time it proved to be fascinating. The level of discussion is invariably very high, the participants are drawn from among top experts on Polish agriculture, and the debate is remarkably free, with no punches being pulled by the discussants.

Essentially the experts can be divided into four groups. The first one, whose views reflect those of Gomułka and whose most able spokesman appears to be M. Mieszczankowski, advocates the circles as the most efficient instrument of socialization.[49] Their ideas were presented above.

The second group is represented by J. Tepicht, one of the most gifted and prolific writers on agricultural affairs and official Party agricultural spokesman before 1956. It favors expansion of contractual deliveries as a means of gradual socialization.[50] Tepicht feels that only a thorough vertical integration of socialized industry and private agriculture through the vehicle of contractual deliveries is likely to result in a highly productive agriculture. The peasants themselves would become a species of semi-industrial workers, using their land simply as one of the factors of

[48] Korbonski, *op. cit.* (in n. 17), pp. 251–255 and 282–286.

[49] M. Mieszczankowski, in a series of articles appearing in *Życie Gosp.* Nos. 11, 15, 18, 20, and 21, (1963) and No. 18 (1965).

[50] Mieszczankowski, *ibid.*, No. 10 (1963), pp. 6–7.

production and not as a sacred piece of property. An important role in this process is assigned to industry which would be obliged not only to purchase the final product but also to ensure the supply of necessary inputs, including credit and equipment. Tepicht and his followers illustrate their program (which they call the "putting-out system") with reference to the close cooperation between industry and agriculture in Western countries, and advocate large expansion of contractual procurements to include all major farm products.[51]

The third school of thought, whose leader seems to be B. Strużek, considers the other two groups to be quite unrealistic and believes that collectivization is the only way to socialize agriculture.[52] Without collective growing of crops and raising of livestock, all other forms are said by this group to be simply a cover-up for private farming. Moreover, they are ideologically incorrect. While Strużek agrees that the past experience was regrettable, he feels that efficient collective farms could be established with the aid of the state and he cites the latest developments in the Soviet Union to claim that cooperative farms can be made to work. It should be mentioned that whatever the views of the other two groups discussed above, they appear to be perfectly united in rejecting collective farms as an instrument of socialist transformation.[53]

The final group with no one in particular to represent its views advocates the so-called "etatization" as the most promising approach to socialization.[54] Its adherents urge the state to start acquiring land owned by old or inefficient peasants in return for an annuity. The land so acquired would be either attached to the existing state farms or used to create new ones. Eventually the process of acquisition would reach the rest of peasantry, and the state farms would become the predominant form of agricultural production unit. The advocates of this approach point with pride to the fact that in this way the intermediate step in the process of socialization (i.e., collective farms) can be jumped over and that the highest form (i.e., state farms) can be reached immediately. The opponents of this school consider it utterly unrealistic in view of the enormous cost involved. They also feel that hardly any of the peasants would be willing to divest themselves of their land in return

[51] According to a recent statement by the Minister of Agriculture in the next few years contractual deliveries are to become the major instrument of accumulation of grain reserves. M. Jagielski, *Nowe Drogi,* XVIII: 12 (December, 1964), 43. See also A. Romanow, *Wieś Współ.*, VIII: 6 (June, 1964).

[52] B. Strużek, *Wieś Współ.*, VI: 7 (July, 1962), and comment on Bodnar's article (see n. 17), *ibid.*, VI: 6, (June, 1962), 48–49.

[53] Bodnar, *op. cit.* (in n. 17), pp. 33–36.

[54] *Ibid.*, pp. 40–43 and Mieszczankowski, *Życie Gosp.*, No. 9 (March 3, 1963).

for an annuity which would not only be smaller than their current income but would also put them entirely at the mercy of the state.[55]

All four groups seem to have at least two things in common. All of them are on record in rejecting the application of force for the purpose of socialization. In addition, they visualize socialist transformation of agriculture as occurring only at the time when industry is able to provide sufficient inputs (including equipment) to make socialist agriculture an efficient and profitable enterprise. They all seem to agree that a rather long period of time would be required before supply problems disappear. For that reason, full socialization of Polish agriculture is likely to be delayed for some time.

The emphasis laid on socialization reflects the changed attitude of Gomułka and the Party. There can be little disagreement as to the change in Gomułka's pronouncements regarding not only agriculture but just about everything else since 1956. From being the leading country in the bloc in the process of general liberalization, Poland found itself lately much in the rear. While the Party has been dragging its feet in economic reforms and individual liberties, it did largely maintain its attitude toward the peasants, both at home and in intra-block relations. Undoubtedly the over-all toughening of the line had to affect agriculture sooner or later. Nevertheless, the main reason for the reopening of the debate on fundamentals concerning socialization seems to be an economic one. The high and growing demand for food, the necessity to import grain, and the threat of hidden unemployment, once again place a heavy burden on agriculture. The Party apparently feels that private farming will be unable to fulfill all the demands put upon it and that only socialized agriculture would be able to accomplish everything, that is, to expand output, to reduce the need for imports, and to provide employment at one and the same time.

In the long run the Party might be correct, although this is by no means certain. But in the short and the medium run there is still ample capacity in private farms to satisfy all the listed requirements, even within the existing restricting limits on individually owned and operated acreage.[56] The Party experts themselves freely admit that consumption

[55] The fact that in many areas the productivity of state farms lagged behind that of individual farms made the acquisition of private farms by the state highly questionable from the economic point of view. J. Poniatowski commenting on Bodnar's paper, *Wieś Współ.*, VI: 6 (June, 1962), 47. Poniatowski was the last Polish Minister of Agriculture before World War II.

[56] M. Mieszczankowski, *Życie Gosp.* No. 15 (April 14), 1963. For an opposing view, see M. Urban, *Nowe Roln.*, Nos. 11–13 (1962).

of fertilizers is still much too low and that increased supplies could easily result in expanded output. Additional fertilizers, improved drainage, and higher quality fodder could alleviate the need for imports while retaining the present structure of agriculture. In addition, medium and large peasant-type farms are, as a rule, more labor-intensive than large, mechanized farms, and they could very likely absorb the surplus population, given additional inputs, improved techniques, and higher incentives.

Thus there is no reason why private agriculture as an alternative to collectivization could not be made to work for quite some time. Past experience should have taught Gomułka and the Party that the Polish peasants should not be underestimated. Their power of resistance and endurance and their ability to read between the lines of official pronouncements were amply proved before 1956. If the Party is genuinely interested in solving the economic problems, the worst possible way to go about it is to discuss, however abstractly, the eventual socialization of agriculture. As stated elsewhere "in terms of the next 10 to 20 years the main problem for the Party is to regain peasant confidence." [57] This still holds true today and although the Party thus far appeared fairly successful in allaying peasant fears, it should not forget the past and become overconfident. Once before in the period 1949–1956, the Party met its match, and the same might well happen again.

APPENDIX TABLE 1

NUMBER, MEMBERSHIP, AND AREA OF COLLECTIVE FARMS, POLAND, 1955–1963

Year	Number of farms	Membership (thousand)	Area (thousand hectares)
1955	9,076	205.2	1,867
1956	1,534	31.6	260
1957	1,527	25.0	211
1958	1,528	24.5	201
1959	1,703	27.3	224
1960	1,668	28.2	228
1961	1,534	26.9	228
1962	1,342	26.3	217
1963	1,295	27.9	216
1964	1,246	29.2	219

SOURCE: *Rocz. Stat.*-1965, p. 254.

[57] Korbonski, *op. cit.* (in n. 17), p. 311.

APPENDIX TABLE 2

MILLINGS AND IMPORTS OF WHEAT AND RYE, POLAND, 1955–63
(thousand tons unless indicated otherwise)

	Wheat			Rye		
Year	Millings	Imports	Imports as percent of millings	Millings	Imports	Imports as percent of millings
1955	1,670	739	44.3	3,186	415	13.0
1956	1,808	664	36.7	3,282	309	9.4
1957	2,186	1,794	82.1	2,945	n.a.	n.a.
1958	2,417	666	27.6	2,616	210	8.0
1959	2,445	1,313	53.7	2,598	2	—
1960	2,600	1,700	65.4	2,690	109	4.1
1961	2,554	1,739	68.0	3,155	313	9.9
1962	2,447	1,504	61.4	2,674	247	9.2
1963	2,800	1,673	59.7	2,210	409	18.5
1964	3,115	2,211	71.0	1,902	—	—

SOURCES: *Rocz. Stat.- 1960*, p. 290; *Rocz. Stat.-1965*, pp. 129, 341

COMMENT

Jacek Romanowski

To socialize or not to socialize, that seems to be the question in Polish agriculture. I have little disagreement with Professor Korboński's presentation except perhaps with his principal conclusion or lack of it. Korbonski has very ably outlined for us the various positions of Polish leaders and economists with respect to the future of Polish agriculture, but he himself prudently refrained from taking a definite stand on any of the positions. Let me therefore be somewhat less prudent in supporting the desirability of socialization of Polish agriculture. By "socialization" I mean the creation of effective control by the state. I am using it because the word "collectivization" is too closely linked to the system and methods found in the Soviet Union.

Korboński states that "the future of individual farming is very closely related to its ability to provide increasing quantities of foodstuffs during the years to come." Although I subscribe to this statement, I think that Polish peasant agriculture, as it exists now, will not be able to provide such increasing quantities of foodstuffs.

It is clear that Polish agriculture today is largely unsocialized; it is also clear that the Party, the ultimate landlord of Poland, has never rejected the desirability of a socialized agriculture. We have thus a disparity between what the Party leadership would like to have and what it actually accepts and supports from day to day. In this disparity, the question when posed honestly is never *whether* to socialize, but rather *when* and *how* to socialize.

We could sit back and delight in the Polish Communists' problems were it not for two factors which render the whole question a crucial one not only for Poland's Communist leadership but also for the welfare of the Polish economy as a whole. These two factors are: (1) The insecurity caused by the disparity between the Party's desires for socialization and the status quo, have kept agriculture in a state of disrepair and lacking in long-range incentives; (2) Polish agriculture is generally inefficient and requires thorough-going remedial action. The fact that it produces better than the agriculture of the Stalinist collective period is just a question of the degree of inefficiency.

This leads to two conclusions: Something decisive has to be done to improve the state of Polish agriculture; and something decisive should be done to stop the ill effects of insecurity on the land.

Now the Hamletean query cannot delight us all that much any more, because, barring unpredictable developments (for example, abolition of the collective credo in the U.S.S.R., or the breaking away of Poland from Soviet domination), Poland's peasant economy seems to have its days numbered. The ultimate goal of socialization can be readily observed in any number of statements, official or unofficial.

The frustration of the Party with its inability to control the peasant sector effectively is also quite evident. There is of course some state control, but it is shockingly inefficient and haphazard. I would consider British agriculture and certainly Dutch and Danish agriculture more socialized than Polish agriculture. This is not borne out in statistics such as the percentage of land under state or collective control but rather in the effectiveness of state measures in the farming sector.

For historical, social, economic, and political reasons, the Polish peasant is a bulwark of willfulness, disrespect for outside authority, ignorance, and poverty. This is not true of all peasants and in all regions of Poland, but it nevertheless is more often true than not. It can be illustrated by relics of the three field system, by rye fields standing in the vegetable-producing Warsaw suburbs on equally desirable land, by grain sowings in the excessively moist Vistula delta, by oversubdivision of strips of land to the point of physical inability to cultivate, and so on.

Blaming all these shortcomings on the peasant would not be fair. Many factors contributed in changing the Vistula basin from a sixteenth-century granary of western Europe to a mid-twentieth century market for American surplus wheat. The reasons for this malaise have to be sought in the economic and political history of the country, including the most recent history of People's Poland.

Poland, as a developing small country is dependent on foreign trade. Before World War II that (inadequate) trade was primarily, and insufficiently, being paid for by agricultural and coal exports. Since World War II, agricultural exports have sharply dropped in favor of domestic consumption. Yet, in its transition from a raw-material-exporting to a manufacturing economy, Poland's industrial produce cannot readily compete in the West nor suffice to pay for the necessary imports from the West. Food exports should continue to secure Western exchange. Meanwhile the country is an importer of food—food that should be grown at home. "Every fourth loaf of bread consumed by the people of the city and village, comes from imported grain." [58] Nothing has changed for the better since the date of that statement.

It seems thus that the welfare of the Polish economy—much more so than just the welfare of the Polish Communists—depends on what will happen to Polish agriculture, if anything will happen at all. Being against communism, and communism being for the socialization of agriculture, we also tend to be against socialization. We quote the peasant's love of *his* land and the proved failures of collectivization in the past. But the backward, stubborn peasant's love of his underfertilized, mismanaged, oversubdivided land? According to British law, many of the Polish farms would be bought out by the state and transferred to more efficient operators if such could be found.

It is here that the agricultural circles seem to promise some hope. Developed in the German part of Poland they had proved to be a most efficient form of Polish peasant cooperation to stem the tide of German colonialism. It is true that the German part of Poland was the most advanced part of Poland in terms of organization, agrotechnical education, and financing, but it had neither the best agricultural land nor were the political conditions perfect.

Polish agricultural economists have been scrutinizing the agricultural cooperative institutions of Denmark and Holland, and some of the functions of these institutions were found to be readily adaptable to the institution of agricultural circles in Poland. The government continues to support these circles. "The circles have made an important and positive contribution to our economy and have aided significantly in the attainment of a number of agricultural gains. The Party is most interested in the development and strengthening of the circles." [59]

As Korboński pointed out, the circles have met with initial approval of the peasant, but the leadership's more open acclaim of the circle's role as an instrument of socialization seems to have cooled peasant interest. Obviously, the leadership has rejoiced at its ruse before the horse has entered the gates of Troy. Yet the agricultural methods of the Polish peasantry, its beautiful Helen, is hardly worth fighting for. We ought to hope that the leadership will manage to redress its horse—the agricultural circles—and render it once more attractive to the peasant.

[58] W. Gomułka's speech at the harvest festivities in Warsaw in September, 1962, as quoted in *Trybuna Ludu,* September 10, 1962.

[59] Gomułka's closing speech before the twelfth plenum meeting of the Central Committee of the Polish United Workers' party, as published in *Nowe Roln.,* No. 5 (1963).

This, should it ever succeed, will no doubt take much effort and time. The Polish economy can, however, hardly afford either another forceful collectivization or the abandoning of the agricultural question altogether. It is therefore that a successful socialization of the peasant sector, through the agricultural circles, promises to be the best chance for a strengthened Polish, albeit Communist, economy.

Index

www.ingramcontent.com/pod-product-compliance
Ingram Content Group UK Ltd.
Pitfield, Milton Keynes, MK11 3LW, UK
UKHW040233290926
15471UKWH00002B/177

9 780520 314795